The Practice of Social Intervention:
Goals, Roles and Strategies

Itasca, Illinois   F. E. PEACOCK PUBLISHERS, INC.

Edited by
Frank M. Loewenberg & Ralph Dolgoff
Council on Social Work Education

THE PRACTICE OF SOCIAL INTERVENTION: GOALS, ROLES & STRATEGIES

A Book Of Readings In Social Work Practice

CONTENTS

PREFACE

CRITICAL THINKING is a basic quality which needs to be developed by all those who plan to become social work professionals. Those unable to think critically (and creatively), as well as those unable to raise relevant questions, tend to become mere technicians. At the same time, there is the danger that questioning and critical thinking, if carried beyond a given point, become ends in themselves and lead to immobilization. Action professionals need to learn to balance their use of questioning and critical thinking with skillful and planful activity.

The present book of readings has been prepared in an attempt to provide students and teachers with just such a balanced mixture. Without sacrificing critical analysis, the focus on the practice of social intervention is always present. This approach to social work grew out of an earlier work of the editors, *The Teaching of Practice Skills in Undergraduate Programs in Social Welfare and Other Helping Services.*[1] A fuller explication of this practice scheme will appear in Loewenberg's forthcoming book, *Social Intervention: Basic Concepts, Strategies and Practice Skills.*[2] Over the years we had many opportunities to work together with social work educators from all parts of the country; their repeated requests for teaching materials led to the present volume.

The list of those whose help should be acknowledged is a long one; fear of omitting some has persuaded us not to mention any by name. It will be obvious to the reader that we have benefited from many and have freely used the thoughts and ideas of others. The errors and misapplications are, of course, our responsibility.

Only those who themselves have edited a book of readings know the many hours and days it takes to complete the task. To our wives, Adeline and Sylvia, and to our children, Joel, Naomi, Chaim, Alisa and Eliana, Shoshana, and Aaron, who paid the price of neglect so that this book could appear go our thanks and appreciation.

F.M.L.
R.D.

June, 1971

[1]New York: Council on Social Work Education, 1970.
[2]New York: Columbia University Press (forthcoming).

SECTION I

Introduction

FRANK M. LOEWENBERG

Social Work, Social Welfare and Social Intervention

Social welfare is one of those words which many use but few really understand. Many identify social welfare with the relief checks provided by the county welfare department to those who do not or cannot work. Others consider social welfare a sort of new-speak for charity and good deeds. Some even equate social welfare efforts with socialism or other radical doctrines allegedly designed to overthrow our country; still others suggest that the real function of social welfare activities is to defend the status quo from the inevitable attack by the victimized populations. Lack of clarity about social welfare is not limited to the general public. A United Nations social welfare consultant, for example, wrote

In no country has terminology been standardized so as to make possible the assignment of precise meaning to such terms as "social welfare," "social service," "social work," and "welfare work." (United Nations, 1950)

And, we may add, there is equal confusion about the concept "social intervention," as we shall see anon.

Under these circumstances it might be tempting to agree with Humpty-Dumpty that a word means "just what I choose it to mean—neither more nor less." Then everybody could be happy with his own definition and the rest of us would continue to misunderstand. But words reflect goals and values; Humpty-Dumpty's advice was designed for a world of confusion. If we want to contribute anything to a better understanding of our society and our role within it, clarity of the concepts we use is absolutely essential.

This introductory chapter was prepared by Frank M. Loewenberg for this reader. This material is based in part on a monograph entitled "Toward a Sociological Perspective on Social Welfare Strategies," to be published by the Council on Social Work Education, New York.

SOCIAL WELFARE

The Constitution of the United States already stated that one of the purposes of the federal government was to ensure the "welfare" of the population. The constitutional "welfare" may or may not have embraced our concept, social welfare, depending on how we define the term. When exactly the term social welfare came into use is not entirely clear; however, Lester Ward already used it at the turn of the century. Certainly, social welfare has moved a long way from the days when all that was needed was a good heart and some money to ensure the welfare of others. Yet, there remains much confusion .about the usage of this and related terms. Perhaps, this confusion and lack of clarity is indicative of a certain degree of bifurcation or value dilemma about the problem, the goals, and even the methods used to achieve these goals.

On the most general level there is agreement that the welfare of all is a desirable societal goal. Yet, despite this, it was not until 1962 that a President of the United States thought it necessary to send to the Congress a message on welfare, for it was only on February 1 of that year that John F. Kennedy sent the first welfare message to Congress, stressing the national desire to eliminate poverty. Poverty was not eliminated but seven years later President Nixon in his message on welfare reform reiterated that "a measure of the greatness of a powerful nation is the character of the life it creates for those who are powerless to make ends meet." Evidently it is easier for Presidents to talk about social welfare than to do something about it.

Social welfare, according to many, is a field, a set of institutions and agencies established by society to provide various kinds of supports; social work, on the other hand, is one of the several helping professions which provide service in the social welfare field. It was Titmuss (1965) who suggested that social welfare services are established either in response to a society's will to survive or in response to society's wish to help individuals to survive. Which services are classified as social welfare services differs from time to time and from society to society because both the actual needs and how these are defined by the various participants differs and will continue to change. Such definitions and perceptions are highly culture bound so that the identical objective situation will be viewed differently by participants located in different spots in the social scene. A fire chief will view a slum hotel through different eyes than a public welfare worker; a tenant differently than a big taxpayer.

In the United States the term "social welfare" is currently used in at least four different ways:

1. Social welfare is the term often used to identify the goal of the various helping professions. Thus Kidneigh (1960, p. 563) observed that social welfare was used to denote "man's humanitarian desire to help his fellow man...." At a recent United Nations meeting of social welfare ministers the term was used to refer "to a state of individual or social well-being." (Wells, 1969, p. 2)

2. Others have used the term to define the parameters of a field or system of service. Thus, Bisno (1959, p. 109) used the term social welfare to define "a social institution, the primary activities of which center about the maintenance and enhancement of the emotional, intellectual, physical and social aspects of human functioning." Many have followed Bisno in using this definition even though reference is primarily to the manifest functions of institutions or of an institutionalized sector of society.

3. In some circles, social welfare has been used as the term to designate the occupation practiced by those working in social agencies who have not earned the master-of-social-work (MSW) degree; however, with the growing recognition of the role of workers with various educational backgrounds in social work, this usage is fast disappearing.

4. University programs designed to study the problems to which social welfare institutions address themselves are in many places designated as social welfare studies or schools of social welfare, possibly in an attempt to distinguish these from other programs which are oriented more toward preparation for practice. In actual fact, the differences in curriculum rarely follow the nomenclature and generally it is difficult to tell apart a school of social work from a school of social welfare.

The variety of definitions can divert us from our real task. We will suggest, therefore, that here social welfare be defined in terms of aims and goals, and not in terms of the administrative auspices which provide the services nor in terms of the methods utilized to offer help. In other words, if the purpose of a children's allowance is to strengthen family life it should be considered a social welfare service regardless of how the grant comes to the recipient; at the present time, most countries do not so consider it if the children's allowances are administered by the same governmental department which handles taxation. Similarly, in the United States some do not consider public education a social welfare service because (1) it is not provided by a "recognized" welfare or social work agency, and (2) it is provided for all children, not exclusively for the poor. The emphasis on auspices makes it difficult for most to view the army as a social welfare institution, even though it performs many functions generally assigned to the social welfare sector; only in Israel where the army was purposefully utilized to promote the integration of the recent immigrants from Oriental countries with the earlier settlers from Europe, has this recognition been frankly accepted.

The use of narrow definitions of social welfare has created some difficulty in identifying social welfare personnel. Both in 1950 and 1960 the U.S. government sponsored a census of social welfare personnel, but the definitions used were in many respects so vague that the results were only of limited use. The rapidly changing social welfare scene, the radical innovations in the service delivery systems, together with the increased utilization of personnel with a variety of educational backgrounds, make the task of identifying social welfare personnel more difficult every day. It is easy to exclude from consideration professionals identified with the law and the clergy since they are basically rooted in other institutional frameworks. But what about nurses, clinical psychologists and teachers? How would one classify a clerk in a social agency who has responsibilities for conducting intake interviews: is she a secretary, a social worker, or what? How does one identify the therapist staff of a narcotic addiction service where therapists trained as social workers, psychologists and medical doctors work side-by-side? What about a congressman's legislative assistant who has earned his MSW degree? By focusing on goals, rather than on institutional auspices, it is possible to handle "difficult jurisdictional" questions such as these.

SOCIAL WORK

Defining the term "social work" presents another set of difficulties. Various attempts have been made to arrive at a definition in terms of a field of work, a method, or the characteristics of those who perform the work. Most generally accepted is the definition proposed by Wilensky and Lebeaux (1958, p. 17n), who suggested that the term signifies "an occupation or profession, a group of people with more or less specified training and skills, who occupy key positions, along with other groups, in the provision of welfare services." The social work profession has developed and is transmitting to social work students a body of knowledge and a set of skills and attitudes considered necessary for the achievement of a professional perspective and of a focus designed to accomplish social welfare goals. In this connection Boehm (1959, p. 54) noted that while social work shared its perspective with most of the other helping professions, its focus on social relationships and on the interaction between man and his environment is its unique and distinguishing characteristic.

These are, of course, days of rapid and even radical change throughout the social system; social work is no exception. Like other units of society, social work has been more responsive to some changes and resistant toward others; some groups within the social work community have been more responsive to change than others as has been the case in all other professional fields. Any discussion of social work in the contemporary society needs to recognize and come to terms with at least three significant types of change: (1) the client, (2) sponsorship and delivery of service, and (3) personnel. These three areas of change will be discussed briefly here since they form, in one way, the very rationale for the relevance of contemporary social work.

1. Until very recently, and in some places still today, social work clients were stigmatized because of the assumption that poverty and dependence were either the results of or symptomatic of personal failure. The principle of "less eligible," inherited from the Elizabethan Poor Laws, mandated that those on "relief" or "welfare" should not be as well-off as the wage earner with the lowest income; symbolically, the "less eligible" principle was transferred to other helping situations. Yet at the very time that the poor and victimized were treated shabbily, they were also abandoned by large elements of the social welfare system, especially by the voluntary agencies (Cloward and Epstein, 1965). Government too provided more for the rich than for the poor, even though the federally assisted social security programs did provide a pittance for many of the poor. Schorr (1969) pointed out, for example, that the federal government's contribution to low-cost housing in 1962 for the bottom fifth of the population was $820 million, while the subsidy to the top fifth in the form of tax deductions for mortgage payments and loans was estimated at $1.7 billion.

One of the unplanned by-products of social work's abandonment of the poor and its subsequent concentration on service to the middle class was the development of the notion that successful therapeutic intervention could occur only when there was a similarity in expectation between clients and workers. Regardless of the correctness of this notion, its widespread acceptance effectively kept most therapy programs from the poor since they were adjudged as "not ready."

However, the poor and victimized were not to be denied. What some have called the "revolt of the client" took many forms in the 1960's: Welfare Rights Organizations, legal services for the poor, maximum feasible participation, etc. With the War on Poverty, the spotlight shifted again on services for the poor; although the "war" was abandoned by a government more concerned with military adventures than with people, it left an indelible imprint on the social scene. Services were no longer limited only to those who were "deserving"; citizens and consumers became beneficiaries of social services made available to all who were legally entitled to them. An equally important development was the shift in service delivery strategies, particularly the shift in focus from the individual to larger collectivities, such as communities and ethnic groups. This shift was based in part on a recognition that the client was only the carrier of problems, not the problem himself.

2. The sponsorship of services is also undergoing important changes. By sponsorship is meant the institution or set of agencies which have undertaken (or been assigned) the responsibility for the delivery of social work services. Originally, in the days of the Elizabethan Poor Law, almost all social work services were provided by local governments; it should be noted however that in other cultural settings, such as Catholic countries, it was the church rather than the municipality which provided social work services. But in the United States the government was always highly involved in social service programs, even during the 19th century when the proponents of laissez-faire doctrines demanded a reduction of government interference in all areas of life. President Pierce's well-known veto of the Million Acres Bill did not argue against governmental participation in social welfare activities (as is commonly suggested) but merely vetoed the involvement of the federal government in activities which he thought belongs to states and cities. However, the public services clearly were unable to cope with the increasing problems accompanying industrialization, urbanization, and large-scale immigration. Starting in the second quarter of the 19th century voluntary agencies began to assume responsibility for providing services not provided by the public sector. In time, the scope of the voluntary

sector by far exceeded that of the public sector; practically all innovations and all progress occurred in voluntary agencies. In fact,
these dominated the scene to such an extent that one can easily
forget the work of public welfare agencies which continued to exist,
though in relative obscurity. Only when society was on the brink of
collapse during the Great Depression did public services expand
sufficiently to assume again a primary role. Some argue that the
expansion of public services in the 1930's was not so much a response to needs as a Machiavellian attempt to preserve the societal
status quo by reducing the most festering problems. One needs to
understand, however, the nature of the New Deal "revolution" in
the social services. Prior to 1929 a large number of states already
operated widows' pension programs as well as other types of categorical assistance programs. The New Deal did not invent a new
type of social service program, but merely assumed for the federal
government some financial responsibility for many of these programs; the actual provision of services continued to remain in state
and local hands.

But the shift in sponsorship services goes beyond the shift from
voluntary to public and from local to state to federal government;
perhaps even more important is the increasing occurrence of innovative settings in which social services are provided. Instead of
delivering social services in "pure" social work agencies or in the
traditional social service departments of hospitals, there is now increasing utilization of natural community settings such as storefronts,
neighborhood clubs, street corners, congressmen's offices, etc. Not
only are social services brought to the client instead of requiring him
to come to a far-off office but deliberate attempts are made to reduce
the social distance between the worker and the recipient of services
by involving recipients in the very sponsorship of social services.

3. A third area of change involved the personnel delivering social
work services. While the days of Lady Bountiful when those who
wanted to do "good" needed only a heart full of good intentions and
a basket full of food are not yet forgotten, in recent decades a
deliberate attempt was made to have social work services provided
only by professional social workers who had earned an MSW degree;
however this goal was never reached since most workers, especially
those employed in public agencies, remained "untrained." But both
trained and untrained workers generally were the products of the
middle class and brought to social work a whole set of middle-class
values and norms. When working with clients who came from a
similar milieu, social distance was no problem; but this was a major

problem when social work resumed large-scale intervention efforts with the poor and rejected. In order to reduce the social distance increasing use has been made of "indigenous workers," i.e., workers who come from the same social background as the recipients. Thus, the Bureau of Indian Affairs has used native American workers, many public welfare agencies have employed ADC mothers, addicts have been used to treat addicts, etc. Utilization of indigenous workers serves to reduce social distance and tends to close the communication gap between the recipient population and the agency decision makers since they can explain each to the other. At the same time new employment opportunities are opened up to many of the hardcore unemployed.

SOCIAL INTERVENTION

Even though there are some who dislike the term "intervention" because of its potential Machiavellian implications, there is increasing recognition that this concept comprises the core of social work activity. Intervention need not mean meddling with someone else's business; thus, one dictionary definition is "to come between as an influencing force; come in to modify, settle, or hinder some action, argument, etc." (*Webster's New World Dictionary*, College Edition, 1964). Gordon (1962, p. 3) defined professional social work as the practice of "interventive action." Crisis theorists, both in social work and in psychiatry, talk of intervention in order to help people in crisis situations avoid the development of chronic disorders and coping patterns. And a recent book on social work stated quite clearly that "the major function of social work [is] the provision of interventive services at the level of the social system and at the level of the action" (Atherton, 1969, p. 421).

We talk of *social* intervention rather than merely intervention in order to highlight two considerations. (1) Since every person is part of a social system, help for an individual requires in some measure social intervention; even where the primary helping method is individualized psychological therapy thought needs to be given to the social environment to which the "cured" person will return. (2) Intervention may serve social as well as antisocial goals; when we use the term social intervention, we refer not only to the area of intervention but also to the goals. This does, of course, raise the basic question of who defines the goals. This question is especially important because social intervention is not viewed as a value-free technique but as a goal-focused process.

CONCLUSION – OR BEGINNING

A conclusion in an introduction is almost a contradiction in terms. Our purpose here has not been to present neat answers but rather to raise questions. All of the questions raised here will be explored in greater detail in the following selections. Because of the present nature of social work practice, the terminology used by various authors will differ – as will their findings. There is, however, a common thread underlying all of the selections – and that is the conviction that social work's task is far more than mending society's little mistakes. While helping people with problems, social workers are ready to address themselves to the roots of these problems. To do this successfully will require conviction, skill, understanding, and clarity of thought.

REFERENCES

ATHERTON, CHARLES R. 1969. "The Social Assignment of Social Work," *Social Service Review*, Vol. 43 (December), pp. 421–29.

BISNO, HERBERT. 1959. *The Place of the Undergraduate Curriculum in Social Work Education* (CSWE Curriculum Study, Vol. II). New York: Council on Social Work Education.

BOEHM, WERNER W. 1959. *Objectives of the Social Work Curriculum of the Future* (CSWE Curriculum Study, Vol. I). New York: Council on Social Work Education.

CLOWARD, RICHARD A., AND EPSTEIN, IRWIN. 1965. "Private Social Welfare's Disengagement from the Poor," in Mayer N. Zald (ed.), *Social Welfare Institutions*. New York: John Wiley & Sons, Inc. Pp. 623–44.

GORDON, WILLIAM E. 1962. "A Critique of the Working Definition," *Social Work*, Vol. 7 (October), pp. 3–13.

KIDNEIGH, JOHN C. 1960. "Social Work as a Profession," in Russell H. Kurtz (ed.), *Social Work Year Book*. New York: National Association of Social Workers. Pp. 563–72.

SCHORR, ALVIN L. 1969. *Explorations in Social Policy*. New York: Basic Books, Inc., Publishers.

TITMUSS, RICHARD M. 1965. "The Social Division of Welfare: Some Reflection on the Search for Equity," in Mayer N. Zald (ed.), *Social Welfare Institutions*. New York: John Wiley & Sons, Inc. Pp. 230–46.

UNITED NATIONS. 1950. *Training for Social Work: An International Survey*. New York: United Nations.

WELLS, LEORA WOODS. 1969. *Training Social Work Manpower*. New York: Council on Social Work Education.

WILENSKY, HAROLD L., AND LEBEAUX, CHARLES N. 1958. *Industrial Society and Social Welfare*. New York: Russell Sage Foundation.

SECTION II

Social Geography

INTRODUCTION

Social intervention generally occurs in response to someone identifying a condition as problematic or faulty. Usually the person who identifies the problem did not create it. But unless a condition becomes identified as a problem, it will not receive attention and will not become the object of any social intervention activity. For example, as long as racial discrimination was accepted as proper, no one did anything about it. It received attention and became the object of various social intervention strategies only after it was identified as a problem.

The manner in which a problem becomes identified will go a long way in determining the type and method of social intervention strategy employed. Assumptions about causation are crucial as is the general knowledge background that the problem definer has about the problem area. Often the problem definers are either too intimately involved with the problem or too far removed from it to adequately define it. Since all of us have grown up in families, we often find it difficult to objectively identify problems, both in our own family and in those of others. On the other hand, and perhaps more serious, many problem definers are too far removed from the victims of social problems to appreciate and understand what and how they suffer. Too often professionals live far away from the problem areas and have little contact with people other than those coming from their own backgrounds. Many beginning social workers have told us that they were quite unprepared for the "smell of poverty" which they faced on their first field trip to the ghetto or barrio.

Before a condition can be defined as a problem, it must be "seen" by someone. Alfred North Whitehead noted that "it requires a very unusual mind to undertake the analysis of the obvious." Many of the conditions now identified as problematic and requiring social intervention have existed for a long time, without being recognized as a problem. Just as it took Thomas Coram a long time to convince his 18th-century contemporaries that infants abandoned upon a dung heap were a social problem, so has it taken contemporary workers a long time to convince Congress that unemployment and underemployment are social problems which require the nation's attention. But the fact remains that a problem is made, not by the facts, but by the definition. Frequently, the identical objective condition will be defined as different types of problems in varying settings; or, in one setting a condition is viewed as a problem and in another it is not. For example, in a society where almost everybody is a high school graduate, the high school dropout constitutes a problem. But in a society where few are high school graduates the dropout presents no problem. When a hurricane strikes and leaves 4,000 families without homes, the nation's attention is mobilized and the federal government responds with crisis aid. But when 1,000 times that many families in our urban ghettos and barrios are virtually homeless, there is little excitement and less intervention. Objective conditions alone do not make for social problems. The facts are a necessary but not a sufficient cause for action.

A problem condition will be identified as a social problem only when it is believed to represent a threat to cherished social values. Societal resources will be mobilized for social intervention efforts only when the consequences of a problem situation are thought to be sufficiently serious for the future well-being of the society. But beyond representing a threat to society and societal values, action toward problem intervention requires that someone or some group assume responsibility for doing something about the problem condition. And unless the problem definer has power and resources or access to these, little will be done about the problem.

Perhaps the most crucial phase in developing a social intervention strategy is the way in which the problem is defined. Whether narcotic addicts are defined as criminals or sick people is basic and crucial in developing the social intervention strategy. And this definition depends not only upon the "facts," but more importantly, upon the knowledge and understanding of the problem definer about the problem and the people involved. Admittedly, people coming from different social classes will view the identical conditions differently. Similarly, people involved in the problem condition will view the problem differently from those who are not involved in it. The differential perception is due not only to different social location but is also the consequence of unlike value systems and assumptions. The Rashamon principle, derived from the Japanese movie by that name, where four people observed the identical crime from different positions, suggests that what the social intervention worker sees may not be what others see.

In order to become more skilled in problem identification it is vital that social workers and other intervention agents become better acquainted with the social geography of the victim population. Problems are not abstractions or theoretical inventions but involve real people in real communities. Those who practice social intervention need to become acquainted with the culture, social structure, and life-styles of those with whom they will work. Though Simmel ascribed certain functional consequences to the role of the stranger, the social intervention worker must not and cannot remain aloof from and strange to the community with which he works.

All communities have unique social and psychological geographies. In "La Raza—I Am You, You Are Me," Richard Yturregui, a VISTA Volunteer, begins to explore the "geography" of the Chicano (Mexican-American) community in Santa Fe, New Mexico. A major focus of "La Raza" is the cultural context which influenced how a helping person could intervene most successfully.

"Who Are the Poor?" explores definitions of poverty, age groups, work experience and the main groups of the poor. This report suggests the poor are mainly in four groups: the elderly, working-age adults who can work including large numbers of female heads of families, working-age adults who cannot work, and children in poor families. What strategy would best eliminate poverty—jobs, income supports, education? By what mechanisms and why has society selected certain groups to suffer poverty? What programs could be effective against the multitude of social ills which affect the poor?

How do American Indians live on reservations? In cities? "Native

Son" by Ellen Urvant highlights the meaning for individual American Indians of the tribe and of the sacred quality of the land; it considers various ways of improving their lives. How can our society redeem the broken promises and help create for American Indians a meaningful and hospitable environment?

A theme examined in "The Social Geography of Poverty" by Harold L. Sheppard is that poverty is associated with place of residence. Since rates of poverty differ in urban and rural settings, the regions in which people live make a real difference. Urbanization tends to reduce poverty for families headed by males, nonwhite as well as white, but not for families headed by females. What are the risks of growing up in a poor community? How much information do we have about the relationship between personality characteristics, family structure, where people live, and poverty?

Dr. Jack Geiger in "Slavery: One Hundred Years Later" indicts our society for the damage done by neglect, omission, hunger, and unemployment. In a devastating catalog of injustices committed on the residents of one Mississippi county, he shows the vulnerability of people who have endured slavery, tenant farming, and an agricultural system which in the end declares them surplus. Must the poor pay the cost of social progress? What is the price our society pays for the degradation and deprivation in this and other counties? What would it take to "turn it around?"

Mary W. Wright in "The Dusty Outskirts of Hope—Public Assistance in the Appalachian South" portrays the everyday realities which face a 45-year-old father of six who asks for help. The cumulative effect of a thousand small decisions prevents him from receiving the assistance to which he and his family is entitled. What support and advocacy can a concerned worker offer? Who is at fault when a man does not get help? What happens to a man when lack of transportation and long waiting lines combine with larger societal forces to defeat a person's best attempts? Should bureaucracies be held accountable for not implementing services to which people are entitled? What does a society lose when it forces a generation of people to live on less than it knows a family needs to survive?

How do poor black people live in a tidewater county in South Carolina? Dr. Donald Gatch in "Hunger in South Carolina" describes how local needs are related to several levels of government and how a local system works for and against people. He goes beyond the nutritional and medical needs of people to show how racism, the economy, housing, are intertwined with the lives of people. What can a county do on its own to guarantee basic subsistence for families? What has location to do with jobs? What responsibilities do professionals have?

Elizabeth Herzog in "Facts and Fictions about the Poor" illustrates the need to view statistical data in context and to avoid oversimplification and misapplication of concepts. In a thoughtful review she examines facts and fictions about out-of-wedlock births and relates these to such concepts as "culture of poverty," school achievement, family norms and forms, and social class. What are the facts? Does one's perspective influence how "facts" are viewed? How do we oversimplify facts? How can we avoid that error and consequent misapplication of facts?

"Family Functioning in the Low-Income Black Community" by Andrew Billingsley moves beyond the "tangle of pathology" hypothesis to an examination and careful reading of family functioning by low-income blacks. He demonstrates the high degree of "copability," self-respect, strength, and the many variations which exist in those families. What strategies for service can be built on the strengths of black communities and black families?

In "Looking for Work" by Edgar May, the attempts of one young man to find work are traced over a year's time. How much courage does it take to persist, to continue, to try day after day? What can society do to help such a young man? In what system can we intervene most effectively? How did society invest in the preparation of work for this young man? Are there two welfare systems—one for the middle class and another for the poor?

The readings selected for this section raise these and other questions without giving definitive answers. But a thorough understanding of the questions is prerequisite to developing appropriate intervention strategies.

· 2 ·

BETTY MURPHY

La Raza—I Am You, You Are Me

Richard Yturregui, 23, of Brooklyn, N.Y., and a graduate of Manhattan College, was a VISTA Volunteer for eight months in the Spanish-American neighborhood of Torreon in Santa Fe, N.M. In May, he was assigned as a VISTA leader in northern New Mexico. Short, stocky, blue-eyed and fair with a slight Brooklyn accent, he is not Latin in appearance but his Spanish background helped him identify with poor Spanish-Americans and establish a close relationship with them. The following is an interview with Yturregui by a VISTA writer.

YTURREGUI: In the city of Santa Fe, New Mexico, there is a section called Torreon. Here Meredith Jones, and I, VISTA Volunteers, started to work on the 7th of August last year. I found that it was difficult to discover where the poverty was. In the Southwest poverty tends to be associated with quaintness—the old adobe homes, the unpaved streets. In Harlem one doesn't walk away thinking how quaint it is.

Poverty in Santa Fe is subtle, a problem of underemployment rather than unemployment, malnutrition rather than starvation. The issues aren't so much racial. Lots of Spanish-Americans are in the city government yet the poor don't start clapping when a Latin gets elected. He doesn't drop his culture or his lodging, but he often learns to use the Anglo culture and, to the poor, he is no longer Spanish-American in feeling. He refuses to look back on what he has left and to the poor people, he is a sell out. In their mind, you can't hold office and be Spanish-American.

There is a feeling of inferiority on the part of most Spanish-Americans. They are different. When a Spanish-American who has made it gets together with another professional who is Anglo, he feel inferior. He's running around with a broken accent and it sets him apart. It is something he has grown up with. Here the merchants are mostly Anglo. The teachers, the doctors, the lawyers. There are not many Spanish-Americans between the poor and those who work in city hall. And the poor naturally have more

SOURCE: Reprinted from *VISTA Volunteer*, September, 1969, pp. 14–19.

contact with the merchants and doctors than city hall. They feel they are being made fun of constantly. They resent their stereotyped image—every Spanish-American has to love chili. They're all fat and dark, sitting with their legs crossed with big hats over their noses. I've met Spanish-Americans who don't like chili. I don't like it, but I'm Spanish too. Spanish Basque. I was born in New York, but I'm first generation here. My family came over in 1939 from Spain, on account of the revolution. They were on the wrong side.

VISTA: Did this background put you on the right side with people in Torreon?

YTURREGUI: Not at first. At that time I had a beard and rode a blue English bicycle.

VISTA: How did you hope to be accepted coming in like that?

YTURREGUI: My philosophy was to let them accept me as I am and I'd accept them as they are and we would work together from a common base of acceptance.

I have had some past experience in this working two summers in Mexico so I knew what had to be done. You try to show the poor what alternatives they have and then you get your sweet head out of there, because otherwise you become a dictator.

VISTA: How did you start out organizing Torreon?

YTURREGUI: With the children. Meredith and I met up with a bunch of kids playing and they started asking us questions. "Where are you from?" "And are you happy? Are you this? Are you that?" I just answered back with questions. "Are you a hippy?" And they'd ask, "What's a hippy?" We had water balloon fights with them in the middle of the street and we played football. One kid was about two foot nothing and I'd give him the football and pick him up and run with him over my head. The kids would be tagging me and I would say you didn't touch the guy with the ball. All this built a rapport with the kids which is still in existence. It wasn't long before people in the neighborhood became aware that I was there. One kid tells another kid. This type of thing, which is kind of irrelevant to the work on poverty but which you need to get established in a community. Pretty soon guys my age—21, and under, started watching us. About nine of them pulled a kind of machismo on me one night.

VISTA: What is a machismo?

YTURREGUI: Rough, brutal, he-man type action. Playing the role of the macho—the John Wayne, Ernest Hemingway image—is their approach to manhood. Yet the Spanish-American himself is easy going, friendly. Internally they are poets. They are very sensitive. Externally, they overact as machos.

These guys wanted to show me they are machos. One guy took out his knife and started to whittle a post and before I knew it, I had nine guys in front of me whittling down the post. I just sat there and looked at them. Finally I went up to them and spoke to them as one human being to another, not down or up to them. "Let's have a meeting," I said. "Let's talk." So we had a meeting and we talked. This was the initial breakthrough.

VISTA: What did you talk about?

YTURREGUI: Girls, sex, politics vaguely. Gradually they opened up with such comments as, "I'm going to the Army." Another guy would say, "I'll never go into the Army. This country has never done anything for me." Then they would all look at me to see what way I swung.

VISTA: Did they think of you as a fellow Spanish-American?

YTURREGUI: At the second or third meeting, after I had enticed them to come visit me as an Anglo, I began speaking Spanish more fluently than they did. I told them that Spanish was my first language and that my family speaks broken English. And I know the frustrations of growing up with parents who can't communicate with the guy in the subway token booth. Also the fact that I went into kindergarten not knowing a word of English. I cried and yelled for two days before a Puerto Rican girl came in to interpret for me. When I told the guys this, I was one of them because I knew what they were up against.

VISTA: Were you also from a poor family?

YTURREGUI: My family is middle class, but I lived in a poverty area on the Lower East Side of New York until the 5th grade. I identify with the Spanish-Americans by being from a minority—not knowing English as a child and eating different foods. My name isn't Jones, it's Yturregui and nobody pronounces it right. Also it begins with Y which means I sat in the last seat in the back row in schools. They feel inferior. Myself, I felt equal, but different.

I know the difficulty of communicating without knowing the language or mispronouncing the language—saying share for chair, shurch for church. I sympathize with their problem of getting along and I feel their poverty syndrome. I feel it in me.

I share their lack of father image. My father was a pantryman with the Merchant Marine and he was at sea most of his life. The Spanish-Americans seem patriarchal, but they are actually matriarchal. Their fathers are really verbalizing the mothers' decisions. Spanish-American males rarely make decisions in the household without consulting the mother, who is usually the stronger of the two.

I feel some of this and it has given me a sensitivity. I've even over-identified and became too cautious because of a fear of turning people off. You get that sensitivity and twist it around and use it in a professional way, like Louis Juarez who is working in Albuquerque with poor Mexican-Americans. He has what it takes to be a community organizer. When he looks at a Mexican-American opening a door he knows. "I was you. You were me."

VISTA: After you established an identity with the nine guys at the whittling post what did you do?

YTURREGUI: The next step was to draw things out. They told me. "I need a high school diploma." "I'm in trouble with the police." "I'm in contempt of court." The guy who wanted the diploma needed a half credit in English.

I took him to the high school principal who did absolutely nothing except direct us to a counselor. The counselor met me on a personal level. "Oh yes. You're Spanish. A Basque from Spain. I'll do anything for you." Just because I'm Spanish Basque. The guy got his diploma after four months of tutoring which the counselor managed.

Another guy had the contempt of court charge for a traffic violation. He was 17 years old, had no money and was scared silly they were going to send him to the pen. We went to see the judge. He reduced the fine from $30 to $5. So all of a sudden I was, "Richard, good buddy. He not only talks but he does things for you."

VISTA: Didn't bestowing favors change your relationship?

YTURREGUI: I think we had established a rapport, a very strong one, but not a real friendship. They saw me — I can't pull any punches about it — much as a private in the Army might look at a sergeant. After a couple of months I asked them to find me a house in the area. They kept saying they were looking but they couldn't come up with anything. I found one, three houses away from where one of the guys lived, an indication that they weren't really looking too hard.

They thought, "Let's not have him in our backyard all the time. We really rip the hell out of that guy behind his back — for his beard, his stupid shoes and so on." I know this happens because I kind of went through it myself. In any event, I moved in and gave them the front room for a club house.

Another time, two of the guys got into a fight over a date. One was beating the other with a chain and kicking him. I stepped in and grabbed him and spun him over a car. Then he started coming at me with the chain. I thought, "This is it, right across the head." He got so close, but dropped it. If I were his friend, I'm sure he would have hit me because he just got through beating on a kid who had been his friend for as long as he knows. But there was kind of a bond created just out of this one incident. After the fight, they all came inside and we had a meeting. The guy who was beaten up sat down and cried, cold sober. The guy who beat him up kept saying, "You ought to go to the hospital, man. Are you hurt?" "No," replied the guy who was crying. "It's not a hurt in the head. It's a hurt down here," he said, pointing to his heart.

They're sensitive guys. A guy who lives in a poverty area, he's as sensitive as maybe an F. Scott Fitzgerald or an Ernest Hemingway or great poets. He just doesn't have the outlet to express it. He cries at the drop of a hat — and here is a sensitive human being. This is what I saw in the people which I think is very important.

VISTA: But how did helping guys in a teenage gang help you to reach the adults?

YTURREGUI: At the same time I was working with the guys, Meredith Jones was running an arts and crafts class for a group of children. She got to know their mothers. Through them and the guys we found out about adults in the neighborhood who had problems.

Some fellow on this street can't pay his hospital bill. Another is having difficulties with the Veterans Administration. A mother and father with kids are having problems with the welfare department. One by one, as with the guys, we tackled these problems, utilizing Santa Fe institutions and special funds to help these people. Word spread up and down the streets—that we were doing things for people, not just making promises. Through this whole thing was the storm that was coming—major issues set up before I got there—Model Cities.

VISTA: What is Model Cities going to do for the people in Torreon?

YTURREGUI: Model Cities is going to spend $5 million, on everything from sewerage to education, in seven areas of Santa Fe. Torreon is one. The city council was going to each area to explain the program. The Torreon meeting was last November 28th.

We went around the neighborhood—myself, Meredith, a couple of community aides and one of the guys I had worked with—and distributed flyers to each of 145 families in the area telling them, "$5 million is going to be spent in Santa Fe in the next five years. Your streets are rotten, your houses are falling apart, your health and education facilities are poor. If you want this changed—if you want some of that $5 million for Torreon—move. Come to the meeting."

Juan Rodrigas, the gang member who was helping us, had lived in Torreon all his life. He knew the people. He knew what they wanted and appealed to their specific needs. "You want more room in your home. Model Cities can build new rooms for you. You've been complaining about not having paved streets for seven years. Model Cities will pave your streets." And so on.

We visited each family four weeks before the meeting and again two weeks later. We held two workshops to explain what Model Cities was. Three hours before the meeting, we went around in a Volkswagen with banners on the side, beeping the horn, yelling at people, "Come to the Model Cities meeting."

We were the last area to meet with the city council. The largest turnout in the six other areas was 60 people. Torreon had more than 90 people. People we had done favors for felt they owed us a favor. But there were others we had not worked for. I think the community was ripe for this type of thing. The people were ready—not for pie in the sky—for Model Cities, $5 million which they knew was a fact.

VISTA: How did you form a firm neighborhood association out of one meeting?

YTURREGUI: It was announced that each area had to have an advisory board representative backed by a steering committee in the neighborhood. So we asked everyone in the area and got seven nominees and held an election. We distributed 187 ballots door to door and collected 143. And who wins but Bob Wilson, an Anglo who owns an electronics company.

I knew why they had done this: the old Spanish patron system where one man looks after all the interests and is supported by the people who look on him as their protector. They felt Bob Wilson lived in the area and he would become their patron.

The next step was to get a group to serve as a steering committee for the neighborhood. With the help of Juan Rodrigas, we selected whom we thought the best people were and invited them to be on the committee by letter. We ended up with 11 members, the majority of whom are Spanish-American. The advisory board representative was directly responsible to the committee for all his actions — which is as it should be. Bob Wilson quit.

VISTA: Who runs the steering committee now?

YTURREGUI: The same 11 people form the core, holding meetings for all the people in the neighborhood. They elected a chairman. He had leadership potential, but like many Spanish-Americans, lacked confidence speaking publicly. He was very quiet and self-conscious at first, but I knew he had it in him to go through the door. He heard me sort of making fun of myself when I started speaking and he adopted it. Now he is not afraid to speak and knows how to put himself and his audience at ease by making little jokes.

The fact of the matter is that these Spanish-American poor have a hell of a lot of good ideas. They have the fight spirit. They just have to learn the value of organization.

So I worked with them. What does Torreon need — so they need streets. If one man goes up to City Hall and says he wants streets, is anybody going to listen? If one man stands on the corner and yells, nobody will turn around. If 100 people are on that corner whispering, somebody is going to hear it. "You don't have a voice. I don't care what you scream about, just get that voice."

At first they were very skeptical about what progress they would make. "So what if we get together?" they would say. "We're not going to be able to do anything anyway." But there was always a fraction of a thought that said, "Gee, maybe we could." They learned. They know now that the essence of their problems is organization. They know that nobody is going to give them something for nothing.

When I saw that they were running their own meetings, fighting their own fight on their own, I dropped out — eight months after I arrived.

VISTA: How is the organization working now?

YTURREGUI: Still struggling. Eleven people fighting for a share in Model Cities. And they're trying to get more people in, because they are finally realizing their political strength — with numbers they can ask.

VISTA: What do you think the group's chances are of developing into a strong, permanent association?

YTURREGUI: People could drift apart. The building could collapse. If the rent's not paid, everything could get thrown out in the street. It could fall flat because of money or disillusionment with the Model Cities system which they have to tackle.

What we did, however, was develop people that in certain cases were apathetic or suspicious and afraid of being taken advantage of. We developed from apathy to activism—from "Gee, I'd really like to do something for my kids, my neighborhood, but I don't know how," to "Here's how." Whether this spirit continues or not, only the future will tell. But even if the group ceases to be an organization, it has given the people a chance to prove their worth—as Spanish-Americans—as human beings.

· 3 ·

SENATE COMMITTEE ON LABOR AND PUBLIC WELFARE

Who Are the Poor?

A strong national commitment to eliminate poverty must be backed by a thoughtful understanding of the nature of the problem. Otherwise, resources cannot be wisely utilized.

The place to start is to realize that the poor are like other Americans in most respects. They have the same human needs and desires: sufficient food, clean air, safe water, decent shelter, satisfactory clothing, good health, adequate medical care, the love and nurture of family life, opportunity for useful work, the feeling of self-worth, the experience of beauty as personally conceived, freedom of action conditioned by social responsibility, and equal justice under law. The poor want a chance to share in the fruits of society and to participate fully in community life. They should be entitled to such opportunities.

To the extent that the poor are unable to fulfill these needs, economic insecurity is a major factor. After all, we live in a money economy, and case income enables a family to satisfy its needs for food, clothing, and shelter, and to obtain medical, legal, and other necessary services. Money provides freedom of choice in housing and patterns of personal consumption, and public programs of com-

SOURCE: Reprinted from "Toward Economic Security for the Poor," a report prepared by the Subcommittee on Employment, Manpower and Poverty of the U.S. Senate Committee on Labor and Public Welfare, Washington, D.C., October, 1968, pp. 7–13. This report was prepared by Howard Hallman and Harold L. Sheppard with the assistance of the subcommittee staff.

modity distribution or free services can never fully provide the flexibility of cash income. Money is not everything, but in our society it is a lot—as both the poor and the nonpoor realize. Poverty has more dimensions than the lack of money, but let us never forget the truism that being poor is not having sufficient income to live as other Americans live.

But let us also be careful that in talking about "the poor" we do not make the mistake of lumping them all in a single, homogeneous group. The poor are not all alike, and as we understand their varied characteristics we will be better able to devise the programs necessary for the abolition of poverty.

A. POVERTY DEFINED

When the poverty program was first proposed in 1964, the poverty line was drawn at $3,000 for families and $1,500 for persons living alone. Since then the Social Security Administration has developed and the Office of Economic Opportunity and other Federal agencies have adopted a poverty index which relates to family size and differentiates between farm and nonfarm families. This index has as its core the economy food plan, developed by the Department of Agriculture, which provides total food expenditure of 75 cents per person per day in a four-person family (1966 prices). The index adds twice this amount to cover all family living items other than food, and makes annual adjustments to allow for rising prices. Farm families are assumed to raise part of their food supply, and their poverty index, including nonfood expenditures, is placed proportionately lower than for nonfarm families. By this measure, the poverty line for a nonfarm family of four is $3,335 and for a four-person farm family is $2,345.

The subcommittee has accepted the SSA poverty index for this report because it is the basis for most of the available Federal statistics. However, the subcommittee has three reservations. First, the poverty line may be drawn too low for what our society can properly afford for all its citizens. Any middle- or upper-income housewife trying to feed her family for 75 cents per person per day will understand why. Second, the differential for farm families seems too great, particularly since the lower food budget is used as a ratio applied to other family expenditures, whereas for many items farm families have to pay the same as nonfarm families and their transportation costs may be even higher. Third, the use of a national average does not account for higher costs of living in some places, such as due to higher rent in cities and greater heating bills in northern regions. When these things are considered, the number who are truly poor is undoubtedly higher than the figures used in this report, but no better data are available.

B. AGE GROUPS OF THE POOR

In 1966 there were 29.7 million poor persons in the United States, according to a survey made by the Bureau of the Census.[1] Of these, 60 percent were too young or too old to work according to our usual concept of working ages. They included 12.5 million children under age 18 living in poor families and 5.4 million elderly persons aged 65 and over, who are past the conventional retirement age. The 40 percent of the poor between ages 18 and 64 consisted of 2.1 million adults living alone, 4.6 million family heads (3 million males, 1.6 million females), and 5.1 million wives and other adult family members. This is illustrated in Figure 3-1.

In a society like ours where employment is the primary source of income, those who are not working are generally the worst off. It is not surprising, therefore, that of all age groups the incidence of poverty is greatest among the elderly since most of them are no longer employed. In 1966, three out of every 10 elderly persons were poor, or about twice the national rate for all ages. Of the elderly persons living in families of two or more persons, 20 percent of them were poor, but of the elderly who were living alone, 55 percent were poor.

Deeper analysis indicates that the situation is even worse. Omitted from the Federal poverty count is the population of institutions, such as nursing homes and homes for the elderly where an estimated 700,000 elderly poor live. Another 1.7 million persons 65 and over have insufficient income of their own to rise above the threshhold of poverty but live with nonpoor families even though the majority of them would probably prefer to live independently. If these were combined with 5.4 million elderly poor of official statistics, the total would be 7.8 million. With these added, the incidence of poverty among the elderly is slightly over 40 percent.

Of all the population groups, the elderly poor have gained the

---

[1]At the end of July, 1968, OEO released preliminary overall figures of the poverty population as of 1967, indicating the decline in that category to 25.9 million. No other detailed numbers or categories were provided.

least in recent years. Their numbers have dropped one-half million since 1959, but there has been no numerical reduction since 1964. Moreover, one group of the elderly poor—women living alone—has increased from 1.8 million in 1959 to 2.1 million in 1966. Each year a higher proportion of the poor consists of the elderly, rising from 15 percent in 1959 to 18 percent in 1966.

FIGURE 3–1
Poor Persons, by Age Groups, 1966
(in millions)

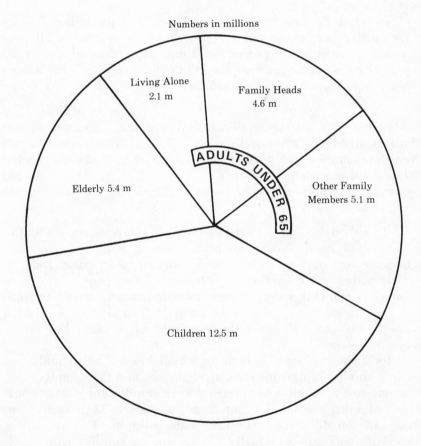

Numbers in millions

Living Alone
2.1 m

Family Heads
4.6 m

ADULTS UNDER 65

Elderly 5.4 m

Other Family
Members 5.1 m

Children 12.5 m

TOTAL 29.7 million

The proportion of children among the poor has held steady at about 43 percent in both 1959 and 1966. However, since most children are in family units, it is more meaningful to examine the situation of poor families rather than considering children alone.

C. HOUSEHOLD TYPES AMONG THE POOR

In 1966, there were 4.6 million families headed by persons under age 65. Of these family heads, 3 million were men and 1.6 million were women.

The trend is toward an increase in the proportion of female-headed families among the poor, from 23 percent of all poor families in 1959 to 30 percent in 1966. The effect of this trend becomes even more apparent when the incidence of poverty among these types of families is examined, as follows:

Chance of Being Poor

All families with head under 65............................11 out of 100
White families with male heads..............................6 out of 100
Nonwhite families with male heads.......................24 out of 100
White families with female heads ....31 out of 100
Nonwhite families with female heads.....................62 out of 100

Thus, although slightly over two-thirds of the poor are white, the incidence of poverty is much higher among nonwhites, most of whom are Negroes but with a sizable number of American Indians. Among male-headed families, the chance of being poor is four times greater for nonwhites than whites. Female-headed, nonwhite families have twice the chance of being poor than do female-headed white families and 10 times the incidence for families headed by white men.

Indeed, the incidence is high for female-headed households, but when a number of persons are considered we find that slightly more than one-half of the poor (52 percent) were found in the conventional family of father-mother-children. Nearly a quarter (23 percent) were living in female-headed families with children. The remaining one-fourth were almost equally divided among families with an elderly head and usually no children (9 percent), elderly persons living alone (9 percent), and persons under age 65 living alone (7 percent). This is shown in Figure 3–2.

FIGURE 3 – 2
Poor Persons, by Household Type, 1966
(in millions)

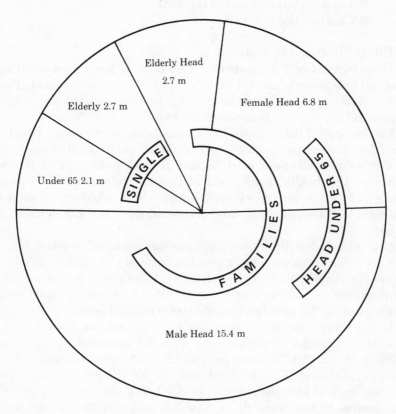

Elderly Head
2.7 m

Elderly 2.7 m

Female Head 6.8 m

Under 65 2.1 m

SINGLE

FAMILIES

HEAD UNDER 65

Male Head 15.4 m

TOTAL 29.7 million

D. WORK EXPERIENCE OF THE POOR

Since three-fourths of the poor are in families headed by a person under age 65, it is important to know to what extent employment provides them their foundation for economic security.

In 1966, the work experience of the heads of these 4.6 million families was as follows:

3.0 million had male heads, of whom —

 1.5 million worked the full year.

 1.0 million worked part of the year.

 0.5 million did not work.

1.6 million had female heads, of whom—
0.3 million worked the full year.
0.5 million worked part of the year.
0.7 million did not work.

This is illustrated in Figure 3–3.

Thus, two out of five heads under 65 of poor families worked full time, all year round; but still their families were impoverished. They were unable to rise above the poverty line because of low wages, large families, or a combination of the two.

Another one-third of these family heads under 65 worked part of the year or in some instances part time all year round. They were unable to find full-time work or not able to hold a job full time because of ill health, family responsibilities, or some other reason. Age was a factor; for among male heads who worked, 62 percent of those under 55 worked full time compared to 42 percent of those 55 to 64.

Altogether 3.3 million poor family heads under 65 worked full or part time. This amounts to 72 percent of such poor families, which shows clearly that they are trying to work their way out of poverty. Furthermore, 1.2 million of these families had two or more wage earners during the year but nonetheless remained poor.

At the same time there were another 1.2 million poor families headed by persons of working age who did not work at all during 1966. Of these, 468,000 were men and 741,000 were women. Of the men, 292,000 were ill or disabled, and 176,000 did not work for other reasons, such as attending school or not being able to find a job. Of the women, 85,000 were ill or disabled, and 656,000 did not work mostly because of family responsibilities, although a number were in school or had other reasons for not working. Thus, of the 1.2 million working-age heads of poor families who did not work in 1966, about one-half had child-care responsibilities and another one-third were ill or disabled.

In addition to the 4.5 million persons under 65 who head poor families, the poverty population includes 2.1 million working-age adults who live alone; 509,000 of them are between the ages of 14 and 24, 743,000 are 25 to 54; and 872,000 are 55 to 64. All told, two-thirds are at the beginning (14-24) or at the end (55-64) of the normal working ages. In comparison, only 30 percent of the family heads are in these younger and older age groups.

In 1966, 1.3 million of the 2.1 million poor single persons of working age were employed at least part of the time. Of these,

FIGURE 3–3
Work Experience of Heads under Age 65 of
Poor Families, 1966
(in millions)

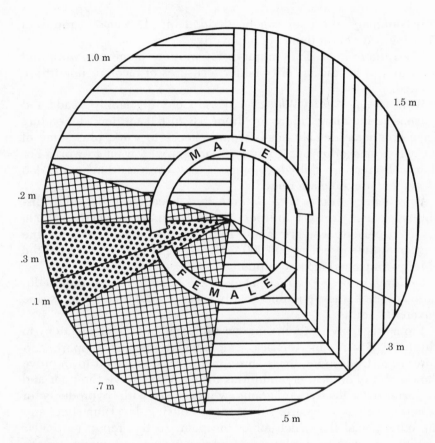

TOTAL 4.5 million

KEY

Didn't Work

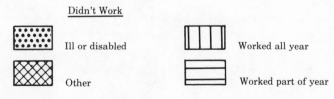

Ill or disabled

Worked all year

Other

Worked part of year

426,000 worked full time for 40 to 52 weeks, and the others worked less. Of the 850,000 who did not work, 290,000 were ill or disabled.

E. MAIN GROUPS OF THE POOR

In summary, the poor can be divided into four main groups in devising ways to lift them out of poverty:

The Elderly Poor. They number 5.4 million. Some can work and want to, but for the majority better measures of income support are needed.

Working-age Adults Who Can Work. Counting family heads and persons living alone, there are from 5.3 to 6.0 million, depending upon how many female heads would choose to work, plus some of the wives and other adult family members who want to work. For them job creation, skill development, day care assistance, and job placement are the main remedies.

Working-age Adults Who Cannot Work because of ill health, disability, or family responsibilities. This group includes nearly 500,000 disabled persons who are family heads or live alone, and a sizable portion of the more than 600,000 nonworking female heads. Like the elderly, they need income support.

Children in Poor Families. They total 12.5 million. For them education of the highest possible quality is essential if they are to escape poverty as adults.

From this analysis, then, emerges the broad outline of a strategy to eliminate poverty in America: employment, income support, and education. Underlying these three main thrusts is need to improve the capability of local communities to reach and serve the poor and to carry out effective programs which deal with byproducts of poverty, such as ill health, substandard housing, legal injustice, and the other social ills which afflict the poor. In this report particular attention is given to employment and income support, which are the major ways of achieving greater economic security for those who are now poor.

·4·

ELLEN URVANT

Native Son

In spite of racial prejudice that has kept the Indian down over the years, in spite of the repeated acts of broken faith by our government, in spite of the brutal treatment of a defeated people and inadequate attempts to return to them pride, dignity and economic well being, Americans are fascinated with Indians.

Because if you are Indian, then you were here on this land before the white man came. Your ties go back to that mysterious time before the "discovery" of America; you are related to the rain and the rocks and trees; you are close to your origins.

This view of man as one with nature is central to the Indian culture. It is predicated on the theory that man is an integral part of an environment, not a creature who has dominance in it. As such it is in conflict with the technological society, which acts on the theory that things are to be used — or mis-used — by man.

Historically, policy has been to stamp out Indian culture, not to preserve it. America simply had no time, no place for Indian-ness. At first, Indians were simply in the way; they were taking up land the settlers wanted. Perhaps co-existence would never have been possible — life styles of some tribes shocked the sensibilities of some of the newcomers, and vice versa. But the moving force in the Indians' dispossession was the white settlers' desire for the Indian land.

The Indians and the settlers represented two entirely opposing concepts of land. The settlers' way of life depended on ownership of land — what he owned was his private wealth, a negotiable asset that added to his person.

To the Indian the land was not something you could get something from, but was something that gave of itself, and was therefore revered. You didn't "have" land, you received from it. In negotiating with the white settlers over territorial rights, the Indian did not intend to open the land up to great numbers who would destroy the

SOURCE: Reprinted from *VISTA Volunteer*, Vol. 5, No. 6 (June, 1969), pp. 3–8.

hunting grounds. And so began the wars and mistrust and misunderstanding.

Andrew Jackson's rationale for the destruction of the Indian way of life, and forced removal of eastern tribes to Indian Territory was expressed in a statement to Congress in the last century.

". . . true philanthropy could not wish to see this continent restored to the condition in which it was found by our forefathers. What good man would prefer a country covered with forests and ranged by a few thousand savages to our extensive Republic, studded with cities, towns, and prosperous farms, embellished with all the improvements which art can devise or industry execute, occupied by more than 12,000,000 happy people, and filled with all the blessings of liberty, civilization, and religion?"

Even after tribes had been destroyed or penned up on reservations, their tribal organizations crippled or broken, there was little appreciation of Indian values or ways. They were not an acceptable part of society. They could not be allowed to interfere with progress.

The Indian is still a shadowy figure in our society despite the fact that today there are more than 560,000 people (some estimate 700,000) classified as Indians because of blood and/or ties to tribes or reservation life.

Three hundred different tribes or bands live in 28 states, on 290 reservations, or on allotted or tribally owned land. All of the land (50 million acres) is held in trust for Indians by our government. Reservations range in size from tiny settlements of only a few acres to the Navajo Reservation of about 14 million acres in Arizona, New Mexico and Utah. Other reservations with as much as 10 million acres are in Arizona, Washington, South Dakota, Wyoming and Montana.

Tribes are technically subordinate and independent nations within our nation. That is, they govern themselves as long as their laws are agreeable to Congress.

It has rarely been recognized how deep-rooted is the tribe in the individual — even in the disorganized state to which many tribes have fallen. Members of various tribes are often lumped together as "Indians," with little recognition for their tribal differences. In the past, the Indian's whole being and concept of himself was tied up with the tribal body of which he was a member. His role as a father, husband, brother was strictly defined. He knew exactly what was expected of him. Anything a member did had an effect on all the others — he could not speak or feel just for himself. For him to turn his back on his people was to take something away from them.

The Indians were offered nothing that could take the place of their tribal membership. Society was not really ready to accept them as they were, to give them a dignified role. In reservation schools run by the government and in public schools, Indians have been taught the white man's version of history, which does little to enhance the Indian's image of himself. Society asked the impossible of him — that he die as an Indian and be born again as a "white" American.

Many Indian children grow up to see themselves as foreigners in their own land. They are torn by the choice between the Indian way or the white way. If you go away and become educated in white schools and return to the reservation or to your family, you may not be accepted. If you stay on the reservation, you are shutting out the other society. Many Indian children feel they have no choice but to stay — with a language difficulty, lagging behind in basic education, they have no place to go.

A Passamaquoddy Indian, whose home base is a reservation in Maine, is one of many Indians who travel the country working on bridges, high construction jobs, other seasonal work, and then return to the reservation to rest, relax, and await a new job.

He is unrecognized by his fellow workers as Indian. Many think he is foreign because of his accent.

"Indian kids grow up to think they are nobody," he said.

A study of the suicide rate in a 10-year period of the Shoshone-Bannock Indians (ending in 1968), revealed the rate in one community to be 10 times the national average. Most of those who took their lives were under 36, most were male. Many young Indians turn to alcohol, and in the words of anthropologist Peter Farb, "die a psychological death at an early age."

Since the time of their ultimate military defeat, the Indians have been at the mercy of the government. In spite of their pleas and need, they have seen their best land taken. Some see themselves as a joke in society. They have seen solemn promises broken again and again. They have never been able to make decisions for themselves, to learn by trial and error. Even though their tribes are technically sovereign nations, they cannot plan a program, spend their tribal money without government approval. The government has always known what was best for the Indian. If the Indian has been uncooperative, it is because he has little desire to help the white man complete this total cultural domination.

Few volunteers are prepared for the cultural differences or the physical isolation that they must often cope with on an Indian reservation. VISTA Volunteers working on Indian reservations have learned that in order to accomplish anything they must adjust to the

Indians' pattern of life. The Volunteer may feel as though he is in another country, where people speak a different language, have different customs and mores.

The 175 VISTA Volunteers working among Indians today are involved in a great variety of activities: tribal newsletters, tutoring programs, craft cooperatives, community action for sanitation, water supplies, better housing, recreation, education, and other issues.

One of the most important roles, and one that all perform, is as liaison for the Indian and the surrounding community. The close proximity of two different cultures makes differences more evident and conflicts natural. There is always a certain amount of prejudice between Indians and whites in nearby communities. Some people who will not listen to or cannot understand the Indian will listen to the VISTA, paving the way for direct communication between the Indian and white communities.

Language itself is often a problem. The Indian who is most eloquent in his own language often finds it difficult to express himself in English. This can be particularly difficult when documents, letters to authorities, resolutions, or papers meant to explain the Indian view to non-Indians are involved. VISTA Volunteers who have good skills in writing or who have training in law serve, upon request, as translators or interpreters in tribal correspondence.

Thus law student VISTA Jon Spack is working with the Three Affiliated Tribes (Arikara, Mandan, Hidatsa) at the Fort Berthhold Reservation in North Dakota, on the revision of their constitution and tribal code. The content is decided strictly by the council members; the Volunteer advises only on wording and technicalities, since the documents must be approved by the United States Government.

"Since I am not a lawyer, the help I can give is limited," Spack said. "The tribes want and need an attorney." One of Spack's main projects, therefore, is to help the tribes apply for a VISTA attorney or an OEO legal aid program. In this case, as in many, the Volunteer's education and experience has given him knowledge of bureaucratic procedure valuable to the Indians.

Indian tribes are looking for more Volunteers with skills in law, medicine, home building, business, and other areas. But the Volunteer who has good knowledge of available resources, both government and private—who knows where to go for help to get various programs started, and who knows how to manipulate red tape—is much wanted and needed.

There are numerous pitfalls for the VISTA among Indians: one of the most common is his being associated with one faction within the tribe, and thus alienating himself from the others. On many Indian reservations, certain families are friends and allies with certain other families; disputes and conflict between different factions can provide friction. If a Volunteer is aligned with a certain faction, he may never gain the trust or confidence of others. When he makes a friend, he is in danger of making an enemy of someone else. His problem is to make it clear that he wants to use his skills, knowledge and know-how for the benefit of the tribe.

Probably the greatest pitfall for the Volunteer is the assumption that the Indian is ready and willing to learn a different culture. The VISTA should understand that the Indian has his own way and manner of doing things, that he likes his way partly because it is Indian and not like middle-class white America.

Before any of the VISTA's own ideas will be considered or accepted by Indians, he will have to respect Indian values and be willing to learn more about them.

There is no one group or person who is spokesman for the American Indian today. But many Indian leaders and individuals agree that most Indians want and have a right to decide whether they will live in a reservation tribal society that, while maintaining its differences, is an integral part of the larger society or whether they will become a part of the mainstream. There is more hope now than ever before that this choice might be possible.

"For the first time in history, people are talking seriously about letting the Indians be free to choose their own life style, to create their own communities," Hal Gross, general counsellor for the National Congress of American Indians, said.

In a speech to the National Congress of American Indians in 1968, President Nixon said,

We must recognize that American society can allow many different cultures to flourish in harmony, and we must provide an opportunity for those Indians wishing to do so to lead a useful and prosperous life in an Indian environment.

The right of self-determination of the Indian people will be respected and their participation in planning their own destiny will be encouraged.

I will oppose any effort to transfer jurisdiction over Indian reservations without Indian consent, will fully support the National Council on Indian Opportunity and ensure that the Indian people are fully consulted before programs under which they must live are planned.

Jobs with the Office of Economic Opportunity, many with the Indian Community Action Programs (ICAP), have given Indians a chance to participate in decisions affecting their tribes. Indians can say no to programs and have done so, much to the wrath of the experts. They can help shape programs to meet their own needs. Through Indian Community Action Programs, tribes are getting training for their members in such varied skills as secretarial work, bronze casting, accounting, weaving, health aids, personnel work, administration and communication, and home building.

Indians rarely have the chance to manage on-reservation business-es, not having control of their resources. Lack of experience is, therefore, a major problem in planning tribal controlled business ventures. Tribes are asking for and getting OEO help in the study of small business development use of business consultants, investment of tribal funds, credit unions and consumer education. In addition, VISTA has recruited Indians to serve as Volunteers on their own reservations.

There is great potential in improving the Indian economy through the further development of such businesses as recreation, tourism, cattle, forestry, factories, and electric power. But much depends on the future. A report released by the BIA in December, 1968, states that there are 150 commercial enterprises on Indian reservations in the United States. Of these, 140 have been established since 1962. They created 10,000 jobs, 4,700 of which are held by Indians.

"In 1962 there were 11,000 unemployed Pueblos alone," Gross said. Those who have great ideas for Indians and Indian land complain of Indian apathy and negativism. Developed by those with the know-how and experience, they say, Indian lands could produce great wealth.

But what Indians want or would do with their land is considerably different from what others would propose. "The tribes are all concerned; they don't want to starve to death," Gross said.

The stand of the National Congress of American Indians (105 tribes) is that land can be developed with respect for land. To the Indians, to ruin a river is sacrilege. They believe it is possible to have a factory and employ people and still put priority on conservation and natural beauty; that it is not necessary to use land, trees, rivers as dispensable objects in order to have economic well being, even in a technological society.

But to try, they need capital. Even though some Indian reservations cover valuable mineral deposits, the tribes have little or no control over these riches. Indians don't qualify for traditional loans because of their poverty, and the fact that their lands are held in trusteeship.

The Indians also have hopes in expanded land bases. Several cases now in litigation involve compensation for, or return of confiscated Indian land. However, even when the Indian Claims Commission rules in favor of the Indian, the settlement takes a long time, often years. The Claims Commission can only make judgment; it cannot make appropriations. Congress must pass one or more bills before the Indian tribes ever see the money or the land.

Money the Indians have received from resources, condemnation of land for dams, right of ways, or for other public purposes, and awards for loss of land have been used to finance services and programs usually provided by local governments. There is never enough left to use as capital in business ventures or economic development projects.

The BIA has credit programs for Indians, but the amount of money is too limited to help much in business ventures. According to the report of the Commission on the Rights, Liberties and Responsibilities of the American Indians (*Indians, America's Unfinished Business*), money from government and commercial sources will always be required to provide the larger capital needs of a resource-development program.

The greatest potential for Indian self-help, according to John Belindo, a Navajo-Kiowa who is director of The National Congress of American Indians, lies in cooperation between tribes which traditionally have been competitive. An example is the Indian Development District of Arizona. Seventeen tribes formed a non-profit organization and entered into contract with the Economic Development Division of the Department of Commerce to develop Indian lands as tribes approve. OEO is providing skill training and technical help, as tribes request it.

The present-day interest in Indians in America and the new government programs are looked upon with both skepticism and hope by most Indians. The need to develop the land has always been the white man's rationale when taking it from the Indians. The Indians would not or could not use land properly and therefore didn't deserve to keep it. So in the name of good use, millions of acres left to the Indians for "as long as the grass grows," have been taken away from him.

HAROLD L. SHEPPARD

The Social Geography of Poverty

What are the rates of poverty according to place of residence in terms of (a) rural-urban locations and (b) region of the Nation? And where are the poor distributed according to these two types of classification? Answers to these questions, too, should provide a major basis for the design of antipoverty programs.

1. While the *rate* of poverty is highest among residents of farm and rural nonfarm areas, we must not lose sight of the fact that most of the poor live *outside* of such areas. But despite the fact that less than 35 percent of all poor persons live in rural areas, it is also crucial to note that a substantial part of the problem of urban poverty stems from the migration of rural poor persons to the urban areas.

This can be dramatically illustrated by referring to the sharp drop from 1959 to 1966 in the number of poor persons living on farms—from 6.8 million to 2.4 million in just 7 years! The difference of 4.4 million is due almost entirely to the migration of poor persons from farm areas. Indeed, the current rate of poverty in *nonfarm* areas would be significantly lower were it not for this mass migration of the farm poor.

This is clearly the case with regard to America's nonwhite poor. Between 1959 and 1966 the number of poor nonwhites living on farms decreased by more than 1.3 million, down to 897,000, but instead of a decrease among the *nonfarm* poor nonwhites, there was actually a slight increase of 204,000 up to 8.7 million. This increase in numbers below the poverty line among nonfarm nonwhites, however, should not obscure a more important point, namely, that the number of *nonpoor* persons in the nonwhite nonfarm population increased during these 7 years by nearly 4.7 million. These additional 4.7 million nonfarm persons constituted a 54 percent increase in the number of nonfarm nonwhites out of poverty since 1959. In sharp

SOURCE: Reprinted from "A Search for New Directions in the War Against Poverty," Appendix of Report to U.S. Senate Committee on Labor and Public Welfare, Washington, D.C., October, 1968, pp. 84–89.

contrast, the corresponding change among nonpoor *whites* in non-farm areas was only 19 percent.

Finally, it should be noted that a major reason—if not *the* major reason—for the slight increase in the number of poor nonwhites living in nonfarm areas is that in the poor nonfarm population, the number of *children* increased by nearly 450,000. But there was an actual *decrease* from 1959 to 1966 in the number of nonfarm, nonwhite poor adults. Furthermore, in 1959, among nonwhite poor persons in nonfarm areas, children constituted exactly one-half of those persons, but by 1966, 54 percent were children. Children, in other words, have become an increasing proportion of the nonwhite poor in the nonfarm areas. *This is not true of nonwhites above the poverty line, or of poor whites.* More pointedly, in our standard metropolitan areas of 250,000 population and larger, children constitute more than 60 percent of the nonwhite poor living in families. Among nonwhites *above* the poverty line, however, less than 40 percent are children.

2. More than one-half of all poor persons in 1965 lived in metropolitan urban areas of 50,000 population or greater. But this varied widely according to region. The following table, based on family heads only, reveals the interregional differences:

Distribution of Poor Families, by Region and Residence

[In percent]

	United States	Northeast	North central	South	West
Total	100.0	100.0	100.0	100.0	100.0
Rural	36.0	14.8	35.8	47.9	22.3
Small Urban [1]	13.1	6.7	14.3	15.2	12.1
Urban [2]	50.9	78.5	49.9	36.9	65.6
50,000 to 250,000	8.6	9.0	5.6	10.5	6.0
250,000 to 1,000,000	18.0	13.8	13.4	19.0	27.8
1,000,000 plus	24.2	55.7	31.0	7.4	31.8

[1] Populations between 2,500 and 50,000.
[2] Standard metropolitan areas (SMSA's).

Source: Derived by H. L. Sheppard from census data for 1965.

This table clearly shows that in the Northeast section of the United States, more than one-half (56 percent) of the poor families lived in the urban areas of more than 1 million population; in the North Central region, the largest proportion (nearly 36 percent) are in rural areas; in the South, nearly one-half (48 percent) are in rural areas; and in the West, nearly one-third (32 percent) were in urban areas with more than 1 million population.

3. As already stated, the risks of poverty are greater in rural areas than in the larger urban centers of the country. For families, the poverty rate is 22 percent in rural areas and declines to 9 percent in the SMSA's of 1 million or more. But once again, the rural and urban rates vary according to region:

Rate of Poverty among Families, by Region and Residence

	United States	Northeast	North central	South	West
Total	13. 4	9. 5	10. 3	21. 4	10. 3
Farm	22. 2	17. 5	14. 6	32. 9	12. 0
Rural nonfarm	22. 4	12. 0	16. 0	30. 9	17. 0
Small urban	13. 2	7. 6	9. 5	20. 6	10. 3
Urban	10. 5	9. 3	8. 5	15. 4	9. 2
50,000 to 250,000	11. 9	9. 9	6. 1	17. 1	11. 1
250,000 to 1,000,000	12. 1	7. 4	9. 6	16. 9	11. 4
1,000,000 plus	9. 2	9. 9	8. 7	11. 2	7. 6

Source: Bureau of Census data for 1965, collected in 1966 survey.

Poverty in rural areas varies by region. The poverty rate among families was as high as 33 percent in the rural farm South and only 12 percent in the rural West. In the urban metropolitan areas, it was as high as 17 percent in Southern areas with 50,000-250,000 population and only 8 percent in areas of more than 1 million in the West.

4. Taking all of the Nation's poor families, where are they to be found? The accompanying table for 1965 shows that 23 percent of all the Nation's poor families were in the rural South; 10 percent in large urban areas of more than 1 million population in the Northeast; 9 percent in areas of 50,000-250,000 in the South; 8 percent in rural areas of the north-central region; 7 percent in the South's very small urban places (2,500 to 50,000 population); 7 percent in 1 million-plus population areas of the north-central region — and the remainder scattered among the categories named in the table.

While the South had nearly one-half of all poor families in the United States, only 30 percent of all the Nation's families — nonpoor and poor combined — resided in that region. Furthermore, nearly two-thirds of poor nonwhite families (64 percent) lived in the South as of 1966, and they were disproportionately concentrated in the rural areas of the South. Nearly six out of every 10 poor nonwhite families in the South lived in rural areas and very small towns as 1966.

5. In large part, the poverty of the Southern Negro is a product of the poverty of Southern agriculture and rural life. This can be seen

Residential and Regional Distribution of Poor Families, 1965

[In percent]

	Northeast	North Central	South	West	All United States
Rural	2.7	7.7	22.8	2.9	36.1
Small urban	1.2	3.1	7.2	1.6	13.1
50,000 to 250,000	1.6	1.2	5.0	0.8	8.6
250,000 to 1,000,000	2.5	2.9	9.0	3.6	18.0
1,000,000 plus	9.9	6.7	3.5	4.2	24.3
Total	17.8	21.6	47.5	13.1	100.0

Total of rows and columns may not add to 100 because of rounding.

from the fact that whereas slightly more than 70 percent of all non-white farm families in the South are poor, the incidence of poverty steadily declines in relationship to degree of urbanization, to less than 27 percent in those few very large urban areas in the South of more than 1 million population. Unfortunately, fewer than 18 percent of Southern Negro families reside in such large urban areas—in contrast to nearly 70 percent of those Negro families living *outside* of the South. But among those few Negro families living in the largest urban areas of the South (with more than 1 million population), the rate of poverty is not much greater than for those living in the large metropolitan areas in the rest of the country. Thus, the decline in the rate of poverty among Negroes is clearly related to degree of urbanization.

6. But a major paradox involved in the positive effects of urbanization upon rates of poverty—*for whites as well as nonwhites*—is one that is apparently not recognized by current students of poverty. The paradox is that *urbanization is definitely a progressive force in the reduction of poverty among those families headed by a male, nonwhite as well as white*—but this is not as true in the case of families headed by a female. For example, the rate of poverty among rural farm families headed by a male is 21 percent and it declines sharply to 6 percent in male-headed families in urban areas of 1 million population or larger. But the corresponding poverty rates for female-headed families are 38 percent in the farm areas and drops only to 31 percent in the largest urban areas. The data are even more dramatic if we concentrate on *children* and the differences in their rates of poverty according to degree of urbanization and whether they live in families headed by a male or female:

Poverty Rate Among Children, according to Sex and Residence of Family
Head, 1955

[In percent]

	Farm	SMSA's 1,000,000-plus	Percentage difference in poverty rates
Living with:			
Male head	34	10	−70.6
Female head	65	56	−13.8

Source: Derived by H. L. Sheppard from census data.

The relatively small impact of urbanization upon rates of poverty
among children in female-headed families, in contrast to its greater
positive impact for those in male-headed families, takes on even
greater significance when we bear in mind that in our large urban
areas of 250,000 and more, children living with a female head number about 4.3 million—and that 2.4 million of these children are
poor. And of this group of 2.4 million poor children living without a
father, more than one-half are nonwhite.

We cannot continue to ignore the fact that urbanization is associated with an increase in the proportion of children living in families
headed by a female (regardless of color) and that the risks of "growing up poor" are tremendously greater when a child is born and/or
reared in such families. As a Nation, we are still confused as to the
exact causes of this impact of urbanism, not to mention the design of
solutions to the resultant social pathologies.

7. In the case of *nonwhite* poverty, the difference it makes to be
born and/or reared in a male-headed family, as opposed to one with a
female head, is magnified according to the extent and size of urbanization. In the rural farm population, it makes very little difference;
but, as one traces the differences in the accompanying table, it is
obvious that the risks of being a poor child if born and/or reared in a
male-headed family dramatically decline the larger the urban setting; but at the same time the risks of poverty among children
without a male head remain as high or even higher *regardless* of
degree of urbanization. Furthermore, the discrepancy between child
poverty rates for male- and female-headed families increases sharply
as one moves along the continuum from rural farm to large urban
metropolitan areas.

The same general point, with slight exceptions and without the
dramatic discrepancies, applies to white poverty.

Discrepancy Between Poverty Rates among Nonwhite Children with Male or Female Head, by Residence, 1966

Residence	Rate among children with male head	Rate among children with female head	Female-male difference
Rural farm	81	79	−2
Nonfarm outside of SMSA's	65	83	+18
50,000 to 250,000 SMSA's	48	86	+38
SMSA's 250,000 plus	31	73	+42
1,000,000 plus only	27	73	+46

An equally critical fact is that both among whites and nonwhites the percentage of white *and* nonwhite poor children living in a female-headed family increases as one moves from the rural farm population on the continuum toward the largest urban concentrations of population:

Percent of Poor Children Living in Female-Headed Families, White and Nonwhite, 1966

Residence	White children	Nonwhite children
Rural farm	3	14
Nonfarm outside of SMSA's	19	29
50,000 to 250,000 SMSA's	32	43
SMSA's 250,000 plus	33	50
1,000,000 plus only	35	54

Source: Derived by H.L. Sheppard from census data collected in 1966, based on 1965 incomes.

The alarming aspect of this type of relationship is made discernible when one considers that it is clear from all of the previous material that (a) *degree* of urbanization (not merely rural versus urban as a totality) affects negatively the integrity of the father-mother type of family; (b) in contrast to the desirable effects of degree of urbanization upon poverty rates for children in male-headed families, urbanization has little, if any, possible effect for children in families without a male head; and (c) degree of urbanization appears to *increase* the proportion of poor children living in families with a female head (the larger the population the greater the percentage of poor children without male heads).

The causes of these deleterious effects of urbanization have not been sufficiently examined to warrant any certain explanations. To speculate at this point would only invite unnecessary and unfruitful polemics. We certainly cannot stem in any major degree the trend toward urbanization, especially when we know that urbanization *in general* reduces the overall poverty rate. But the reasons for the three effects summarized in the previous paragraph must be systematically sought through careful research and analysis, in order to determine the effective solutions.

We do know, however, some of the consequences of growing up poor in female-headed families in a megalopolis. Many of these consequences are social-psychological in nature and they, in turn, have a bearing on the educational, occupational, and economic achievements of such children. Unfortunately, and to repeat, there is no clear understanding of the forces that are brought into play as a result of increased conglomerations of persons in urban areas, which in turn engender the disruptive and crippling effects implied here.

· 6 ·

H. JACK GEIGER

Slavery: One Hundred Years Later

In this area—the Mississippi Delta—in which we have worked the past 3 years are some of the poorest and sickest populations in the United States. Our turf is northern Bolivar County, 500 square miles. The population of that area is overwhelmingly black, and the black population, which is approximately 15,000 people, is overwhelmingly poor.

We are, of course, open to anyone in poverty. I think at latest count we have 12 white patients. But all the rest of our patients are black. This is a self-segregation and self-selection process, and I

SOURCE: Reprinted from Statement made before Subcommittee on Employment, Manpower, and Poverty of the Committee on Labor and Public Welfare, U.S. Senate, 91st Cong. (April–June, 1969), pp. 261–64.

think a choice which we regard as unfortunate on the part of poor whites. By and large in the Mississippi Delta, however, poverty is enormously concentrated in the black population and there are not that many poor whites as can be found in other areas of Mississippi outside the delta. So all of the data I am about to present relates to this black population in this northern Mississippi county.

Among these 15,000 people the median rural family income is $900 per family per year. That is about $2.50 per day for every family need—food, clothing, shelter, housing, the works. The average family is four and a half people, so it comes to something like 50 cents a day to survive on. Ninety percent of the housing is what I would call unfit for human habitation. The Census Bureau calls it either dilapidated or deteriorated.

Seventy percent of the housing has no piped water. Most of it has no safe water supply of any kind. Seventy-five percent of the black population is unemployed or underemployed; and this problem has been increasing for two decades. As a consequence of the mechanization of agriculture, one double-row, cotton-picking machine replaces 70 field hands.

This area, as a consequence, has been among those that have been the source of the massive migration of rural southern Negroes to the urban North in search of survival jobs, education, food, some viable way of life.

The infant mortality rate for years in this area among the black population has hovered officially at about 60 per 1,000 live births. It is about three times the white rate in the same area.

I have to immediately agree completely with Mr. Choate and say on the basis of our own experience this is underreported. There are infants that are born and die with no record, particularly among the most deprived and the most isolated.

I suspect that the real figures are higher than that. I agree, further, that many of these deaths are significantly related to malnutrition, both maternal and infant. We will be coming back to that subject in a moment.

Indeed, the factors of neglect, omission, hunger, unemployment, the rest of what is lacking in the environment, often manage to see to it that the children don't get born at all.

There is indirect evidence of very high spontaneous miscarriage and abortion rates in this population which we think might be significantly related to prenatal and maternal nutrition.

Twelve percent of the black women in north Bolivar County who have ever been pregnant have no living children. That is the combination of miscarriage and infant mortality. Every 10th child now is out of school for lack of shoes, clothing, or some of the other necessities of life. The median educational level for the whole black population in our target area is less than 6 years, and many are functionally illiterate; 13 percent of the households, when we first came to the area, reported they ate only one meal a day and those on one meal a day were on the worst diets. We found people trying to subsist on pecan nuts, on hunting rabbits and fishing, on biscuits and sirup as a basic diet.

The out-migration of the past two decades has, if anything, made the process worse by skewing the population distribution. As in all migrations, able-bodied, younger people, particularly males, leave first, leaving behind high concentrations of children, women of child-bearing age, and the elderly, which is a definition of those at highest risk.

There is no adequate or easy way to describe this environment. The life of the 8-week-old infant whose picture I have submitted can be saved by adequate nutrition and skilled medical care, only to be returned to the same miserable shack, the same filthy, contaminated water supply, the same lack of fuel, the same rags for clothing, the same lack of bedding, the same lack of any prospect of a decent education, the same lack of basic sanitary facilities that made him sick in the first place, and will see to it that this cycle will recur.

The new evidence that I have to present today, new in the sense that much of what I have just described, I am sure, is familiar to the committee from evidence submitted in the past, has to do with a study of black children in northern Bolivar County between the ages of 1 month and 36 months. A very great deal has been said about the possible effects of malnutrition and other kinds of deprivation on intellectual development. The period of greatest vulnerability to this kind of damage is the period between birth and 36 months, the period of most rapid growth of the brain and the central nervous system.

We know, as a result of this, a combined nutritional and psychological testing study, that 90 percent of the children were anemic. We are still looking at the rest of the nutritional data. But what I want to present today is the result of the intellectual performance testing which demonstrated to us that before our eyes, starting at about 18 months of age and very, very evident by 3 years of age, one can see and measure the deterioration of the mental performance and abilities of these children. We studied—"we" really refers to Dr.

Florence Helpern, a most distinguished psychologist on the faculties of New York and Columbia Universities, who has for the past 2 years been part of the staff at the health center, and Dr. Roy E. Brown, pediatrician and epidemiologist—344 children between the age of 1 month and 36 months of age. We measured the developmental quotient, which is the equivalent of the intelligence quotient that we are familiar with at later ages. It is based on tests of motor performance, verbal performance, and adaptive functioning.

On the average, these black children, for the first 4 or 5 months of life, scored 17 percent above the national norm, the national norm for white children is 100. Their score was 117. Why is this, given the terrible environment I have talked about?

I think quite clearly this is because we are dealing with the survivors of a cruel selection process, given that infant mortality rate, that miscarriage and abortion rate that I have talked about. The weaker children have already been killed off and you find stronger, better children surviving in the first 4 or 5 months of life.

At 1 month to 5 or 6 months in particular, this accelerated development beyond the national norm for whites was evident in this population. I think it is a result of this selection process.

Over the first year this decayed rapidly to about the national norm for whites, 100 or so, and by 13 months a process began that looks on the graph like falling off the cliff. At 36 months the norm for these children was 85, 15 to 20 percent in many cases below the national norms, in children, babies, infants that had started out ahead.

We found a 20-percent lag in verbal skills, an 11-percent lag in motor skills and something close to an 11-percent lag in adaptive functioning. We feel very strongly that this may be related to nutritional impairment.

It is also clearly related to experiential deprivation, to the lack of anything in the home that we regard as normal for children—lights, toys, books, objects in the environment to manipulate and play with, and time for parent or parents to stimulate and interact with their children.

In short, I think this is a situation that would be helped substantially by food, but nobody should fool themselves that food alone will make up for all of the depreciation that black children in areas like this suffer.

Nonetheless, to my knowledge this is the first clear evidence of how drastic a change is and can be taking place in a very vulnerable population.

I suspect that it is astonishing indeed that Headstart makes as much difference as it does, because it is beginning after significant amounts of damage have already been done, if our evidence is generalizable to larger populations.

This data does give, I think, some flavor of the hopeless subsistence level, the miserable flavor of life in a population struggling to hang on at the very edge of survival. The reasons for this are multiple and not very complex. This was a population that lived in slavery for almost 100 years past the Emancipation Proclamation, the Civil War, and Reconstruction. The label changed in these great cotton-growing areas of the rural South, from slave to tenant, but very little else about life changed.

In particular, the experience of managing one's own affairs, developing the capacities that are central to survival in the American economy, shopping for your own food, taking care of your own family, were systematically denied this population. You lived on the plantation. You got your food at the plantation store. Major purchases were negotiated by the plantation management at the county seat and deducted from what you were supposed to be earning. So was medical care. These accounts were often inaccurate and were never in any case explained to the individual worker.

The system was one of total social, economic, educational, political, and environmental control. It didn't begin to change until about two decades ago with the advent of the mechanical cotton-picking machine in the area and chemical herbicides. You didn't need to chop cotton with a hoe any longer because you could spray from a plane, and you didn't need to pick cotton because you had a mechanical cotton picker that was more efficient. So people became useless, surplus.

MARY W. WRIGHT

The Dusty Outskirts of Hope — Public Assistance in the Appalachian South

Are there perhaps some individuals in need in Appalachia who do not now avail themselves of help "already theirs for the asking?" Why are there cases of serious deprivation which are not in contact with appropriate agencies of assistance?

I know a man, I'll call him Buddy Banks. He lives in a ravine in a little, one-room pole-and-cardboard house he built himself, with his wife, their six children, and baby granddaughter. Mr. Banks, 45 years old, is a sober man, a kindly man, and a passive man. He can read and write a little, has worked in the coal mines and on farms, but over the years he's been pretty badly battered up and today is "none too stout." Last fall, when he could no longer pay the rent where he was staying, his mother-in-law gave him a small piece of ground, and he hastened to put up this little shack in the woods before the snow came. If, as you rode by, you happened to glance down and saw where he lives, and saw his children playing among the stones, you would say, "White trash." You would say, "Welfare bums."

When the newspaper announced the new ADC program for unemployed fathers, I thought of Buddy Banks. There is not much farm work to be done in the wintertime, and Mr. Banks has been without a job since summer. Here in their ravine, they can dig their coal from a hole in the hill and dip their water from the creek, and each month he scratches together two dollars for his food stamps by doing odd jobs for his neighbors, who are very nearly as poor as he is. Other than this, there is nothing coming in. I thought, maybe here is some help for Buddy Banks.

Since Mr. Banks does not get a newspaper or have a radio, he had not heard about the new program. He said, yes, he would be interested. I offered to take him to town right then, but he said no, he

SOURCE: Reprinted from *Mountain Life and Work*, Spring, 1964, © 1964 by the Council of the Southern Mountains, Inc. Berea, Ky.

would have to clean up first, he couldn't go to town looking like this. So I agreed to come back Friday.

On Friday he told me he'd heard today was the last day for signing up. We were lucky, eh? It wasn't true, but it's what he had heard, and I wondered, suppose he'd been told last Tuesday was the last day for signing up, and I hadn't been there to say, well, let's go find out anyway.

Buddy Banks was all fixed up and looked nice as he stepped out of his cabin. His jacket was clean, and he had big rubber boots on and a cap on his head. I felt proud walking along with him, and he walked proud. (Later, in town, I noticed how the hair curled over his collar, and the gray look about him, and the stoop of his shoulders. If you had seen him, you'd have said, "Country boy, come to get his check.")

When we reached the Welfare Office, it was full of people, a crowd of slouchy, shuffly men, standing around and looking vaguely in different directions. I followed Buddy Banks and his brother-in-law, who had asked to come with us, into the lobby, and they too stood in the middle of the floor. Just stood. It was not the momentary hesitation that comes before decision. It was the paralysis of strangeness, of lostness, of not knowing what to do. A girl was sitting at a table, and after a number of minutes of nothing, I quietly suggested they ask her. No, they told me, that was the food stamp girl. But there was no other. So finally, when I suggested, well, ask her anyway, they nodded their heads, moved over, and asked her. I wondered how long they might have gone on standing there if I'd kept my mouth shut. I wondered how long the others all around us had been standing there. I had an idea that if I hadn't been right in the way, Buddy Banks just might have turned around and gone out the door when he saw the crowd, the lines, and that smartly dressed food stamp girl bending over her desk.

Yes, he was told, and after waiting a few minutes, he was shown behind the rail to a chair beside a desk, and a man with a necktie and a big typewriter began to talk with him. They talked a long, long time, while the brother-in-law and I waited in the lobby. (They had asked the brother-in-law if he had brought the birth certificates. No, he hadn't, and so they said there wasn't anything they could do, to come back next Tuesday. He said nothing, stared at them a moment, then walked away. He stood around waiting for us all day long and never asked them another question. He said he would tend to it some other time. Fortunately, they got Mr. Banks sitting down before they inquired about the birth certificates.)

I knew what they were talking about: I have talked long times with Mr. Banks myself, and they were going over it again, and again, and I could imagine Mr. Banks nodding his head to the question he didn't quite understand, because he wanted to make a good impression, and it would be a little while before the worker realized that he hadn't understood, and so they would go back and try again, and then Mr. Banks would explain as best he could, but he would leave something out, and then the worker wouldn't understand, so that, in all, their heads were bent together for almost an hour and a half. It seemed a long time to take to discover Buddy Banks's need—a visit to his home would have revealed it in a very few minutes, but of course 12 miles out and 12 miles back takes time too, and there are all those eligibility rules to be checked out, lest somebody slip them a lie and the editorials start hollering, "Fraud! Fraud!" Actually, I was impressed that the worker would give him that much time. It *takes* time to be sympathetic, to listen, to hear—to understand a human condition.

At last he came out, and, with an apologetic grin, he said he must return on Tuesday, he must go home and get the birth certificates. Then they would let him apply. (How will you come back, Mr. Banks? Where will you get the $3 for taxi fare by next Tuesday? Perhaps you could scrape it up by Monday week, but suppose you come on Monday week and your worker isn't here? Then perhaps you won't come back at all . . .)

While Mr. Banks was busy talking, I was chatting with one of the other workers. Because I am a social worker too, I can come and go through the little iron gate, and they smile at me and say, "Well, *hello* there!" We talked about all the work she has to do, and one of the things she told me was how, often, to save time, they send people down to the Health Department to get their own birth records. Then they can come back and apply the same day. I wondered why Mr. Banks's worker never suggested this. Maybe he never thought of it. (Maybe he doesn't live 12 miles out with no car, and the nearest bus eight miles from home. And no bus fare at that.) Or perhaps he *did* mention it, and Mr. Banks never heard him, because his head was already filled up with the words that went before: "I'm sorry, there's nothing we can do until you bring us the birth certificates," and he was trying to think in which box, under which bed, had the children been into them . . .?

So I tried to suggest to him that we go now to the Health Department, but he didn't hear me either. He said, and he persisted, I'm going to the Court House, I'll be right back, will you wait for me? I tried to stop him: let's plan something, what we're going to do next, it's almost lunchtime and things will close up—until suddenly I realized that after the time and the tension of the morning, this was no doubt a call of nature that could not wait for reasonable planning, nor could a proud man come out and ask if there might not be a more accessible solution. And so, as he headed quickly away for the one sure place he knew, I stood mute and waited while he walked the three blocks there and the three blocks back. I wonder if that's something anybody ever thinks about when they're interviewing clients.

Mr. Banks and I had talked earlier about the Manpower Redevelopment Vocational Training Programs, and he had seemed interested. "I'd sure rather work and look after my family than mess with all this stuff, but what can I do? I have no education." I told him about the courses and he said, yes, I'd like that. And so we planned to look into this too, while we were in town. But by now, Mr. Banks was ready to go home. "I hate all this standing around. I'd work two days rather than stand around like this." It wasn't really the standing around he minded. It was the circumstances of the standing around. It took some persuading to get him back into the building, only to be told—at 11:30—to come back at ten to one. (Suppose his ride, I thought, had been with somebody busier than I. Suppose they couldn't wait till ten to one and kept badgering him, "Come on Buddy, hurry up, will you? We ain't got all day!")

I tried to suggest some lunch while we waited, but they didn't want lunch. "We had breakfast late; I'm not hungry, really." So instead, I took him around to the Health Department and the Circuit Court and the County Court, and we verified everything, although he needed some help to figure which years the children were born in.

At ten to one, he was again outside the Welfare Office, and he drew me aside and said that he'd been thinking: maybe he should go home and talk this whole thing over a little more. He felt that before jumping into something, he should know better what it was all about. This startled me, for I wondered what that hour and a half had been for, if now, after everything, he felt he must return to his cronies up the creek to find out what it all meant. So we stood aside, and I interpreted the program as best I could—whom it was for, what it required, and what it would do for him and his family—while he stood, nodding his head and staring at the sidewalk. Finally, cautiously, almost grimly, he once again pushed his way into that crowded, smoke-filled lobby.

"Those who are to report at one o'clock, stand in this line. Others in that line." Mr. Banks stood in the one o'clock line. At 1:15, he reached the counter. I don't know what he asked, but I saw the man behind the desk point over toward the other side of the building, the Public Assistance side, where Mr. Banks had already spent all morning. Mr. Banks nodded his head and turned away as he was told to do. At that point I butted in. "Assistance for the unemployed is over there," the man said and pointed again. So I mentioned training. "He wants training? Why didn't he say so? He's in the wrong line." I don't know what Mr. Banks had said, but what *does* a person say when he's anxious, tired, and confused, and when a crowd of others, equally anxious, are pushing from behind, and when the man at the counter says, "Yes?" I butted in, and Mr. Banks went to stand in the right line, but I wondered what the man behind us did, who didn't have anybody to butt in for him.

While Mr. Banks was waiting, to save time, I took the birth certificates to his worker on the other side. I walked right in, because I was a social worker and could do that, and he talked to me right away and said, "Yes, yes, this is good. This will save time. No, he won't have to come back on Tuesday. Yes, he can apply today. Just have him come back over here when he is through over there. Very good."

At 1:30, Buddy Banks reached the counter again, was given a card and told to go sit on a chair until his name was called. I had business at 2:00 and returned at 3:00, and there he was, sitting on the same chair. But I learned as I sat beside him that things had been happening. He had talked with the training counselor, returned to his welfare worker, and was sent back to the unemployment counselor, after which he was to return once more to his welfare worker. I asked what he had learned about the training. "There's nothing right now, maybe later." Auto mechanics? Bench work? Need too much education. There may be something about washing cars, changing oil, things like that. Later on. Did you sign up for anything? No. Did they say they'd let you know? No. How will you know? I don't know.

At last his ADC (Unemployed) application was signed, his cards were registered, his name was in the file. Come back in two weeks and we'll see if you're eligible. (How will you get back, Buddy? I'll find a way.)

It was four o'clock. "Well, that's over." And he said, "I suppose a fellow's got to go through all that, but I'd sure rather be a-working than a-fooling around with all that mess." We went out to the car, and I took him home. "I sure do thank you, though," he said.

While I'd been waiting there in the lobby, I saw another man come up to the counter. He was small and middle-aged, with a wedding band on his finger, and his face was creased with lines of care. I saw him speak quietly to the man across the desk. I don't know what he said or what the problem was, but they talked a moment and the official told him, "Well, if you're disabled for work, then there's no use asking about training," and he put up his hands and turned away to the papers on his desk. The man waited there a moment, then slowly turned around and stood in the middle of the floor. He lifted his head to stare up at the wall, the blank wall, and his blue eyes were held wide open to keep the tears from coming. I couldn't help watching him, and when suddenly he looked at me, his eyes straight into mine, I couldn't help asking him — across the wide distance of the crowd that for just an instant vanished into the intimacy of human communion — I asked, "Trouble?" Almost as if he were reaching out his hands, he answered me and said, "I just got the news from Washington and come to sign up, and . . . " But then, embarrassed to be talking to a stranger, he mumbled something else I couldn't understand, turned his back to me, stood another long moment in the middle of the crowd, and then walked out the door.

Disabled or not disabled. Employed or not employed. In need or not in need. Yes or no. Black or white. Answer the question. Stand in line.

It is not the program's fault. You have to have questionnaires, and questionnaires require a yes or no. There is no space for a maybe, but . . .

Nor is it the people-who-work-there's fault, for who can see — or take time to see — the whole constellation of people and pressures, needs and perplexities, desires and dreads that walk into an office in the person of one shuffling, bedraggled man — especially when there are a hundred other bedraggled men waiting behind him? You ask the questions and await the answers. What else can you do?

Then perhaps it is the fault of the man himself, the man who asks — or doesn't quite know how to ask — for help. Indeed, he's called a lazy cheat if he does, and an unmotivated, ignorant fool if he doesn't. It must be his own fault.

Or maybe it's nobody's fault. It's just the way things are . . .

Yes, there are reasons why some in need among us do not avail themselves of the help that is "already theirs for the asking."

Which of us, I sometimes wonder, will know which counter to go to in Heaven, and after the first few questions, will we too be tempted to turn around and go out the door and try to catch us a ride back home — even if it is just a one-room pole shack buried in a dank ravine?

· 8 ·

DONALD E. GATCH

Hunger in South Carolina

DR. GATCH: I am a private physician in a little town in the lower end of South Carolina. The town that I live in has a population of maybe 500. My total patient load is maybe 5,000 or 6,000. I draw from a much larger area.

Medicine today is no longer just writing a prescription for drugs. Before a doctor can become effective in treating patients, he is going to have to be able to write a prescription for a house that doesn't leak and that has some windows, that has floors, and he is going to have to be able to write a prescription for food. He is going to have to be able to write a prescription for electric lights, for a toilet of some kind so they don't have to use the woods. In other words, it is impossible to practice medicine today without a tremendous support from the Federal Government. We are just a poor area there, especially in the South, and we aren't going to face the facts and be able to deal with them until the Federal Government pours a huge amount of money into the South.

MR. SCHERLE: If hunger exists, as you mention, what would your recommendation be to reach these people?

DR. GATCH: It can't be a food stamp program. It has to be food. The food stamp program is worthless for the people who really need it. They don't have the money to pay for the initial cost. We have—I have patients that literally have no food in their house today, and maybe have one meal, if they can scratch it out.

MR. SCHERLE: In a community where you have a population of 20,000, and that is a good-sized city, why is it that poverty exists in an area that large? Why don't the citizens of that community help these people?

DR. GATCH: You mean the leaders of the community, or the people themselves?

MR. SCHERLE: You have welfare programs, social programs, you have leaders in the community.

DR. GATCH: First of all, they are unaware.

MR. SCHERLE: Couldn't you make them aware of it?

SOURCE: Reprinted and abridged from "Malnutrition and Federal Food Service Programs," Hearings before the Committee on Education and Labor, House of Representatives, 90th Cong. 2d sess. (Washington, D.C.: U.S. Government Printing Office, June, 1968), pp. 967–971.

DR. GATCH: I have tried. It is very difficult for a community to accept the fact that people are dying and are hungry, and live with it without doing something about it. So you either deny that [it] exists, or you do something about it, and so far most of the South denies that it exists.

MR. SCHERLE: But they know that it does.

DR. GATCH: Not actually. It is a funny thing what the automobile has done. The automobile takes you past these houses. It doesn't take you in them, and it takes you past these people. Most white people have not seen the inside of those shacks ever.

MR. SCHERLE: In a community of 20,000 all the social services and welfare programs must be available. Are you telling me that this community to which you have reference completely closes their eyes to the situation and have become so hardened that they don't care? Are you trying to tell me that your city has no heart?

DR. GATCH: It isn't a matter of heart. It is a matter of living with one's self. It is no different with them than you all.

MR. SCHERLE: This is not a true statement as far as the communities in the district I represent are concerned. I can guarantee you this, that if we knew a family in our community that was hungry, they would be supplied with food immediately.

DR. GATCH: I bet I could go into your community today and as a doctor, and seeing these kinds of patients, that I can see conditions that are intolerable, and I am certain that there are hungry people in your community. There is not a single community that I have ever been in, and I have been all over the United States at one time or another, that does not have this problem. It is not limited to the South. It is much worse in the South.

MR. STEIGER: *Esquire* magazine in 1968, made the statement in Columbia, that in Beaufort County people were dying of starvation, and that they were allowed to start starving before they were born, and that you personally presided at eight deaths which could be honestly attributed only to hunger. Of those dead, three in one family all were Negroes, the article goes on to say, whose strength had been sapped by worms. It says that if white children had died of parasites, something would have been done eons ago. Do you believe that?

DR. GATCH: Yes.

MR. STEIGER: Hunger exists today?

DR. GATCH: I sent some pictures up.

MR. STEIGER: May we see the pictures? The Board that you testified before was the hearing on which the "Hunger USA" report is based. Is that correct? Do you want to talk about these pictures? Here is one looking at the woman.

DR. GATCH: Yes. This is an elderly colored woman that has severe rheumatoid arthritis. She lives in a house without electricity, without water, without windows, without, literally, doors that work. You can open them, but there are no hinges on them.

You go into her room and it is so dark you can't see her. Nobody, I think, within the last 2 or 3 weeks one of the Public Health nurses has been going in to see her, but up until that time — I think she gets $30 a month.

MR. STEIGER: How much?

DR. GATCH: Thirty dollars a month, she and her sister. I am not exactly certain of the figure they give.

They often have grits or rice with maybe a little greens in it. They don't have any medicine, money for medicine, money for doctors.

She can't move. She can't take care of herself. Her sister can't, and she is hungry every day.

MR. STEIGER: What about this family? [Indicating picture.]

DR. GATCH: This is a family in which I think 17 or 18 people live in the house. This is one of the rather unusual families in that the father is trying to get a job. The night that we took this picture, he was drunk, but he had been working all week.

CHAIRMAN PERKINS: What did he work at?

DR. GATCH: Works on a county maintenance crew, I think. He works with the county. I think it is with the maintenance crew. And he gets — I don't remember the figure, but a couple of hundred dollars a month, something like that.

But this is the problem you run into when you say you are going to deal with this kind of problem.

The child sitting here is a hydrocephalic. She has never walked. She can't talk. They brought her into the office for the first time a couple of months ago. She has a hemoglobin of eight, she has intestinal parasites — she is a happy little child, but she is sick, and she is hungry. They never have three meals a day. They have sometimes breakfast and always supper. Some of the kids get lunch programs, some of them don't.

Another child, her whole face has a birthmark, and she is really a rather tragic child. She has had some work on it done by the medical college.

Another boy here only has one eye. The other eye got shot out, I think, with a BB gun. It needs some care.

I haven't seen any of the rest of the family, but other than just when I was at their home, but I am sure they all have worms, they are all — most of the kids — are anemic.

The mothers, two of the daughters have children, and they both look rather anemic to me. I am sure they have a protein deficiency, not enough milk, which in this country is called anemia.

ELIZABETH HERZOG

Facts and Fictions about the Poor

Anyone who tries to ferret out and report facts about the poor—to tell it like it is—encounters some statements that are simply not true and some that are true and not true at the same time. They may be true as far as they go but misleading if viewed out of context, or partly true but distorted into falsehood by oversimplification.

This article is limited to two examples, one concerning the need to view statistical data in context and the other concerning oversimplification and misapplication of a convenient concept.

BIRTHS OUT OF WEDLOCK

We constantly see references to "the alarming rise" in illegitimate births. Alarm could be directed to the sheer increase in numbers, or the assumed causes of the increase, or to the consequences and implications—actual or potential. And the word "alarming" could reflect either unadulterated fear, or fear compounded by hostility and resentment.

Because hostility and fear are so often associated with the crisis view, it is useful to consider the difference between seeing illegitimacy figures in and out of context (Chart 9-1). The trend line for births out of wedlock from 1940 to 1965 shows that during those years the numbers more than tripled to about 291,000 in 1965 from about 89,000 in 1940. This tremendous number and increase is the picture most often impressed upon the public. When this same trend line is shown as part of all live births, the rise is still clear, but it can be seen as part of a rise in the total number of births (Chart 9-2).

There is some question about the extent to which the greater rise in illegitimacy before 1961 was real and to what extent it resulted from improved reporting and better estimates—for all our national illegitimacy figures are estimates, based on reports from about 35

SOURCE: Reprinted from *Monthly Labor Review*, February, 1969, pp. 42–49.

CHART 9-1
Births out of Wedlock, United States, 1940–65[1]

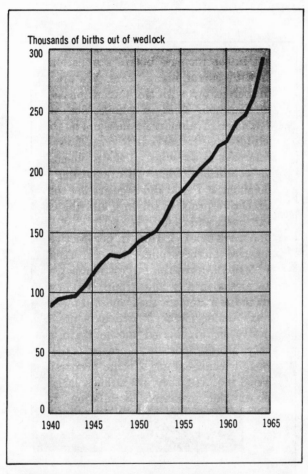

Thousands of births out of wedlock

[1] Beginning 1959, includes Alaska; beginning 1960, includes Hawaii.

SOURCE: *Vital Statistics of the United States, 1964, Vol. 1—Natality,* table 1–26 (1966) and *Vital Statistics of the United States, 1965, Vol. 1—Natality* (U.S. Public Health Service, National Center for Health Statistics).

states. However, the main point is that even if births out of wedlock had not increased faster than births in wedlock, the bulk of the problem would still be with us. The problem is not in the increase

CHART 9-2
Total Live Births and Estimated Live Births out of
Wedlock. United States, 1940–65[1]

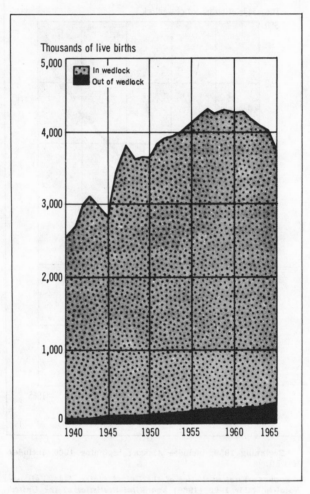

[1] Beginning 1959, includes Alaska; beginning 1960, includes Hawaii.

SOURCE: *Vital Statistics of the United States, 1964, Vol. 1—Natality,* tables 1–1 and 1–26 (1966) and *Vital Statistics of the United States, 1965, Vol. 1—Natality* (U.S. Public Health Service, National Center for Health Statistics).

but in a situation that has been with us for many years. We are faced not with a crisis but with the current phase of a long term situation. This, of course, does not reduce the number of unmarried mothers or the number of children to be served. It does, however, make a difference in our view of the problem which, in turn, conditions what we are willing and able to do about it. Panic and rage are not conducive to constructive problem-solving, and the crisis view breeds panic and rage.

One more brief exercise in perspective concerns unmarried mothers under twenty. Teenage girls, age 15 to 19, have the largest number of illegitimate births in any age group. This event often leads to the statement that "most unmarried mothers are under twenty," which is not true. The majority of unmarried mothers are not under twenty. More important, however, is the fact that, although teenagers are a large proportion of unmarried mothers, they are a much larger proportion of the principal population for whom unmarried motherhood is a risk—unmarried, widowed, divorced and separated women. Among the Nation's unmarried mothers, teenagers are a smaller proportion of the total than they are of the total unmarried female population.

With the generation gap yawning before us, it is well to remember that 20 years ago teenagers produced a larger proportion of nonwedlock births than today, and that the illegitimacy rate among teenagers is lower and has risen less than among women in their twenties and thirties.

That word "rate" demands a passing bow, for clarity about the difference between illegitimacy rate and illegitimacy ratio is as necessary as it is rare. The ratio is the number of illegitimate babies per 1,000 live births. The rate is the number of births per 1,000 unmarried women of childbearing age. The ratio talks about babies, the rate talks about mothers. The ratio is useful for planning services, but worse than useless for considering trends, since it depends on the age and marital composition of the population, illegitimacy rate, and the fertility of married women. For example, the ratio among girls under 18 is bound to be high in comparison with older women, since few are married mothers. However, the illegitimacy rate is relatively low.[1]

There are two reasons for dwelling on this point. One is that ratios are surprisingly often published under the name of rates. The other

---

[1]Arthur A. Campbell, "Illegitimacy," in Clyde V. Kiser, *et al., Trends and Variations in Fertility in the United States* (Cambridge, Mass., Harvard University Press, 1967).

is that the overall illegitimacy rate, after increasing substantially
from 1940 to 1957, has more or less leveled off during the years
1957–66, oscillating within one or two points.[2] What it may do next
remains to be seen. But, on the whole, the main reason for the
increase in numbers of illegitimate births since 1957 is that there are
more women. Since numbers, rates, and ratios are estimates, and
since there is reason to suspect overreporting in some groups and
underreporting in others, yearly oscillations of one or two points are
best disregarded.

THE "CULTURE OF POVERTY"

A prime example of what is partly true and partly not true is the
"culture of poverty." It is also an example of the dangers inherent in
setting up a half-true label and then mistaking it for an explanation or
using it as a substitute for thought.

The culture-of-poverty concept provides a reminder that, in some
ways, different groups live in different worlds and respond to
different imperatives. Perhaps this should not have been necessary,
but it was. Disraeli thrust such a reminder upon the attention of his
fellow countrymen when a character in his novel, *Sybil*, declared
that Queen Victoria was reigning over not one Nation, but two:
". . . two nations between whom there is no intercourse and no sympathy; who are as ignorant of each other's habits, thoughts, and
feelings as if they were dwellers in different zones or inhabitants of
different planets; who are formed by a different breeding, are fed by
a different food, are ordered by different manners, and are not governed by the same law – The Rich and The Poor."[3] Michael Harrington, more than a century later, was referring to that conversation
when he called his book *The Other America*, and called the last
chapter "The Two Nations." And Oscar Lewis, at about the same
time, expressed a similar, though by no means identical, idea in
referring to the culture of poverty.

The culture-of-poverty idea, for the short time in which it was
being looked at with new eyes, did set up a ripple of fresh com-
prehension, and this is a contribution to be respected. What is to be
deplored about the concept lies less in its original thoughtful formulation than in the way it has been applied by others.

---

[2]*Monthly Vital Statistics Report: Highlights, June 14, 1966* (U.S. Public Health
Service, National Center for Health Statistics).

[3]Benjamin Disraeli, *Sybil: or The Two Nations* (London: H. Colburn, 1845).

Lewis pointed out that in some ways the poor of any industrialized country resemble each other more than they resemble the prosperous in their own society. He mentioned, for example, a number of economic traits, including "the constant struggle for survival, unemployment and underemployment, low wages, a miscellany of unskilled occupations, . . . the absence of savings, a chronic shortage of cash, the absence of food reserves in the home, the pattern of frequent buying of small quantities of food as need arises, the pawning of personal goods, borrowing from local money lenders at usurious rates of interest, spontaneous informal credit devices . . . organized by neighbors, and the use of second-hand clothing and furniture."[4]

He also mentioned a number of social and psychological characteristics, including: " . . . living in crowded quarters, a lack of privacy, gregariousness, a high incidence of alcoholism, frequent use of physical violence in the training of children, wife beating, early initiation into sex, free unions or consensual marriages, a relatively high incidence of the abandonment of mothers and children, a trend toward mother-centered families and a much greater knowledge of maternal relatives, the predominance of the nuclear family, a strong predisposition to authoritarianism, and a great emphasis on family solidarity — an ideal only rarely achieved. Other traits include . . . a sense of resignation and fatalism based upon the realities of their difficult life situation, a belief in male superiority which reaches its crystallization in *machismo* or the cult of masculinity, a corresponding martyr complex among women, and finally, a high tolerance for psychological pathology of all sorts."[5]

Much of what he said has been documented as a description of traits commonly found among the poor in any industrialized society. A few points have been sharply challenged. But the basic question is whether this much similarity of traits does indeed constitute a culture; and the basic problem lies in the applications and implications that others have derived from assuming that it does. Before grappling with the concept in general, a few examples are in order of the specifics that make the idea of a culture of poverty difficult either to accept or to reject without reservation.

With regard to economic patterns and the social habits derived from them, one may question whether these patterns and habits are culture traits or merely pragmatic responses to real life exigencies. If

[4]Oscar Lewis, *The Children of Sanchez: An Autobiography of a Mexican Family* (New York, Random House, Inc., 1961), p. xxvi.

[5]*Ibid.*, pp. xxvi–xxvii.

the latter, then they are not necessarily culture traits – that is, learned ways of life, transmitted from generation to generation – but rather responses of each generation to the circumstances in which it grows up. Some psychosocial characteristics often attributed to the culture of poverty can also be viewed as a response to reality, ready to change if reality fosters or at least permits change. It can be argued further that certain psychological attitudes commonly attributed to the poor are in fact the products of physical reality; and that some ascribed attitudes and values are erroneously ascribed.

For example, some psychological attributes often attributed to the culture of poverty are intertwined with the effects of hunger and malnutrition in such a way that they operate both as cause and as effect. The most familiar effects of extreme malnutrition are loss of weight, weakness, and anemia. In addition, according to one authority, various functional changes occur that are often mistaken for neurasthenic manifestations, including "excessive fatigueability, disturbances in sleep, inability to concentrate."[6] Other symptoms cited in connection with prolonged malnutrition are "depression, loss of ambition, apathy, lethargy, impotence, and a sensation of being old."[7] Obviously, some characteristics that nutritional experts attribute to diet deficiency are the same ones often ascribed to the culture of poverty.

SCHOOL ACHIEVEMENT

Poor school performance by children of the slums is often attributed to the low esteem in which book learning is held by the culture of poverty, and the consequent lack of interest by parents in the schooling of their children. That inadequate diet can contribute to poor school performance has been established by systematic studies as well as by unsystematic observation.

Poor school performance is also promoted by lack of sleep, a deficiency which is caused in some instances by staying up late to watch television, but often is the result of overcrowded housing. To raise the subject of housing leads into an array of traits often associated with the culture of poverty, yet often produced by physical condition. Among those that have been described are pessimism and

---

[6]Norman Jolliffe, "The Pathogenesis of Deficiency Disease," in Norman Jolliffe, F. F. Tisdell, Paul R. Canon (eds.), *Clinical Nutrition* (New York, Harper & Brothers, 1950), p. 33.

[7]Alvin L. Schorr, "The Nonculture of Poverty," *American Journal of Orthopsychiatry*, October, 1964, p. 909.

passivity, stress to which the individual cannot adapt, a state of dissatisfaction, pleasure in company but not in solitude, difficulty in household management and child rearing, and relationships that tend to spread out in the neighborhood rather than deeply into the family.[8] The effects of poor housing on physical health have been widely discussed, including safety, respiratory and skin diseases, lead poisoning, and rat bites.[9]

Because school achievement has been so important a focus of poverty problems and of efforts to solve them, it is especially appropriate for illustrating the possibility that features often ascribed to the culture of poverty may in fact be reflections of middle class behavior and attitudes. One such attitude, namely, the expectation of the teacher with regard to the child's ability to learn, has had some attention and is likely to receive more.

Scattered evidence is piling up in support of Kenneth Clark's thesis that ghetto children do poorly in school because the teachers expect them to do poorly.[10] In Washington, D.C., for example, the academic average in the public schools has been reported as far below the national norm. However, one school in a very poor neighborhood stood out far above the average for the city. According to newspaper accounts, the difference was that the school principal would not accept the proposition that ghetto children could not learn, and would not allow the teachers in her school to accept it. And the children did learn, as attested by the academic scores.[11] This kind of evidence was reinforced by an experiment in another city, where teachers in a very poor neighborhood were told that—on the basis of psychological tests—certain children in their classes were likely to show remarkable intellectual gains. The children, in fact, had been selected at random. Nevertheless, during the year those particular children did make gains significantly greater than those of their classmates. Apparently, because the teachers expected them to learn, they did learn.[12]

Another characteristic often attributed to the culture of poverty is

---

[8]Alvin L. Schorr, *Slums and Social Insecurity* (U.S. Social Security Administration, 1963), Research Report 1.

[9]R. C. Griggs, *et al.*, "Environmental Factors in Childhood Lead Poisoning," *Journal of the American Medical Association*, March, 1964.

[10]Kenneth B. Clark, *Dark Ghetto* (New York, Harper & Row, 1965).

[11]*Washington Post*, April 16, 1967, and April 26, 1967.

[12]Robert Rosenthal and Lenore Jacobson, "Self-Fulfilling Prophecies in the Classroom: Teachers' Expectations as Unintended Determinants." (Paper presented at the Annual Meeting of the American Psychological Association, Washington, D.C., September, 1967.) 14 pp. Mimeographed.

lack of motivation. But motivation is a product of multiple ingredients and not a unitary trait. Moreover, it is a response as well as
an attribute and is affected, as we have just seen, by nutrition,
general health level, and other life circumstances that influence
energy and ability to concentrate. It includes, also, aspiration and
expectation, and the stronger of these is expectation. If expectation is
very low, aspiration can be crippled. At one time, it was assumed
that ghetto parents had very low educational aspirations for their
children. A number of studies have made it clear, however, that the
educational aspirations of very low-income parents for their children
are often as high as, or higher than, those of the affluent.[13] Their
expectations, on the other hand, had not been high. Nor have they
seen themselves as playing any role in helping their children to
actual educational achievement. A great deal of the effort to involve
parents in school and preschool activities has been directed toward
convincing them that home and parents play a vital part in a child's
school performance, and in demonstrating to them ways of making
their part constructive.

FAMILY NORMS AND FORMS

Of all the features ascribed to the culture of poverty, perhaps the
most deplored is family instability with all its concomitants—
including female-headed families, illegitimacy, and dependence on
public assistance, especially Aid to Families of Dependent Children
(AFDC). Our census data assure us that family instability does characterize the poor in this country: Divorce and separation are on the
whole inversely correlated with income.[14] Yet there is abundant
evidence that the norms of stable family life are preferred by the
poor as well as by the prosperous.

This point embodies and illustrates one of the chief problems
about the culture of poverty concept. To be acceptable at all, the
culture of poverty must be viewed, not as a culture but as a "subculture," a culture within a culture, existing within and as part of our
prevailing culture of the middle class. With regard to family norms
and forms especially, there is ample and increasing evidence that

---

[13]Melvin H. Kohn, "Social Class and Exercise of Parental Authority," *American
Sociological Review*, June, 1959, pp. 352–366. Hylan Lewis, "Child-Rearing Practices
among Low-Income Families," in *Casework Papers, 1961* (New York, Family Service
Association of America, 1961).

[14]Arthur A. Campbell, "The Role of Family Planning in the Reduction of Poverty,"
Journal of Marriage and the Family, Vol. 30, No. 2 (1968), pp. 236–245.

stable marriage and family life are accepted as a preferred ideal by most poor people, white and nonwhite. Such evidence was offered by Hylan Lewis' study of childrearing practices among low-income families,[15] has been supported by the investigations of Hyman Rodman,[16] by numerous reports and studies of AFDC clients—including that conducted by Greenleigh Associates,[17] and has recently been reinforced in a number of research and demonstration projects conducted under grants from the Department of Health, Education, and Welfare.

According to these and other reports, middle class standards of sex and family life do not rank as high on the value pyramid of the poor as on that of the prosperous. But they are preferred as luxuries one would gladly be able to afford—just as certain business men prefer certain forms of honesty, while considering them unrealistic for practice in daily life. This ability to believe in one set of values while practicing a different set is by no means unique to the poor. Many of us experience something like it occasionally or frequently. However, like the mote in the eye, or the spot in the middle of the forehead, it's easier to see on the other fellow.

The exigencies that prompt the poor to depart from preferred norms of family life and sex behavior include, among many things, early marriage, lack of education, employment problems, and welfare regulations. The man who is not a provider loses status in the eyes of the community, his family, and himself. He may leave because of this or because his family cannot obtain public assistance while he is present.

The vicious cycle is aggravated by the fact that the poor have larger families than the nonpoor. Not because large families are their choice. Overall, the preferred American family size is about the same at all economic levels, about three children.[18] However, the nonpoor have greater access to means of limiting the family and of averting extramarital pregnancy. It is by now a familiar fact that large families are more likely to be poor than small families, and that families which are both large and nonwhite run double risk of poverty.[19]

Illegitimacy is more frequent among the poor than the nonpoor.

---

[15] Hylan Lewis, *op. cit.*

[16] Hyman Rodman, "On Understanding Lower-Class Behavior," *Social and Economic Studies,* December, 1959, Vol. 8, pp. 441–450.

[17] *Facts, Fallacies and Future—A Study of the Aid to Dependent Children Program of Cook County, Ill.* (New York, Greenleigh Associates, Inc., 1960).

[18] Arthur A. Campbell, *op. cit.*

[19] Mollie Orshansky, "Recounting the Poor: A Five-Year Review," *Social Security Bulletin,* April, 1966, pp. 20–37.

But the preferred norms include birth in wedlock for poor and non-poor, white and nonwhite. On this point also, evidence piles up from many sources, and sometimes it is very poignant evidence. We hear of a child taunted by classmates for not knowing who his father is, punished by a teacher for reporting as reality his fantasies about a nonexistent father, sidling up to a strange man on the street in the hope of being called "Son."[20] The evidence also indicates, however, that at different economic levels, birth status occupies a different rank in the value hierarchy.

The different ranking of values is illustrated by Hylan Lewis' study, which was conducted in the District of Columbia. The mothers in his sample, white and nonwhite, dreaded unmarried motherhood for their daughters, prayed that it might not happen, and were devastated if it did. Yet they were equally emphatic, all of them, that if it did happen they would not try to persuade the young couple to marry—not unless they really loved each other.[21] A good marriage they viewed as one of life's chief blessings and certainly one of its rarest blessings; but a bad marriage, in their eyes, was worse than none. A study of the Detroit area reports greater readiness of white girls than of Negro girls to marry because of pregnancy.[22] It does not, however, report the economic status of the girls who were pregnant before marriage. Therefore, once again, a question remains, whether differences in illegitimacy rates are associated primarily with socioeconomic status or with color.

It is unfortunate that the white-nonwhite category is so much easier to apply than a socioeconomic classification, since it has led to reporting some figures (such as illegitimacy) only in terms of age and color. This habit of reporting, in turn, leads to overrating of ethnic factors and underrating of other factors. It has been estimated that if illegitimacy statistics could be controlled for income, the difference between white and nonwhite illegitimacy rates would dwindle dramatically.[23]

---

[20]Dick Gregory, *Nigger* (New York, E. P. Dutton & Co., Inc., 1964); John H. Roher and Munro S. Edmonson, *The Eighth Generation* (New York, Harper & Brothers, 1960).

[21]Hylan Lewis, "Culture, Class and Family Life among Low-Income Urban Negroes," in Arthur Ross (ed.), *Employment, Race and Poverty* (New York, Harcourt, Brace & World, Inc., 1967).

[22]William F. Pratt, "Premarital Pregnancies and Illegitimate Births in a Metropolitan Community—An Analysis of Age and Color Differentials." Unpublished manuscript cited in Stephanie J. Ventura, *Recent Trends and Differentials in Illegitimacy* (U.S. Department of Health, Education, and Welfare, Natality Statistics Branch, April 1968).

[23]Arthur A. Campbell, "Illegitimacy," *op. cit.*, and Elizabeth Herzog, "Unmarried

THE SLAVERY HERITAGE

In other respects also, the habit of reporting by color rather than by income fosters the habit of attributing to ethnic background differences that may in fact derive chiefly from socioeconomic status. For example, the differences in family life patterns between non-whites, and whites in poverty are dwarfed by the resemblances, if comparisons are made within specified income levels. Myron Lefcowitz, among others, has shown[24] that differences by income are more striking than differences by color, when controlled even very roughly by income; and that when Negro and white children with similar family incomes are compared, differences between them in educational achievement diminish and differences by class appear more striking than differences by color. Description of families in northern white slums could easily be mistaken for descriptions of families in the Harlem ghetto, whether one reads Lloyd Warner (1941) Hollingshead (1949) or Walter Miller (1959).[25]

This leads to a paradox: The culture of poverty concept bumps against the thesis that low-income Negro patterns of family life and sex behavior are primarily the heritage of the slavery years. The patterns so often described as a cultural legacy of slavery are to a large extent the patterns ascribed to the culture of poverty among people who have never been slaves. Yet those who invoke the slavery-specific thesis use it to document differences between Negroes and whites, and offer it as *the* explanation of behavior patterns among low-income Negroes.

With regard to the features ascribed—for example, family instability, woman-based households, overt sex antagonism, illegitimacy, large families, interpersonal violence, depression, apathy, sense of lacking control over one's own fate—no inconsistency is involved. Slavery, in fact, can be viewed—for some slaves and to some extent—as an extreme version of poverty with a few repulsive

Mothers: Some Questions to Be Answered and Some Answers to Be Questioned," in *About the Poor: Some Facts and Some Fictions* (U.S. Department of Health, Education and Welfare, 1968), Children's Bureau Publication No. 451, pp. 55–57.

[24]Myron Lefcowitz, *Poverty and Negro-White Family Structures*. (Background paper for White House Conference, "To Fulfill These Rights," Washington, D.C., November 1965.)

[25]Lloyd W. Warner and Paul S. Lunt, *The Social Life of a Modern Community* (New Haven, Conn., Yale University Press, 1941); August B. Hollingshead, *Elmstown's Youth—The Impact of Social Classes on Adolescents* (New York, John Wiley & Sons, Inc., 1949); Walter B. Miller, "Implications of Urban Lower-Class Culture for Social Work," *Social Service Review*, September, 1959, pp. 219–236.

additions. The inconsistency lies in attributing to the heritage of slavery the same behavior patterns that, for other groups, are attributed to poverty, and then assuming that the slavery heritage, in itself, accounts for those behavior patterns when they occur among Negroes.

The point has been made that the differences between very low-income whites and Negroes are dwarfed by the similarities, with regard to characteristics so far investigated. This is not to argue against the existence of differences. It is also arguable, however, that such differences could be attributable to a century of prejudice, discrimination, and persecution as much as or more than to the preceding years of slavery.

The argument is complicated by the fact that, in our society, economic status to a large extent determines culture, so that it is very difficult to disentangle what we mean by culture and what we mean by class. This intertwining is, of course, built into the culture-of-poverty concept.

SUBCULTURE OR CULTURE

The various specifics mentioned illustrate considerations that point to two conclusions concerning "the culture of poverty": If the concept is to be useful at all, it must be explicitly recognized as a subculture rather than a culture; but under any name, poverty lacks the essential elements of a culture.

With regard to the first point, the poor, like the nonpoor, on the whole accept the norms and standards of what has come to be called the mainstream culture. Any subculture coexists and competes with a number of other subcultures. Most citizens of the United States are members of a good many subcultures: Family, peers, colleagues, organizations, and so forth, each with its own norms and imperatives. Which set wins out at any given moment depends on the personal makeup and history of the individual, on the nature of the situation and on coincidental circumstances. The complexity of this mixture makes doubly inappropriate what I have called the "cookie-cutter concept of culture"—the idea that a culture produces individuals as identical as cookies cut from the same mold.[26]

A subculture of poverty, to the extent that it exists, can explain

---

[26]Elizabeth Herzog, "Some Assumptions about the Poor," *About the Poor: Some Facts and Some Fictions, op. cit.,* pp. 35–51.

relatively little about a specific individual at a specific moment. It can, however, offer a pat phrase: "It's the culture," as a substitute for thought and for action. To the extent that this substitute is accepted, the concept jeopardizes both thought and action. "It's the culture," can mean "they don't mind, that's the way they like it, and anyway it's built-in, so you can't do anything about it."

The second point is that, under any name, poverty lacks some essential elements of a culture. The chief one is a matter of identification. Members of a culture, or a subculture, have a sense of belonging to a culture entity with institutions, patterns, and shared beliefs. Committed members have a sense of allegiance as well as of identity. Even those who want to break away have the feeling that they are separating themselves from an entity that exists and claims them as members. Corollary to this is the sense of participating in the life of a broad group, sharing in a system of beliefs and practices. This positive aspect of culture, the sense of belonging, with its corollary elements of sharing and of participating, has not characterized the people who served as models for the culture of poverty concept.

On the contrary, some of the closest students of slum life emphasize the unincorporated quality of life in the slums. There are gangs and cliques, but their subculture is the gang or the clique. The neighborhoods consist of people who happen to live near each other. A salient characteristic of AFDC mothers and of many other slum dwellers is their social isolation. The lack of worldly goods, according to these observers of large city slums, does not create a sense of community, of common institutions and customs, practices and beliefs. The life-ways of the slum dwellers represent, not a system of culturally evolved patterns, but rather a series of adjustments to exigencies perceived as unpredictable and uncontrollable.

It may be asked, is a culture of poverty evolving from the civil rights movement and the Poor People's Campaign? If so, it is by no means what has been meant hitherto by the culture of poverty. Some salient traits of the movements now on the march represent the most conspicuous lacks in the so-called culture of poverty: Commitment, energetic motivation, hope. It may well be that these movements will shoulder aside preoccupation with and arguments about the culture of poverty. What they produce to supersede it remains to be seen. But no development will free us of the need to subject simple and easy generalizations to cautious and continuous checking against available evidence.

ANDREW BILLINGSLEY

Family Functioning in the
Low-Income Black Community

No task of the social worker and social planner is more imperative today than the development of a sensitive appreciation of the structure and functioning of black families. For despite the rapid and sometimes cataclysmic social changes now taking place, the family remains the basic unit of society and the most important social institution for the welfare and the healthful development of children. Elsewhere I have outlined a theoretical framework within which to view the structure and the functioning of family life in the black community.[1] According to that formulation the black family should be looked at as a social system imbedded in the black community; in turn, the black community is surrounded by the largely white community and its institutions. The structure of family life in the black community is a product of forces in the wider white society, though it is to some extent shaped by the conditions of life to which black people have been subjected. In my view, the extent to which black families are able to meet the needs of their members and the requirements society places on all families depends heavily on the extent to which the institutions of the wider society meet the needs of black people in general and black families in particular.

In a very real sense, all black families live in Michael Harrington's "other America," apart from the mainstream of what Kenneth Galbraith has termed *the affluent society*, in which two-thirds of all families in this nation dwell. In this society it is a curse to be poor, and it is a double curse to be poor and black. Being black but not poor is no picnic! For in every facet of American life, black families fare worse at the hands of society than do their white counterparts.

Families may be described according to their capacities for carrying out instrumental and expressive functions. Instrumental func-

---

SOURCE: Reprinted from *Social Casework*, December, 1969, pp. 563–72.
[1]Andrew Billingsley, *Black Families in White America* (Englewood Cliffs, N. J.: Prentice-Hall, Inc., 1968).

tions are those functions concerned with the provision of the basic necessities of life, such as food, clothing, shelter, health care, and the acquisition of occupational skills. Falling within the realm of expressive functions are the establishment of relationships with relatives; the structuring of the patterns of love, friendship, and affection; and the subtle determination of the intimate but intricate ways in which family members relate to each other, teach each other, and enhance or deflate each other's dignity and sense of worth. The family does not function well or poorly as a whole. Rather, it performs its functions well or poorly in certain specific realms of life. For example, child rearing is only one realm in which the family functions either well or poorly. It is also one area in which the literature about the dysfunctioning of black families is inaccurate and the views expressed are distorted.

THE TANGLE OF PATHOLOGY

It is nearly five years since a governmental report concluded that family life in the black community constitutes a "tangle of pathology ... capable of perpetuating itself without assistance from the white world,"[2] and that "at the heart of the deterioration of the fabric of Negro society is the deterioration of the Negro family. It is the fundamental *source* [italics mine] of the weakness of the Negro community at the present time."[3] I believe that this is an incorrect analysis of the relationship between black families and white society. Weakness in the family does not cause poverty, nor does black racism constitute the source of the pathology that afflicts black people. Quite to the contrary: the family is a creature of the society, and the greatest problems facing black families are problems that emanate from our *white* racist, militaristic, and materialistic society. Ours is a society that places higher priority on putting white men on the moon than putting black men on their feet on this earth. But Daniel Moynihan's analysis, which placed the responsibility for the difficulties faced by black people on the family unit, was eagerly received by the American reading public as a key to understanding black people. Although Moynihan has subsequently modified his position in some respects, one of the unfortunate consequences of

---

[2]*The Negro Family: The Case for National Action . . .*, Office of Policy Planning and Research, U.S. Department of Labor (Washington, D.C.: U.S. Government Printing Offce, 1965), 47.

[3]*The Negro Family*, 5.

his report is that it has given rise to similar analyses by other white students of the black family.

Now, nearly five years later, two white social scientists who call themselves "militant integrationists" have written a book based on their observations during a nine-month sojourn in a black community.[4] It includes a chapter entitled "The Negro Ghetto Non-family," which perpetuates the incorrect analysis made so famous by Moynihan but which has been thoroughly discredited by more careful social analyses.[5] Henry Etzkowitz and Gerald Schaflander state candidly their view of black people:

It is our own belief that there are practically no plusses in Negro ghetto culture. We see nothing but bitterness and despair, nihilism, hopelessness, rootlessness, and all the symptoms of social disintegration in the poor speech, poor hygiene, poor education, and the lack of security resulting from a nonfamily background in which the stabilizing paternal factor is absent and where there is no stable institution to substitute for the family.[6]

They go considerably beyond the Moynihan thesis of disintegrating family life in asserting without qualification "that love, warmth, hygiene, education and family stability are absent for most Negroes."[7] They add that "booze, gambling, drugs, and prostitution are the inevitable result of the absence of a stable family institution."[8]

These men are as insensitive and arrogant as they are incorrect in their analysis. They insist that the line of causation runs from the family to the society. After describing in extremely negative terms what they consider "momism" — represented by the harassed, cranky, frustrated, church-going, overworked mothers who dominate their nonfamilies by "driving young children into fierce competition" — these white liberal social scientists conclude that "the damage *resulting* [italics added] from this *typical* nonfamily life often leads to young dropouts and unwed mothers, and to crime, violence, alcoholism and drug addiction."[9]

Despite the incorrectness of their analysis of the relationship be-

---

[4]Henry Etzkowitz and Gerald M. Schaflander, *Ghetto Crisis: Riots or Reconciliation?* (Boston: Little, Brown and Company, 1969).

[5]See, for example, Elizabeth Herzog, *About the Poor: Some Facts and Some Fictions*, Children's Bureau Publication No. 451 (Washington, D.C.: U.S. Government Printing Office, 1967).

[6]Etzkowitz and Schaflander, *Ghetto Crisis, op. cit.,* p. 15.

[7]*Ibid.*, p. 14.

[8]*Ibid.*, p. 14.

[9]*Ibid.*, p. 16.

tween black family life and the white society, their views are similar
to those held by many persons, including some members of the
social work profession. The authentication of such views by social
science scholarship supported by generous foundation grants serves
to perpetuate this erroneous thinking. As a consequence enlightened
people are stopped from getting on with the task of analyzing and
helping to remove the crippling consequences of institutionalized
racism that the *Report of the National Advisory Commission on Civil
Disorders* so correctly identifies as the most important cause of the
difficulties black people face in this country and the most important
cause of their outrage against oppression.

For scholars and students trying to understand family functioning
in the black community, the chief faults of the type of analysis
described above lie in the reversal of the cause and effect relationship between the black family and society and in the ignoring of the
forces of institutionalized racism. For social work practitioners and
social planners, an additional problem is that this type of analysis
ignores the variety and complexity of black family and black community life while concentrating on its negative features. Analyses of this
kind are made from the narrow perspective of white-Anglo conformity by which black people are judged outside the context of their
unique anchor in history, their treatment in this country, and their
contemporary social conditions. More important, such analyses ignore both the existence of a black subculture and the strengths of the
black community and the black family that have enabled black
people to survive in a hostile environment for more than three
hundred years.

Unfortunately, analyses of black families by well-educated,
well-meaning white liberal integrationists are based more on their
own perspectives and prejudices than on the realities and complexities of life in the black community. The continuation of the
white-middle-class-outsider perspective — born out of a combination
of ignorance and arrogance — not only obscures the realities of black
family and black community life but performs a downright disservice
to the understanding the wider society so desperately needs.

The truth of the matter is that most black families in most communities of any size meet the American test of stability. Contrary to the
impression generally circulated by white students of the black family, most black families, even those who live in the ghetto, are headed
by men. And most of the men are still married to their first wives.
Furthermore, most of them, and many black women, too, are employed full time but are still unable to lift their families out of

poverty. What we need to know more about is how these families manage. How do they function? How do they meet the needs of their children? My own research, as well as an increasing number of other studies, suggests that black family life—even that of the lower-class ghetto family—is much more varied than is generally recognized.

A BUNDLE OF COMPLEXITY

I have discovered, for example, that the lower class consists of at least three groups rather than one.[10] Some lower-class black families are managing well both economically and socially; these are the *working nonpoor*. The vast majority of the black lower class form a middle layer I have termed the *working poor*. The third segment is composed of the relatively large number of families who are economically dependent, termed the *under class* or *nonworking poor*. The latter two groups of poor families account for nearly half of all black families and nearly one-quarter of all poor families in the United States.

The complexity of family life in the black community has been emphasized by Ralph Ellison.[11] When asked by a group of young black writers to comment on how they might more truly reflect the complexity of the human condition, using their own experience as a theme, he replied:

If [the Negro writer] accepts the clichés to the effect that the Negro family is usually a broken family, that it is matriarchal in form and that the mother dominates and castrates the males, if he believes that Negro males are having all of these alleged troubles with their sexuality, or that Harlem is a "Negro ghetto" . . . —well, he'll never see the people of whom he wishes to write. . . .[12]

Ellison's observations are not confined to fictional descriptions of black family life. He continues:

I don't deny that these sociological formulas are drawn from life, but I do deny that they define the complexity of Harlem. . . . I simply don't recognize Harlem in them. And I certainly don't recognize the people of Harlem whom I know. Which is by no means to deny the ruggedness of life there, nor the

---

[10]Billingsley, *Black Families in White America*, 136–42.

[11]"A Very Stern Discipline," interview with Ralph Ellison, *Harper's Magazine* (March, 1967), 76–95.

[12]"A Very Stern Discipline," 76.

hardship, the poverty, the sordidness, the filth. But there is something else in Harlem, something subjective, willful, and complexly and compellingly human. It is "that something else" that challenges the sociologists who ignore it, and the society which would deny its existence. It is that "something else" which makes for our strength, which makes for our endurance and our promise.[13]

Josephine Carson, a highly sensitive white female writer who went into the South to study the role of black women today, came to a similar conclusion.[14] She found a strong attachment to familism in black communities.

They are together, the link is not broken. Black is intimate. Whatever the broken family is, one feels unbrokenness here more than brokenness: *My sister ... My cousin ... My mother keeps him while I work ... This is a picture of my son ... My daddy was a preacher ... My granddaddy bought my grandma ... Listen, with a man you has to put up with a heap o' thangs to stay, like you said you would, till death ... The chillrun stops by my aunt's place till I comes home ...*[15]

"There is," she concludes, "a chain of black being."[16] Her description of the black women among whom she lived is quite in contrast to that of Etzkowitz and Schaflander:

The impression left is of a formidable woman: a worker, a believer; one who is patient, enduring, full of wit. A fortress. A matriarch by default. Someone had to mother that estranged white South and try to bind the sundered black family. Negro society is no more matriarchal, no more addicted to her healing power than the South itself.[17]

And the black woman of her acquaintance "rarely fails to describe her mother with love and admiration," "a woman who is loved, needed; who is sometimes sacrosanct, often exploited; who endures."[18]

It may be that Josephine Carson's analysis is more sensitive, and therefore more correct, in part at least because of who she is and how she behaved in the presence of black people. She is a woman who

---

[13]"A Very Stern Discipline," 76.
[14]Josephine Carson, *Silent Voices: The Southern Negro Woman Today* (Delacorte Press, New York, 1969).
[15]Carson, *Silent Voices*, 7–8.
[16]Carson, *Silent Voices*, 7–8.
[17]Carson, *Silent Voices*, 263.
[18]Carson, *Silent Voices*, 265.

got very close to the subjects of her study. More important, perhaps, she was not inhibited by some of the strictures of the more professional and scholarly social scientists who rely so heavily on their own intelligence, their instruments, their tape recorders, and their white faculty advisors. Miss Carson seemed to be aware of her limitations as a white person living among black people. She rode the bus with black domestics returning from a long day's work in the white part of town and commented: "The presence of Miss Ann on this bus at this hour is enough to stop the seriousness, if there is any, of the exchanges. Miss Ann manages to break the domestic barricade, nothing more. *Mr. Charley would do even less* [italics added]."[19]

Rather than considering black families to be the cause of the poverty they experience, Josephine Carson observes and remarks on the amazing ability of black families to survive and maintain stability in the face of poverty and other overwhelming odds: "Love and family solidarity sometimes survive the siege [of poverty]. In this neighborhood, with all its bitter poverty, the statistics show that only one-third are broken homes. Hard to believe."[20] Nor is she confused about the relationship among family structure, poverty, and racism. It is not the female family head, but racism, that causes the poverty. For although it is true that black families headed by women are more likely to be in poverty than black families headed by men, it is also true, and even more relevant, that black female family heads who work earn considerably less than white female family heads who work and therefore are even more likely to be living in poverty. Josephine Carson observes this interrelated complex of forces and comments: "When the black family was headed by a woman [in 1966], 61.8 percent were living in poverty," which is "more than twice the percentage of white families headed by women and living in poverty!"[21] Obviously, then, it is not the family structure that *causes* poverty!

At another point she notes some of the positive attributes of the black experience. "A family," she observes, "is not two parents with children in a housing tract, in a housing project. . . . A family is kin. The black woman's milieu is among kin."[22] And she writes, "When one speaks of poverty and dejection and misery, one forgets to say that the most humor and affection for life, the most sheer creature vitality to be found in this country are surely in the young black

---

[19]Carson, *Silent Voices*, 11.
[20]Carson, *Silent Voices*, 51.
[21]Carson, *Silent Voices*, 266.
[22]Carson, *Silent Voices*, 8.

face."[23] This fact has escaped the notice of many white experts on black people.

Josephine Carson's sophisticated analysis of the relationship between poverty and family life in the black community has benefited from her ability to listen to the voices and the spirits of her subjects, including the voice and the spirit of that amazing black woman in the Southern Liberation Movement, Mrs. Charity Simmons, who could well have been the co-author of *Silent Voices*, sharing in its rewards as she did in its labors.

I have referred at some length to Josephine Carson's work in part because it is a more correct analysis than the ones referred to earlier and in part because it demonstrates that not all white people are completely insensitive or unable to learn about the complexities of the black experience. Fortunately, her views are not idiosyncratic but are supported by a growing body of careful research.

THE CARE AND PROTECTION OF CHILDREN

The extent to which a black family functions adequately in protecting its children depends chiefly on the social supports it is given by society and on its position in the social-class structure. Thus, the working-class family, the middle-class family, and the upper-class family in the black community each provides a higher level of instrumental protection than does the lower-class or the under-class family, owing not so much to the family structure as to the nature of the resources available. A husband and father is an important figure, but his presence in the family is neither necessary nor sufficient to insure the instrumental well-being of children. Particularly in the black community other family members, relatives, friends, neighbors, and other role models provide the screens of opportunity that enable some families to function better than others.

Even among the lowest social classes in the black community, families give the children better care than is generally recognized, and often the care is better than that given by white families in similar social circumstances. Black people are not nearly as alienated from their families, from their children, or from themselves as white people are. They have not become as victimized by the debilitating forces of American-style "success," which requires utter lack of regard for others unless they happen to be powerful. Perhaps this is why black families still consider children important and why they go

---

[23]Carson, *Silent Voices*, 53.

to such great lengths to protect their children and try to meet their basic economic, social, physical, and psychological needs.

It is not generally appreciated, for example, that child neglect and abuse are much more common in white families than in black families. Child neglect is much more common among lower-class white families than among lower-class black families. Child abuse is much more likely to occur in white families than in black families who live in similar, or even worse, economic circumstances. In a study of physical neglect and abuse of young children in low-income families in New York State, Leontine Young found that even though black families were overrepresented in the population she sampled [public welfare clients], neglect and abuse were much more prevalent among white families. She found a similar phenomenon in a series of studies she conducted in various cities across the nation.[24]

A second set of data comes from the 1960 United States census. Although black children were overrepresented in institutions for delinquents, they were underrepresented in institutions for neglected and dependent children; only 8.4 percent of all children in institutions for the dependent and neglected were black, considerably less than their proportion in the population.[25]

It is possible, of course, that some of the underrepresentation of black children in institutions for neglected children is due to the nature of the system itself and how it operates. Since, in general, institutions for neglected and dependent children are a shade superior to institutions for delinquents, there may be a tendency for black children to be more readily categorized as delinquent rather than neglected as compared with white children. There is no doubt, however, that there is something about black culture that is also operative and is in part responsible for this phenomenon. For in the black community a child's or a youth's striking out at society in ways considered antisocial is not only justified but is an exceedingly healthy expression of his reaction against the constraints placed upon him by an uncaring society. It is quite another thing, however, for parents to deliberately mistreat their children or to refuse to feed, clothe, and shelter them when they have these resources available.

A third study was part of my own research. In a randomly selected sample of 40 white and 40 black low-income families headed by

---

[24]Leontine R. Young, "The Behavior Syndromes of Parents Who Neglect and Abuse Their Children," doctoral dissertation, Columbia University School of Social Work, 1963.

[25]U.S. 1960 Census of Population, *Inmates of Institutions*, P.C. (2) 3A, table 31, p. 44.

women, the researchers found that the physical abuse of children was over twice as common among white mothers as among black mothers; 38 percent of the white mothers but only 13 percent of the black mothers abused their children.[26] And in a study of 206 white and 239 black families in public welfare caseloads, it was found that 63 percent of the white families as compared with 43 percent of the black families were found to neglect or abuse their children.[27]

Finally, in a study of 371 low-income mothers who delivered babies at San Francisco General Hospital between September and December 1966, it was found that black families were more likely to have taken advantage of prenatal care than were low-income white families.[28] Thus, 26 percent of the black mothers as compared with 5 percent of the white mothers were in the group that had received the most adequate care.

These data are not to be viewed as evidence that all black families function well in meeting the instrumental needs of their children. Rather, the point to be made is that there is what Robert Coles terms *sinew* in the black family; many unrecognized positive attributes and coping patterns have been generated in order to provide a measure of protection to children, although the coping behavior varies greatly. Many black families function very well indeed, all things considered. For these families, a little bit more money would solve whatever problems they have. Other families do not manage quite so well, and the care they give their children is marginal. Still others seem to be in a constant state of chronic dysfunction, and their children are likely to be grossly neglected.

PATTERNS OF CHILD CARE

When Hylan Lewis and his associates analyzed the attitudes and behavior of 41 parental figures in 39 households in Washington, D.C., they found a high degree of conformity to middle-class norms of child rearing among very-low-income black mothers.[29] They also

[26]Barbara Griswold and Andrew Billingsley, "Personality and Social Characteristics of Low-Income Mothers Who Neglect or Abuse Their Children" (unpublished manuscript, 1967).

[27]Andrew Billingsley, "A Study of Child Neglect and Abuse" (unpublished, School of Social Welfare, University of California, Berkeley, 1967).

[28]Jeanne Giovannoni and Andrew Billingsley, "Social Determinants Affecting Prenatal and Well Baby Care," paper presented to Western Society for Pediatric Research, Los Angeles, California, 1967.

[29]Hylan Lewis, *Culture, Class and Poverty*, three papers from the Child Rearing Study of Low Income District of Columbia Families (CROSSTELL), sponsored by the Health and Welfare Council of the National Capital Area, Washington, D.C., February 1967.

found, however, a high degree of vulnerability to "unguided, un-planned influences outside the family,"[30] which play an inordinately important role in the socialization of children.

These researchers identified three patterns of family functioning with respect to the adequacy of child-rearing behavior in these low-income families. One group of parents not only showed great concern for their children's health, education, and welfare but also behaved in such a manner as to assure the care and protection of their children. They were adequate parents. Lewis writes, "Working with what they have, [these adequate parents] show high 'copabil-ity,' self-reliance, and self-respect."[31]

A second group of parents also had great concern for the welfare of their children, but they seemed unable to behave appropriately; their verbalized concern was accompanied by behavior that was inconsistent with their stated goals. These parents tended to be highly self-centered and demanding; they seemed to love their children, but they could not view them as individuals in their own right. The children were in constant danger of being neglected.

A third group of parents seemed unconcerned for the welfare of their children, and their patterns of behavior toward and on behalf of the children were dysfunctional. The result was the classic picture of child neglect; the children were undernourished, their physical ailments were untreated, and they were exposed to violence, harsh treatment, and arbitrary punishment. The parents tended to use their children as scapegoats for the frustrations they experienced in their own lives. Dependent and lacking in self-confidence, self-reliance, or self-esteem, these parents seemed to resent their children's dependence on them.

A study made by Joan Gordon and her associates of low-income black families in central Harlem also supports the view that some of these families function amazingly well, others function marginally well, and others are characterized by inadequate social functioning.[32] This study also suggests some of the factors that make the difference: when the forces of the larger society fail these families, many of them are able to call upon the resources of their neighbors and their relatives to support the expressive functions of family life and to enable them to meet the needs of the children. These are rich

---

[30]Lewis, *Culture, Class and Poverty*, 3.

[31]Lewis, *Culture, Class and Poverty*, 6.

[32]Joan Gordon, *The Poor of Harlem: Social Functioning in the Underclass*, A Report to the Welfare Administration (Office of the Mayor, Interdepartmental Neighborhood Service Center, New York, 1965).

resources for the very survival of many poor black families in a hostile society.

In her study Dr. Gordon used black interviewers to conduct intensive interviews with 46 black mothers, most of whom were recipients of Aid to Families with Dependent Children. Although a great deal of attention has been focused on the presumed disorganization, estrangement, and alienation to be found in low-income black families in the ghetto, this study did not find these phenomena but rather several levels of social integration. Sixteen of the 46 mothers were considered to be highly integrated into the neighborhood system. Their behavior included helping each other in time of trouble, helping each other in time of illness, minding each other's children, and lending and borrowing food, money, and clothes. These highly integrated mothers also exchanged information with each other about the best place to shop, how to raise children, problems on the block, and problems with the public welfare department. Twelve of the mothers were considered to be moderately well integrated; they were involved in at least two of the four areas of mutual aid and at least two of the four areas of information exchange. Thus, almost two-thirds of the mothers were involved in a network of informal relations with their neighbors. The authors found a similar patterning with respect to kinship ties.

The researchers had not expected to find such a high level of group cohesion. "It is remarkable," they concluded, " . . . that given how little they have in the way of income or material resources and how beset they are with problems, so many, nevertheless, share what they have and try to help in critical times."[33] Fifteen of the 46 mothers did, however, reveal the classical picture of isolation and estrangement; they gave and received no aid or information.

In the area of child rearing, the researchers examined three dimensions of attitude and behavior: (1) the mothers' behavior, knowledge, and standards with respect to the education of their children; (2) the mothers' attitudes about selected child-rearing items; and (3) the mothers' preferences for child care arrangements. Again, the research found no support for the claim of universal ignorance, apathy, and absence of standards in the area of child rearing.

Both the Lewis and the Gordon studies have shown that family functioning, even among those attenuated nuclear families with the lowest incomes in the urban black ghetto, is far from uniform. Many families are given by their immediate society, their neighbors, and

---

[33]Gordon, *The Poor of Harlem*, 42.

their relatives the resources that enable them to do an amazingly good job in caring for their children. Others are given fewer of these resources. And still other families seem to have been utterly deserted, so that both the families and the wider society suffer the consequences.

MAN IN THE HOUSE

Surely one of the more important resources for the care and protection of children is the presence of "a man in the house." Most studies of low-income black families are focused almost exclusively on the mother as a source of data and also as an object of analysis, in spite of the fact that most black families are headed by men. In 1966 R. C. Stone and F. T. Schlamp reported to the California State Department of Social Welfare on their study of 1,200 intact low-income families, 316 of which were black.[34] The study comprised families supported by AFDC and other low-income families who were self-supporting. The men in the families were the major source of data. The comments that follow are based on the findings concerning the role relations in the 316 black families.

Role relationships in the black family are highly affected by the family's level of economic functioning and the pattern of its participation in the world of work. The division of labor for selected household and childrearing tasks in the black families studied by Stone and Schlamp is shown in Table 10–1.

It is obvious from this table that the family division of labor falls into a variety of patterns, and that husbands are more likely to help their wives with child care tasks than with household chores. It is of special interest that in more than two-thirds of these families the husband and wife are jointly active in disciplining the children and taking them on outings. And in two-fifths of the families there is joint participation in basic child care and in helping the children with schoolwork. Among these low-income black families, the dominant pattern of controlling the use of money is equalitarian; nearly 48 percent of these married couples report that the husband and wife make decisions jointly.

But having a man in the house is not always an unmixed blessing for the children who need care and the other family members who

---

[34]R. C. Stone and F. T. Schlamp, *Family Life Syles Below the Poverty Line*, Report to the State Social Welfare Board for Social Science Research (San Francisco State College, San Francisco, California, 1966).

must provide that care. David Schulz, in a study of five families in a public housing project, found three different patterns of relationships the fathers maintained to meet the instrumental needs of their families and children.[35] One pattern he termed the *indiscreet free man*, a pattern in which the father shared openly his personal, financial, and other resources with one or more families outside his main household. He observed: "Such a father's interests reverberate upon his children, creating an intensified kind of sibling rivalry with his 'outside' children, who, in some instances, are known personally by his legitimate children. Life within such families is thus one of constant conflict and bickering."[36] The second pattern, the *discreet free man*, is a relationship in which the father also has outside family responsibilities, but they are secondary and are not used to antagonize his wife and children. The third pattern is the *traditional monogamous* one in which the man's "home and family are his major concerns and receive his constant attention."[37] Since the study sample consisted of only five families, it is difficult to be sure that these three patterns are the only ones that characterize black fathers' relationships with their families.

TABLE 10-1
Family Division of Labor

Kind of task	Usual performers (in percent)			
	Wife only	Husband only	Husband-wife jointly	Husband-wife plus others
Household				
Laundry	59.8	3.4	18.4	18.4
Cooking	59.5	0.0	22.6	17.9
Dishes	38.6	1.2	14.5	45.7
Cleaning	33.7	2.4	20.9	43.0
Shopping	27.7	7.3	57.8	7.2
Child care				
Child care	37.0	0.0	40.7	22.3
Child discipline	22.6	3.6	67.8	6.0
Child outings	18.8	2.5	68.7	10.0
Help with schoolwork	34.9	12.7	39.7	12.7
Control over				
Spending money	36.9	14.3	47.6	1.2

---

[35]David A. Schulz, *Coming Up Black: Patterns of Ghetto Socialization* (Prentice-Hall, Englewood Cliffs, New Jersey, 1969).
[36]Schulz, *Coming Up Black*, 127.
[37]Schulz, *Coming Up Black*, 128.

STUDY OF FAMILY LIFE

Camille Jeffers spent 15 months studying child rearing and family life in a low-income housing project composed primarily of black families.[38] Her study provides further examples of patterns in family functioning and in child rearing in the black community. Her overall findings were much more positive than those of many observers who have spent briefer periods of time making their studies and have used more formal techniques of observation. "My impressions after 15 months," she observes, "were that the overwhelming majority of parents cared deeply about, and were concerned about, the welfare of their children. Their concern took many forms and had many dimensions. Concern about children might be focused on attempting to obtain the basic necessities of life for them. . . . There was seldom total absence of concern about a child or children on the part of parents."[39]

The three major patterns of family life she found were reflected in the well-being of the children. One group of families held themselves aloof from the other families in the housing project. Their reference group was made up of people who lived outside the project, and they aspired to be upwardly mobile. Usually, the husband had a secure job. They were more likely than other families to control the size of the family, and the children were generally well cared for. A second group consisted of families not unlike the first group in their orientation toward the children, but they were more interdependent with other families in the project. In these families the husband's employment ranged from very stable to very unstable. Life was a bit more precarious for these families, but they maintained a considerable degree of control over the children. A third group of families included, but was not confined to, one-parent families. Income was uncertain and jobs unstable; money was constantly in short supply. These parents spent most of their time in the housing project; yet the children had more freedom of movement than those in other families and were less closely supervised. "As early as their second or third years, children from this third group of parents could be seen outside playing alone without adult supervision but, supposedly, under the watchful eye of a brother or a sister not much older than themselves."[40]

---

[38]Camille Jeffers, *Living Poor: A Participant Observer Study of Choices and Priorities* (Ann Arbor Publishers, Ann Arbor, Michigan, 1967).

[39]Jeffers, *Living Poor*, 53.

[40]Jeffers, *Living Poor*, 19.

This research also underscored the importance of mutual-aid relations with friends, relatives, and neighbors as a resource for child care. "It was impressive to see how quickly some mothers could parcel out their children and just as impressive to see the way some neighbors would rise to the occasion when such demands were made. . . . Some mothers had three or four persons upon whom they could call in an emergency" to care for their children.[41]

SUMMARY

A series of careful and sensitive studies of family life in the low-income black community lends support to the theoretical perspective advanced at the beginning of this article. Even in the black under class, family life is considerably more varied than many of the negative generalizations made by well-meaning social scientists would suggest. Furthermore, these studies lift the veil from the mystery of why some families function better than others. Three patterns of family functioning have been identified. Some families manage well to hold themselves together and to meet the children's needs. Others function marginally, and the children are constantly on the verge of difficulty. Still other families are involved in an almost perpetual state of dysfunctioning. And it is the children of these families who are most likely to suffer the scars of racism, poverty, and family disruption.

Several clues emerge from these studies about the factors that are likely to enhance family functioning. Economic viability is, of course, the most crucial element. Education of the family head is another, and it helps if there is a man in the house. Some families manage to hold themselves together by a network of intimate interrelationships of mutual aid and social integration with their neighbors and kin. These are the "screens of opportunity" available to some families and denied to others that help to account for the various kinds of functioning in black families. Rather than relying on the gross generalizations that have emanated from limited studies, social workers should take leadership in creating intervention strategies and building programs based on the resourcefulness and strengths of black communities and black families.

---

[41]Jeffers, *Living Poor*, 21.

·11·

EDGAR MAY

Looking for Work

[*The sequence of events described in the following selection occurred to a young man within one year's time. A welfare recipient
living in a large urban county, this man received "help" from a
program which may have had adequate goals. The perseverance of
the young man may be praiseworthy but his efforts were less than
successful, possibly because of a faulty choice of intervention strategies.*]

Job-hunting efforts of this boy will be frequent and sporadic, and
as he gets older and acquires a family, more difficult. Exactly how
difficult they may become can be seen by glancing at the job record
of a welfare recipient in the generation ahead of this boy. The record
comes from the files of the Cook County Department of Public Aid's
Industrial Training Center, which prepares relief recipients for work
and runs its own employment program. It begins March 3, 1961, after
the recipient was assigned to the training center.[1]

3/3/61:	States that he wants a job very badly in order to support his two young children.
4/10/61:	Rfd. to Johnson's Restaurant as cook's helper.
4/17/61:	Rfd. as porter-dishwasher to Charlie's Snack Shop.
5/5/61:	Rfd. as porter to Swift Candy Co.
6/2/61:	Appointment for 6/5/61.
6/2/61:	Rfd. to National Time Co. as porter.
6/5/61:	Rfd. as porter to Standard Hotel.
6/7/61:	No suitable opening.
6/9/61:	Rfd. to Joe's Drive Inn as porter.
6/13/61:	Client hired on above referral, but stated that he had difficulty obtaining transportation from that address after 2:00 A.M. He was picked up by police and questioned regarding being in

SOURCE: Reprinted from pp. 81–83 in *The Wasted Americans* by Edgar May.
Copyright © 1964 by Edgar May. Reprinted by permission of Harper & Row, Publishers, Inc., and Curtis Brown, Ltd.
[1]The real names of companies in the record have been changed.

	the neighborhood and was threatened by a motorist. Client did not return to job. He is to report 6/14/61 for a day's pay.
6/20/61:	Rfd. to ISES [Illinois State Employment Service].
6/23/61:	Rfd. as porter to Rosa Restaurant.
6/27/61:	Rfd. as dishwasher-porter to Lefferts Restaurant.
6/30/61:	Client is in today saying that he could not find the place where he was referred.
7/5/61:	No suitable opening.
7/6/61:	No referral.
7/12/61:	Complained of toothache.
7/20/61:	Complained of post-dental complications.
8/3/61:	Sent to ISES.
8/10/61:	No employment available.
8/17/61:	No suitable opening.
9/5/61:	Transfer to another load. Record held in ITC over 60 days after graduation.
9/25/61:	Referred for current evaluation of employability. Still registers physical pain on left side.
9/28/61:	Is employable and restricted to medium-light-type work.
10/13/61:	No suitable opening. Referred to Work Relief.
11/2/61:	Telephoned—left message with landlady. Referred as dishwasher, Lake Isle Restaurant.
11/3/61:	Hired as dishwasher—Lake Isle Restaurant @ $40 per week—72 hr. work week—6 day week (includes meals and uniforms).
11/15/61:	Worked 1 day on the above job—earned $4.50. To continue on Work Relief Project.
12/5/61:	Intensive dish washing and pot washing job solicitation made, but to no avail. Return Appt. 12/8/61.
12/7/61:	Could not be reached by telephone. Telegram sent—referred as bus boy to Sam's Restaurant.
12/7/61:	Sent wire to Sam's.
12/8/61:	Was not hired at Sam's today, however, was told to return next week for possible openings.
1/8/62:	Employed (City Restaurant) to telephone 1/9/62—3:00 P.M. re: possible opening.
1/12/62:	Referred as dishwasher and kitchen helper to Delfin Restaurant.
2/9/62:	No suitable opening.
3/30/62:	Telegram sent. Referred as machine dishwasher to Tip Top Restaurant.
4/3/62:	Telegram sent. Referred as dishwasher to Carla Rest Home.
4/4/62:	Hired to start 4/5/62 @ $35.00 per week.

Employment records like this will be written with increased frequency in the sixties. They may be briefer, because there just will not be as many places to send people.

And they will include more and more young people consigned to the welfare rolls, because on the day when they looked for their first job, they were obsolete.

And they were obsolete, in part, because we are assuming that their desires from life are the same as ours, even though their parents may have never experienced them, could not talk about them, and therefore did not teach them to their children.

And they are obsolete, in part, because they have been plunged into a school system largely designed for middle-class Americans, where an academic high school diploma is a matter of course and in many neighborhoods the question of college only a matter of choice.

SECTION III

Goals for Social Intervention

INTRODUCTION

The importance of problem identification was noted in the previous section. We observed that the way a problem was defined determined in large measure the type of intervention activity selected. For example, it makes a difference in planning intervention strategies whether a given group of people is viewed as hungry, as unemployed, or without money. Clearly, through the process of identifying and defining the problem we already are suggesting goals and strategies. Yet goal setting should become an explicit activity rather than take place implicitly.

It is relatively easy to suggest that something is a problem, that something is wrong. For example, how often have we said that the Smith family has a problem or that our city has many problems. However, unless we can specify goals, social intervention activity may be meaningless and pointless. Undoubtedly there are many things wrong with the Smith family and quite certainly our community has many problems. But mere concern or unhappiness about these provides insufficient direction for social intervention activity. An integral part of the problem definition and the development of the social intervention strategy is the determination of social intervention goals. In this connection one is reminded of Alice, who in her travels in Wonderland asked, "would you tell me, please, which way I ought to go from here?" To which the cat replied, "that depends a good deal on where you want to go." Where we want to go (goals) is, however, prescribed and limited by cultural values, availability of resources, and the skill of the social intervention agent.

Failure to achieve a desired outcome may be due to a variety of factors including the following:

1. Incorrect or faulty problem definition
2. Incorrect or faulty specification of goals or failure to specify the goal with sufficient clarity
3. Incorrect or faulty strategy selection
4. Incorrect target for strategy application
5. Incorrect or faulty application or implementation of the strategy

Though the error may occur in any one of these steps, an error in one of the earlier steps is more serious and will make certain that the outcome will be less than successful, no matter how perfect the techniques and means employed. Clear and correct identification and specification of goals is or should be the cornerstone of any social intervention activity. Good motivations or the intention to do good does not constitute a goal. Neither is the desire to do "something" about a pressing problem sufficiently clear or precise enough a goal to give direction to program designers and evaluators.

In developing goals, there is need to distinguish between direct and indirect goals, short-range and long-range goals, as well as nominal and fundamental goals. In specifying goals for any given problem, we must be aware that any specific goal may only be a step toward the realization of a long-range or ultimate goal. Effective social intervention activity will often require a division of the problem into subproblems where the achievement of each goal leads to further intervention activity. But very often, a desired goal cannot be achieved by direct intervention efforts; instead the worker will specify an indirect goal which may be responsive to intervention activity in order to ultimately effect another goal. The reduction of teenage pregnancies may require greater stability in the families in which these teenagers live. One of the ways to ensure greater family stability is to provide jobs so that fathers can earn an adequate income sufficient to take care of their families. These goals then may be viewed as follows:

Goal 1 – Provision of jobs
Goal 2 – Increasing family stability
Goal 3 – Reduction of teenage pregnancies

Initially Goal 1 will be considered the direct goal and Goals 2 and 3 the indirect goals.

Quite often the resolution of a problem or the reduction of its impact will involve both short-range and long-term goals. One type of strategy may be devised to achieve short-range goals and a different one to effect long-range goals. In working with a poor and victimized population, the short-range goals may include (1) to organize sufficient strength in the community so that the people can undertake further action and (2) to provide enough resources to meet the most emergent needs; the long-range goal may be to restructure society so that no community will find itself in the situation that this community is in. Clearly different strategies will be developed for each level of goals. The possibility of achieving success in short-range goals while experiencing failure in the long-range goals is not uncommon. In mental hospitals, for example, the short-range goal may be to cure patients sufficiently so that they can be returned to their community while the long-range goal would be to cure patients sufficiently so that they can function permanently in the community. The increasingly shorter hospital stays occurring at the same time with increasing rates of readmission suggest success in achieving short-range goals but failure in the long-range goal.

Perhaps a more crucial question concerning goals is whether nominal or fundamental change is necessary to achieve the desired goals. Should we attempt (1) to change people so that they will fit into the society as it exists or (2) should we attempt to change the society which initially caused the problem. The intervention strategy used will depend largely on the type of goal stipulated. Project Head Start, for example, was a strategy designed in response to a nominal change goal; it attempted to give disadvantaged children the skills necessary for better access to the existing opportunity structure but made no attempt to widen the opportunity structure or to introduce other basic changes in society. Generally social intervention efforts are directed toward nominal change goals. Failure to achieve any real success will occasionally result in the realization that fundamental rather than nominal change is required. Thus, the Mobilization-for-Youth experiment, after five years of attempting nominal change intervention activities, discovered that the problems of New York's Lower East Side were so severe that only basic societal changes, particularly income redistribution, would be successful (Weissman, 1969, p. 201).

It is an American tradition to meet problems only after they have become acute. This approach has contributed to the establishment of many unrelated services and to the avoidance of establishing basic problem-solving policies. It has also resulted in intervention efforts which generally are geared to treating symptoms rather than basic causes. Social scientists usually regard symptomatic treatment efforts with little respect since they tend to leave basic problems unresolved. Etzioni (1968) made the interesting suggestion, however, that this need not be true since quite often symptomatic treatment does result in desirable goal achievement. He noted that opposition to symptomatic treatment may be the result of long-held prejudices or deeply ingrained value position; thus, he suggested, that the opposition to methadone treatment for heroin addicts may be the result of our "puritanical feelings" that addicts should suffer. Too often, insistence on basic intervention efforts has resulted in no treatment at all. Although we need to realize that intervention efforts aimed at symptoms may not cure the cause, they should not be disregarded.

The question of who shall or should be involved in goal setting for specific social intervention activity will be covered more fully in the next unit. There are however certain overriding societal goals which give direction to the specific goals necessary for social intervention activity. In recent years social indicators have been utilized to quantify where we, as a society, are and whither we should move. Social policy and priorities for action can then be determined and based on statistical data. This permits focused intervention, directed social change, and measurable change.

Wilbur J. Cohen, former Secretary of Health, Education, and Welfare, listed potential societal goals for a congressional committee in "Social Indicators." From another point of view, the Kerner Commission described the dysfunctional consequences of a massive social intervention effort ("The Welfare System"). The selection develops basic strategies and programs for change; a minimum standard of decent living for all is explored as a societal goal. Will money alone solve the massive problems of our dependent populations?

The Family Service Association of America in "Families in Extreme Jeopardy: A Position Statement" suggests that more than money is needed; it calls for a national policy to help meet the needs and aspirations of millions of families who have been placed in extreme jeopardy. In succinct fashion, the statement focuses sharply on the relationship between family life, institutional arrangements, and societal pressures.

What are the crucial social goals for our society? Would everybody agree on the same priorities for social intervention? Is direct intervention always the most effective means toward goal achievement? What are the basic strategies and programs which can best be used by our nation to meet the needs of those who are victims of prejudice and discrimination?

Goals are often specified without adequate attention to facts; there is need to consider what people desire for themselves and for their families. "Employability of AFDC Family Heads" by Leonard J. Hausman examines the employment status of welfare family heads with particular attention to how definitions alter who is and how many people are employable. How can we encourage families to "take-off" for independence? Should this become the goal for all families? What kinds of child-care programs are needed? What bearing does the minimum wage and the availability of jobs have on public assistance programs? What is the relationship of public assistance programs on minimum wages and job availability?

Daniel P. Moynihan's "Policy vs. Program in the '70's" argues against programmatic perspectives and for a social policy approach because of the latter's potential and comprehensive nature. Complex systems have complicated "inputs" and "outputs." A policy framework, it is suggested, can be helpful because it encourages a more real view of a complicated series of interrelationships which accompany social systems and social interventions. Can policy be viewed separate from programs? How can we define success? What policies would you promulgate? What programs?

The late Samuel Mencher in "Ideology and the Welfare Society" takes us beyond "the end of ideology," pointing out that welfare problems do not arise out of technical problems. He demonstrates how ideological differences continue to determine answers to important questions such as income distribution and social wealth, the balance of social and individual interests, and the goals of state policy. What are the ideologies which today influence social agencies, social policy and social interventions? How are practitioner interventions determined by social policy and ultimately by ideological considerations? What is social welfare? What is social "dis-welfare?" How is ideology related to social goals and social costs?

REFERENCES

ETZIONI, AMITAI. 1968. " 'Shortcuts' to Social Change?" *The Public Interest,*
    Vol. 12 (Summer), pp. 40–51.
WEISSMAN, HAROLD H. (ed.). 1969. *Justice and Law.* New York: Association
    Press.

·12·

WILBUR J. COHEN

Social Indicators

The following goals, which are expressed in measurable terms,
represent specific indicators of social change. Some deal with areas
of health, education, and welfare – others with social trends, such as
women coming into the labor force and vacations and leisure time in
our society. (See p.99.)

Obviously, people assign different priorities to these and other
items of public policy. The goals are designed as a point of departure – to help in opening up the dialogue and debate which must
take place before social action is possible. They will test our resolve,
as individuals and as a Nation, in the years ahead. If we reach them,
we can climb to heights beyond our present ability to envision.

SOURCE: Full Opportunity Act. Hearings before Special Subcommittee on Evaluation and Planning of Social Programs of the Committee on Labor and Public
Welfare, U. S. Senate, 91st Cong. July 7, 8, 10, 18; December 18, 1969; and March 13,
1970. (Washington, D.C.: Government Printing Office, 1970).

Indicator	Present Experience	1976 Goal
1. Infant mortality (per 1,000 live births)	22.1 (1967)	12.6.
2. Maternal mortality (per 100,000 live births)	28.9 (1967)	15.
3. Family planning services for low-income women 15 to 44	1,000,000	5,000,000.
4. Deaths from accidents (per 100,000 population)	55.1 (1967)	50.
5. Number of persons in State mental hospitals	426,000 (1967)	50,000.
6. Expectancy of healthy life	68.2 years (1966)	70.2 years.
7. 3- to 5-year olds in school or preschool	35.2 percent (1967)	100 percent.
8. Persons 25 and older who graduate from high school	51.1 percent (1967)	65 percent.
9. Persons 25 and older who graduate from college	10.1 percent (1967)	15 percent.
10. Persons in learning force	100,000,000 (1967)	150,000,000.
11. Percent of major cities with public community colleges	65 percent	100 percent.
12. Number of 1st-year students in medical schools	10,000 (1967)	18,000.
13. Handicapped persons rehabilitated	208,000 (1968)	600,000.
14. Average weekly hours of work – Manufacturing	40.6 (1967)	37.5.
15. Labor force participation rate for women aged 35 to 64	48 percent (1967)	60 percent.
16. Average annual paid vacation – Manufacturing	2 weeks (1967)	4 weeks.
17. Housing units with bath tub, or shower	85 percent (1960)	100 percent.
18. Percent of population illiterate	2.4 percent (1960)	0.
19. Voters as a percentage of voting age population	63 percent (1964)	80 percent.
20. Private philanthropy as a percent of GNP	1.9 percent (1967)	2.7 percent.
21. Public and private expenditures for health, education, and welfare as a percent of GNP	19.8 percent (1968)	25 percent.
22. Percent of population in poverty	11 percent (1968)	0.
23. Income of lowest 1/5 of population	4 percent (1967)	10 percent.
24. Persons who work during the year	88,000,000 (1967)	110,000,000.
25. Life expectancy	70.2 years (1966)	72 years.

NATIONAL ADVISORY COMMISSION ON CIVIL DISORDERS

The Welfare System

INTRODUCTION

The Commission believes that our present system of public assistance contributes materially to the tensions and social disorganization that have led to civil disorders. The failures of the system alienate the taxpayers who support it, the social workers who administer it, and the poor who depend on it. As Mitchell Ginsberg, head of New York City's Welfare Department, stated before the Commission, "The welfare system is designed to save money instead of people and tragically ends up doing neither."

The system is deficient in two critical ways:

First, it excludes large numbers of persons who are in great need, and who, if provided a decent level of support, might be able to become more productive and self-sufficient;

Second, for those who are included, it provides assistance well below the minimum necessary for a decent level of existence, and imposes restrictions that encourage continued dependency on welfare and undermine self-respect.

In short, while the system is indispensable because for millions—mostly children—it supports basic needs, drastic reforms are required if it is to help people free themselves from poverty.

The existing welfare programs are a labyrinth of federal, state and local legislation. Over 90 percent of national welfare payments are made through programs that are partly or largely federally funded. These reach an average of 7.5 million persons each month:

- 2.7 million are over 65, blind or otherwise severely handicapped.
- 3.6 million are children in the Aid for Dependent Children (AFDC), whose parents do not or cannot provide financial support.
- 1.2 million are the parents of children on AFDC. Of these, over one million are mothers and less than 200,000 are fathers; about

Reprinted from Report of the National Advisory Commission on Civil Disorders (Kerner Commission) (Washington, D.C.: U.S. Government Printing Office, March 1, 1968), pp. 252–56.

two-thirds of the fathers are incapacitated. Only 60,000 fathers are in the special program called "Aid to Families with Dependent Children (Unemployed Parents)" (AFDC-UP) operating in 22 states.

Among all welfare programs, AFDC and AFDC-UP have clearly the greatest impact on youths and families in central cities areas; for this reason, it will be the principal focus for discussion here.

States and local governments contribute an average of about 45 percent of the cost of supporting the AFDC program, with each state setting the level of grants for its own residents. Monthly payments vary widely from state to state. They range from $9.30 per AFDC recipient monthly in Mississippi to a high of $62.55 in New York. In fiscal year 1967, the total annual cost of the AFDC program, including federal, state and local contributions, was approximately $2.0 billion, providing an average of about $36 monthly for each recipient.

This sum is well below the poverty subsistence level under any standard. The National Advisory Council on Public Welfare has commented:

The national average provides little more than half the amounts admittedly required by a family for subsistence; in some low-income states, it is less than a quarter of that amount. The low public assistance payments contribute to the perpetuation of poverty and deprivation that extend into future generations.

Over the last six years, despite the longest sustained period of economic progress in the history of this country, the AFDC caseload has risen each year while the unemployment rate has fallen. Cases increased nationally by 319,000 during fiscal year 1967 and will, under present HEW estimates, increase by another 686,000 during fiscal year 1968. The burden of welfare—and the burden of the increases—will fall principally on our central cities. In New York City alone, 525,000 people receive AFDC support and 7,000 to 10,000 more are added each month. Yet, it has been estimated in 1965, nationwide, over 50 percent of persons eligible to receive assistance under welfare programs were not enrolled.

In addition to the AFDC program, almost all states have a program of general assistance to provide minimum payments based largely or entirely on need. During calendar year 1966, the states spent $336 million on general assistance. No federal funds have ever been available for this program. In fact, no federal funds have ever been available for men or women, however needy, who are neither aged, severely handicapped nor the parents of minor children.

The dimension of the "pool" of poor but unassisted individuals and families—either ineligible under present programs or eligible but unenrolled—is indicated by the fact that in 1966 there were 21.7 million nonaged persons in the United States with incomes below the "poverty level" as defined by the Social Security Administration. Only a third of these received assistance from major public welfare programs:

[T]he bulk of the nonaged poor live in families where there is a breadwinner who works either every day or who had worked a part of the year, so that the picture that people have of who the poor are is quite a different thing from an analysis of the poverty population. And what we have done in effect is carve out, because of our categorical approach to public assistance, a certain group of people within that overall poverty population to give help to.

Seventy per cent of the nonaged poor families were headed by men, and 50 per cent of these held full-time jobs and 86 per cent of them worked at least part of the year, so that the typical poor family is much like the typical American family, except they don't make enough money. And they have been historically excluded from the AFDC program.[1]

The gaps in coverage and low levels of payments are the source of much of the long-term dissatisfaction with the system. The day-to-day administration of the system creates even sharper bitterness and dissatisfaction, because it serves to remind recipients that they are considered untrustworthy, ungrateful, promiscuous and lazy. Among the most tension-producing statutory requirements, administrative practices and regulations are the following:

First, in most states benefits are available only when a parent is absent from the home. Thus, in these states an unemployed father whose family needs public assistance in order to survive, must either abandon his family or see them go hungry. This so-called "Man-in-the-House" rule was intended to prevent payments to children who have an alternative potential source of support. In fact, the rule seems to have fostered the breakup of homes and perpetuated reliance on welfare. The irritation caused by the rule is aggravated in some states by regular searches of recipients' homes to ferret out violations.

---

[1]Testimony before the Commission of Lisle C. Carter, Jr., Assistant Secretary for Individual and Family Services, Department of Health, Education and Welfare.

Second, until recently *all* amounts earned by adult welfare recipients on outside jobs, except for small allowances for expenses, were deducted directly from the welfare payments they would otherwise have received. This practice, required by federal law, appears to have taken away from many recipients the incentive to seek part- or full-time employment. The 1967 amendments to the welfare laws permit retention of the first $30 earned by a recipient each month and one-third of all earnings above that amount. This is a start in the right direction but does not go nearly far enough. New York City has, for example, begun experimenting with a promising program that allows welfare mothers to keep the first $85 of earnings each month and a percentage of amounts above that.

Third, in most states, there is a residency requirement, generally averaging around a year, before a person is eligible to receive welfare. These state regulations were enacted to discourage persons from moving from one state to another to take advantage of higher welfare payments. In fact, they appear to have had little, if any, impact on migration and have frequently served to prevent those in greatest need—desperately poor families arriving in a strange city—from receiving the boost that might give them a fresh start.

Fourth, though large amounts are being spent on social service programs for families, children and young people, few of these programs have been effective. In the view of the Advisory Council on Public Welfare, the inadequacies in social services:

are themselves a major source of such social evils as crime and juvenile delinquency, mental illness, illegitimacy, multi-generational dependency, slum environments, and the widely deplored climate of unrest, alienation, and discouragement among many groups in the population.

A final source of tension is the brittle relationship that exists between many welfare workers and the poor. The cumulative abrasive effects of the low levels of assistance, the complicated eligibility requirements, the continuing efforts required by regulations to verify eligibility—often by means that constitute flagrant invasions of privacy—have often brought about an adversary relationship between the case worker and the recipient family. This is intensified by the fact that the investigative requirements not only force continuing confrontations but, in those states where the same worker performs both investigative and service functions, leave the worker little time to provide service.

As was stated by Lisle Carter, Assistant Secretary of Health, Education and Welfare, in testimony before the Commission:

[W]e think [it] is extremely important that welfare recipients begin to feel that the welfare worker is on their side instead of on the side of the agency. There have been statements made that the welfare workers are among the most hated persons in the ghetto, and one of the studies shows that the recipients tend to feel that what the workers says is something that cannot be challenged. Nowhere do you get the feeling that . . . the worker is there to really go to bat for recipients in dealing with the other pressures that they face in the community. . . .

One manifestation of the tension and dissatisfaction created by the present system has been the growth of national and local welfare protest groups. Some are seeking to precipitate a national welfare crisis, in part by bringing on the welfare rolls so many new recipients that America will be forced to face the enormity of its poverty problem. Others, often composed of welfare recipients or welfare workers, seek expanded welfare programs and attack day-to-day inequities in the administration of the system.

On the other hand, many Americans who advocate better housing, better schools, and better employment opportunities for dis- advantaged citizens oppose welfare programs of all kinds in the belief that they "subsidize" people who should be working. The fact is, as we have pointed out, that all but a small fraction of welfare recipients are disabled because of age, ill health or the need to care for their children. Even more basic is the fact that the heads of most poor families who can work are working, and are not on welfare. For both of these groups of people in need—those who cannot work and those who can and do—the problem in at least one vital respect is the same: lack of sufficient income to provide a base on which they can begin building a path out of poverty, if not for themselves, at least for their children.

An altered and expanded welfare system by extending support to more of those in need, by raising levels of assistance on a uniform national basis, and by eliminating demeaning restrictions, could be- gin to recapture the rich human resources that are being wasted by poverty.

BASIC STRATEGIES

In framing strategies to attack welfare problems, the Commission recognizes that a number of fundamental questions remain to be answered. Although many of the present inadequacies in the system can be identified, and specific changes recommended, long-term measures for altering the system are still untested.

A first strategy is to learn more about how welfare affects people and what its possibilities for creative use are. We endorse the recommendation of the Advisory Council on Public Welfare for greatly expanded research. We also commend the experimental incentive programs being carried out through the Department of Health, Education and Welfare and the Office of Economic Opportunity, as well as the Model Cities Program through which some cities hope to develop integrated programs of income supplementation, job training and education. We further commend the President's recent creation of a Commission on Income Maintenance Programs, which may provide answers to the complex problems here presented.

Despite the questions left open, we believe that many specific inadequacies in the present structure can and should be corrected.

The most important basic strategy we would recommend is to overhaul the existing categorical system to:

(*a*) provide more adequate levels of assistance on the basis of uniform national standards.

(*b*) reduce the burden on state and local government by financing the cost of assistance almost entirely with federal funds.

(*c*) create new incentives to work and eliminate the features that cause hardship and dependency.

(*d*) improve family-planning and other social services to welfare recipients.

Our longer-range strategy, one for which we can offer only tentative guides, is the development of a national system of income supplementation to provide a basic floor of economic and social security for all Americans.

SUGGESTED PROGRAMS

Overhauling the Present System

To repair the defects in the existing categorical system is not simply a matter of changing one or two aspects. Major changes are needed in at least seven areas.

1. Standards of Assistance.—The federal government should develop a minimum income standard for individuals and families enrolled in AFDC. The standard should be at least as high as the subsistence "poverty" level periodically determined by the Social

Security Administration. Only a few states now approach this "poverty" level, which is currently set at $3,335 for an urban family of four. The amending legislation should, if feasible, also permit cost of living variations among the states and within "high-cost" areas in each state.

As a critical first step toward raising assistance levels, the Commission recommends that the present provision under which the federal government pays fifteen-eighteenths of the first $18 of AFDC monthly payments be amended to provide that the federal government assume the entire first $15 and the same proportion of payments beyond $15 presently applied to that above $18. Taken together with existing legislation that requires the states to maintain levels of support when federal assistance rates are increased, the effect of this change would be to raise by over one-third the monthly welfare payments in eight states of the Deep South. In Mississippi, payments would be more than doubled.

2. *Extension of AFDC-UP.* — The Commission strongly urges that the temporary legislation, enacted in 1961, which extends the AFDC programs to include needy families with two unemployed parents be made permanent and mandatory on all states and that the new federal definition of "unemployment" be broadened. This program, which reaches the family while it is still intact, has been put into effect in only 22 states. Even in states where it has been implemented, the numbers participating have been small, partly because many states have narrowly defined the term "unemployment" and partly because the number of broken homes makes many children eligible under the regular form of AFDC.

3. *Financing.* — Because the states are unable to bear substantially increased welfare costs, the federal government should absorb a far greater share of the financial burden than presently. At least two methods are worth considering. The first would be to rearrange payment formulas so that, even at the highest levels of payments, the federal government absorbed 90 percent or more of the costs. A second method would be to have the federal government assume 100 percent of the increment in costs that would be encountered through raising standards of assistance and rendering AFDC-UP mandatory. Under either of these approaches, the share of costs presently imposed on municipal governments should be removed to release their limited resources for other uses.

4. *Work Incentives and Training.* — In three important ways, steps were taken in the 1967 amendments to the Federal Welfare Act to encourage — or compel — welfare recipients to seek employment.

Each of these controversial steps had some salutory aspects but each requires substantial further attention:

(a) Job Training.—The amendments provide substantially greater funds for job training. This was in principle a wise step. The amendments also, however, require the states to condition grants to "appropriate" adult welfare recipients on their willingness to submit to job training. Though the Commission agrees that welfare recipients should be encouraged to accept employment or job training, we strongly disagree with compelling mothers of small children to work or else lose welfare support. Many mothers, we believe, will want to work. A recent study of about 1,500 welfare mothers in New York indicated that 70 percent of all mothers—and 80 percent of Negro mothers—would prefer to work for pay than stay at home.

(b) Day-Care Centers for Children.—The 1967 amendments provide funds for the first time for day-care programs for children of working mothers. Further expansion is desirable to make centers an effective means of enabling welfare recipients to take advantage of training and employment opportunities. Efforts should be made to ensure that centers are open in the evening and that more education features are built into center programs. State and federal standards that prevent centers from employing subprofessional workers, including welfare recipient mothers, should be removed.

Welfare mothers themselves should be encouraged to set up cooperative centers with one or more mothers tending children of other mothers and with welfare funds available for salaries. Such "living room" day care can only be effective if the mother taking care of the children can be paid without losing any substantial portion of her welfare check.

(c) Retention of Part of Earnings.—The amendments permit an AFDC or AFDC-UP recipient to retain the first $30 of earned income monthly and one-third of the balance. Both the sums that can be kept without penalty, and the percentage of the balance that can be retained, should be raised substantially to maximize incentive to work. To determine the appropriate level and, indeed, to determine how job training and welfare programs can best interrelate, call for experimental programs to test different combinations and approaches. These programs should be supported at all levels of government.

5. *Removal of Freeze on Recipients.*—The 1967 welfare amendments freeze, for each state, the percentage of children who can be covered by federal AFDC grants to the percentage of coverage in that state in January 1968. The anticipated effect of this new restric-

tion will be to prevent federal assistance during 1968 to 475,000 new applicants otherwise eligible under present standards. In the face of this restriction, states and cities will have to dig further into already depleted local resources to maintain current levels. If they cannot bear the increased costs, a second alternative, less feasible under existing federal requirements, will be to tighten eligibility requirements for everyone or reduce per capita payments. We strongly believe that none of these alternatives are acceptable.

6. *Restrictions on Eligibility.* — The so-called "Man-in-the-House" rule and restrictions on new residents of states should be eliminated. Though these restrictions are currently being challenged in the courts, we believe that legislative and administrative action should be taken to eliminate them now.

7. *Other features of the program which can strengthen the capacity of welfare recipients to become self-sufficient and which deserve increased federal support are:*

(a) Clear and Enforceable Rights. — These include prompt determinations of eligibility and rights to administrative appeal with representation by counsel. A recipient should be able to regard assistance as a right and not as an act of charity.

Applicants should be able to establish initial eligibility by personal statements or affidavits relating to their financial situation and family composition, subject to subsequent review conducted in a manner that protects their dignity, privacy and constitutional rights. Searches of welfare recipients' homes, whether with or without consent, should be abandoned. Such changes in procedures would not only accord welfare recipients the respect to which they are entitled but also release welfare workers to concentrate more of their time on providing service. They would also release a substantial portion of the funds spent on establishing eligibility for the more important function of providing support.

(b) Separation of Administration of AFDC and Welfare Programs for the Disabled. — The time that welfare workers have available for the provision of services would be increased further by separating the administration of AFDC and general assistance programs from aid to aged and physically incapacitated. The problems of these latter groups are greatly different and might better be handled, at the federal level, through the Social Security Administration. Any such change would, of course, require that programs for the disabled and aged continue to be paid out of general funds and not impair the integrity of the Social Security Trust Fund.

(c) Special Neighborhood Welfare Contact and Diagnostic Centers.—Centers to provide the full complement of welfare services should be combined into the multi-purpose neighborhood service facilities being developed by the Office of Economic Opportunity and the Department of Housing and Urban Development. Federal funds should be provided to help local welfare agencies decentralize their programs through these centers, which would include representatives of all welfare, social, rehabilitation and income-assistance services.

(d) Expansion of Family-Planning Programs.—Social workers have found that many women in poverty areas would like to limit the size of their families and are simply unaware of existing birth control methods or do not have such methods available to them. Governments at all levels—and particularly the federal—should underwrite broader programs to provide family-planning information and devices to those who desire them. Through such programs, the Commission believes that a significant contribution can be made to breaking the cycle of poverty and dependency.

TOWARD A NATIONAL SYSTEM OF INCOME SUPPLEMENTATION

In 1949, Senator Robert A. Taft described a system to provide a decent level of income for all citizens:

I believe that the American people feel that with the high production of which we are now capable, there is enough left over to prevent extreme hardship and maintain a minimum standard floor under subsistence, education, medical care and housing, to give to all a minimum standard of decent living and to all children a fair opportunity to get a start in life.

Such a "minimum standard of decent living" has been called for by many other groups and individuals, including the AFL-CIO, major corporate executives, and numerous civil rights and welfare organizations. The study of the new Commission on Income Maintenance Programs, and the Model Cities Program will be of particular importance in providing direction. We believe that efforts should be made to develop a system of income supplementation with two broad and basic purposes:

• To provide for those who can work or who do work, any necessary supplements in such a way as to develop incentives for fuller employment;
• To provide for those who cannot work and for mothers who decide to

remain with their children, a system that provides a minimum standard of decent living and to aid in saving children from the prison of poverty that has held their parents.

Under this approach, then, all present restrictions on eligibility—other than need—would be eliminated. In this way, two large and important groups not covered by present federal programs would be provided for: employed persons working at substandard hours or wages, and unemployed persons who are neither disabled nor parents of minor children.

A broad system of supplementation would involve substantially greater federal expenditures than anything now contemplated. The cost will range widely depending on the standard of need accepted as the "basic allowance" to individuals and families, and on the rate at which additional income above this level is taxed. Yet if the deepening cycle of poverty and dependence on welfare can be broken, if the children of the poor can be given the opportunity to scale the wall that now separates them from the rest of society, the return on this investment will be great indeed.

·14·

FAMILY SERVICE ASSOCIATION OF AMERICA

Families in Extreme Jeopardy:
A Position Statement

The growing crisis in our city slums—a crisis marked by civil disturbances, violence, suffering, and despair—impels the Family Service Association of America to call for a national policy to protect and strengthen American families. This policy must be translated

This position statement was accepted by the board of directors of the Family Service Association of America and is reprinted with permission from *Social Casework*, January, 1968, pp. 44–45.

into effective action to remove the obstacles that block the urban poor from achieving healthy family life.

As an association of more than 335 member agencies working to prevent family breakdown and promote family development, we are in a position to understand the threats to urban families and to recommend constructive action. We now exercise our moral responsibility to speak out again on principles and programs that are basic to meeting the needs and aspirations of millions of families whose poverty and status in a minority group—Negro, Puerto Rican, Mexican, Indian, or other—place them in extreme jeopardy.

CALL TO NATIONAL COMMITMENT

We call for a total national commitment to the eradication of racial and ethnic discrimination and the causes of poverty so that *all* families may have the opportunity to participate fully in a democratic society. To initiate the programs needed for the long battle to reach these goals, a commitment must be made by all levels of government and by all other sectors of our society.

To this end, we urge a reordering of the priorities of our nation, states, and communities. The task demands the allocation of resources equal to the magnitude of the problems. It challenges all instruments of social and economic life to effect basic legal, economic, and social changes. It demands the moral force of strong leadership.

Although the principal funding of a national effort so vast in scope must be governmental, private enterprise and voluntary philanthropy also must make a substantial contribution of their skills and resources. Business, industry, labor, organized religion, citizen and professional groups must be directly involved in this effort. They must exert leadership to influence the allocation of national resources. And they must redouble their efforts to eliminate all obstacles to equality of opportunity within their own domains.

Basic to all other measures are legal, economic, and other arrangements that will provide a guarantee against poverty and social deprivation for all people. Equally necessary is elimination of *all* discriminatory practices. Programs to enable people to take advantage of their potential for self-support must be accompanied by acceptance of and provision for the people who have no such potential. When full rights and opportunities are available to all, society can then expect families and individuals to respond responsibly to the obligations of good citizenship.

Immediate and substantial movement in all the following areas is urgent:

• Creation of a national program in which government in co-operation with business and labor assures work opportunity at a living wage for all employable people.

• Creation of extensive training programs to equip the unskilled for productive employment.

• Provision of adequate financial aid available to all who need it as a matter of enforceable legal right. An adequate floor must be established and maintained and appropriation of funds required in every state to provide an income below which no family or individual will have to exist.

• Rehabilitation of deteriorating cities and erection of housing open to all and designed for wholesome family and community living.

• Development of educational programs geared to the current and future needs of socially or economically deprived children and young people.

• Development of adequate services for the prevention and treatment of illness, physical or mental.

• Expansion of social services essential to enable people to make effective use of their own strengths and opportunities. Outreach programs of counseling, group education, day care, family planning, consumer education, recreation must be widely available. They must be manned by staff sensitive to the need of people to be heard, skillful in helping people to involve themselves, and free of stereotyped approaches to individuals or groups.

Problems that cry out for solution are multiple and interrelated. Each attack upon a problem is affected by and has an effect upon proposals that approach the situation from other angles. Institutional interests are threatened by new or redirected programs. An overview of these reciprocal effects and their social, economic, and political aspects, plus co-ordination of the proposed measures into a comprehensive plan, is an absolute requirement.

APPEAL TO CONSCIENCE

The survival of strong family life for *all* citizens demands the highest priority. The stamina, ingenuity, determination, and adapt-

ability of human beings constitute our greatest national resource.
Active involvement of all our citizens—of all races, classes, and
conditions—is a vital ingredient of constructive planning and
effective programs.

We deplore the often irrational public response to civil disturbances. Too much reliance is placed on repressive measures that
ignore the basic problems of the slums. Prejudice and discrimination, now pervasive in our society, cruelly assault human
dignity and breed hate.

Blocked by inequality and deprivation, families in extreme jeopardy have psychological as well as material needs that must be met.
We believe that our nation has the resources, the knowledge, and the
skills to eradicate poverty and discrimination. What is lacking is the
will to do so. The nation has demonstrated that it can fulfill its
commitments in an emergency. Witness other national crises such as
the Great Depression, World War II, and the rebuilding of Europe
after that war. We cannot afford to say that meeting today's crisis is
too costly. Whatever is required must be done. The history, the
ideals, and the conscience of America demand that we do no less.

·15·

LEONARD J. HAUSMAN

Employability of AFDC Family Heads

Given the probable inability of most AFDC family heads to meet
the minimum income needs of their families by working at jobs in
which they have some experience, there is still a question of how
much work effort on their part can reasonably be expected. How

SOURCE: Reprinted from *Manpower Research Monograph No. 12* (Washington,
D.C.: Manpower Administration, U.S. Department of Labor, 1969), pp. 9–15.

many can work if some of the obstacles that now keep them out of the labor market can be removed?

Welfare departments generally define employability by reference to the absence of handicapping characteristics, such as physical or mental illness or the presence of young children; the possession of certain attributes, such as recent work experience or skills; and the state of the economy.

The City of Detroit Department of Public Welfare states: "Relief claimants are considered employable if they pass a physical examination and are not needed at home for the proper care of the members of the family unit."[1]

The Cook County (Ill.) Department of Public Aid identifies as "potentially employable" those AFDC mothers who were employed for 3 or more months within the 5 preceding years and who had no physical limitations, and notes that employability is also a function of the individual's "economic milieu" and of personal characteristics.[2]

The New York State Department of Social Welfare uses two criteria: (1) A welfare recipient is deemed unavailable for employment if he is "attending day school on a full-time basis," or is an "adult with household responsibilities," "incapacitated," or a "person with acute illness." (2) He is regarded as employable if, "in the judgment of the caseworker, [he is] designated as placeable based upon [his] skills and personal characteristics . . . as well as employment opportunities in the community."[3]

Such definitions may provide simple ways of dividing the AFDC caseload between those who "ought" and "ought not" to be in the labor force. However, they do not permit distinctions within the former category between those who could be hired at a market wage only if they acquired more skills or were rehabilitated and those whose employment hinges on such nonpersonal factors as increasing aggregate demand and day-care facilities, or reducing the welfare tax rate and racial discrimination. For this purpose, a better definition might be: An employable individual is one who, at a very high level

---

[1]Edward D. Wickersham, *Detroit's Insured Unemployed and Employable Welfare Recipients: Their Characteristics, Labor Market Experience, and Attitudes* (Kalamazoo, Mich.: The W. E. Upjohn Institute for Employment Research, April 1963), p. 8.

[2]Deton J. Brooks and others, *A Study to Determine the Employment Potential of Mothers Receiving Aid to Dependent Children Assistance* (Chicago: Cook County Department of Public Aid, June, 1964), p. 88.

[3]New York State Department of Social Welfare, Forms RS– 121 (6/65) for "Quarterly Statistical Report on Employability Status," published in the department's *Social Statistics*.

of aggregate demand, has a high probability of finding one or more hours per week of suitable work at some market wage.

Under this definition, recipients who require immediate rehabilitation and training would be classified as unemployable. Those who require day-care facilities, available jobs, or greater financial inducements to expand their work effort would be classed as employable. Being employable does not imply that a recipient ought to be able to earn enough to be financially independent at a reasonable income. Thus, even employable recipients who "ought" to work may merit upgrading and further rehabilitation.

The practical effect of the difference between this definition and those commonly used by welfare departments on the interpretation of "employability" is demonstrated in a comparison of survey results.

WELFARE DEPARTMENT STUDIES

The only employability data for AFDC-UP recipients come from California and New York State, which now account for more than half of all AFDC-UP cases. In July 1965, half of all AFDC-UP fathers in California were judged to be employable; men were considered unemployable if they were "older than age 50, illiterate," or had "acute or permanent physical or mental handicap." In September 1965, close to three-fifths of all AFDC-UP fathers in New York State were deemed employable, since they were both "available for employment" and "placeable." The data are weak in some respects. Surely some 51-year-old, illiterate men could hold part-time jobs, but no doubt some literate AFDC-UP fathers under 50 are not employable unless they can acquire new skills. The New York State data were gathered when the unemployment rate in that State exceeded 4.5 percent.[4] A crucial unanswered question is, how many of them would have been "placeable" at a 3 percent or 3.5 percent unemployment rate?

Nevertheless, the welfare department data indicate that a large proportion of AFDC-UP fathers are not to be thought of as being excluded from the labor market. Other types of data support this contention. In California, roughly 360 per 1,000 active AFDC-UP cases were closed between January 1, 1965, and June 30, 1965, because of the increased earnings of the AFDC-UP father. For the national AFDC-UP caseload, data for 3 months between December

---

[4]*Manpower Report of the President* (Washington: U.S. Department of Labor, April 1968), p. 282.

1964 and February 1966 yield a similar rate of "cases closed because of earnings."

That welfare departments may encounter difficulties in discovering disguised employables because the welfare tax rate is 100 percent or more is well illustrated by the case of an incapacitated father who was receiving Aid to Needy Children (ANC, now AFDC) in California.

> ... Mr. P., aged 46, has a wife and eight children, ranging from 3 to 13 years. Until 1951 he had a good work record, mostly in laboring jobs. His last job, as a pavement smoother, brought in a weekly wage of $70. Arthritis of the hip forced him to quit work. He received treatment at the county hospital, and the family received aid to needy children [ANC].
>
> Because of his disability, age, work record, attitudes, and level of intelligence, the type of work he can do is very limited. A caseworker at the Bureau of Vocational Rehabilitation counseled Mr. P. and developed a sedentary job for him on the assembly line of an electric products company.
>
> The dilemma which this case presents is that, once Mr. P. has proven his ability to work, the family will be removed from the ANC rolls. The ANC payment has amounted to $305 a month for the family of 10. On his new job, Mr. P. cannot hope to net more than $210 per month. Under the law, ANC cannot supplement his income since such supplementation is permissible only for a woman recipient, nor is it probable that general relief will be granted to supplement earnings.
>
> The Bureau of Vocational Rehabilitation was concerned about this case on medical grounds and pointed out to the State Department of Social Welfare:
>
> > There is no question in our minds that, as soon as these facts of life are brought home to him, he is going to develop subjective complaints which will make it impossible to continue on the job on which he is placed. Furthermore, none of us really believes that 10 people can even eat satisfactorily on $210 a month let alone maintain a decent standard of living.
>
> Cases like this one present a very real problem, and they are a significant factor in limiting rehabilitation work. The Bureau of Vocational Rehabilitation suggested to the Department that motivation toward rehabilitation could be provided by supplementing wages after treatment, where the parent's earnings have in any way been affected by his disability.[5]

This illustration is not used to imply that further investments in

---

[5]Margaret Greenfield, *Self-Support in Aid to Dependent Children* (Berkeley, Calif.: Bureau of Public Administration of the University of California, February, 1956), pp. 94–95.

the skills and health of welfare recipients are either unnecessary or undesirable; nor does it suggest that further efforts are not needed to raise the level of demand and thus open more opportunities to these individuals. It does imply that a larger proportion of AFDC-UP fathers, and perhaps even of "incapacitated" AFDC fathers, are employable than welfare data show, and that this employability may be revealed by changing nonpersonal factors such as the welfare tax rate.

How many AFDC mothers are employable, under the kind of criteria conventionally used by welfare departments? One or two careful studies are available to help answer this question.

In the 1965 survey of its AFDC caseload, the California Department of Social Welfare counted as "probably unemployable" those mothers who were either "older than age 50, illiterate, [limited by] any acute or permanent physical or mental handicap, or [by] more than 6 children." Using these criteria, 62.6 percent of the mothers were considered to be "probably unemployable." Of the remaining 37.4 percent, over half were considered by their caseworkers to be "needed in home as full-time homemakers." Thus only 17 percent of the California AFDC mothers were either employed or considered fully available for employment.

In New York State, the percentage of AFDC mothers who were either employed or employable, according to the criteria noted earlier, came to roughly 7 percent. If the determination of employability had not included a judgment as to how "placeable" a welfare client is, the 7-percent figure might have been a couple of percentage points higher.

From a random sample of 278 mothers in the AFDC caseload in early 1962, the Cook County Department of Public Aid selected as "potentially employable women" those who had 3 or more months of work experience within the previous 5 years and who were not handicapped by visible physical limitations. Not counting six women who were employed, 82, or 29.5 percent of the total sample, were found who satisfied both criteria. However, the imposition of a third criterion of no preschool-aged children reduced the employed and employable mothers to roughly 8 percent of the total sample. Yet some women who had been absent from the labor market for the past 5 years may no longer have been inhibited or handicapped by personal factors which necessitated previous inactivity; surely many young mothers return to the labor market after long inactivity. Also, some of the women who had preschool-aged children indicated that they could obtain cost-free child care if they began to work or retrain.

They may well have revealed limited employability if they believed the net wages they could earn would make employment profitable for them. The researchers made no effort to speculate about the actual market behavior of these women at full employment.

A nationwide study of AFDC mothers classed as having "no marketable skills" those "not needed as homemakers, who are unemployed because they have no work training or experience and whose potential for employment is poor, regardless of the conditions of the labor market." (See Table 15–1.) The employable women, according to the criteria used by the Bureau of Family Services of the U.S. Department of Health, Education, and Welfare (HEW), included those employed, either part time or full time, and those classified under "suitable employment not available," that is, women who met the conventional definition of the term "unemployed." Nationally then, roughly 22 percent of all AFDC mothers were either employed or considered employable in 1961.

TABLE 15–1

Employment Status of AFDC Mothers in the Home, Late 1961

Employment status	Number	Percent
Mother not employed:		
Needed in the home as full-time homemaker	411,300	55.3
No marketable skills	52,300	7.0
Suitable employment not available	43,500	5.9
Physically or mentally not able	85,600	11.5
None of the above factors apply	34,000	4.6
Mother employed full time	41,300	15.7
Mother employed part time	75,200	
Total	743,200	100.0

[1] Roughly 45,000 of the 743,200 mothers are in AFDC-UP families. Since those families are usually quite large—they average close to four children per family—most of the 45,000 mothers would be needed in the home. Thus the proportions of employable and unemployable mothers in the AFDC families only would be somewhat different.

SOURCE: *Study of Recipients of Aid to Families With Dependent Children, November-December 1961: National Cross-Tabulations* (Washington: U.S. Department of Health, Education, and Welfare, Bureau of Family Services, August 1965), table 23.

AN INDEPENDENT SURVEY OF
AFDC MOTHERS

A different picture of the extent of employability among AFDC mothers emerges from a small survey conducted for this study in New York during the late summer and early fall of 1966. An attempt was also made to determine what impact changes in the welfare tax rate would have on their employability. For this purpose, survey results are, of course, not as desirable or reliable as observations of actual labor market behavior. Employability involves consideration of both the demand for and the supply of an individual's labor, and only an experiment with a variety of net wage rates and with ample day-care facilities would permit strong statements about the mothers in the sample. But the survey data do contribute some tentative conclusions on the employability of AFDC mothers.

If an AFDC mother is capable of increased work effort, and if the welfare department is able to determine such a capability, her eligibility for assistance may be jeopardized. Such a woman might well be reluctant to answer questions pertaining to her employability for anyone whom she suspects of being affiliated with the welfare department.

Consequently, for this survey, the researchers enlisted the aid of the local chapter of a national organization that is organizing welfare recipients to represent them in dealings with local assistance agencies. This organization not only supplied four interviewers and gave the interviewers letters of introduction to the respondents, but also allowed the study directors to be introduced and questioned at one of its meetings and spread the word that the study directors were in no way connected with the New York City Department of Welfare. Nevertheless, some respondents—who clearly indicated to the interviewers that they believed the welfare department was resorting to more subtle means of investigation—undoubtedly were unwilling to answer questions freely and honestly. In sum, the survey estimates of the employability of AFDC mothers—while far above those based on investigations by the local welfare department—are probably below estimates that would be derived from absolutely free and honest answers to the same questions.

Although the small sample was not designed to represent any population larger than that of the area surveyed, a number of characteristics of the heavily Negro sample were remarkably similar to those of Negro AFDC mothers in the major cities of the Nation. The two groups were closely matched as to educational attainment level, employment and labor force status, and occupational distribution, as well as ages of the mothers and children, number of children per family, and proportion of families with children of preschool age.

The most important characteristic on which there was a substantial divergence between the two groups was "length of time on AFDC since most recent opening of case." This divergence may be due to shortcomings in data collection for the smaller study, or relaxed eligibility requirements and higher benefits levels in some States may have resulted in increased long-time dependency since 1961, when the national study was made. If the divergence on this characteristic is merely a data problem, then the study group closely resembles Negro AFDC mothers in other major cities. If welfare dependency has in fact risen, then the conclusions on the extent of employability among the respondents and on the possible impact of reduced welfare tax rates on employability would seem to hold, a fortiori, for some larger group of AFDC mothers. Generalizations from data yielded by the small sample should, however, be made with great caution and skepticism.

Potential Response to Changes in Welfare Tax Rate.—The responses of the 131 AFDC mothers interviewed indicated that many of them may be "disguised employables" and that their work effort may be influenced by the welfare tax rate. Again, though, under the most liberal assumptions made about their skills and the state of the labor market, they were overwhelmingly incapable of self-support.

Under the assumptions and definitions conventionally employed by welfare departments, a large majority of them would be classed as unemployable. If the employable category is limited to those mothers who are presently in the labor force, 16.8 percent is the relevant figure. (See Table 15–2.) If the employable category is expanded to encompass those mothers who claim they are now able to work, the proportion reaches 22.9 percent.

Most of the mothers, 65 percent, claimed to be unemployed or not in the labor force because they were unable to find suitable child care or because they were not physically well. A few, 5 percent, stated that their skills were inadequate, while others boldly replied that they did not like to work, that they preferred to be on welfare, or that mothers on AFDC were not supposed to work (10 percent).[6] When asked why she was unable to work, one woman said, "Because I worked before and I know what it's like working 8 hours a day." Another explained, "If I get off welfare, I couldn't make enough to support my family." Still another responded, "If the pay was good for a decent job, I would take one for sure. But the jobs they [the welfare

---

[6]The distribution of these mothers by their reason for not working is very similar to that of the Chicago AFDC mothers. In the Chicago sample, roughly 76 percent of the entire sample explained their nonemployment similarly. Most of the difference between the two figures is probably traceable to the fact that the Chicago study was conducted by the welfare department and thus the AFDC mothers were less prone to explain their behavior frankly.

TABLE 15-2
Employability of 131 Mothers in New York Survey, by Different Criteria

Definition of employability[1]	Percent employable
Mothers who—	
Are employed or looking for work	16.8
Are employed or claim ability to work, and have available child care	22.9
Have no health problems	25.2
Have no children under 6	35.9
Have free child care available	10.7
Had job within past 5 years	18.3
Indicate job interest and possession of skills	27.5
Appear employable in general evaluation of responses	38.9

[1] The categories are not mutually exclusive.

department] expect us to take aren't good. They don't pay enough and you're never sure how long you're going to be working." A woman, who later volunteered that she had recently completed one sales job at which she worked for 18 successive months and, just prior to that, one at which she worked for 8 months told the interviewer, "I'm not good at working. Just can't seem to hold a job. You know, I can't work with my hands too well and my education is limited."

When employability was defined as having recent employment experience and no health problems or preschool-aged children — roughly the criteria applied in the Chicago study — the proportion of employable mothers in the New York study was slightly higher than the Chicago figure: 10.7 percent compared with about 8 percent. However, just under 25 percent of the mothers in the sample indicated that if they had to work and got a job next week, they would be able either to find nonpublic, cost-free child care or to work while their children were in school.[7]

[7]In discussions with the AFDC mothers who were the leaders of the welfare recipients' organization that aided the study, one got the impression that a larger proportion of mothers could obtain cost-free child care on a part-time basis — if it paid for the mothers to work. They spoke as if they were quite sure of this fact and claimed

A series of questions was designed to probe the effect of the welfare tax rate on the mothers' revealed employability. Just over 37 percent of the 131 women replied affirmatively to the first question: "Have you ever felt that it didn't pay you to work?" Over 80 percent of this group—or more than 30 percent of the entire sample—either explained that expenses incurred in working, including child-care expenses, made employment financially senseless, or, implicitly noting that the high tax rates on their benefits restricted their choice of work or welfare, explained that they were financially better off on welfare. Of the 17 women who complained about employment-related expenses, one said: "Right now it really doesn't pay for me to work unless I get a decent salary. After all, when you work you have to have lunch, dress nice, spend money for carfare, and those things cost a lot of money. By the time you're through with all the expenses there's hardly nothin' left." One of the 25 women who chose welfare on economic grounds explained her reasoning this way: "Because I would make less working than what I get from welfare. If I worked, I'd get about $50 a week. When on welfare, I get $62 a week."

The questions that followed were:

1. Do you think, if the Welfare Department let other AFDC mothers keep most of what they earned and didn't budget their earnings, that this would influence or do anything to the amount of work they did every week?
   a) Why do you think so?
      or
   b) Why don't you think so?
2. A few months ago the New York City Welfare Department decided to allow AFDC mothers to keep $40 of what they earned every month; they no longer budget that amount of money or deduct it from the assistance check.
   a) Did you know about this new rule before I told you about it?
   b) What do you think of it?
   c) Do you think this will influence the amount of work that people do?

---

that outsiders were not aware of the potential informal child-care resources available to AFDC mothers. It should be noted, though, that the respondents were quizzed on what they would do if they *had* to work; some may have answered differently if the question had implied that the women had a greater degree of choice over their work behavior. Thus, it is hard to judge the probable direction of the error in this estimate. In the Chicago study, a number of the mothers indicated that they had cost-free child care available to them, if they were to be retrained or to find work. What is clear is that by no means all women with young children are prevented, for that reason, from working.

To question 1, about 72 percent responded affirmatively; and one-sixth of the remaining women explained their "no" or "not sure" answers in a manner that indicated they would have responded affirmatively if they had understood the question. Roughly 15 percent said that they and/or others would respond to a large earnings exemption by going to work; roughly 30 percent found the prospects of an added income attractive; and another 15 percent indicated that working would no longer be futile. For example:

"I know if I could work and not be afraid of getting caught while I'm getting my check, I'd work."

"If I could work, I know I'd find something, if that meant I could still collect from the welfare department."

"Because that way they won't feel that their working is futile. Why work when they're gonna take it from you?"

"Some women or most women need that money real bad and being on welfare wouldn't be so bad if a woman could work and keep her dignity."

Most mothers were not aware of the (then) new earnings exemption rule in New York City, and just over half thought it was a good idea. Only 36 percent, however, indicated that this kind of earnings exemption would motivate mothers to seek work and another 27 percent were unsure of its effects. It was quite clear that the women thought of the $40 per month as their earnings for a month of full-time work; thus for many, the implied low net wage rate meant that work would still not be a financially sensible alternative to "full-time leisure." The proportion who thought that mothers would be sensitive to a "low" net wage rate was about half of the proportion who thought that mothers would work at a "high" net wage rate. Many of the responses to question 2 offer interesting contrasts with those to question 1:

"Personally, I wouldn't go to work for $40 a month unless I was working one hour a day."

"Well, I have six kids and in a way the extra $40 would come in handy, but I couldn't see going to work every day for that."

"Well, personally, I wouldn't go to work for that; but looking at it broad-mindedly, I'd imagine many mothers would take advantage, but I doubt if they'd all report their incomes to the welfare department."

The responses to this series of questions show that less than one-fourth of the mothers believed that a lower welfare tax rate would not induce greater work effort. About one-third felt that any moderate or reasonable earnings exemption or any reasonable change in their potential net wage rates would motivate mothers to work. Another two-fifths felt that only a substantial change from the status quo would be effective in motivating AFDC mothers to greater work effort.

Overall Estimates of Employability.—From the results of this series of questions and other data obtained in the interviews, it appears that 27.5 percent of the mothers were either working or were interested in jobs and had marketable skills. Those who were not working were regarded as likely to look for a job—provided lower welfare tax rates were to bring their net wage into line with their market wage. This proportion rises to 38.9 percent if the term "employable" is redefined to exclude only those clearly uninterested in working under any circumstances, obviously without marketable skills, or definitely prevented from working because of poor health or a large number of children. Another 14.5 percent of the 131 mothers were marginal or questionable cases, given the available data. Thus, less than half could be considered clearly unemployable under the simple definition proposed earlier in this section.

The survey responses suggest that, given favorable welfare tax rates, more AFDC mothers are employable than is frequently believed. Of course, the women were not asked whether *they* would work under different net wage rates or if they personally would want to work at various net wage rates, so their responses may not predict their behavior under the stated conditions. Even if all of the mothers who implied that they or others would want to work actually would search for jobs, it is by no means certain that they could find employment at market wage rates, even at high levels of aggregate demand. In short, conclusions drawn about employability and work effort changes in response to changes in the welfare tax rate or net wage rates among these AFDC mothers from this survey must be highly tentative. The most reasonable conclusion from this small survey is that reduced welfare tax rates and increased child-care facilities will substantially increase labor force participation, if not employment, among these mothers.

DANIEL P. MOYNIHAN

Policy vs. Program in the '70's

One of the anomalies of the 1960's is that a period of such extraordinary effort at social improvement should have concluded in a miasma, some would say a maelstrom, of social dissatisfaction.

What went wrong?

Well, countless things went wrong. But I believe one of the more important things is that the structure of American government, and the pragmatic tradition of American politics, too much defined public policy in forms of *program,* and in consequence has inhibited the development of true *policy.* In simpler times a simple programmatic approach was an efficient way to go about the public business. The problem comes with complexity. More specifically, the problem comes when society becomes ambitious and begins to seek to bring about significant changes in the operation of complex systems such as the society itself. There is nothing the least wrong with such ambitions. What is wrong is a pattern in which the ambitions are repeatedly proclaimed, and just as repeatedly frustrated—especially when the source of the frustration lies not in the malfeasance of individuals but in the limitations of the *program* approach to issues which demand the disciplined formulations and elaborations of public *policy.*

These are terms that rightly call for definitions. Here I think the temptation is to be too clever. As increasingly we perceive and begin to understand the social system as just that, a system, it is possible, and for many purposes necessary, to be meticulous about classifying various forms of system intervention. But, my rough purpose is more readily served by a simple distinction. Programs relate to a single part of the system; policy seeks to respond to the system in its entirety.

The idea of policy is not new. We have for long been accustomed to the idea of foreign policy, including defense policy. Since 1946

SOURCE: Reprinted with permission from *The Public Interest,* No. 20 (Summer, 1970), pp. 90–100. © National Affairs, 1970.

Congress has mandated an employment and income policy more or less explicitly based on a "general theory" of the endlessly intricate interconnections of such matters. Yet our ways of behavior resist this: only great crises, great dangers seem to evoke the effort. Or have seemed able to do so in the past. I believe, however, that a learning process of sorts has been going on. Increasingly the idea of system-wide policies commends itself to persons of responsibility in public affairs as an approach both desirable and necessary. We can expect it to be one of the formative ideas of the 1970's.

CONSTITUENCIES AND MASTERS

As in most times, it is the style, the approach of the incumbent administration that has most to do with such matters. The first official act of President Nixon, taken his third day in office, was to establish the Urban Affairs Council, a cabinet level body. The first task assigned the council was to "advise and assist" the President in the formulation of a National Urban Policy. This was something new. It had not been done before; no one was certain it could be done. No one is as yet certain it can be done successfully. Certainly there did not exist anything like Keynes' General Theory which guided our development of national policy on employment and income. Nor were there any Admiral Mahans or George Kennans to provide a master theory of an urban policy comparable to previous formulations of foreign and defense policy. Even so, the process went forward with fair dispatch, so that for anyone caring to know the general outlines of the urban policy of the present administration there is at least a document. Not a definitive one, nor even perhaps a comprehensive one; but an existing one. (I do not infer that this urban policy has had any great consequence. It has not. Only a small element in either the political or career bureaucracy of the federal government has grasped the policy concept, and where it has been understood it has on the whole been opposed. It will be years—if ever—before the Presidential initiative will have any real consequence. Changing the federal system is immensely difficult. Thus, the PPBS system [Planning—Programming—Budgeting System] was introduced in the mid-1960's with great energy and visibility, and strong Presidential support. By the end of the decade it had all but disappeared as an element in decision-making, at least at the higher levels of government. For purpose of provoking a discussion, I would be prepared to assert that the McNamara colonization of the domestic departments of the federal government with the system of

Moynihan: Policy vs. Program in the '70's

127

benefit-cost analysis developed in the Pentagon failed. A primary source of failure was the lack of talent to carry out the analyses involved. Other sources were the resistance of the program bureaucracies, and probably also the insensitivity of PPBS analysis to the actual complexities of social interventions, a point argued in this paper.)

It is not my purpose here to discuss urban policy, but rather to suggest some of the principles which distinguish policy formulation from program formulation. The rules of the latter are, I should think, fairly well laid out in the descriptive political science of our time. The defining characteristic of a program is that it is directed to a specific situation with the purpose of maintaining or changing that situation in some desired fashion. We have programs to build roads, subsidize the growing of cotton, cure cancer, retrain the unemployed. To be sure there are programs that are quite general in their outlook; but here, with respect to the federal government and indeed to all levels and forms of government within the United States with which I am familiar, any tendency toward universality is immediately constricted by the structure of government. Doubtless there are even programs that would wish to evolve into policies, but reality is quickly enough imposed on them by the fact that one bureau in one department is responsible for performing the function involved; one branch of one division in the Bureau of the Budget handles the appropriation request; one super-specific subcommittee of one special committee of the Congress handles the substantive legislation, and an equivalent subcommittee handles the provision of funds. These are the constituencies of the program, and also its masters. It is a wise program that knows its place, and does not aspire beyond its station.

It would be foolish to be disdainful of such enterprises. Burke's dictum that the law sharpens the mind by narrowing it may be usefully applied to the program approach to social problems. Social commitments are not easy to sustain, certainly not over the long span of time which most social problems require. The program approach is designed to enhance the capacity of the enterprise to survive by narrowing its range of activity and intensifying the support for it. Come hell or high water, come Republicans, Democrats, or Free Silverites, the Bureau of Disabled Appalachian Urban Agronomists gets its appropriation and does next year the job it did last year. A quality, I repeat, not to be disdained.

But for all the plain-as-stick practicality about such arrangements, in the end they are self-defeating. They are in their way "realistic," but they do not adequately reflect a large enough part of reality. In fact, they will usually end by distorting reality. This is the essence of the problem.

By contrast, a policy approach to government does at least begin by seeking to encompass the largest possible range of phenomena and concerns. This has its dangers, its difficulties. But I shall argue that increasingly there is no respectable alternative. Knowing what we do about the nature of society and of social interventions, we have no option but to seek to deal in terms of the entire society, and all the consequences of intervention. One might wish for a simpler time when such knowledge was not available, but the loss of innocence is an old experience to mankind, and not perhaps to be avoided. Certainly not to be reversed.

THE ASSUMPTIONS OF A POLICY APPROACH

Let me then propose three propositions—I shall call them master propositions—that relate to a concept of government by policy as distinguished from government by program.

First is the familiar proposition that everything relates to everything. This is the fact that defines a system. Taken too literally it can be a bit traumatizing, but fortunately some things relate more than others. And it usually is possible to identify those components that in fact have the greatest influence.

The second master proposition is that from the fact that everything relates to everything it follows that there are no social interests about which the national government does not have some policy or other, simply by virtue of the indirect influences of programs nominally directed to other areas. These are *the hidden policies* of government.

This is not such a familiar proposition. The interconnections of programs directed to one area with outcomes in another are sometimes seen. Most of us have by now got it fairly straight that, for example, agricultural research can lead to the migration of farm populations, which has consequences for cities. But by and large these connections need to be pretty evident for much note to be taken of them, and ability to detect them is much influenced by intellectual and political fashion. It is fashion that dictates that some activities are interesting; others not. And if a subject is not interesting, it can have consequences all over the place of which no one is likely to take much heed.

Permit me an example. One of the received truths of contemporary liberal history is that no domestic initiatives of any consequence occurred during the Eisenhower Presidency. I will not contest the general point that was a period of relatively "low governmental profile," as the phrase now goes, following twenty years of the alarums and exertions of the New Deal and Fair Deal. Even so, there was one program of truly transcendent, continental consequence. This was a program which the twenty-first century will almost certainly judge to have had more influence on the shape and development of American cities, the distribution of population within metropolitan areas and across the nation as a whole, the location of industry and various kinds of employment opportunities (and, through all these, immense influence on race relations and the welfare of black Americans) than any initiative of the middle third of the twentieth century. This was, of course, the Interstate and Defense Highway System. It has been, it is, the largest public works program in history. Activities such as urban renewal, public housing, community development, and the like are reduced to mere digressions when compared to the extraordinary impact of the highway program.

Once approved and begun, one would imagine it would have become the object of extraordinary interest, comment, and critique. If nothing of the sort occurred, the explanation would seem evident. Highways have never been a subject of any very great interest among persons given to writing or speculating about government. Certainly they have rarely been associated with social welfare issues, save in the early days of "getting the farmer out of the mud." Further, the politics of getting the Interstate Highway program enacted decreed, or at least indicated, the narrowest possible definition of its purpose and impact. This was altogether agreeable to the Bureau of Public Roads, the slightly obscure organization established in the 1930's as a unit of the Department of Agriculture and shifted by degrees to the shadowy recesses of the Department of Commerce. The permanent staff of the Bureau of Public Roads had neither the inclination nor training to assert that they were doing anything more than obeying the narrow terms of their project descriptions. As bureaucrats, their instinct was faultless. Had anyone realized what they were in fact doing, the sheer magnitude of the interests they were affecting, it is nigh impossible to imagine that they would have won acceptance. Indeed a bare fifteen years after the Interstate program commenced, it is just about impossible to get a major highway program approved in most large American cities. But it is too late: most systems have already been built. In the process—such at least would be my view—quite appalling mistakes were made, but they were mistakes having to do with issues nominally altogether unrelated to the highway program itself, and so no one was responsible for them.

Surely it is possible to hope for something more. Government must seek out its hidden policies, raising them to a level of consciousness and acceptance—or rejection—and acknowledge the extraordinary range of contradictions that are typically encountered. (To the frequent question "Why don't government programs work?" it is often a truthful answer that they do work. It is just that so frequently the effect of a "hidden" program cancels out the avowed one.) Surely also it is possible to hope for a career civil service that is not only encouraged but required to see their activities in the largest possible scope. There are few things that ought more to annoy us than the misuse we make of such splendidly competent organizations as the Bureau of Public Roads. It is fully capable of the most complex calculations of the effects of its programs (and increasingly does just that) but for many a long decade the word from the political world on high was to stick to building roads and to see that not too much sand was used in the concrete.

The third master proposition is clearly the least familiar of all; the one least likely of acceptance. It is not a matter that can be confidently demonstrated, or so at least would be my impression. It is rather the best available explanation for recurrent phenomena which increasingly demand explanation. I refer to what Jay Forrester has termed the "counter-intuitive" nature of social problems. We learn to think, Forrester assures us, in simple loop systems. But social problems arise out of complex systems. The two are not alike, or so it is asserted by men who ought to know. They have fundamentally different properties, such that good common sense judgment about the one will lead with fair predictability to illusions about the other. Thus Forrester: "With a high degree of confidence we can say that the intuitive solution to the problems of complex social systems will be wrong most of the time."

GRASPING COMPLEX SYSTEMS

Whatever the absolute nature of a proposition such as that, one surely can agree with Forrester that social systems have internal regulatory mechanisms that are, in effect, incentives (or disincentives) to behave in various ways. Just as surely, changing those incentives is an extraordinarily complex job. Surely also, too many programs of social intervention in the 1960's went about this extraordinarily complex task in a fairly simpleminded manner, usually just adding a few counter-incentives to the prevailing incentive system. Stated perhaps too simply: the federal government has typically entered a situation in which most actors manifestly had strong incentives to act in ways which were not thought good for the larger society, or for the individuals involved, or both; incentives were offered to reverse the undesired behavior; but too commonly these incentives proved weak and ineffective when compared to the original set.

We should be clear, I think, that if this third proposition proves to be unavoidably the case, there are contained within it rather serious implications for the democratic direction of society. It is the old—or new—question of the expert again. I have gone on record as having a certain suspicion of intellectuals myself, and I think we all should, whatever the shape of our heads. Still, we have grown accustomed to depending on experts in science, and have developed reasonably appropriate ways of translating scientific and technological knowledge into forms of public action by statesmen. The problem arises with regard to social knowledge because, while most everyone will accept that he or she doesn't know much about implosion, everyone thinks he knows a lot about what makes a good school. And now men of unquestioned competence and good will are coming along with the information that what everyone knows about schools is almost precisely what is *not* the case. What do we do about that? What confidence are the people to have in their own judgment if such events multiply, as almost certainly they will?

I believe there is an answer to this. We must develop a new journalism, and political leadership, capable of handling information and of translating it into valid terms of public debate. But this will not be easy. I cannot imagine it happening inside a generation.

In the meantime, the one thing most likely to help us through the period of transition is the practice of thinking in terms of policy rather than of program. The policy-frame-of-mind may not grasp all the interrelations and surprises implicit in social problems, but it does at least start out with the expectation that there are such, and so is not only more on the alert for signals of such problems, but also is least resistant, least unbelieving in the face of the evidence. That is no small thing.

Neither is it any small thing that we should begin to try to take this large view of events. If there is a tendency in our land, as in any, to complacency about many of the conditions of our lives, there is also, I would submit, an almost equal and very nearly opposite tendency to alarm. If man is a problem solving animal, *homus Americanus* is also a problem-discovering one. The fact is that in our eagerness to draw attention to problems, we do frequently tend to make them seem worse than they are. In particular we tend to depict things as worsening when in fact they are improving.

This tendency arises from any number of sources. Three at least come to mind. There is surely a Protestant tendency to be dissatisfied with what might be called normal human behavior. On top of this we have of late had to learn to live with the burden of affluence. (Robert Nisbet frequently reminds us that boredom is the most underrated force in history. Heaven protect the land whose privileged classes get bored with their privileges, as clearly ours has done!) And there is also the tyranny of fashion: a mysterious force, but an open enough one. Fashions of thought get set, and for a period at least they prevail. Evidence to the contrary is treated not as information but as wrongdoing, and woe betide the bearer of such news. The more, then, should we welcome a policy approach to social issues, simply because it insists on setting all specifics in a general context.

THE TREND OF RACE RELATIONS

An example of surpassing importance—or so it would seem to me—concerns the state of race relations in the United States at this moment. Are things getting better as most of us would define that term—namely, are we moving away from a past of racism and caste exclusion—or are they getting worse? I would believe it fair to say that the fashion of late has been to believe things are getting worse, and I can attest that it is costly to argue otherwise. And yet the data, such as they are, argue that indeed things are *not* getting worse. To the contrary, the *Newsletter* of the University of Michigan Institute of Social Research recently summarized the findings to this effect by Angus Campbell and others of the University's Survey Research Center, which we would all, I think, acknowledge as one of the four or five leading institutions of its type in the world.

The white backlash and the deterioration of white and black attitudes toward integration which have been noted by many social observers do not show up in the findings of a recent Survey Research Center nationwide survey.

"There is evidence that, in some respects, blacks and whites are in closer contact and more friendly contact than they had been for years earlier," Angus Campbell, director of SRC, reports.

The SRC data, gathered during the 1964 and 1968 election studies represented possibly the only carefully designed academic study of national attitudes before and after the 1967 riots. They stand in marked contrast to the conclusion drawn by the Kerner Commission appointed by President Lyndon Johnson to study the riots. The Commission reported in March of 1968 that, "Our nation is moving toward two societies, one black, one white— separate and unequal."

In comparing racial attitudes over the four-year period, the SRC survey notes that whites favoring desegregation in 1968 outnumbered strict segregationists by a ratio of nearly two to one (31 and 16 per cent respectively). Four years earlier whites had been about evenly divided on the question of desegregation or strict segregation (27 to 24 per cent).

Although the doctrine of black separatism has been increasingly voiced by some members of the black community, it still has only minority support; and there has been little change in black attitudes toward desegregation over the four-year period. For example, in 1964 some 72 per cent of the blacks questioned said they were in favor of desegregation (with only 6 per cent favoring strict segregation) and four years later 75 per cent were favoring desegregation (with only 3 per cent for strict segregation).

Campbell indicates that not only were the attitudes toward desegregation more positive, actual contact between the races seem to have increased. Whites and blacks were less likely in 1968 than in 1964 to say their neighborhoods or their schools were completely segregated. And whites were less likely to work and shop in all-white areas.

The per cent of whites who said they live in all-white neighborhoods dropped from 80 to 75 per cent, while the number of blacks living in all-black neighborhoods went from 33 per cent to 25 per cent.

In 1964, 43 per cent of whites reported that the high school nearest them was all white.

That figure had dropped to 27 per cent by 1968. Similarly, blacks reporting their nearest high school as all black dropped from 36 per cent to 21 per cent over the four years.

Whites who reported working in an all-white environment totaled 54 per cent in 1964, but that number had dropped to 42 per cent by 1968.

One might account for the reported increases in contact between the races on the grounds that they don't represent real shifts in neighborhood and school population—just more awareness of each other's presence. The increase in publicity surrounding racial issues might have changed people's perception.

Campbell doesn't think so: "People now are more sensitive than they were four years ago but it's highly unlikely that the figures represent purely imaginary increased contact."

POVERTY AND POLICY

Similarly, a policy approach to government has profound consequences on the kinds of programs which are supported and pursued. I would suggest to you that this has been the case with respect to the problem of poverty and racial isolation in the nation. During the 1960's a quite extraordinary commitment was made by the national government to put an end to poverty. Yet the effort to do so went forward in entirely too fragmented a manner. In effect, a collection of programs was put together and it was hoped these would somehow add up to a policy. I don't believe they did. Nor do I believe there was any way we were likely to have found this out save by the route we did in fact follow. But after a point this became evident enough, and it became possible for the government to respond in terms of large-scale policy, and to fit programs to that policy.

The two basic networks of a modern society are the family structure and the occupational structure. A stable society attends to each. The preeminent arbiter of family stability is income. If social science has taught us anything, it is that. Income typically derives from employment, but also typically there are individuals and on occasion groups in the society whose income is not sufficient either because employment is spasmodic, or their skills insufficient to earn an adequate wage. Whatever the case, an effective war on poverty requires a strategy that deals first of all with problems of jobs and income. Once that became clear, it was relatively easy for the national government to develop programs in response.

Let me offer you an almost absurdly simple example. The federal government has had since 1965 a formal policy of abolishing poverty. The Office of Economic Opportunity was established with that purpose in mind. But until this year almost a third of the expenditures of OEO were provided, in effect, by income taxes collected from the poor! Since it has been in the nature of the "services strategy" so much in evidence in early OEO programs to hire middle-class persons to be of assistance to poor persons, the actual *income transfer effect* of many of these OEO programs was to take money from farm laborers and give it to college graduates. No one intended it that way, but that was the unintended consequence of programs being operated in the absence of policy. Almost the first measure President Nixon proposed in this area upon taking office was to abolish income taxes for the poor, and this was done with the completely willing cooperation of the Congress once the absurdity of the previous arrangement was pointed out.

In a similar vein is the Family Assistance Plan which has, properly I would think, been termed the most important piece of domestic legislation to come before the Congress in four decades. The principle of the program is simple and it derives from policy. Families must have an adequate income, and this should be provided them with a minimum effect on their status as stable, self-determining units in society, and with maximum incentive to earn by their own efforts as much a proportion of their needed income as they possibly can. The President has accordingly proposed to place a floor under the income of every American family with children, to provide within that context a specific incentive to work, specific opportunities for work training and placement, and the absolutely crucial provision that this assistance will not be conditioned on dependency. A family does not have to be down and out, busted and broken to get help, when often as not all that was needed at a particular moment was a relatively small bit of help at the margin.

DEFINING SUCCESS

Will FAP succeed? None of us could say right now. But there is one essential aspect to such a question—a question directed to a program that derives from a policy. Namely, that the question can be answered. Family assistance will have succeeded if, over the course of the 1970's, the steadily rising number of dependent families in the nation begins to level off and then to turn down, both in terms of actual numbers and over-all proportions. It is as simple as that to define success for a policy. Yet such definition is the one thing that often defies all effort when applied to programs.

This is the final point I would make about the concept of national policy with respect to social programs. It is a concept most explicitly outlined in the President's recent message to the Congress on Elementary and Secondary Education. *The test of a program, when this program is part of a policy, is not input but output.* It is interesting, and at times important, to know how much money is spent on schools in a particular neighborhood or city. But the crucial question is how much do the children learn. Programs are for people, not for bureaucracies. This is the final, as I say, and probably also the most important lesson of the policy approach to government.

·17·

SAMUEL MENCHER

Ideology and the Welfare Society

The welfare state has frequently been considered the heir of the mercantilist mantle. There are some superficial resemblances between the sixteenth- and seventeenth-century society that bridged the evolution from feudalism to the commercial era and the welfare society that may be the transitional phase in the replacement of individualism and economic self-interest by social and humanitarian values. The mercantilist state, although actively concerned with the national welfare, as compared to its immediate predecessors and successors, identified the national welfare with a static concept of society and with the values of the privileged members of society. The welfare society—in principle at least—has been oriented to progess and egalitarianism.[1]

What is striking, however, in both earlier mercantilist and contemporary welfare doctrines is their ideological looseness. There was no clear text or school of mercantilism as there was, for example, in the case of its latter-day chief rival, classical economics or, more broadly, liberalism. Similarly, the ideology of the contemporary welfare society may be loosely defined as falling somewhere between liberalism and socialism, but it is difficult to find any clearly recognizable or conscious school of social and economic thought providing the foundation of welfare thinking. This may reflect to some degree the experience of contemporary idealists and reformers who found only too recently that identification with too-well-defined social movements can be personally disillusioning and practically embarrassing, if not dangerous. This would account for a strong rejection of ideology in current thinking, its consequence being indicated by relegation of ideology to the past or to underdeveloped areas and the viewing of issues of policy as largely, if not wholly, in the comfortable realm of strategy and the neutral sphere of expertise.[2]

SOURCE: Reprinted with permission of the National Association of Social Workers, from *Social Work,* Vol. 12, No. 3 (July, 1967), pp. 3–11.

[1]Gunnar Myrdal, *Beyond the Welfare State* (New Haven, Conn.: Yale University Press, 1960), pp. 59–61.

[2]Ideology as used here follows Bell's definition of a total ideology: "It is an

BASIC IDEOLOGIES

But the problem is a difficult one. The emphasis on means with assumed agreement on rarely specified ends is complicated for the advocates of a welfare society, for in practice they reject the philosophical *modus vivendi* of liberalism and socialism that permitted an avoidance of speculation about the projected society. Liberalism looked to the natural law of the harmony of individual interest and social good as categorically resulting in the Great Society. Marxism, starting from the opposite premise, assumed that the conflict between private and public interest was the foundation of dissatisfaction. If the class conflict rising out of antagonistic economic interests could be removed, then society would naturally take on its desired dimensions. Once the proper conditions were established, the Marxists assumed, like the liberals, that harmony of interest would obviate the need for intervention and the state would eventually wither away or its functions diminish much as the liberals had, at least abstractly, pressed for at the start.

Thus, the two basic ideologies influencing the welfare society have emphasized establishing the conditions that by themselves would produce the ideal society. However, the supporters of what has been called by Myrdal the "welfare culture" have relied neither on natural law nor on historical necessity for the fulfillment of their goals. Welfare thinking has an essential utilitarian core, and it shares with the utilitarians their abandonment of natural and historical explanations. Like the utilitarians, the welfare state's advocates set the goal of maximum satisfaction shared broadly or democratically among the citizenry. Like the utilitarian, the welfare culture relies heavily on "artificial" or "created" harmony. Such harmony is the result of social policy that keeps the potentially irrational and antisocial desires of the members in accord with the welfare of the whole. The welfare of the whole must then be clearly defined. It is not the outgrowth of the liberal passion for individual interest nor the socialist faith in a classless symphony. The welfare society, with no fixed or deterministic means, is exposed to more ideological conflict than societies that, by the establishment of the preconditions for the maintenance of their values, avoid an elaborate range of conflict positions over ends. As Bell has succinctly noted:

The ladder to the City of Heaven can no longer be a faith ladder but an

all-inclusive system of comprehensive reality, it is a set of beliefs, infused with passion, and seeks to transform the whole of a way of life." Daniel Bell, *The End of Ideology* (New York: Free Press, 1960), p. 400.

empirical one: a Utopia has to specify *where* one wants to go, *how* to get there, the cost of the experience, and some realization of and justification for the estimation of *who* is to pay.[3]

Perhaps what is deceptive to those who emphasize the ideological absence or blandness of the welfare society is their overidentification of ideology with the issues or the wording of the issues that earlier set the tone for the dispute between the liberal and socialist points of view. There has no doubt been some erosion of the former lines of conflict although not as sharp an erosion as some would insist. Some of the terms associated with ideological difference have been changed, some of the emphases shifted, and some of the issues conveniently repressed. However, even if the philosophical differences between liberalism and socialism were accommodated in the welfare society, there is no reason to assume that these span the whole of possible value conflict. To suggest that there is a fundamental consensus and that the policy issues are largely matters for administrative or technical differences is to ignore the vital interrelationships of policy and administrative action or, more broadly, the indissoluble nature of means and ends. It should be noted that the utilitarian followers of Bentham who were identified with administrative reform and the objective assessment or calculus of satisfaction had complementary roles as philosophical radicals.

The tendency to dismiss ideological conflict as anachronistic and to substitute technical decision-making has been affirmed by reference to organizational strategies for establishing policy. Under this form of reasoning, if policy is determined in the administrative process, then the conventional definition of administrative process is policy-making. Reference may be made to such devices as "muddling through," the "branch" or "incremental" approach, or the "theory of the second best" to demonstrate that policy is a matter for technical expertise rather than ideological dispute. This is a confusion of battle strategy with the war.

INCREASED STATUS OF THE EXPERT

Thus, a primary problem for the advancement of the welfare society is the dismissal of or inattention to fundamental differences and the growing authority in the hands of the professional elite who view themselves as neutral instruments for optimal achievement of already determined goals. There is no question that the increasing

---

[3]*Ibid.*, p. 405.

complexity of society and the advance of technological competence alone would have increased the status of the expert. The assumption that policy is nonpartisan has strengthened the decision-making function of the expert within the organizational structure and as the transmission agent of government policy to the citizenry served.

However, the function of the expert in organizational matters cannot be seen as lacking in value. Every instrument to fulfill a policy goal is an organic part of the policy decision.[4] As the problems of society become more complex, the charges of legislative leaders and other democratically representative agents of the citizenry become loose and require more exacting definition and detailed formulation by those responsible for their execution. For each level of government in the process of administering a program, the administrative decision on one level functions as policy for the next.[5] As the issues become more complex and the interests involved more widespread and sensitive, there is greater and greater tendency for major consideration of important policy changes to be made within that nine-tenths of the bureaucracy that is submerged from the public view. The bureaucratic organization has its own protective camouflage of confidentiality, which frequently denies to those politically responsible knowledge of the conflicting range of potential policies as well as protects them from public awareness of the issues.

The response to the efforts of some within the poverty program to open the policy-making process on the local level to popular participation is indicative of the degree to which the closed structure reacts with discomfort to the idea of bringing welfare policy into the public forum. It is questionable whether the poverty program as a welfare measure would have become as vital a subject for public debate if it were not so closely connected with the civil rights struggle, which at least up to the present has resisted subjection to the authority of technical expertise and administrative structure.

BROADENING RESPONSIBILITIES OF PROFESSIONALS

On the general level, policy has often been viewed as a choice among neutral alternatives, and administrative process has expanded into the sphere of practical decision-making. On the individual level, the role of the professional or technical expert has had comparable

---

[4]Herbert Simon, *Administrative Behavior* (New York: Macmillan Co., 1957).
[5]Piet Thuenes, *The Elite in the Welfare State* (London: Faber & Faber, 1966), p. 155.

development. To an increasing extent the staffs of welfare agencies are playing an adjudicative role in the lives of the citizenry under the guise of clinical expertise. As in the political sphere, the traditional democratic institutions remain in existence but a different balance has resulted in professional or expert discretion when previously such control was exercised by agencies or individuals specifically vested with legal or judicial responsibility. In the business or commercial world the drift toward expert decision-making was clearly marked by the establishment of administrative commissions, such as the Interstate Commerce Commission or Federal Trade Commission, with adjudicative procedures. Thus, in effect, the potential conflict between the regulating role of the state and private interests was recognized and an effective system of institutions was devised to expedite the solution of conflict.

In the social field, the growing decision-making role of technical and administrative personnel and the conflicts of interest with the citizenry have been neglected. Only recently have the legal rights of clients of public welfare agencies been given serious attention, and a variety of issues have been noted in the practice of public assistance as well as in other agencies in which the legal rights of clients have been infringed upon by policies or practices of social welfare agencies.

The examination here of the role of technical expertise is not for the purpose of criticizing bureaucratic or professional behavior, but to suggest that the broadening responsibilities of the professional within the administrative structure are not evidence of the absence of ideological or value conflict. The movement of policy-making from the institutions and areas previously identified with ideological differences does not necessarily mean that such basic issues no longer exist. The avoidance of open differences, the political popularity of mainstream strategies, and the immersion of conflict resolution in the less observable layers of the system are not synonymous with the absence of significantly different philosophical positions about the nature and goals of society. The interplay of technical expertise is frequently a disguise for essentially conflicting value orientations.

DANGERS OF EXPERT AUTHORITY

In fact, the authority of expertise in itself presents one of the fundamental value problems of the welfare society. While the application of expertise or technical proficiency to inanimate aspects of the culture—the efficient production of material goods—has enriched the available resources, its application to human problems presents some clear dangers. The threat that Titmuss has remarked upon in the growth of a "new authoritarianism in medicine" holds true as well as for the other professional services.[6] There is the authority that the professions are given as a result of scientific competence and the authority that they take to themselves in their own endeavors for status and the assumption of a self-protective mystique.

The functioning of the welfare bureaucracy on the American scene has, according to a recent analysis, weakened the influence of low-income people on public policy.[7] By expanding its own sphere of control in the political process, the welfare bureaucracy has removed much decision-making from the sphere of public accountability and reduced public sensitivity to policy-making. More directly, through its focal power over the influential benefits of the welfare system the bureaucracy can exert strong controls over those who need such benefits and defend itself against their dissatisfaction or opposition.

The issue of professional authority in the welfare society is not to be resolved by the sacrifice of the role of scientific expertise. Since the welfare society itself represents an evolution from earlier orders, it would not be realistic to revive the Jacksonian "spoils system" in place of the benefits of qualified specialists. The broadening of the concept of justice in many aspects of the law through its supplementation by social and psychological expertise is creating a system of justice to parallel the changes in society as a whole from earlier traditional devices in other important institutions of society.

GOVERNMENTAL INVOLVEMENT IN WELFARE

It should not be assumed that the problems of expertise and bureaucracy are indigenous to the welfare state alone. They are rather the normal correlates of organization in modern society, whether public or private. In fact, it is likely that bureaucratic influences over major policy choices are more prevalent in the private than in the public sphere. In the latter, there is at least a nominal identification with democratic values and procedures and at best a

---

[6]Richard Titmuss, *Essays in "The Welfare State"* (London: Allen & Unwin, 1958), p. 202.

[7]Richard A. Cloward and Frances Fox Piven, "The Professional Bureaucracies Benefit Systems As Influence Systems," in *The Role of Government in Social Change* (New York: Columbia University School of Social Work, 1966).

real encouragement of citizen participation. The private sphere, despite the great publicity given to the democratic spread of industrial ownership, entirely limits the cost of democratic involvement to the annual luncheon meeting for stockholders.

On the other hand, attention to welfare goals by government does not in itself guarantee a democratic value system. It need only be recalled that the pioneering efforts of Bismarck in the social insurances in Germany were neither the outgrowth of nor the introduction to great democratic change. The purpose was rather much the reverse: the maintenance of the stability of an elite society. A recent analysis of the factors associated with the expansion of social security programs indicated that economic advance was essential to their development and may provide both the necessary and sufficient foundation for social welfare. Although a combination of economic development and political representation was more favorable, economic development rather than political democracy was the key variable. The people of less democratic nations were often provided equally with the benefits of social security programs.[8] Government policy, it was concluded, might be viewed as

. . . intimately related to the problem of maintaining motivation and order in societies as well as being a response to the democratically organized demands of the population. . . . Governments may ignore human needs, but there are rather tight limits on the extent to which they may ignore organizational requirements.[9]

Thus, it would appear that many of the attributes normally associated with the welfare state may not be the symbols of a new society or any particular society, but are the prerequisites of certain stages of technological and economic development. Like transportation and urbanization, a state's involvement in welfare may merely indicate the complexity of its social and economic structure.

BALANCE OF SOCIAL AND INDIVIDUAL INTERESTS

Careful examination of welfare programs and their consequences has raised some serious questions about the reality termed the welfare state. When the score is tabulated, the welfare state falls far short

---

[8]Phillips Cutright, "Political Structure, Economic Development, and National Social Security Programs," in Mayer N. Zald (ed.), *Social Welfare Institutions* (New York: John Wiley & Sons, Inc., 1965), pp. 123–140.

[9]*Ibid.*, p. 138.

of the ideals for which it is praised by its advocates and damned by its critics. To some extent, these failures may be attributed to limited technical competence in achieving the desired goals. Understanding, selecting, planning, and controlling the variables necessary for effective social programs is still a relatively primitive science. However, the degree of success cannot be attributed entirely or even primarily to the nation's skills in social engineering. The consequences have been heavily influenced by conflicting forces or interests acting on the core choices for social policy. The existence of a significant amount of poverty, the absence of adequate health, education, and housing resources, the continuation of discriminatory practices toward ethnic groups cannot be totally accounted for by the weakness of expertise. Rather, they reflect ideological differences that contest the comfortable notion that the welfare state is a uniform and universal ideal with variations reduced to the level of tactics and strategy.

Of the ideological issues, one of the most fundamental today is the balance between social and individual interests. On the one hand, there is the belief that the welfare state is itself already outdated, that it satisfied a relatively brief moment when critical economic conditions required the ·meeting of individual needs through the expansion of social instruments. However, the difficult conditions that culminated in such drastic social welfare developments as the New Deal in the United States and the Beveridge report and the expansion of the social services in Great Britain immediately following World War II are no longer present. The great emphasis on social decisions and social choice is no longer necessary in an affluent society, it is maintained, and the free market system of supply and demand should again govern the economy. Like Milton Friedman, those who support such a position would be willing, although reluctantly, to meet the minimum budgetary needs of those with clearly insufficient income rather than be accused of inhumanity. Friedman, along with other advocates of reducing social intervention to providing for the needy alone, has seen this as the primary strategy for moving from a welfare-oriented society.

In effect, the current supporters of laissez-faire have reversed the position of their predecessors, who considered the supplying of income outside the recognized institutions of the private economy as the most dangerous threat to a free economy. The growth of the social services as distinct from direct income provision during the nineteenth century may be attributed in large measure to the desire to avoid distributing income in any fashion that would compete with or confuse what were considered the normal sources of income. In the case of the poor, this was labor. A second and closely related motivation for social service rather than social income was the objection to permitting those whose existence was supported or subsidized by public funds to make the free consumer choices acknowledged as the right of those who earned their income in the approved way. Closely linked to this was the belief that those who could not support themselves independently were not fit to make wise consumer decisions in their own behalf. Thus, for a variety of closely related reasons, providing in-kind—whether the direct commodities of shelter, clothing, and food or the services of health, recreation, and education—was viewed as the most effective means of meeting the needs of those who were completely indigent or those whose indigency might be limited to more complex needs such as health or education.

SHIFT IN WELFARE POLICY

This preference for the social services over substitute income, however, has resulted in a vast expansion of the social services and has been associated with a major shift in welfare philosophy. The service system has moved welfare from its identification with the poor and those of low status to a broad system of provision for a wide spectrum of society. Early income assistance schemes were replaced by a growing system of universal services. The charitable and temporary have now given way to the permanent and institutionalized. The social services, as the Webbs recommended in the Minority Report of the 1905 English Poor Law Commission, were freed from their confining association with pauperism. The pattern of the welfare services and their related goals has suggested that society was a social and economic organism whose interests and wealth were to be the subject of social rather than individual decision-making. The expansion of the social services signified that an increasing proportion of the wealth of society could be viewed as social wealth to be removed from private consumer or investment judgments and to be invested in commodities that reflected social goals.

Under these circumstances, there are those who would reorient society to supplying the income needs of those beneath a defined minimum and replacing social provision with the interplay of private interests. The argument runs that since all or almost all can now afford to meet their needs they should be able to express their choices independently rather than in the collective fashion of the socially provided services. Even when the problem of conflicting individual and social interests is avoided such a direction presents some difficulties. First, how well are the general run of consumers able to evaluate and make choices among the complex of services currently sponsored publicly. Experience with less essential products does not suggest that basic needs can rely on consumer sophistication. Second, opening the market to private choice has the counterpart of private supply. What faith is there that private suppliers will be sufficiently favorable to public needs to give them priority over the private interests of the suppliers? Then, too, leaving the control of supply to individual consumer power orients the market to the demands of the most wealthy or most powerful consumers. This is especially true in the case of scarce resources, as is generally true in welfare, in which a mass-market commodity is not easily produced and quality differences are of critical importance. Thus, a wholly private medical market, for example, places the medical expertise in exceedingly short supply in the hands of those who can most comfortably meet the cost. The program of Medicare for the aged received such support on the grounds that the aged could not afford to compete in the open market for medical care. It would have taken a vast increase in social security income to put them in this position. Closely related is the fact that production of welfare services cannot easily be increased to meet market demand. It is clear that the major problems of the services today are not so much the absence of financial means to purchase them as the absence of resources to be purchased. Professional expertise is a scarcity and its appropriate distribution will depend on rational social planning. Only when society has a surplus would it appear possible to consider letting the market control the distribution.

GOALS OF STATE POLICY

In effect, the rationale behind reducing the role of social planning and programming to its residual responsibilities in the early part of the century has little validity. The era of private entrepreneurship and self-interest, whose values have been emphasized by the critics of the welfare society, existed for only a relatively short time in the history of Western society. Even for much of the period identified with laissez-faire the concept was more of an abstract economic principle than a relevant symbol of political reality. Its most active supporters recognized the need for governmental intervention, and the nineteenth century—the heyday of laissez-faire both in England

and the United States—was marked by considerable government social and economic policy. Thus, the fundamental issue is not state action, for this is not the radical innovation to the welfare society, but the goals to which state policy is to be addressed.

At the present time these goals are centered in several issues of ideological conflict. (1) To what extent should the distribution of income resulting from the private economic market be permitted to be the final determinant of the distribution of income among the members of society? (2) To what extent should the use of national income be dominated by private or public choices? (3) What roles or opportunities must be provided so that all may enjoy dignified and creative lives? (4) How can the security and rationality of social planning and intervention be harnessed to effect the maximum advantages for individual freedom of thought and action?

Sincere and effective attention to these issues would make as significant a change in contemporary society as the earlier shift from a moralistic concern with pauperism to an appreciation of the reality of poverty. The move toward a national minimum standard for all and the abolition of the major wants so eloquently described by Beveridge must now give way to a fundamental reconsideration of the nature or quality of society itself. By the end of the nineteenth century the poor were recognized as human and by the middle of the twentieth century the presence of poverty itself in Western industrial societies was no longer acceptable. However, the issue for contemporary society is no longer reducing or eliminating the inequities of the past—goals already established in the early part of the century. Such policies would require a relatively small investment of national income and would not be the cause of deep controversy. Rather, what is needed is the kind of reorientation signaled by the civil rights movement—a re-examination of the essential premises of American social life. This has stimulated a white backlash in race relations just as a threat to the vested or believed vested position of the privileged or "more equal" may result in firm opposition to major reforms in the social and economic life that affect more than enlightened public philanthropy.

ROLE OF THE PROFESSIONS

The role of the social professions will be strategic in the growth of the new society. Their expertise will be essential to the formulation of social policies made possible by expanded economic resources. The "affluent" society is a greater challenge to social imagination than the limitations imposed by its parsimonious progenitors who made all goals subservient to increasing productivity and economic demand. The ideals previously designated as utopian are within realistic reach if we are ready to think in terms of major reforms in society rather than piecemeal programs. The direction before us encompasses far greater revisions than merely placing the less advantaged on the rungs of the ladder to success. The ladder itself requires reconsideration, and the new society may involve a radical re-evaluation of the functions and status of the well-to-do, as well as of their less fortunate neighbors. In effect, society must be looked upon holistically by the social professions if effective social policies are to be introduced. This conception of society must involve consideration of the demands of the greater universe or what Kenneth Boulding calls the "superculture," which, growing beyond national limits, will influence at an increasing rate the viability of traditional national cultures in the eras ahead.

Along with goals or direction the social professions must be deeply concerned with the methods or processes through which these goals are implemented. On the political side, the issues of ideological controversy must be identified so that they permit appropriate democratic action and decision-making. On the administrative side, programs must be so constituted that they permit maximum freedom of expression and satisfaction by those being served.

CONCLUSION

The welfare state as it is constituted today has by no means established the full foundation for the society ahead. The major questions of income distribution, social wealth, individual and social values, and the independence of individual and social choices within the welfare society have not been examined in depth. These involve ideological differences, and the growing controversy over the most effective approaches for accomplishing social change suggests that fundamental conflicts that symbolized periods of recognized ideology are still present.

SECTION IV

Social Services, Welfare Colonialism, and Community Control

INTRODUCTION

Traditionally, professionals and community influentials have determined goals and selected social intervention activities. The view attributed to Max Weber at the turn of the century that he would consider himself "a very poor bureaucrat" if he did not believe himself "to know better than those blockheads what is really good for them" reflects the feeling of many (cited by Michels, 1959, p. 230n). Of course, participation in decision making requires an awareness of decision opportunities and a modicum of knowledge about the problem; in the past, this awareness and this knowledge were believed to be restricted to relatively small groups of professionals and influentials. Knowledge and skill in decision making were usually not available to the poor, the victimized and the underprivileged. Social welfare professionals, like professionals generally, claimed the right to make decisions for their clients and even though the really big decisions were not made by social workers, as far as the recipients of service were concerned, most of the decisions were made by the social workers.

More recently we have witnessed "a revolt of the clients." A new stage in the relation between workers and recipients is developing. The recipients are questioning the legitimacy of a system which ostensibly was designed to provide services for their benefit but which has failed to achieve positive results and which is now considered by many to be part of the problem rather than part of the solution. Because services and intervention strategies in the past had been planned without the involvement of the recipients of service and intended beneficiaries, these groups are now demanding accountability. Where professionals have been unable to meet these demands for accountability, there have followed calls for community control.

Social workers generally have come from communities and social groups far removed from those of the recipients and beneficiaries of services. The relation of the social worker to the recipient community may or may not be problematic for the worker. But the perception of this relationship by those receiving services makes this a problem area in any event. Too often those coming from "the other side of the tracks" have been unable to see how life is really lived. They have failed to understand the sense of desperation and frustration which is so pervasive in many client communities. Further they have failed to perceive how the social services are viewed in that community. Hard questions need to be raised even though no easy answers are available. Is "power" the answer? What are the implications for practice of such concepts as accountability, community control, and decentralization?

As recipients of services, particularly lower class and nonwhite recipients, become involved in strategy developments and decision making, a different order of questions becomes apparent. What are the consequences of involving lower class recipients of service on middle-class or upper class boards of directors? What happens to the communication process and the decision-making process when people from vastly different cultural backgrounds fail to understand each other? On what societal level can action toward involvement of recipients best take place? What organizational structures facilitate this involvement? And what structural obstacles need to be removed? How can professional integrity and autonomy be maintained in the face of increasing demands for community control and community accountability?

Robert Blauner in "Internal Colonialism and Ghetto Revolt" suggests that white-black relations and conflict (and, by implication, those with other minority groups) in America can only be understood in terms of a model of colonialism. The social system of colonialism is made possible in part because of the functional roles played by the social welfare institution and the profession of social work. Blauner suggests that the anticolonial and community control movements want to assume control in their "turf" of business, social services, schools, and the police. If the social problems of the black community will be solved ultimately by people and organizations from that community, several questions are raised: What should be the role of whites in the decolonization process? What are the implications of the colonial model for social service organizations? For black and white social workers? How shall our society arrange for community control, abolish white instruments of control and exploitation, and simultaneously provide for full participation by minority group members in the institutions of the mainstream? Finally, what of the future for social welfare institutions and social work as a profession?

In "The 'Rights' of the Poor: Welfare Witch-hunts in the District of Columbia," Winifred Bell illustrates how the constitutional rights of AFDC mothers were disregarded because of their lack of power. Are the protection of human dignity and constitutional rights of secondary importance to "saving" tax funds? If one is poor and the recipient of public assistance, should he be deprived of due process of law and fundamental citizen rights? Why do such "witch-hunts" most often focus on those who are most vulnerable?

Community control is often suggested as a panacea for solving the problems of the poor. Bertram Beck suggests in "Community Control: A Distraction, Not an Answer," that the real problem is how to make bureaucracies more responsive to the poor. Although he holds that professionals are not the "enemy," he urgently demands that professionals and bureaucracies become more accountable to the consumers of service. How can consumer preference be utilized to institutionalize this accountability? Will emphasis on accountability reduce and diminish the positive results of professionalism? Are there other means for encouraging professionals and bureaucracies to be more responsive to the poor? Is local community control always consistent with democratic principles?

Given the characteristics of the urban poor, a number of program strategies toward the "Participation of Residents in Neighborhood Community Action Programs" are reviewed by Frances Piven. Barriers to such participation are formidable; nevertheless, proposals are made for organizational forms of participation. Regardless of organ-

izational patterns developed to enhance resident participation, a
number of questions arise. Who should participate? Under what
conditions? How can participation by specified groups be elicited
and maintained? What are the political arrangements and social values which can support or deter participation by the poor?

Edward J. O'Donnell and Catherine S. Chilman, in "Poor People
on Public Welfare Boards and Committees: Participation in Policy-Making?" point out that the involvement of local people in planning governmental programs has a long history. Their review of the
arguments and research literature on participation by the poor is
organized around four themes: reducing alienation, opportunities to
influence decisions, improving communication, and socialization.
Should participation be advice giving or policy making? Who represents the poor? What are the various options available for involvement of the poor?

Sumati N. Dubey reviews various rationales for "Community Action Programs and Citizen Participation: Issues and Confusions."
After an examination of the patterns of participation, he describes
various methods of promoting participation. Several issues are identified, including the question of consensus on goals, degree of participation, and sanctions; he asks whether or not representation by the
poor is a diversionary tactic. Can local control be viewed apart from
the overall national policy? Are institutional changes needed? What
are the relationships between various policy-making governmental
jurisdictions and how do these influence patterns of power and influence?

How far can a government go toward supporting the powerless in
their challenge of the powerful? In "Federal Support for Citizen
Participation in Social Action," Melvin Mogulof traces the gradual
evolution of federal policies supporting community involvement in
decision making in such programs as juvenile delinquency prevention, community action, and model cities. Among the themes
explored by Mogulof are integration and separatism, social brokerage, neighborhood technical assistance, and selection of leadership.

The development of community leadership is crucial if social
services are to become more accountable to local residents and
recipients. Several issues emerge for consideration once a decision
has been made to support greater citizen responsibility and community involvement. Shall participation be segregated along racial
lines? Can we build ghetto communities through community development and encourage integration at the same time? How can the
apparent co-optation of local leadership be minimized or avoided?

REFERENCE

MICHELS, ROBERT. 1959. *Political Parties: A Sociological Study of the Oligarchical Tendencies of Modern Democracy.* Trans. by Eden and Cedar Paul. New York: Dover Publications, Inc.

·18·

ROBERT BLAUNER

Internal Colonialism and Ghetto Revolt

It is becoming almost fashionable to analyze American racial conflict today in terms of the colonial analogy. I shall argue in this paper that the utility of this perspective depends upon a distinction between colonization as a process and colonialism as a social, economic, and political system. It is the experience of colonization that Afro-Americans share with many of the non-white people of the world. But this subjugation has taken place in a societal context that differs in important respects from the situation of "classical colonialism." In the body of this essay I shall look at some major developments in Black protest—the urban riots, cultural nationalism, and

SOURCE: Reprinted from *Social Problems*, Vol. 16 (September, 1969), pp. 393–408. With permission by the Society for the Study of Social Problems.

This is a revised version of a paper delivered at the University of California Centennial Program, "Studies in Violence," Los Angeles, June 1, 1968. For criticisms and ideas that have improved an earlier draft, I am indebted to Robert Wood, Lincoln Bergman, and Gary Marx. As a good colonialist I have probably restated (read: stolen) more ideas from the writings of Kenneth Clark, Stokely Carmichael, Frantz Fanon, and especially such contributors to the Black Panther Party (Oakland) newspaper as Huey Newton, Bobby Seale, Eldridge Cleaver, and Kathleen Cleaver than I have appropriately credited or generated myself. In self-defense I should state that I began working somewhat independently on a colonial analysis of American race relations in the fall of 1965; see my "Whitewash over Watts: The Failure of the McCone Report," *Trans-action*, 3 (March–April, 1966), pp. 3–9, 54.

the movement for ghetto control—as collective responses to colonized status. Viewing our domestic situation as a special form of colonization outside a context of a colonial system will help explain some of the dilemmas and ambiguities within these movements.

The present crisis in American life has brought about changes in social perspectives and the questioning of long accepted frameworks. Intellectuals and social scientists have been forced by the pressure of events to look at old definitions of the character of our society, the role of racism, and the workings of basic institutions. The depth and volatility of contemporary racial conflict challenge sociologists in particular to question the adequacy of theoretical models by which we have explained American race relations in the past.

For a long time the distinctiveness of the Negro situation among the ethnic minorities was placed in terms of color, and the systematic discrimination that follows from our deep-seated racial prejudices. This was sometimes called the caste theory, and while provocative, it missed essential and dynamic features of American race relations. In the past ten years there has been a tendency to view Afro-Americans as another ethnic group not basically different in experience from previous ethnics and whose "immigration" condition in the North would in time follow their upward course. The inadequacy of this model is now clear—even the Kerner Report devotes a chapter to criticizing this analogy. A more recent (though hardly new) approach views the essence of racial subordination in economic class terms: Black people as an underclass are to a degree specially exploited and to a degree economically dispensable in an automating society. Important as are economic factors, the power of race and racism in America cannot be sufficiently explained through class analysis. Into this theory vacuum steps the model of internal colonialism. Problematic and imprecise as it is, it gives hope of becoming a framework that can integrate the insights of caste and racism, ethnicity, culture, and economic exploitation into an overall conceptual scheme. At the same time, the danger of the colonial model is the imposition of an artificial analogy which might keep us from facing up to the fact (to quote Harold Cruse) that "the American black and white social phenomenon is a uniquely new world thing."[1]

During the late 1950's, identification with African nations and other colonial or formerly colonized peoples grew in importance among Black militants.[2] As a result the U.S. was increasingly seen as

---

[1]Harold Cruse, *Rebellion or Revolution*, New York: 1968, p. 214.

[2]Nationalism, including an orientation toward Africa, is no new development. It has been a constant tendency within Afro-American politics. See Cruse, *ibid*, esp. chaps. 5–7.

a colonial power and the concept of domestic colonialism was introduced into the political analysis and rhetoric of militant nationalists. During the same period Black social theorists began developing this frame of reference for explaining American realities. As early as 1962, Cruse characterized race relations in this country as "domestic colonialism."[3] Three years later in *Dark Ghetto*, Kenneth Clark demonstrated how the political, economic, and social structure of Harlem was essentially that of a colony.[4] Finally in 1967, a full-blown elaboration of "internal colonialism" provided the theoretical framework for Carmichael and Hamilton's widely read *Black Power*.[5] The following year the colonial analogy gained currency and new "respectability" when Senator McCarthy habitually referred to Black Americans as a colonized people during his campaign. While the rhetoric of internal colonialism was catching on, other social scientists began to raise questions about its appropriateness as a scheme of analysis.

The colonial analysis has been rejected as obscurantist and misleading by scholars who point to the significant differences in history and social-political conditions between our domestic patterns and what took place in Africa and India. Colonialism traditionally refers to the establishment of domination over a geographically external political unit, most often inhabited by people of a different race and culture, where this domination is political and economic, and the colony exists subordinated to and dependent upon the mother country. Typically the colonizers exploit the land, the raw materials, the labor, and other resources of the colonized nation; in addition a formal recognition is given to the difference in power, autonomy, and political status, and various agencies are set up to maintain this subordination. Seemingly the analogy must be stretched beyond usefulness if the American version is to be forced into this model. For here we are talking about group relations within a society; the mother country—colony separation in geography is absent. Though whites certainly colonized the territory of the original Americans, internal colonization of Afro-Americans did not involve the settlement of whites in any land that was unequivocably Black. And unlike the colonial situation, there has been no formal recognition of

---

[3]This was six years before the publication of *The Crisis of the Negro Intellectual*, New York: Morrow, 1968, which brought Cruse into prominence. Thus the 1962 article was not widely read until its reprinting in Cruse's essays, *Rebellion or Revolution, op. cit.*

[4]Kenneth Clark, *Dark Ghetto*, New York: Harper and Row, 1965. Clark's analysis first appeared a year earlier in *Youth in the Ghetto*, New York: Haryou Associates, 1964.

[5]Stokely Carmichael and Charles Hamilton, *Black Power*, New York: Random, 1967.

differing power since slavery was abolished outside the South. Classic colonialism involved the control and exploitation of the majority of a nation by a minority of outsiders, whereas in America the people who are oppressed themselves were originally outsiders and are a numerical minority.

This conventional critique of "internal colonialism" is useful in pointing to the differences between our domestic patterns and the overseas situation. But in its bold attack it tends to lose sight of common experiences that have been historically shared by the most subjugated racial minorities in America and non-white peoples in some other parts of the world. For understanding the most dramatic recent developments on the race scene, this common core element—which I shall call colonization—may be more important than the undeniable divergences between the two contexts.

The common features ultimately relate to the fact that the classical colonialism of the imperialist era and American racism developed out of the same historical situation and reflected a common world economic and power stratification. The slave trade for the most part preceded the imperialist partition and economic exploitation of Africa, and in fact may have been a necessary prerequisite for colonial conquest—since it helped deplete and pacify Africa, undermining the resistance to direct occupation. Slavery contributed one of the basic raw materials for the textile industry which provided much of the capital for the West's industrial development and need for economic expansionism. The essential condition for both American slavery and European colonialism was the power domination and the technological superiority of the Western world in its relation to peoples of non-Western and non-white origins. This objective supremacy in technology and military power buttressed the West's sense of cultural superiority, laying the basis for racist ideologies that were elaborated to justify control and exploitation of non-white people. Thus because classical colonialism and America's internal version developed out of a similar balance of technological, cultural, and power relations, a common *process* of social oppression characterized the racial patterns in the two contexts—despite the variation in political and social structure.

There appear to be four basic components of the colonization complex. The first refers to how the racial group enters into the dominant society (whether colonial power or not). Colonization begins with a forced, involuntary entry. Second, there is an impact on the culture and social organization of the colonized people which is more than just a result of such "natural" processes as contact and acculturation. The colonizing power carries out a policy which constrains, transforms, or destroys indigenous values, orientations, and ways of life. Third, colonization involves a relationship by which members of the colonized group tend to be administered by representatives of the dominant power. There is an experience of being managed and manipulated by outsiders in terms of ethnic status.

A final fundament of colonization is racism. Racism is a principle of social domination by which a group seen as inferior or different in terms of alleged biological characteristics is exploited, controlled, and oppressed socially and psychically by a superordinate group. Except for the marginal case of Japanese imperialism, the major examples of colonialism have involved the subjugation of non-white Asian, African, and Latin American peoples by white European powers. Thus racism has generally accompanied colonialism. Race prejudice can exist without colonization—the experience of Asian-American minorities is a case in point—but racism as a system of domination is part of the complex of colonization.

The concept of colonization stresses the enormous fatefulness of the historical factor, namely the manner in which a minority group becomes a part of the dominant society.[6] The crucial difference between the colonized Americans and the ethnic immigrant minorities is that the latter have always been able to operate fairly competitively within that relatively open section of the social and economic order because these groups came voluntarily in search of a better life, because their movements in society were not administratively controlled, and because they transformed their culture at their own pace—giving up ethnic values and institutions when it was seen as a desirable exchange for improvements in social position.

In present-day America, a major device of Black colonization is the powerless ghetto. As Kenneth Clark describes the situation:

Ghettoes are the consequence of the imposition of external power and the institutionalization of powerlessness. In this respect, they are in fact social, political, educational, and above all—economic colonies. Those confined within the ghetto walls are subject peoples. They are victims of the greed, cruelty, insensitivity, guilt and fear of their masters. . . .

The community can best be described in terms of the analogy of a powerless colony. Its political leadership is divided, and all but one or two of its

---

[6]As Eldridge Cleaver reminds us, "Black people are a stolen people held in a colonial status on stolen land, and any analysis which does not acknowledge the colonial status of black people cannot hope to deal with the real problem." "The Land Question," *Ramparts*, 6 (May, 1968), p. 51.

political leaders are shortsighted and dependent upon the larger political power structure. Its social agencies are financially precarious and dependent upon sources of support outside the community. Its churches are isolated or dependent. Its economy is dominated by small businesses which are largely owned by absentee owners, and its tenements and other real property are also owned by absentee landlords.

Under a system of centralization, Harlem's schools are controlled by forces outside of the community. Programs and policies are supervised and determined by individuals who do not live in the community. . . .[7]

Of course many ethnic groups in America have lived in ghettoes. What make the Black ghettoes an expression of colonized status are three special features. First, the ethnic ghettoes arose more from voluntary choice, both in the sense of the choice to immigrate to America and the decision to live among one's fellow ethnics. Second, the immigrant ghettoes tended to be a one and two generation phenomenon; they were actually way-stations in the process of acculturation and assimilation. When they continue to persist as in the case of San Francisco's Chinatown, it is because they are big business for the ethnics themselves and there is a new stream of immigrants. The Black ghetto on the other hand has been a more permanent phenomenon, although some individuals do escape it. But most relevant is the third point. European ethnic groups like the Poles, Italians, and Jews generally only experienced a brief period, often less than a generation, during which their residential buildings, commercial stores, and other enterprises were owned by outsiders. The Chinese and Japanese faced handicaps of color prejudice that were almost as strong as the Blacks faced, but very soon gained control of their internal communities, because their traditional ethnic culture and social organization had not been destroyed by slavery and internal colonization. But Afro-Americans are distinct in the extent to which their segregated communities have remained controlled economically, politically, and administratively from the outside. One indicator of this difference is the estimate that the "income of Chinese-Americans from Chinese-owned businesses is in proportion to their numbers 45 times as great as the income of Negroes from Negro owned businesses."[8] But what is true of business is also true for the other social institutions that operate within the ghetto. The educators, policemen, social workers, politicians, and others who adminis-

---

[7]*Youth in the Ghetto, op. cit.*, pp. 10- 11; 79–80.

[8]N. Glazer and D. P. Moynihan, *Beyond the Melting Pot,* Cambridge, Mass.: M.I.T., 1963, p. 37.

ter the affairs of ghetto residents are typically whites who live out-side the Black community. Thus the ghetto plays a strategic role as the focus for the administration by outsiders which is also essential to the structure of overseas colonialism.[9]

The colonial status of the Negro community goes beyond the issue of ownership and decision-making within Black neighborhoods. The Afro-American population in most cities has very little influence on the power structure and institutions of the larger metropolis, despite the fact that in numerical terms, Blacks tend to be the most sizeable of the various interest groups. A recent analysis of policy-making in Chicago estimates that "Negroes really hold less than 1 percent of the effective power in the Chicago metropolitan area. [Negroes are 20 percent of Cook County's population.] Realistically the power structure of Chicago is hardly less white than that of Mississippi."[10]

Colonization outside of a traditional colonial structure has its own special conditions. The group culture and social structure of the colonized in America is less developed; it is also less autonomous. In addition, the colonized are a numerical minority, and furthermore they are ghettoized more totally and are more dispersed than people under classic colonialism. Though these realities affect the magni-tude and direction of response, it is my basic thesis that the most important expressions of protest in the Black community during the recent years reflect the colonized status of Afro-America. Riots, pro-grams of separation, politics of community control, the Black revolu-tionary movements, and cultural nationalism each represent a different strategy of attack on domestic colonialism in America. Let us now examine some of these movements.

---

[9]"When we speak of Negro social disabilities under capitalism, . . . we refer to the fact that he does not own anything—*even what is ownable in his own community.* Thus to fight for black liberation *is to fight for his right to own.* The Negro is politically compromised today because he owns nothing. He has little voice in the affairs of state because he owns nothing. The fundamental reason why the Negro bourgeois-democratic revolution has been aborted is because American capitalism has prevented the development of a black class of capitalist owners of institutions and economic tools. To take one crucial example, Negro radicals today are severely hampered in their tasks of educating the black masses on political issues because Negroes do not own any of the necessary means of propaganda and communication. The Negro owns no printing presses, he has no stake in the networks of the means of communication. Inside his own communities he does not own the house he lives in, the property he lives on, nor the wholesale and retail sources from which he buys his commodities. He does not own the edifices in which he enjoys culture and entertain-ment or in which he socializes. In capitalist society, an individual or group that does not own anything is powerless." H. Cruse, "Behind the Black Power Slogan," in Cruse, *Rebellion or Revolution, op. cit.,* pp. 238–39.

[10]Harold M. Baron, "Black Powerlessness in Chicago," *Trans-action,* 6 (Nov., 1968), pp. 27–33.

RIOT OR REVOLT?

The so-called riots are being increasingly recognized as a preliminary if primitive form of mass rebellion against a colonial status.
There is still a tendency to absorb their meaning within the conventional scope of assimilation-integration politics: some commentators stress the material motives involved in looting as a sign
that the rioters want to join America's middle-class affluence just like
everyone else. That motives are mixed and often unconscious, that
Black people want good furniture and television sets like whites is
beside the point. The guiding impulse in most major outbreaks has
not been integration with American society, but an attempt to stake
out a sphere of control by moving against that society and destroying
the symbols of its oppression.

In my critique of the McCone report I observed that the rioters
were asserting a claim to territoriality, an unorganized and rather
inchoate attempt to gain control over their community or "turf."[11] In
succeeding disorders also the thrust of the action has been the attempt to clear out an alien presence, white men and officials, rather
than a drive to kill whites as in a conventional race riot. The main
attacks have been directed at the property of white business men and
at the police who operate in the Black community "like an army of
occupation" protecting the interests of outside exploiters and maintaining the domination over the ghetto by the central metropolitan
power structure.[12] The Kerner report misleads when it attempts to
explain riots in terms of integration: "What the rioters appear to be
seeking was fuller participation in the social order and the material
benefits enjoyed by the majority of American citizens. Rather than
rejecting the American system, they were anxious to obtain a place
for themselves in it."[13] More accurately, the revolts pointed to alienation from this system on the part of many poor and also not-so-poor
Blacks. The sacredness of private property, that unconsciously accepted bulwark of our social arrangements, was rejected; people who
looted apparently without guilt generally remarked that they were

---

[11]R. Blauner, "Whitewash over Watts," *op. cit.*

[12]"The police function to support and enforce the interests of the dominant political,
social, and economic interests of the town" is a statement made by a former police
scholar and official, according to A. Neiderhoffer, *Behind the Shield*, New York:
Doubleday, 1967 as cited by Gary T. Marx, "Civil Disorder and the Agents of Control," *Journal of Social Issues*, forthcoming.

[13]Report of the National Advisory Commission on Civil Disorders, N.Y.: Bantam,
March, 1968, p. 7.

taking things that "really belonged" to them anyway.[14] Obviously the society's bases of legitimacy and authority have been attacked. Law and order has long been viewed as the white man's law and order by Afro-Americans; but now this perspective characteristic of a colonized people is out in the open. And the Kerner Report's own data question how well ghetto rebels are buying the system: In Newark only 33 percent of self-reported rioters said they thought this country was worth fighting for in the event of a major war; in the Detroit sample the figure was 55 percent.[15]

One of the most significant consequences of the process of colonization is a weakening of the colonized's individual and collective will to resist his oppression. It has been easier to contain and control Black ghettoes because communal bonds and group solidarity have been weakened through divisions among leadership, failures of organization, and a general disspiritment that accompanies social oppression. The riots are a signal that the will to resist has broken the mold of accommodation. In some cities as in Watts they also represented nascent movements toward community identity. In several riot-torn ghettoes the outbursts have stimulated new organizations and movements. If it is true that the riot phenomenon of 1964–68 has passed its peak, its historical import may be more for the "internal" organizing momentum generated than for any profound "external" response of the larger society facing up to underlying causes.

Despite the appeal of Frantz Fanon to young Black revolutionaries, America is not Algeria. It is difficult to foresee how riots in our cities can play a role equivalent to rioting in the colonial situation as an integral phase in a movement for national liberation. In 1968 some militant groups (for example, the Black Panther Party in Oakland) had concluded that ghetto riots were self-defeating of the lives and interests of Black people in the present balance of organization and gunpower, though they had served a role to stimulate both Black consciousness and white awareness of the depths of racial crisis. Such militants have been influential in "cooling" their communities during periods of high riot potential. Theoretically oriented Black radicals see riots as spontaneous mass behavior which must be re-

---

[14]This kind of attitude has a long history among American Negroes. During slavery, Blacks used the same rationalization to justify stealing from their masters. Appropriating things from the master was viewed as "*taking* part of his property for the benefit of another part; whereas *stealing* referred to appropriating something from another slave, an offense that was not condoned." Kenneth Stampp, *The Peculiar Institution*, Vintage, 1956, p. 127.

[15]Report of the National Advisory Commission on Civil Disorders, *op. cit.*, p. 178.

placed by a revolutionary organization and consciousness. But despite the differences in objective conditions, the violence of the
1960's seems to serve the same psychic function, assertions of dignity and manhood for young Blacks in urban ghettoes, as it did for
the colonized of North Africa described by Fanon and Memmi.[16]

CULTURAL NATIONALISM

Cultural conflict is generic to the colonial relation because colonization involves the domination of Western technological values over
the more communal cultures of non-Western peoples. Colonialism
played havoc with the national integrity of the peoples it brought
under its sway. Of course, all traditional cultures are threatened by
industrialism, the city, and modernization in communication, transportation, health, and education. What is special are the political and
administrative decisions of colonizers in managing and controlling
colonized peoples. The boundaries of African colonies, for example,
were drawn to suit the political conveniences of the European nations without regard to the social organization and cultures of African
tribes and kingdoms. Thus Nigeria as blocked out by the British
included the Yorubas and the Ibos, whose civil war today is a residu-
um of the colonialist's disrespect for the integrity of indigenous
cultures.

The most total destruction of culture in the colonization process
took place not in traditional colonialism but in America. As Frazier
stressed, the integral cultures of the diverse African peoples who
furnished the slave trade were destroyed because slaves from
different tribes, kingdoms, and linguistic groups were purposely separated to maximize domination and control. Thus language, religion,
and national loyalties were lost in North America much more completely than in the Caribbean and Brazil where slavery developed
somewhat differently. Thus on this key point America's internal
colonization has been more total and extreme than situations of
classic colonialism. For the British in India and the European powers in Africa were not able – as outnumbered minorities – to destroy
the national and tribal cultures of the colonized. Recall that American slavery lasted 250 years and its racist aftermath another 100.
Colonial dependency in the case of British Kenya and French Algeria lasted only 77 and 125 years respectively. In the wake of this

---

[16]Frantz Fanon, *Wretched of the Earth,* New York: Grove, 1963; Albert Memmi, *The
Colonizer and the Colonized,* Boston: Beacon, 1967.

more drastic uprooting and destruction of culture and social organization, much more powerful agencies of social, political, and psychological domination developed in the American case.

Colonial control of many peoples inhabiting the colonies was more a goal than a fact, and at Independence there were undoubtedly fairly large numbers of Africans who had never seen a colonial administrator. The gradual process of extension of control from the administrative center on the African coast contrasts sharply with the total uprooting involved in the slave trade and the totalitarian aspects of slavery in the United States. Whether or not Elkins is correct in treating slavery as a total institution, it undoubtedly had a far more radical and pervasive impact on American slaves than did colonialism on the vast majority of Africans.[17]

Yet a similar cultural process unfolds in both contexts of colonialism. To the extent that they are involved in the larger society and economy, the colonized are caught up in a conflict between two cultures. Fanon has described how the assimilation-oriented schools of Martinique taught him to reject his own culture and Blackness in favor of Westernized, French, and white values.[18] Both the colonized elites under traditional colonialism and perhaps the majority of Afro-Americans today experience a parallel split in identity, cultural loyalty, and political orientation.[19]

The colonizers use their culture to socialize the colonized elites (intellectuals, politicians, and middle class) into an identification with the colonial system. Because Western culture has the prestige, the power, and the key to open the limited opportunity that a minority of the colonized may achieve, the first reaction seems to be an acceptance of the dominant values. Call it brainwashing as the Black Muslims put it; call it identifying with the aggressor if you prefer Freudian terminology; call it a natural response to the hope and belief that integration and democratization can really take place if you favor a more commonsense explanation, this initial acceptance in time crumbles on the realities of racism and colonialism. The colonized, seeing that his success within colonialism is at the expense of his group and his own inner identity, moves radically toward a

---

[17]Robert Wood, "Colonialism in Africa and America: Some Conceptual Considerations," December, 1967, unpublished paper.

[18]F. Fanon, *Black Skins, White Masks*, New York: Grove, 1967.

[19]Harold Cruse has described how these two themes of integration with the larger society and identification with ethnic nationality have struggled within the political and cultural movements of Negro Americans. *The Crisis of the Negro Intellectual*, op. cit.

rejection of the Western culture and develops a nationalist outlook that celebrates his people and their traditions. As Memmi describes it:

Assimilation being abandoned, the colonized's liberation must be carried out through a recovery of self and of autonomous dignity. Attempts at imitating the colonizer required self-denial; the colonizer's rejection is the indispensable prelude to self-discovery. That accusing and annihilating image must be shaken off; oppression must be attacked boldly since it is impossible to go around it. After having been rejected for so long by the colonizer, the day has come when it is the colonized who must refuse the colonizer.[20]

Memmi's book, *The Colonizer and the Colonized,* is based on his experience as a Tunisian Jew in a marginal position between the French and the colonized Arab majority. The uncanny parallels between the North African situation he describes and the course of Black-white relations in our society is the best impressionist argument I know for the thesis that we have a colonized group and a colonizing system in America. His discussion of why even the most radical French anti-colonialist cannot participate in the struggle of the colonized is directly applicable to the situation of the white liberal and radical vis-à-vis the Black movement. His portrait of the colonized is as good an analysis of the psychology behind Black Power and Black nationalism as anything that has been written in the U.S. Consider for example:

Considered *en bloc* as *them, they,* or *those,* different from every point of view, homogeneous in a radical heterogeneity, the colonized reacts by rejecting all the colonizers *en bloc.* The distinction between deed and intent has no great significance in the colonial situation. In the eyes of the colonized, all Europeans in the colonies are de facto colonizers, and whether they want to be or not, they are colonizers in some ways. By their privileged economic position, by belonging to the political system of oppression, or by participating in an effectively negative complex toward the colonized, they are colonizers. . . . They are supporters or at least unconscious accomplices of that great collective aggression of Europe.[21]

The same passion which made him admire and absorb Europe shall make him assert his differences; since those differences, after all, are within him and correctly constitute his true self.[22]

The important thing now is to rebuild his people, whatever be their

---

[20]Memmi, *op. cit.,* p. 128.
[21]*Ibid.,* p. 130.
[22]*Ibid.,* p. 132.

authentic nature; to reforge their unity, communicate with it, and to feel that they belong.[23]

Cultural revitalization movements play a key role in anti-colonial movements. They follow an inner necessity and logic of their own that comes from the consequences of colonialism on groups and personal identities; they are also essential to provide the solidarity which the political or military phase of the anti-colonial revolution requires. In the U.S. an Afro-American culture has been developing since slavery out of the ingredients of African world-views, the experience of bondage, Southern values and customs, migration and the Northern lower-class ghettoes, and most importantly, the political history of the Black population in its struggle against racism.[24] That Afro-Americans are moving toward cultural nationalism in a period when ethnic loyalties tend to be weak (and perhaps on the decline) in this country is another confirmation of the unique colonized position of the Black group. (A similar nationalism seems to be growing among American Indians and Mexican-Americans.)

THE MOVEMENT FOR GHETTO CONTROL

The call for Black Power unites a number of varied movements and tendencies.[25] Though no clear-cut program has yet emerged, the most important emphasis seems to be the movement for control of the ghetto. Black leaders and organizations are increasingly concerned with owning and controlling those institutions that exist within or impinge upon their community. The colonial model provides a key to the understanding of this movement, and indeed ghetto control advocates have increasingly invoked the language of colonialism in pressing for local home rule. The framework of anti-colonialism

---

[23]*Ibid.*, p. 134.

[24]In another essay, I argue against the standard sociological position that denies the existence of an ethnic Afro-American culture and I expand on the above themes. The concept of "Soul" is astonishingly parallel in content to the mystique of "Negritude" in Africa; the Pan-African culture movement has its parallel in the burgeoning Black culture mood in Afro-American communities. See "Black Culture: Myth or Reality" in Peter Rose, editor, *Americans From Africa*, Atherton, 1969.

[25]Scholars and social commentators, Black and white alike, disagree in interpreting the contemporary Black Power movement. The issues concern whether this is a new development in Black protest or an old tendency revised; whether the movement is radical, revolutionary, reformist, or conservative; and whether this orientation is unique to Afro-Americans or essentially a Black parallel to other ethnic group strategies for collective mobility. For an interesting discussion of Black Power as a modernized version of Booker T. Washington's separatism and economism, see Harold Cruse, *Rebellion or Revolution, op. cit.*, pp. 193–258.

explains why the struggle for poor people's or community control of poverty programs has been more central in many cities than the content of these programs and why it has been crucial to exclude whites from leadership positions in Black organizations.

The key institutions that anti-colonialists want to take over or control are business, social services, schools, and the police. Though many spokesmen have advocated the exclusion of white landlords and small businessmen from the ghetto, this program has evidently not struck fire with the Black population and little concrete movement toward economic expropriation has yet developed. Welfare recipients have organized in many cities to protect their rights and gain a greater voice in the decisions that affect them, but whole communities have not yet been able to mount direct action against welfare colonialism. Thus schools and the police seem now to be the burning issues of ghetto control politics.

During the past few years there has been a dramatic shift from educational integration as the primary goal to that of community control of the schools. Afro-Americans are demanding their own school boards, with the power to hire and fire principals and teachers and to construct a curriculum which would be relevant to the special needs and culture style of ghetto youth. Especially active in high schools and colleges have been Black students, whose protests have centered on the incorporation of Black Power and Black culture into the educational system. Consider how similar is the spirit behind these developments to the attitude of the colonized North African toward European education:

He will prefer a long period of educational mistakes to the continuance of the colonizer's school organization. He will choose institutional disorder in order to destroy the institutions built by the colonizer as soon as possible. There we will see, indeed a reactive drive of profound protest. He will no longer owe anything to the colonizer and will have definitely broken with him.[26]

Protest and institutional disorder over the issue of school control came to a head in 1968 in New York City. The procrastination in the Albany State legislature, the several crippling strikes called by the teachers union, and the almost frenzied response of Jewish organizations make it clear that decolonization of education faces the resistance of powerful vested interests.[27] The situation is too dynam-

---

[26]Memmi, op. cit., pp. 137–138.

[27]For the New York school conflict see Jason Epstein, "The Politics of School Decentralization," New York Review of Books, June 6, 1968, pp. 26–32; and "The New York City School Revolt," ibid., 11, no. 6, pp. 37–41.

ic at present to assess probable future results. However, it can be safely predicted that some form of school decentralization will be institutionalized in New York, and the movement for community control of education will spread to more cities.

This movement reflects some of the problems and ambiguities that stem from the situation of colonization outside an immediate colonial context. The Afro-American community is not parallel in structure to the communities of colonized nations under traditional colonialism. The significant difference here is the lack of fully developed indigenous institutions besides the church. Outside of some areas of the South there is really no Black economy, and most Afro-Americans are inevitably caught up in the larger society's structure of occupations, education, and mass communication. Thus the ethnic nationalist orientation which reflects the reality of colonization exists alongside an integrationist orientation which corresponds to the reality that the institutions of the larger society are much more developed than those of the incipient nation.[28] As would be expected the movement for school control reflects both tendencies. The militant leaders who spearhead such local movements may be primarily motivated by the desire to gain control over the community's institutions — they are anti-colonialists first and foremost. Many parents who support them may share this goal also, but the majority are probably more concerned about creating a new education that will enable their children to "make it" in the society and the economy as a whole — they know that the present school system fails ghetto children and does not prepare them for participation in American life.

There is a growing recognition that the police are the most crucial institution maintaining the colonized status of Black Americans. And of all establishment institutions, police departments probably include the highest proportion of individual racists. This is no accident since central to the workings of racism (an essential component of colonization) are attacks on the humanity and dignity of the subject group. Through their normal routines the police constrict Afro-Americans to Black neighborhoods by harassing and questioning them when found outside the ghetto; they break up groups of youth congregating on corners or in cars without any provocation; and they continue to use offensive and racist language no matter how many intergroup understanding seminars have been built into the

---

[28]This dual split in the politics and psyche of the Black American was poetically described by Du Bois in his *Souls of Black Folk*, and more recently has been insightfully analyzed by Harold Cruse in *The Crisis of the Negro Intellectual, op. cit.* Cruse has also characterized the problem of the Black community as that of underdevelopment.

police academy. They also shoot to kill ghetto residents for alleged crimes such as car thefts and running from police officers.[29]

Police are key agents in the power equation as well as the drama of dehumanization. In the final analysis they do the dirty work for the larger system by restricting the striking back of Black rebels to skirmishes inside the ghetto, thus deflecting energies and attacks from the communities and institutions of the larger power structure. In a historical review, Gary Marx notes that since the French revolution, police and other authorities have killed large numbers of demonstrators and rioters; the rebellious "rabble" rarely destroys human life. The same pattern has been repeated in America's recent revolts.[30] Journalistic accounts appearing in the press recently suggest that police see themselves as defending the interests of white people against a tide of Black insurgence; furthermore the majority of whites appear to view "blue power" in this light. There is probably no other opinion on which the races are as far apart today as they are on the question of attitudes toward the police.

In many cases set off by a confrontation between a policeman and a Black citizen, the ghetto uprisings have dramatized the role of law enforcement and the issue of police brutality. In their aftermath, movements have arisen to contain police activity. One of the first was the Community Alert Patrol in Los Angeles, a method of policing the police in order to keep them honest and constrain their violations of personal dignity. This was the first tactic of the Black Panther Party which originated in Oakland, perhaps the most significant group to

---

[29]A recent survey of police finds "that in the predominantly Negro areas of several large cities, many of the police perceive the residents as basically hostile, especially the youth and adolescents. A lack of public support—from citizens, from courts, and from laws—is the policeman's major complaint. But some of the public criticism can be traced to the activities in which he engages day by day, and perhaps to the tone in which he enforces the 'law' in the Negro neighborhoods. Most frequently he is 'called upon' to intervene in domestic quarrels and break up loitering groups. He stops and frisks two or three times as many people as are carrying dangerous weapons or are actual criminals, and almost half of these don't wish to cooperate with the policeman's efforts." Peter Rossi *et al.*, "Between Black and White—The Faces of American Institutions and the Ghetto," in Supplemental Studies for The National Advisory Commission on Civil Disorders, July 1968, p. 114.

[30]"In the Gordon Riots of 1780 demonstrators destroyed property and freed prisoners, but did not seem to kill anyone, while authorities killed several hundred rioters and hung an additional 25. In the Rebellion Riots of the French Revolution, though several hundred rioters were killed, they killed no one. Up to the end of the Summer of 1967, this pattern had clearly been repeated, as police, not rioters, were responsible for most of the more than 100 deaths that have occurred. Similarly, in a related context, the more than 100 civil rights murders of recent years have been matched by almost no murders of racist whites." G. Marx, "Civil Disorders and the Agents of Social Control," *op. cit.*

challenge the police role in maintaining the ghetto as a colony. The Panthers' later policy of openly carrying guns (a legally protected right) and their intention of defending themselves against police aggression has brought on a series of confrontations with the Oakland police department. All indications are that the authorities intend to destroy the Panthers by shooting, framing up, or legally harassing their leadership — diverting the group's energies away from its primary purpose of self-defense and organization of the Black community to that of legal defense and gaining support in the white community.

There are three major approaches to "police colonialism" that correspond to reformist and revolutionary readings of the situation. The most elementary and also superficial sees colonialism in the fact that ghettoes are overwhelmingly patrolled by white rather than by Black officers. The proposal — supported today by many police departments — to increase the number of Blacks on local forces to something like their distribution in the city would then make it possible to reduce the use of white cops in the ghetto. This reform should be supported, for a variety of obvious reasons, but it does not get to the heart of the police role as agents of colonization.

The Kerner Report documents the fact that in some cases Black policemen can be as brutal as their white counterparts. The Report does not tell us who polices the ghetto, but they have compiled the proportion of Negroes on the forces of the major cities. In some cities the disparity is so striking that white police inevitably dominate ghetto patrols. (In Oakland 31 percent of the population and only 4 percent of the police are Black; in Detroit the figures are 39 percent and 5 percent; and in New Orleans 41 and 4.) In other cities, however, the proportion of Black cops is approaching the distribution in the city: Philadelphia 29 percent and 20 percent; Chicago 27 percent and 17 percent.[31] These figures also suggest that both the extent and the pattern of colonization may vary from one city to another. It would be useful to study how Black communities differ in degree of control over internal institutions as well as in economic and political power in the metropolitan area.

A second demand which gets more to the issue is that police

---

[31]Report of the National Advisory Commission on Civil Disorders, *op. cit.*, p. 321. That Black officers nevertheless would make a difference is suggested by data from one of the supplemental studies to the Kerner Report. They found Negro policemen working in the ghettoes considerably more sympathetic to the community and its social problems than their white counterparts. Peter Rossi *et al.*, "Between Black and White — The Faces of American Institutions in the Ghetto," *op. cit.*, chap. 6.

should live in the communities they patrol. The idea here is that Black cops who lived in the ghetto would have to be accountable to the community; if they came on like white cops then "the brothers would take care of business" and make their lives miserable. The third or maximalist position is based on the premise that the police play no positive role in the ghettoes. It calls for the withdrawal of metropolitan officers from Black communities and the substitution of an autonomous indigenous force that would maintain order without oppressing the population. The precise relationship between such an independent police, the city and county law enforcement agencies, a ghetto governing body that would supervise and finance it, and especially the law itself is yet unclear. It is unlikely that we will soon face these problems directly as they have arisen in the case of New York's schools. Of all the programs of decolonization, police autonomy will be most resisted. It gets to the heart of how the state functions to control and contain the Black community through delegating the legitimate use of violence to police authority.

The various "Black Power" programs that are aimed at gaining control of individual ghettoes — buying up property and businesses, running the schools through community boards, taking over anti-poverty programs and other social agencies, diminishing the arbitrary power of the police — can serve to revitalize the institutions of the ghetto and build up an economic, professional, and political power base. These programs seem limited; we do not know at present if they are enough in themselves to end colonized status.[32] But they are certainly a necessary first step.

THE ROLE OF WHITES

What makes the Kerner Report a less-than-radical document is its superficial treatment of racism and its reluctance to confront the colonized relationship between Black people and the larger society. The Report emphasizes the attitudes and feelings that make up white racism, rather than the system of privilege and control which is the heart of the matter.[33] With all its discussion of the ghetto and its

---

[32]Eldridge Cleaver has called this first stage of the anti-colonial movement *community* liberation in contrast to a more long-range goal of *national* liberation. E. Cleaver, "Community Imperialism," Black Panther Party newspaper, 2 (May 18, 1968).

[33]For a discussion of this failure to deal with racism, see Gary T. Marx, "Report of the National Commission: The Analysis of Disorder or Disorderly Analysis," 1968, unpublished paper.

problems, it never faces the question of the stake that white Americans have in racism and ghettoization.

This is not a simple question, but this paper should not end with the impression that police are the major villains. All white Americans gain some privileges and advantage from the colonization of Black communities.[34] The majority of whites also lose something from this oppression and division in society. Serious research should be directed to the ways in which white individuals and institutions are tied into the ghetto. In closing let me suggest some possible parameters.

1. It is my guess that only a small minority of whites make a direct economic profit from ghetto colonization. This is hopeful in that the ouster of white businessmen may become politically feasible. Much more significant, however, are the private and corporate interests in the land and residential property of the Black community; their holdings and influence on urban decision-making must be exposed and combated.

2. A much larger minority have occupational and professional interests in the present arrangements. The Kerner Commission reports that 1.3 million non-white men would have to be upgraded occupationally in order to make the Black job distribution roughly similar to the white. They advocate this without mentioning that 1.3 million specially privileged white workers would lose in the bargain.[35] In addition there are those professionals who carry out what Lee Rainwater has called the "dirty work" of administering the lives of the ghetto poor: the social workers, the school teachers, the urban development people, and of course the police.[36] The social problems of the Black community will ultimately be solved only by people and organizations from that community; thus the emphasis within these professions must shift toward training such a cadre of minoritity personnel. Social scientists who teach and study problems of race and poverty likewise have an obligation to replace themselves by bringing into the graduate schools and college faculties men of color who will become the future experts in these areas. For cultural and intellectual imperialism is as real as welfare colonialism, though it is

---

[34]Such a statement is easier to assert than to document but I am attempting the latter in a forthcoming book tentatively titled *White Racism, Black Culture,* to be published by Little Brown.

[35]Report of the National Advisory Commission on Civil Disorders, *op. cit.,* pp. 253–256.

[36]Lee Rainwater, "The Revolt of the Dirty-Workers," *Trans-action,* 5 (Nov., 1967), pp. 2, 64.

currently screened behind such unassailable shibboleths as universalism and the objectivity of scientific inquiry.

3. Without downgrading the vested interests of profit and profession, the real nitty-gritty elements of the white stake are political power and bureaucratic security. Whereas few whites have much understanding of the realities of race relations and ghetto life, I think most give tacit or at least subconscious support for the containment and control of the Black population. Whereas most whites have extremely distorted images of Black Power, many—if not most—would still be frightened by actual Black political power. Racial groups and identities are real in American life; white Americans sense they are on top, and they fear possible reprisals or disruptions were power to be more equalized. There seems to be a paranoid fear in the white psyche of Black dominance; the belief that Black autonomy would mean unbridled license is so ingrained that such reasonable outcomes as Black political majorities and independent Black police forces will be bitterly resisted.

On this level the major mass bulwark of colonization is the administrative need for bureaucratic security so that the middle classes can go about their life and business in peace and quiet. The Black militant movement is a threat to the orderly procedures by which bureaucracies and suburbs manage their existence, and I think today there are more people who feel a stake in conventional procedures than there are those who gain directly from racism. For in their fight for institutional control, the colonized will not play by the white rules of the game. These administrative rules have kept them down and out of the system; therefore they have no necessary intention of running institutions in the image of the white middle class.

The liberal, humanist value that violence is the worst sin cannot be defended today if one is committed squarely against racism and for self-determination. For some violence is almost inevitable in the decolonization process; unfortunately racism in America has been so effective that the greatest power Afro-Americans (and perhaps also Mexican-Americans) wield today is the power to disrupt. If we are going to swing with these revolutionary times and at least respond positively to the anti-colonial movement, we will have to learn to live with conflict, confrontation, constant change, and what may be real or apparent chaos and disorder.

A positive response from the white majority needs to be in two major directions at the same time. First, community liberation movements should be supported in every way by pulling out white instruments of direct control and exploitation and substituting technical assistance to the community when this is asked for. But it is not enough to relate affirmatively to the nationalist movement for ghetto control without at the same time radically opening doors for full participation in the institutions of the mainstream. Otherwise the liberal and radical position is little different than the traditional segregationist. Freedom in the special conditions of American colonization means that the colonized must have the choice between participation in the larger society and in their own independent structures.

·19·

WINIFRED BELL

The "Rights" of the Poor: Welfare Witch-hunts in the District of Columbia

On October 5, 1961, the District of Columbia commissioners approved the proposal of the D.C. Department of Public Welfare for a Special Investigation Project (SIP) and the assignment of five experienced investigators from the Office of Investigations and Collections (OIC) to conduct an intensive field investigation of a random sample of Aid to Dependent Children (ADC) and general public assistance cases to determine the "validity of the case loads."[1]

This action launched one of the most exhaustive attempts in this century to weed out all possible "ineligibles" from the public assistance rolls. Men with special investigative skills were to make sur-

SOURCE: Reprinted with permission of the National Association of Social Workers, from Social Work, Vol. 13, No. 1 (January, 1968), pp. 60–67.
[1]More recently the name of the program has been changed to Aid to Families with Dependent Children (AFDC).

prise night searches in efforts to prove that fathers were not really absent—a condition necessary to receive AFDC in the District of Columbia—or to unearth other reasons for ineligibility. Collateral sources—friends, neighbors, relatives, ministers, stocks and bonds, postal savings accounts, banks, possible employers, credit firms, disability and veterans' benefits, workmen's compensation, accident claims, children, ad infinitum—were to be checked to turn up skulduggery among the poor.

Now, six years later, two mothers have challenged the D.C. Department of Public Welfare's right to invade their privacy and look under their beds without search warrants. They have engaged lawyers from the Neighborhood Legal Services Project, funded by the Office of Economic Opportunity in behalf of Washington's poor families. So, finally, the department's methods are being scrutinized as closely as AFDC families have been. As in any other critical moment, some surprising documents have come to light. Among them are all the department's regulations regarding the use of special investigators and the first full report of the 1961–62 Special Investigation Project.

The SIP began its work on November 13, 1961. Assigned to it were the investigations and collections officer, five OIC investigators, a case evaluator, and two clerks. On February 4, 1962, five additional investigators were assigned. On March 1, 1962, the D.C. commissioners requested the chairmen of the House and Senate subcommittees of the D.C. Committees on Appropriations to provide additional staff. Ten more investigators were therefore assigned on March 12, 1962, from the General Accounting Office. By that date, 115 ADC cases had been fully investigated; with the additional staff, another 121 cases were completed by June.

The ADC random sample was selected by the Department of Public Welfare's chief of research and statistics from the 5,601 cases active as of September 30, 1961. A 10 percent sample was selected, then divided into two 5 percent samples by placing odd-numbered cards in one pile, even-numbered cards in another pile; the former group, consisting of 280 cases, was used for the SIP.

Case attrition began immediately. By the time the 280 cases were read, 9 were already inactive, 33 others had been closed by the regular public welfare worker before the SIP staff could embark on their investigation, and one had moved into the D.C. Residential Training Center. One was erroneously marked closed and was excluded because of this fact. This left SIP with 236 cases and a sample that was no longer random. Four of the 236 cases were found to

contain errors and were immediately sent back to the welfare workers for correction. These four cases, representing 1.4 percent of 280,
were the only ones clearly identified as erroneous eligibility decisions since they were the only ones known to have been based on
the facts known to the welfare worker at the time of his decision.

Since one of SIP's claims, later repeated by OIC, is that the
1961–62 investigations revealed the inadequacy of normal eligibility
determination processes, specifically the public welfare workers' decisions, it is necessary to examine precisely what the "normal" eligibility process was in the District of Columbia prior to the fall of
1961. One thing becomes clear: the OIC was very much involved in
this normal process.

"NORMAL" REFERRALS TO OIC

According to a Public Assistance Handbook release dated October
25, 1955, a specialized unit of trained investigators was established
for the purpose of determining eligibility when "assistance is applied for on the basis of an absent parent." The investigators were to
concentrate on "problem ADC cases." Specifically, referral of applications was to be made.

when the field social worker has conducted the initial application interview
and in his judgment the applicant has been purposely vague or is so limited
mentally as to be unable to grasp the explanation made to her of the action
requested of her. . . .

Active cases were to be selected for referral as follows:

. . . those in which the worker has a reasonable suspicion that the
man – either the husband, father of one or more of the children, or some
other male person – is present in the home or has free access to the home but
in the handling of the case has been unable to obtain sufficient evidence to
arrive at a reasonable conclusion as to "presence or absence."
. . . those in which the question as to the current presence of the man in
the home does not arise but where existing clues have been insufficient to
arrive at determination as to the exact whereabouts of the absent man.
. . . those in which there is a suspected resource which the worker has
been unable to establish exists or does not exist, such as employment, illegal
money-making activity, or the existence of material possessions of unusual
value, the means of acquisition being unexplained or unknown.

In Manual Release No. 381, dated July 25, 1956, the cases to be referred from the active case load were expanded to include the following:

1. Any case that has been closed because of misrepresentation on the part of the recipient, fraud, husband or other man in home, or concealed resources before the new application for public assistance can be approved.
2. Any case in which the recipient claims that a mother, husband or a father of her child or children is missing, any case of pregnancy in which the father is alleged to be absent from the home.
3. Any case in which a child was born in the last two years while the husband was out of the home for over one year prior to the birth of the child, where there has been neither court action nor signing of a voluntary support agreement.
4. Any case in which it appears that the recipient is living in a manner or has use of material possessions which do not appear compatible with the known resources of the family or in which there is a suspected resource which the worker has been unable to establish exists or does not exist, such as employment, illegal money-making activity.
5. Any case in which a complaint or denunciation, anonymous or otherwise, of a recipient's eligibility for public assistance is received is to be *immediately* referred for investigation of the validity of the complaint. The source of all such complaints or denunciations must be kept confidential and under no circumstances revealed to the recipient.
6. Cases in which the worker has a reasonable suspicion that the man — either the husband, father of one or more of the children, or some other male person — is present in the home or has free access to the home but in the handling of the case has been unable to obtain sufficient evidence to arrive at a reasonable conclusion as to "presence or absence."

As Manual Release No. 465, dated December 2, 1957, documented, the functions of the special investigation service had expanded to include routine verification of "miscellaneous resources" — the collateral sources previously mentioned. In addition, it listed thirteen types of situations that should be referred for special investigation, four of which would swell the earlier lists.

1. Any case (ADC, GPA, ATD, OAA) in which there is reason to believe that client is not eligible for assistance or that there are

factors in the case affecting eligibility which cannot be proved by the social worker.

10. All cases except OAA and AB in which the landlord lives in the same premises as recipient, or recipient's home is rented in another person's name, unless the landlord is a relative of the recipient or is a recipient.

11. All cases except OAA and AB in which the recipient shares the rent of a home or an apartment with another family, who are not relatives or recipients, and has lived with the same family at a previous address.

12. Any case in which the recipient has a roomer of the opposite sex.

13. An active or closed case when there is a hearing (appeal) pending, and the social worker needs additional information for the hearing.

Essentially the same cases described during previous years and in this last release were to be referred to special investigators, according to Manual Release No. 59, dated January 12, 1960. In other words, what was initiated as a special service had now become a routine part of the procedure to establish and review eligibility.

What is the significance of this large-scale referral to OIC prior to the fall of 1961? Clearly, since practically all difficult or "absence" cases were routinely referred, this means that OIC had approved them if they were active on September 30, 1961. In a memorandum from OIC to the director of the Department of Public Welfare, dated July 27, 1962, and titled "Report by Special Investigation Project on ADC Random Sample Cases Investigated," there were twenty-four detailed case surveys appended. In fourteen of the cases explicit mention of investigations prior to the beginning of SIP were made. Some examples follow:

No. 5. In 1955–56 "an exhaustive investigation" was made prior to approval on March 1, 1956. Four night visits were made in 1961 resulting in a report on July 12, 1961, "that there was no evidence of the presence of any man in the home."

No. 8. In August 1961 the Agency requested the Investigation Service to locate the father of the oldest child. Referral was also made to the Investigation Service in August 1961 to establish whether H.W. or any other man and the mother were involved in a continuing relationship. On October 9, 1961, Investigation Service gave the agency an address for the older child's father. He failed appointments and finally on December 8, 1962 [should undoubtedly read 1961] the social worker suspended assistance because the father's contribution to the family could not be verified.

No. 24. In October 1956 a referral was made to Investigation Service to locate father. . . . Again in April 1961 Investigation Service was requested to determine whether father was living in the home; and to ascertain the number of persons living in the household and their identity. The reply from Investigation Service was that visits made to the home on June 11, June 13, and June 18 revealed that recipient was living at the address with her two children. No other people were living with her and during these visits father was not seen in the home.

No. 32. Her first application in December 1956 was in the process of termination in February 1957 because Investigation Service established the presence of a paramour in the home who had previously denied continuing relationship. . . . Mrs. G's second application in March 1958, due to Mr. G's incarceration was approved because of evident need and the fact that Investigation Service reported no man in home. . . . The second Investigation Services referral (1959) proved negative and assistance was continued to Mrs. G and the children until February 1962 when the Special Investigation Unit found a man in the home and the case was closed.[2]

In other words, when SIP claimed a given percentage of error in eligibility determination, it was not the work of regular public welfare workers that was found inadequate, but the work that was the special investigators' specific responsibility for approximately six years prior to the fall of 1961. Failure to turn up men consistently, despite the diligence of the search, suggests that the only reliable method of assuring the "true" absence of all men from AFDC homes is to move the special investigators into the homes on a twenty-four-hour, seven-days-a-week basis.

WHAT INVESTIGATIONS DID NOT REVEAL

Exactly what did the arduous investigations by SIP and OIC in subsequent years reveal about the ADC case load that might not otherwise have turned up? First, let us examine what they did *not* reveal.

1. *That the normal eligibility determination process was faulty or inadequate in the District of Columbia.* The ADC random sample was selected from the active case load as of September 30, 1961. SIP did not begin work until November 13, 1961 and completed its job

---

[2]The twenty-four cases cited underwent, in addition to regular welfare workers' investigations and special investigations, a visit by child welfare workers concerned about children when aid was discontinued during SIP's, and then another visit by SIP staff to verify that no harm had been done and that families were managing. The last two visits followed the pleas of some families not to be harassed again.

about 6½ months later. Special investigators, except for the four cases subjected only to desk audit, did not review the accuracy of previous eligibility decisions. Instead they looked for current "facts." In late 1961, yearly reviews in ADC were as necessary as they were in the adult categories. This means that about one-twelfth of a randomly selected sample (23.3 cases per month in a sample of 280) would come up for review in normal agency procedure, assuming that applications were distributed evenly over the year. So about 210 of the 280 cases would have been due for review during the 7½ months from the time the sample was selected until the investigations ended. In fact, the normal reviews must have continued during this period or the agency would risk being found out of conformity with the Social Security Act by the U.S. Department of Health, Education, and Welfare (HEW).

In the administrative reviews that the Department of HEW routinely makes of local eligibility decisions (now known as Quality Control or QC), the requirement is for immediate review of the workers' decisions so that the reviewers will make their decisions, as nearly as possible, from the same circumstances prevailing when the grant was approved. Any other method of validating agency decisions assumes that life stands still for AFDC families and the public welfare agency.

As a matter of fact, life is changeable and circumstances fluid among AFDC families. They come on and go off assistance quickly. In Baltimore in 1961, for example, 26 percent of AFDC cases closed in a three-month period. If the character of the case load remained constant, it could be estimated that as high as 52 percent might terminate within a six-month period. (This percentage is very close to the 57 percent cited in SIP reports as being closed "subsequent to its investigations.") The Baltimore case load is similar to the District of Columbia case load: it is essentially nonwhite and composed of families with "absent" fathers. In a nationwide study of the AFDC case load made in 1961 by the Department of HEW, it was found that 17 percent of the cases were on the rolls less than six months, 15 percent for six months but less than one year, and another 17 percent for a year but less than two years.[3]

The point was best made, perhaps, by Senator Henry M. Jackson (D-Washington) at the Senate Permanent Subcommittee on In-

---

[3]Robert H. Mugge, "Aid to Families with Dependent Children: Initial Findings of the 1961 Report on the Characteristics of AFDC Recipients," *Social Security Bulletin*, Vol. 26, No. 3 (March, 1963).

vestigations' hearings on February 3, 1953, in which he referred to his experience as a home visitor for a county welfare department:

Well, for 5 months I was a home visitor for the welfare department: and I do not know much about it, but I do know that you cannot tell from looking at a file whether they (ADC families) are eligible. . . . For example, let us take a typical case, where people are living on a little farm, a stump ranch, we will say, out in our state. They may have a cow or two. When the cow goes dry, they are eligible. When the cow is fresh, they are ineligible.[4]

Translated into urban terms, recovery from an illness can make a family ineligible (in the District of Columbia where employable mothers are not eligible for AFDC) although a grant was previously legal. Or a day's visit by a father from New York, if it coincides with a special investigator's surprise call, can mean there is a "man in the home" although he leaves that night and is not heard from for months.

Given fluid circumstances in the lives of the poor, when one crisis pushes them onto AFDC and a stroke of luck lifts them off, it is only possible to obtain a valid check of the public assistance worker's decision if investigations proceed immediately after the worker's decision, and even then there must be some room for error. Otherwise, changed circumstances will inevitably affect the findings and, in doing so, they become a reflection of the fluidity of life among the poor rather than the inaccuracy of the agency.

2. *The investigation did not reveal that the OIC was solely, or even primarily, responsible for case closings subsequent to special investigative efforts.* AFDC cases are closed in the District of Columbia and elsewhere (when special investigators are involved) as the result of (1) information freely provided by clients, (2) information learned by workers, and (3) unknown facts revealed by special investigators. It is only for the last group of facts that special investigators can validly claim credit. But at no time, in no published source so far available, does the OIC staff protect itself by listing systematically the sources of information that were crucial to the case closing. Hence there is no basis for a judgment about the significance of their activity.

The case surveys appended to the 1962 SIP report show that all three sources could claim credit for closing the sample cases. In all

---

[4]United States Senate, *Hearings on Eligibility Audit*, given before the Senate Permanent Subcommittee on Investigations, Committee on Government Operations, February 3, 1953, p. 14.

OIC reports, the phrase "subsequent to the special investigation" is used to define those cases for which it claims sole credit.

In Baltimore, where another special investigative effort occurred in 1961, everyone involved protected against errors of this nature by keeping a precise count of the source (client, worker, special investigator) that revealed the fact or facts that led to an ineligibility decision. It turned out that 22.5 percent of the randomly selected cases were closed during a three-month period because of facts contributed by workers and clients, while the special investigators unearthed information that led to the closing of 3.9 percent of the cases, making a total of 26.4 percent closed in this sample. Subsequently, a further 3.5 percent were closed by normal review procedures *made immediately after the special investigator's approval.* In the words of John R. Schneid, then research analyst for the Baltimore Department of Public Welfare:

The findings with regard to closings in Washington (in the SIP report) were classified as to technical reasons for ineligibility — not . . . how the factors were obtained, or . . . whether those possessing the factors were "freeloaders." The Baltimore study . . . classified its results according to who produced the factor which closed the sample case — the client himself, the worker who had the necessary fact, or the investigator who turned up the unknown fact. After all, this is the question at issue. If it is assumed from the start that unknown ineligibility exists [that slips] through the net of ordinary determination, the logical question is: Exactly how much heretofore unknown ineligibility is revealed by the use of a different method. The classification scheme used in the Washington [D.C.] report appears to imply that all ineligibility was the product of the investigation. Breaking the total by technical reasons begs the question implied in the charge to the Department. . . .[5]

So only one valid generalization of the SIP or OIC work remains: any AFDC case load changes continually — new cases open, others close. Poor people are, in fact, exceedingly vulnerable to every manner of change: in the surrounding community, their own personal lives, the lives of their families, the health of their children, a shift in bus fares, accidents, and birth and death themselves. In a jurisdiction like the District of Columbia, in which so much of the routine work of the public assistance staff has been transferred to special investigators, it can be anticipated that some workers become careless

---

[5]John R. Schneid, "Research Responsibilities in Public Assistance Eligibility Check Studies," unpublished manuscript prepared for the National Conference on Social Welfare, Cleveland, Ohio, 1963, pp. 8–9. (Mimeographed.)

in their initial exploration and develop a "trained incapacity" to listen perceptively as well as to fit into their busy schedules numerous telephone calls to check "miscellaneous resources." So the volume of closings that OIC might validly claim is, of course, swollen when compared to other jurisdictions in which welfare workers discharge their full responsibilities.

But the "witch-hunt" aura pervading public welfare in Washington, D.C., where seventy-seven investigators now work for OIC, is dramatized by the utter failure of either public welfare leaders or OIC staff members to clarify what percentage of closings or denials is based on information freely provided by applicants and recipients.[6] While this information is not required by the Department of HEW, it would seem that in an agency with any degree of service orientation, when clients have sustained such long attack and have been subjected to such suspicion and harassment, the least the agency could do would be to clarify this factor routinely. When it was clarified in Baltimore, it was decided that the small amount of ineligibility owing to the special investigative efforts made in 1961 was not worth the cost to taxpayers.

SELF-ADMINISTERED QUESTIONNAIRES

When self-administered questionnaires were introduced by the West Virginia Department of Public Welfare for use in OAA reviews, the aged turned out to be more accurate than public welfare workers had been: there were fewer defective case actions resulting from information based entirely on questionnaires than when information was gathered by workers. Full investigation was carried out on 10 percent of the cases. The rate of defective actions, it was learned, did not reflect on the rate of ineligibility but rather the enormous complexity of eligibility requirements. So the state decided it must first simplify eligibility if it wished to reduce the rate of error. In California, the experience with self-administered questionnaires in the aged program similarly resulted in a decision to use this method statewide. When the public welfare strike occurred in New York City in January 1965 and it became necessary to forego home visits, the same proportion of negative decisions in the AFDC program turned up for eligibility decisions made during January as for the two preceding months when home visits were routinely scheduled. New

---

[6] In November, 1967, an additional ten investigators were authorized by the Senate Subcommittee on D.C. Appropriations.

York City has recently initiated a project using self-administered questionnaires as the basis for eligibility decisions for all programs in several district welfare offices.

It may be true that in Washington, D.C., which does not have AFDC for unemployed parents, a general assistance program for employable adults, or AFDC for employable one-parent families, but does have an ever increasing pride in reducing "absence of parent" as a reason for qualifying for AFDC and a long history of exhaustive night searches, the poor are under special pressure to dissemble and withhold information, especially when parents love each other and hope to stay together. But in jurisdictions in which public assistance programs wish to keep families intact and help in this process by providing public aid promptly, there is evidence from many sources that the poor report their needs and circumstances forthrightly. If dishonesty is prevalent among the poor in the nation's capital, the failure of Congress to permit an adequate assistance program and to treat the poor with respect are probably the most responsible factors.

INACCURATELY DENIED GRANTS

Finally, the tragedy of failing to study the accuracy of denied and discontinued grants with the same ardor brought to the task of searching for freeloaders cannot help but raise disturbing questions about American value systems. For years, underpayments in AFDC have outweighed overpayments and the federal administrative reviews have documented the denial of assistance to many perfectly eligible families. Yet when the Department of HEW designed the national eligibility review of AFDC, ordered by the Senate Committee on Appropriations in 1962, to include a study of denied and discontinued grants as well as a study of the problems and needs of these rejected families, the committee concluded that these portions of the design were not responsive to its charge. It is difficult to escape the conclusion that at that moment in time, tax money was important—human rights and suffering were not.

From the constitutional viewpoint, the equitable treatment of applicants and recipients is at least as important, if not far more so, than saving tax funds. So being certain that rights are not denied without due process of law becomes by far the graver public charge. Similarly, from a social point of view, learning what needs and problems those families rejected by public programs still have is of vast significance in planning corrective measures. Instead of shedding light on these issues, approximately $4 million were spent in the national eligibility review of AFDC to learn that an estimated 5.4 percent of families had become ineligible and that public welfare workers make errors in computing the size of the grant (the budgeting process is horrendous). But no effort was expended to learn if constitutional rights had been denied vulnerable poor families, as experts knew *was* happening in jurisdictions that had restrictive public welfare programs such as the Congress of the United States had willed for the nation's capital.

·20·

BERTRAM M. BECK

Community Control:
A Distraction, Not an Answer

Only the most insulated worker could fail to recognize the need to alter the power relationship between the social worker and the client involved in the giving and receiving of social services. Achievement of such an alteration is the most promising path toward making social welfare institutions more responsive to the needs of their clientele.

The problem of the nonresponsive institution is a crucial one, affecting all institutions and all people without regard to class, economic status, or ethnicity. The attention of social workers is riveted on the effect of nonresponsive institutions on the poor and on those who have been shut out of society by discrimination. This is as it should be. It is, however, important to recognize the pervasiveness of the problem throughout society to achieve an awareness of the heroic nature of the measures that will be required of all professions and institutions to cope with the problem.

SOURCE: Reprinted with permission of the National Association of Social Workers, from *Social Work*, Vol. 14, No. 4 (October, 1969), pp. 14–20.

CONSENSUS AND CONTROL

Any effort to equalize the power of social worker and client through formal means must involve a modification of the bureaucratic structure that, of course, determines formal assignment of power. This goes right to the heart of a crucial issue, since rampant disenchantment with the functioning of social institutions is, in fact, disenchantment with bureaucratic structure as a means of organizing human activity.

The essence of bureaucracy is the effort to control human behavior through delegated authority to reward and punish. Recent rebellions have demonstrated that no system of social control short of total military rule will work without basic assent of the participants.

This assent is usually based on a genuine acceptance not of a goal or method of achieving it, but of role. As long as exploiter and exploited accept their roles, social calm prevails. Once consensus concerning acceptance of social role is dissolved, rebellion ensues. However righteous the cause, the rebellion poses a special hazard to problem-solving in a democracy, since the process of redressing the just cause of rebellion demands a large degree of consensus and control. Meetings for deliberation, discussion, and decision-making, for example, are a necessary ingredient of the democratic process. A group intent on disrupting a meeting can do so, and although repressive measures can be used, the milieu in which democratic procedures can flourish cannot be regained. If a sufficient degree of consensus for social control based on assent cannot be maintained, the natural consequence will be a society in which social control is based on repressive measures — a society based on tyranny.

One of the commentators on Etzioni's recent volume dealing with consensus and control points out that

the possibility of achieving a balance between [consensus and control] . . . is clearly very much affected by the size and nature of the social groupings of which [the larger units of society] . . . are composed. The problem that concerns Etzioni here is how to maintain a "community of publics" in what is increasingly a "mass society." . . . the individual [can] hardly hope to affect the larger society by his private acts. Public policy can only be influenced by intermediate sized collectivities, but in our society such collectivities seem unable to achieve much influence unless they become so large that they are virtually as unresponsive to the needs of their constituents as the society itself. . . . An active society must have reliable channels for transmitting data concerning a developing consensus upward to the elites, so that a responsive policy can be maintained. Thus the nature of the intervening collectivities participating in consensus formation and communication is clearly crucial.[1]

Arnold Toynbee, after studying the decline of major civilizations in the history of mankind, came to the conclusion that when the elites do not receive data concerning the developing or shifting consensus, or when they are not responsive to such data, society crumbles and the forces of barbarism take over. The decline of a civilization is marked by the violence of barbarians at home and abroad. Obviously, in our own society it is not the lack of data, but the difficulty in achieving an adequate response to conflicting interests that has led to the current impasse.

THRUST TOWARD COMMUNITY CONTROL

Social work's response to the crisis caused by rebellion against the nonresponsive institution has been preoccupation with the notions of community control or client participation in decision-making. Both bear some relationship to the central problem, but the exact nature of this relationship remains unexplored. Most often, the words themselves are put forward as substitutes for thinking, bearing out, perhaps, an observation by Hutchins, who recently claimed:

No existing theory of politics, society, or international relations can explain or account for the facts of contemporary life. Our situation has changed too fast for our ideas. And so our ideas have degenerated into slogans—forms of words that pass through the mind without putting any strain on it and that cause only imperceptible mental disturbance.[2]

The thrust toward community control is obviously an effort to reduce the size of collectivities, to temper the power of professions and make them more responsive to human needs. What is ignored, however, is the whole history of political administration, which teaches that small political subdivisions tend to place power in the hands of a few who tyrannize the many. Moreover, the insular quality of administration in small political units leads to debased standards and parochial concerns. Major social advances in this country

---

[1]Edgar Z. Friedenberg, in a review symposium on Amitai Etzioni's *The Active Society: A Theory of Societal and Political Processes* (New York: Free Press, 1969). The symposium discussion appeared in *American Sociological Review*, Vol. 33, No. 6 (December, 1968), p. 965.

[2]Robert Hutchins, "Report of the President" (Santa Barbara, Calif.: Center for the Study of Democratic Institutions, 1965–67).

have always and inevitably required the application of federal power. Strident cries for community power and community control cannot help us deal with the fact that our concern must be for the health, welfare, and education of every child and every adult in every state and every township. If this is so, we cannot rest content with the notion that giving power to the community in Greensborough, North Carolina, Jackson, Mississippi, or the Lower East Side of New York City will automatically usher in the good life.

Moreover, those who are infatuated with the notion of community power bypass the difficult problem of defining just who or what "the community" is. One often encounters the exhortation to respond to the wishes of "the community," or the inevitable person who says he represents "the community," all in the face of the fact that there is no one community, there are only communities. Surely for the purposes of community control, the community must be seen as a group of people with some sense of affinity; merely living in one geographic area or being poor does not necessarily result in a sense of community.

When this simple sociological fact is ignored by social workers trying to respond to the new era, the consequence is that power is inadvertently transferred from one affinity group to another by social workers who assume an identity of interest among the poor. The tremendous tension between working-class whites and minority groups in our cities is a consequence in part of the effort to redress the intolerable wrongs done to blacks and other minority groups without consideration of the consequences of the social action. Obviously, injustice should not be tolerated, but those who accept responsibility for social leadership in their professional capacities cannot merely endorse the panacea of the day and excuse themselves from the pain of thought.

BUREAUCRATIC STRUCTURE REMAINS

In terms of whether social workers and clients can be coequals in policy-making and administration, it is important to note that when a community takes control of a health, welfare, or educational service, the clients and the professionals are still not coequals, because bureaucratic structure remains. The social work revolutionaries inevitably use the word bureaucracy in the pejorative sense, but can offer no other way of organizing major complex structures for service delivery. This is not at all surprising. After Max Weber had defined the nature of bureaucracy, many perceptive students of social structure emphasized the nonfunctional characteristics of bureaucratic organization—its ritualism, its rewards for mediocrity and over-conformity, its lack of adaptability, its protectiveness. Many proposed means for minimizing these negative qualities. None proposed a complete substitute. Participatory democracy can work in small voluntary efforts characterized by face-to-face communication such as block organization. It cannot work, however, as the major means of organizing human activity required to deliver health, welfare, and education services to the American people.

Consequently, when a community takes over a health, welfare, or education service, members of that community take over the policy-making functions at a top level. When difficulties ensue, they are in part a result of the fact that the members of that community did not necessarily desire to play the role of board members. They rebelled against the nonresponsiveness of the institution to their need. As board members, they can make the organization more responsive if they are successful in fulfilling the board member role. If they are not successful because of lack of interest or lack of training, capable personnel leave and the service deteriorates. This is by no means always the case. It happens frequently enough, however, to demonstrate that service delivery in a bureaucracy will fail when members of the bureaucratic structure either do not accept or cannot function within their roles.

The deterioration of service is of no concern to those who see participation as an end in itself and who expect that through the mere act of participating there will be some type of social renaissance. The deterioration of service is also of no concern to those modern revolutionaries who view society as so debased and so corrupt that the decline of its institutions can only usher in a better day. It is of great concern, however, to the masses of poor people in America who subscribe to no abstract ideology and merely want for themselves a fair share of the American dream. The deterioration of service must, therefore, be a key concern of social workers.

ARE PROFESSIONALS THE ENEMY?

Frequently those concerned with the notion that community control ensures responsiveness of social institutions see social workers, physicians, teachers, and other professionals as the enemy. In one sense, this view is correct. Professions are by definition self-defining and self-policing. Greenwood says that the hallmark of a profession is the possession of special knowledge and skill to guide interventions of public as well as private importance.[3] When lawmakers are convinced of the existence of this special knowledge, they are prone to give a monopoly over certain acts of intervention to the profession concerned. The profession, in turn, develops a code of ethics and attempts to control the behavior and practice of its members. Professionals therefore tend to be accountable to other professionals rather than to the consumers of their services. Any effort to humanize social institutions dominated by a profession has to deal with this fact and has to find a way to ensure that the professionals are more responsive to their clients.

Heightening the responsiveness of the social agency to its clients is not to be achieved by making client and social worker coequal. As noted, client control of the board may heighten responsiveness but certainly does not equalize clients and social workers. It gives the client power over the social worker, but this is formal power. To influence the informal power structure so that true equality is achieved between the helped and the helper is more to the point and involves nothing short of the destruction of the concept of profession. There are those who view professions as essentially exploitative and selfish and who would welcome a homogenized service structure in which the very notion of professions would be eliminated.

Such persons place more emphasis on the limitations of professions than on their unique and irreplaceable role in the democratic process. Frankel, in writing of that role, states that the profession as a social institution rests on three principles: (1) individual merit as the determinant of the right to practice, (2) self-criticism, and (3) moral impartiality.[4] He makes clear that the last involves the willingness to describe reality as perceived. This is in contradistinction to the twisting of perceived reality to fit an ideological framework. It is not moral indifference.

Frankel is quick to agree that no profession abides by these three principles in toto, but that is not the point at issue. Rather, the question is whether society *needs* professionals chosen on the basis of merit who are self-appraising and free to take whatever stand seems right in the light of their professions' knowledge and values. If so, then the concept of profession must be strengthened, not destroyed, and the notion of professional and client as coequals is an

---

[3]Edward Greenwood, "Attributes of a Profession," *Social Work,* Vol. 2, No. 3 (July, 1957), pp. 45–55.

[4] Charles Frankel, "Social Values and Professional Values," *Journal of Education for Social Work,* Vol. 5, No. 1 (Spring, 1969), pp. 29–35.

absurd nonsequitur, since by definition they can only be equal in certain respects, not in all respects.

As a matter of fact, one social work scholar concerned with the uses of authority in treatment stated that the client must grant "psychological authority" to the social worker before service can be given.[5] The client must, in effect, come to the conclusion that the social worker has some means of being of assistance to the client before anything of significance can happen. In this light, then, there can be no coequality in treatment but different roles, with the client granting to the social worker special abilities to assist in the problem-solving at hand. Without this inequality, there would be no social worker-client relationship, but a joint endeavor of coequals in problem-solving such as might exist between friends or within a social movement. Such coequality is possible, but redefines profession in such a way as to destroy the essence of professionalism.

FALSE RESPONSE TO A REAL NEED

Because social workers employed in health and welfare agencies have confusing and sometimes conflicting responsibilities to their clientele, agency, and society, and because health and welfare agencies are reluctant to respond with repressive measures to attacks from their clientele, social workers, public health workers, and the like are increasingly attacked by the new militants as if they were the archenemies of social progress. Meanwhile, more important targets are spared. This appears to be an instance of what Etzioni calls "inauthenticity" — a false response to a real need.

The need is real because the clients in rebellion are seeking a response to which they are entitled and that they must demand. The social leaders who seek to steer the needful into activities in which the chief target is the relatively humanizing forces in society are bringing about a false response.

Etzioni explains this phenomenon by describing alienation as a consequence of the early phases of industrial capitalism. In the later stages of industrial development, in the age of public relations, gimmicks are created that look like responsiveness to the real need of all people for incorporation in the sense of community. These responses are superficial, essentially false, and thereby debasing.

This would appear to be a proper characterization of much of the

---

[5]Elliot Studt, "An Outline for Study of Social Authority Factors in Casework," *Social Casework*, Vol. 35, No. 6 (June, 1954).

antipoverty movement, much of the agitation for community control, and the make-believe confrontations between the new militants and the liberal managers of weak but relatively benign social institutions. An antipoverty program that does not concern itself with redistribution of wealth, that has meager resources and a great deal of ballyhoo, is obviously not a real response to the problem of poverty and thus can only result in greater social alienation. The fundamental obstacle to the development of health, welfare, and educational services in America is not the difference between professionals and laymen, but the lack of a national commitment to provide a decent standard of living. Without universal health insurance, community control of health services is not going to make a great deal of difference to the sick, and most especially the poor sick: When the attention of the poor is taken from basic social injustice and riveted on issues of community control, important and fundamental social change is avoided. When persons of only average venality are held up as the archenemies, the more venal are left unscathed.

If one subscribed to a conspiratorial view of American society, one might well imagine the most powerful figures in the military-industrial complex designing an anti-poverty program whereby poor people who do not participate in standard political processes would be diverted to toy elections and to fighting among themselves over the control of pitifully inadequate sums of money. One could well imagine the leaders of such a complex encouraging the drive for community control with the knowledge that local sovereignty has always been the rallying cry of the reactionaries. An effective diversion of America's gross national product into social measures can only take place on a federal level. How ironic it is to see those who think of themselves as proponents of revolutionary change playing into the hands of the most reactionary forces in America.

MAKING THE PROFESSIONAL MORE ACCOUNTABLE TO THE CLIENT

The most effective way of making the professional more accountable to the client and thus bringing about a greater equality in policy-making and administration is to imitate the means whereby the attorney or physician serving the rich is made more accountable to his client than is the professional person serving the poor: through the pocketbook.

The United Fund, for example, is the key point of distribution for voluntary contributions to health, welfare, and education services. At the present time, distribution of funds is presided over by representatives of various institutional interests. What would happen if instead of distributing these funds to different services, there was a distribution of scrip or some type of credit card to potential consumers? Funds would then be dispersed to services based on consumer preference. Institutions dependent on voluntary funds would soon become more responsive to client need.

The neighborhood school is obviously a thing of the past, born at a time when transportation was a major problem. Suppose parents and teachers were encouraged to develop within each school an educational style and methodology unique to that school. Persons who send their youngsters to private schools today carefully assess their methodology and attempt to select a school that fits the needs of the child. No one school is suitable for all children, and yet the public school system has a standardized approach and a standardized curriculum. Suppose parents were free to select the school best suited to their children's needs and funds were allotted based on consumer selection. Teachers and other school authorities would soon become quite responsive to parent need.

Medicaid, for all its terrible inadequacies, has moved in this direction in the health field and the impact is already seen on health practitioners in neighborhoods where there are large numbers of eligible persons. It even becomes possible for persons with Medicaid to join with professional people and organize their own health service in a way that does make patient and professional coequal, not in knowledge or responsibility, but in partnership for the provision of health service.

There is every reason to believe that job training programs for the unemployed and the underemployed would be vastly superior if support for these programs were related, at least in part, to the programs persons elected to use. At present, funding is dependent on the grantsmanship of the fund-seeker as well as on the professional judgment of the fund-giver. While professional judgment of productivity could not be eliminated, surely the man in the street can make a valuable judgment as to the program he thinks most benefits him.

In other words, equalizing the power of client and professional can best be achieved by reducing the power of the professional to give or withhold service without suffering the consequence of nonresponsiveness. Expansion of social insurances to include an income maintenance program is, of course, a major step in this direction, as is the institution of national health insurance. The problem of professional accountability is not an acute one in the social security system, in which benefits are a matter of right. The development of legal services for the poor as part of the antipoverty program is another step in this direction, since professionals are forced to be accountable within a body of law rather than accountable to their peers within the professional culture. Even though the class bias of jurists has impeded this development, the knowledge that a poor person can and will seek his rights through the courts tempers professional judgment.

Within such a context, the provision of means to attain a credential for practice in addition to formal education will make service systems more responsive by blurring the line between service-seeker and service-giver. This does not mean forsaking the notion of merit as entrance to the profession. For example, in the social work profession the MSW should not be the only acceptable evidence of competence to practice. The addition of program participants or consumers to policy-making boards is still another means of helping those responsible for top policy to understand the way in which services impinge on those they are designed to serve. The organization of clients to press for their rights as evidenced by the welfare rights movement is an effective way of achieving greater responsiveness.

The need to change cannot be met by empty slogans providing shallow answers to complex problems. If organizations in which social workers are the dominant professionals cannot point the way toward altering the power relationship of client and professional, then it is doubtful if it can be done. The hallmark of social work is its commitment to a set of values. The tension between cause and function in social work has been manifest throughout the evolution of the profession and has been documented at length. The most valuable contributions social workers have made to the functioning of bureaucratic structures such as hospitals and schools has been through the irresolvable conflict between professional and organizational values. Of course, social workers have compromised, have overemphasized individual change as contrasted with social change, and have been and must be instruments of the society of which they are a part. A profession is not, cannot be, and never will be identical to the movement for social reform. Social work is, however, the profession that comes closest to being a social movement, and as such it behooves members of this profession to seek such social changes as will increase resources available for health, welfare, and education in America. At the same time, it is of desperate importance that changes are sought within the institutions that employ social workers that will improve the quality of service and at long last make those services and the professionals responsive not to *the* community, but to *a* community of persons who stand in need of the specific service offered.

·21·

FRANCES PIVEN

Participation of Residents in Neighborhood Community Action Programs

The widespread advocacy of participation by residents of local communities in public programs by no means reflects agreement regarding the goals of such participation, the forms it should take, or the means for its effectuation. Some of the different concepts comprehended by "resident participation" and the problems these entail are suggested by a review of recent experiences with urban renewal and the early community action projects, predecessors of the antipoverty program.[1]

Both urban renewal and the antipoverty program can be viewed as policies for under-developed areas. They represent a new move forward in the developmental functions of government, as distinguished from its more traditional regulatory functions. It follows from the tasks of these programs that they have extraordinary — and differential — impact on selected local communities.

SOURCE: Reprinted with permission of the National Association of Social Workers, from *Social Work*, Vol. 11, No. 1 (January, 1966), pp. 73–80.

[1]Community action projects were initiated by the Ford Foundation's "Grey Areas Program" and by the President's Committee on Juvenile Delinquency and Youth Crime several years before the current spate of projects funded under Title II of the antipoverty legislation, according to which a "community action program means a program which mobilizes and utilizes resources, public or private of any . . . 'community' . . . in an attack on poverty." Public Law 88–452, Title II, Part A, Section 202.

AN ISSUE IN URBAN RENEWAL

Resident participation became a major issue in local areas earmarked for rebuilding under urban renewal programs. The dilemmas regarding resident participation followed in part from the fact that although local areas were selected as targets for redevelopment they were to be redeveloped in terms of assumptions about the welfare of "the city as a whole." Whatever diffuse benefits such a program might indeed come to have for the larger community, an immediately disruptive impact was felt by groups residing in the target area.[2] It was these groups that were hit most sharply by the costs of renewal, but it was not necessarily these groups that were to benefit from the new development. Economic and cultural revitalization of inner city areas was spelled out for slum residents by clearance and dislocation. The new developments chiefly included high rental housing. Existing residents in areas scheduled for renewal were confronted with the distress of upheaval, the loss of neighborhood, and the prospect of greatly increased rentals.[3] In consequence, adamant local protests came to be an earmark of renewal programs, often spelling political turmoil for the projects.[4] These experiences resulted in a growing concern with resident participation in renewal and also influenced the kinds of participation that were advocated and solicited by those responsible for the programs. In order to avoid local protests, which often rocked the projects when they were already well under way, steps were taken to initiate resident groups at an early stage in order to educate and win them to the plans.

Efforts to bring about resident participation in urban renewal were thus marked by an irony reflecting the dilemmas of renewal policy. Programs for resident participation were developed to offset the spontaneous — but disruptive — participation of local protest groups. Critics came to describe such programs cynically as a mere "cooling-off" tactic. However, so long as renewal plans were oriented to

[2]Considerable outrage has been occasioned among the advocates of government action in housing and urban renewal by publication recently of an extremely critical study of urban renewal by a conservative economist. See Martin Anderson, *The Federal Bulldozer* (Cambridge, Mass.: MIT Press, 1964). For a general but more judicious review of urban renewal policies and problems, see Herbert J. Gans, "The Failure of Urban Renewal," *Commentary*, Vol. 39, No. 4 (April, 1965), pp. 29–37.

[3]For a review of problems in relocation, see Chester Hartman, "The Housing of Relocated Families," *Journal of the American Institute of Planners*, Vol. 30, No. 4 (November, 1964), pp. 266–86.

[4]For a discussion of the political dilemmas created by renewal programs, see James Q. Wilson, "Planning and Politics: Citizen Participation in Urban Renewal," *Journal of the American Institute of Planners*, Vol. 29, No. 4 (November, 1963).

the welfare of the city as a whole they would almost surely generate acute protest and conflict in local areas. Only the most blithe and happy faith in the democratic consensus could permit a program geared to the community as a whole to promote participation by *and influence of* local residents in renewal areas. It was virtually inevitable that educational forms of participation would be emphasized in renewal programs.

DIFFERENCE IN POVERTY PROJECTS

The community-based poverty projects that are already under way also emphasize the place of resident participation. These projects have, however, been given a different public mandate than renewal programs in that they are oriented to the problems of the poor in the project community rather than to the larger urban community. Moreover, they have developed at a time when the civil rights movement has lent new force and meaning to political and organizational activity among the minority groups that form the bulk of the urban poor.

The new concern with resident participation reflects a characterization of the low-income urban community as disorganized and politically ineffective. Low-income people tend not to belong to organizations and do not participate in community affairs. They are relatively uninfluential in the formation of policies and practices of the major institutions that affect the course of their lives. This kind of social and political inactivity is viewed as an aspect of social disorganization and is closely linked, therefore, with many of the problems of the low-income community—having to do particularly with socialization of the young and also with the social preconditions for individual and family effectiveness generally.

Consistent with this characterization, new objectives and strategies are being associated with resident participation in the antipoverty projects. Three interrelated objectives can be identified:

1. Fostering the participation of low-income people in a variety of local associations.
2. Enhancing the effective influence of low-income people on the policies and practices of institutions that serve the low-income community.
3. Establishing the conditions for effective individual and family life by altering the social context of individual behavior.

These objectives for resident participation reflect the concern of the poverty programs with political problems pertaining to democratic participation and influence, as well as concern with the social welfare problems to which the programs are principally addressed. The conception attributed to urban renewal programs, in contrast, emphasizes another kind of political problem—that of integrating local groups to the support of a larger public policy. It should be noted, however, that the poverty programs are only less immediately charged with the problem of reconciling divergent group interests. To the extent that the programs do pursue objectives oriented specifically to the interests of the poor they will, as they develop, require changes and accommodations from larger institutions. Problems of political conflict and integration will inevitably arise and rebound on the objectives of local resident participation and influence.[5] Recent contests between city officials and neighborhood leaders for control of the local poverty program structures may be an anticipation of these developments.

CHARACTERISTICS OF THE URBAN POOR

While the poor are obviously composed of diverse groups, certain attributes can be identified that are pertinent to any efforts to encourage resident participation among the poor, in terms of the objectives outlined above.[6] The discussion which follows is addressed specifically to the urban poor. The problems and potentialities in involving the rural poor would appear to be quite different and to require examination in their own right. Several aspects of low-income urban life contribute to disorganization and political ineffectiveness.[7] Low-income people are overwhelmed by concrete daily needs. Their lives are often crisis ridden, deflecting from any concern with community issues. They often have no belief in their ability to affect the world in which they live, and so they are not

---

[5]There is already evidence of such problems in the controversy over Mobilization For Youth, an action-research project on New York's Lower East Side. Recent testimony from local leaders before a Congressional committee suggests, moreover, that such problems may smolder without becoming so publicly evident.

[6]For a discussion of the different class and status factors used to identify the lower class, see S. M. Miller, "The American Lower Classes: A Typological Approach," in Frank Riessman, Jerome Cohen, and Arthur Pearl (eds.), *Mental Health of the Poor: New Treatment Approaches for Low Income People* (New York: Free Press of Glencoe, 1964), pp. 139–54.

[7]For a review of the sociological literature on the lower class, see Herbert Gans, "A Survey of Working Class and Lower Class Studies," in Riessman, Cohen, and Pearl, *ibid.*, pp. 119–27.

easily induced to try to affect it.[8] Frequently they lack the necessary resources of knowledge and information to enable them to scrutinize social policies. Leadership capabilities are also scarcer among the poor. Moreover, when leaders do emerge, the poor have few incentives to offer them and means of controlling them are scarce. Potential leaders therefore tend to take advantage of opportunities for their own advancement that move them quickly away from low-income concerns. Finally, the institutions whose services might offer incentives for low-income interest and activity are often effectively insulated from the low-income community by their structure, practices, and cultural style.[9]

These several aspects of low-income life are interrelated and cumulative in their effects. Thus, lower-class interpretations of the world stress the inability of most men to affect the conditions under which they live.[10] These beliefs take form in a sense of political inefficacy, which discourages political participation and thus further reinforces conditions of actual powerlessness. Low-income people have little to offer in the way of material resources as political inducements, and they are separated by their social location from the exercise of personal influence on decision-makers. Therefore they are not easily able to obtain the benefits of political influence that might serve as inducements for political participation and to overcome the disadvantages in education and skill that inhibit participation.

The organizational life of the low-income community both reflects these individual attributes and serves also to maintain the conditions

---

[8]See Walter B. Miller, "Lower Class Culture as a Generating Milieu of Gang Delinquency," *Journal of Social Issues,* Vol. 14, No. 3 (July, 1958), pp. 5–19; and Albert Cohen and Harold Hodges, "Characteristics of the Lower Blue-Collar Class," *Social Problems,* Vol. 10, No. 4 (Spring, 1963), pp. 303–34.

[9]This has been a major theme in recent criticism of social welfare services, and a problem that the employment of "indigenous" or "nonprofessional" workers in neighborhood service centers is designed to alleviate, by helping to bridge the cultural and bureaucratic gaps between client and agency. For a description of public welfare practices and how they are countered by such a service center, see Richard A. Cloward and Richard M. Elman, "The Storefront on Stanton Street," to be published in *Commentary.* For a critique of the service patterns of the private social welfare agency, see Richard A. Cloward and Irwin Epstein, "Private Social Welfare's Disengagement from the Poor: The Case of Family Adjustment Agencies" (New York: Columbia University School of Social Work, 1964). (Mimeographed.) See *also* Herbert J. Gans, "Redefining the Settlement's Function for the War on Poverty," *Social Work,* Vol. 9, No. 4 (October, 1964), pp. 3–12.

[10]For a discussion of the interrelationships between real powerlessness and attitudes of powerlessness, see Warren C. Haggstrom, "The Power of the Poor," in Riessman, Cohen, and Pearl, *op. cit.,* pp. 205–23.

that produce them. Participation and influence do not consist only of the relations between disparate individuals and official decision-makers. The influence of individuals is mediated by organizations. It is through organizations that diverse individual resources are co-ordinated into coherent patterns of effective influence. But lower-class people have few of the requirements out of which stable organizations are generated: they have less organizational skill, less professional expertise, less money, and fewer personal relations with officials.[11] In any case, they do not have the resources lent by a stable livelihood that are required merely for regular participation in organizations. The instability of lower-class life and the character of lower-class beliefs further discourage the poor from organizational participation.[12] It is, in turn, partly because of the meagerness of organizational life that the poor community is so little able to retain or control its potential leaders.[13]

This characterization of low-income urban life may be modified or even overcome when, for example, a community is bound by a strong ethnic culture.[14] It is a characterization that tends to apply to vast numbers of the urban poor today, however, and one that marks those groups who share least in organizational and political life. The meager success of traditional approaches to involving the poor, which rely on exhorting them to participate or on civic education, can be understood in terms of the interlocking and reinforcing relationships between actual powerlessness, apathetic beliefs, and scarce skills and resources. These circumstances, in turn, both produce and are maintained by the paucity of organizational life in the low-income community.

---

[11]For a political scientist's discussion of the requirements for organizational influence in city affairs, see Wallace L. Sayre and Herbert Kaufman, *Governing New York City* (New York: Russell Sage Foundation, 1960), pp. 481–515.

[12]In fact, instability in occupational or family life has frequently been the criterion used to distinguish the lower class, or the poor, from the working class. See, for example, S. M. Miller, *op. cit.;* and S. M. Miller and Frank Riessman, "The Working-Class Subculture: A New View," *Social Problems*, Vol. 9, No. 1 (Summer, 1961), pp. 86–97.

[13]The sparse social texture of the poor community is suggested by a survey conducted by Mobilization For Youth on the Lower East Side of New York City. Over half the residents reported no informal group participation and only 15 percent got together with a group more than once a week "just to talk, play cards, go bowling, or something else like that." "Codebook: Mobilization For Youth. Vol. I. Adult Survey" (New York: Research Center, Columbia University School of Social Work, 1962). (Mimeographed.)

[14]See, for example, Herbert J. Gans's study of an Italian community in Boston in *The Urban Villagers: Group and Class in the Life of Italian-Americans* (New York: Free Press of Glencoe, 1962). See *also* William F. Whyte, Jr., *Street Corner Society* (Chicago: The University of Chicago Press, 1955).

PROGRAM STRATEGIES

The antipoverty projects can address these problems in resident participation in two different contexts. They can attempt to facilitate resident participation in a variety of areas of community life and with regard to a variety of institutions. This is typically the approach of community organization efforts. The antipoverty project is, however, also itself a public policy arena. The focus may, therefore, be specifically on resident participation in the policy and program of the local project.

Various strategies for facilitating resident participation in community life generally are being used by projects already under way. These can be identified and reviewed in terms of early experiences.

1. Concrete services are provided, such as help in processing housing complaints or in consumer problems. These services are located in places easily accessible to local people and are expected to attract low-income people as recipients. The effort, however, is to induce recipients to take on more active roles through associations formed around the provision of service. Thus tenant associations may be organized in housing clinics, with the aim of interesting tenants in sponsoring and operating the clinic and the hope that eventually, as a group, they will become more articulate and aggressive concerning the issues in housing policy that their daily problems reflect. Mobilization For Youth, for example, opened storefronts where residents could get not only advice on housing problems, but the intervention of staff in dealings with landlords and housing agencies. The staff first gave individual help and then attempted to induce the tenants in a building to get together in order to register joint complaints and in some instances for joint withholding of rent. These different building organizations were, in turn, invited to join a neighborhood-wide tenants' council for further group action.

2. Existing low-income organizations in the project area are helped with staff and facilities. It is expected that adding to the resources of these groups will enable them to attract more participants and will also encourage them to take more alert and forceful positions on social issues of concern to the membership. The Haryou-Act project in New York's Harlem tries to do this by subcontracting many of its programs, with the idea that program resources can thus serve in building local organizations.

3. A short-term approach to the problem of scarce leadership resources in the community is the engagement of professional staff in community organization activity. This is, of course, not a new role for

social workers. Whether the engagement of professionals in this role is indeed merely an interim solution depends on success in the development of local leadership.

Potential leadership is sought among local people. Efforts are made to interest persons who seem to show leadership qualities in organizing activity and to educate these persons about issues considered critical to low-income people. These individuals may be paid as a kind of "community worker," or they may be coached and encouraged to perform actively as volunteers. Some projects have actually developed "community action institutes" to train neighborhood people who will be employed as block workers or organizers.

4. The social contiguity provided by ethnic, religious, occupational, or residential groups is a natural basis for affiliation and therefore is a reference in organizing group activity. Residential groupings—the building or block association—and racial or ethnic groupings seem particularly important among the poor. Many projects are located in ghetto neighborhoods and therefore work only with a racially and ethnically homogeneous client population. In a mixed community such as the Lower East Side of New York, however, groups are often formed according to the racial and ethnic lines along which people divide themselves.

5. Participation in social protest action is sometimes encouraged by staff assigned to local organizations. Facilities required to pursue such actions may also be provided to these organizations or even to formally unaffiliated individuals who seem to play a leader role. These protest actions may range from participation in nationwide or city-wide events to demonstrations over specific grievances involving perhaps only a few residents.[15]

BARRIERS TO PARTICIPATION

Some early experience with these program strategies reveals persisting problems in overcoming barriers to low-income participation and influence in community affairs.

When concrete services are the incentive for initial participation they tend to remain the focus of activity. The extent of need for such service among the poor seems to overwhelm any less urgent acti-

---

[15]It should be noted that while protest actions by the poor have received wide interest and attention, they have not generally been risked by the community action projects. Mobilization for Youth in New York City and the Syracuse University training program for community organizations, inspired largely by Saul Alinsky, are two exceptions.

vities and the provision of services consumes the energies of staff and recipients alike. Thus staff assigned to help with housing or welfare problems find that emergency housing violations or delayed welfare checks are so widespread and compelling as to require their direct and continuing efforts at obtaining service, deflecting them from organizational activities.

Existing low-income organizations are weak and seem often to be mere emblems of power for leaders whose personal ambition is tied, not to a low-income following that has little to offer them, but rather to the service organization. Thus these organizations may use facilities or funds they receive to acquire the furbishings of respectability: typewriters, furniture, and the like. And new resources can merely precipitate bickering among leaders, deflecting rather than impelling their attention to membership.

The role of professionals in community organization remains problematical. Local people tend to regard them with uneasiness, as strangers. The professionals themselves must accommodate a strain between the style and actions indicated by their role in low-income organizations, the dictates of their professional training, and the organizational requirements of the antipoverty project itself. Thus the professional worker is expected by the community group with whom he works to take clear and supportive positions on issues that arise. If instead he defers to directives from his supervisors or to the dictates of professional neutrality, he may lose the confidence of the community group.

Other problems seem to reside in the strategies for selecting and cultivating indigenous leadership. When these individuals are paid, in an effort to compensate for the absence of incentives for leadership in the low-income community, they tend to orient themselves predominantly to the organization that pays them. Volunteers, when they can be cultivated, come to expect similar compensation.

Social protest actions, because they offer simple and dramatic definitions of problems, may penetrate apathy and override the puzzled disengagement bred of lack of information. These actions also require less personal and economic stability than sustained organizational participation. It should be noted that urban renewal programs elicited protest action from local groups in response to the threats posed by renewal. Social protest is likely, however, to incur hostile and repressive reactions from other groups in the community and from public authorities. Low-income groups may in consequence be even further cut off from channels to influence and also from the services that can serve as a basis for more stable organization. Experience with antipoverty programs testifies dramatically to this risk.

DIFFERENT WAYS OF PARTICIPATING

The antipoverty project itself is a potential arena for resident participation. This has lately become something of a public issue and several different organizational forms of participation are being recommended:

1. Residents should participate on policy-making structures — ordinarily the board — either on the city-wide or local level. These residents are regarded as representatives of the resident population in the areas served. It is this kind of participation that has usually been associated with the legislative mandate for "maximum feasible participation of residents." A certain proportion of the seats on these structures are allocated to residents, with different schemes — elections, appointments, or conventions — for selecting them. These arrangements have often been the occasion for tugging and hauling among various groups, local and city-wide, for controlling influence.

2. Residents should participate as staff. These programs, generally referred to as the employment of indigenous or nonprofessional workers, are among the most widely used of the poverty program strategies.[16]

3. Residents should be formed into active constituent groups. These groups are sometimes recommended as a program resource for professional staff, providing feedback for program evaluation, or they may be regarded as pressure groups that properly influence the project in its activities.

The "neighborhood boards" of Haryou-Act, planned also by the Youth-In-Action project in Brooklyn, are organizational devices intended to provide for all three of the foregoing forms of participation. These boards are supposed to be independent of the parent project — though funded by it — and governed by neighborhood people. The boards are supposed to develop service functions and will presumably make policy in that regard (at least within the limitations set by the terms of their contracts with the parent project and within the over-all limitations set by the city's poverty structure). The boards

---

[16]They are often interpreted in terms of other goals than resident participation, however: they provide employment for local people, for example, or intermediaries to bridge the cultural and organizational gap between clients and service bureaucracies.

will employ local people in service-giving functions. And, finally, since the boards are composed of independent groups of residents they are potentially active constituents for the parent project.

These proposals can be reviewed for problems and potentialities in the light of the foregoing characterization of low-income urban life:

1. Persons from the resident community who are selected to participate in policy-making structures will, if they are to be effective, ordinarily be distinguished by superior abilities or resources. To this extent their representative character is qualified. Moreover, what has been said about the scarce resources for control of leaders in the low-income community applies to the control of these representatives as well. The community has little in the way of an alert and able citizenry or organizational resources to review, control, and direct what its ostensible spokesmen do. The anti-poverty program, on the other hand, and the organizations with which it is affiliated constitute an active source of pressure and inducement to the presumed representatives.

2. To some extent these problems also pertain when residents are employed as staff. Their sense of themselves as employees, however—facilitated by unionization—may create something of a bulwark enhancing resident identity. The tendency of supervising professionals to become overly protective and directing with resident staff, usually in the name of professional guidance and training, may also strain against the goals of participation and influence. This may be mitigated if the resident staff are organized in cadres enhancing their resident identity and providing group support.

3. When constituent groups are restricted to "feedback" participation there may be little incentive for their continuing viability. Feedback in the form of more active pressure and influence by these groups, in the course of which the project could deliver incentives for continued engagement, might be more successful. This requires organizational arrangements that try to insure the project's responsiveness to constituent groups. For example, local public hearings can be held on various program practices provided these practices are deemed appropriately reviewed and changed in response to constituent groups.

CONCLUSIONS

Whatever patterns are developed in the antipoverty projects for resident participation will reflect answers to two sets of questions:

1. Who should participate? In what actions should they participate? Where should this participation be located in the organizational structure? What conditions should govern this action?

2. How can participation by the specified groups, and in the prescribed forms, be elicited and maintained; i.e., what are the effectuating mechanisms for the forms of participation prescribed by the answers to the first set of questions above?

Decisions made in antipoverty programs will initiate patterns of participation and influence, and these questions should be confronted. Decisions pertaining to program activities designed to foster resident participation in community life generally will imply answers that properly vary with the kinds of participation considered and the institutional contexts of participation. The full scope of such decisions will reflect the political philosophy of the anti-poverty program, as well as a range of assumptions regarding the conditions of social action. Insofar as these decisions pertain to participation in the project themselves, they will imply answers that describe the antipoverty program as a political subsystem and the place of residents of the local community in this political subsystem.

The answers to these questions must reflect some of the fundamental ambiguities of our political values and must take account of the fluidity of social and political arrangements. Moreover, they require knowledge of processes of social and political change that does not yet exist. For these reasons, the questions will not be answered entirely explicitly or comprehensively.

The essential dilemma in gaining participation, however, and the problem that underlies many of the difficulties detailed here, is that participation and influence depend on a range of social and economic capabilities. Strategies intended specifically to induce participation may set directions. Sustained and effective participation, however, will finally depend on the allocation to these communities of the social and economic benefits that are the resources for participation and influence in a complex society.

·22·

EDWARD J. O'DONNELL and CATHERINE S. CHILMAN

Poor People on Public Welfare Boards and Committees: Participation in Policy-Making?

Social agencies are unmistakably moving toward involving low-income persons in planning and carrying out service programs that affect their lives. Yet the objectives of such participation and the extent to which they can be achieved are obscure. Despite confusion about the goals and probable outcome of such involvement, the movement is gaining numerous adherents and its principles are being reflected in the policies of many health, education, and welfare agencies and in recent Federal legislation and administrative guidelines.

Although the movement goes far beyond the programs of the U.S. Department of Health, Education, and Welfare (HEW), our discussion in this article centers on the trend in public welfare—specifically on the trend toward including low-income persons as advisers to and policy-makers in public welfare programs.[1]

BACKGROUND OF THE MOVEMENT

The idea of citizens serving as advisers and policy-makers in Federal programs is not new.[2] The U.S. Department of Agriculture

SOURCE: Reprinted from *Welfare in Review*, May-June 1969, Social and Rehabilitation Service, U.S. Department of Health, Education, and Welfare, pp. 1–10.

[1]For a useful contribution to this topic, see William Friedlander, "Client Involvement in the Public Welfare System," Technical Assistance Project, American Public Welfare Association, August, 1967. See also Cynthia R. Nathan, "Involving All Citizens in Public Welfare," paper prepared for the Southeast Regional Conference of the American Public Welfare Association, Lexington, Ky., Sept. 19, 1968. For a recent general review, see Vincent Mathews, "Citizen Participation: An Analytical Study of the Literature," Community Relations Service, U.S. Department of Justice, June, 1968. See also Richard H. P. Mendes, "Bibliography on Community Organization for Citizen Participation in Voluntary Democratic Associations," *President's Committee on Juvenile Delinquency and Youth Crime*, June, 1965.

[2]For discussions of the evolution of the idea of community action and participation,

has involved local people in planning its extension service programs for decades.[3] The Federal Housing Administration, predecessor of the U.S. Department of Housing and Urban Development, fostered the principle of citizen participation in urban renewal programs – an idea greatly enlarged in the model cities program. The Office of Economic Opportunity (OEO) enlists the participation of low-income people in the war against poverty and emphasizes the principle that poor people have a right to help plan and staff programs affecting them.

In the last year HEW took several steps to promote the effective involvement of citizens in its activities. In response to the Poor Peoples Campaign (summer 1968), the former Secretary of Health, Education, and Welfare, Wilbur J. Cohen, called for the active participation of recipients and other poor people in a broad range of HEW programs. A number of national committees of the poor have since been established to serve in advisory capacities to Federal agencies. In a task force report on parent participation, the Department recommends that all parents, but particularly low-income parents, take part as advisers and employees in its programs.[4] HEW's administrative guidelines for Title I of the Elementary and Secondary Education Act require applicants to indicate that local advisory committees will be set up to plan, operate, and evaluate compensatory education programs.[5] In January 1968 HEW established an Office of Citizen Participation in the Social and Rehabilitation Service (SRS) to coordinate programs and to serve as a clearinghouse and as a focal point for developing the idea of recipient involvement in SRS programs and services. SRS guidelines for the 1967 amendments to the Social Security Act require States to set up advisory committees for aid to families with dependent children (AFDC) and child welfare programs and to insure that committee members have

see Peter Marris and Martin Rein, *Dilemmas of Social Reform* (New York: Atherton Press, 1967), pp. 7–32; and Lillian Rubin, "Maximum Feasible Participation – The Origins, Implications, and Present Status," *Poverty and Human Resources Abstracts,* November–December, 1967, pp. 5–18.

[3]See, for example, J. Neil Raudabaugh and Ward F. Porter, "Sociological Bases for Program Planning and Development," Federal Extension Service, U.S. Department of Agriculture, paper prepared for the Southern Sociological Society Annual Meeting, Asheville, N.C. April, 1964.

[4]"Parents as Partners in Department Programs for Children and Youth: A Report to the Secretary of Health, Education, and Welfare" by the Task Force on Parent Participation, Office of the Secretary, U.S. Department of Health, Education, and Welfare, August 1968 (Catherine S. Chilman, chairman).

[5]ESEA Title I Program Guides # 46, Office of Education, U.S. Department of Health, Education, and Welfare, July 2, 1968.

adequate opportunity for participation in both policy development and program administration.[6] SRS policy also stipulates that an advisory committee on day care service be set up and that at least a third of its members be drawn from recipients or recipient representatives.[7]

THE ARGUMENT FOR PARTICIPATION

Cogent arguments can be made for having low-income persons and public assistance recipients serve as members of advisory committees and boards of public welfare. Generally, the persons for whom programs operate are not represented at policy-making and planning levels. A 1962 survey found that welfare agencies had little experience with recipient participation in their programs. Professors of social work and agency administrators were generally opposed to the appointment of recipients to public welfare boards because of alleged incompetence, high turnover, and conflict of interest. They favored appointment of low-income people to State and local advisory committees, but they did not agree on how to organize such committees.[8] Presently, recipients serve on welfare boards in only a few States; these include Maine, Massachusetts, and Delaware.

A study sponsored by the American Public Welfare Association proposes to investigate the extent to which citizens—particularly low-income people and the recipients of services—are participating in the work of State and local public welfare boards and committees and the extent to which their participation contributes to effective administration.[9]

The movement to extend greater power to people in public welfare programs is closely associated with changes in our social institutions. Leaders of poor people's groups and recipient organizations are demanding more representation in institutions affecting their lives. Efforts like the Poor Peoples Campaign and the Welfare Rights Movement point up the determination of such groups to wield

---

[6]"The Welfare and Child Health Provisions of the Social Security Amendments of 1967—Legislative History and Summary," *Welfare in Review*, May-June, 1968, p. 25.

[7]"State Plan Requirements for Service Programs to Children and Families Under Parts A and B of Title IV of the Social Security Act" (Fifth Issuance), Office of the Administrator, Social and Rehabilitation Service, U.S. Department of Health, Education, and Welfare, June 10, 1968, pp. 8–9.

[8]Jerome L. Schwartz and Milton Chernin, "Participation of Recipients in Public Welfare Planning and Administration," *Social Service Review*, March, 1967, p. 22.

[9]"A Study of Boards of Public Welfare and Advisory Committees," American Public Welfare Association, November, 1968.

power and influence.[10] They are no longer willing to be shut out of the community as a whole and cut off from resources necessary to survival in a competitive world.

A society that is increasingly urban, centralized, materialistic, and impersonal threatens the humanity of all men, but particularly those who are poor. Worldwide violence, conflict, and demands for "confrontation and significant dialog" are probably related to the many kinds of pressure put on all people, but especially on those on the fringe of society. The movement toward the "participation of the poor" is but one aspect of the revolution against the obliteration of individuality, one more attempt to establish greater interaction between institutions that have grown so very large and individual persons who feel so very small.

THE MAJOR OBJECTIVES OF PARTICIPATION

Although the rational basis for increasing the opportunities of poor people to take part in planning and operating social service programs is ample, confusion regarding the program and policy objectives of participation, as we have said, is considerable. Confusion shows itself in several ways: the wide range of antipoverty programs set up in different neighborhoods and communities, the different kinds of action reported in the mass media and professional literature, the varying methods followed and goals held by different antipoverty and minority group organizations, and the varying bodies of social science theories and research findings used to support different points of view.

The participation of the poor has different meaning to different people and even different meaning to the same people at different times. There are, nevertheless, generally accepted objectives, specifically these four:

1. To help poor people feel less alienated from the institutions that purport to serve them.
2. To provide poor people with an opportunity to influence the decisions that affect them.
3. To improve communication between low-income persons and other persons in the community.
4. To provide poor persons with an opportunity for socialization into the ways of the community at large.

---

[10]See, for example, the analysis of Joseph E. Paull, "Recipients Aroused: The New Welfare Rights Movement," *Social Work*, April, 1967, pp. 101–106.

REDUCING ALIENATION

That the poor feel alienated from social institutions, there is no doubt. Indeed, alienation is increasing in many segments of society.[11] The fact that poor people have been virtually excluded from organizational life is indisputable.[12] Efforts made so far to include low-income people in community programs have mostly been token and sporadic. Many institutions are criticized as being excessively if not exclusively oriented to the middle-class and as being impervious to the needs of minorities. Schools, medical and social agencies, and police and welfare departments are prime targets for such criticism. Studies of community power structures, traditional agency boards, and voluntary associations attest to the fact that small elitist groups exercise considerable power and influence[13] and that tight control by such groups has greatly contributed to the hostile disaffection of minority groups. But these conditions have also led to the development of counter-measures to surrender more power to minority groups and low-income people through decentralized operations and the establishment of neighborhood organizations.

To what extent these countermeasures will reduce the alienation of the poor is an open question. Neal and Seeman have shown that members of labor organizations have a stronger sense of control over events than unorganized laborers, and they suggest that such organizations may provide a bulwark against the development of alienation in mass society.[14] Dare, in a study of the boards of directors of

---

[11]A Louis Harris survey found that between 1966 and 1968 the number of U.S. Negroes who felt alienated increased from 34 to 54 percent, *Washington Post*, April 15, 1968.

[12]See, for example, Howard E. Freeman, Edwin Novak, and Leo Reeder, "Correlates of Membership in Voluntary Associations," *American Sociological Review*, October, 1957, pp. 528–533; Charles R. Wright and Herbert H. Hyman, "Voluntary Association Membership of American Adults: Evidence from National Sample Surveys," *American Sociological Review*, June, 1958, pp. 284–294; and Murray Hausknecht, *The Joiners* (New York: The Bedminster Press, 1962).

[13]See Floyd Hunter, *Community Power Structure: A Study of Decision Makers* (Chapel Hill: University of North Carolina Press, 1953) for the pioneer study in this field. See also Peter H. Rossi, "Community Decision Making," *Administrative Science Quarterly*, March, 1957, pp. 415–443; Robert A. Dahl, "A Critique of the Ruling Elite Model," *American Political Science Review*, June, 1958, pp. 463–469; Peter H. Rossi, Robert A. Dahl, and Lloyd Rodwin, in Charles R. Adrian (ed.), *Social Science and Community Action* (East Lansing: Institute for Community Development and Services, Michigan State University, 1960); and Charles Press, *Main Street Politics: Policy Making at the Local Level* (East Lansing: Institute of Community Development and Services, Michigan State University, 1962).

[14]Arthur G. Neal and Melvin Seeman, "Organizations and Powerlessness: A Test of the Mediation Hypothesis," *American Sociological Review*, April, 1964, pp. 216–226.

Atlanta's economic opportunity program (EOA), compared the characteristics of a sample of members serving in 1965 with a sample serving in 1966. He found that the advisers from low-income groups who had been chosen by a combination of selection and election — selection by persons influential in the community and election by members of the community the advisers would represent — were more alienated and had fewer organizational memberships than the 1965 advisers who had been chosen by the EOA staff. In fact, the 1966 advisers had many more of the characteristics associated with the poor than the 1965 advisers. How effective participation on the EOA boards was in reducing alienation was not determined.[15]

Because the individual person has become increasingly powerless to control his destiny and the institution too large and impersonal to be effective, bureaucracies are likely targets for activity and change — both from within and without. The participation of the poor in the work of bureaucracies potentially provides people with an increased sense of worth and power and the bureaucracies with an increased sense of purpose and effectiveness.

Two broad methods of effecting change in bureaucracies through organization are apparent: from within — through the decentralization of authority — and from without — through persuasion and protest. But Glazer observes: "Our bureaucracies are more difficult to adapt to new needs than those in Europe, and reformers, progressive administrators, and clients alike despair of making any great impact upon them, and so prefer to set up competing organizations, or to attack bureaucracies to force them into change."[16]

The middle ground between pushing from within and pulling from without is that occupied by the opinion and influence represented in boards and committees attached to institutions and organizations. Such board and committee activity, however, is still carried on within a bureaucracy. The extent to which public welfare departments offer realistic opportunities for participation or present peculiar problems has yet to be determined. Friedlander suggests that the structure of the public welfare system precludes useful citizen or client participation and cites the "impermeability" of the system as a major reason for the development of the Welfare Rights Movement.[17] The maze of legislative and administrative rules and

---

[15]Robert Dare, "Involvement of the Poor in Atlanta," *Quarterly Report No. 5: A Comprehensive and Systematic Evaluation of the Community Action Program and Related Programs Operating in Atlanta, Georgia,* Emory University, January–March 31, 1968.

[16]Nathan Glazer, "Paradoxes of American Poverty," *Public Interest,* Fall 1965, p. 80.

[17]Friedlander, p. 18.

regulations and policies and procedures that govern public welfare agencies is well known.

In contrast, Appleby suggests that the very rigidity of the system lends itself to the pursuit of the legal rights of welfare recipients. He says: "The most significant institutional change has occurred in the public welfare system where a clear set of standards and an impartial appeal system made effective legal advocacy possible."[18]

Reviews of programs that include the principle of "participation of the poor" indicate that conflict almost invariably arises over lack of clarification regarding differences between policy-making and advisory functions. In a study of community action programs in five California communities, Kramer observed just such disagreement.[19] Ideally, the distinctly different functions of policy-making boards and advisory committees should be made clear and consistent. Boards usually have broad power to make policy decisions; committees merely advise and make recommendations.[20] Yet many committee members press for, and think they have, the powers of board members. Board member powers also necessarily have their limitations in respect to the details of decision-making.

The line between setting a broad course of action by boards and the administration of programs is thin. Generally, though a board has broad policy-making powers, administrators reserve the right to hire and fire staff members and to make specific day-to-day decisions about operations. Some of the problems caused by citizen participation on boards and committees arise partly because professional and lay persons fail to understand their legitimate responsibilities or inappropriately attempt to usurp each other's authority.

A board or committee member is affected by the constituency he represents. His response to and feeling of responsibility toward the board or committee will be different, depending on whether he was selected by the agency or elected by the people he represents. Dare, for example, reports that the Atlanta EOA election led the board members to believe that they had a mandate from the people of their neighborhoods for assuming authority and taking decisive action.[21]

The prospects for effective citizen involvement through member-

---

[18]Michael Appleby, "The Practice of Poverty Law: A Case Study of a Neighborhood Legal Service Program," unpublished doctoral dissertation, Massachusetts Institute of Technology, 1968.

[19]Ralph M. Kramer, *Participation of the Poor: Comparative Community Case Studies in the War on Poverty* (Englewood Cliffs: Prentice-Hall, 1969).

[20]For a discussion of some of these differences, see *Parents as Partners*, pp. 9–19.

[21]Dare, p. 5.

ship on boards and committees in larger issues, though slim, are not hopeless. The experience of at least one State board of public welfare seems to attest to the feasibility of moving beyond purely administrative problems. Despite "some controversy" and "strong resistance," the board is exploring the question of how the welfare system meets the general problems of the poor and has successfully augmented the work of its staff in this regard.[22]

Some claim, however, that a public social service agency cannot become involved in larger social and economic problems, that an agency's attempts to mix service and social action can result in chaos, and that either one function or the other becomes lost or submerged. Kramer found that the agencies he studied were confused about goals and the means to achieve them.[23] Studies by Kirschner Associates, Hallman, and Gilbert also attest to the difficulty of carrying on social action and service programs in the same agency.[24]

Marris and Rein draw this conclusion: it is unlikely that a community action project dependent on the approval and economic support of the government and of foundations can champion radical democracy.[25] And Glazer believes that "using government funds for . . . controlled revolution will turn out to be too demanding for both Federal administrators and local community-action organizers."[26] Perhaps the chief issue is the extent to which public programs can pay for, speed up, and legitimate the pressure for participation and change and the extent to which the pressure will find its way to extralegal and extragovernmental channels through riots, demonstrations, protests, or militant social action.

Apparently, many obstacles are likely to stand in the way of effective change through the membership of low-income persons on public welfare committees and boards. To the extent such change

---

[22]David G. French (ed.), "Planning Responsibilities of State Departments of Public Welfare," *Proceedings of the Conference on Planning Responsibilities of State Departments of Public Welfare*, Brandeis University, Waltham, Mass., Nov. 16–18, 1966, American Public Welfare Association, 1967, p. 64.

[23]Kramer.

[24]Kirschner Associates, "A Description and Evaluation of Neighborhood Centers," *A Report* for the Office of Economic Opportunity, December, 1966; Howard W. Hallman, "The Community Action Program—An Interpretative Analysis of 35 Communities," *Examination of the War on Poverty*, Vol. IV, U.S. Senate Committee on Labor and Public Welfare, September, 1967, U.S. Government Printing Office, Washington, 1967, pp. 897–915; Neil Gilbert, "Clients or Constituents? A Case Study of Pittsburgh's War on Poverty," unpublished doctoral dissertation, University of Pittsburgh, Feb. 1968.

[25]Marris and Rein.

[26]Glazer, p. 80.

fails to occur, it seems likely that the alienation of the poor from the welfare agency and middle-class society will increase. As the functions and powers of boards, committees, and social action groups are better defined, their limitations, as well as potentialities, should be better understood: whether they will be better accepted by the poor is another matter. However, such clarification may reduce their feeling of being misled. Although clarification of limits and of responsibilities is likely to induce resistance and anger, field observations suggest that clarity and consistency in the face of pressure may appear as evidence of respect for one's self and for others: an important influence in reducing alienation and frustration.

THE OPPORTUNITY TO INFLUENCE DECISIONS

Research concerning social organizations indicates that the patterns of community organizations broadly reflect community social structure.[27] Even within individual agencies and organizations, boards and committees can be differentiated according to the power and prestige they confer on members.[28] It is probably safe to assume that within the affiliations available to the poor hierarchies will develop whereby upwardly mobile persons will move from one organizational rung to another. But the pertinent question here is what opportunities are available to the poor to reach the first rung.

Particularly in the past 5 years, the Federal Government has taken the lead in "attempting to open up the opportunity system" for disadvantaged and handicapped persons, including the poor, particularly Negroes. The public is confused as to the meaning of the term, and it is not clear how far most Americans are willing to go in this direction. Both of these conditions are apparent in the diverse programs launched under the Economic Opportunity Act. These programs range from those emphasizing changing the person through education, job-training, and job placement to those emphasizing

[27]See, for example, Mhyra S. Minnis, "The Patterns of Women's Organizations: Significance, Types, Social Prestige Rank, and Activities," in Marvin B. Sussman (ed.), *Community Structure and Analysis* (New York: Thomas Y. Crowell Company, 1959), pp. 269–287.

[28]See Aileen D. Ross, "Philanthropic Activity and the Business Career," *Social Forces*, March, 1954, pp. 274–280; Nicholas Babchuk, Ruth Massey, and C. Wayne Gordon, "Men and Women in Community Agencies: A Note on Power and Prestige," *American Sociological Review*, June, 1960, pp. 399–403; Arnold J. Auerbach, "Aspirations of Power People and Agency Goals," *Social Work*, January, 1961, pp. 66–73; and Charles V. Willie, Herbert Notkin, and Nicolas Rozak, "Trends on the Participation of Business Men in Local Voluntary Affairs," *Sociology and Social Research*, April, 1964, pp. 289–300.

"changing the system" through community social action. The system itself is charged with robbing the poor of power.

Membership on a board or committee means little or nothing if the member is without power. As suggested by Dahl and Rossi, power and influence can derive from a number of sources: control over money and credit; the mass media; groups with mutual interests; and knowledge, values, and "prestigeful interaction."[29] To be effective, people must have access to such resources and be willing to take advantage of them.[30] Unfortunately, the poor have had few resources and little opportunity to mobilize what they have. Conventional political and social methods of organizing have been severely limited in low-income communities. Such communities lack the individual, as well as the organizational, resources associated with social participation. The people who live in them are not usually the kind who take part in organizational activities.

Gans points to the transience of poor people and to their suspicion of landlords, storeowners, policemen, and politicians and suggests that their "involvement in the neighborhood is at best neutral, and more often, negative."[31] Foskett says that participation is greatly facilitated by the opportunity for communication with participants from other social and economic levels; the ability to articulate; the means to afford the time and expense involved; and the awareness of the relevance of participation to one's personal situation or value system.[32] Poor people are unlikely to have opportunities, abilities, attitudes, and values like these.

Poor people have fewer of the kinds of resources that favor effective participation. Poverty fosters life styles oriented toward physical action rather than verbal communication and toward authoritarian rather than democratic interpersonal relations.[33] Furthermore, the conditions of poverty deprive poor persons of the resources necessary for organizational life and bring out rejecting and scornful attitudes in the prosperous members of organizations. Thus,

---

[29]Robert A. Dahl, "The Analysis of Influence in Local Communities" in Charles R. Adrian, *Social Science and Community Action,* pp. 25–42; and Peter H. Rossi, "What Makes Communities Tick?" *Public Health Reports,* February, 1962, pp. 117–124.

[30]Dahl, pp. 32–34.

[31]Herbert J. Gans, "Social and Physical Planning for the Elimination of Urban Poverty," in Bernard Rosenberg, Israel Gerver, and F. William Howton (eds.), *Mass Society in Crisis* (New York: The Macmillan Company, 1964), pp. 629–644.

[32]John M. Foskett, "The Influence of Social Participation on Community Programs and Activities," in Marvin B. Sussman, *Community Structure and Analysis,* pp. 311–330.

[33]Catherine S. Chilman, *Growing Up Poor,* Welfare Administration Publication No. 13, U.S. Department of Health, Education, and Welfare, May 1966.

the people who most need effective organizations are those least likely to have them.

Specht says that barriers to the effective participation of poor people in organizational life come from four sources: the people themselves—their self-defeating attitudes; community attitudes—such as discrimination toward minority groups; the organization—characteristics that discourage participation; and the political structure—the opposition of the dominant political machine to admitting new members.[34] Thus, participation by low-income persons is severely limited by lack of organizational and individual assets and environmental supports.

The sheer burden of survival in low-income communities often prevents low-income persons from participating in organized activity—and, when they do, from being effective. "Many have heavy debts, physical illness and suffer the consequences of broken, disrupted homes. Many are poorly or inadequately educated. Some ... distrust and are hostile toward professionals, sponsoring agencies—and sometimes themselves."[35]

Kramer found that splinter groups frequently formed in community action programs and that factional strife consumed much time and energy. Conflict occurred when differences arose among ethnic groups and between lower class members and staff members and staff members and directors. The issues varied from community to community, but few programs were free from strife.[36]

The fundamental issue in most struggles was the scramble for jobs. Because they have few resources, persons in low-income neighborhoods and organizations are particularly susceptible to intense competition. Ghetto life increases the likelihood that such feeling will be turned inward. According to Rainwater, aggression directed within the group is one of the things that make it difficult to have any continuing organization (within the ghetto). It is one of the reasons why it is possible to organize people around specific crises that have an immediate impact that permits momentary focus on the fact that the outside world imposes these constraints. This quickly falls apart, however, and the group returns to the same old way of doing business.[37]

---

[34]Harry Specht, *Urban Community Development: A Social Work Process*, Contra Costa Council of Community Services, Nov. 1966, pp. 27–28.

[35]Harry Specht, *Community Development in Low-Income Areas: Its Relevance to Problems of the Negro Community*, Contra Costa Council of Community Services, Feb. 1966, p. 43.

[36]Kramer.

[37]Lee Rainwater, "Neighborhood Action and Lower-class Life-styles" (discussion),

The highly vulnerable low-income community feels organizational discontinuity more intensely than any other. Cunningham indicates that the problem of the poverty program was not so much in mobilizing participation as in sustaining it.[38]

The problem of sustaining motivation and peaceful relations is not peculiar to lower class organizations, of course. Every group has within-group and between-group rivalries. Conflict in middle-class groups, though usually subtle and covert, can also alienate group members. "The main problem in voluntary associations is to maintain motivation. To sustain high commitment for long periods of time is, understandably, an even more difficult task."[39]

Except for a handful of "select" leaders, poor people are systematically excluded from organizations. When they are allowed to participate, they feel "uncomfortable" and "treated as special." They see participation "as highly competitive," and "they feel that they are left out by their inability to dress well, to speak correctly, and so on. . . . Lower-class people expect to be manipulated, looked down upon and exploited by organizations."[40]

The severe problems involved and the very limited prospects for the participation of the poor in the work of public welfare boards and committees notwithstanding, experience does provide some perspective on the current situation. At best, few people participate actively in organized efforts—even in middle-class organizations. Information concerning individual participant characteristics is very limited. Perlman and Jones report: "No data are available on who actually participates in neighborhood organizations. . . . Information about participation in terms of either total number of or proportion of the target population is also scanty."[41] Organized participation in neighborhood centers provides such a point from which to view the people involved. The Kirschner Associates' early study of neighborhood centers found that one common thread appeared "through all forms of participation . . . it is the upper stratum of the poor which is involved and the 'problematic' and 'disreputable' poor are almost totally uninvolved except on an emergency basis . . . most of the poor

---

in John B. Turner (ed.), *Neighborhood Organization for Community Action* (New York: The National Association of Social Workers, 1968), p. 41.

[38]As cited in Mathews, p. 60.

[39]Mathews, p. 7.

[40]Rainwater, p. 32.

[41]Robert Perlman and David Jones, *Neighborhood Service Centers*, Welfare Administration, Office of Juvenile Delinquency, U.S. Department of Health, Education, and Welfare, 1967, p. 54.

have no involvement whatsoever."[42] Just as most traditional community organizations have an upper middle-class bias, apparently most innovational neighborhood organizations have an upper lower class bias.

The experience of OEO programs also provides information about the participation of the poor in policy-making decisions. Mathews reports: "During the first years of the program 'only an inconsequential number of emblematic poor' served on Boards dominated and controlled by a social welfare-education-civic elite."[43] The Kirschner Associates' study found that "poor" board members were inarticulate and ineffective, that they felt frustrated, that their views were not respected, that they had no real control, and that they were "inadequate to cope with the complexity of affairs confronting them."[44] Representatives of the poor were conservative "company men" who did not want to "rock the boat."[45] Role conflict and reference group theory suggest that at least the socially mobile representatives of low-income neighborhood groups tend to overidentify with their middle-class colleagues on boards and committees and in the process alienate the groups they represent.[46] The problems of recruitment and representation obviously loom large; the potential for formal or informal cooptation of the poor by the "establishment" is great.

Though most of the poor have been involved as advisers only, the pressure for more active and influential roles in policy-making continues.[47] Similar pressure will probably be put on public welfare boards and committees.

Most representatives of the poor have thus far been appointed by mayors, city councilmen, or boards of county supervisors. Although OEO programs have used both selection and appointment, programs in several cities have held elections. According to Levitan, the participation rate in these elections ranged from 1 to 5 percent of the eligible voters. He concludes that, "since these elections were widely publicized, particularly in low-income neighborhoods, it was

---

[42]Kirschner Associates, p. 46.

[43]Mathews, p. 56.

[44]Kirschner Associates, p. 46.

[45]_____, p. 21.

[46]For a discussion of this issue as reflected in the employment of neighborhood workers, see Charles F. Grosser, "Local Residents as Mediators Between Middle-Class Professional Workers and Lower-Class Clients,"*Social Service Review*, March, 1966, pp. 56–63.

[47]Kramer; Dare.

apparent that the vast majority of the poor did not participate."[48] In contrast, Shostak points out that in Philadelphia voter interest was high and that the greatest interest and heaviest voting occurred in the poorest communities.[49]

Despite the great handicaps under which the poor have labored, cautious optimism may be in order. Shostak says that the 12 spokesmen for the poor on the Philadelphia Antipoverty Action committee often voted together. They did not appear to be "overwhelmed" by the professional members; and they "successfully pressed for concrete and swift results, keeping up strong pressure to move proposals through the unfamiliar. . . bureaucratic channels and red-tape procedures that confront every antipoverty proposal." He concludes that the contributions of these representatives of the poor far outweighed the problems raised by their participation.[50] On the basis of a study of some 35 community action agencies, Hallman concludes that "after two years of experience, representatives of the poor are beginning to be influential in the governing boards. . . . At first these representatives did not understand board proceedings and were inarticulate, but in recent months they have been more expressive and more forceful."[51]

There are serious questions as to whether the participation of poor people on boards and committees will effectively increase the power and influence of low-income members. Their lack of access to the economic and organizational sources of community power, the poverty in which they live, and the life styles that do not favor cooperation and commitment to long-term goals seem to block their organizational effectiveness. Evidently, only a few low-income people try to become advisers and policy-makers. But there is also evidence that low-income people do produce leaders who can with experience become effective and influential.

IMPROVING COMMUNICATION

Communication between the poor and other members of the com-

[48]Sar A. Levitan, "Is This Poverty War 'Different'?" *The Use of Social Research in Federal Domestic Programs*, Part II: *The Adequacy and Usefulness of Federally Financed Research on Major National Social Problems*. A Staff Study for the Research and Technical Programs Subcommittee of the Committee on Government Operations, U.S. Senate, Apr. 1967, p. 283.

[49]Arthur B. Shostak, "Promoting Participation of the Poor: Philadelphia's Antipoverty Program," *Social Work*, January, 1966, p. 68.

[50]Shostak, p. 69.

[51]Hallman, p. 908.

munity is not and will not be easy. Citizen board and committee members representing different social and cultural backgrounds will probably find it hard to understand and accept each other. Staff members of public welfare agencies will be confronted with conflicting viewpoints and challenges to their prerogatives. They will probably be hampered by their inexperience and lack of training in communicating with citizen groups. "The field of public welfare has created boards but many times has shown no skill in how to use them. There is no point in having a board unless you have professionals involved in making the board active and effective."[52]

Findings from research related to small groups provide leads that may be useful in considering the issue of communication. Because these findings are drawn from studies of middle-class groups in structured settings, they may be only indirectly applicable.[53] In our discussion we assume that representatives of the poor on public welfare boards and committees are of lower social and economic status than other members and are drawn primarily from minority groups.

Studies of group behavior suggest that high status members of organizations are usually more active and influential and take more responsibility for the success of the group than others.[54] In large boards and committees, members of the same ethnic groups usually interact exclusively with each other and exhibit similar patterns of behavior.[55] Without a close working relationship, Negroes often withdraw from situations in which they must compete with white persons.[56] In experimental studies Negro college students displayed

---

[52]French, p. 64.

[53]For an excellent review of the research literature, see A. Paul Hare, *Handbook of Small Group Research* (Glencoe: The Free Press, 1963). See also Harold B. Gerard and Norman Miller, "Group Dynamics," in Paul R. Farnsworth, Olga McNemar, and Quinn McNemar (eds.), *Annual Review of Psychology*, Vol. 18 (1967), pp. 287–332.

[54]See, for example, F. L. Strodtbeck, Rita M. James, and C. Hawkins, "Social Status in Jury Deliberations," *American Sociological Review*, June, 1957, pp. 179–185; and H. Medow and A. Zander, "Aspirations for the Group Chosen by Central and Peripheral Members,"*Journal of Personality and Social Psychology*, March, 1965, pp. 224–228.

[55]See J. Gyr, "Analysis of Committee Member Behavior in Four Cultures," *Human Relations*, Vol. 4, No. 2 (1951), pp. 193–202, and Irwin Katz, Judith Goldston, and L. Benjamin, "Behavior and Productivity in Bi-racial Work Groups,"*Human Relations*, Vol. II, No. 2 (1958), pp. 123–141; see also T. M. Newcomb, "Stabilities Underlying Changes in Interpersonal Attraction," *Journal of Abnormal and Social Psychology*, April, 1963, pp. 376–386; and P. F. Secord and C. W. Backman, "Interpersonal Congruency, Perceived Similarity, and Friendship," *Sociometry*, June, 1964, pp. 115–127.

[56]H. M. Lefcourt, and G. W. Ladwig, "The Effect of Reference Group Upon Negroes'Task Persistence in a Biracial Competitive Game," *Journal of Personality and Social Psychology*, June, 1965, pp. 668–671.

marked social inhibition and impairment of intellectual ability when working with white students at cooperative problem-solving.[57] Yet the opportunity to work repeatedly and successfully with the same persons increases the likelihood of Negroes and white persons participating equally.[58]

To the extent that representatives of the poor are in the minority, they are likely to be under great pressure to conform to the will of the group. Whether a member conforms, however, may depend on whether he is accepted by other members. Neither the highly accepted member nor unacceptable member tends to conform: the one because he feels secure; the other because he sees no point in conformity.[59] In general, an individual member of a board or committee may feel great pressure to conform when the issue is comparatively ambiguous; when his judgment will be made public; when most members hold the same view; and when he highly values membership in the group.[60]

Individual members, particularly persons from minority groups, may reach outside the board or committee for strength and support. Welfare rights organizations and other groups will probably lend considerable power and influence to them.[61] Low-income members may compensate for what they lack in organizational skill and resources by their knowledge and experience as poor persons or as the recipients of services.

In general, board and committee members will be most satisfied and collective efforts most productive when the group is task-oriented and is able to accomplish specific results[62] in an equalitarian, democratic climate. Open discussion and decision-making in a group with full participation will also make the committee more effective.[63] A democratic attitude in and self-confident behavior from

[57]Irwin Katz, "Desegregation or Integration in Public Schools? The Policy Implications of Research," prepared for the National Conference on Equal Educational Opportunity in America's Cities, U.S. Commission on Civil Rights, Washington, D.C., Nov. 16–18, 1967, pp. 473–500.

[58]Lefcourt and Ladwig.

[59]See for example, C. A. Kiesler, "Attraction to the Group and Conformity to Group Norms," Journal of Personality, December, 1963, pp. 559–569; and J. E. Dittes and H. H. Kelley, "Effects of Different Conditions of Acceptance Upon Conformity to Group Norms," Journal of Abnormal and Social Psychology, July, 1956, pp. 100–107.

[60]Hare, p. 48.

[61]Shostak, p. 68.

[62]Hare, p. 271.

[63]See for example, K. Lewin, "Frontiers in Group Dynamics: Channels of Group Life; Social Planning and Action Research," Human Relations, Vol. 1, No. 2 (1947), pp. 142–153; L. Coch and J. R. P. French, Jr., "Overcoming Resistance to Change," Human Relations, Vol. 1, No. 4 (1948), pp. 512–532; and B. Willerman, "The Relation of Motivation and Skill to Active and Passive Participation in the Group," Journal of Applied Psychology, October, 1953, pp. 378–390.

the staff will improve communication. Informal reports of successful staff-committee relations in public welfare agencies suggest that frankness, informality, and flexibility in working with low-income groups are important to communication. Low-income people usually prefer direct, specific, clear statements to abstractions. Poor education and action-oriented life styles are likely to hamper their ability to understand and to make themselves understood when an intellectual, impersonal method is followed.[64]

One special problem that may arise when recipients and staff members participate together on boards and committees is this: they are likely to carry over attitudes and feelings originally developed within the worker-client relationship.[65] The staff member, feeling that he and he only is an expert on public welfare, may play down the potential contribution of the recipient. The recipient may feel ill at ease—ambivalent or hostile toward the staff member—and may suffer from a feeling of subservience. Briar found that most welfare recipients saw themselves as dependent supplicants and not as citizens with rightful legal claims.[66]

True communication with the board's constituency—including the poor—is vital to public understanding and support of the organization. In part, understanding will depend on the support available in the community to the poor serving on boards and committees, whether they are elected or selected and by whom, and the extent to which they maintain the base on which they were chosen.

Apart from the access to and use made of these sources, low-income people generally rely on informal channels of communication and interaction.[67] Dare reports that the chairman of the EOA's board of directors told members that "attempting to communicate with the city's poorer areas by radio and newspaper was less effective than working through ministers and their pulpits, knocking on doors, and using other types of personal contact."[68] Specht also underscores the importance of ministers and churches for Negro communities. "The Negro church still remains the most formidable institution involving significant numbers of lower-class Negroes and

---

[64]Chilman.

[65]For a discussion of this general issue, see Edward J. O'Donnell, "The Professional Volunteer Versus the Volunteer Professional," *Community Mental Health Journal* (June 1970).

[66]Scott Briar, "Welfare from Below: Recipients' Views of the Public Welfare System," *California Law Review*, May, 1966, pp. 370–385.

[67]Chilman.

[68]Dare, p. 1.

is the only indigenous institution of the community that also has its own personnel, facilities, and established means of communication."[69]

SOCIALIZATION THROUGH PARTICIPATION

The life styles of low-income persons represent an adaptation to but not an escape from poverty, and to this extent poor people remain inappropriately socialized.[70] A large body of social and pyschological research and theory indicates the importance of involving all members in the processes of the group if their motivation for changing and ability to do so are to be aroused and kept alive. Anthropologists point out that cultural change is unlikely unless the need for and advantages of change are clear to all members of a society and its leaders endorse and act to effect such change. Although social and behavioral scientists vary in detail, they agree that learning does not occur unless the person takes active part in the learning process and feels rewarded for his participation.

Thus, if poor people are to learn how to adapt to society, if they are to be motivated to become full-fledged members, if they are to acquire the competence needed for social and economic independence, they must participate in society's group processes and their participation must result in clear rewards such as more income, better jobs, better housing, and a fair share of economic abundance.

Increased participation in the planning and carrying out of public welfare programs appears to hold out some promise. It reflects a recognition that our social and economic systems are significant in contributing to economic dependency and that poor people have a right to share in the shaping of social programs, especially those affecting them. It rests on the principle that active and effective involvement in community affairs rather than passive acceptance of adversity may counteract fatalistic and alienated life styles.

Although participation in the work of boards and committees is likely to involve only a small proportion of the poor, potentially it can provide the participant with a creative learning experience that can affect others in his neighborhood. However, if the participant has an unfavorable experience, he is just as likely to communicate his hostile or fatalistic attitude.

---

[69]Harry Specht, "Community Development in Low-Income Negro Areas," *Social Work*, October, 1966, p. 81.

[70] Chilman.

Revolutionary social changes demand that all people acquire new values and attitudes. Among the changes to which they must adapt are the demands of poor people for real equality. Through participation in group meetings with disadvantaged people, middle-class members of boards and committees may acquire new knowledge and insight. Whether they do depends on many aspects, including the quality of group leadership and whether leadership promotes open communication.

SUGGESTIONS FOR RESEARCH

The need for research concerning the effectiveness of the participation of low-income people in the work of the boards and advisory committees of public welfare agencies is obvious. A wide range of investigations, including surveys, informal evaluations conducted with group members and staff people, and formal program research must be undertaken. The major question is this: Have the objectives of the participation of the poor in the work of boards and committees as discussed here been attained in whole or in part? Answers might be sought through research concerning these specific questions.

● Has the welfare department made program and policy changes suggested by the board or advisory committee? What changes? How have the views of public assistance recipients changed? Those of agency staff members? Those of the community as a whole?

● Do low-income board and committee members believe that through membership they have attained rights and acquired power equal to other members of the board? Do other members think their rights and powers have been reduced? If so, how have they responded?

● Does the existence of participatory boards and committees affect the sense of powerlessness low-income groups often feel? Do such boards and committees make low-income members feel they have more influence in the operation of the welfare system than they had before they were on the boards?

● Does participation on such boards and committees by people from all socioeconomic levels promote communication and greater understanding between members? Do the attitudes of members toward each other and the group they represent change? Does increased information and understanding spread to the agency administrator and staff? To the community?

● Do public assistance recipients, in general, know about such boards and committees? How do they view them? To what extent do they believe that the "poverty members" represent their views? Are they aware of communication channels that could keep them informed about board and committee activities? Do they belong to groups in contact with board or committee representatives?

● Is the community as a whole aware of boards and committees? What is the attitude toward them? Does the attitude shift in time?

● What effect does board and committee membership have on the social skill of low-income members? Do they increasingly identify themselves with such middle-class values as commitment to long-term, abstract goals? Do they acquire greater skill in verbal communication and in organizational behavior? Does their employment status change?

● What kinds of change are better undertaken through organized efforts outside of the existing welfare system?

Attempts to obtain dependable answers to questions like these are far from simple. Many problems present themselves, particularly concerning these points: the reliability of answers obtained from questionnaires or interviews; the validity of answers obtained; and whether results are associated with the existence of boards and committees.

In conducting studies concerning these points, a careful accounting must be kept of several aspects, including these: program input—for example, the kind of leadership provided for committees or boards; the community and agency situation in which the board or committee operates; and the composition of the board or committee. Such aspects are likely to affect the results. Without taking into account mitigating circumstances, the research might reach biased conclusions about boards and committees as such.

Studies on such subjects might lend themselves to informal evaluations by staff members to find ways to increase the effectiveness of an agency board or committee. Of course, only formal research would give confidence to the results as they related to the community. A series of carefully designed studies conducted in several communities would have to be completed before generalizations could be drawn.

Studies conducted over a long time (3 years or more) to permit fair assessment of the effects of a continuing program are greatly needed. Public welfare boards and committees, newly constituted to include a cross-section of the community and a large proportion of low-income people, would likely face several difficulties at first that could be reduced through experience and mutual accommodation. Thus, studies that allow for analysis of changes in group behavior and change over a period of time are needed. If patterns of group movement are observed and analyzed in a number of situations, helpful conclusions might turn up as to how to improve the long-range effectiveness of such groups.

Other studies might aim at finding out what blocks and what promotes effective committee and board action, using the methods of small group research. Information from such studies should be useful to the agencies directly involved and might provide information for other, similar organizations.

Questions might arise in many communities as to which of several programs aimed at increasing the participation of poor people would be the most effective. We have indicated that ways to promote participation include employing them in human service programs, using them as volunteers, and giving them membership in agency-independent social action groups. The study topics suggested might be expanded to include questions about other forms of participation. These questions might concern what forms of participation respondents know, which they prefer, and which appear to have the greatest effect on socialization, employment, and family stability.

WHERE DOES PARTICIPATION STAND?

Although government action is opening the way for increased participation by poor people in the work of public welfare boards and committees and the reasons for their participation are strong, the question of whether participation works is unanswered. Can participation lead the way to power and real involvement in society for those now excluded by poverty and failure? Can it bring about changes that will reduce the amount of poverty or only changes that adjust the nature of social services and the way in which they are delivered? Can it bridge the gap in communication between the rich and the poor? Can poor people acquire the skill, understanding, and flexibility they need to have a greater share of power, resources, and opportunities? More specifically, can the Nation provide opportunities for people to effectively engage in community decision-making through participation in the work of public welfare boards and committees?

We can at least offer tentative answers to these questions. Leaning heavily on the theory and evidence we have cited, we tentatively conclude that the poor will have restricted opportunity to take part in the work of welfare boards and committees, that participation will take the form more of advice-giving than of policy-making, that the poor moving upward socially will be selected for participation, and that participation will be conservative and traditional and probably not very effective. But we also believe that, in time, the representatives of the poor will more actively reflect the needs and aspirations of the people they represent, will more aggressively assert themselves during board and committee deliberations, will press for radical reform of the social welfare system, and will be more effective in organizations.

Considerable conflict and pressure are likely to attend these changes, as members from low-income and minority groups strive with increasing determination to get their share of democracy's blessings. Such conflict will be reduced if real participation is encouraged; if agencies are ready to listen to and communicate with constituent groups; if the limits of power and the functions of advisory committees, policy boards, and independent social action groups are clearly defined; if agencies become more responsive to demands for change; and if other opportunities are simultaneously opened to poor people to attain full membership in the social and economic system. If, however, participation is denied and opportunities are blocked, the Nation can expect increased alienation, hostility, withdrawal into separation, and a widening of the gulf between the justifiably resentful poor and the rest of society.

·23·

SUMATI N. DUBEY

Community Action Programs and Citizen Participation: Issues and Confusions

The Community Action Program (CAP) of the Economic Opportunity Act of 1964 is defined in the act as fighting poverty by (1)

SOURCE: Reprinted with permission of the National Association of Social Workers, from *Social Work*, Vol. 15, No. 1 (January, 1970), pp. 76–84.

providing service assistance and conducting other activities that give promise of bettering the conditions under which people live, learn, and work, (2) mobilizing and utilizing public and private resources, and (3) developing, conducting, and administering such programs with the maximum feasible participation of the neighborhood residents (i.e., low-income individuals, families, and groups upon whose needs the programs are focused). The central preoccupation of CAPs, consequently, is the planning and development of relevant activities and services as well as effective and efficient allocation of resources. This is to be accomplished through organizational operations whereby the target population participates in setting goals, developing strategies, defining policies, and establishing structures for reaching the legislative objectives.[1]

The mandatory requirement of enlisting the active participation of indigenous people in shaping decisions affecting their own welfare distinguishes the CAP from earlier attempts to involve local groups. In urban renewal projects, for example, citizen participation was sought in order to avoid, or at least to handle, protests that arose among the residents of the areas scheduled for renewal. In other words, whether intentionally or not, programs for resident participation were often used to offset the spontaneous but disruptive activities of local protest groups.[2]

The President's Commission on Juvenile Delinquency and Youth Crime may be the closest forerunner of the CAP from the point of view of resident participation. Administrative guidelines issued by the committee in 1963 called for the involvement of "individuals and organizations in the target community." Local organizations formed to carry out social development programs came to be called "community action agencies." Perhaps the difference between the committee's efforts to involve residents and the CAP's requirement of participation is more a matter of magnitude than of substance.[3]

From the point of view of its ideology and methods of operation,

---

[1]Simon Slavin, "Community Action and Institutional Change," in *Social Welfare Forum, 1965* (New York: Columbia University Press, 1965), p. 148.

[2]Frances Fox Piven, "Participation of Residents in Neighborhood Community Action Programs," *Social Work*, Vol. 11, No. 1 (January, 1956), pp. 73–74.

[3]Robert F. Kennedy, then attorney general, pointed up the similarities between the juvenile delinquency and CAP programs: "The Juvenile Delinquency Programs . . . created under the [Juvenile Delinquency Control] Act are similar to the Community Action Organization of Title II. So are the techniques, although, of course, the Community Action Program's aims are much broader and will use many more and different techniques." Hearings before the Subcommittee on the War on Poverty Program, March 17–April 14, 1964 (Washington, D.C.: U.S. Government Printing Office, 1964), pp. 304–305.

the CAP can best be conceptualized as a contemporary blend of social action and community development (as defined by the United Nations[4]). The basic similarities between the CAP and the community development concept seem to be that both emphasize involvement of local communities as units of action and decision-making and both require the participation of governments to help these communities in their efforts.

However, there are also some differences. The main one is that in community development (as conducted in developing countries) the greatest emphasis is placed on utilization of surplus human labor as a resource for economic development, while in the CAP the action agenda deals with the inequitable distribution and application of actually and potentially available resources. The CAP objective is to rechannel resources into those local communities suffering most from deprivation, social dislocation, and individual incapacity to meet basic human needs, in order to grant them a substantial share in society's goals and services.[5]

RATIONALES FOR RESIDENT PARTICIPATION

Various rationales for resident participation in CAP antipoverty programs are advanced depending on beliefs about the causes of poverty, commitment to the ideology of social action stemming from the civil rights movement, the degree of commitment to the American value of rugged individualism, and the concern about and belief in the value of coherence and co-ordination among social welfare services.[6] Four basic rationales are given to defend the requirement of resident participation. Each has its own proponents, who do not always agree on a given issue even among themselves.

1. *Program Irrelevance and Inadequacy.*—Programs intended to assimilate the poor into the mainstream of American society, such as public welfare, public housing, social settlements, and social work with hardcore families, are usually initiated and supported from

---

[4]According to the United Nations, the term community development designates the utilization, under a single program, of approaches and techniques that rely on local communities as units of action and attempt to combine outside assistance with organized local self-determination and effort, and that correspondingly seek to stimulate local initiative and leadership as the primary instrument of change. *See Programme of Concerted Action in the Social Field of the United Nations and Specialized Agencies,* Document E/CN/5/291 (New York: United Nations, 1963).

[5]Slavin, *op. cit.,* p. 148.

[6]Daniel P. Moynihan, "What Is Community Action?" *The Public Interest,* No. 5 (Fall, 1966), pp. 3–8.

outside the neighborhood and are in effect imposed on the poor.[7] Lacking the basic involvement of the people they try to serve, these programs are generally insufficient, inappropriate, fragmented, and unsuitable to the life-style of the poor, especially of minority groups. Some services even mitigate against the escape of the recipients and their families from the cycle of poverty.[8] In other words, the programs fail to make any lasting positive impact on the conditions of poverty; the majority of service recipients remain poor, live in an atmosphere of apathy and disorganization, and consequently feel hostile toward the very programs supposedly designed to rescue them.[9]

It is therefore considered important to involve the poor in order to obtain a realistic perspective on the appropriateness and effectiveness of social services—a perspective free from biases stemming from considerations of careerism, political interests, and the public relations needs of agencies and their personnel. It is argued that the poor are in the best position to define their own needs and to suggest appropriate uses of federal funds to meet these needs. Inclusion of the poor in the antipoverty programs, from this point of view, will help overcome a long-standing "colonialism" in both public and private sectors of the social welfare field.[10] The new antipoverty legislation represents a significant breakthrough insofar as it officially recognizes the rights of the poor to participate as policy-makers and program developers, operators, and evaluators, in contrast to their more traditional role of passive consumers.[11]

2. *Creating a Power Base.*—Poverty is conceptualized as a situation of enforced dependency and powerlessness wherein the poor have little control over events and decisions affecting them.[12] Banfield observes that concerted action for any purpose necessitates creation of a more or less elaborate system of influence: appropriate people must be persuaded, coerced, inveigled, or otherwise induced

---

[7]Warren C. Haggstrom, "The Power of the Poor," in Frank Riessman and Jerome Cohen (eds.), *Mental Health of the Poor* (New York: Free Press, 1964), pp. 214–225.

[8]Frank Riessman, "The New Anti-Poverty Ideology," *Poverty and Human Resources Abstracts,* Vol. 1, No. 4 (July, 1966), pp. 5–11.

[9]Haggstrom, *op. cit.*, p. 214.

[10]Richard A. Cloward, "Are the Poor Left Out?" *The Nation* (August 2, 1965), pp. 55–60.

[11]Riessman, *op. cit.*, p. 6.

[12]*See* Kenneth S. Waterman, "Local Issues in the Urban War on Poverty," *Social Work*, Vol. 11, No. 1 (January, 1966), pp. 57–63; Kenneth B. Clark, *Dark Ghetto: Dilemmas of Social Power* (New York: Harper & Row, 1965), pp. 11–12; and James Baldwin, *The Fire Next Time* (New York: Dial Press, 1963).

to do what is required of them.[13] Where does this influence come from? According to Dahl the possible bases of influence are large, but the most important are money and credit; control over jobs; control over information; social standing; knowledge and expertise; popularity, esteem, or charisma; legality, constitutionality, and officiality; ethnic solidarity; and the right to vote.[14] Rossi points out that the major sources of power with which to induce social change are wealth and other physical resources, control over prestigious interactions, control over values, threats to property (such as take place in civil disobedience, demonstrations, and so on), and the backing of solidarity interest groups either as voting blocks or as potential votes.[15] The poor, as these authorities imply, do not possess these resources and therefore have relatively little power.

The poor are dependent for their survival on powerful persons and organizations such as slum landlords, public welfare departments, the public housing authority, and local political machines. Welfare payments, exorbitant rent for poor housing, and racial discrimination all contribute toward a condition of impoverishment in which the individual feels worthless and powerless. The poor are not able to deal with the community power structure on equal terms. Their inability to enter into successful negotiation with powerful persons and organizations is due mainly to the lack of necessary re-sources — expert knowledge, organizational skills, and coercive pow-er — associated with the lowest socioeconomic status. Whenever the poor press their demands by the threat of disruption or other means, the community power structure withholds access to economic re-sources and brings coercive power to bear through the police, the courts, and administrative regulations in order to defeat such threats.

This [coercive] power has been and can be mobilized at any time as a direct force to defeat the efforts of self-help organizations [of the poor]. The com-munity can impose direct sanctions — such as use of police violence, refusal to rent land to tenant farmers, eviction from a public housing project, and harrassment of welfare clients — on members of these organizations as a means of resisting change efforts.[16]

---

[13]Edward C. Banfield, *Political Influence* (New York: Free Press of Glencoe, 1961).

[14]Robert A. Dahl, "The Analysis of Influence in a Local Community," in Charles Adrian (ed.), *Social Science and Community Action* (East Lansing, Mich.: Michigan State University, 1960), pp. 24–42.

[15]Peter Rossi, "Theory, Research and Practice in Community Organization," in Adrian (ed.), *op. cit.*, pp. 9–24.

[16]Arthur Blum, Magdalena Miranda, and Maurice Meyer, "Goals and Means for Social Change," in John B. Turner (ed.), *Neighborhood Organization for Community Action* (New York: National Association of Social Workers, 1968), p. 114.

The CAP aims at creating a power base for the poor by delivering to them control over the programs and funds to be funneled into slum and ghetto communities. Cloward points out that under the antipoverty program billions of dollars are likely to be assigned to depressed neighborhoods for use in a wide range of services. To manage these services, huge organizations must be set up. Thousands of jobs are likely to be created and whether these are filled by professionals or by the poor, the new workers will owe allegiance to those who manage the operation. The organizations to be created or expanded, if manned by the poor, are likely to constitute a potentially important source of power for them.[17]

3. *Improved Service Delivery.* — A third rationale lies in the administrative and therapeutic potential of involvement of the poor. One area of increasing concern in the health and welfare field is the problem of service delivery and utilization. In many instances social welfare services seem to be utilized least by those who need them most. Consequently, ways must be found to make these services more available to persons in the lower socioeconomic classes. One such way may be use of area residents as nonprofessional helpers. This has obvious advantages: such indigenous workers tend to bridge the gap between middle-class personnel and the poor — a common obstacle to service delivery — and they supplement the manpower resources that are so scarce in the social welfare field.[18] Riessman observes that the helper therapy principle — the use of people with a specific problem or handicap to help other people with the same problem, with positive results for both — can be especially workable with the poor, since this is culturally congruent with co-operative trends within the lower socioeconomic groups.[19] It is further hoped that nonprofessional staff members, because of their understanding of the culture of poverty, would be able to provide information on the needs and problems of the poor from which realistic programs can be planned.[20]

4. *Value of Participatory Democracy.* — It is usually assumed that every citizen should contribute to the working of the society to the

[17]Cloward, *op. cit.*

[18]Alfred H. Katz, "Application of Self-Help Concepts in Current Social Welfare," *Social Work*, Vol. 10, No. 3 (July, 1965), pp. 68–74.

[19]Frank Riessman, "The 'Helper' Therapy Principle," *Social Work*, Vol. 10, No. 2 (April, 1965), pp. 27–32. See also Katz, *op. cit.*; and George Brager, "The Indigenous Worker: A New Approach to the Social Work Technician," *Social Work*, Vol. 10, No. 2 (April, 1965), pp. 33–40.

[20]Frank Riessman, "The New Anti-Poverty Ideology"; George Brager and Harry Specht, "Mobilizing the Poor for Social Action," *Social Welfare Forum, 1965* (New York: Columbia University Press, 1965), pp. 197–210.

fullest possible extent. In slum communities the primacy of the individual's welfare is generally overshadowed by the interests and manipulations of the "down-town" political apparatus, whose decisions are frequently inconsistent with the values and aspirations of the slum residents. Consequently, new opportunities and channels are needed to enable people to participate in the affairs of *their* community and to express their own opinions.

PREDOMINANT PATTERNS

The term "maximum feasible participation" is subject to various interpretations, and the participation of poverty area residents in CAPs has followed various patterns. Programs differ with respect to the number of residents involved, the level of their participation in the organizational structure (e.g., service on an advisory, policy-making, or constituent body), and in the methods used to promote participation (e.g., election, political appointment, or the like). Although information is not available for the entire country, three patterns of participation seem to be emerging:

1. Residents have become involved as policy-makers on boards of directors—either at the city or local level—that define program goals and means. By and large, however, such participation has not taken place to any substantial degree.

2. The poor have performed staff functions in antipoverty programs, generally being referred to as "indigenous" or "non-professional" workers. This is the most prevalent form of participation.

3. They have acted as constituent groups, providing the professional staff with feedback for program evaluation or acting as pressure groups to influence the project's activities.

A number of issues, based on the assumptions discussed previously, are raised with respect to these patterns of participation, among them the following: (1) To what extent and in what ways can and should the poor help determine program goals and the means to achieve them? (2) What is the nature of the partnership among the representatives of the poor, the public interest, the planning expert, and the political bureaucracy?[21] These will be discussed later.

METHODS OF PROMOTING PARTICIPATION

The diversity of methods for involving the poor in the CAPs stems from the lack of specificity in the prescription of maximum feasible

---

[21]Piven, *op. cit.*, pp. 73–80.

participation, from the relative willingness or unwillingness of local politicians to risk a threat to their positions, and from the coalesced strength of the poor in different geographic areas. Shostak identifies three predominant modes of involvement: containment, co-optation, and codetermination.[22]

Containment is designed to keep the aggressive element among the poor under control. This is the predominant mode, for example, in Atlanta and Chicago. The poverty board in Atlanta consists of a majority of whites and a few Negro businessmen—all political appointees— who dictate policy to welfare department personnel. Although two-thirds of Atlanta's poor are Negroes, none of the city's antipoverty programs is run by them. Advisory councils of the poor attached to neighborhood centers are severely limited in their authority over programs. In the case of Chicago's Committee on Urban Opportunity—a city-wide board with ninety members—seven persons (the chairmen of the advisory councils of the seven urban progress centers) represent the poverty neighborhoods. The remaining eighty-three members are high-level public officials, corporation executives, welfare officials, labor leaders, clergymen, and so on.

In cities where *co-optation* is the primary mode, the middle-class members of the active ethnic and racial communities (especially the Negro community) are appointed to antipoverty boards to advise politicians on programs. For example, Detroit's antipoverty board consists of indigenous leaders who work with welfare professionals and influential community leaders to provide guidance for the mayor's antipoverty program. The mayor formulates policy with the apparent support of the middle-class Negro community and business and labor leaders.

Codetermination with the poor, the rarest model, is approximated in Philadelphia, where elected spokesmen for the poor join welfare professionals and community leaders in running the city's antipoverty programs. The Philadelphia Anti-Poverty Action Committee consists of elected representatives of the poor, delegates from welfare agencies, religious bodies, organized labor, the business community, NAACP, CORE, and the Urban League. Inclusion of the poor among the decision-makers has had three major effects: (1) Spokesmen for the poor are able to press for an important role for the community action councils. As a result, the councils now recommend

---

[22]Arthur B. Shostak, "Containment, Co-optation or Co-determination," *American Child*, Vol. 44, No. 4 (November, 1965), pp. 15-19. The examples that follow are taken from this paper.

candidates for nonprofessional jobs and review the qualifications of professional appointees. (2) The elected representatives have also been able to bring about certain reforms or changes in antipoverty programs. (3) The spokesmen have successfully pressed for swift and concrete results by exerting strong external pressures that help move proposals through the unfamiliar maze of bureaucratic channels and red tape that confront every antipoverty proposal.

LACK OF CONSENSUS ON GOALS

One issue clearly emerging with regard to citizen participation is a lack of consensus on the goal of participation. Is it to promote better utilization of social welfare services by achieving better co-ordination among them? to provide opportunities for participation by the poor in order to enable them to gain power whereby they can personally escape from poverty? to bring about significant social change and eliminate poverty itself?

The issue stems from a theoretical controversy about the causes of poverty and the resultant strategies to deal with it. Where do the causes of poverty rest—in the individual's inabilities, in the social institutions dealing with the poor, or in the social structure that fosters or permits poverty? The Committee on Education and Labor of the House of Representatives identified, in its report on the poverty bill (HR 11377), lack of education, poor health, the absence of marketable skills, and the unstable family life of the poor as causes of their poverty.[23] Accordingly, the bill directed attention to such components of the CAP as expanded and improved services, increased assistance, and necessary facilities in the fields of education, employment, job training and counseling, health services, vocational rehabilitation, housing, home management, and social services.

This conception carries an implicit assumption in the program strategy that the poor are responsible for their poverty, i.e., the defects to be remedied are located within the individual. Consequently, attention is focused on inadequacies of the poor rather than of social institutions and their policies.[24] Participation is thus viewed as a form of social therapy to treat social disintegration and apathy among the poor through self-help.

Those who believe that the causes of poverty lie in the in-

[23]Report of the Committee on Education and Labor, 88th Cong., 2d Sess., June 3, 1964, p. 2.
[24]Slavin, op. cit., pp. 148–150.

stitutional structure of society see participation of the poor as a means of building up a new political force to bring about significant social change. On this basis, militant groups in a number of cities have organized to protest against city administrations.

DEGREE OF PARTICIPATION

Another issue is related to the degree of resident participation as well as the amount of authority vested in participants. *Community Action Program Guide,* the first policy document issued by the Office of Economic Opportunity, states that a vital feature of every CAP is involvement of the poor (and/or residents of the area) in planning, policy-making, and program operation.[25]

It is widely understood, although not explicitly stated, that OEO expects one-third of the local poverty board members to be drawn from the poor.[26] The direction of the program is to help the poor to help themselves. The guide strongly urges direct involvement of the poor in block elections, petitions and referenda, and neighborhood legal aid associations. This policy is not always adhered to. Deviations from the policy seem typically to have been forced by local politicians (i.e., mayors and governors) who see a potential threat to their political power. Carter reports that OEO no longer emphasizes representation of the poor on poverty boards, in appeasement of the mayors of Syracuse, Chicago, and Atlanta, who vehemently opposed participation of the poor in the CAPs.[27]

There have also been conflicting pronouncements by OEO officials. "Are the poor supposed to make up a third of poverty boards?" Shriver was asked. "No," he replied on November 5, 1965. Yet only two weeks earlier OEO had sent a memorandum to all its regional directors announcing that "we are proposing as a guide that the representatives of the poor be approximately one-third of the membership of a [community action] governing body."[28] On January 12, 1966, Shriver reiterated:

[25]*Community Action Program Guide,* I (Washington, D.C.: Office of Economic Opportunity, October 1965), p. 7.

[26]Barbara Carter, "Sargent Shriver and the Role of the Poor," *Reporter,* May 5, 1966, pp. 17–20.

[27]*Ibid.* Interestingly, in contrast to this above assertion, OEO slashed poverty funds to Los Angeles on the ground that the poor did not have any voice in the poverty board. This policy was again reversed when OEO granted funds to the Atlanta poverty board, which did not have a single poor person on it. When asked about this, Mr. Shriver compared the role of the poor to that of an architect's client who participates in the planning but does not actually design the house.

[28]*Ibid.*

There is no requirement in this statute that persons have to be poor to serve on a Community Action Committee. The phrase "the poor" is an elliptical way of describing the statutory language. You do not have to be poor to fulfill the statute, and we are not trying to get poor people as such. Is this clear enough?[29]

Pressures from groups that have traditionally presided over public welfare have also been forcing OEO to retreat from its policy of innovation, especially from the technique of arming the poor with power to force a changed institutional structure and/or delivery of services.[30] It is clear that with respect to participation of the poor in CAPs, OEO needs to state its policy firmly and clearly and follow it in a consistent fashion.

RIGHT TO SANCTION POLICY

The right of the poor to sanction a policy must also be clarified. This is important since the poor may be involved for different purposes: they may be involved in policy-making bodies as representatives of the groups a CAP seeks as constituents, they may be target area residents serving on an ad hoc or continuing basis as advisers, or they may be asked to give local sanction to policy created at a higher level. The difference between advice and sanction in dealing with representatives of the poor is critical.[31] In CAPs, involvement of the poor has appeared to represent an attempt to gain legitimation and support of policy, but the poor are rejected when they challenge the central goals and methods of traditional welfare programs. The controversy over the rights of the poor to make decisions is, in fact, the question of distribution of power between the poor and the social welfare network.[32] The dilemma is that a genuine, free, and effective political instrument cannot be created or guaranteed by OEO or any other public program. It will be up to the churches, foundations, and other active organizations to provide "seed money" for the poor to build effective organizations—if they are to be *of* the poor, and not dominated by or dependent on the goodwill and services of agencies

---

[29]*Ibid.*

[30]Jules Witcover and Erwin Knoll, "Politics and the Poor: Shriver's Second Thought," *Reporter*, December 30, 1965, pp. 23–24.

[31]Melvin B. Mogulof, "Involving Low-Income Neighborhoods in Antidelinquency Programs," *Social Work*, Vol. 10, No. 4 (October, 1965), pp. 51–57.

[32]See the statement made by Kenneth B. Clark, Hearing of the Subcommittee on Employment, Manpower, and Poverty, 90th Cong., 1967, p. 391.

and professionals. When a grass-roots organization of the poor comes into being, it might then contract with government programs to operate services for the poor.[33]

The fear of sanctions from the power structure, the lack of expert knowledge, poor formal communication skills, deficiency in organization skills, preoccupation with survival, and lack of confidence in organizational means as a way of effecting change in their life situation are some of the factors that make participation of the poor in CAPs highly problematic, if not impossible.[34] Verba points out four main conditions for political participation: (1) resources such as information about politics, issues, communication channels, and rules of political participation; skills in written and oral expression; and material and social resources, (2) motivation to participate, (3) structural conduciveness, by which is meant the availability of formal participatory structures, the presence of regularized procedures for participation such as Ombudsmen to process citizen complaints, and the availability of such procedures as periodic elections, and (4) cultural conduciveness such as support of the general norms of democracy. He further points out that these conditions are inequitably distributed in American society—lower-class Americans, especially Negroes, do not possess these resources. Consequently they participate to a significantly lower degree than do the white middle and upper classes.[35]

It has been observed in Cleveland, for example, that those who are struggling to make both ends meet cannot take a fight to the city hall or use coercion or other sanctions. The poor are afraid of going to jail, cannot afford to lose their jobs, and cannot hire lawyers to protect their rights vis-à-vis the police or the public housing authorities. It may be wondered how, with all of these limitations, the poor can participate in social action. Waterman observes that the poor

are politically disconnected and emasculated. Consequently it is almost inevitable that the dominant control and planning of even the Community Action Programs of the War on Poverty, which is to be done at the local level, will not represent those who are poor.[36]

---

[33]Waterman, *op. cit.*, p. 61.

[34]See Blum, Miranda, and Meyer, *op. cit.*, p. 18; and Lee Rainwater, "Neighborhood Action and Lower-Class Life-Style," in Turner (ed.), *op. cit.*, pp. 25–39.

[35]Sidney Verba, "Democratic Participation," *Annals*, Vol. 373 (September, 1967), pp. 53–78.

[36]Waterman, *op. cit.*, p. 60.

IS REPRESENTATION A DIVERSIONARY TACTIC?

Another issue is whether the representation of the poor on anti-poverty councils is a diversionary tactic. The effort to involve the poor may be primarily an attempt to divert attention from a far more fundamental problem confronting the poor in this society. In the event the poor take control of the antipoverty programs (and this has not happened), what would they win? They would win control over employment programs — which is not the same as control over the processes that create employment. Participation is therefore irrelevant to the solution of their problems. Many feel that the solution lies in institutional change. The local power structures, although they can affect the lives of individuals, have little freedom to create policies that affect the whole poverty group. Decisions at the local level involve the implementation of national and regional policies rather than the creation of policies that affect major resource allocation.[37]

WHO SHOULD BE INVOLVED

The final issue is whom to involve on the antipoverty boards: spokesmen for the poor, residents of the poverty areas who may not themselves be poor, or the poor themselves? There is a tendency in community action agencies to involve self-appointed spokesmen for the poor. Under the guise of involvement some projects have selected Negroes who have only the dimmest notion of what poverty is like. Projects that appoint middle- or upper-class Negroes as representatives of poor Negroes perform a ritual to fulfill the statutory requirements.[38] Kramer's study of CAPs in San Francisco substantiates this assertion:

The main critical issue among the members of the action system [consisting of welfare professionals, city officials and others] was the identification of appropriate representatives of the poor in the Community Action Program. Although the legislation explicitly prescribed a geographic target area as the basis for representation, this provided few guidelines for the community plan. . . . Usually, some criterion of association with the poor was used, circumventing direct involvement of residents or recipients.[39]

---

[37]Blum, Miranda, and Meyer, *op. cit.*

[38]Mogulof, *op. cit.*, pp. 53–54.

[39]Ralph M. Kramer and Clare Denton, "Organization of a Community Action Program: A Comparative Case Study," *Social Work*, Vol. 12, No. 4 (October, 1967), p. 78.

Even when representatives of the poor have been elected,

in no case were elected poor influential or taken seriously in any major civic decision and in very few cases were they competent or capable of any genuine rather than condescending involvement.[40]

SUMMARY

The basic rationales advanced for resident participation in CAPs include irrelevance and inadequacy of current programs in regard to the needs of the poor, creation of a power base for the poor, improvement in the service delivery system, and the need of a populace to participate in the democratic process. Residents have been involved in CAPs in the capacity of policy-makers, as staff workers, and as sounding-boards for the welfare organizations. The main issues that have arisen in regard to citizen participation in CAPs are the lack of consensus on goals and degrees of participation of residents, their right to sanction policy, and credentials of participants. These issues have considerably affected the workings of the program.

---

[40]Clark, *op. cit.*, p. 392.

· 24 ·

MELVIN B. MOGULOF

Federal Support for Citizen Participation in Social Action

An analysis of the many negotiating sessions and the reams of memoranda issued in the early days of the Office of Economic Op-

---

SOURCE: Reprinted with permission of the National Conference on Social Welfare from *The Social Welfare Forum 1969* (New York: Columbia University Press, 1969), pp. 86–107.

portunity's (OEO) community action program (CAP) would suggest to the reviewer one issue of overriding importance. That issue was how poor people and their representatives were to be included in, or excluded from, the local authority structures which were being established as part of the program.

In this year 1969 one may not be too surprised that in the early days of the antipoverty war there was greater concern with who would determine the program's direction than with what that direction would be. It was as if a shrewd decision had been made to the effect that the greater the involvement of those who were poor, the more likely was their poverty to be ameliorated or lifted. Now the notion that the involvement of the client is a crucial factor in his own healing is a central idea in many individually oriented therapies. A stress on client involvement can also be seen as ideologically close to the idea that the poor are to blame for their misfortune. The argument could be read: "If we could only engage him in desiring a better lot for himself, he would learn to make better use of available resources, and his poverty would soon come to an end."

The reader is hardly asked to believe that the focus on citizen involvement in CAP owed its existence to those whose model of poverty causation was an ineffectively functioning poor person surrounded by adequate resources. Rather, we are suggesting that there was a confluence of those who saw involvement as instrumental toward the lifting of poverty with those whose notions of poverty causation were much more environmentally based. To this latter group, the conditions of the poor, and more particularly the black poor, rested in a misallocation of resources. Further, this group saw that even those resources which were allocated to the poor were delivered through organizations controlled by middle-class whites in such a way as to sustain the interests of that class. The purpose of involvement, then, was to win control of the resource-allocating mechanisms and/or to establish pressure points by virtue of involvement, and in so doing change the way in which resources were delivered to poor people.

We are much less interested in the influence of those who conceive of involvement as somehow essential to successful therapy with poor people. The issue of involvement no longer belongs to this school of therapists. It is not defined by leaders of the black and other minority group poor who see sickness in the controlling elements of the society. When the problem is so defined, the purpose of involvement becomes the wresting of power from such controlling elements; or, at the very least, involvement becomes a means of forcing these elements to new kinds of accommodations affecting poor people and the black community.

The three federal programs under consideration—the juvenile delinquency demonstration program; CAP; and the model cities program—in the six years which span their history have provided the principal grounds for the evolution of the ideas of involvement. These programs have been influenced by a parallel movement in the black community away from integration and toward development of an independent black community. It seems clear that the programs themselves influenced the evolution of a national focus on community self-determination for minorities and for the black community in particular.

Certain commonalities between the three programs may make even sharper the evaluation of the issue of involvement for the purpose of influence:

1. In each program there was established a central organization which would define the nature of the problem locally and its causes. Only after such definition would intervention take place, and it was to be an intervention which in some way could stand the test of "comprehensiveness." In effect, in all three efforts action was to be preceded by planning.

2. In each program the emphasis was on local development of program to meet the assumed local differences in the problem.

3. Each program had a clearly defined population or area of service. In CAP the legislative phrase "maximum feasible involvement of groups and areas to be served" is generally perverted to "maximum feasible involvement of the poor."

4. Each program became primarily occupied with areas in which the black poor predominated to the point that "poor" became a euphemism for "Negro." One of the cautions in any exposition of the issues of involvement in these programs is that the evidence in large part has its best fit in black-white relations. Indeed, it can be argued that the too easy transfer of the argument to the Mexican-American may impede exercising the option of integration which is clearly much more alive for the Mexican-American than for the Negro.

5. No matter who sponsored the program, in each one the sponsoring agent formed a policy-making coalition of representatives from some or all of the following sectors: the public governing bodies (city, county, schools, the state); community elites; voluntary agency representatives; the organized middle-class minority community; the poor and their selected representatives.

6. Each program in some fashion encouraged the affected citizenry to come together.

In examining the issue of involvement, the last two commonalities will provide the thread. The strength (or the mere presence) of neighborhood representation on the coalition has shown marked change in the three federally supported programs. Perhaps the outer limits of this evolution are shown in two examples: (a) the Los Angeles delinquency demonstration (Youth Opportunities Board), governed by a joint powers arrangement between the city, the county, the schools, and the state of California; and (b) the Oakland model cities format, where a neighborhood congress with its own staff resources must review and approve all programs before the city council will consider them for purposes of funding.

THE DELINQUENCY DEMONSTRATION PROGRAM

The policy guide to the presentation of proposals for funding under Public Law 87–274 said nothing about the composition of the governing body of a delinquency demonstration program. But what this guide does have to say about neighborhood organization represents a bold conception to the effect that the strength or weakness of a community can itself be a factor in whether its children become "delinquent." The policy guide suggests that a major learning area in the demonstration will be the "process by which the competence of local community residents is increased so that they become a more potent factor in the lives of their youth."[1] To facilitate this learning the guide notes:

In a project's consideration of means of intervention, evidence must be shown that careful thought was given to plans for increasing the competence of target area residents and organizations. Such competence will be expected to increase the capacity to participate more effectively in decisions affecting their welfare and that of their youth. In all likelihood, such a capacity would facilitate the attainment of the project's goals.[2]

Here specifically and clearly is the assumption that involvement of a community can be an instrument toward achievement of a goal such as the prevention and control of delinquency. It would seem that this

---

[1]Department of Health, Education and Welfare, *Policy Guides to the Presentation of Proposals for Funding under P.L. S7.274* (undated), p. 1.
[2]*Ibid.,* p. 7.

assumption became a guiding concept in utilizing the much greater energies that were to be expended in bringing about neighborhood involvement in CAP.

While all the federally supported delinquency projects sought to bring affected populations into policy formulation, such involvement was more frequently in an advisory than decision-making capacity. Further, the selection of representatives was always at the discretion of the sponsoring agent, with no formal attempt to have the neighborhood actually select its own representatives. Of the three programs under examination it was only in this one that we could find governing coalitions which included *no* significant neighborhood representation. The following appear to have been the dominant modes of policy-making coalitions in the delinquency projects.

1. Strong mayor model: appointed by, and responsible to, the Mayor; included "elite" leadership plus key figures of those agencies seen as relevant to the development and implementation of the plan
2. Government-centered coalition: separately incorporated and autonomous in policy; composed primarily of key public agency figures
3. Cause-oriented and voluntary coalition: board generally a "mix" of those oriented to the problem plus representation from public and voluntary agencies who were seen as controlling resources critical to the project's success.

In none of these policy-making coalitions did the neighborhood representatives approximate more than 10 percent of the governing body. In all cases, they were selected by the coalition's sponsor, sometimes in consultation with community civil rights groups.

Six years have made the quality and quantity of neighborhood involvement in the program's policy-making seem at best minimal. Yet those were important steps, clearly linked in sequence to the quasi-governmental units which seem now to be emerging in various black communities as part of the Model Cities effort. Many of the factors which made the delinquency projects sensitive to the issue of neighborhood involvement continued and intensified in CAP and the model cities program.

In the delinquency program and in CAP, the governing boards were often new *ad hoc* arrangements, with ill-defined authority and a frail legitimacy. The projects needed a constituency if they were to influence existing agencies to attempt new programs. In the search for a constituency the neighborhood became a likely source. This involvement of neighborhoods was abetted when project staff came from social work, a profession which prizes the client's participation in decision-making as a goal in itself. Many projects also found a powerful ally in the civil rights movement. In the most recent years, of course, increasing black militancy was further to spur the interest of projects in seeking alliances with neighborhood leadership.

In retrospect, none of the delinquency demonstration policy coalitions would meet any current test of adequacy with regard to representativeness and sufficiency of "clout" for the neighborhood. Yet, the experience was such that in 1964 I could note that

the experience of the committee demonstrations [juvenile delinquency projects] is clear: all boards of directors are chosen by some notion of representation. It is unthinkable that boards of projects concerned with problems of poverty will not allocate certain places in their policy structures to bona fide representatives of the poor.[3]

As we know, CAP more than validated this observation.

Neighborhood Organization. — In retrospect, it seems ironical that the juvenile delinquency programs in their conception were much more concerned with neighborhood organization than with means of including neighborhood residents on their governing coalitions. The irony is that the issue of neighborhood presence on the governing coalition was to predominate in the early years of the anti-poverty program. Even more interesting is the fact that in 1969 it appears that the "elitist" planners in the program who gave a priority to neighborhood organization were better predictors of the future. The development of a self-determining black community and some of the program's notions of neighborhood organization can be seen as compatible ideas. On the other hand, participation in a governmentally sponsored coalition has more in common with the notion of integration than it does with separatism, and to that extent it may have lost some of its earlier importance.

Without claiming that the neighborhood organization conceptions of Mobilization for Youth (MFY) were typical of all the juvenile delinquency projects, they are worth restating because of their clarity and because MFY was the first project to have its conceptions tested in action. This testing led to a rapid reappraisal by the federal

---

[3]Melvin B. Mogulof, "Involving Low-Income Neighborhoods in Antidelinquency Programs," *Social Work*, X, No. 4 (1965), 54.

funding source of the degree to which it might support the organization of affected populations into action groups. MFY stated the
following objectives:

1. To increase the ability of local residents to participate in and influence the
social and political life of their community. This will have the further
objective of providing an example for adolescents of a means of handling
alienation constructively
2. To identify, document, and dramatize community needs
3. To widen channels of communication between lower-class persons and
institutional personnel or decision-makers, and thereby to increase both the
institutions' responsiveness to lower-class needs and the residents' knowledge and use of community resources
4. To increase community integration and the effectiveness of social controls
5. To improve the confidence of local leaders to deal with grievances and to
defend their constituents' right and privileges.[4]

The proposal speculates about the consequences of success with
the above approach:

The uniqueness of our approach to community action is in the encouragement of autonomy among lower-class participants. There is, of course, a
contradiction inherent in the proposal to establish lower-class community
organizations under Mobilization sponsorship. Mobilization is responsible to
a wide variety of groups. Issues with which lower-class organizations deal
may threaten some of these groups.... Unless they are formed spontaneously under the impetus of an inflammatory issue, lower-class groups cannot be organized without the financing and support of such established (i.e.,
middle-class) organizations as Mobilization. The fact that Mobilization constitutes a new structure partially mitigates the problem of control. So, too,
does the Mobilization intent to protect the organizations' independence from
both outside pressure and Mobilization's own opinions about their mistakes.
This is no real solution, however; it will be necessary for Mobilization to
divest itself of responsibility for the project as soon as feasible. Encouraging
the organizations to raise their own funds will be a step in that direction.[5]

The reader may be forgiven his nostalgia for those not-so-long-ago
days when white planners could speculate about the consequences
of *their* unleashing the affected population. Perhaps nothing so well
mirrors the movement of events as MFY's brave words of eight years
ago which now in *concept* seem so dated. (The *practice*, of course, in

    [4]*A Proposal for the Prevention and Control of Delinquency by Expanding Opportu-
nities* (New York: Mobilization for Youth, Inc., 1961), pp. 328–29.
    [5]*Ibid.*, pp. 136–37.

most communities today still makes MFY years ahead of the times, both current and past.)

Shortly after the summer of 1964, the Wagner administration in New York City was in hot pursuit of MFY because of its neighborhood organization activities, with attendant pressures on the Department of Health, Education, and Welfare (HEW) to curb MFY's approach to neighborhood organization. As a result of the federal reappraisal, the following key points were made in an HEW guideline to federal support for continuing efforts to "increase the competence of neighborhood residents." The first point was a strong affirmation of the legitimacy of neighborhood organization: "Amelioration of social problems like delinquency is not possible without attention to the development of the capacity of neighborhoods to become more potent forces in their communities."[6]

But as a means of control, the federal guide stipulated that

projects should be asked to indicate (a) the issues, problems or other content areas in which it anticipates groups becoming involved, and (b) the levels of activity, channels and strategies which are open to groups. It must assure that groups will not work exclusively or mainly outside of established, existing channels.[7]

After specifying a list of neighborhood action tactics that it could support, the HEW guideline goes on to specify that "projects must indicate which of these lawful strategies it sees as possible and usable and why. . . . The Government cannot fund projects which will use *only* the protest route."[8]

The facts in the juvenile delinquency demonstrations did not justify the anxiety apparently felt by federal officials when they issued these words of constraint. Few of the demonstration projects shared the more militant perspectives of MFY. Only in MFY were there continuing efforts to create groups which sought to deal with and influence the imbalance of resources flowing into the neighborhood *independently* of the efforts of the demonstration. Perhaps the more usual neighborhood organization in the juvenile delinquency program fitted into one or both of the following conceptions:

1. Neighborhood groups should be formed to serve as an ally of the delinquency demonstration in helping it to implement its various programs. The role of neighborhood groups was to help this new

---

[6]*Suggested Guidelines for Federal Support of Neighborhood Organization Efforts* (U.S. Department of Health, Education and Welfare; undated), p. 1.
[7]*Ibid.*, p. 7, in original.
[8]*Ibid.*, p. 8.

input of effort into the neighborhood to be successful. Such groups become a natural constituency for the project and, in turn, feed back information to the project policy-makers as to how the program is being delivered and received. The appropriate analogy might be to a PTA which is seen by the school as supportive of the educational process, as a constituency for the particular school in helping to protect its resources, and as a device for keeping the school's program in balance with community needs as these needs are defined by PTA members.

2. A second distinctive function for neighborhood organization is the creation of working units which may identify and develop the skills to work on common problems. Through programs of self-help, neighborhoods are seen as developing the potential for changing those conditions which cause their problems, and in particular the problems that underlie the deviant behavior of their youth. The focus of this organization is inward, with an emphasis on cooperative action between neighbors rather than on confrontation with the political system and with the key public agencies that control resources for the neighborhood.

One must respect the integrity of the other Delinquency Demonstration projects in *not* seeking to imitate MFY's neighborhood organization style. MFY's militancy on paper, soon to be translated into action, fitted neither the mood nor the sponsorship of most of the other projects, and it would have been an unfulfilled gesture had they all chosen to parrot MFY.

What these projects did do was to make clear that the building of communal action entities, organized around the grievances and needs of poor people, was an essential part of dealing with the problem of delinquency. This lesson was not lost on the soon-to-emerge CAP, almost all of which saw neighborhood organization as a central program item. These same CAP organizations were to take the juvenile delinquency program's slender beginnings in sharing policy authority and move them to a level far from the foregoing description of such governing coalitions.

THE COMMUNITY ACTION PROGRAM

The failures of citizen participation in the antipoverty program were noted by a British critic: "The guts of the programme, a sneaky little clause in the legislation which requires 'participation of the poor to the maximum extent feasible' in planning and operating the various poverty battles, . . . has never been followed in anything but form."[9] Apart from misquoting the language of the legislation, as did virtually every commentator, the *New Statesman's* verdict seems strangely out of joint in 1969.

Expectedly caustic in an analysis which calls the war on poverty "political pornography," Saul Alinsky correctly anticipates developments in CAP and the model cities program:

I have serious doubts about any really meaningful program to help and work with the poor until such time as the poor, through their own organized power, are able to provide legitimate representatives of their interests to sit at the programming table and have a strong voice in both the formulation and the running of the program.[10]

Policy Board Participation.—The OEO's guide to CAP was issued some three months after the start of the program, during which time it had become clear in community after community that the composition of CAP policy boards was to be a major issue. If anyone in OEO or elsewhere in the federal administration harbored hopes that "maximum feasible involvement" was to be satisfied by jobs in the program, he quickly learned otherwise. Aroused minority leadership in many communities, abetted by an OEO leadership committed to testing the boundaries of "maximum feasible involvement," made a battleground over the creation of CAP policy boards in a way that had never been witnessed in the delinquency demonstration program. Unlike HEW's guide to the delinquency program, the OEO guide made clear that neighborhood residents were to be part of the program's policy apparatus: "To be broadly-based, a community action agency must provide ample opportunity for participation in policy-making by . . . . the population to be served by the community action program."[11] In a later paragraph, the guide indicated minimum standards for representation as being "at least one representative selected from each of the neighborhoods, or areas in which the community action program will be concentrated.[12]

The mere issuance of an administrative guide is no assurance that policy will be adhered to. In the antipoverty legislation hearings of

[9]Andrew Kopkind, "Not So Great Society," *New Statesman and Nation,* August 6, 1965, p. 177.

[10]Saul Alinsky, "The War on Poverty—Political Pornography," *Journal of Social Issues,* XXI, No. 1 (1965), 45–46.

[11]*Community Action Program Guide* (Washington, D.C.: Office of Economic Opportunity, 1965), p. 17.

[12]*Ibid.,* p. 18.

that year (1965), Representative Adam Clayton Powell castigated one city after another for failing to seat poor people on the top municipal antipoverty councils. In retrospect, it seems that the legislative language which spoke of "maximum feasible involvement," when translated into administrative policy which set a minimum of one representative per neighborhood, invited a period of testing and conflict. This conflict was to be somewhat resolved legislatively by the Quie amendment, adopted in 1966, requiring at least one third of the CAP board to be representative of the poor.

In its guidelines to construction of a CAP policy-making body, OEO had introduced the idea of a "three-legged stool"—a policy body with three categories of representation: (a) public and private agencies responsible for services or programs concerned with poverty; (b) elements in the community as a whole; and (c) the population to be served by CAP. The Quie amendment supplied legislative assurance that the population to be served would be represented by at least a full leg of that three-cornered stool. Parenthetically, the amendment had come at a time when the boards of many large city CAP agencies had moved to *majority* control by the neighborhoods.

In a remarkably short time, as measured from the start of the delinquency program to the Quie amendment, there had been a radical shift in the notions of legitimacy for decision-making bodies affecting the lives of poor people (or at least of those decision-making bodies funded federally). Coincident with this movement toward numerical control of policy bodies by affected populations was an equally important movement to democratize the way in which such representatives were chosen. In 1967 this author suggested two phases for CAP, in the first of which neighborhood representatives would be chosen by "downtown" figures and by those who "speak for the poor," followed by a later period in which board representation would be selected by the beneficiary groups themselves.[13] This metamorphosis was encouraged by the CAP guidebook, which said:

The selection process should be designed to encourage the use, whenever feasible, of traditional democratic approaches and techniques such as group forums and discussions, nominations, and balloting. This will minimize the possibility that a representative does not command the support or confidence of the group or area that he represents.[14]

---

[13]Melvin B. Mogulof, "A Developmental Approach to the Community Action Program Idea," *Social Work*, XII, No. 2 (1967), 19.

[14]*Community Action Program Guide*, p. 18.

This incipient focus on a constituency for policy board representatives (or if not constituency, at least the stated desire that a selection process must try to insure that a representative in fact represents somebody) was to abet a counterpart focus in CAP on neighborhood councils and neighborhood organization. From such efforts could come the base for a representative system in which policy-makers were held accountable by a neighborhood constituency.

Neighborhood Organization. — In a 1966 memo to OEO field staff this writer noted the following areas of concern with regard to the representation of poor people on policy boards:

1. Low-income representation should approximate one third, and such representation should be selected by those being served by the program or who are potential beneficiaries. Where such a plan has not been developed, it is equally important to develop some means of interim representation immediately.

2. We need to continue to stress that representation from the key minority groups is not necessarily representation from the low-income sector; rather it should more appropriately be seen as part of our general community representation sector.

3. We are clearly embarked on the path of stimulating neighborhood councils which will have a role in the way community action agency decisions are made. The fact that we have mandated the establishment of such councils in Los Angeles can be seen as further indication of the direction that OEO is going in. Clearly, we are seeking to push decision-making as close to the groups concerned as possible. It should also be noted that invariably ... we have moved from the concept of representatives of the poor to the concept that the poor themselves need to be placed on these councils. In addition, we have almost invariably seen a 51% figure as the breaking point for the participation of low-income people on neighborhood council boards.[15]

Given the focus on policy board representation in the poverty program, and the parallel concern with the matter of selecting representatives, the neighborhood council was an expected development. The council not only provided another means for citizen involvement; it provided a constituency base for those who represented the neighborhood on the CAP policy body.

In many CAP activities the first funding efforts were toward establishing a central administrative structure and something which generally passed as an action component labeled "neighborhood organ-

---

[15]Office of Economic Opportunity mimeographed memo; not publicly available.

ization." Some communities vaguely saw this as a means by which they would find neighborhood representatives to put on their boards, thus satisfying OEO. Others thought that neighborhood organization was really "brokerage" (a concept popularized by MFY), a process by which organizers find clients for agencies, or help clients redress their grievances with agencies.

As with the juvenile delinquency demonstrations, some CAPs saw neighborhood organization somewhat like a grand "self-help" party where people do things for each other, as well as prevent their kids from being too difficult. If one can visualize a neighborhood as a closed box, this kind of organization deals with the reorganization of resources inside that box.

However, there was also a style of neighborhood action in CAP which could trace its conceptual lineage to MFY. This kind of neighborhood organization was much more focused on affecting the resources which got fed into the box (the neighborhood) by public and private agencies. To this observer, a project's willingness to focus on the external tasks of neighborhood organizations was somewhat dependent upon whether the leadership of the population was both black and militant.

The formation of multiservice centers and other neighborhood-based service deliveries was a common feature of CAP. Simultaneously, neighborhood organization often was occupied with setting up local policy boards for these neighborhood-based services.

In the delinquency program, the "target area" was prevalent—a place *to which* something was done. In CAP, the neighborhood began to emerge as a partner and, in some of the projects, as a controlling force in the decision-making process. In the Western region of OEO it was not many months before in three large cities CAP gave to the neighborhood councils veto power over any CAP activities to be funded in their neighborhood.

Much neighborhood organization in CAP, as in the delinquency program, was concerned with linking people to services and building a constituency for the program. But it was the activity which saw the organizational needs of the neighborhood as distinct and separate from those of the larger community and even from the CAP agency itself that was the most distinctive part of CAP. Interestingly, the sanction for this kind of "separatist" activity rested in the guidebook, which noted:

Providing staff services and other resources, including equipment and facilities, to existing local organizations in order to enable them to advise and inform the community action agency and other institutions about the needs, problems, and concerns of the poor. *Where these are absent or without the confidence of the poor, staff can be made available for the purposes of developing local autonomous associations and organizations.*[16]

It is this writer's impression that the success of CAP's neighborhood organizational activity was to provide a different kind of base for model cities efforts than had been provided by the delinquency demonstrations for the CAP agencies. Undoubtedly, the different mood of the black community in 1967 as compared to that in 1964 had a great deal to do with the readiness of certain model cities to concede a different role in decision-making to their aggrieved neighborhoods.

THE MODEL CITY PROGRAM

Citizen Participation. — It is far too early to tell what the model city program will do in the area that the CAP guide calls "resident participation." Given the sponsorship of model city programs by city governments, one might not expect to find much focus on the organization of neighborhoods for protest activities, particularly those aimed against established public agencies. There was no great emphasis on sharing authority with neighborhood leadership. Nevertheless, the best clues as to what may be expected do not lie in the verbal promises of proposals. Rather, they lie in the structures that result from a city's experience in trying to develop a decision-making system which has legitimacy in the eyes of the people who are to be affected by the intervention. In most instances, such a system has emerged through hard bargaining with the community *after* the writing of proposals.

A survey of ten proposed model city decision structures suggests that cities hardly meant to surrender *on paper* the authority which they thought government had won as a result of the outcries over "rampant" neighborhood control of the poverty program. Further, the guidebook issued by the Department of Housing and Urban Development suggests nothing more violent than that "means of introducing the views of area residents in policy-making should be developed."[17] The guide is much less explicit about what these means might be; a vagueness which might be seen as extremely

---

[16]*Community Action Program Guide*, pp. 27–28.
[17]Department of Housing and Urban Development, *Improving the Quality of Urban Life* (1967), p. 20.

appropriate to a demonstration program. As a result, the ten proposals presented a variety of approaches to whether or how to include
neighborhood residents on policymaking bodies. The following facts
are worthy of note:

1. Two of the ten proposals were so ambiguous that it was difficult
to tell what the intent was with regard to neighborhood participation.

2. All the proposals made clear that any coalition involving neighborhood people would be only advisory in nature; the final authority
would always rest with the mayor and/or the city council.

3. Five proposals chose to form a community-wide coalition as an
advisory body. The number of neighborhood people on these coalitions ranged from a token in three cases to equality or simple majority in two. Two of these five established a counterpart advisory group
composed solely of agency technicians.

4. Three proposals sought to form an advisory group made up
solely of neighborhood people, counterbalanced by another advisory
group made up solely of technicians.[18]

It should be noted that in three instances the adversary notion was
embodied in the proposed decision structure. In these three, city
government placed itself in the position of having to deal with the
concerns of a body of neighborhood people in that the body was
made a legitimate part of the decision system. From the point of
view of the neighborhood as an adversary, it is likely that the two
coalition advisory bodies dominated by neighborhood members
could also come to play an adversary role in model cities decision-making, should these structures be implemented.

The reader must note that this analysis deals only with what was
proposed. It should further be noted that despite model city guidebook injunctions to plan together with neighborhood residents, these
proposals were primarily the product of those employed by city
government.

Some eight months after some of these proposals were funded, the
reality seems radically different. In *every* case in the Western region
where the model cities neighborhood population is black, the governing coalition is numerically dominated by neighborhood residents. In almost every case where there is a parallel advisory group
of technicians, this group has merged with, and come under the
domination of, neighborhood residents. While in every case the role
of policy bodies was conceived of as advisory, the decision system

---

[18]Melvin Mogulof, "Policy-making Structures in Model Cities Communities" (unpublished).

which has evolved has given to such advisory groups a *de facto* veto over the model cities program. This veto is accomplished by a procedure which blocks the city council or mayor from acting on funding for the program until it has been approved by the advisory group dominated by neighborhood representatives (or, as in two of the Western region model cities, composed *solely of neighborhood representatives*). As a further augur of things to come, two of the cities have given to the neighborhood-dominated group a technical planning staff of its own.

It seems apparent that there has been a marked increase in the power of neighborhood-dominated groups between making the proposals and establishing actual decision-making systems. It further seems clear that these changes were made because the sponsoring city *had* to make them as the price for winning legitimacy for the programs from neighborhood leadership. These radical changes were accomplished in the eight months since the implementation of model cities planning grants.

Based upon the experience to date, one can speculate on the further diffusion and acceleration of changes in black-dominated neighborhoods within the model cities program. Very probably neighborhood councils or congresses will emerge as quasi-governmental units for their areas with jurisdiction gradually spreading to other expenditures. These groups will be given their own staff resources with which to develop their own program plans and with which to refine and counter plans drawn for their neighborhood by other sectors of the community.

In the delinquency program, one of the boldest of these efforts, MFY conceived of itself as social broker—a friendly third party linking the neighborhood to the bureaucracies supplying it with resources. In six years we have come to the point in our major cities where it is not conceivable that a third party could stand between the aspirations of the black community and the local government. Whether city government and an emerging black neighborhood government can reach an accommodation which will produce significant new resources and options for Negroes in our cities remains to be tested as part of the model cities program. Equally important is whether any such accommodation will stimulate or check the move toward apartheid in America.

THEMES CENTRAL TO THE THREE PROGRAMS

We can hardly pretend that everything is of a piece with regard to neighborhood participation. We risk some generalization in an attempt to gain understanding of what we have achieved in these six years. Some of the obvious questions, the answers to which may explain differences of which the reader is aware, may rest in the following:

1. In what section of the country is the community located?
2. Are all Negroes, no matter what their class, concentrated in a particular area, or are there ghetto separations by class?
3. Has the community had the experience of all three federal programs?
4. What is the density of the black population — its percentage of the larger community and how close it is to becoming the larger community?
5. Has the community had a major riot?

Needless to say, there are many other variables, concerned with historical relationships between the black and white communities, style of political life, economic base of community, and the like, which may help to explain differences.

Perhaps there should be another word of explanation as to why we have transposed the subject of neighborhood and citizen participation to the issue of black and white. I think it is time to stop using one concept — neighborhood, or poor — as a euphemism for the other — black. We have at least two major domestic issues, one of which can be subsumed under problems of caste and the other under problems of class. In the antipoverty program we may have discovered that one does not deal with problems of class by using caste-oriented strategies. On the other hand, the poverty program's greatest successes may have been its caste-oriented strategies, those dealing with problems of participation and connection as opposed to the amelioration of poverty.

Integration and Separatism. — In the Delinquency program the Harlem proposal for action, written under the leadership of Dr. Kenneth Clark, used the concept of "tangles of pathology." It was a concept particularly appropriate to the lives of black youth in the ghetto. The delinquency program intuitively sought the tangles, and not surprisingly wound up in areas of minority group concentration. The poverty program ostensibly was interested in the poor wherever they were. But perhaps the notion of "groups and areas to be served" as part of "maximum feasible" betrayed the program's real intention to deal with minority groups. In 1967, at the start of the model cities program, one frequently heard the model cities idea referred to as a "gilding-the-ghetto strategy." The target was, clearly, areas of great minority group concentration. Black militants to the contrary, there was no consensus in the black or white communities as to whether we meant to contain and preserve these areas of minority concentration. Even the model cities program in its short life span seems conceptually to have moved from a policy of containment to one where the provision of living options, in and outside the neighborhood, is the primary goal. From the delinquency program to model cities we finally have arrived at the point where representative black leaders will be able to deal as peers with government on issues of separateness and integration.

The Social Broker. — From this vantage point it seems clear that the Delinquency programs were all "elitist" third-party operations. They were meant to be that and they need no apology. But unlike MFY, few of the juvenile delinquency projects understood that the "broker" needs two forces to broker between. The minority neighborhood as a coherent set of forces did not seem to exist in 1962 and 1963. MFY set out to build a neighborhood force so that its broker role could become feasible. CAP took some of the emerging neighborhood leadership and made it part of its third-party broker coalition. Simultaneously, it put a great deal of effort into organizing the neighborhood. In black areas, it is clear that the riots and new leadership of 1965, 1966, and 1967 were major supporting forces of black communalism. In 1967 and 1968 the model cities experience indicated that the idea of third-party planning groups (coalition or not) was on the wane. In some fashion, the black neighborhood groups and city government would have to learn to live with each other without benefit of intermediary.

Neighborhood Technical Assistance. — In the juvenile delinquency program the technical staff resembled that of a social agency established to do good things for the downtrodden. Only one of the original seventeen project directors was a minority group member. Few of the projects contemplated the kind of assistance to neighborhood groups that MFY proposed. It was part of the MFY plan to render technical advice to newly formed neighborhood groups by aiding them to deal with the establishment. In CAP there emerged the capacity to find many additional minority group professional staff members. Parenthetically, a number of the second generation juvenile delinquency project directors were also of minority status. CAP also provided more staff resources to emerging neighborhood groups. In the model cities program, there seems to be an even greater capacity to find minority group staff, but the greatest potential is the insistence that the "citizen participation structure" of the program shall receive technical assistance in a manner acceptable to it. As of this writing some of the concepts in this formulation remain ambiguous, at least as interpreted by the model cities Administration in Washington, but the direction is clear. When the city of Oakland is prepared to give 44 percent of its planning budget to the neighborhood organization in its model neighborhood area, to hire technical staff responsible to this organization we have the emergence of the idea of a professional secretariat (paid for with federal funds and agreed to by the city) for a black neighborhood government in the making.

Selection of Leadership. — Wherever neighborhood leadership appeared in the juvenile delinquency project coalitions, their presence was approved by those elites who established the policy board. Needless to say, many such coalitions were carefully put together with the hope that the people selected would link the project to key groups in their neighborhood.

Even though the CAP guide called for "traditional democratic approaches" in selecting representatives to policy boards, many of the early leaders were hand-picked, and on occasion were deemed representative by virtue of their color rather than the fact that they lived in the target neighborhood. As the poverty program matured, the issue of representative selection became central, with an early move toward elections and other devices which sought to insure that control of representatives would rest in the neighborhood. In the model cities program where the relationship between the neighborhood and city government often had an adversary theme, it was difficult to see as legitimate any system in which one adversary (the city) determined whom it would deal with on behalf of the other (the neighborhood); hence the increasing popularity of elections or the selection of representatives by neighborhood forums and other devices completely under control of the neighborhood.

Perhaps no theme mirrored as sharp a movement in these six years and three programs as the "who" and the "how" of representation for the black community in its dealings with the establishment. In fact, in one Western city there is evidence that a lower class black community will reject black middle-class leadership as representative of its interest if this middle-class leadership lives elsewhere. This may be evidence that the issues of class and caste remain separable.[19]

---

[19]For further comments on this issue, see James Wilson, "The Urban Unease," *The Public Interest*, Summer, 1968, pp. 25–39.

Whatever the local peculiarities, we have clearly entered a period where old notions of community and neighborhood are being buried. We are no longer talking of a neighborhood in a geographic sense; we seem to be talking of a community of black people who have finally claimed for themselves the difference which has been thrust upon them by hundreds of years of American racism. We are dealing with relationships of black and white where any attempt by white to tamper with who represents the black makes the legitimacy of that representation suspect. That the form of relationship between the races may lead to a compartmentalization of communities along racial lines is a real possibility. That it may also hasten the day in which certain cities become all black is also possible. The trends in these three federal programs and the current state of what is meant by "citizen participation" makes some of these events predictable and perhaps tragic. Whether we can build the ghetto and break it at the same time, as one observer has suggested, remains moot in the face of this accumulated experience.

What is not moot is the fact of organized black communities, increasingly able to bargain and negotiate in their own behalf. It is around these facts of black communalism and its focus on self-interest and determination that future issues of citizen participation will have to be agitated and decided. One might suggest that this thought is both very close to, and very far from, MFY's initial conception of citizen organization.

SECTION V

Social Intervention Systems: Agencies and People

INTRODUCTION

An oversimplified model of the helping relationship includes only the worker and the client. A more realistic presentation would include not only worker and beneficiary but also the target, the problem condition, and the agency from which the worker comes. We will call this system the social intervention system. To obtain a more complete picture of the intervention process one might think of two intersecting circles with one circle representing the social intervention system and the second, the social welfare system. The worker would be located at the point where the two circles intersect since he is part of both systems. The social agencies and institutions of the social welfare system are, for the most part, prime examples of bureaucratic operations. Tradition and self-interest, as much as the needs of the victimized population, dictate their boundaries and population. The gap in services and the biases resulting from these traditional boundaries are well known but need to be reexamined for each new generation of bureaucrats.

The worker, who functions in both systems, brings to the action arena certain assets and handicaps which need to be identified.

Here, we are concerned primarily with those consequences, both functional and dysfunctional, which arise out of the worker's status in the agency setting and in the social welfare system, not those deriving from any of his personal characteristics. For example, the social distance between the typical worker, on the one hand, and the beneficiary, on the other, introduces a number of problem conditions which need to be recognized in developing a strategy.

Even though differences and similarities between bureaucratic and professional organizations have been examined previously by others (Litwak, 1961; Blau, 1962; Vinter, 1959; Corwin, 1961), the question of professional autonomy within bureaucratic organizations needs further exploration. There are examples where a high degree of professional autonomy coincides with a high degree of bureaucratic organization; this is particularly true of certain medical practices. On the other hand, there are other situations where a low degree of professional autonomy coincides with a relatively low degree of bureaucratization; social work in some settings would be an example of the latter. The degree of professional autonomy may not be directly related to the level of bureaucratic control, as many had previously assumed. Instead, it may relate much more to the level of skill or supposed skill attributed to the practitioner; few laymen think that they can duplicate a doctor's skill but most feel that they can do everything a social worker can do.

The relation of worker to client is also problematic because of conflicting role expectations. On the one hand, people will relate only to workers who appear to them as persons who want to help; on the other hand, there is a professional tradition which suggests that aloofness and noninvolvement are desirable qualities. The worker who "overidentifies" with his clients is suspect by his colleagues. A further complication occurs when the client fails to understand what is expected of him by the worker and by the agency. Becoming a client is hazardous since the client role violates the cultural imperatives of self-reliance and independence. Furthermore, the client role is also culturally disadvantageous because by becoming an agency client one publicly declares his disability. In fact, in his own community, assuming a client role may be frowned upon. The awareness of these dilemmas by workers as well as by potential consumers of service would be desirable.

What is needed for relevant social work practice are not antiseptic professionals but people who are sympathetic to the problems presented to them. Essential skills of social intervention agents include the ability to listen, to learn, to separate problems into their parts, and to mobilize resources in an effort to implement social intervention activity.

In an "Odyssey through the Agencies" the difficulties and some methods for dealing with unapproachable bureaucratic organizations are described. With a caring and persevering worker who is able to assume the advocacy role, a significant and pressing problem which affects a young person's life is worked on with some success. Are all bureaucracies unreceptive to people in need? What are the differences between responsive and unresponsive organizations? Should all social workers become advocates?

Knowledge of the language and the cultural context play a part in solving problems when a social worker helps a Navajo woman institutionalized for 20 years. Inez M. Tyler and Sophie D. Thompson in "Cultural Factors in Casework Treatment of a Navajo Mental Patient," confirm that a worker needs a thorough knowledge of a person's milieu and culture before she can be of help. At what points in the interventions described was specific knowledge of the unique culture essential? What might have happened if the worker had ignored the cultural context?

Since a growing share of welfare services are provided under governmental auspices, Charles Grosser in "Community Organization and the Grass Roots" suggests that grass-roots populations be involved as citizens in policy determination and planning. He also explores community organization strategies and processes which can make bureaucracies more accountable to those they serve. Along these lines, Edward J. O'Donnell and Marilyn M. Sullivan, in "Service Delivery and Social Action through the Neighborhood Center: A Review of Research" review research findings which have influenced the provision of more effective services. Can social services be improved by involving the consumers in decision making? Or does the structure of the service delivery system determine in large part whether a service is effective? Among the alternatives considered are administrative direction and neighborhood control, service and social action, specific functions and general activities, professional and nonprofessional services, information/referral and advocacy/follow-up, cooperative methods and conflict tactics, and others. Each choice carries with it certain consequences. In a given situation, one or the other might prove to be more effective. Why?

Donald Schon in "The Blindness System" reviews services to the blind and shows how an entire delivery system can mismatch services and clients. He indicates why various strategies for service were selected and how they are related to relevant constraints. This study raises questions as to how institutions and agencies choose interventive strategies. What is the appropriate level for intervention if changes are desired in services for the blind?

Do black clients prefer black caseworkers? Even if a white worker were more skillful? What are the worker characteristics most desired by black clients? These questions and others are explored by Donald Brieland in "Black Identity and the Helping Person." Carmen Normandia explores the "Characteristics and Role of Indigenous Workers." This latter selection defines the strengths and limitations of indigenous workers in social welfare services. How can indigenous workers maintain their connections with the community and at the same time become fully involved in the agency? This question is further explored by Harry Specht, Arthur Hawkins, and Floyd McGee in "Excerpts from the Casebooks of Subprofessional Workers."

Frank Loewenberg in "Social Workers and Indigenous Nonprofessionals: Some Structural Dilemmas" illustrates how structural variables rather than personality factors are primarily responsible for some of the difficulties experienced by social workers in a nonsocial work oriented antipoverty program. Similarly, structural variables will affect the functioning of all other levels of workers. Suggestions are made for dealing constructively with the problems identified. How can teams of people with different educational backgrounds successfully work together? What can agencies do to create structures which provide for maximum cooperation and teamwork by staff members and simultaneously support qualitative service delivery? Loewenberg also introduces in "Toward a Systems Analysis of Social Welfare Manpower Utilization Patterns" a preliminary paradigm for the evaluation of staff utilization patterns. These patterns determine whether services will be adequate, available, relevant, and high quality. What staff utilization model seems to be most effective? Is the evaluation paradigm presented helpful in understanding a system? What is the relation between manpower utilization and services for people? Is any part of the system more important than others in determining whether people receive services?

REFERENCES

Blau, Peter M., and Scott, Richard W. 1962. *Formal Organizations.* San Francisco: Chandler Publishing Company.

Corwin, Ronald G. 1961. "The Professional Employee: A Study of Conflict in Nursing Roles," *American Journal of Sociology,* Vol. 66, pp. 604–15.

LITWAK, EUGENE. 1961. "Models of Bureaucracy That Permit Conflict," *American Journal of Sociology*, Vol. 67, pp. 177–84.

VINTER, ROBERT D. 1959. "The Social Structure of Service," in A.J. Kahn (ed.), *Issues in American Social Work*. New York: Columbia University Press, pp. 242–69.

· 25 ·

COUNCIL ON SOCIAL WORK EDUCATION

An Odyssey Through the Agencies

"O.K., you're right," Joe said, "I've gotta get outta my house."

I was so happy to hear him say this. I had been trying for weeks now to get him to see it. I was literally afraid of murder if he stayed home much longer.

"Last night, Pa come home drunk again. He was throwing things, and I started hittin' back. Lucky he passed out before it got worse. But, I swear, he lay a finger on me tonight, I'm gonna give it to him."

"But you won't be there," I said. "It's really the only way. Look, you're 17, you're smart, you can make it. You know that the two of you together are going to destroy each other. Start fresh while you can!"

Joe agreed. All the work I and the Center had done was paying off. He really wanted to make it. "Where should I go?" he asked.

I hadn't really thought about it. But this was a fair-sized city, with a number of social services. There would surely be a place for a 17-year-old high school senior who had to get away from a destructive situation. He had the marks on his body to show just how bad things were.

SOURCE: Reprinted with permission of the Council on Social Work Education, Inc., from *Working with the Poor*, Unit II: *Role of the Worker* (New York: Council on Social Work Education, 1968), #68-340-101B.

I called Mr. Baker at the Center and explained the situation. Where could he go? Mr. Baker was not as helpful as I expected. He said it would not be that easy . . . the Family Service might help.

Joe and I walked to the Family Service. The receptionist said no one could see us without an appointment. I said we wanted to make an appointment for right now. She said appointments are usually made on the phone. I asked if she would prefer if I went outside and called her. Finally, she got one of the caseworkers to talk to us. The caseworker said she had only 10 minutes before her next appointment. And there were complications. Family Service did not give financial aid. They *did* find foster placements. But you couldn't find one that easily for a 17-year-old. Besides, Joe was still a minor in this state until his next birthday. He should have his father's permission, even to begin with Family Service. I tried to explain that Joe's father was incompetent, drunk, and brutal, and that was why Joe was here. In that case, said the caseworker, maybe the school authorities could start legal action to remove Joe from his father's custody. Or maybe Legal Aid could help. But their office was across the river, in Bigsville.

Bigsville! Suddenly I thought of the model Teen House I had read about there. We took the bus. Once there, we created more of a sensation than at Family Service. The receptionist was all flustered. The lady she called immediately called another person to see us. He seemed very flustered, too. He piled us high with forms and told us to mail them in. Right now, Teen House was full. But I reminded him of the feature in last Sunday's paper—how Teen House had just opened and was seeking applicants.

"Well, you just fill out the forms," he said, half pushing us out the door. I was still too new to know what was going on. Joe had to explain that they were reacting to the fact that he is a Negro. I was furious. I called Mr. Baker again. He knew all about Teen House; that's why he didn't send me there. Sure, something could be done about it—there was already a court case pending and the color line would be broken—in six months or a year.

We took the bus back to town and went to the Welfare Department. They had all kinds of technical questions, too, but they *did* have a temporary shelter and said Joe could use it until they figured out what to do. He walked there. In the lobby, an old man was vomiting. From the odor, he was not the first that day. Joe took one look at the "dormitory" and ran down. "I'd be better off home," he said.

By now we were both chilled, hungry, and low on funds. We went to my place for something to eat. I knew that a single female volunteer worker entertaining a young man alone in her apartment was not strictly according to Hoyle, but I was too mad and too tired to care. As we sat over coffee, Joe suggested that if he quit school, he might earn enough to live somewhere. "But one of the main reasons for all this is so you can finish school!" I said.

I made some other calls from home. The Christian Aid Society only served those over 21. Social Service at the hospital could see Joe only if he were a hospital patient.

"There's always the hospital clinic. If I do something real nuts they gotta take me in." Joe was trying to joke, but there were tears in his eyes. I knew if we skipped this moment of decision, the whole deal might be lost. I began to do mental arithmetic. If I paid for a room for Joe somewhere for a few days, could I get by until my next payday? And what about all the orientation at the center that said if you start giving handouts, that's real bad? Then the phone rang. It was Artie. He had been in the citywide volunteer orientation with me. He had been trying to date me, but we never could find time. He was working on the new School-Work project of the Vocational Service. Then it hit me! "Artie, isn't your program for kids who have to earn money, but want to finish school?" When he said yes, I told him we were coming right over. He protested that on Thursdays everything was closed down early due to staff meeting. I told him we were coming and would sit there until someone took care of us, so he'd better get someone.

The man who saw us was a little annoyed by my insistence, but once he and Joe got talking, he seemed to get interested. He promised Joe that when school re-opened Monday, he would try to arrange for a change of schedule which would allow Joe to work three hours a day. If he were accepted in the special work program, he could earn $6 a day and more on Saturdays.

Joe was delighted. The money wasn't much, but it would help till the end of his senior year. The man recommended a decent, cheap rooming-house nearby. Forgetting all the rules, I told Joe I would stake him until Monday.

Next morning I asked Mr. Baker why he didn't refer me to the Vocational Service's project.

"Didn't know of it. That must be one of the new O.E.O. contracts. Look, I've been in this business almost 20 years, and I still can't make my way through the maze. Fact is, it gets harder to keep up every year."

26

INEZ M. TYLER AND SOPHIE D. THOMPSON

Cultural Factors in Casework Treatment of a Navajo Mental Patient

Planning aftercare service for a non-English-speaking Navajo Indian who has been a long-term mental patient presents the social worker with two specific kinds of problems. Not only must he deal with the usual problems associated with the discharge of a mentally ill patient, but, in addition, he must deal with problems that are unique to the Indian culture. The case discussed in this article illustrates the importance of the worker's understanding the Navajo language and culture.

The Navajo woman who returned home had been a mental patient for twenty years in a hospital located at a great distance from her family and homeland. The worker showed unusual skill in utilizing her knowledge of the patient's cultural background to help the patient and her family achieve a realistic view of her return home. In this case it is of special interest to note the process by which certain specific cultural beliefs were incorporated in the patient's symptomatology. Before a discussion of the case is presented, however, information is given about the Navajos and their mode of living in order to provide some understanding of their orientation to problems involving health and medical care, and how this sociocultural orientation may affect casework treatment.

CULTURAL BACKGROUND

With an estimated population of 90,000 the Navajo is the largest Indian tribe in the United States, living on 14,450,369 acres of land in the states of Arizona, New Mexico, and Utah. Their complex social

SOURCE: Reprinted from *Social Casework*, Vol. 46 (April, 1965), pp. 215–20.

The authors wish to acknowledge the advice and help of Katherine Spencer, Ph.D., Professor of Social Work Research, Boston University, Boston, Massachusetts, and Elizabeth Wheeler, Supervisor and Caseworker, Social Service Department, Massachusetts General Hospital, Boston, Massachusetts, both of whom reviewed the manuscript of this article.

and economic problems are compounded by cultural and language barriers that separate them from the dominant society. Their poor roads, their inadequate transportation facilities, and their low educational attainment further serve to increase their isolation. During the past ten years, however, there has been great progress in making available to the Navajos an opportunity to be educated in local day and boarding schools and in the public schools of "bordertowns" that lie outside the reservation.

Traditionally, the Navajos are a semi-nomadic people whose principal livelihood is gained from herding sheep. They are accustomed to move with the sheep to new grazing land. They live in octagonal hogans, built of logs and mud; the floors are dirt, and a smoke hole is cut in the roof. The one-room hogan may shelter an entire family composed of from two to twelve or more persons. The Navajos do not live in villages, and the family groups are often separated from one another by long distances. In many instances the members of a traditional matrilineal extended family, including grandparents, parents, and daughters and their husbands are still found living near one another. In general, however, no more than four or five hogans are located in one place. The hogans lack indoor sanitary facilities and electricity. Neither water nor wood is readily available, and each family must haul its water from a distance, perhaps so much as twenty miles. The storage of hauled water has become less a threat to the Navajo's health since the people learned in a sanitation program supported by the Public Health Service to build platforms for the steel water containers.

The traditional Navajo religion is oriented primarily to maintaining health and curing illness. One of the simplest and clearest statements of Navajo religious thought and its relationship to health was made by Mary and John Collier, Jr.:

The basis of Navajo religious thought is that the universe and all the earth peoples function according to rules. The misfortunes of sickness and premature death are the result of not following the rules. Navajos hold ceremonials to restore order in the individual by performing exact rituals which will require supernatural forces to withdraw their punishment, or the sickness, from the individual. To be well you must obey the ancient rules, and the chants and ceremonies are routines to re-establish the broken routine.[1]

---

[1]Mary and John Collier, Jr., "The Basis of Navajo Religion," in I. Sanders and others (ed.), *Societies around the World*, Vol. I (New York: Dryden Press, 1953), p. 300.

MEDICAL AND PSYCHIATRIC FACILITIES

In 1955 the responsibility for the medical care of Indians living on reservations was transferred from the Bureau of Indian Affairs to the Division of Indian Health, a part of the U.S. Public Health Service responsible for all health services to Indians and Alaskan natives. Six hospitals, three field health centers, and a number of health stations provide preventive and curative health care to Navajos living on the reservation.

The staff of the Division of Indian Health is especially concerned about the high rate of illness among mothers and children and the high rate of infant mortality; they are also concerned about the high incidence of accidents and the identification and care of people suffering from emotional problems and mental illness. Providing comprehensive health services to patients on the reservation is complicated by problems of communication, shortage of staff, and other factors already mentioned.

The Public Health Service contracts with state and private mental hospitals to provide psychiatric care for the Navajos, since psychiatric services are not available on the reservation. In past years mentally ill Navajos were committed to federal hospitals located hundreds of miles from their homes, where, because of the language barrier, they received only limited care. Some Navajos have remained in such institutions for as long as twenty years, or even longer. Recently emphasis has been placed on using psychiatric facilities that are near the reservation. Efforts have been made, when medically feasible, to arrange for patients previously sent to distant hospitals to return to their reservation. Mrs. Y was one such patient, whom the caseworker helped to return home after a long absence. In this instance, the caseworker was the only trained Navajo caseworker on the reservation.

CASE ILLUSTRATION

In the late 1930's, Mrs. Y was living with her children in her mother's extended family kinship group. Following the death of one of her relatives in this camp, she was accused—apparently by an aunt and a sister with whom she had quarreled—of killing the relative. The court records do not contain a clear statement of the circumstances surrounding the death of the relative. Mrs. Y was hurriedly convicted, and her mother was unable to see her before she was taken from the reservation.

Mrs. Y could not converse in the prison because no one there understood the Navajo language. She became depressed and resistive and developed symptoms of emotional disturbance, such as vomiting and refusal to eat. As a result she was transferred, within a few months after her imprisonment, to a mental hospital in the East. At this hospital the patient spoke to no one for many years and lay huddled, in a fetal position, in a blanket on the floor. She continued to be resistive and apprehensive, spoke to no one, and refused to be examined. Attempts to speak to her through an interpreter were unsuccessful, but it was not clear whether the problem stemmed from the inadequacy of the interpreter or the inability of the patient to communicate with him.

Gradually Mrs. Y began to show improvement and became less resistive. She spoke her native language, began to smile, ate well, slept well, and was quiet and pleasant. She showed some interest in others about her, and as she continued to improve, she began to take care of herself and to eat her meals with a group of other patients. By then twenty years had passed since she had been imprisoned, and she was over fifty years of age.

After the hospital staff inquired at the Division of Indian Health regarding plans for discharging Mrs. Y, the caseworker on the reservation contacted her daughter, who was by then an adult with a family of her own. She also contacted Mrs. Y's mother and sister in order to include them in the planning for her return to the reservation. The family members were pleased to receive news about the patient, and they were also pleased at the possibility that Mrs. Y might return home after such a long separation. During a visit to the social worker's office they tape recorded a message to Mrs. Y, and the tapes, along with photographs taken that day, were sent to her.

THE CASEWORKER VISITS THE PATIENT

It was hoped that Mrs. Y could be either discharged or transferred to an institution closer to her home. The reservation caseworker visited her at the hospital on a number of occasions in an attempt to arrive at an accurate evaluation of her condition. On the first occasion the patient eyed the worker apprehensively. The worker said hello in Navajo and told Mrs. Y she had come from the Navajo country to see her. The patient continued to look at the worker and remained silent. The worker asked the patient if she were a Navajo. She replied yes, and then tested the worker's Navajo origin by asking her to name the clan to which she belonged. Because the worker was able to speak in Navajo and understand the patient's feelings and cultural background, Mrs. Y could express her feelings to her freely.

The worker learned that Mrs. Y strongly resented her removal from her home, and she held her family and relatives responsible. With each succeeding visit to the patient, her feelings about having been "hauled away" seemed to increase. "They destroyed me, trampled me in the dirt, stripped away my clothing, took me apart joint by joint." At this moment she pointed to her knees, shoulders, and elbows. "They brought me to shame, they made me nothing. I crawled, begging to go back, I had no pride [self-respect]. I am nothing, only a stranger here, I have no will, no thinking, no right to say yes or no, to decide. . . ."

To questions regarding her wish to return home, she replied, "I'm not in authority; that's not for me to decide." Who was the authority? "I don't know." The doctor asked her if she would return home if *he* said she could do so. Again she said it was not for her to decide. She had no right; she was only there. Then she said, "It costs money. How will I pay?" Assurance that her transportation would be paid did not help her make a decision.

The doctor asked her if she knew she was in a hospital. She replied, "*Hwo'la* (I don't know)." Was she aware of the nature of her illness? "*Hwo'la.*" The caseworker asked whether she knew that she had been sick in her "thinking process." Again she replied "*Hwo'la.*" The doctor then asked her if she had ever killed anyone. She promptly shook her head and replied, "No, no." Would she kill anyone? Again her answer was, "No, no." Whenever her family was mentioned, she began a monologue. She spoke about them in a rapid, breathless way, and her set speech sounded like something she might have memorized, something she was repeating automatically. When the worker asked her which members of the family were responsible for her imprisonment, she replied, "All of them." The only members of her family whom she exempted were her children, whom she thought of as small and helpless. She showed her feeling for them when she said she had "nearly died for them." The worker and the doctor thought that if the patient could change or moderate her attitude, she could be discharged and return home. To help her mother's family understand her illness and attitude, they decided that the worker should visit them.

THE CASEWORKER VISITS THE FAMILY

On the reservation the caseworker discussed the plan to discharge

Mrs. Y with the patient's mother, her daughter and son-in-law, and her two sisters and their husbands. They showed interest in the plan and were anxious to have the patient return to them. The women in the family were an impressive group, attractive, healthy, and friendly; each of them had an excellent sense of humor. Mrs. Y's mother, old but alert and intelligent, was obviously the matriarch of this extended family group. Her rule was not rigidly authoritarian. Instead, she exercised a guiding influence on each of the independent families in the camp. The worker was impressed by the dignity, pride, and self-assurance displayed by the family; it seemed that they might have been descendants of an influential and ancient lineage of medicine men.

The women were very interested in hearing about the patient and asked many questions about her: How did she look? Was her hair turning grey? Did she look "as old" as her sisters at home? What kind of clothes did she have? Could she still speak Navajo? Did she remember them or the children? What had she said about coming home? Had she commented on their photographs and the tape recordings of their voices? The worker reported her observations of the patient and the feelings she had expressed about the family. They, in turn, told the worker a little of the history of the patient's departure from home. The mother, as head of the household, then took proper steps to call together community leaders and councilmen and learn their reactions to her daughter's proposed return and to help them understand her illness.

THE PATIENT'S RETURN TO THE RESERVATION

It took several months to arrange for the transfer of the patient to a general hospital on the reservation. Mrs. Y was given appropriate clothes and was accompanied on the flight by an attendant. She recognized the caseworker at the airport. From the beginning she was cheerful and in good contact. On the ride from the airport to the hospital she talked in Navajo about her trip: "A morning cab ride to the airport, boarded an airplane, three stops en route, scared, and near the end of the trip, vomited." This experience seemed to remind her of her abrupt separation from her family when she had been taken to prison. She conversed well and spoke of her family when the worker told her that she was on her way home. Mrs. Y said, "I didn't know where we were going, but I just stayed right behind her [the attendant]." She said she had suffered "for nothing" for many years and recalled that her mother had not witnessed her removal from home. An aunt had delivered her to the "wolves" to destroy her mentality. They cast a spell over her and took complete possession of her mind to the extent that she could no longer think or feel. In her own words, "I just gave up to them."

Wolf is a colloquial Navajo term meaning *witch*. Clyde Kluckhohn and Dorothea Leighton emphasize the strength of witch-craft beliefs among Navajos, even today, and the deep-seated fears associated with them: "What counts is that belief in witches is universal and that there are deep fears, much gossip and countless and widely current anecdotes."[2]

Throughout her stay at the hospital on the reservation, Mrs. Y's adjustment was satisfactory. She was assigned to a ward occupied by other Navajo women. At first she sat by her bed most of the day, but soon she began to exchange a few words with the women. Later, in talking to them, she said that she had been away from home a long time. She wondered whether she still owned any sheep and whether she retained authority to make decisions in her own home. She enjoyed a ride with the worker around the reservation to look at flocks of sheep, people riding horseback, an occasional wagon on the road, and, of course, the hogans. She said that these sights brought back memories of her people. They stopped at the store, and the worker permitted the patient to make her own purchases so that she could learn whether or not Mrs. Y was capable of making decisions by herself. Mrs. Y purchased cookies and candies and paid the correct amount to the clerk.

The patient became aware of the difference between her short hair and the long hair of the other Navajo women, which was plaited in the traditional Navajo knot. Navajo women feel that long hair adds to their attractiveness, and it enhances their self-image. Several times the patient made reference to her hair, and the worker felt that long hair would help her regain her self-esteem.

Mrs. Y's mother, sister, niece, daughter, and two small grandsons visited her the day after she arrived at the hospital. Mrs. Y had no difficulty in recognizing her mother, but the other members of the family had to introduce themselves to her. She readily accepted her grandchildren, hugged the baby occasionally, and inquired about the identifying characteristics of her son-in-law—his parents, clan, origin, and so forth. She was obviously happy to see her family. She said that until then she had been afraid to believe that she was really

---

[2]Clyde Kluckhohn and Dorothea Leighton, *The Navaho* (Cambridge, Mass.: Harvard University Press, 1946), p. 172.

home. Her mother gave her information about her brothers and sisters and her other relatives and her neighbors. Although Mrs. Y's ability to express herself in Navajo was somewhat limited, she conversed rationally and coherently with the family. When they attempted to plan for her return home and asked her how she would like her clothes made, she kept saying, "I have no authority; I cannot decide." Her daughter told her that her refusal to make decisions was part of the past life that she had left behind her. Now she was home, among her people, and she was again entitled to all her rights and privileges. She was a person again. She could now make decisions, and the family would help her.

Mrs. Y, however, still feared members of "the old regime" who had taken her away from her home. Her mother explained that "the old regime" no longer exercised authority over the Navajos, but Mrs. Y did not quite understand this. The patient continued to refer to the aunt who had sent her away, and her family reassured her by telling her that this aunt had died. Mrs. Y asked the worker to tell the officials of her return in order to learn about their reaction. She also talked about a bracelet taken from her when she had been imprisoned.

Mrs. Y was confused about the reasons for her imprisonment. She believed that she was the victim of the jealous, now deceased, aunt who had sought to bring evil upon her. She spoke again of "Navajo wolves" (human beings in wolf skins) turned loose upon her, crawling upon her hogan, and running riot in her mind. Her daughter, who had been ten years old at the time of her mother's imprisonment, remembered these animals crawling on the hogan at night and scaring the whole family. The worker surmised that these ideas, rather than being manifestations of the patient's illness, were a part of the Navajo culture. Kluckhohn described the way the Navajos believe these "witches" behave:

Witches are active primarily at night, roaming about at great speed in skins of wolf, coyote and other animals (bear, owl, desert fox, crow). This is one bit of witchcraft lore with which even the youngest Navajo is familiar. Indeed, ["wolf," in the Navajo language] I have found to be the most common colloquial term for "witch."[3]

Since Mrs. Y was able to adjust to life on the reservation successfully, the worker believed she would be able to adjust to living

---

[3]Clyde Kluckhohn, *Navajo Witchcraft* (Boston: Beacon Press, 1962), p. 26.

among her people without great difficulty. She still needed help with the unresolved problems of "the wolves," symbolic in Navajo culture of everything evil and to her of her fear in connection with her traumatic separation from her people. She also needed assurance that she had a secure place with her family and in the community. The family could help her with this problem, but the worker thought it advisable to request support from community agencies for both the patient and her family.

Two months later the worker made a home visit and found Mrs. Y baby sitting for her niece. She had just finished feeding four children, aged four, three, two, and one, and washing the dishes. She apologized to the worker for not giving her something to eat, explaining that she was not in her own home. She was cheerful and talked of helping her mother with the cooking and other chores; she also helped to prepare the wool for weaving. Mrs. Y was anxious to weave, but her mother had advised her to wait, because she still suffered from nocturnal episodes of vomiting and diarrhea. At night she was afraid of something she could not identify, but during the day she had no problems. These symptoms may well have indicated her persisting fear of witchcraft. Her family had arranged for some ceremonies to be performed that were designed to cure Mrs. Y of her illness, and they were planning for more of them. These ceremonies are the basic Navajo method of curing illness, including illness caused by witchcraft. Kluckhohn and Leighton state:

The most efficacious reassurance for victims of witchcraft is provided, therefore, by the unusual, complicated, and costly prayer ceremonials, with many relatives and friends in attendance, lending their help and expressing their sympathy.[4]

The particular ceremony recommended by the Navajo diagnostician depends on his identification of the supernatural cause of the illness. The ceremonies vary in length from one to nine days. Many relatives and friends gather to participate in them, bringing together the efforts of the community for the well-being of the patient. In this way they provide a positive emotional support for the member of the community who is ill. The Public Health Service doctors have come to recognize the continuing importance to the Navajos of their ceremonies, and in some cases they encourage the use of native methods of treatment along with those of modern medicine.

---

[4]Kluckhohn and Leighton, op. cit., p. 175.

In a second home visit the worker learned that Mrs. Y had made marked improvement. She was living in her own home and taking full responsibility for herself. She had woven a number of rugs and was pleased to be back on the reservation. Mrs. Y spoke of the "voices inside her," but she recognized them as part of the past and they no longer guided her in her actions.

SUMMARY

The case discussed in this article illustrates some of the problems social workers encounter in the rehabilitation of patients who have been hospitalized for long periods. Long-term care of patients in hospitals located at considerable distances from their families and communities often fosters the development of symptoms associated with institutionalization. Although the patient's illness may be in remission, his ability to relate to family and community is thwarted by his isolation from them. Members of minority groups may, of course, be even more isolated than patients who are members of the dominant culture.

Some of the problems the social worker encountered in helping a Navajo Indian return to her home after an absence of twenty years were resolved because the worker understood the patient's cultural beliefs and customs and was able to communicate with her in her native language. The worker helped the family understand Mrs. Y's illness and her attitude toward them, which was essential in securing the family's participation in planning for her return home.

Casework service is especially needed in helping mental patients who have been hospitalized for a long time to bridge the gap between living in the hospital and living in the community. It is especially important to involve the patient's family and community agencies in planning for the discharge of such patients.

27

CHARLES F. GROSSER

Community Organization
and the Grass Roots

Richard Titmuss has stated that the central problem of today's urban-industrial poor is not poverty but inequality.[1] The benefits of the welfare state accrue in the main to the middle and stable working classes. Thus, the major social issue of the day is the extension of rights provided by the welfare state so that the lower classes may share fully in these benefits. Such an objective, Titmuss suggests, will entail both alterations in the existing social structure and cost to the affluent in the community. The effect on the total population of what is essentially a redistribution of the nation's resources will be different from and greater than the effect of strategies directed specifically toward the poor.

WELFARE STATE BENEFITS

That the welfare state's resources are distributed differentially along class lines can be illustrated by any number of governmental programs. It has been established, for example, that the typical slum school (1) has a smaller ratio of staff to children than does the suburban school, (2) provides fewer hours a day of actual instruction, (3) spends half as many dollars per pupil per year, (4) operates in older, more crowded, and dilapidated buildings with fewer library, recreational, and special instructional facilities, and (5) employs less adequately trained teachers.[2] Yet public education is perhaps the best established and least controversial of the services provided by government. It is offered not merely as a matter of right, but under

---

SOURCE: Reprinted with permission of the National Association of Social Workers, from *Social Work*, Vol. 12, No. 4 (October, 1967), pp. 61–67.

[1]Richard Titmuss, "Poverty vs. Inequality in the Welfare State," *The Nation*, Vol. 200, No. 6 (February 8, 1965), pp. 130–133; and Titmuss, "The Role of Redistribution in Social Policy," *Social Security Bulletin*, Vol. 28, No. 6 (June, 1965), pp. 14–20.

[2]See, for example, James B. Conant, *Slums and Suburbs* (New York: McGraw-Hill Book Co., 1961); and Patricia C. Sexton, *Education and Income: Inequalities of Opportunity in Our Public Schools* (New York: Viking Press, 1961).

the compulsion of legislation that makes attendance mandatory for all children with no restrictions, qualifications, or eligibility requirements.

Other welfare state benefits are provided under systems of eligibility that often categorically exclude those who most need them. Benefits under the Social Security Act such as OASDI and the unemployment and disability insurances are cases in point. Based on equity rather than adequacy, and modeled on private insurance plans designed to show a profit, they provide benefits to the temporarily unemployed, stable working class rather than to the chronically unemployed or the marginally or seasonally employed. Further, these benefits are designed to provide submarginal assistance over short periods of time, which are viewed as interruptions in a state of continuous employment, rather than substantial assistance over long periods of chronic unemployment. In the years since the enactment of social security, continuous modification of the original legislation has tempered, but not eliminated, this aspect of the program.[3]

In other categories of welfare state benefits—public housing, federal mortgage assistance, and such "social utilities" as museums, libraries, and beaches—the demand for service far exceeds the available resources.[4] The administering agencies are therefore required to use discretion in selecting from the total population those who may take advantage of each program. Because of such factors as the tendency of organizations to avoid abrasive or problem-producing circumstances, the ethnocentricity of the professions, which limits the perception of their members, and the tendency of both organizations and professions to avoid antagonizing those who have the power to demand redress, choices of the population to be served discriminate against the large family, unstable community, isolated neighborhood, and wage earner without collateral. In these programs, too, it is equity rather than adequacy that is sought. Thus instance after instance is seen in which local, state, or federal jurisdictions provide benefits to limited numbers of citizens. The poor, minority group members, ghetto residents, migrant workers, and female-headed families are dramatically underrepresented or totally unserved.

In excluding the poor from general benefits of the welfare state,

---

[3]See Eveline Burns, "Social Security in Evolution: Toward What?" *Social Service Review*, Vol. 39, No. 2 (June, 1965), pp. 129–140.

[4]See Alfred Kahn, "New Policies and Service Models: The Next Phase." Paper presented at the Annual Meeting of the American Orthopsychiatric Association, March 18, 1965. (Mimeographed.)

government has provided them with such programs as public assistance that were designed especially for them. It has been amply
documented that these programs characteristically place the burden
of proving eligibility on the recipient, stigmatize him as a failure,
provide meager benefits, and otherwise discourage eligible persons
from availing themselves of their entitlements.[5]

Private social service has in large measure ignored the problems of
the impoverished rejects of the welfare state.[6] Thus the tasks identified by Andrews, among others, as the province of voluntary
agencies—"filling gaps and inadequacies . . . covering many additional needs now not met by government"—are performed on the
same exclusionary basis as are the functions of welfare state programs.[7]

PRIVATE SERVICE AND
PLANNING AGENCIES

Traditionally, the community organizer, operating through a welfare council made up of agency representatives and influential citizens, undertook to plan for the community and to co-ordinate the
activities of private health and welfare agencies.[8] The provision of
services to the needy has not been his major function. Rather, his
activity was limited by the agencies that employed him to facilitating
and co-ordinating existing resources.

Speaking of the leaders of community health and welfare planning
agencies, Burke notes:

Frequently, . . . their view is completely at variance with the desires and
needs of those who are clients of social welfare agencies. Even more sadly,

---

[5]Edward Sparer, "The Role of the Welfare Client's Lawyer," *UCLA Law Review*,
Vol. 12, No. 2 (January, 1965).

[6]See August B. Hollingshead, *Elmtown's Youth* (New York: John Wiley & Sons,
Inc., 1949), chap. 12; William F. Whyte, *Street Corner Society* (2d ed.; Chicago:
University of Chicago Press, 1955); H.C. Bredemeier, "The Socially Handicapped and
the Agencies," in Frank Riessman, Jerome Cohen, and Arthur Pearl (eds.), *Mental
Health of the Poor* (New York: Free Press of Glencoe, 1964), pp. 88–109; Richard A.
Cloward and Irwin Epstein, "Private Social Welfare's Disengagement from the Poor:
The Case of Family Adjustment Agencies," in Meyer Zald (ed.), *Social Welfare
Institutions* (New York: John Wiley & Sons, Inc., 1965), pp. 623–644.

[7]F. Emerson Andrews, *Philanthropic Giving* (New York: Russell Sage Foundation,
1950), p. 113.

[8]"There is usually an even greater concentration of the business elite or their
representatives on the boards of central fund-raising agencies than in service
agencies; a nationwide study . . . found Chest Fund and Council Boards to be composed 40% of employers and business representatives." *Ibid.*, p. 271.

their conventional wisdom has not been able to understand the needs of the large numbers who are denied access to all the health, welfare and recreation services they need.[9]

This unresponsiveness or unawareness of the needs of a large section of the population has been possible because the poor, in addition to being "invisible," have also been without voice, vote, power, and influence. The local social welfare planning council has suffered no consequences and endured no sanctions by failing to serve them.

The poor, after all, are those who were stigmatized in an earlier era as "undeserving" and designated as the responsibility of the county rather than of private welfare. Those who financially supported the private agencies derived no satisfaction from serving this group. Furthermore, since their numbers were so large, the poor represented a vast burden on already overloaded agency budgets. In addition, this client group tended to be unresponsive to the type of service offered by the agency, alienated more-desirable clients, reduced the status of professional service staff, and tarnished the image presented in fund-raising appeals. As a result, the planning organizations, which had to be responsive to the interests of professionals in welfare and influential laymen, were discouraged from attending to the needs and wishes of the poor.

NEW FORMS OF PUBLIC AND
VOLUNTARY WELFARE

The inception of the urban, slum-based, comprehensive delinquency-prevention projects supported by President Kennedy's Committee on Juvenile Delinquency and Youth Crime marked a new phase in the development of the welfare state. For the first time large-scale, diversified social change-oriented welfare programs were introduced under public auspices, funded with public money, and based in local neighborhoods. Although these programs were still designed specifically for the poor, they provided new and expanded patterns of service. They both created new agencies (the "quasi-public" or, if you will, "quasi-private" social agency, such as Mobilization For Youth, Community Progress, Inc., and HAR-YOU-Act) and affected existing agencies by providing them with monies to fund specific programs. Both functions have profoundly

---

[9]Edmund M. Burke, "The Road to Planning: An Organizational Analysis," *Social Service Review*, Vol. 39, No. 3 (September, 1965), p. 268.

changed the traditional patterns of community organization and social planning.

The Continuing Voluntary Agency — Although the terms "private"
and "voluntary" are commonly used interchangeably, it is the author's position that the evolution of the welfare state in the public
sector was accompanied by a transition of no less importance in the
nonpublic sector. The emergence of large-scale delinquency-prevention projects marked the point when public support of
"private" social welfare could no longer be ignored; thus nonpublic
social welfare became "voluntary."

It had generally been assumed that the emerging pattern in voluntary social welfare financing was centralized fund-raising and that
this technique was the means by which the economic problems of
such agencies would ultimately be solved. These assumptions reinforced the domination of social welfare planning by the community
elite because planning patterns always follow funding patterns in
obeisance to the adage: "He who pays the piper calls the tune."
Until recently, scant attention was paid to the fact that voluntarism in
social welfare has depended for survival in the past several decades
on substantial support from such public agencies as, for example, the
New York City Youth Board and the New York City Department of
Welfare, and the indirect support offered through federal tax ex-
emptions. With the increase in population, income, and cost of service over the last two decades,

... voluntary giving buys no more service per person today than it did in
1945. ... But *in relation to their income,* the American people seem to be
giving for voluntary welfare services only two-thirds of what they did in
1945.[10]

It can be argued whether the welfare community has been well
aware of this situation. There can be no dispute, however, that until
recently community planning agencies and community organizers
have failed to acknowledge the public source of their support by
neglecting to solicit the participation of the general electorate or
public agency in the health and welfare councils' activities.

Because public monies were dramatically injected into voluntary
programs to meet burgeoning critical needs, the separatist strategies
of the antidelinquency and poverty programs were connected to the

---

[10]Alvin L. Schorr, "The Future Structure of Community Services," *Social Welfare
Forum, 1965* (New York: Columbia University Press, 1965), pp. 136–137.

welfare state itself. Although services were still separate, the projects' policies were in the mainstream of community life, which was evident from the development of competition within the voluntary welfare community and between it and the public sector. As this competition became more overt, the poor gained visibility, not through any explicit change in their status, but through their increasing viability as a political issue. As a result of the public debate stirred up initially by the programs of the President's committee and intensified by the Office of Economic Opportunity's programs, particularly those under Title II of the Economic Opportunity Act, community planners began to consider such inclusionist strategies as the participation of service recipients, the general electorate, and the poor in the planning process.

NEW WELFARE AGENCIES

The new service and planning agencies created by direct federal subsidy through the Office of Juvenile Delinquency and the OEO, with their community planning and community development sections, have been most persuasive in directing community organizers to new constituencies. Since the programs of the new delinquency projects were comprehensive in design and embraced a variety of services (including those contracted with numerous pre-existing public and voluntary agencies), the projects undertook to co-ordinate and plan the use of these various services to control and prevent delinquency. In addition, these agencies viewed the participation of low-income residents as crucial to the success of their efforts. Under Title II of the Economic Opportunity Act, local communities were encouraged to set up autonomous planning and co-ordinating devices — "poverty operations boards" — that would screen and determine the nature of the poverty programs in each community. The OEO specified the inclusion of the recipients of service in its now famous requirement that the new programs provide for the "maximum feasible participation of the residents of the areas to be served" (later determined to be one-third). Such directives were more than simple admonitions — funds actually were withheld when such participation did not occur. The anomalous result was that essentially separatist programs again were serving inclusionist purposes.

The often deceptive and ineffectual ways in which local communities met the federal directive are not at issue here. The author just wants to emphasize that the mandate was given and that overt attempts were made to comply with it. Communities have been torn by conflict between various contenders for the public largess. Harris describes this phenomenon as follows:

No program has had harder birth pains, or a stormier infancy. Neighborhood groups, grasping at the chance to get control on the local level, fight each other, or strike an uneasy truce and fight City Hall. City-wide social agencies maneuver against each other for supremacy in the Poverty councils and fight City Hall. City officials struggle to keep the Poverty reins in their own hands. Charges and countercharges of politics, bad faith, and poor accountability are hurled back and forth and made in the press and at Congressional hearings.[11]

Public debate abounds. Agencies whose only public contact has been an appeal for support find their fiscal practices open to public scrutiny, programs open to public appraisal, and both subjected to essentially public or political judgments. Although much confusion and disorder reign, it is clear that *total* community planning, however inadequate and confused, has emerged as both a high-priority issue of social policy and an area of practice.

WELFARE COUNCIL AND
NEIGHBORHOOD ORGANIZATION

The author has noted that although much support of local social welfare agencies came from public sources, the voluntary community welfare council apparently has felt no pressure for the systematic inclusion of the "public" in the planning process. It is not surprising, then, that the newly created delinquency-prevention and anti-poverty programs often have bypassed the existing local welfare council and its constituents. In city after city, acrimony developed between the new and continuing programs when the new projects refused to give over the planning, co-ordinating, and community-organizing functions to the established agencies. In a few instances the council and the new agency have joined forces. In New Haven, for example,

council staff and lay leadership enjoyed the confidence of the key leadership of CPI (Community Progress, Inc.). Council planning became part of CPI planning. Conversely, CPI planning begins to become part of council plan-

---

[11]Helen M. Harris, "Annual Report of the Executive Director," Vol. I (New York: United Neighborhood Houses of New York, Inc., May 11, 1965). (Mimeographed.)

ning. . . . Council advice and suggestions are welcomed with respect to CPI programs . . . (when) its knowledge and ability to relate the various components and their effect upon people has great value.[12]

When such co-operation exists, it is only because the project needs the council's expertise in dealing with the health and welfare community. In this instance, council practice is directly applicable and can continue to operate as usual, without adaptation or change, while co-operating with the project.

In a variation of this pattern, the local welfare council does not join with the project in a common cause, but receives project funds to continue or expand its ongoing work. The project concurrently creates new community organizations to meet the new planning and participation demands of its programs. In addition, as a result of the support provided by public funds, congressional subcommittees, city councils, councils of the poor, civil rights organizations, and trade unions — to name but a few — also became active in the social welfare planning process and have undertaken and expanded the functions heretofore conceded to the welfare council.

The new public welfare programs offer service to segments of the population previously neglected by both the welfare state and voluntary social agencies. That new groups have been formed to do community work with these groups is understandable since the experience and methodology of existing community organization agencies have failed to meet the needs of the diverse settings and new client population in today's social welfare complex. The newly created project agency, particularly since it sees itself as impermanent, is able to experiment with new forms of neighborhood community organization.

These new forms of organization have raised issues that go far beyond the scope of the projects that initially gave them impetus to suggest entirely new concepts of planning and accountability. For example, organizing public agency clients has now become a method of social planning and insuring agency accountability. It can no longer be dismissed as "outside agitation" or stirring up "people not yet ready for freedom," as it was characterized by a public agency supervisor only two years ago. In its early stages, the stance of such grass roots organization may well be militant and its voice strident, but ultimately it is likely to become institutionalized as part of a new

---

[12]Frank W. Harris, "A Modern Council Point of View," *Social Work*, Vol. 9, No. 4 (October, 1964), p. 36.

style of assistance. Community organization methods for social planning of this kind do not as yet exist.

Not infrequently in the new scheme of things, one social welfare agency becomes engaged in community organization activities with citizens receiving benefits from another agency, which may be a target of community planning change. When this is the case, the target agency usually responds with a vituperative attack against the planning agency and accuses it of betraying the social work profession.[13] Methodology is not yet sufficiently diverse or sophisticated to deal with such problems.

SOME STRATEGIES

The development of a new type of social welfare service has been described—a service sponsored, funded, and held accountable by government. It is not contended that this phenomenon is fresh on the welfare scene, but the emergence of the comprehensive antipoverty project has dramatically and inescapably exposed to public scrutiny that the government is the major purveyor of all social welfare services, public and voluntary. To recognize this is to acknowledge also that as far as social welfare is concerned, this nation is a functioning welfare state. The model of private social welfare as largess distributed by the elite for the benefit of the poor can no longer be defended.

In the arena of private charity, the poor were mere supplicants, but in the arena of democratic politics the poor have the vote and the power which can come from the organization of masses of votes. Thus, when welfare decisions are moved to government and the sphere of democratic politics where the poor are not merely recipients, new forces should become decisive in social welfare policies and practices.[14]

That social welfare planning within this construction is a function of governmental and political processes alters the client's role. Once a separated, isolated beneficiary, he is or can become a voter, demonstrator, taxpayer, or rioter. Thus, community organization has come around full cycle, from dealing almost exclusively with elites to

---

[13]Charles F. Grosser, "Community Development Programs Serving the Urban Poor," *Social Work*, Vol. 10, No. 3 (July, 1965), pp. 15–21.

[14]Frances Fox Piven, "Private Benevolence and the Welfare State." Paper presented at the Alumni Conference of the Columbia University School of Social Work, New York, April 23, 1966. Dr. Piven goes on to argue that this promise has not been fulfilled because the programs keep the poor in continued powerlessness.

organizing the citizen recipients of public or voluntary services to use whatever resources they have for the provision of services as enforceable rights.

The ramifications of this state of affairs are just beginning to be felt. Work at the grass roots and with the unaffiliated is no longer justified simply on the therapeutic ground that organization of such groups will help to overcome the pessimism and apathy that keep the poor impoverished. Nor is justification sought on the grounds that the mandate of the enabling legislation is merely being met. (It appears that so far as Title II is concerned, Congress has all but removed the mandate.) It is because social welfare is moving to the point at which it serves a total community of citizen-clients that community organization should concern itself with organizing the grass-roots population to participate in welfare planning. Planning should include such goals as exercising the franchise and establishing integration — in short, such efforts to insure any and all of the rights under the welfare state.

Such activity calls for new techniques. In the public political arena controversy and conflict abound. Social workers shall have to learn to understand and use them. Out of the concern for the powerless (rather than the elite) methods must be developed to utilize powerlessness (rather than influence) to effect planning decisions on behalf of the new constituents. Methods may have to be sought in such sources as the nonviolence of Ghandiism, which utilized the powerlessness of an impoverished peasantry in the method of passive resistance. A creative application of this method is the welfare rights movement, which utilizes eligibility for public welfare as an instrument of social organization and change.[15]

For the new clients new allies must be sought from among the civil rights, student, and trade union movements (in addition to the old ones from commerce, business, academe, and the professions). Finally, continuous government sponsorship of welfare must be accepted, understood, and shaped, because this is clearly the pattern of future human service. It may be that by implementing the conception of total population involvement in community planning and organization we can not only extend the benefits of the welfare state to all but maintain the very substance of a pluralistic democratic society in the face of ever increasing institutionalization and complexity.

---

[15]See, for example, Richard A. Cloward and Frances Fox Piven, "A Strategy to End Poverty," *The Nation*, Vol. 202, No. 18 (May 2, 1966), pp. 510–17.

· 28 ·

EDWARD J. O'DONNELL and MARILYN M. SULLIVAN

Service Delivery and Social Action through the Neighborhood Center: A Review of Research

The star of the "income strategy" is ascending.[1] And it is high time. Poor people need money; ours is a money economy and "money talks." Poor people need power, too; they must organize and act. Some want to; a few will. People need money and people need power. Service is a poor substitute.[2] A "service strategy" is not at all fashionable; some say not at all relevant. Kravitz, for one, argues: "To talk about new forms of delivery of service ... is to offer smelling salts when the patient is strangling, band-aids when the patient is bleeding to death ... Building ... new neighborhood centers amid slum squalor is immoral."[3] Perhaps so. But Specht reminds us of the "many needy people who may only want more and better service—who may not want to organize or protest, but simply to find alternatives to fighting City Hall and Bureaucracy."[4] The neighbor-

SOURCE: Reprinted from *Welfare in Review*, Vol. 7, No. 6 (November–December, 1969), pp. 1–12.

[1]President Nixon's proposed family assistance plan is one indication of this, as is the interest in the negative income tax, children's allowances, and the income supplementation plan of the President's Commission on Income Maintenance Programs. See "Poverty Amid Plenty: The American Paradox," *Report of the President's Commission on Income Maintenance Programs*, Nov. 12, 1969.

[2]See "Special Report: Sick Cities—and the Search for a Cure," especially Daniel P. Moynihan, "The Urban Negro Is the 'Urban Problem'," pp. 36–38, and Lee Rainwater, "The Services Strategy vs. the Income Strategy," pp. 40–41, *Trans-action*, Oct., 1967.

[3]Sanford Kravitz, "Issues and Opportunities Facing Public Welfare," *Public Welfare*, Vol. XXVI, No. 1 (Jan., 1968), pp. 5–6.

[4]Harry Specht, "Community Development in Low-Income Negro Areas," *Social Work*, Oct. 1966, p. 78. It is interesting to note that the Heineman Commission sees the neighborhood center as a worthy vehicle for service delivery at the local level: "We recommend that the basic services provided through Federally-aided programs be included in multi-purpose urban neighborhood service centers which would provide a single location from which social services could be dispensed. These neighbor-

hood service center holds promise of doing both — of providing better service and effecting social change. This article examines that promise.

The traditional organizations and institutions designed to provide services have, increasingly, come under fire. They have been swept along by social currents to the point of their being too big, too distant, and too self-serving. The traditional agency has been criticized as formal, fragmented, impersonal, officious, and timid; as alienating and intimidating people; as insuring long delays and expecting those it serves to accept its policy without question. But the neighborhood center has been championed as informal, integrated, personal, courteous, and courageous; as making people feel they belong; as offering instant service and promoting the active participation of the neighborhood in its program. Such, at any rate, is the rhetoric of the advocates of neighborhood centers.

THE IMPETUS BEHIND IT

The development of the neighborhood center owes much to a number of forces and movements — not the least significant of which has been the long-term migration of low-income Negroes and members of other minority groups to the cities, the out-migration of the more affluent white people to the suburbs, the increasing irrelevance of community agencies to the problems of poor people,[5] and the gradual decline of machine-dominated city politics. All but gone is the neighborhood ward "healer" and his patronage system for obtaining jobs, welfare, and legal advice for the poor.

The neighborhood center is an attempt to institutionalize many of the services performed by local political bosses. The neighborhood service system has become the functional equivalent of the old political ward system. The ward man has become the neighborhood worker; the political club, the neighborhood center. "People came to . . . (the ward man) to inquire about welfare payments, to get their relatives into public institutions, to get something done about neighborhood nuisances. . . . and to make complaints about the police or other city departments."[6] "He had to know his neighborhood thor-

---

hood service centers also could provide information and referral services, have outlets for manpower programs, and provide space for clinical services." See "Poverty Amid Plenty: The American Paradox," p. 162.

[5]See, for example, Albert Rose, "The Social Services in the Modern Metropolis," *Social Service Review*, Dec., 1963, pp. 375–389.

[6]Edward Banfield, *City Politics* (Cambridge, Mass.: Harvard University Press,

oughly . . . catering to local interests and problems. He found jobs for
needy families, or loaned them money. . . . For businessmen and
saloon-keepers, he granted relief from some law or city ordinance;
for gamblers, prostitutes, and gangsters in trouble, he found bail,
or . . . he could arrange for the 'right' lawyer and the 'right' judge,
who would arrange for the 'right' sentence."[7]

"If the ward leader was shrewd, he made his ward clubhouse
into a pleasant place where a tired Manure Inspector or an Assistant
Health Warden could find relaxation at the billiard table or at the
bar where he could chew over the latest political gossip. If he was
particularly canny, he would create a neighborhood espirit de
corps . . . by having his club sponsor clambakes, picnics, summer
outings . . . at least two 'balls' a year . . . torchlight parades and ral-
lies . . . Deeply political as it was . . . it served as a social institution
as well. The clubhouse, like the saloon, was a haven for recreation
and good fellowship, and a refuge from wives. And the club itself
provided a means by which the native poor, or an immigrant Irishman or German, could advance to some social standing."[8]

Obviously, the comparison between the neighborhood service
center and the old political club stops far short of many of the
wardheeler's "services"; and though there are no more "tired"
manure inspectors and neighborhood centers do not typically offer
billiards and bars, the idea of a center's being a "pleasant place" and
the effort to "create neighborhood espirit de corps" are not unalike.
And though the center is no longer a "refuge from wives" (indeed,
more likely a refuge from children), it can be "a haven for recreation
and good fellowship." And, finally, though the "social standing and
status" of "an immigrant Irishman or German" is no longer relevant,
the advancement of the Appalachian, the Negro, the Puerto Rican,
and the Mexican-American most certainly is. Just as the political club
replaced the saloon as *the* grassroots center for neighborhood activity, so perhaps the neighborhood service center will eventually assume this role and responsibility.

But understanding the impetus behind the rise of the neighborhood center does not clarify all questions about its goals. These
questions particularly stand out: Is the neighborhood service center

---

1963), as quoted in Robert Perlman and David Jones, *Neighborhood Service Centers*,
Office of Juvenile Delinquency, Welfare Administration, U.S. Department of Health,
Education, and Welfare, 1967, p. 8.
    [7]Alexander B. Callow, Jr., *The Tweed Ring* (New York: Oxford University Press,
1966), pp. 104–105.
    [8]Callow, pp. 105–106.

primarily a means for making the best use of services by overcoming geographic and psychological distances? Can it successfully promote social action and institutional change? Is it merely a fact-gathering operation concerned with the identification of inadequacies in the welfare system and other traditional agencies? Can the center change services for the better? Can it provide better services itself? What is the best mix of service and action efforts?[9]

By examining some research evidence we can perhaps shed some light on these questions and raise still other issues.

ITS ORGANIZATIONAL STRUCTURE

Potentially, the settings of neighborhood service centers are as diversified as the programs they offer and the people they serve. "Such centers could be located in a variety of places, including public housing projects . . . settlement houses, neighborhood stores and shopping centers. They would be pleasant places to come to, open weekends and some evenings, with . . . overriding courtesy."[10] The continuing involvement of residents in the planning and staffing of programs is one of the center's innovations. Typically, area residents participate in center activities both as members of boards and committees and as staff workers. "Except for the very poor, the most militant, and the established political leadership, the boards represent a reasonable cross-section of the neighborhood."[11]

Neighborhood center staffs vary greatly in size — from one-man operations to those employing over a hundred. The median size of the 20 centers Perlman and Jones studied was 14;[12] a Brandeis University study of 54 centers found a median size staff of 15.[13] The proportion of workers from the neighborhood varies from center to center; however, virtually all try to employ some neighborhood people.

The neighborhood service center study by Kirschner Associates,

---

[9]See, for example, Perlman and Jones, p. 37.

[10]"The Advisory Committee on HEW Relationships with State Health Agencies," *Report to the Secretary*, U.S. Department of Health, Education, and Welfare, December 30, 1966, p. 53.

[11]"OSTI Revised Decentralized Training Paper," *Organization for Social and Technological Innovation*, Apr. 30, 1969, p. 53.

[12]Perlman and Jones, p. 82.

[13]"Neighborhood Organizational Units of the Community Action Agency," *Community Representation in Community Action Programs*, Report No. 4, Florence Heller Graduate School for Advanced Studies in Social Welfare, Brandeis University, Nov. 1968, p. 8.

and the studies of community action programs by Brandeis University and Hallman, indicate that more women than men were involved as staff employees and that, except in small towns and rural areas, more Negro than white women.[14]

Though the evidence on the employment of neighborhood workers indicates reasonable success, that on the participation of residents on boards and committees is less than compelling.[15] Kirschner Associates found that "the participation of the poor as employees . . . seems to be well advanced and largely successful . . . Participation of the poor as policymakers and administrators seems to have been achieved on a quantitative basis but there appears to be little effective involvement due to a lack of training in some cases and a lack of authority in others."[16] Similarly, in reporting on the findings of a study of 12 community action programs, Clark writes that "the poor were involved as staff in all effective programs and as participants in voter registration drives, rent strikes and the like, but the degree of their participation was guided and to a large extent controlled by leaders not themselves poor . . . In no case of an effective program were elected poor influential in major decisions, though several programs envisioned gradual involvement of neighborhood boards at policy-making levels."[17]

THE SERVICES IT OFFERS

First and foremost, neighborhood service centers provide social services. Many combine services and social action, but all of them provide service in some form.

Kirschner Associates found wide variations in the kinds of services offered, ranging from centers concentrating on one service such as employment counseling to centers offering many different kinds of

---

[14]Kirschner Associates, *A Description and Evaluation of Neighborhood Centers*, A Report for the Office of Economic Opportunity, Dec. 1966, p. 69; "Community Representation in Community Action Programs," *Report No. 5, Final Report*, The Florence Heller Graduate School for Advanced Studies in Social Welfare, Brandeis University, Mar. 1969, pp. 74–75; Howard W. Hallman, *The Community Action Program—An Interpretive Analysis of 35 Communities, Examination of the War on Poverty*, Vol. IV, U.S. Senate Committee on Labor and Public Welfare, September, 1967, p. 908.

[15]Edward J. O'Donnell and Catherine S. Chilman, "Poor People on Public Welfare Boards and Committees," *Welfare in Review*, May-June, 1969, pp. 1–9.

[16]Kirschner Associates, p. 47.

[17]Kenneth B. Clark, "Urban Crises—Gimmicks vs. Serious Programs," paper presented at the Annual Forum of the National Conference on Social Welfare, New York City, May 26, 1969, pp. 6–7.

services to many different kinds of people. Almost all offered employment counseling and job placement services. Next came welfare, primarily through the aid to families with dependent children (AFDC) program. At least half provided educational and health services. Housing, recreational, consumer education, and legal aid services were offered in decreasing order with decreasing frequency.[18]

A study of neighborhood service programs undertaken by Abt Associates noted that "family life, welfare assistance, health, legal aid, and education programs" were generally offered to residents of the areas served.[19]

A sample of cases studied by Perlman and Jones at the Roxbury center in Boston found that the problems people presented, in order of frequency, were employment, legal, economic, housing, family, and health[20]—all consistent with services that centers generally make available.

REQUISITES FOR GOOD SERVICE

Though the neighborhood service center has the obvious potential of being all things to all men, a reasonable list of requisites would include the following:[21]

Accessible. The center should be easy to get to. It should be open evenings and weekends and should provide emergency telephone service 24 hours a day.

Acceptable. The center should be clean, comfortable, and informal; its operation should be consistent with the neighborhood's way of life. Neither its employees nor its services should be foreign or alien. Faces should be familiar, and workers should be friendly and courteous.

Immediate. The center should provide prompt, efficient, immediate service. It should be able to respond to day-to-day problems without long hours of waiting and many rounds of appointments.

Comprehensive. The center should offer a full range of usable, on-the-spot

---

[18]Kirschner Associates, p. 32.

[19]"Summary and Recommendations," A Study of the Neighborhood Center Pilot Program, prepared for the Executive Office of the President, Bureau of the Budget, Abt Associates Incorporated, vol. 1, Apr. 30, 1969, p. 11.

[20]Perlman and Jones, p. 27.

[21]See Hobart A. Burch and Edward Newman, "A Federal Program for Neighborhood Services," paper presented at the National Conference on Social Welfare, San Francisco, May 27, 1968; Thomas H. Walz "The Emergence of the Neighborhood Service Center," Public Welfare, Apr., 1969, pp. 147–156; and Michael S. March, "The Neighborhood Center Concept," Public Welfare, Apr., 1968, pp. 97–111.

services or easy access to other resources by available transportation. It should gear itself to the needs that people have—especially poor people—and provide for the simultaneous handling of problems where possible.

Integrated. The center should insure the coordination and integration of services so that they might be more effectively brought to bear on all the problems that people present.

Responsive. The center should reflect the needs and desires of the neighborhood. It should provide ways in which residents can shape the program and continue to contribute to its course and development. It should be relevant and ready to respond to changing needs.

These categories are neither mutually exclusive nor exhaustive. Several overlap. And though still others could be used, these seem to provide an analytically useful way to approach the literature.[22]

RESEARCH FINDINGS AND PERFORMANCE CRITERIA

These characteristics are criteria against which the achievements of the center can be measured. Together they are one basis for assessing centers and for organizing the findings of a variety of studies.[23]

Are Centers Accessible?—Centers are located in low-income areas and, by virtue of their physical location, are at least more accessible than traditional agencies. Kirschner Associates note that the center is a way of introducing conventional community services to people for whom they have been previously unavailable.[24] Perlman and Jones report that, "in general, neighborhood centers serve people who live within walking distance or on transportation lines."[25] Data from their

---

[22]See also Kirschner Associates, pp. 41–42, and "An Approach to Measuring the Impact of Existing Service Systems on Problems of Urban Poverty," Greenleigh Associates, Inc., New York, Chicago, pp. 1–8, for still other schemes for evaluation.

[23]Obviously, the major studies reviewed here vary considerably: for example, Perlman and Jones studied 20 centers operating six major programs; Kirschner Associates studied 20 OEO centers; Abt Associates studied 13 centers sponsored jointly by five Federal Departments; and Brandeis University studied 54 OEO centers as part of its study of resident participation in community action programs. Thus, these preliminary findings reflect the experience of neighborhood centers supported through Federal programs—primarily OEO. They do not necessarily speak to the long experience of traditional settlement houses, for example, and should be regarded as tentative pending the outcome of such further systematic research as is underway in the Social and Rehabilitation Service, U.S. Department of Health, Education, and Welfare, and the Office of Economic Opportunity.

[24]Kirschner Associates, p. 15.

[25]Perlman and Jones, p. 30.

centers indicated that most clients were "walk-ins." In only one did the number referred from other agencies exceed that of those who came in on their own or who were referred by family, friends, or neighbors.[26] A number of centers have set up outreach operations. But some have had to cut back such efforts because of heavy demands on resources.[27] Most have found no shortage of persons to serve.

Nevertheless, the proportion of residents served varies greatly. Perlman and Jones' estimates suggest that their centers contacted from less than 2 percent of the area population of the Mobilization for Youth program in New York City to as many as 20 percent of the service population of Community Progress, Inc., in New Haven.[28] Based on figures from 10 to 20 sample centers, Kirschner Associates estimate that some 18 percent of the people in their neighborhood areas were reached.[29]

The number reached, however, may not reflect the actual number served. One neighborhood program, for example, contacted about 10,000 people but served fewer than 500.[30]

Great effort is going into reducing the psychological distance between client and service unit by employing neighborhood people and making them visible and accessible in and out of the center. They typically provide outreach service and otherwise encourage agency-shy persons to use the center. Though it may be argued that centers are doing all they can to make their services accessible, it is clear that there are many more clients who need to be served and that clients will continue to overrun as many centers as are established.

Are Services Immediate?—There is little evidence that centers as yet offer "instant" service. However, to the extent that they are at convenient locations, are open evenings and weekends, provide transportation, employ generalist receptionists and intake workers, have a range of on-the-spot services or access to such services through links to community agencies, the centers probably can rather promptly attend to client problems, particularly the day-to-day criti-

---

[26] Perlman and Jones, p. 30.
[27] Perlman and Jones, p. 41.
[28] Perlman and Jones, p. 81.
[29] Kirschner Associates, p. 24.
[30] "An Evaluation of the Thirteen Neighborhood Service Programs," A Study of the Neighborhood Center Pilot Program, prepared for the Executive Office of the President, Bureau of the Budget, Abt Associates Incorporated, Vol. 2, part 2, Apr. 30, 1969, p. 41.

cal problems of poor people. Perlman and Jones describe the prospect for immediate service this way: "A receptionist, most often a woman who handled incoming calls and some clerical work, greeted the client, took her name and address, and arranged an appointment with one of the workers within a matter of minutes; rarely was there a wait of more than fifteen or twenty minutes. If an answer could be given . . . the receptionist would give the information; otherwise she would refer the client to another worker."[31] "In Roxbury, 74% of the clients were seen immediately by one of the services, 14% were seen by appointment, and 12% were not recorded."[32]

Centers are usually inundated with demands on their scarce resources and find themselves having to make the same hard choices as traditional agencies. Perlman and Jones note that "going beyond" instant service "requires the investment of a substantial amount of staff time with clients who require intensive and extended service" and raise this issue: "Should quick service to ten clients take precedence over intensive service to one?"[33] Given the great demand and the relatively few resources at their disposal, their centers soon responded in either of two ways. They continued to do what they could to serve individual clients and families by stretching or expanding resources and by cutting back on client recruitment, or they played down individual services and organized neighborhood groups to demand more and better services from other agencies.[34]

The second recourse—community action—becomes problematic, however, when the client's perception of the neighborhood center is taken into account. "In their view the purpose of the center is to help people by providing them with the services they need . . . the idea of organizing the poor to help themselves is not very prominent in the client's perceptions."[35]

The question of whether neighborhood centers have the ability to respond promptly to resident needs remains open. They may be able to serve a few and to cut redtape for a few others but for the rest—a prompt reception may stop far short of much-needed service. A client cutback is no solution. Is an invitation to "come let us organize together" any better?

---

[31]Perlman and Jones, p. 26.
[32]Perlman and Jones, p. 26.
[33]Perlman and Jones, p. 33.
[34]Perlman and Jones, p. 40.
[35]Kirschner Associates, p. 17. See also, Charles F. Grosser, "Helping Youth—A Study of Six Community Organization Programs," Office of Juvenile Delinquency and Youth Development, Social and Rehabilitation Service, U.S. Department of Health, Education, and Welfare, 1968, p. 57.

Are Services Acceptable?—Services should be in keeping with neighborhood life styles. Perlman and Jones observed an "easy and friendly atmosphere" in the centers they visited,[36] and Kirschner Associates refer to the "modest size and relatively simple organization" of most of their sample centers. "There is every indication that people . . . found them warm and welcoming."[37]

Though most centers have the kind of casual and informal atmosphere that appeals to poor people, Kirschner Associates observed that in some cities, the very large centers have assumed an unattractive institutional quality.[38] Abt Associates found that in nine of the 13 programs they studied, core service facilities were inadequate due to cramped space and lack of privacy. Large meeting rooms within the center itself were not generally available but were provided by schools and churches; in any event, poor facilities apparently had not hindered program effectiveness.[39] Generally, the facilities available for neighborhood centers have been more or less adequate and relatively acceptable to residents.

As we have indicated, the presence in the program of workers from the neighborhood, people with whom the residents can readily identify, also makes the center more acceptable. In commenting on the phenomenon that a few residents came from considerable distances to the center, Perlman and Jones allude to psychological proximity. "Some find the centers less formidable than large, impersonal offices of agencies that may actually be closer to them; some Negroes or Puerto Ricans feel more at home in an agency where they find people of their own ethnic group on the staff."[40] In the Kirschner Associates study, the characteristics of both the people served and the center staffs were similar. In fact, the only differences between the two were that the residents had larger families and the staffs more education.[41] The characteristics of the nonprofessional staff members of the community action program reported in the Brandeis study were also similar.[42] To the extent that such similar characteristics contribute to the client's ability to identify with workers and feel more "at home," neighborhood centers seem to be acceptable to the people served.

[36]Perlman and Jones, p. 31.
[37]Kirschner Associates, p. 26.
[38]Perlman and Jones, p. 26.
[39]Abt Associates, Vol. 2, part 2, pp. 52, 110.
[40]Perlman and Jones, p. 30.
[41]Kirschner Associates, pp. 24, 27.
[42]Brandeis University, Report No. 5, pp. 74–75.

Are Services Comprehensive? — One sign of a comprehensive center is the variety of its programs and activities. The 54 centers in the
Brandeis study offered from four to 10 services. Half were locally
developed, direct services, 25 percent were "national emphasis" and
other programs, and the rest were neighborhood organization and
self-help activities.[43] The specific services most often provided
focused on health, recreation, counseling, employment, and education; the economic programs on buyers' clubs and tenant unions; and
the special projects on neighborhood clean-up campaigns and voter
registration drives. Four of every five centers promoted these programs and projects,[44] and most provided some combination. The
neighborhood service programs reported on by Abt Associates were
heavily weighed toward service. Few programs had developed community action to the point where neighborhoods were able to manage their own affairs and develop their own areas.[45] Among the
component programs of the neighborhood service programs, about 60
percent emphasized social service; some 35 percent "opportunity
enhancement;" and 10 percent community mobilization.[46]

Kirschner Associates found a very broad range of social services in their centers. Though programs in the smaller communities
and rural areas were more diversified, most provided several
different services. A highly specialized center was unusual.[47] The
method of providing service varied greatly — from information and
referral to on-the-spot service. "The bulk of their service functions
involve . . . traditional services . . . very few . . . are 'new inventions'."[48] What is novel is the neighborhood package of public
and private services.

In examining the extent to which center services approach comprehensiveness, the relative mix of services becomes crucial. Kirschner Associates' findings are relevant here: 60 percent of their centers
offered employment and welfare services *or* employment and health
services, and 40 percent linked four services together — education,
employment, welfare, and health.[49]

But the fact that centers offer a range of services does little to
insure their use. In fact, data from the Roxbury center raise serious

---

[43] Brandeis University, Report No. 4, p. 9.
[44] Brandeis University, Report No. 4, Appendix C.
[45] Abt Associates, Vol. 2, part 2, p. 22.
[46] Abt Associates, Vol. 2, part 2, p. 101.
[47] Kirschner Associates, p. 14.
[48] Kirschner Associates, p. 15.
[49] Kirschner Associates, p. 33.

questions about the comprehensiveness of service—from the client's view. The service outcome of a 15 percent sample of clients served in 1965 was as follows: of 92 cases presented at intake, 36 were referred to social service, 33 to employment, and 19 to the legal unit. The receptionist handled one case; the fate of three others is not clear. Of those referred fully 69 had contact with one unit only. Of the 23 recipients who had subsequent contact with another unit, 16 had direct contact with two and seven with three.[50] Thus, it appears that fewer than three of 10 clients were able to use more than one service. The Roxbury data seem consistent with those of the Kirschner Associates study, which found that clients are oriented to a single service and "often do not even know that it is a neighborhood service center as such."[51]

If the neighborhood center merely provides increased accessibility to selected services, it is possible that single-service agencies decentralized into a neighborhood center would accomplish the same purpose. At any rate, the case for comprehensive, one-stop service in the neighborhood center is less than persuasive. It is not enough for services to be accessible, even immediately available, if they cannot meet the different needs that people have. Moreover, they are only potentially comprehensive unless the different services can be effectively coordinated and made meaningful and usable.

Are Services Integrated?—Proximity of itself may facilitate but cannot insure coordinated services,[52] a point Perlman and Jones make about the presence of staff representatives of other agencies in neighborhood centers, holds for center staffs, too. Abt Associates note that, though core service activity was relatively successful in coordinating the movement of clients through the system of the neighborhood service programs, in four the core service unit was separate from other service units and that this separation contributed greatly to service fragmentation and lack of coordination.[53] Even where staff members are present together, problems of communication and coordination exist and are exacerbated when the center director has no effective administrative control over workers from other agencies. In eight of the 13 neighborhood service programs, the directors had no control over other agency workers.[54] When center workers are responsible to other agencies, problems in communication and

---

[50]Perlman and Jones, p. 34.
[51]Kirschner Associates, p. 45.
[52]Perlman and Jones, p. 37.
[53]Abt Associates, pp. 52–54.
[54]Abt Associates, p. 144.

effective service coordination are more likely to occur. But, just as physical proximity does not guarantee integrated services, neither does administrative control.

Perlman and Jones found that, in the Roxbury center, "barriers to interdisciplinary cooperation were serious within . . . core staff . . . under the same administration."[55] Such a problem is fairly widespread. The Kirschner Associates study suggests that linked services do not automatically insure coordination. They found little evidence of "carefully planned efforts to present well coordinated service programs. This is something often talked about but rarely achieved."[56] Abt Associates also found that the integration and coordination of services was a major problem.[57] Few formal coordinating mechanisms had been set up, and workers mostly relied on informal relations and communications.[58] Kirschner Associates found some successful "case" coordination, but at a cost of considerable time and effort.[59] Perlman and Jones note that "commitment to the goals of marshalling resources for the benefit of clients seems to be most crucial in these arrangements" and that such commitment must be shared by both agency and worker.[60] Though centers have devised some means for coordination — the rotation of intake, the anchor worker, the case conference, the central file system, the case coordinator — none of them have been wholly effective.

As pointed out, most center contacts are with one service only. Of the 23 cases provided with two or more services in the Roxbury sample, only four were the subject of a "review conference." The service coordinator was often pressed into providing direct service and could not spend enough time in interservice coordination.[61] Abt Associates found a similar situation.[62] The Roxbury center concentrated multiservice activity on proportionately few cases. In one month's period, 5 percent of the recipients had 30 percent of the contacts.[63] Thus, even when multiservice activity takes place, only a few recipients can be served. It is clear that neighborhood centers suffer from some of the traditional problems of specialization and fragmentation. Just as different agencies strive to maintain au-

---

[55]Perlman and Jones, p. 37.
[56]Kirschner Associates, p. 34.
[57]Abt Associates, Vol. 2, part 2, p. 40.
[58]Abt Associates, Vol. 2, part 2, p. 145.
[59]Kirschner Associates, p. 44.
[60]Perlman and Jones, p. 37.
[61]Perlman and Jones, p. 34.
[62]Abt Associates, Vol. 2, part 2, p. 90.
[63]Perlman and Jones, p. 40.

tonomy and independence, so do different center services. Organizational sovereignty and professional ideology both contribute to this condition, as does the need for organizational survival and professional status. "Each service tends to perceive problems in its own terms and is reluctant to 'surrender' its clients or share them with another service."[64] Because services are "different," they are likely to draw on different resources, use different people, perform different functions, and serve different needs in different groups of people.

In the Kirschner Associates centers, though education and employment services were linked in some 60 percent of the centers, there was no evidence of their coordination. "To the contrary, the two services deal with different clientele."[65]

The attempt to coordinate and rationalize services is at many levels: within the center's service units, between the center and participating agencies, and between the center and all other agencies serving the neighborhood. As one of their tasks, centers try to coordinate and improve community services. The Brandeis study found, in fact, that some 14 percent of their centers saw coordination as a primary objective — taking precedence over the provision of direct service, community organization, and case finding and referral.[66] Kirschner Associates found, however, little marked success in this regard.[67] Because few centers provide "new" services, they are left trying to use, coordinate, and improve traditional community services. The Abt Associates study reports that, at first, residents in many communities did not want to work with traditional agencies, which had neglected them for years, and were reluctant to share their few resources with the community.[68] The strain between neighborhood centers and community agencies is an obvious obstacle to effective coordination.

But still other functions of the center may also block the coordination of services: "Some centers concentrate on developing an informal atmosphere that is inviting to the poor people of the neighborhood. These centers are less concerned with service integration or refinements. Other centers encourage attitudes and organizational arrangements associated with aggressive community action and these

---

[64]Perlman and Jones, p. 34.
[65]Kirschner Associates, p. 34.
[66]Brandeis University, Report No. 4, p. 12.
[67]Kirschner Associates, p. 44.
[68]Abt Associates, Vol. 1, p. 14.

appear antithetical to close collaboration with traditional agencies."[69] Either stance militates against effective integration. Coordination of services remains an elusive objective, if not the major challenge.

Are Services Responsive? — One way to judge the responsiveness of centers to neighborhood needs is to look at the response of the residents to the centers. Such response has far exceeded expectations.[70] Moreover, the services provided seem to be more or less consistent with the problems. Abt Associates report that residents were generally consulted about their most pressing problems and that these problems were those the programs attempted to handle.[71] Though some centers have shifted programs to meet resident needs and demands, others have done so for want of funds and resources. In all neighborhood service programs, activity has been limited by lack of money, staff, and proficiency. They have not been fully responsive to resident needs for employment, job training, and housing. But, in general, they "have addressed themselves to the most salient needs of the community, where they had the resources to do so."[72]

Perlman and Jones report that their centers apparently served people who both racially and ethnically represented the neighborhood. Moreover, by and large, these centers attracted the kinds of people who could best be helped, given the kinds of service offered.[73]

Though few centers are set up for formal, systematic review and followup, recipients can take part in center programs and policymaking in several ways — principally through board, committee, staff, and volunteer work. Abt Associates found an overriding desire in residents for a larger voice in neighborhood service programs. But, of 13 programs, "only in five of the cities have the residents really had a voice in setting policy."[74] Here the staff positions open to neighborhood people promised rapid advancement and opportunity to effect key decisions; participation on boards, committees, and neighborhood corporations was rewarding and residents could influence program activities.[75] The opportunity for rewarding involvement in the other eight centers, however, apparently left much to be desired. As

---

[69]Kirschner Associates, p. 53.
[70]Perlman and Jones, p. 75.
[71]Abt Associates, Vol. 2, part 2, p. 22.
[72]Abt Associates, Vol. 2, part 2, pp. 76, 79.
[73]Perlman and Jones, p. 29.
[74]Abt Associates, Vol. 2, part 2, p. 126.
[75]Abt Associates, Vol. 2, part 2, p. 127.

we have seen, the evidence for effective resident participation on center boards and committees is hardly persuasive; the obstacles are many and hard to overcome; and, though there is reason for optimism about participation by neighborhood workers, the limits of their role circumscribe their contribution.

To the extent that the center's responsiveness is assessed by the opportunity neighborhood people have for shaping policies and programs, most centers could be much more "responsive." But to the extent that centers have moved at all to facilitate resident expression and to make programs accessible and acceptable, they have made a beginning.

But Are They Effective? — Assuming that services are accessible and acceptable — which they are — and assuming that they are responsive and comprehensive — which they may well be — and even assuming that they are immediately available and well integrated — which they are not — the question remains: Are they effective?

The evidence for the effectiveness of neighborhood centers is based at this point on gross impressions and guesswork. Until data are available on the ways in which centers help solve the problems people have or strengthen their capacity for dealing with them and until we learn whether and how centers improve the quality of neighborhood life and influence community agencies and institutions, there is really little to say. Nevertheless, we can review and summarize the prevailing impressions.

Abt Associates report that in most of the cities they studied, programs have been reasonably effective. In the few cities where they have not been, the neighborhood service program "has proved to be yet another program that promises many benefits and produces few results."[76]

In general these centers have provided an impressive array of services and, though quality varies greatly, service is now available, and all within a short time.[77] Specifically, eight of the neighborhood programs had improved neighborhood services and had begun to meet resident needs. They had introduced new resources and had begun to coordinate and integrate others. Traditional agencies had become more responsive and were modifying hiring policies to the advantage of poor people. These centers have gained the confidence of the people they serve and have demonstrated that neighborhood people can develop and operate their own programs.[78]

---

[76]Abt Associates, Vol. 2, part 2, p. 43.
[77]Abt Associates, Vol. 2, part 2, p. 6.
[78]Abt Associates, Vol. 2, part 2, p. 42.

Kirschner Associates interviewed some 189 clients and neighborhood residents. The responses of those interviewed to two questions
are especially pertinent in assessing how helpful the centers were.
When asked what the centers had done for them and their families,
three out of 10 said "nothing." Though 70 percent mentioned receiving one or another service, the fact that nearly a third of those
presumably served replied "nothing" rules out any great enthusiasm
for the centers.[79] Yet a question tapping whether residents felt better
off because of the center yielded less equivocal findings. Some 60
percent of the respondents in medium-sized and large cities and
fully 95 percent in small towns and rural areas felt "much better off"
because of the centers.[80] These centers were mostly service oriented
and were, by virtue of their small size, less forbidding than large,
bureaucratic urban organizations.[81]

In summing up, Kirschner Associates say that neighborhood centers have undoubtedly contributed to change: several public and
private agencies have become more flexible and have modified practices to make them more relevant; political institutions have become
more alert and, in some instances, more sensitive. But economic
institutions and the neighborhood environment appear to be little
affected. The poor people employed by the centers appear to have
changed the most, and many seem to have acquired confidence and a
sense of having made worthwhile contributions. Some board members share this enthusiasm, but others are disillusioned. Of the persons served in general, they note "that most have not yet been
reached in a meaningful way at all; that some have become clients
for services and perceive the centers as givers of services and themselves as recipients of services; and that a still smaller number
regard themselves as active members of society with the right and
ability to influence it. To the extent that these feelings represent
shifts from apathetic, helpless attitudes they are significant and appear to relate to some involvement with the center."[82]

Perlman and Jones found that neighborhood centers were able to
identify pressing needs and were moving toward meeting them.
They also observed that centers were instrumental in stimulating
traditional service agencies to change and had found rather creative
ways to make full use of their scarce resources.[83] Given their relative

---

[79]Kirschner Associates, p. 25.
[80]Kirschner Associates, Appendix V, table 7.
[81]Kirschner Associates, p. 26.
[82]Kirschner Associates, p. 50.
[83]Perlman and Jones, p. 78.

youthfulness and the many constraints under which they function, even small successes are impressive.

SOCIAL ACTION

Neighborhood service centers always include a service component—it is their reason for being. However, the "package deal" offered may or may not include a social action component. Implicit in describing social action efforts in centers are these questions: What type of social action can be promoted? and What is its relative weight in the program? Data from the Brandeis study indicate that, though community organization projects absorbed only about 25 percent of the center's activities, 43 percent of the centers saw the organization of residents as their primary objective.[84]

Social action is difficult to define; its methods may run from complete cooperation with other groups to all-out conflict. "Social action . . . means and demands the stimulation of concern among individuals who share a common predicament; who are victims of long standing community problems and injustices, who can be induced not only to identify their problems but to seek to determine the methods by which they can be resolved, and who are able to develop and sustain the initiative for the type of collective action, which, in fact, does resolve or ameliorate these problems."[85]

Perlman and Jones explicate four goals for social action: delivering social services more effectively; fostering concrete self-help efforts; providing for the poor the social and psychological benefits of taking part in organizational life; and changing policies and practices among relevant agencies and institutions.[86]

The Kirschner Associates study found no clear evidence of the effectiveness of social action. Attempts were made to develop new service programs and activities such as tutoring programs, day-care centers, thrift shops, and recreation programs. And half of their centers had conducted cleanup campaigns, but these were invariably started by community action officials. "This type of community action is not a spontaneous thing for poverty area residents. Rather it is a middle-class concern . . ."[87]

Clark suggests "that the threshold of tolerability for significant

---

[84]Brandeis University, Report No. 4, p. 12.
[85]HARYOU-ACT, quoted in Perlman and Jones, p. 53.
[86]Perlman and Jones, pp. 49–51.
[87]Kirschner Associates, p. 17.

changes in the predicament of the poor is rather low for politicians and may be somewhat higher but not particularly high for middle-class professionals and even those staff members who are charged with the responsibility for directing community action and other programs in behalf of the poor . . . This . . . tends to result either in the maintenance of the status quo or in the restriction of community action programs to techniques and methods acceptable to the middle class, thereby limiting the rate or the amount of change permitted the poor."[88]

The problems inherent in the development of citizen organizations are how to stimulate and how to sustain interest. Research shows that poor people are physical, visual, problem-centered, and action-oriented rather than verbal. Committee meetings, written reports, and abstract discussions may not accomplish specific goals.[89]

Perlman and Jones say: "Neighborhood groups find it difficult to move from a situation of shared individual interests to a common concern for larger social issues."[90] Bread-and-butter issues are necessary. Unless there are immediate rewards, rank-and-file participants quickly lose interest.

Abt Associates found less resident interest in community mobilization than in some of the more concrete social services; and few of their centers tried to foster community organization.[91]

Organizing for more effective delivery of social services and stimulating self-help are directed toward amelioration and not change. For this reason, residents may see such goals as demeaning and palliative and as "put-offs." Nevertheless, they can offer invaluable educational benefits and a point of departure for residents.

Another rationale for social action is the social and psychological benefits derived from participating in organizational life. Ideally, participation in collective social action may "reduce alienation and anomie; provide opportunities for self-fulfillment; overcome feelings of powerlessness; improve the individual and group self-image of those who participate; and generally increase community integration and control."[92] But we have little evidence to suggest that it does all or any of these. [93]

---

[88]Clark, p. 15.

[89]Catherine S. Chilman, *Growing Up Poor*, Welfare Administration Publication No. 13, U.S. Department of Health, Education, and Welfare, May, 1966.

[90]Perlman and Jones, p. 51.

[91]Abt Associates, p. 91.

[92]Perlman and Jones, p. 51.

[93]For a recent attempt to measure changes in participants, see Louis A. Zurcher, Jr.,

Institutional change is usually only a small aspect of a center's program. We have little data on the success of efforts in this direction. Wharf's recent study of the Roxbury Multi-Service Center found that the center had minimal effect on its "target agencies" and could not achieve significant organizational change.[94] This objective is sometimes directed at other than service institutions and is often put into operation with conflict-oriented social action methods. Here, the keys are money and power; the kinds of technique range from non-violent protest marches and economic boycott of merchants and public transportation to more violent demonstrations such as "sit-ins," work stoppages, and riots. Explicit goals are usually "against" rather than "for" something—mobilizing voter registration to defeat a racist candidate, for instance.

Perlman and Jones identify two central issues in promoting social action:

• The centers cannot create and hope to control autonomous and independent groups.
• The groups may threaten the sponsor or other relevant reference groups in the community.[95]

Such problems inhibit the widespread development of neighborhood and community action efforts.

Is it any wonder that few if any neighborhood service centers engage in conflict-oriented social action? Hallman says: "Except for a very small number of communities, the Community Action Program does not involve a predominant commitment to the strategy of giving power to the poor, of deliberate confrontation with established power, of purposefully created conflict."[96]

Similarly, Kirschner Associates found conflict-oriented social action against the political power structure in few of the rural centers and in only about 25 percent of the urban centers partly because of the relationship to the sponsor.[97] Marris and Rein, in commenting on

"Social-Psychological Changes among OEO Indigenous Leaders as a Result of 'Maximum Feasible Participation,'" paper presented to the Society for the Study of Social Problems, American Sociological Association Meetings, Boston, Aug. 25, 1968.

[94]Brian W.H. Wharf, "Boundary Personnel: An Exploratory Study of Their Role Responsibilities in the Interorganizational Relationships of a Multi-Service Center," unpublished doctoral dissertation, Brandeis University, June 1969.

[95]Perlman and Jones, p. 61.

[96]Hallman, p. 900.

[97]Kirschner Associates, p. 97.

this dilemma, say: "If the sponsors cannot disdain responsibility for the organization they create, and if . . . they defeat their own purpose in seeking to control it, only a sponsor free from other commitments can afford to support his organization in whatever course it chooses . . . It is not unlikely that participants who are encouraged to take action . . . may challenge the sponsor's basis of allocating resources; and the 'citizens' organization may want to utilize tactics and develop strategies which the sponsor may find incompatible with its own principles."[98]

Realize, though, that the question of what type of social action to be implemented is not merely a this-or-that position; even highly cooperative community development efforts can have undesirable consequences for the center. Clearly, however, conflict-oriented social action methods are not usually followed under the guise of the neighborhood service center, and collaborative and cooperative efforts for change only operate successfully within a defined sphere of influence. Cohen suggests: "I think of these service type operations as a range within which there can be certain levels of social action, but I don't think it is a mechanism through which we can get at the larger question."[99]

Thus, the social action component in the neighborhood service center tends to be a self-help, community development effort based on cooperation and collaboration and the use of mild protest and peaceful demonstration only in certain circumscribed situations to obtain immediate and concrete goals.

SERVICES OR ACTION?

What exactly is at issue in weighing social services against social action?

Rainwater says: "In the services business it is easy to forget about . . . the things that people need and want that aren't provided by services. . . . The minute you adopt a service strategy . . . for dealing with the problem of poverty . . . you're setting priorities for the families involved. . . . Poor people would rather make these decisions themselves."[100] Social service and social action programs often

---

[98]Peter Marris and Martin Rein, *Dilemmas of Social Reform* (New York: Atherton Press, 1967), p. 168.

[99]Nathan E. Cohen, "Building a Social Movement Among the Poor," (discussion) in John B. Turner (ed.), *Neighborhood Organization for Community Action*, National Association of Social Workers, New York, 1968, p. 71.

[100]Lee Rainwater, "Neighborhood Action and Lower-class Life-styles" (discussion) in Turner, p. 72.

aim at different goals: the first at having "the professional" decide what the poor person needs and administering the right measure; the second at giving the poor enough power and leverage to decide and to act to get what they want and need.

Overlying both goals are the organizational problems raised by a neighborhood service center. The limitation of resources, both of staff time and program funds, almost intrinsically demands a choice of service or action as the major program goal. All too often "agencies try to cover too much ground; . . . they are good neither in service nor in . . . social action."[101]

Perlman and Jones found that in five programs they studied, three deemphasized social services and stressed community organization. The others continued to emphasize services but had to cut back programs by either stretching resources or providing special services or closing intake at several points until the caseload became manageable.[102]

Grosser, in a study of community organization in six youth programs, found that "social action and service components may exist either as part of a comprehensive project, or more desirably, as separate cooperative entities. The separation of the services and action functions into discrete organizations is suggested because the two functions are frequently in disharmony . . . and because the dispensers of public agency services are congenitally and organizationally unable to distinguish between the protest and service function when practiced by the same organization."[103]

Findings from the Brandeis study further suggest "that it is not possible to give equal attention to both of the objectives . . . in a single unit and that most frequently service delivery requirements take precedence over . . . action."[104] Kirschner Associates make a similar point: "The evidence indicates that it is extremely rare to find both aggressive community action and well executed service programs within the same center."[105]

Perlman and Jones further suggest that the form of the services-action relationship in a center depends both on the activities involved in each and on what the community is willing to accept.[106] To ease tension between the two, they suggest that a center become

---

[101]Cohen in Turner, p. 71.
[102]Perlman and Jones, p. 40.
[103]Grosser, p. 58.
[104]Brandeis University, Report No. 4, p. 5.
[105]Kirschner Associates, p. 22.
[106]Perlman and Jones, p. 72.

primarily an instrument of social action, that its services act only to attract participants and to help them with their problems.

The Kirschner Associates study supports the method of attracting the poor to the center with the offer of services. They found that "the idea of community action in which the poor organize to deal with their problems themselves is not very prominent in their thoughts about the neighborhood centers. The poor, however, do understand the idea of services."[107]

Combining services and action in one center, as we have seen, is not without its problems, however, because of the difficulty of coordinating center programs and those of other community agencies. The autonomy of the center, its interest in community action, and the participation of residents are, as noted, key influences contributing to lack of service coordination between the neighborhood center and the "downtown" agency.

Hallman reminds us, however, that the "variation found among the communities does not reflect a choice between services and citizen organization. Those who follow the most activist approach to resident participation also provide services, and many but not all of those with effective service programs pursue certain forms of resident participation. The crucial difference is the approach to institutional change and to planning coordination."[108]

Although Hallman is undoubtedly correct in suggesting that a broad overlap exists between services and action and in specifying that the choice in the world of the neighborhood service center is usually one of method rather than policy, nevertheless, methods do ultimately contribute to program emphasis and action.

Thus, the durable services-action issue is one that each center must inevitably confront.

ISSUES WITHOUT ANSWERS

In this section we will attempt to indicate some of the more salient issues to be confronted — if not completely resolved. The main issues revolve around questions of organizational sponsorship; the specification of goals; the kinds of interventions developed; the types of workers employed; and the implications of any or all of these for the

---

[107]Kirschner Associates, p. 25.
[108]Hallman, p. 900.

survival and success of the neighborhood center. Though some of these questions can be cast as either-or-dilemmas, it is not necessary that one preclude the other. In fact, both will be present in some form; it is a question of relative emphasis and of possible trade-offs between the two. These options are, of course, unduly simplified, even arbitrary, not necessarily contradictory, certainly not exhaustive, and in many ways artificial.

A center may emphasize professional direction and administration *or* resident participation and neighborhood control. If *administration,* programs and services may be run more smoothly and efficiently—but may not be entirely relevant to the needs and desires of residents; if *participation,* the center may be more responsive to neighborhood wants—but lack the administrative sophistication and organizational skill to operate effective programs.

A center may emphasize the provision of service *or* social action. If *service,* individual needs may be better satisfied—but some of the larger community issues may be neglected; if *action,* collective needs may be fully addressed—but the particular problems that people have may not be solved.

A center may emphasize special functions *or* general activities. If *special,* unusual and particular functions may be carried out with dispatch—but the effective integration of activities will be weak; if *general,* the center may be better coordinated—but no one aspect will receive the kind of attention required to make a real contribution.

A center may emphasize professional service *or* nonprofessional services. If *professional,* a relatively few clients may be competently served—but many potential clients may not be reached; if *nonprofessional,* many more neighborhood residents will be attracted to the center—but deeply personal problems will not be presented and complicated problems may not be adequately handled.

A center may emphasize information and referral *or* client advocacy and followup. If *information,* existing agencies may become more widely known and used—but questions of service modification and agency practice will not be sufficiently dealt with; if *advocacy,* traditional services may be challenged and different patterns of relationships hammered out—but fewer clients may be actually served and other problems may be created in the process.

A center may emphasize collaborative and cooperative methods *or* contest and conflict tactics. If *cooperative,* the good will and resources of other agencies and institutions may be more readily available—but the center may become preoccupied with the process to the neglect of hard results; if *conflict,* the center may be able to force some issues and achieve some action — but may have to go it alone and run the risk of diminishing resources and community support.

A center may emphasize neighborhood development and resident self-help *or* community change and political action. If *development,* residents may gain a sense of satisfaction, pride, and confidence — but the broader institutions that impinge on the neighborhood may remain untouched; if *change,* important political issues may be confronted — but the immediate effect on the neighborhood and its residents may be less than obvious.

A center may emphasize the problems and prospects of one particular group or institution *or* many different groups or institutions. If *one,* the group or institution may become better known and more surely helped or influenced — but others may remain unaffected if not disaffected by the center's work; if *many,* a number of different groups or institutions may be touched but perhaps no one in particular will become sufficiently well identified and changed by the center.

Again, these alternatives are not so much choices to be made as they are chances to be taken and risks to be run. In practice, both may be pursued simultaneously; indeed, the pursuit of one may lead to the other. But, at some point, the fact that they often require different resources, point in different directions, and have different costs and consequences may mean, to the extent these alternatives are attempted in the same center, that one or the other emphasis will eventually be given primacy.

In describing the experience of one of the early neighborhood service centers sponsored by Mobilization for Youth, Cloward and Elman sum up their impression this way: "The storefront on Stanton Street has been in existence a little less than four years and its work has increased tenfold. . . . It is still too early to evaluate its permanent contributions to life in the community. Its powers have been limited. It has not yet been able to change substantially the terms of economic dependency when it still seems to be the consensus among most legislators and their constituents that such dependency is to be discouraged, abhorred, and punished. Many more people from Stanton street are on welfare than before. The storefront's clients are better clothed, better housed, and better fed than they were four years ago. Many now have telephones, quite a few have washing machines and television sets. Are they better people? Are they worse? Such questions seem like the supreme irrelevancy. For if they are not better for their improved economic circumstances, the society is better for their actions against it." [109] And so it is.

This is the bottom line: the extent to which we help people is the ultimate test. We must ask—as a result of the center—are people better off? And we must, sooner or later, be able to answer—yes—or stand to abandon the idea.

[109]Richard A. Cloward and Richard M. Elman, "Advocacy in the Ghetto," *Trans-action*, Dec., 1966, p. 109.

· 29 ·

DONALD A. SCHON

The Blindness System

THE MISMATCH OF SERVICES AND CLIENTS

There has been, since the turn of the century, a significant change in the makeup of those people identified as blind. In the period between 1900 and the 1930's, the blind were identified primarily as children and adults of working age. The dominant causes of blindness were war, industrial accident, and disease, and the blind were likely to have only the single handicap of blindness. During the 1930's, federal and state aid to the blind came into being on a significant scale, carried along on the wave of New Deal social legislation. This period of change saw the establishment of certain major programs for the blind. *The sheltered workshop*, publicly or privately supported, trained blind adults for occupations thought to be particularly appropriate to the blind—piano tuner, for example, or broom maker, or vending stand operator. *The school for the blind* provided separate track, physically segregated education for the blind child. And in the early 1940's, state *vocational legislation*

SOURCE: Reprinted from *The Public Interest*, No. 18 (Winter, 1970), pp. 29–33.

promoted rehabilitation for adults of working age. All such programs treated fitness for work and economic independence through employment as the central tests of rehabilitation.

Today, the makeup of the blind has changed. The population of the severely visually impaired in the United States is now heavily weighted toward (1) the aged blind; (2) the multiple-handicapped, especially among children; (3) the poor ethnic minorities, especially the low-skilled; (4) those with significant residual vision. All sources indicate that a high percentage of the blind are persons over 65, although the estimates vary from 40 per cent (MRA) to 65 per cent (NHS, which uses a broader, functional definition of blindness). The dominant causes of blindness today are senile degeneration, diabetes, and other multiple etiologies characteristic of old age and, among children, genetic and prenatal influences which tend to be associated with other disabilities in addition to blindness. The overall pattern, both for the aged and for children, is one of multiple disability. Projections of the prevalence of blindness and the makeup of the blind to 1970 and 1985 suggest that, with the increase in the numbers of persons over 65, these trends will continue.

These developments mean that, for an increasing majority of the blind, economic employment is an unrealistic goal. *Nevertheless, agencies for the blind continue to behave as though this shift in the blind population had not taken place.* In the selection of clients and the provision of services, their programs are oriented to work or to education leading to work. They measure the success of their services in terms of their clients' achievement of some measure of economic independence. Only a small number of significant exceptions to this general pattern exist within the blindness system.

At the time of its inception, each of these work-oriented programs represented a significant innovation in what was considered humane treatment for the blind. Yet each has tended to become established and frozen in place as an aspect of the way services to the blind "must" operate. Thus, the blindness system today is an array of agencies and services dating from different periods, based on different assumptions concerning the character of the blind population, pursuing different goals, and using different technologies. The effect is rather like complex geological strata in which substances of widely varying origins and characters exist side by side.

The result is that the official blindness system provides services to only a relatively small fraction of those who are actually blind and eligible for assistance. Since the services offered are largely education, rehabilitation, and care, *only about 20 per cent of the total blind population are actually being served today.* In general, these 20 per cent are either children with the single handicap of blindness or adults of working age and potential for employment. The 80 per cent who receive no services tend to be those without apparent potential for employment or educational advancement: the aged, the multiple-handicapped, the poor, and the low-skilled. Such persons are shunted off to other systems which provide minimal income-maintenance or custodial care, or are ignored. A substantial portion of the 80 per cent may receive some form of support from the informal system of family, friends, and community.[1]

Why have the design and mix of official services been so unresponsive to changes in the needs and capacities of the blind? The answer is that, for good bureaucratic reasons, agencies tend to behave as if they believed that the blind need, or should have, *the services which happen to be offered by the agencies* rather than that agencies should modify services in response to changing characteristics of the blind population. This is true both of the kinds of services offered and of the methods or techniques by which such services are delivered. To be sure, there are exceptions. But in the case of services designed specifically for the "newer" categories of the blind, the exceptions do not exceed three agencies in each category. And even in the case of services designed for more traditional categories of the blind—mobility training, comprehensive rehabilitation, or training in the use of low vision aids—only a few agencies have shown themselves to be innovative in any significant degree. Taken together, these exceptional, change-oriented agencies constitute only a tiny fraction of the entire official blindness system. The overwhelming pattern remains firmly based on the assumption that "the blind" are employable adults, children with the single handicap of blindness, and the totally blind. The shifting population of the blind has falsified that assumption, yet the pattern of programs remains.

STRATEGIES, CONSTRAINTS

Why does this blindness system behave in such a fashion? One important factor is to be found in the purposes of the organizations and individuals who serve the blind. Now, because the system is in

---

[1]See the study conducted by the Bureau of Labor Statistics for the American Foundation for the Blind, "National Survey of Personnel Standards and Personnel Practices and Services for the Blind—1955."

reality a *non*system, there is no group or institution capable of setting a common objective for all elements of the blindness system. Nevertheless, it is clear from the statements of participants and observers that there are three main objectives which enjoy widespread currency, in practice or in rhetoric, within the blindness system:

1. Minimize the cost to the blindness system of providing services to the blind. This is the principle of "least cost to the system itself."
2. Minimize the cost to the nation of providing services.
3. Optimize human functioning for the blind. This objective, frequently voiced by professionals within the system, focuses on what services may enable the blind to *do* or *become*, rather than the economic criteria of performance.

Each of these objectives implies a different strategy for allocating resources and defining configurations of service and coverage.

Least Cost to the Blindness System. — If it were to operate under this principle alone, the blindness system would provide services only to those blind people who are likely to be able to enter the labor force. This way, the system encounters only those who can be trained to leave the blindness system quickly, thereby maximizing turnover rates and minimizing the cost to the blindness system. Hence, the system would select children with the single handicap of blindness and adults of working age and would provide them with education and instrumental and vocational services. The others — multiple handicapped children, adults over 44, etc. — it would either shunt off to other systems or provide with minimal care or maintenance.

Least Cost to the Nation. — Under this principle, the system would operate much as it does under the first principle. The main difference is that, under this second objective, it would be far less selective in providing educational, instrumental, or vocational services. The cumulative costs of income maintenance or custodial care are so great that it is cost-effective to give job-oriented services to all individuals for whom there is *any* finite chance that they will be able to leave the system. The first objective, which does not require the blindness system to bear the costs of long-term maintenance or support of those blind who are unable to work, provides the system with no incentive to behave this way.

Here, the analysis touches on a peculiar and interesting feature of the blindness system. *Those who must decide whether or not to*

*provide services to an individual are institutionally separated from
those who stand the cost and trouble of long-term maintenance and
care.* The current system's fragmentation removes the incentive to
provide services so as to avoid later maintenance and care.

Optimize Human Functioning. — This objective implies that, even
if there is no possibility of his gaining economic independence, it is
worth devoting resources to a blind person in order to make him
function somewhat more independently. This means, in other words,
that an additional benefit — personal independence — counts in
offsetting costs incurred in the system. The consequence of such an
objective, of course, is to increase the cost of operating the system. In
1966, for example, an additional $1 billion (on a base of about $446
million) would have been needed for a blindness system which
attempted to maximize human functioning. A very large portion of
that increase would have gone for services to the aged.[2]

In terms of these three models, the current blindness system is a
hybrid. With respect to the way in which it determines what categories of the blind shall receive services, it functions according to
the principle of the least cost to the system itself. Those blind
without high potential for gainful employment are either ignored or
shunted off to other systems (such as welfare, veterans' care, etc.).
But with respect to those whom it *does* select training or care, the
blindness system tends to behave as if its purpose were to optimize
their human functioning. Its expenditures on the blind it chooses to
encounter are high.

---

[2]Although the money costs of this third system are important, the problem of
manpower resources constitutes an even more powerful constraint.

30

DONALD BRIELAND

Black Identity and the Helping Person

The growing emphasis in this country on "black identity" raises many important questions for agencies in the fields of health, education, and welfare. The large demand in the inner city areas for maternal and child health services and for public assistance under the program of aid to families with dependent children makes the following questions of special interest to agencies serving mothers and children. Do residents of black inner city neighborhoods consider competence more important than race in the provision of services? Are white members of service staffs still welcome in black neighborhoods? Is the preference in these neighborhoods for black service-givers great enough that white persons ultimately will not be accepted? If so, would public agencies be able to comply with the Civil Rights Act? These questions are of interest not only to service agencies but also to professional schools, since their students – black and white – often serve as interns in the inner city.

In their discussions of these questions, white professional persons and black community leaders often express widely differing views that are rarely reported in print. Except for the results of a small study conducted in Cleveland, Ohio, virtually no data exist on attitudes of black persons seeking or receiving service.[1]

The University of Chicago School of Social Service Administration, with support from the Children's Bureau, in 1968 conducted a feasibility study of the operations of a social services center. One part concerned the preferences of the residents of a black neighborhood in Chicago regarding the race and competence of persons providing them with services. The rationale was that agencies plan-

SOURCE: Reprinted from *Children*, Vol. 16, No. 5 (September-October, 1969), pp. 170–75.

[1]Eight social work students assisted in the design, data gathering, and analysis of the study reported here – Merle Becker, Robert Grimm, James Kallmyer, Bernard Hannon, Vivian Loseth, Mary McDavitt, Ruth Chitlik, and Patricia Steiner. Esther Silverman supervised the data analysis.

ning or providing services need to be aware of the attitudes of the people they intend to serve.

The opinions in the neighborhood under study may or may not be typical of other neighborhoods and probably vary from time to time. Also, in any opinion research, expressed opinions may not always be valid indicators of actual opinions or future conduct. Respondents may tell the interviewer what they think he wants to hear. Those who say they will not accept service from a white person may or may not actually refuse to be served by a white person, depending upon the strength of their conviction and the intensity of their need for service. The School of Social Service Administration has plans to repeat the study in at least one other neighborhood, and perhaps more, with different kinds of civil rights activities and interracial services. Its method may also be useful for similar studies in other cities.

METHOD AND SAMPLE

Thirty-eight items were developed as a questionnaire to be administered in a 10-minute interview with each participant. Six items had to do with identifying data such as place of birth, age, sex, and length of residence; 32 items were concerned with the participants' experience with services and their attitudes toward the race of the persons giving them.

The study was conducted in the Woodlawn area of Chicago's South Side, a neighborhood inhabited by persons of low income, 98 percent of whom are black. The sample included 380 black persons—85 men and 295 women. All participants were seeking or receiving service from at least one Woodlawn social or health agency.

The participants were told that questions were being asked of Woodlawn residents so that "more effective services could be developed for a new center being planned." Each person was assured that participation was completely voluntary and that he did not have to give his name. Less than 5 percent of the persons approached refused to participate.

The participants were selected at random from persons waiting to see staff members in two public aid offices, an Urban Progress Center supported by the Office of Economic Opportunity, a maternal and child health station, and a legal aid office. More women were available than men, since the agencies operated during hours when men are usually at work. The number of interviews in each of the locations ranged from 52 at the legal aid clinic to 109 at the Urban Progress Center.

The sample was composed predominantly of younger adults: 304, or 80 percent, were under 40 — 170 were between 20 and 29, 88 were between 30 and 39, and 46 were under 20.

About 60 percent of the persons interviewed were born in the South and 35 percent in Illinois. Their length of residence in Chicago varied widely. Thirteen percent had been in Chicago fewer than 5 years, but 17 percent had been in the city 30 years or more. Eighteen percent had lived in the Woodlawn neighborhood less than a year, but 59 percent had lived there from 1 to 9 years.

Because race of the interviewers could be an important variable in the study, both black and white interviewers were used and a large enough sample of respondents were included to make a valid comparison of their findings. Black interviewers conducted 291 interviews and white interviewers, 89. Data gathered by black interviewers and white interviewers on questions involving attitudes were analyzed separately and compared.

Another variable might be the participant's racial self-referent—the term he uses to designate his race. Therefore, the participant was asked which term he preferred—"black," "Negro," or "colored." The term selected was used by the interviewer in asking all subsequent questions that required the participant to choose between one race or the other. The point was to discover not only the popularity of the newer term "black," but also whether persons choosing "black" had different preferences than others in regard to service-givers.

ISSUES AND FINDINGS

Self-Referent.—In response to the question "Which term do you prefer?" 53 percent said "Negro," 24 percent "black," 19 percent "colored," and the rest "no preference." Preferences were not significantly associated with the race of the interviewer or the ages of the participants. Also, those who preferred the term "black" did not have a stronger preference than others for being served by black persons.

Service Experience.—Questions were included regarding the participant's actual experience with five types of helping persons—physicians (referred to as "doctors"), caseworkers, teachers, lawyers, and leaders of parents' child-care discussion groups. Very few of the respondents had had experience with more than three of the five kinds of service-givers, but nearly all had had experience with more than one type.

Doctors. — Half the persons interviewed did not have a private physician. The rest had received some service for their families in medical clinics where there was no choice of doctor at the outset, though some clinics tried to have the patient see the same doctor for a series of visits. Twenty-two percent of those interviewed had private physicians who were black and 22 percent had private physicians who were white. Four percent said their families were served by private physicians of both races. Two percent said they were served by private physicians but did not indicate race.

Caseworkers. — Fifty-three percent had never been served by a social caseworker. Twenty-four percent had been served by a black caseworker and 19 percent by a white caseworker. One percent had been served by both black and white caseworkers and three percent did not indicate race. About one-sixth of the sample had received casework service for less than 6 months. The same proportion had received it for more than 2 years. Among the latter group, turnover of caseworkers was often mentioned as a problem. The participants' interpretation of social casework clearly included service from public assistance workers.

Lawyers. — Sixty-seven percent had had no legal service in the last 5 years. Ten percent had had a black lawyer and 21 percent a white lawyer. Lawyers of both races had been used by 2 percent. These percentages included both lawyers in private practice and lawyers provided by legal aid service.

Teachers. — Forty-six percent had no children in school at the time of the study. The children of 11 percent of the total sample had been served only by black teachers and 3 percent only by white teachers. Thirty-five percent had had teachers of both races. Two percent did not indicate race and 3 percent did not know.

Parent Group Leaders. — Sixty-eight percent of the persons interviewed had not attended any parent groups — a smaller percentage than the study planners had expected. Ten percent had participated in such group discussions with a black leader, 2 percent with a white leader, and 20 percent with leaders of both races.

The data on experience with service suggest that the participants' actual contact with service personnel of the two races differed considerably from one type of service to another. As many had been served by white as by black private physicians. Experience with both races was most common in the case of teachers. Only one-third of the participants had had any experience with lawyers, but among those who had, the lawyers usually had been white.

Service Persons Preferred. — The interviewers asked the following question in referring to each of the five types of service-givers: "If both were equally good, would you prefer that they be Negro (black, colored) or white?" All but 2 percent of the persons interviewed responded to this question, but there was a greater tendency to hesitate in answering among the participants who had white interviewers. Table 30–1 presents the results.

TABLE 30–1

Race Preference for Service-Givers

(percentage distribution)

Preference	Doctor		Caseworker		Teacher		Lawyer		Parent group leader	
	WI	BI	WI	BI	WI	BI	WI	BI	WI	BI
Black	18	66	17	55	13	55	15	51	27	64
White	8	11	25	24	8	10	16	26	7	5
No preference	74	23	58	21	79	35	69	23	66	31

WI = White Interviewer
BI = Black Interviewer

Responses to white interviewers piled up in the "no preference" category. Respondents having black interviewers showed a preference for being served by black persons from 2 to 4 times as great as those who had white interviewers, the size of the difference depending upon the type of service under consideration. For each of the helping professions, the odds are less than one in 1,000 that the differences between responses to white and black interviewers would occur by chance.

The strongest preference was expressed for black physicians and the least for black lawyers. However, a majority still favored black lawyers. The highest percentage of "no preference" was for teachers.

The participants were then asked why they preferred to be served by persons of the race they designated. Data on reasons for preferences must be interpreted carefully. Asking a person why he expresses a certain preference stimulates responses without indicating their intensity or validity. Some people state reasons that reflect their basic values, but others come up with superficial answers just to have something to say. With a wide range of responses, there also is difficulty in categorization.

Three general classifications were developed in analyzing the findings: racial identification; emphasis on understanding personal problems; and technical competence. The rest of the responses constitutes a miscellaneous group, since they could not be coded. Obviously, the latter two place no primary emphasis on race. In the case of racial identification, the subject wanted to be with members of his race, liked black people better, felt more at ease with them, or wanted them to provide the service because he believed in patronizing members of his own race. The second classification stressed the need for someone who had had similar experiences to the participants and therefore understood him. The third referred to the skill of the service-giver.

TABLE 30–2

Major Reasons for Race Preference for Service-Givers

(percentage distribution)

Service personnel	Racial identification	Understanding of problems	Competence	Miscellaneous
Doctor	34	13	27	26
Caseworker	18	32	21	29
Teacher	16	20	31	33
Lawyer	21	14	24	41
Parent group leader	16	32	23	29

Findings differed for the various helping roles as can be seen in Table 30–2. Although the questions asked preferences as to race among service-givers who were equally skillful, competence was still a major element in the statement of reasons for preference.

Importance of Qualifications. — Those who preferred to be served by black persons were then asked for each type of service, "Would it make a difference in your choice if a white person were better qualified?" Competence proved to be more important to the respondents than race, regardless of the race of the interviewer, as can be seen in Table 30–3.

In all categories except parent group leader, over 90 percent of the respondents interviewed by white persons said that qualifications would make a difference in their choice. In responses to black interviewers, the range was from 63 to 88 percent in favor of competence. Only about 10 percent of the total sample made the choice in terms of race in spite of qualifications, except in regard to parent group leaders. For that category, the percentage still preferring to be served by their own race was doubled, but, nevertheless, was only 20 percent.

TABLE 30–3

Persons Preferring Service from Blacks for Whom Qualifications Would Alter Choice

(percentage distribution)

Qualifications alter choice	Doctor		Caseworker		Teacher		Lawyer		Parent group leader	
	WI	BI	WI	BI	WI	BI	WI	BI	WI	BI
Yes	94	83	93	74	100	69	92	76	70	63
No	6	17	7	26	0	31	8	24	30	37

WI = White Interviewer
BI = Black Interviewer

Acceptance of Service. — Another series of questions on the race of service-givers was asked only of persons who said they preferred to receive service from members of their own race: "Would you accept service from a white person?" Only 30 persons or 8 percent of the total sample said "No." Two persons said they would not accept service from a white person in any of the five professional roles, three rejected whites in four roles, one in three, six in two, and 18 in one. Rejection was greatest for white parent group leaders, with 25 persons answering "no" in their regard, and least for white case-workers and physicians, with only six and five persons respectively answering "no." Eleven persons said they would reject white teachers; only eight would reject white lawyers.

The questions on preference were analyzed to discern the attitudes of the 58 subjects who had had more than 2 years of social casework service. Twelve had been interviewed by white interviewers and 46 by black interviewers. The effort was to learn whether a relatively long experience with a helping service made any difference in the respondents' preferences concerning the race of the serving person. The responses to the black interviewers showed that among persons who had had 2 or more years of casework service, 41 percent preferred having a white caseworker; 33 percent, a black caseworker; and 26 percent had no preference. And among the 149 respondents who had had less than 2 years of casework service or none at all, 59 percent said they would prefer a black caseworker; 21 percent, a white caseworker; and 20 percent had no preference. The number of persons interviewed by white interviewers was too small for such a comparison.

Thus, 2 years or more of casework service is associated with a significantly smaller preference for black caseworkers, but this is true only of such longterm service. Dividing the rest of the sample into persons who had some casework service, but less than 2 years, and those who had none showed no differences in preferences. The study did not obtain data for a similar analysis of the other professions.

Characteristics of Helping People. — The respondents were asked several questions concerning their opinions of the characteristics of service-givers.

"Even though there may be only a slight difference between them —

"Who understands better what it means to be poor, Negro (or other preferred term) or white?"

"Who expects people to feel more grateful to them?"

"Who gives people more of a feeling of hope?"

"Who makes people they help feel that they don't amount to very much?"

"Who talks down to people?"

"Who is more interested in your problems?"

The results are summarized in Table 30–4.

In each case, the majority chose black persons for the more favorable answer. Although this choice was more common for the group interviewed by black interviewers, the differences in responses according to the race of the interviewer were not statistically significant. The greatest consensus was obtained on blacks' "best knowing the meaning of being poor" and the least consensus on "who expects more gratitude." In this, as in other aspects of the study, the black interviewers received fewer indefinite responses.

In general, these results indicate that black people seeking or receiving service in one low-income black neighborhood prefer to be served by members of their own race, all other things being equal. But when competence is introduced as a factor, it becomes more important in determining preferences than does race. The race of the

TABLE 30-4

Characteristics of Service-Givers

(percentage distribution)

Race of helping person	Best knows meaning of poverty		Expects more gratitude		Gives more feeling of hope		Makes people feel they don't amount to very much		Talks down to people		More interested in your problems	
	WI	BI	WI	BI	WI	BI	WI	BI	WI	BI	WI	BI
White	12	8	48	53	37	31	40	66	49	66	36	22
Black	78	87	31	43	52	63	34	28	29	28	51	75
It depends	10	5	21	4	11	6	26	6	22	6	13	3

WI = White Interviewer
BI = Black Interviewer

interviewer affects results, the black interviewers eliciting significantly fewer undecided responses and stronger preferences for black service-givers.

IMPLICATIONS OF STUDY

This study does *not* show that white helping persons are unwelcome in black neighborhoods. However, the results suggest the need to provide black service-givers in service agencies — especially so to serve persons who reflect the community leadership's concern with the development of pride in black identity. It also emphasizes for white people who work in predominantly black neighborhoods the importance of being sensitive to the broad implications of the emerging emphasis on black identity.

The study came up with a rather complex set of results. Not only does it show that strength of preference for black people as service-givers differs from one service role to another, but also that the proportion of rejection of whites also differs among the roles. These differences suggest that each agency must look at its own situation not only in relation to the kind of personnel it has and the clients it serves but also in relation to the goals of the community leadership. The study also reinforces the importance of competence as the first requirement in selection of staff members.

31

CARMEN NORMANDIA

Characteristics and Role
of Indigenous Workers

Any attempt to describe the role of the indigenous worker as a specific pattern to be followed gives rise to serious difficulties. The meaning of the term "indigenous worker" is unclear and the role itself has different meanings for different people. Experience with programs of community action does not yet warrant an extensive analysis of the indigenous worker's role. This paper, therefore, only attempts to describe what it is on the basis of the writer's experiences as an indigenous worker during the past three years.

CHARACTERISTICS OF THE INDIGENOUS WORKER

The indigenous worker is in direct contact with the community and with the poor whom he serves.

He relates closely to the community because he is like the people of which it is composed. He is personally involved with the problems of those he serves and he devotes his best efforts to solving them. To solve problems for his clients is as important to him as having his own problems solved.

He is able to get the members of the community to participate in collective action in finding suitable solutions of their common problems since he is closely identified with the community and is in constant contact with those who come to him for help. He is more effective in doing this if he lives in the community in which he works.

He is able to organize social action acceptable to his neighbors because he lives where they do, shops and finds entertainment in the

SOURCE: Reprinted with permission of Council on Social Work Education, Inc., from *Anti-poverty Programs: Implications for Social Work Education* (New York: Council on Social Work Education, 1967), pp. 63–66.

same places, and has been a victim of the same bureaucracy that oppresses them all.

GROUP ACTION

It is not difficult for the indigenous worker to organize groups since he understands the problems and feelings of the people with whom he is working and the issues involved. He encourages imme-diate action since he is eager to see results.

The professional worker, by contrast, insists on drawing up a program, and this takes time. He conducts a series of meetings to plan the course of action. He begins, with the best of intentions, to suggest ideas. These may be good, but they will be wasted if he does not get down to the level of understanding of the people with whom he is working. Finally, people get bored and withdraw from the group. Even if they remain in the group and are kept together by the professional worker, formalities and parliamentary procedure tend to limit their participation and restrict their activities.

RELATIONS BETWEEN INDIGENOUS AND PROFESSIONAL WORKERS

The indigenous worker has a full-time job. This does not mean an eight-hour day and a five-day week. It means that he is on duty whenever he is called upon, and whenever there is an emer-gency—including after five o'clock on weekdays, and on Saturdays and Sundays. The community knows that he is being paid to provide services. People come to him at any time because emergencies do not arise only during office hours; they do not stop at the close of work on Friday. The agency office may be closed, but the indigenous worker is responsible to the community and the people of the com-munity know this. So, naturally, they expect him to be on hand to help them solve their problems at any time.

Because the community feels this way, the indigenous worker does not like to punch a time card at 9 A.M. and at 5 P.M. Often he simply cannot leave a client in distress while he runs back to the office to punch out. Unfortunately, some supervisors pay more atten-tion to this administrative procedure than to the service the worker is giving at the moment when he is supposed to be at the office check-ing out.

Keeping records is also difficult for the indigenous worker—one of the hardest things he has to do. Being with people and working with them sets up a relationship that cannot be conveyed in words. Most of the time, the essence of what takes place cannot be put down on paper. The indigenous worker knows that it is a great achievement to get his client's trust and that most of what is said is confidential. Why, he feels, should he share it with someone else?

At the start, the indigenous worker sees the professional supervisor as part of the structure that has always been telling him that he is wrong. It takes time for him to accept the concept of supervision, but he responds gradually to constructive criticism. Once this type of relationship is established, the worker benefits from supervision and carries out his tasks with ease and efficiency.

A change in supervisory staff is likely to create difficulties if the new supervisor demands that things be done in a different way. The worker feels that the purpose of supervision should be to guide him to perform better, rather than to control his way of acting. He believes in action and that this is more important than filling out forms.

TRAINING AND USE

The indigenous worker should be trained to become an effective advocate for his community. Part of this training should focus on better understanding of the existing power structure, with emphasis on how to deal with it without losing his identity.

He should be trained to be articulate, informed, and militant.

He should be taught how to be politically articulate.

He should be used to bridge the gap that often separates clients and professional social workers.

He should be used as an advisor in gaining a better understanding of community problems, since he has firsthand knowledge of them.

He should not be absorbed by the professional workers, since his potential contribution is distinct from theirs.

He should be looked upon as a source of positive values which bring people together and, when properly developed, lead to better understanding and better community relations.

In essence, he is the most effective public relations force an agency can have.

· 32 ·

HARRY SPECHT,
ARTHUR HAWKINS, and
FLOYD MCGEE

Excerpts from the Casebooks of Subprofessional Workers

Contra Costa Council of Community Services in Walnut Creek, Calif., is finding the use of subprofessional workers drawn from the poor people in the community at whom welfare services are directed more than rewarding. These workers are serving the poor people of the community as subprofessional workers through the Richmond Community Development Demonstration Project, a program made possible by a grant from the Office of Economic Opportunity. The project, which serves the city of Richmond, Calif., aims at demonstrating the means by which public agencies can incorporate these new workers into their operations. Two of the authors of this article are subprofessional workers with the project; the third was formerly the director of the project.

The idea of using subprofessional or paraprofessional workers in the human services is not new. However, the current widespread use of "indigenous" workers, that is, persons drawn from the neighborhoods and the kinds of people the program serves, as staff members of social agencies is a radical change in social service programs. The major impetus to this development came from the commitment of the Office of Economic Opportunity (OEO) to finding new means of bringing about "maximum feasible participation" of the poor themselves in the operation of the poverty program. At present, as a result of OEO's commitment, about 125,000 subprofessional workers are serving throughout the country in community poverty programs.[1] Recent major Federal legislation such as the 1966 amendments to the Economic Opportunity Act, the Safe Streets Act, the Juvenile

SOURCE: Reprinted from *Children*, Vol. 15, No. 1 (January-February, 1968), pp. 7–12.

[1] F. Riessman, "The New Careers Concept," *American Child,* Winter, 1967.

Delinquency and Youth Offenses Control Act, the Elementary and Secondary Education Act, the Law Enforcement Assistance Act, and the Demonstration Cities and Metropolitan Development Act is increasing the use of subprofessional workers drawn from the people served.

For the past 5 years a good deal has been written about the use of neighborhood people as subprofessional workers in the human services.[2-4] However, much of this writing does not substantially describe what these workers do. Rather, they center on describing the development of "new careers" — employment methods, problems of organization, and relations between subprofessional and professional workers — and the personal characteristics of persons going into these "new careers."

DIFFERENCES AND SIMILARITIES

Because of their concern with employment methods and job development, agencies have tended to use subprofessional workers to perform tasks ordinarily done by professional workers but for which professional training is not required. Or they have tended to use subprofessional workers for tasks that offer service not being given by anyone else. One reason why agencies only assign such tasks as these to subprofessional workers may be that they want to neutralize the objection of professional workers to having subprofessional workers perform tasks similar to those carried out by professional workers.

Descriptions of the personal characteristics of those in the "new careers" have tended to stress the *differences* between them and professional workers and the *similarities* between them and the clients. These differences and similarities are nearly always interpreted as assets in that they enable the subprofessional worker to "bridge" the gap between the client and the agency, to serve as a communicator who is better able than the professional worker to help clients put their anger and frustration into words and, as a result, make better use of available services or organize to demand services not available. Stressing differences and similarities might

―――――――
[2]A. Pearl and F. Riessman, *"New Careers for the Poor"* (New York: The Free Press 1965).

[3]F. Riessman, "The 'Helper' Therapy Principle," *Social Work*, April, 1965.

[4]R. T. Barker and T. L. Briggs, *Trends in the Utilization of Social Work Personnel: An Evaluative Research Study of the Literature* (New York: National Association of Social Workers, 1966).

also be another way of neutralizing the opposition of professional workers to programs using subprofessional workers because recognition of the similarities between the subprofessional and professional workers (and there is evidence that there are similarities)[5] might also be problematic.

In their method of creating jobs and in their concern with differences and similarities, agencies emphasize defining the jobs of new "careerists" on the basis of the tasks they perform. However, this will very likely prove to be an insufficient basis on which to define jobs for and to assess the performance of the subprofessional worker. In the human services, most tasks are similar. Certainly, when we look at the day-to-day work of subprofessional workers in our project who are serving as school aides, police community relations aides, probation aides, and community organizers, we find that they, like professional workers, interview, make referrals, consult other agencies, serve as resource people for clients, and counsel individual clients, groups, and organizations. Ultimately, the distinction between professional and subprofessional workers and their right to carry responsibilities and claim status will have to rest not only on the tasks performed but also on the extent of the knowledge different workers bring to their tasks and the degree of skill with which they perform them.[6]

At present, these distinctions and rights are largely judged by credentials. Unfortunately, in the absence of clear and tested measures of skill and knowledge, most of the human service professions must base these distinctions on the academic degree. Two results of this condition are evident. First, in nearly all cases, subprofessional workers have been relegated to carrying out the tasks professional workers find the least gratifying. Second, at present, there is little hope that professional associations such as the National Association of Social Workers will admit the subprofessional worker without an academic degree.

TWO CASES

It is our contention that the resolution of the problems of advancement to professional status either on the job or in the professional

---

[5]C. F. Grosser, "Local Residents as Mediators Between Middle-class Professional Workers and Lower-class Clients," *Social Service Review*, March, 1966.

[6]B. M. Beck, "A Professional Approach to the Use of the 'Non-professional,'" paper presented at the American Psychological Association and National Association of Social Workers Conference on Non-professionals, Washington, D.C., 1967.

association must be based on an assessment of the knowledge and skill the job requires. As a first step toward this goal in our project, we gathered case records prepared by subprofessional workers that could be used to evaluate their use of skill and knowledge. Two casebooks of these records have already been published.[7,8] Our next step will be to analyze the records. The following excerpts are from two records included in these casebooks. Each excerpt is followed by the worker's comments about his record.

The first of these cases involved a 16-year-old unmarried mother who lived with her mother, two brothers, and two sisters. The family was receiving public assistance. The baby, a boy, was 16 months old at the time his mother's case was handled by the worker. The girl's mother tended the baby 2 days a week; a paternal aunt, the other 3 days while the mother was at school. The mother and daughter got into a heated argument that led the girl to run away to the baby's paternal grandmother. The mother called the police to report that her daughter had run away from home; the girl's sister let her know what the mother had done. The neighborhood worker entered the case at this point.

The [paternal] grandmother knew that I worked with the Welfare Rights Organization [a group of welfare clients organized by two community aides] so she contacted me for advice. I told the [paternal] grandmother that if the police came for the girl, she was to turn her over to them. I assured the [paternal] grandmother and the girl that I would do everything I could to help.

On Monday morning, I picked the girl up and took her to my office. My first step was to contact my supervisor to bring him up to date. My second was to contact one of the police community relations aides at the police department, who told me there was a warrant out for the girl's arrest and that a policewoman was handling the case. The officer in charge was not present, so I informed the aide that I would bring the girl to the police station on that day.

My next step was to contact the Contra Costa County Department of Social Services to talk with the girl's social worker. The worker was on vacation so I talked with the worker's supervisor. I explained the situation and asked what the welfare department's position would be at this point. I

[7]Allee Ester, *et al.*, "School Community Workers," *Richmond Community Development Demonstration Project New Careerist Casebook No. 1.* Contra Costa Council of Community Services, Walnut Creek, Calif., March, 1967.

[8]Noble E. Coleman, *et al.*, "Police Community Aides and Probation Aides," *Richmond Community Development Demonstration Project New Careerist Casebook No. 2.* Contra Costa Council of Community Services, Walnut Creek, Calif., May, 1967.

was informed by the supervisor that the department's primary concern at this point was that the girl, since she was only 16 years of age, would have to be supervised by an adult blood relative. I then asked if the baby's [paternal] grandmother and aunt, both of whom are over 21 years of age, would fit the category of a blood relative. The supervisor stated that they would be acceptable in this case. The supervisor also stated that before the welfare department would take any action the probation department would have to approve the person who would be supervising the girl.

I then took the girl to the intake officer at the probation department and explained the situation to the intake officer. He said that the probation department would have no objection to the girl living with someone else over 21 as long as the mother consented. He said that the probation department had no jurisdiction at this point because the police department had not turned the girl over to Juvenile Hall [the residential agency of the probation department] as yet. He also stated that if the girl was picked up she wouldn't have to spend more than 1 or 2 days at Juvenile Hall.

I then took the girl to the police department and surrendered her. The policewoman in charge listened to the girl's story, then called the girl's mother and asked her if she still wanted her daughter picked up. The mother said she did. The policewoman then said that she would have to take the girl to Juvenile Hall. I asked the officer if the girl could be released in my custody for an hour so she could get the baby some clothing. The officer consented with the provision that I have the girl back at the station by 1 o'clock. I took the girl to her house to pick up the clothes and then to the aunt's house.

My main concern was seeing that the girl wasn't locked up. With this concern in mind, I bent the law slightly. Instead of returning the girl to the police department, I called the intake officer at the probation department once again. I told the intake officer what had happened at the police department. I asked the officer if it was possible for the probation department to order the release of the girl into their custody and to allow the girl to be retained in the aunt's house, pending a court decision. The intake officer checked with her supervisor and found that what I had requested was permissible, and she said she would confirm our conversation with the police department. I then asked the intake officer if she wanted to talk with the baby's aunt. The officer said that would not be necessary since I had given my word that the aunt was over 21 and that she could provide a place for the girl and the baby to live.

I took the girl back to the police department where the policewoman in charge had received the confirmation from the probation department. The girl was then released.

The worker then arranged with the welfare department to send the girl's grant to the paternal aunt as her guardian, pending a court hearing. The next day, the intake officer at the probation department called the worker to say that the girl's mother had come in to see her and that she objected to the girl's living with the aunt. The officer said she would have to determine whether or not the aunt met the qualifications necessary to act as guardian for the girl and her baby. A meeting was set up for Wednesday at the probation department. The worker's record continues:

Meanwhile, the girl's mother came in to see me. She voiced her disapproval of what I had done to help her daughter. She felt that I had done her daughter more harm than good. I tried to explain to the mother that my primary concern was to see that the girl was not detained in Juvenile Hall. I made it clear that I had no jurisdiction over whether or not the girl would be sent to Juvenile Hall. I told her that the probation department had ordered that the girl be detained in the home of the aunt. The mother was not satisfied and left rather angry.

On Wednesday morning, I took the girl and the aunt to the probation department to meet the intake officer. The intake officer questioned the aunt on her qualifications to supervise the girl. The officer was satisfied with the aunt's qualifications and ordered that the girl be detained in the home of the aunt, pending a detention hearing. The officer stated that the girl would not have to attend the hearing, but the aunt and mother would. The officer also stated that if the girl was ordered by the court to live with the baby's aunt, she would be a ward of the court and placed on probation until she reached the age of 18.

After hearing testimony from a representative of the probation department, the girl's mother, and the aunt, the judge at the detention hearing ordered that the girl be placed in the aunt's custody until she reached the age of 18.

The worker followed his account of the case with these comments:

This is one of the two or three hundred cases the Welfare Rights Organization (WRO) has handled. It also is an example of the individual direct service that WRO offers. If WRO had not existed, this girl would not have been given individual service. No other agency exists that would have handled this case as I did. Another important factor is that our services are free.

I think that it is a direct and personal service that I offer my clients. I live in the community I serve; I am available at all hours and on weekends. By living in the community, I am available to provide the same resources as is common in our middle class communities which often have doctors, lawyers, and other professionals living next door to each other.

Individuals such as myself have never been available for the poor community to take advantage of. I believe that my style of handling clients' problems who live in the poor community is the most effective way possible. I'm from the community I serve, I know most of the people, they know me, I know their problems because they are mine also, and I understand the poor people because I am one, and a part of them.

The other case concerns the work of a subprofessional worker in helping a family cope with an emergency. In this case, Mr. and Mrs. T, the parents of three school-age children—Saul, Cora, and Tess—were injured in an automobile accident and confined to the hospital for a few weeks. A friend, Mrs. S, who was riding in the automobile when the accident occurred but who received only slight injuries, offered to take the T children into her home.

The subprofessional neighborhood worker was called in by Mrs. T to talk with her concerning the help that she would need for the children during her absence from home. She called this particular worker because he had worked with Saul at his school concerning truancy and delinquent behavior. The worker describes the case in these words:

I talked to Mrs. T and asked her what she would like for me to do. First she wanted to know how Saul, Cora, and Tess were doing. I told her that Saul and Cora were doing fine in school, and that, although they had been worried at first about the accident, after talking with me about everything they had calmed down. She told me that the children would be staying with their friend Mrs. S at her home in Point Richmond. She asked if there was any way that they could get from Point Richmond to their school. I said that I would pick up Saul and Cora and bring them to school and take them home in the evening until she could work out another way. I also talked to Mrs. S about whether it would be hard for her to take care of the T's kids until Mr. and Mrs. T were out of the hospital. She said she could do this.

I returned to the hospital and told Mrs. T that Mrs. S could take care of the kids until she returned home. She asked if I could get some assistance for the kids because the money that would be coming in to her would not be enough to cover their needs. I told her that I would look into this. I also told Mrs. S to call me if she needed to. About 10:30 that night she called me and said she was having trouble getting Tess to come over there like her mother said. She wanted to know if I could talk to Tess and show her why she should come there to stay because her mother was in the hospital. I asked her if Tess was there, and she said that Tess was at home. I told her I would talk with Tess and for her to call me back later. I called Tess. I asked her how come she didn't want to stay with Mrs. S and she said because she "didn't want to." "Well, Tess," I said, "you know the struggle right now that your mother and father are in. With all the worries that they have by being in the hospital and they worry about you children too, their minds would be more at ease if they knew you were staying with Mrs. S instead of being by yourself." Tess asked me, "Well, do I have to?" I said, "Well, Tess, I think you should. But I will leave it up to you to make up your own mind whether you should stay with Mrs. S because there are a lot of things that could happen to you in a lonely house by yourself." She paused for a moment and then said, "Well, OK, I'm going." She then asked me whether I was going to call and find out if she got there and I told her no and that as she had given me her word she would go why should I call to find out whether she was going to lie to me or not. About 11:20 that night Mrs. S called me again and told me that Tess had come. She also told me she wanted to talk to me the next day about Tess because Tess had two or three places she wanted to go over the weekend. She felt that Tess shouldn't be out late at night. She asked me to talk to Tess about this. I told her I would, and I did the next day.

Mrs. S explained that the money was low and that [the children] didn't have any lunch money and she said she didn't know whether Mrs. T had any money. I told her not to worry, that I would give them lunch money.

On Wednesday evening, I got permission from Mrs. T to talk with her doctor. I called him and told him who I was and what my duties were concerning Mrs. T and also the reason why I would like information about the T's. He told me that Mrs. T would be in the hospital for approximately 3 weeks. Mr. T at that time was still in intensive care. I haven't had a chance to talk with him. But as soon as they remove him from intensive care into one of the rooms, I will be able to. He also may be in the hospital for at least 3 weeks, and when released he probably won't be able to go back to work for at least another 3 weeks.

The protective services worker told me that Mrs. S would have to have some kind of license to keep the kids at her home because it would be such a long time. I asked her would this present any complication and would she be able to do this because I felt the kids were in a place they liked and were being very well taken care of. She told me that there was a good possibility that they might remain with Mrs. S. She then told me that she would call social service to see what could be done and she would call me back and give me the information.

The rest of the worker's record describes his continued contacts with all of the people concerned and with the protective services worker responsible for Saul. This worker helped him get assistance for the T's from the welfare department to supplement their resources. He continued his activities during the time it took Mr. and Mrs. T to recuperate in the hospital.

The worker's comments on this record are as follows:

In crisis people must have someone with whom they can talk. I was there in the school, close to the home, within walking distance. The youngsters in the family knew I was concerned. They needed someone to listen to them and explain what had happened and what would happen to them.

Giving is part of my job. To be able to give service or a small amount of money was very gratifying for me. Besides, why bother a family with serious problems about a few cents?

Later when I thought the time was right, I asked about the T family's financial standing because not only did the kids need lunch money but the family keeping them also needed money for expenses.

It's very important that school officials be informed of changes in a family situation. In this case, with both parents in the hospital, the kids would be upset for a while.

Contacting the welfare agency, I found I had to get more information about the family. I was familiar with the social services procedures so this helped me explain it to the family. The parents gave me their permission to talk with the doctor for they were glad someone was doing something.

I kept close contact to make certain everyone had what they needed, and, most important, enough food.

The doctor was very cooperative. I received a special permission slip to see the father. There was hospitalization insurance for the father only. When the social worker made her visit, I asked to go along with her. I wanted the family to know they had somebody working with them at all times.

Although the mother is in a wheelchair, the father is now back on the job. I am still working with this family and their problems. The children know now how important a *united* family is. They have lived through a misfortune and have been helped by friends. They now understand what a school community worker is really needed for.

AN EXISTING CHALLENGE

To make use of the records in our work requires the creation of a scale by which to measure practice and to compare the efforts of these workers. However, there are several observations we can make about the records in themselves.

First, the subprofessional workers obviously provided important and significant services. Can one help feeling wonder and shock that the services given to these families were not available before? Yet tasks of the *kinds* the workers are carrying out are not really new; rather, these tasks extend the *kinds* of services we have the knowledge and means to give clients not being served. Second, in providing these services the workers perform a "community building" service since they are enabling families in low-income areas to make use of the institutions set up to serve them. The workers represent an important bridging or communicating mechanism. Third, as the number of such workers increases and their skill and ability improve with experience and training, their effect on the institutions and on professional workers may become increasingly abrasive. And fourth, the records show that the workers are using knowledge and skill in interviews, diagnosis, referral, advocacy, and "brokerage."

Unless we develop means of measuring competence other than academic credentials, we shall soon find that we have created a large group of subprofessional workers who are locked into low-paying, unrewarding jobs with no chance for advancement, however great their skill and competence. The fact that the majority of these workers will be Negroes or of Spanish extraction will only further point up the built-in injustice of our system for awarding status and prestige and fixing salary.

The two records selected for this article are not essentially different from those of other subprofessional workers in our project. Both of the workers had had approximately a year's experience with the project and the benefit of education through in-service training, seminars, and formal courses. They showed evidence that they were acquiring the knowledge and skill of professional workers and using them creatively. The records of these workers suggest the possibility that the development of professional knowledge and skill can take place in settings other than academic. The continuation of this kind of effort to identify and measure competence in performance in subprofessional workers is an exciting challenge to people in the human services, as well as to educators, we believe.

FRANK M. LOEWENBERG

Social Workers and Indigenous Nonprofessionals: Some Structural Dilemmas

Employment of persons without a master of social work degree to fill responsible positions in social welfare programs is not a recent development. Hospital social service departments have used case aides and other nonprofessionals for decades, group service agencies traditionally have relied on volunteers and untrained leaders, selected prisons have experimentally assigned correction officers as group therapists, and the new multiservice agencies have employed nonprofessionals in various important jobs. Until recently, however, these nonprofessionals were generally college graduates or young people with some college training. Usually they were employed because of the continuing manpower shortage and were assigned to specific subprofessional tasks.[1] For the most part, professional social workers would have preferred to hire MSW's for all social work positions; the employment of nonprofessionals was not viewed as a permanent solution to the social welfare manpower problem but rather as a temporary stopgap. Their employment, according to Mencher, represented "at best a grudging delegation of inconsequential

SOURCE: Reprinted with permission of the National Association of Social Workers, from *Social Work*, Vol. 13, No. 3 (July, 1968), pp. 65–71.

[1]Laura Epstein, "Differential Use of Staff: A Method to Expand Social Services," *Social Work*, Vol. 7, No. 4 (October, 1962), pp. 66–72; Marcella Farrar and Mary L. Hemmy, "Use of Nonprofessional Staff in Work with the Aged," *Social Work*, Vol. 8, No. 3 (July, 1963), pp. 44–50; Gertrude S. Goldberg, "Job and Career Development for the Poor . . . The Human Services," *IRCD Bulletin*, Vol. 2, No. 4 (September, 1966), pp. 1–5; Elinor Stevens, "Aides, Volunteers and the Indigenous Nonprofessional Worker," paper presented at the 1965 NASW Southern Regional Institute, Nashville, Tenn. (mimeographed); Verne Weed and William H. Denham, "Toward More Effective Use of the Nonprofessional Worker: A Recent Experiment," *Social Work*, Vol. 6, No. 4 (October 1961), pp. 29–36; Judith G. Benjamin *et al.*, *Pros and Cons: New Roles for Nonprofessionals in Corrections* (Washington, D.C.: Welfare Administration, U. S. Department of Health, Education, and Welfare, 1966).

functions" so that the nonprofessional became "the handmaiden for widening the sphere of professional performance."[2]

USES OF INDIGENOUS WORKERS

Within the past decade a different type of nonprofessional, the indigenous worker, has emerged on the social welfare scene. This new worker must not be confused with the traditional nonprofessional worker; unlike the latter, the indigenous worker is recruited from the target neighborhood and the risk population served by the employing agency. Indigenous workers (and there are reported to be about 24,000 working in programs of the Office of Economic Opportunity[3]) are not employed because of a shortage of professional manpower but for one or more of the following reasons:

1. *Service Delivery.*—Indigenous workers function as "expediters" or "mediators" so that social welfare programs become more compatible with and more readily available to the poor.

2. *Helper Therapy.*—The therapeutic effect of employment on the indigenous worker himself may be more important than his effectiveness on the job; for those who have always been losers, gaining self-respect, identity, and skill is no small achievement.

3. *Participation.*—Federal law requires "the maximum feasible participation of the poor." Some agencies believe that this prerequisite is met by employing indigenous workers; others believe that by employing indigenous workers it will be easier to involve the bona fide poor in decision-making.

4. *Employment.*—The development of new employment opportunities is, according to many, a crucial task in the antipoverty effort. They believe that many million new employees with relatively low skills can be absorbed by the "human services" (health, education, and welfare).[4]

For years nonprofessionals were employed only as subprofessionals and assigned to inconsequential tasks. More recently, social

---

[2]Samuel Mencher, "Social Policy and Welfare Manpower," in Edward E. Schwartz (ed.), *Manpower in Social Welfare: Research Perspectives* (New York: National Association of Social Workers, 1966), pp. 39–40.

[3]Goldberg, *op. cit.*, p. 3.

[4]Charles F. Grosser, "Local Residents as Mediators between Middle-Class Professional Workers and Lower-Class Clients," *Social Service Review*, Vol. 40, No. 1 (March, 1966), pp. 55–63; Frank Riessman, "The 'Helper' Therapy Principle," *Social Work*, Vol. 10, No. 2 (April, 1965), pp. 27–32; Arthur Pearl and Frank Riessman (eds.), *New Careers for the Poor* (New York: Free Press, 1965).

work-oriented community agencies such as New York City's Mobilization For Youth have pioneered in utilizing nonprofessionals in a variety of different ways, not always on the subprofessional level; yet even in these innovative agencies crucial policy-making and training positions are generally manned by professional social workers.[5] For some of the culturally deprived, however, this job has become a means of access to professional status.

Problems arising out of the employment of nonprofessionals have been discussed with increasing frequency in the social work literature.[6] Professional social workers who train and supervise indigenous workers have reported, for example, that nonprofessionals often question social work's basic assumptions, some resent the professional method, and others challenge the commitment of the professionally trained staff. These reports are generally based on the problems faced by social workers who work in traditional agencies or in the newer social work-oriented community agencies.

There is yet another type of setting that is rarely mentioned in the social work literature but that needs to be considered. A social agency that is *not* influenced by social workers and in which social work professionals generally do *not* participate in policy-making or on the executive level is a recent development that has occurred in many cities under the umbrella of the Economic Opportunity Act. These agencies employ many indigenous workers and it is in these settings that career opportunities for the poor arise most frequently. Professional social workers who practice in these agencies face somewhat different problems from those faced by their colleagues in the traditional agencies.

If the relationship between professionals and nonprofessionals poses generic problems, little new will be learned from an analysis of the problems occurring in one of these newer community action agencies. Yet there is much in contemporary social science theory to support the idea that the setting in which the interaction takes place affects the interaction process; to understand the relationship pattern, one must understand the organizational environment and the social system of the work setting.[7] Although the specifics of the

[5]The social work-oriented community agency continues to serve as an important model for social work's participation in the antipoverty effort. *See* Salvatore Ambrosino, "A Family Agency Reaches Out to a Slum Ghetto," *Social Work,* Vol. 11, No. 4 (October, 1966), pp. 17–23.

[6]The literature is too extensive for footnoting. *IRCD Bulletin,* Vol. 2, No. 4 (September, 1966), contains a seven-page bibliography on "The Nonprofessional in the Human Services."

[7]Peter M. Blau and W. Richard Scott, *Formal Organizations* (San Francisco: Chandler Publishing Co., 1962), pp. 87–115.

organizational environment will differ from agency to agency, knowledge gained from an analysis of one situation should be useful to social workers in other settings.

NEIGHBORHOOD CENTER

Neighborhood Center is one of a series of multiservice centers opened with OEO funds during the past two years by the community action agency of a large midwestern metropolis. The immediate neighborhood served by Neighborhood Center has a population of nearly 10,000 families, 80 percent of whom are nonwhite and 30 percent of whom have an annual income of less than $3,000. Half the adults have less than an eighth-grade education, the infant death rate is almost 35 per 1,000 live births, and one of every three dwelling units has been classified substandard. Neighborhood Center employs a relatively large staff to work with this high-risk population group, including a director, a community action division (CA) with four full-time and thirty part-time workers, an employment division with five full-time workers, and a social service division (SS) with four full-time workers. In order to simplify the analysis here focus will be only on the relationship between the CA and SS workers.

The only professional social worker is the SS director. Most staff members can be classified as indigenous workers. Almost all live in the neighborhood served by the center and all but two are nonwhites. Nearly half the full-time workers and most of the part-time workers did not complete high school. Only the SS director and one of his assistants have completed college; although both are nonwhite, neither lives in the target area.

PROBLEMS ENCOUNTERED BY STAFF

Interviews with various staff members revealed several problems that are relevant to the question of professional-nonprofessional relations.

1. CA workers held expectations of SS workers that social workers were unwilling or unable to accept. CA workers felt that the SS staff was not performing adequately, nor did they understand why SS workers spent so much time in the office rather than on the street.

2. Social workers had great difficulty in understanding the informal work habits and apparent planlessness of the CA staff; for example, appointments were rarely kept and staff meetings were called or canceled without advance notice. Not only did CA workers

demand "the impossible," but they also tended to criticize the SS workers' efforts in front of clients.

3. The Neighborhood Center's administrators also did not understand what social workers were trying to do. The center director made administrative decisions involving SS staff on the basis of criteria that were not relevant to social work.

4. The program emphasis of the center was on rendering concrete services, but no funds were available for these. Instead, SS workers were expected to "co-ordinate" concrete services provided by other public and private agencies. However, social workers were not adequately prepared for this difficult task.

5. Social work practitioners in the center felt isolated from the mainstream of professional social work. Within the center social work was generally evaluated negatively; at the same time their social work colleagues in other agencies tended to stereotype the "nonprofessional" setting in which the center staff were currently working. SS workers in Neighborhood Center found that they could no longer rely on the traditional professional model but needed to develop a new one.

SOCIAL SYSTEM ANALYSIS

A social systems model will be utilized to analyze these problems and place them in their proper perspective, with "role" and "position" used as key concepts.[8] *Role* is defined as the set of normative expectations held by others for the occupants of any given position; these expectations include the rights, duties, taboos, and responsibilities incumbent on those who occupy the position. *Position* specifies a location in a social system. *Role performance* is the actual behavior of the occupant of a position.[9] Several assumptions underlie these definitions:

---

[8]Borgatta suggested that "a meaningful study of role is implicitly a study of a social system." Edgar F. Borgatta, "Role and Reference Group Theory," in Leonard S. Kogan (ed.), *Social Science Theory and Social Work Research* (New York: National Association of Social Workers, 1959), p. 17.

[9]These definitions and the discussion below were stimulated by J. Milton Yinger, *Toward a Field Theory of Behavior* (New York: McGraw-Hill Book Co., 1965). For an analysis of the different ways in which the role concept has been used in the social science literature, *see* Neal Gross, Ward S. Mason, and Alexander W. McEachern, *Explorations in Role Analysis: Studies of the School Superintendent Role* (New York: John Wiley & Sons, 1958), chap. 2; Daniel J. Levinson, "Role, Personality, and Social Structure in the Organizational Setting," *Journal of Abnormal and Social Psychology,* Vol. 58 (1959), pp. 170–180; Yinger, *op. cit.*, pp. 132–133. Social workers will be

1. Role is not behavior but expectation for behavior normatively associated with a given position.

2. Role expectations are held for a position, not for the occupant of the position; thus, the role expectation for the position "social worker" holds regardless of whether the position is occupied by a man or a woman, by an experienced worker or a novice, by an MSW or a nonprofessional worker. Even when the position occupant's actual behavior does not fit the role expectation, the normative role expectation tends to remain fixed.

3. Role expectations are held by specific others who do not always agree among themselves. Clients and colleagues may hold different role expectations for the position of "social worker"; two clients need not have identical role expectations for that position.

4. Role performance may fall short of role expectation because the position incumbent has failed to internalize successfully the relevant role or because he has internalized only one of several roles. When, for example, clients and supervisors have conflicting role expectations for the position of social worker, the occupant of that position cannot meet both sets of expectations with equal success.

5. A set of role expectations internalized for one position may be inappropriate for a second position occupied by the same individual. Thus, the role performance appropriate for the position "child" is not appropriate for the position "husband." In this society position changes are sometimes so swift that there is insufficient opportunity to internalize new roles.

STRUCTURAL DILEMMAS

Social workers at Neighborhood Center face a variety of problems. This analysis will attempt to show that these problems arise out of the agency setting and the profession's structure and are not the result of personality limitations of the workers currently employed. Although some practitioners are more skillful than others, the problems they face arise primarily out of structural dilemmas, not personality flaws.

Social interaction is one of the basic human needs. Generally people require two position networks to meet this need adequately:

especially interested in Andie L. Knutson, *The Individual, Society and Health Behavior* (New York: Russell Sage Foundation, 1965), pp. 117–131; and Bruce J. Biddle and Edwin J. Thomas (eds.), *Role Theory: Concepts and Research* (New York: John Wiley & Sons, 1966), pp. 3–63.

a set of persons before whom they can act out role-conforming behavior patterns and another set of colleagues for assistance in meeting role expectations and for providing opportunities for "collusive intimacies and backstage relaxation."[10] Social workers usually interact with two distinct networks: the client and the peer networks. In Neighborhood Center, however, SS workers generally were limited to one interaction network. The peer network consisted of the CA workers who, it will be remembered, were indigenous nonprofessionals recruited from the client group and who remained part of the client group. The fact that staff and clients did not represent two separate networks was not accidental. While in traditional social agencies indigenous workers rapidly assimilate some professional patterns of behavior, in the innovative antipoverty organizations emphasis is placed on preserving the indigenous characteristics of the nonprofessional staff because it is believed that only those who come from and remain part of the target population can mobilize the community for action.[11] For the SS workers there is little that distinguishes colleague from client. At the very time when SS workers need the help of a collegial group to internalize unfamiliar and new role expectations they find themselves without teammates.

Lower-class clients sometimes exhibit a high level of spontaneity, an unfamiliarity with bureaucracy, a devaluation of education, and an animosity toward social workers. To meet these responses among colleagues is a new experience for social workers, yet these patterns were characteristic of many Neighborhood Center staff members. When indigenous workers were asked what they would do if the center budget were cut, they commonly suggested the firing of social workers and other college graduates. This open antagonism toward social workers and other professionals created a morale problem among the SS staff.

The spontaneous work habits of the indigenous workers and their lack of adherence to bureaucratic work patterns often created difficulties; for example, appointments were routinely forgotten, some staff meetings were called on a moment's notice, statistical activity reports were practically unobtainable, and so on. Spontaneity extended to such areas as hours of work and assignments so that it was difficult to determine when work hours ended and personal

---

[10]Erving Goffman, *The Presentation of Self in Everyday Life* (Garden City, N.Y.: Anchor Books, Doubleday & Co., 1959), p. 206.

[11]George Brager, "The Indigenous Worker: A New Approach to the Social Work Technician," *Social Work*, Vol. 10, No. 2 (April, 1965), p. 39.

business commenced. The SS workers, accustomed to a more bureaucratic work style, were not only appalled by the seeming planlessness and waste of manpower, but the unpredictable behavior of their colleagues interfered with the social workers' performance. Because indigenous workers did not meet any of the role expectations traditional in social agencies, SS staff members were often puzzled; CA workers' role behavior fit the pattern of neither the subordinate nonprofessional worker nor the compliant client. When, for example, a CA worker barged in on a critical session with clients in order to recruit pickets for a demonstration, the SS worker's reaction was one of hostility and shock.

A basic role expectation for professional colleagues calls for reciprocal support in front of those who are not professionals. When correction is necessary this should be handled "backstage" so that clients do not become aware of the professional's mistakes. Disagreement about professional matters can be discussed with fellow professionals but not with the clients. At Neighborhood Center, however, staff members were generally not aware of these professional norms. CA workers felt a stronger bond with clients than with their social work colleagues; consequently they had little hesitation about criticizing social workers in front of clients. Public discussions of "secrets" were, in fact, encouraged by the structure of the center, especially the imperative of maximum involvement of the poor.

When examining the division of labor within any organization, functional as well as status implications must be recognized. In most social agencies employing nonprofessional workers the more difficult cases are assigned to fully trained social workers while aides handle routine cases or assist professional workers with routine details. This division corresponds to the status hierarchy of the traditional agency where social workers outrank nonprofessionals. When many professions practice in one organization the professional group most closely identified with the primary goal achievement ranks highest (e.g., physicians in hospitals, educators in universities, line officers in the armed forces, and so on); those in high-status positions are almost always members of a professional group while those without professional status rank lower. It is difficult to think of examples in which nonprofessionals outrank professionals, but Neighborhood Center is one such example of status-reversal since there the apex of the status pyramid is occupied by the CA workers, an occupational group that does not meet the conventional criteria of a profession. Social workers are accustomed to function in subordinate positions to members of other professions, but to be outranked by nonprofessionals is a new experience for which few professional social workers have been prepared. Those who practice in these newer settings will need to adapt, adjust, and learn new roles.

As a result of their professional training and experience, social workers have developed specific role expectations for the position of "supervisor"; for example, the supervisor is expected to ease the strain between professional and bureaucratic norms.[12] When a specific supervisor is unable to meet this role expectation, the social worker in the counterposition, the supervisee, will attempt to resolve the strain by developing a new set of variant role expectations and/or will arrange consultations with professional colleagues. The Neighborhood Center director had neither the background, skill, nor time to function as a social work supervisor; instead the SS director began to lean heavily on the social work consultant who was on the staff of the city-wide community action agency. This informal relationship appeared to be legitimated by the city-wide meetings of all SS directors, which were chaired by the consultant. At the time of the study, the relationship between the center's SS director and the consultant was more significant than the relationship between the SS director and his direct supervisor, the center director. When, for example, a conflict between the SS workers and the CA workers came to a head, the consultant backed the SS director while the center director supported the CA director and his staff. The failure to establish a working relationship between the SS director and the center director may be yet another aspect of the professional-nonprofessional problem, since the center director stressed throughout that he was an indigenous worker.

Organizational pressures and structural dilemmas resulting from conflicting professional and bureaucratic demands can also be reduced if the professional's primary reference group is located outside the organizational system.[13] Drafted army doctors, for example, tend to place greater emphasis on their medical affiliation than on their army rank; in part this adaptive behavior is designed to avoid the pressures of the military bureaucracy. This process, however, is successful only when the professional group legitimates the extra-professional position; if doctors generally believed that army doctors did not practice medicine, then army doctors would find it futile to stress the MD above their military rank.

---

[12]Henry J. Meyer, "The Effect of Social Work Professionalization on Manpower," in Schwartz (ed.), *op. cit.*, pp. 74–75.

[13]Blau and Scott, *op. cit.*, p. 74.

By the same token, if the mainstream of professional social workers viewed social work positions in antipoverty agencies as too far off the beaten path, social workers in these positions could not use their professional affiliation to resolve their occupational dilemmas. In fact, SS workers felt isolated from other social workers and believed that the profession was not helpful in resolving their dilemmas. The "alienation" from the profession was felt doubly by the SS workers since they realized the need for professional support and recognition. They also knew that their own professional advancement within professional social work depended in large measure on how their professional peers evaluated their present activity, yet they were aware that many of their colleagues did not approve of the innovative setting in which they currently practiced.

SUMMARY AND CONCLUSIONS

There is need to re-examine the relationship between the social work profession and the newer social welfare programs that have sprung up in recent years under OEO auspices. Many have observed that the profession has been "reluctant to accept new policies and patterns of services which displace the traditional concepts of function."[14] The absence of social workers from the War on Poverty has been noted repeatedly; although some social workers have made notable contributions, social work as a profession did not become involved with Great Society projects until after the present policies had been formulated. Similarly, relatively few social workers have manned practice positions in local antipoverty agencies. If there is merit to the professional credo that social workers can make a unique contribution to solving human problems, it is important to understand why they have done so only in limited fashion until now. In this paper the writer has attempted to examine the experiences of some professional social workers who are practicing in these innovative settings; understanding their problems will, it is hoped, help other social workers to face the issues involved.

The thesis developed here is that structural variables rather than personality factors are primarily responsible for the difficulties experienced by professional social workers practicing in antipoverty programs that are not social work oriented. The problems examined involved the following areas: (1) indigenous workers were unaware

---

[14]Mencher, *op. cit.*, p. 41.

of the "rules," (2) professional social workers found themselves without colleagues in the agency, (3) to some extent professionals were isolated from their professional peers outside the agency, (4) professional social workers found themselves in positions subordinate to nonprofessionals, and (5) the normal supervisory relationships were nonexistent.

The structural variables examined seemed to cluster into two sets: one involved the organizational environment of the anti-poverty agency, the other the organizational structure of the social work profession. Neighborhood Center and similar agencies need to become aware that their policies and routines have dysfunctional as well as functional consequences; even when these policies have positive results, the dysfunctional consequences may interfere with goal achievement. The professional group, on the other hand, needs to re-examine its attitude toward these newer programs; new role models for workers and services need to be developed and new structures need to be devised if social work and social workers aim to fill leadership positions in social welfare planning and programming.

· 34 ·

FRANK M. LOEWENBERG

Toward a Systems Analysis of Social Welfare Manpower Utilization Patterns

The shortage of qualified manpower in social welfare agencies has been with us for decades. Instead of showing signs of decreasing, the problem becomes more serious year by year. Our affluent society

SOURCE: Reprinted from *Child Welfare*, Vol. 49, No. 5 (May, 1970), pp. 252–59.

needs and expects more and better social services than are currently available. With the identification of an increasing number of "new" social problems, larger (but still insufficient) sums of public and voluntary money have been allocated to begin to deal with them. Yet services still are not available to many who seek or need them. Despite our best efforts to recruit and train additional personnel, things are getting worse rather than better.

Admittedly, the manpower shortage is only one of several problems that make for the current crisis in service delivery. But empty desks and high turnover rates are clearly visible. Increasingly we hear calls for the abandonment of professional requirements on the basis that it will be impossible in the foreseeable future to fill all social work positions with M.S.W. workers. Bronfenbrenner reflected this note when he condemned the "too-exclusive reliance on professional help" as unwarranted because it results in too little service becoming available.[1]

It is a fact that workers who have not earned a professional social work degree man more than 80 percent of the direct service positions in public and voluntary agencies. Sometimes these so-called nonprofessionals are employed on a planned basis; more often they are "emergency appointees" who become permanent employees. It is not uncommon that workers with and without the M.S.W. degree are assigned to the same kinds of tasks.[2]

Increasingly, professional social workers recognize that the demand to fill every position in social work with an M.S.W. worker is neither feasible nor desirable. Pins points out that "there is general agreement today that, even if there were no shortage of professionally educated social workers, not all jobs in social welfare need to be or should be filled by a person who is equipped with 2 years of graduate professional education."[3] However, the employment of workers with other educational backgrounds will do little to solve the service delivery problem unless such workers are utilized in an efficient and effective manner. Shockingly high turnover of new

---

[1]Urie Bronfenbrenner, "Damping the Unemployability Explosion," *Saturday Review*, Jan. 4, 1969, p. 109.

[2]Robert L. Barker and Thomas L. Briggs, *Differential Use of Social Work Manpower* (New York: NASW, 1968), p. 108. Jones reported that 86 percent of the nonprofessional child care workers in her sample were assigned to the same kinds of jobs as professional caseworkers. Betty Lacy Jones, "Nonprofessional Workers in Professional Foster Family Agencies," unpublished D.S.W. dissertation, University of Pennsylvania, 1966, p. 288.

[3]Arnulf M. Pins, "Undergraduate Education in Social Welfare," in *The Social Welfare Forum 1967* (New York: Columbia University Press, 1967), pp. 148–149.

workers, generally among those who have not earned an M.S.W. degree, suggest that utilization rather than recruiting represents the real priority. When, for example, more than a fourth of all child welfare workers in the United States leave their jobs each year, the quality of the service received by children must be somewhat less than excellent. And the turnover rates in public assistance agencies are even higher.[4]

In addition to employing M.S.W. workers, many, if not most, social welfare agencies today employ workers with other educational backgrounds. With this in mind, there is urgent need to analyze manpower utilization patterns. Though the literature is extensive, the explorative and comparative study of utilization patterns has remained "mostly uncharted territory."[5] Those examining the deployment of social work personnel often have not been aware of what others had already discovered; instead of building on the findings of others, almost every student of manpower utilization patterns feels the need to start almost from the beginning. Administrators and others charged with implementing manpower utilization plans understandably are confused by this seeming repetition. Some feel that they tested and abandoned years ago the "experiments and innovations" they read about today. Others report that the specifics tested elsewhere cannot be applied to their own agencies. What is needed is a general paradigm that can be applied in evaluating various manpower utilization approaches in the light of specific local agency needs. The development of such a general paradigm will be attempted here, after a brief review of several manpower utilization patterns.

UTILIZATION PATTERNS

Every social welfare agency has a manpower utilization pattern that matches specific jobs or sets of tasks with different staff groups. This statement should be no more startling than the discovery of

---

[4]*Child Welfare Statistics 1966* (Washington, D.C.: U.S. Children's Bureau Statistical Series 88, 1967), Tables 17 and 20.

[5]Barker and Briggs, *op. cit.*, p. 52. Barker and Briggs provide an extensive bibliography. An early report on this subject is by Susan M. Boyd, "An Experiment with Case Aides," *CWLA Bulletin*, XXII, No. 8 (1943), pp. 12–13. In 1945, the Family Service Association of America issued a report on "Case Aides in Private Member Agencies," *Highlights*, VI, No. 4 (1945), pp. 34–36. More recent articles include Werner W. Boehm, "The Differential Use of Personnel—The Contribution of Education," *Child Welfare*, XLVII, No. 8 (1968), pp. 455–460, and Selma Cohen, "Utilization of the Subprofessional," in *Proceedings, Tri-Regional Workshop on Community Health Services for Mothers and Children* (Pittsburgh: University of Pittsburgh, 1968), pp. 53–64.

elementary school children that they already know how to talk in prose. In most agencies the janitor does one type of job, the secretaries are skilled in something else, and the social workers have responsibility for still another area of work. Of course, the division of responsibilities may not be sharp or clear—and in some agencies it is not unusual for a social worker to sweep out her office.

Here our focus will be more specific, limited to an analysis of tasks connected with and related to the provision of direct services to clients. Who carries responsibility for direct services? On what basis are these responsibilities assigned to one or another group of workers? To simplify the analysis, only two groups of social workers will be considered: those with an M.S.W. degree and those with a B.A. degree. A fuller analysis would, of course, include other groups such as social work technicians with an A.A. degree, indigenous workers without any college education, workers with a doctoral degree, and those with education in professions other than social work.

Manpower utilization patterns can conveniently be classified by how the differentiation, if any, in assignments occurs. Chart 34-1 suggests three such classifications: (1) no differentiation, (2) differentiation of cases according to established criteria, and (3) differentiation by service activities. By indicating to which group or groups of workers assignments are made, five types of manpower utilization patterns can be identified. These patterns represent, of course, "ideal types."[6] In practice various combinations of those types will occur.

1. Classical Model

All direct social work services are provided exclusively by M.S.W. workers. In some agencies using this pattern, the M.S.W. may be assisted by one or more aides or assistants who work under his direction, but the M.S.W. always carries full responsibility for the cases assigned to him. This is true even when he assigns to an aide

---

[6]The identification of five types, and not six or seven or eight, is somewhat arbitrary. A common variant, the utilization of specialists, has not been identified as a separate model since it can be used in connection with all of the models identified here. When specialists are used, responsibility for the case remains with the worker and the specialist works under the social worker's direction. A common example of specialists would be the use of homemakers in family agencies. The specialists variant differs from the team model in that the specialist is concerned only with his specialty and usually has no long-term involvement with the case.

CHART 34 – 1

Classification of Manpower Utilization Patterns

	(1) No Differ- entiation	(2) Cases Assigned Differentially	(3) Tasks or Activities Assigned Differentially
Direct services by M.S.W. workers only	I	—	—
Direct services by both			
M.S.W. and B.A. workers	II	IV	V
Direct services by B.A. workers only	III	—	—

specific auxiliary tasks, such as obtaining information from a secondary source or completing administrative reports.

II. Undifferentiated Model

Service to clients is provided by both M.S.W. and B.A. workers. B.A. workers may originally have been employed on an emergency or stopgap basis. Although there may be formal differentiations in title, pay, and even assignments, in practice the two groups of workers do pretty much the same job.

III. Two-Level Model

All direct social work services are provided by B.S. workers, while M.S.W. workers supervise B.A. workers and devote their time to reviewing and correcting the work of the B.A. workers. In some agencies decisions about the type of service to be provided may be made by the M.S.W. supervisors, yet the direct contact is always between client and the B.A. workers.

IV. Differential Model

When cases are differentially assigned, the criteria used usually attempt to direct the more difficult cases to workers with more education (M.S.W.) and the easier ones to workers with less education (B.A.). The unit of differentiation may be the case (for example, cases including difficult problems and cases including easier problems), the tasks required for successful intervention (for example, complex tasks and simple tasks), or the service required by the client (for example, therapeutic services and program services). Once a case has been assigned to a specific worker, that worker has full responsibility for the case and does everything that needs to be done; the crucial assignment decision is made at intake, though theoretically it is possible to reassign a case when it is determined that it requires a worker with a higher (or lower) level of skill than the original diagnosis indicated. Since clients often have a variety of problems, the assigned worker will be responsible not only for services directed at the presenting problem on which the case was assigned, but for all other services necessitated by problem situations that are identified subsequently.

V. Team Model

In agencies using the team approach to staffing, a group of workers with various educational backgrounds work together as a team, with case assignments going to the total team. The team manager or director, usually the M.S.W. worker, coordinates the use of all manpower required to accomplish the goal for each specific case. In one variant of the team pattern, different team members are responsible for fulfilling the specific goals assigned to them, so that a number of skilled workers may be working with the same family at the same time or over a period of time; each team member will be responsible for achieving the specified goal with this family. In another variant, the team manager assigns specific tasks to various team members who have expertise in the particular area; decisions on outcome goals are made by the total team. In still another variant, every team member functions as coordinator for a given number of cases; the coordinator for the particular case calls on other team members for expert assistance whenever necessary.

AN APPROACH TO THE ANALYSIS OF UTILIZATION PATTERNS

In analyzing the various manpower utilization patterns (both those identified here and others described in the literature) we need to distinguish between the motivation that led to their inauguration (presumably, though not necessarily, better utilization of manpower resources in order to deliver services more effectively) and the objective consequences. Since equivalences cannot be assumed in a social system as complex as contemporary society, it is necessary to specify the units for which the consequences of any given patterns are to be observed.[7] Blum has suggested that manpower utilization patterns should be examined on the basis of "how best to serve clients, not on present professional definitions and organizational patterns."[8]

However, limiting the analysis to the consequences for clients not only is too simple a procedure, but disregards the well-established observation that a given phenomenon or utilization pattern will have different consequences for different units of the social system. We suggest, therefore, that a full analysis of manpower utilization patterns include at least the following components of the social welfare system:

(a) *The Clients.* — Those who receive agency service: How effective is the delivery of service?

(b) *Potential Clients.* — Those on the agency's waiting list, as well as others requiring the agency's service but without access to it: How effective, accessible, and universal is the delivery of service?

(c) *The Community.* — The larger social system of which the agency and clients are subsystems: How effective is the agency in protecting the community from the potential "dangers" resulting from the presence of unserved and untreated clients? (This "danger" may be real or imaginary, physical or economic, etc.)

(d) *Qualified Manpower.* — Does this utilization pattern result in more effective recruiting and in more effective retention of qualified staff?

(e) *Agency.* — Are there sufficient resources available to implement this utilization pattern? Is this the most effective and efficient use of available resources? Is the pattern effective in meeting the mandate and goal of the agency?

(f) *Social Work Profession.* — Does this pattern result in professional satisfaction and other concrete rewards (e.g., higher salary levels) for those who have completed graduate professional studies? Does it result in status gains for the profession?

It will be necessary to examine the functional and dysfunctional consequences of each manpower utilization pattern for each of the specified units of the social welfare system before one can assess the overall effectiveness of any one pattern. A plan, for example, that was highly effective in treating a limited number of clients but that was not conducive to recruiting and retaining sufficient qualified staff

---

[7]Robert K. Merton, *Social Theory and Social Structure,* revised edition (Glencoe, Ill.: Free Press, 1957), pp. 60, 30.

[8]Arthur Blum, "Differential Use of Manpower in Public Welfare," *Social Work,* XI, No. 1 (1966), p. 16.

would not be rated as desirable in some circumstances. A utilization plan that was effective in recruiting a large number of untrained workers who were then assigned to all kinds of complex professional activities would not be only harmful to the social work profession but highly dysfunctional for both the agency's clients who need skilled workers and for the community that expects a high level of professional skill. Chart 34-2 attempts a preliminary and summary analysis of the functional and dysfunctional consequences of each of the five manpower utilization patterns in terms of the various units of the social welfare system.

CHART 34-2

Preliminary Analysis of Functional Consequences of Various Manpower Utilization Patterns

	I	II	III	IV	V
			Patterns		
Consequences for					
a. Individual client	xxx	xx	xx	xx	xxx
b. Individual not receiving service	x	xx	xxx	xx	xxx
c. Community	x	xx	xx	xx	xx
d. Staff	x	x	xxx	xxx	xxx
e. Agency	x	x	xx	xxx	xx
f. Profession	x	x	xx	xx	xxx

x Dysfunctional consequences outweigh functional consequences.
xx Functional consequences outweigh dysfunctional consequences.
xxx Functional consequences greatly outweigh dysfunctional consequences.

A PRELIMINARY ANALYSIS OF UTILIZATION PATTERNS

It must be remembered that this is a provisional and preliminary analysis, using gross measures as indicators for functional and dysfunctional consequences. More important than the accurate determination in any specific instance is the procedure, which can be easily duplicated in any local community. In Chart 34-2, the "XXX" suggests that the pattern results in obvious functional consequences for the particular unit, the "XX" indicates that the functional consequences outweigh the dysfunctional consequences for that unit, and the "X" denotes that dysfunctional consequences seem to outweigh any functional consequences. Since accurate measuring tools to determine consequences are not yet available, the rating scale represents only estimates on the basis of "practice wisdom" and insight. The disciplined use of this kind of procedure, however, does lead to more useful and clearer planning and evaluation.

Chart 34-2 suggests that the *Classical Model* manpower utilization pattern (Type I), in which the M.S.W. worker provides all direct services, generally results in superior service to those clients fortunate enough to receive casework services. The relatively small number of M.S.W. workers available, however, limits service to few of those who need to be served. The community will not be protected from the potentially damaging activities of those not receiving service. At the very time when it has been most difficult to recruit a sufficient number of M.S.W. workers, this pattern makes the recruitment and retention of workers with other backgrounds even more difficult, since the action and the glamour are with the M.S.W. The cost per case of this utilization pattern is relatively high. The continual frustrations and lack of satisfactions resulting from large caseloads and constant pressures in agencies following this pattern probably contribute little to enhance the status of the profession generally, although workers employed in high-status agencies with limited intake may enjoy a high degree of community prestige.

In agencies using an *Undifferentiated Model* (Type II), in which both groups of workers deliver all direct services, some clients will receive excellent service while others will receive poor or inappropriate service. Waiting lists may be small and access to service may be open to a relatively large proportion of those needing and requiring service. This may serve to "protect" the community. However, the level of service is uneven and it is a matter of chance whether clients with serious and complex problems will receive service from skilled workers; this staffing pattern may, in the end, be highly dysfunctional for clients, prospective clients, and the community.

Agencies using this model will find that the recruiting and retention of B.A. workers, as well as M.S.W. staff, will be difficult. Although B.A. workers may be attracted initially in large numbers, they soon encounter the inevitable frustration resulting from carrying cases too difficult for them. Competent M.S.W. workers will tend to avoid agencies that do not appear to use professional standards. High staff turnover will require the agency to invest heavily in training and supervision, so that any savings made by hiring B.A. workers at low salaries will be erased quickly. The undifferentiated utilization pattern will do little to enhance social work's professional status in the eyes of the public, since it appears that all workers, trained as well as untrained, engage in the identical "professional" activities; though professional social workers can distinguish between agencies that utilize professional methods and those that fail to do so, this distinction has not yet been conveyed successfully to the community.

The *Two-Level Model* (Type III) is generally functional for all system units. However, since all direct services are provided by B.A. workers, some clients will not receive the skilled services their complex problems require. Similarly, the community may not be protected from difficult or potentially dangerous cases if it does not receive service from skilled workers. Agency resources may be overtaxed if M.S.W. supervisors need to spend too much time in rectifying mistakes made by B.A. workers required to serve cases too difficult for them, or if high turnover requires constant training programs for new workers. The clear differentiation of tasks and the direct involvement of B.A. workers in service delivery will be functional for recruiting and retaining workers. Since all M.S.W.s will be in supervisory positions, social work may enjoy a high status; however, the removal of all professionally trained workers from direct client involvement may have dysfunctional consequences for the further development of social work's knowledge and skill base.

The functional consequences for all units of the social welfare system also appear to be high in the *Differential Model* (Type IV). Dysfunctional consequences may occur when a particular client initially assigned to a given worker on the basis of the presenting problem must remain with this worker even though his problems change drastically. As a consequence, the community may not receive the kind of protection it requires and expects. Neither the client nor the community in general may understand the basis on which cases are assigned to different types of workers, so that it may appear that both B.A. workers and M.S.W. workers are performing the same tasks. However, rigid definitions or inappropriate application of the differentiation criteria may prevent a more flexible utilization of personnel by the agency.

On paper the *Team Model* (Type V) is scored with the greatest number of functional consequences, appearing highly functional for all units of the social welfare system. There are, however, a number of questions that must be considered in connection with this utilization pattern. Salary costs may be higher for this pattern than for any of the others. Human relations between workers loom more important here than elsewhere; the "lone eagle" who could render outstanding service in other patterns may not fit on a team. Some

team operations have resulted in administrative problems, others
have confused clients because seemingly the workers played musical
chairs.

CONCLUSION

It must be pointed out again that these estimates are highly provisional. Further analysis and experience with various manpower utilization patterns may reveal that what was believed to be a functional
consequence turns out to be a dysfunctional one. A utilization pattern that appears functional today or in one setting may be dysfunctional tomorrow or in another setting because the demands for service differ.

For the present, we suggest that the significance of this paradigm
is not in any specific estimate, but in the general approach to evaluating utilization patterns. Instead of limiting the analysis to the
consequences experienced by any individual client, our paradigm
suggests that all units of the social welfare system be considered and
analyzed.

SECTION VI

Social Intervention Strategies: Levels, Targets, Roles

INTRODUCTION

Everybody has had experience in working with other people. As a result, every layman assumes that he is able to deal even with the most complex of human problems, something he would never claim when it comes to the medical or physical sciences. Nevertheless, it needs to be emphasized that a high order of skill and expertise is required to deal in the human arena and particularly in planning and developing social intervention strategies. We have already observed that the first steps in developing a social intervention strategy include defining the problem and specifying the goal. Mistakes made at those points are all but irreversible.

We are not using the term "social intervention strategies" as a code word for the classical social work methods such as casework, group work, and community organization. These "method labels" do not represent strategies. In fact, they are almost meaningless labels since they relate neither to the problems identified nor to the techniques or strategies to be developed. Instead they primarily tell us about the number of people involved in the target population. "Group work" cannot be considered a social intervention strategy or a technique but it merely tells us that the target population consists of more than one person. As Bisno (1969, p. 8) correctly noted, the names of the traditional social work methods "hint at neither the purpose of the intervention nor the operational procedures."

Strategy selection should not be predetermined by the agency's or the worker's preferred modality of service but by the problems, goals and the needs of the beneficiary population. When a person presents a problem to a worker in a group work agency, it should not be assumed a priori that group work services will provide the most effective intervention strategy. Kaplan's "law of the hammer," (1964, p. 28) which suggests that a small boy who has received a hammer as a present will find that everything he encounters needs pounding, should not be applied in social work. But all too often social intervention workers formulate problems in such ways that they will always require the very strategies in which they are most skilled, or, even worse, they will apply these strategies in which they are most skilled, regardless of whether or not they fit the problem.

Applying an incorrect or ineffective strategy may not be "bad" but may not achieve the goals dictated by the problem. A doctor who discovered half a dozen cholera cases should not merely treat these six sick patients but should suspect the possibility of an epidemic and set in motion public health efforts to cope with the potential epidemic; anything less is a strategy that does not "fit" the problem even if his cure results in the recovery of his six patients. It should be noted that we do not require the doctor himself to apply public health measures; we merely indicated his professional responsibility to "set in motion efforts."

Those who design social intervention strategies need to decide early whether to intervene at the case level, the class level, the system level or the institutional level. Given the same social problem, intervention is possible (though not always feasible) at any one or all of these levels. The strategic choice depends upon the resources available, the goals, and the wishes of the decision makers. Although in any given situation, with any given problem, many levels of intervention may be appropriate, we need to remember that in the United States most major problem areas ultimately require intervention at the systems level. Dean Mitchell Ginsberg, the former head of the New York City Human Resources Administration, noted that major changes in public welfare and social service programs are brought about only through major changes in federal and state financial support.

Social intervention strategies need to be evaluated in terms of efficiency, effectiveness, cost, availability, equity and inclusiveness. Intervention strategies need to be *efficient* in terms of goal achievement; given two strategies, the more efficient one should be selected, all other factors being equal. The *effectiveness* of the strategy relates to whether the strategy will achieve the desired outcome. A strategy which does not achieve the desired goal is not effective, no matter how little it costs. The *cost* of the strategy relates to the resources available and necessary. When two alternate strategies are available to meet a problem, the less costly will be more efficient and more desirable. However, cost is not only a question of dollars but would involve other factors such as time, human resources, functional and dysfunctional consequences, and so on. Availability refers to the means necessary for implementing a strategy. Are the techniques and knowledge necessary for the strategy *available*? Have they been developed? *Equity* addresses itself to the question of whether the strategy can redress both individual and group inequities. *Inclusiveness*, finally, refers to the question whether the strategy covers all of the victimized population or only a selected or favored segment. In evaluating intervention strategy all of these criteria should be considered although it may not be possible to maximize all at the same time.

All social interventions necessitate a worker actively entering ongoing systems in order to help create change or to sustain people, groups, or communities. The choice of strategy, the level on which change is to be sought, the specific targets for interventions, and worker roles need to be chosen prior to entry, but in many cases will be altered when the worker learns more about the particular system. Assessment, in other words, is an ongoing process.

R. Alex Sim's "Stranger in the Community" is a selection which sensitively traces the feelings, communications, relationships and work of a professional as he enters a new community. The role of stranger is a difficult one, but one that workers need to master as they enter social systems to explore and to help. Are the feelings, questions, and observations identified in this article also relevant for working with individuals, groups, families, and organizations?

What are the roles workers can constructively play? Charles F. Grosser in "Changing Theory and Changing Practice," contrasts worker roles which derive from residual and institutional approaches to social welfare. Are workers and clients co-citizens and co-equals? How do our views of the function of social welfare as a social institution influence our interventive roles and methods?

Qualitative social interventions are dependent upon individualization of people, situations, and methods for helping. In "Making Casework Relevant to Black People: Approaches, Techniques, Theoretical Implications," Dorcas D. Bowles illustrates how the physical setting and specific type of family suggest varied techniques for intervention. Engagement and the selection of helping roles are dependent on the particular people involved. Can special helping roles and techniques be selected for use with people of varying economic, racial, familial, neighborhood, and other backgrounds?

The question of worker role is further explored by Fred W. Christie in "The Gang Fight," an excerpt from Irving Spergel's *Street Gang Work, Theory and Practice.* The worker is especially familiar with the local culture and is involved deeply with the people. Is this a case of overidentification or an idiosyncratic but successful social intervention technique?

B. Harold Chetkow's "So Go Fight City Hall: A Community Work Record" demonstrates how a knowledgeable citizen-professional with information about a system successfully intervenes in a complicated situation primarily through the use of phone calls. If you were working in such a community, what different approaches might you have pursued in order to be of help?

"How the Federal Government Caused the Welfare Crisis" by Frances F. Piven and Richard A. Cloward reviews the background of the antipoverty programs and federal social welfare interventions of the 1960's on a national scale. They correct misinformation and myths about the reasons for rises in the number of people receiving public assistance. New services offered the poor information about their entitlements; litigation enabled people to obtain resources; and new organizations of the poor pressured for change and also created an environment which undermined partially the "stigma" of public assistance. What skills were needed to accomplish these feats? Do you need special expertise to influence another social welfare agency on behalf of a person or group? A government department? A legislative body? How can a worker locate where decisions are made?

In what ways were the national interventions of the 1960's successful and in what ways were they less successful? If you were intervening, and had the requisite power, what kind of public welfare system would you design? Would you emphasize social services, including information and referral; legal class actions and other legal advocacy; community organization; higher income provision; government-created jobs; others?

If there is a cardinal rule in social intervention, it might well be "know who you are dealing with." "A Preview of the Migrant as a Rehab Client" by Myrtle R. Reul amply illustrates the importance of understanding the cultural and other background of those with whom you work. What are the special characteristics of groups of migrants which she has identified? How do these characteristics play a part in determining what intervention strategies can be employed? Are there general characteristics of all migrants which could influence one's work with them?

Hettie Jones, in "Neighborhood Service Centers," examines the role of concrete services as an intervention technique. The "packaging" and the availability of these centers distinguish these from the classical efforts. Should all neighborhoods regardless of economic class have such centers? H. Jack Geiger's statement in "Medical Services: Digging Wells and Building Privies," also describes a multifaceted approach to services. He highlights the interconnectedness of problems. Intervention strategies, like problems, need to address themselves to the total problem configuration. Starting with medical problems, Geiger identifies a problem set which requires intervention. Why is Geiger's strategy so unlike most approaches to medical problems? What additional resources are needed for strategies which attempt to cope with problem sets?

Legal intervention is often thought of as among the most effective techniques. In "The Consequences of Florida's Suitable Home Law: A Study of Ineffective Intervention," Roland Chilton explores one attempt at legal intervention which proved to be highly dysfunctional for the target population. Evidently there was a lack of clarity in defining the problem and in setting goals, two prerequisites for any type of intervention. What alternative strategies might be employed to achieve one or the other objective? Can laws ever be employed as an effective intervention technique? What can or should be the worker's role in attempting a change in the legal structure? How much change can a worker or group of workers make in such a situation? What options are available for action if they wish to alter the law?

"Damping the Unemployability Explosion" by Urie Bronfenbrenner suggests a national plan for restoring a sense of community, offering all families and children the sustenance they need. Is his view utopian? Why does he select a national approach to change? What alternatives are available? How does a society ultimately pay for the deprivations of its poor citizens? What would you do about the problems he identified?

When change is suggested, many times we are told "that's just a patch-up job or first-aid." Amitai Etzioni in " 'Shortcuts' to Social Change?" reviews what we know and what we do not know about several potential shortcuts for dealing with drug addiction, gun control, and other problems. Can such problems be "solved"? If not, then how shall we approach them? At one point with one strategy? At many points with several approaches? What information is needed to decide how to intervene?

In the final selection, Mary Rabagliati and Ezra Birnbaum report on their experiences with "The Campaign for Minimum Standards." A group of welfare recipients work within the system to get what they are entitled to as recipients according to the law. Why does the worker assert his own opinions at several points in the process? What skills did the group members have and which skills did they learn? When does the worker choose a less active leadership role in the group? Why does he choose the less active role?

REFERENCES

BISNO, HERBERT. 1969. "A Theoretical Framework for Teaching Social Work Methods and Skills," *Journal of Education for Social Work*, Vol. 5 (Fall, 1969), pp. 5–17.
KAPLAN, ABRAHAM. 1964. *The Conduct of Inquiry*. San Francisco: Chandler Publishing Company.

· 35 ·

R. ALEX SIM

Stranger in the Community

The professional worker or volunteer who is sent, or who goes of his own volition to work in a community or institutional setting is

SOURCE: "Stranger in the Community" originally appeared in the November–December, 1969, issue of *Canadian Welfare*, published by The Canadian Council on Social Development (formerly the Canadian Welfare Council).

aware, or should be aware, that he is entering an established social system. The skills required and the dangers encountered are not peculiar to community work. In an age of high mobility more and more adults are experiencing the acts of entry into operating social systems: new jobs, new places to live, conferences, school and training experiences. Man is on the move.

Examples of more complex occasions of entry are recorded by anthropologists, travellers and espionage agents. The primitive society, tradition-bound and close-knit, had its own language and dialect, customs, style of behavior. The outsider, quickly visible, was a threat to the balancing of relationships. He had to be dealt with. Even though there might be elaborate rituals of receiving a visitor, and proffering him hospitality, he might not be aware of all the niceties, or of the precariousness of his position. But if he decided to stay that was another matter. Though the instances are rare of outright cannibalism, every anthropologist knows or should know, there are more ways than one of having a stranger for dinner.

PREPARATION

Entry has to do with the impact of an outsider upon an operational social system, and reciprocally it has to do with the effects upon the entering person of the experience. My concern at the moment is the impact of entry on social systems as it applies specifically to community work.

Ahead of departure, the worker's duty will be to inform himself about his destination. It is hoped he will have already acquired some acquaintance with the theory of culture and community structure. A good library will yield additional helpful information. Historical background, travellers' accounts, local histories will prepare the worker for the general cultural environment to which he is to go. If it is a distinctive culture with a rich history there will be art, poetry and fiction to bolster his knowledge. These sources will give him some expectations about the style and quality of life he may expect to find.

If the worker is assigned to a small area, an Indian reserve, or an urban neighbourhood, there will still be statistical data available, possibly on a census tract basis, but should such sources be scarce or hard to find, he can look up studies and reports on similar locations on which data are available.

We hope agencies sending workers forth do so with gusto and bustle. It is not a matter for casual assignment. In the process of selection and training, questions have been asked about the worker's suitability and preparation. The steps toward gaining answers to these questions are arduous; they should not be matters of arbitrary decision, for the worker should ultimately select or de-select himself from the field. The training instrument should lead him to reach that decision. Having equipped himself emotionally and intellectually for his work, nothing remains but to see that his medical shots are in order; that he is provided adequately but without ostentation with material necessities.

A PERSONAL RISK

The worker knows he is now with a certain agency and that he is assigned to a particular place. He may go alone, or he may go with others into a field location without an advance party and without following other established workers. He may be one of those who go out into a situation well prepared by those who have pioneered. Whatever the case, if the position is really exposed to the unprotected force of community feeling, inertia, push and pull of events, his entry is a personal individual commitment, a testing and risky experience.

David Reisman in a Peace Corps Communique has this to say of what he calls a terrifying and illuminating experience:

These volunteers, like most of those engaged in community development, had had to find their own jobs. Many had become self-trained anthropologists in villages whose complicated networks of influence, malice, and rare benevolence no one had mapped yet, and where any small mistake could have catastrophic consequences for the Volunteer and his project and perhaps for the whole cadre of Volunteers. Even those who go out to apparently more structured jobs, as teachers do, may discover that the schools to which they have been sent haven't been built yet, or have fallen in, or are embroiled in the kinds of struggles over authority that are not unknown in school systems elsewhere. A change of government in a host country can topple a program, and indeed any one of a thousand things can go wrong, even in the most well-endowed society, and probably do go wrong in the areas where Volunteers work.

In a society where some people desperately want and need them, while others fear and resent them, they have perforce to become diplomats without portfolio, in a language in which they feel awkward, among customs easily and unknowingly violated. They can take nothing for granted, not the promises of officials nor the smiles of their co-workers, nor yet their own reaction to occasions of betrayal, disappointment, or misunderstanding of their work. . . .

The physical hardships turn out not to be a problem: if anything, the reverse, since such hardships provide a self-evident obstacle and one that is readily surmounted. The graver hazards are emotional and interpersonal. They may include the risk to one's psychic balance of living at once alone and in a crowd for two years; the risk to one's self-confidence in encountering one's first significant failure after years of success at home and in school; the risk to one's sense of values of coming to question, in a strange environment, the virtues of democracy, charity, accomplishment, perhaps even life itself. . . .

ON ARRIVAL

If communities had well-laid mine fields in their outer boundaries, the worker would find it easier to avoid danger than when required to negotiate the cultural and psychological hazards which surround and protect the places where people live. The modern community unlike the mediaeval city, is not encircled by moat and walls. The present-day community seems defenceless. The community worker can walk in without opposition. If he is not visibly different in dress, deportment and skin color, he will not be opposed. But he will be noticed. It may be months or years later that he will discover some error in judgment at the early stages has prejudiced key figures in the community against his work, or opened the way to his success.

The community worker arriving for the first time in his place of work will be much more alert to all his sensory impressions than ever again. The color, the sounds, the odors of the place will strike him forcibly then. Weeks later he will take most of them for granted, and they will pass unnoticed to him as to the more settled resident.

HOUSING

During his first twenty-four hours the worker must find a place to sleep. It may be a temporary abode, and if it is he will only defer the final question of where he is to live.

There is a question of principle as to how closely he should be identified with the people, and how his capacities match the principle. There is one view that the worker should share fully the life and vicissitudes of the people with whom he works. If he lives in comfort in one quarter of the city and commutes into a centre of dire poverty, how can he empathize with those he wishes to help? He should enter fully into their suffering and only then will he understand their life. *This view has validity in certain situations.* The desirability of moving directly into the community must be balanced against the worker's emotional stability, his health, and his commitments to others, say his wife and children. Ideally the worker should be mature and his wife and children robust, but this is not always the case.

There is another argument that the worker can be too close physically to the people with whom he works. Michel Blondin[1] for instance, sees many disadvantages to a location in the centre of the community. In his work in St-Henri he does not give people in the community his telephone number. He has told them, "When you need me, I will help you." He appears regularly at certain places in the community where people can find him or leave messages for him. As he puts it: "I am there to help, but not to operate a first-aid station." He needs some privacy. This measure of detachment gives him the strength he needs to meet the demands put upon him. He also thinks that if he is too close to every day problems and emergencies, the people can become too dependent upon him. Then he would become another leader competing with those already there.

NON-VERBAL COMMUNICATION

The newcomer might wish that he could be inconspicuous when he first arrives in a new place. It is a vain hope. Simply keeping quiet may help but there is non-verbal communication to consider. Here are some of the factors that will signal information: the way he dresses, his grooming and general appearance; the place he selects for living quarters, and the spot designated as his headquarters; whether or not he drinks and if he drinks — where, what brand, and in what quantity; apparatus: the items he brings with him, if he is empty-handed without so much as a bed-roll or a suitcase, will be as eloquent as if he carries an expensive camera, tape recorder and other gadgets typifying affluence and perhaps ostentation.

The worker can expect that his gestures, manner of speech, dress and general appearance will be noted, discussed, commented upon. They may be the cause of laughter and amusement. Yet all of this may occur covertly behind his back or behind closed doors. He must acknowledge that he is being examined from head to toe, even if he cannot observe it directly. Indeed such covert interest is the first step toward wider acceptance. He must decide for himself about his deportment under this scrutiny.

---

[1]Notes from a conversation with an "animateur social" in St-Henri, Montreal.

A detached worker in an area of high delinquency took a stand on such matters of behavior and dress that was his own conclusion and part of his identity. He chose to avoid situations where he would be in competition with the youths, and hence did not participate in activities such as billiards. He took a stand on fighting so that he would not become an opponent, by simply announcing that he was not a fighter. He further stated that he would fight to protect them if necessary, but not to protect himself, for he would rather run away or call the police. (No one called him "chicken").

In dress he always wore a tie and a coat for this was his normal mode of dress: there was no need to alter his style. In this situation there seem to have been other less easily identifiable items such as facial expressions, movements, gestures which convinced the youths initially that the worker had a continued interest (without participating) in what they were doing and that he cared about what happened to them.

A worker may become uncomfortable under the probing eyes of the community and wish he could disappear. No such luck and fortunate too, for the very fact that he is different is part of the worker's charm and attraction. Many workers faced by unblinking and unsmiling scrutiny will wish to hide, or wish they could buy invisible paint. A colleague of mine on a rural community study in Ontario, affected knee boots and a flannel shirt. He then took lessons in tractor driving, "in case someone says to me 'get up on the seat and show me what you can do'."

The good people in the country found his costume rather bizarre. He had made himself more conspicuous than if he had dressed in the business suit that corresponded more closely to his role. As for driving a tractor: they were much too courteous to wish to humiliate him, and much too fond of their tractors to have chosen that means of putting him down. The fact was he was afraid, and it was his vulnerability that made him appealing to these people who soon grew to like and accept him. They saw through his act, and fortunately for all and for the study, they liked what they saw. For indeed he had a deep human sympathy, and an interest that was not spoiled by idle curiosity.

By the same token, a worker who tries to hide feelings of superiority, arrogance, or shock, cannot hide these either. The truth comes out in telltale gestures, and inflections of speech that are slightly off key.

On the other side of the coin, the worker should be aware of his own observations, and he should record them (provided he has a secure place to keep such jottings). If he finds the people strange, exotic, different, enchanting, repulsive, it is quite possible they have quite similar views of him.

LANGUAGE AND DIALECT

Even where the worker knows the language of those he is working with, it is possible he will have problems of dialect and special vocabulary. A clergyman with an urban background in a parish of farmers or fishermen has this problem.

The novice has no choice but to learn how to talk with the people about matters that affect them most deeply. This is not a manipulative tool, but a means of sharing a universe of discourse, and it should be motivated by genuine concern.

The extent to which the local vocabulary is adopted may be a matter of taste, and of deciding how much social distance to maintain between the worker and the people. For instance, when the detached worker is conversing with a gang of boys, does he call a policeman "a fuzz"? Does he adopt the language of the street for a functionary who may be in some respects a colleague, or does he use a more respectful term and risk the loss of rapport with the boys? The detached worker mentioned above settled this problem for himself, again by using his customary style of speech, appropriate to his professional status, which he had interpreted to the boys. This seemed quite satisfactory to the youth, because when he used an occasional swear word, there were expressions of shocked surprise.

The exploration of a foreign tongue, or of a dialect within a familiar language, is a fascinating means of identifying the inner recesses of a culture. Through this exploration a culture, or a sub-culture, may be examined and understood. Language is therefore not simply the means of transmitting messages between two individuals; it is the key to understanding cultural values. Within a language family, differences of dialect reveal basic differences in the definition of things, and of social facts. The community worker who is a student of language becomes, through the sharpening of his perception of sound differences, a sensitive student of the people he seeks to serve.

BEGINNING THE JOB

We have been trying to suggest how an outsider who enters a

social system as a change agent should behave. Of particular interest
is the intense continuing, supportive role that an outsider can play
who acts as instigator, not as leader. The chemical term "catalyst,"
the French expression "animateur" are both suggestive without
fitting exactly into the definition we seek.

To begin with the worker must be able to maintain himself as an
integrated person in the social system. It is important for the worker
to maintain his equilibrium, and to find release from tension created
by the difficult role he is playing. The trip "out" has more than one
advantage. It allows the worker to get away, and it permits members
of the community to appreciate his status more realistically: besides,
a rest may be due them as well!

NEW RELATIONSHIPS

The worker entering the field will find himself caught in a network of relationships that bind him with other outsiders who have
duties in the community. These are, in a sense, his colleagues and
the usual rules, obligations, and rivalries which operate among colleagues in other settings will operate here too.

The person who is entering the community, who must find a place
in the interlocking social systems, is a novitiate and must learn to
suffer and learn from the introductory rites that accompany this role.
He will have problems: one is the accommodation to others already
established in the field. The new worker must be slow to condemn
or accuse other seasoned workers who are caught helpless (or hap-
pily) in the coils of policy and official incomprehension within which
they work. On the other hand, he may feel he is quite justified in
keeping himself aloof, as politely as he can, from the demands of
their sub-culture. If he does this he must be prepared to pay the
price such exclusive behavior will exact; above all, he must not fall
into the ready trap of stereotyping these workers who are in fact his
colleagues.

He may stay aloof, but to do so completely would be a mistake, for
he will find in due course it is not as cohesive a group as it may have
appeared to be at first. In time he will find individuals who are
sympathetic to his point of view. They will seek him out and share
their thoughts with him. If he judges too harshly at first, he will have
alienated himself from resources that he requires and the community
needs, and from an outlet for talk and action with these new colleagues.

On the other hand, if there is a battle line drawn between the local bureaucracy and the residents or "natives," the change agent who is looking for a middle ground may find himself in no-man's land, a target for a destructive crossfire. There should be a middle ground, which may be hard to find, but he must find it in his first days and weeks or his lot will be difficult and lonely.

ON BEING A STRANGER

There is no better way to describe the community worker: he is a "stranger within the gates." The role of the stranger may sit ill with many field workers; they would much prefer to be an "insider" or be "with it." Moreover, the conception of social distance in the context of social space, may suggest to them that artificial barriers can easily be ignored, "if I'm friendly enough."

The urge to "go native" in the best sense of the word (for there are other meanings to this expression) should be resisted for many reasons, the most obvious being that there are probably enough natives there as it is. There is no justification for a change agent "going native" in the worse sense either. If the community needs a worker, one presumes it is because there is a requirement for new resources. So the act of maintaining some distance has its utility, for it gives the worker the perspective which may make him a useful and helpful participant in community affairs.

"DOING NOTHING"

Community work will appear to most people as nothing-work. Nor does the pressure come from the middle class alone. A worker in an area where the people seem to have rejected contemporary work habits and routines, will reveal their own basic lack of acceptance of that behavior by criticizing a worker among them who appears to have no identifiable production goals. At least they would like to watch him work. By the same token, criticism comes readily from those functionaries who are busily engaged in doing for others what they should be doing for themselves. Job-saving and ego-saving are always readily evoked.

The worker must begin carefully, he must become thoroughly familiar with his environment. He must do this before he commits himself to any group or any course of action. Moreover if he begins too soon to do things himself he will have fallen into the trap of so many other workers in the past.

Doing nothing is not a justification for a worker who is genuinely disoriented and confused. But for a well-trained, well-prepared worker, we can expect him to have enough poise and personal resources to go slowly at the beginning. He will know his environment better, and he will not be sucked into a cycle of false starts and busy work that will yield no measurable return.

WHAT HE ACHIEVES

The roots of a worker's power are simple. He becomes a force in the new community because he cares. The people he is working with may be Indians on a reservation, villagers in a new African state, a group of adolescents many of whom are on parole, or upper middle class housewives in a suburban neighbourhood. They become more introspective, they think more about their place in the world, their destiny, because there is a stranger among them. He does not tell them what to do, and this puzzles and intrigues them. They consider privately what his motives are, they test his sincerity, they begin to imagine interesting items and bits of information that they can tell him.

From this behavior, which has an infantile quality to it, there is a beginning of independent autonomous thought. Soon people begin to make decisions independently of the interesting person in their midst who came to help. They may even act contrary to his known desires but such action is not rebellious or demonstrative, it is a mature act for which they take full responsibility. At this stage the worker's own maturity and integrity will be tested. If he has worked toward a true state of independence, the growing freedom of the group from his own support and encouragement will not threaten his own personal security. He will welcome these indications of the results of his method. Now they know how *he* would react to a problem they are facing alone.

What we speak of is not a new idea, yet in recognizing fully its subtlety, the insight, tolerance, and personal security it calls for, it is not surprising that we are still trying to understand and practice a concept of leadership Lao-Tzue spoke of centuries ago:

Of the best leaders
The people only know that they exist;
The next best they love and praise;
The next they fear;
And the next they revile.

When they do not command the people's faith

Some will lose faith in them,
And then they resort to recriminations.
But of the best, when their task
Is accomplished, their work done,
The people all remark,
We have done it ourselves.

· 36 ·

CHARLES F. GROSSER

Changing Theory and Changing Practice

The extraordinary developments of the past few years set off the sixties as a period of unprecendented political, social, cultural, and economic change. It is a period that marks the emergence of this nation as a welfare state. For social work, continually engaged in "agonizing reappraisal," the impact of the sixties has produced a more profound and more far-reaching examination of practice than the profession has undergone since it first struggled with the implications of psychoanalytic theory.

During earlier periods of self-assessment in the face of external change, social work had not yet reached its maturity. Changes in the profession were developmental; although reflective of their time they were largely self-induced attempts to polish and define an evolving profession. Today social work shares with other institutions that play a significant part in national life the urgent need to redefine its practice in order to deal with a newly emerging national community.[1] Perhaps because this imperative has been thrust on the profes-

SOURCE: Reprinted from *Social Casework*, Vol. 50, No. 1 (January, 1969), pp. 16–21.
[1]Gordon Hamilton, *Theory and Practice of Social Casework*, 2nd ed. rev. (Columbia University Press, New York, 1951), 123. See also Samuel Mencher, "Ideology and the Welfare Society," *Social Work*, 12:3–11 (July, 1967).

sion by outside forces — sometimes hostile and often beyond professional control — and because such externally generated demands are more sweeping, less orderly, and more imperious than internally generated change, the ensuing impact on the social work field appears more profound and dramatic than any before. Nevertheless, the stage through which social work is currently passing, although alarming to some observers, is a normal component of the development of all social movements, professions, and fields of practice. In every such endeavor there comes a time when theories, methods, ideologies, and technologies developed in an earlier period must be modified, more or less drastically, to suit changed circumstances. Inevitably a schism develops between those who cling to the forms of the past and those who wish to meet the imperatives of the moment. Ultimately a new entity emerges, which while retaining features from the past incorporates substantial innovation.

Although this process of cleavage and eventual synthesis is, as noted, a normal stage in the evolution of a profession, those for whom the viability of tradition is a matter of immediate professional relevance are understandably concerned. As each side struggles to uphold its point of view in the face of attack, polarization develops and rigidifies. Years may be spent in battle, as the traditionalists offer stanch resistance to change and thus prompt the innovators to refuse obstinately to acknowledge what they know is worth retaining in the old ways.

In this article the position is taken that the issues in the current dispute in the field of social work, between those who espouse a doctrinaire point of view and those who advocate change, are portents of an emerging new practice.[2] This new practice, the resultant of a long series of events and experiences, reflects recent changes in the society at large as well as in the field of social work. The changes of the sixties, in particular, have precipitated and shaped the development of the new social work method.

The complexities and ramifications of current methodological issues have been carefully and thoughtfully considered by a number of scholars and practitioners.[3] The issues have by no means been re-

[2]This article is based on material that will be elaborated in a volume on contemporary community organization practice, sponsored by a grant from the Russell Sage Foundation.

[3]See Scott Briar, "The Current Crisis in Social Casework," *Social Work Practice* (Columbia University Press, New York, 1967), 19–33; Alfred J. Kahn, "The Societal Context of Social Work Practice," *Social Work*, 10:145–55 (October, 1965); John B. Turner, "Relation of Health and Welfare Planning to Social Change and Social Development," in *Social Work and Social Planning* (National Association of Social Workers, New York, 1964), 11–19; Helen Harris Perlman, "Casework Is Dead," *Social Case-*

solved, and it is clear that the best interests of the social work field will be served by a continuation of the debate. It is in this spirit that this article deals with several nonmethodological consequences of the sociology of the sixties for social work. Specifically, the impact of the sixties on residual perspectives of the history and practice of social work will be acknowledged; the relevance of the institutional view and some consequences of this view on assumptions customarily made regarding the relationship between worker and client will be asserted; finally, possible applications of an institutional perspective of the field will be suggested.

RECAPITULATION OF THE ISSUES

According to the residual view of social work, the profession is a source of supplementary rehabilitative services to be utilized when regular social processes break down. It is assumed that problems necessitating social work intervention are anomalous, accidental, and temporary.According to the institutional view, on the other hand, social work is an integral part of a social welfare network, which, in turn, is part of a complex social system composed principally of formally organized collectivities.[4]

The residual perspective has led to a historical view of social welfare as a largely ineffectual attempt to deal with needs that far outstrip its meager resources. Social welfare is placed outside the mainstream of the social system, attempting by education, moral persuasion, religious witness, and rational positivism to persuade the dominant groups in the society to provide, as a matter of conscience, some measure of support to the unfortunate poor. Social welfare, according to this view, is an entity that exists to assist those who, as a result of their own failings, are unable to deal with various social exigencies. Thus, it makes up for temporary failures in regularly

---

work, 48:22–25 (January, 1967); Frances Fox Piven, "Professionalism as Political Skill: The Case of a Poverty Program," in *Personnel in Anti-Poverty Programs: Implications for Social Work Education* (Council on Social Work Education, New York, 1967), 37–50; Alvin Schorr, "Poverty, Politics, and People: The Education of Social Workers," in *Personnel in Anti-Poverty Programs . . .*, 29–36; George Brager, "Advocacy and Political Behavior," *Social Work*, 13:5–15 (April, 1968); and Shirley Cooper and Barbara Krantzler, "A Polemic in Response to a Tribute," *Social Work*, 13:3–4, 117–19 (April, 1968).

    [4]Harold L. Wilensky and Charles N. Lebeaux, *Industrial Society and Social Welfare* (Russell Sage Foundation, New York, 1958), 138–40; and Alfred J. Kahn, "The Function of Social Work in the Modern World," in Alfred J. Kahn (ed.), *Issues in American Social Work* (Columbia University Press, New York, 1959), 3–38.

functioning social institutions. The social work practice that logically evolved from this perspective was directed at helping individuals—by therapy, education, counseling, and other restorative and rehabilitative techniques—to overcome their inadequacies and to achieve a modicum of social equity. This was a practice that assisted communities by emphasizing coordination, efficiency, collective funding and planning, and other consensual, rational devices to improve the functioning of existing social welfare institutions.

At the core of this residual approach is the notion that the inequities being addressed by the field came into being unintentionally. Although it is conceded that callousness, inefficiency, ignorance, and pathology may have played a part, their creation was nevertheless unwitting. It is argued that institutions that are insensitive, callous, inept, or ignorant can be improved through logic, education, appeals to morality, and rational planning; and society's citizens who are damaged as a result can be made whole.

Many recent and ongoing modifications in social work practice are clearly not contained by the rationale just outlined. In order to provide a historically relevant context for the substantive innovations of social work practice of the sixties, an institutional structural perspective on the evolvement of social welfare is necessary. Such an alternate view takes as its point of departure the opposite core position, to the effect that the inequities addressed by the field are created by intentional, knowing acts on the part of individuals and institutions, for such purposes as maintaining a source of mobile, cheap labor. It posits, further, that although many of these inequities have been and will be resolved, the solutions themselves have created and will create new problems; therefore, neither the institutions of society nor its citizens have reached, or will ever reach, a fixed point of restoration.

According to the institutional-structural view, social welfare is a permanent device that ensures societal stability by alleviating the oppressive consequences of such conditions as unemployment, pathology, broken homes, and environmental deprivation. And if inadequate social welfare resources are considered in such structural terms—as a matter of deliberate, planful, conscious action (or inaction)—it follows that the critical factor to any solution of social inequities is power. Whereas the residual practice of social work in the face of institutional problems makes social work an instrument of control—an attempt to avoid precipitous, unpredictable, radical change—an institutional perspective provides a basis for partisanship and advocacy, aimed at overcoming the vested interests that have a stake in maintaining inequities.

This position does not preclude the altruistic and humanitarian practices that have graced the social work profession from its inception. Quite the contrary; it is posited that the institutional-structural perspective enables the field to fulfill these objectives more completely. Social work is not seen as the agent that mitigates the effects of inequity enough to prevent either the collapse of the status quo or revolution against it; rather, social work is seen as the agent that maximizes change by making it the price of stability and structurally integrates significant changes that are achieved. Thus, social work will educate its constituents to extract substantial, permanent, unstigmatized concessions for whole classes of citizens, instead of individual, temporary, means-test benefits for those who can present themselves in that state of grace that welfare systems and social agencies define as eligibility.

It is basically through such an interpretation and application of welfare history that it is possible to reconcile doctrines that call for partisanship, advocacy, social brokerage, policy-making by clients, and accountability through public ownership of welfare organizations.

WORKER'S ROLE

A residual view of social work history and practice casts the practitioner into an other-oriented role. Social work characterizes itself as a helping profession, and it is seen as such by the larger community, except, probably, by those persons who are public agency clients. Recruitment of social workers has been based largely on a perception of the profession as offering a rich opportunity to help people. The giving of service, as an ethical, moral, and personally gratifying objective, has been integral to the method and the life style of our profession. Helping the client to overcome his physical, emotional, economic, and social inadequacies so as to cope more effectively with life's problems has been the *raison d'etre* of social work practice.

But such a view creates a schism between clients and nonclients. And the field's conscientious respect for the integrity of the client and its careful adherence to the principle of self-determination and the doctrine of meeting the client at his own level of readiness to cope have been necessary because clients, from a residual perspective, are necessarily classified as helpless. The social worker is, of course, a "nonclient"; he comes to the profession able to help himself and then develops skill in helping others to help themselves. Both the process and the shibboleths of the profession have reflected this differential in the status of client and worker.

An institutional-structural view precludes such distinctions. Since individual pathology is seen as a function of social disorganization, the invidious characterization of the client as helpless and the distinctions between client and nonclient are substantially mitigated. It should be noted that in this view the existence of pathology is not denied; but the categorical designation of all social service beneficiaries as impaired is avoided. Nor are differences between clients and nonclients denied; but a pluralistic concept is applied that calls for both groups—equal albeit different—to share in planning and other social welfare processes.

The virtually universal nature of social welfare services in a welfare state precludes maintenance of a firm distinction between client and nonclient. A historical perspective that persists in drawing this now irrelevant distinction is as out-of-date and dysfunctional as the geocentric theory of the universe. The concept of institutionalism and the emergence of the welfare state have made the term *client* virtually obsolete. The ubiquity of coverage under the Social Security Act ensures that a beneficiary of Old-Age, Survivors, and Disability Insurance will not be distinguishable in the total population of which he is a part. The term *client*, as we are accustomed to use it, is inadequate to describe the association between citizen and OASDI, which takes on various forms as the citizen makes contributions, receives benefits, or is a dependent of a contributor or recipient.

Beneficiary designations apply without modification to those who work within the Social Security Administration; thus, a social worker employed by it is working for himself as well as for others. The practitioner is literally a client, or a potential client, as well as a dispenser of service; thus, he can be said to be helping himself as he advances the interests of clients in general. And a conception of the worker as having something to gain or lose as a result of his own practice can be incorporated into social work only through an institutional-structural perspective.

A view of worker and client as having different but equal roles is not simply a theoretical concept; it is a practical prerequisite to operationalizing such innovations as worker partisanship and client participation. The sharing of policy-making by agency staff and client is viable only if predicated on this concept of equality, along with a concept of welfare benefits as a right.[5]

Many examples can be cited that suggest that the current development of client participation in policy-making is endemic, brought about by events beyond the control of social work or any single profession. Even self-serving and profit-motivated industry reflects a similar state of affairs, not only in the tendency for stockholders to participate in policy-making but also in management-initiated employee participation. The demands of students for a role in determining academic policy have led to a searching review of the theoretical and ideological premises of the university; the demands of parents for a role in the management of the school have led to similar reviews of public education.

The resistance of social work and other professions to incursions on policy-making functions by the beneficiaries of service is symptomatic of an ingrained residualism, within which philosophy such participation is indeed inconceivable. According to the structural view, on the other hand, both worker and client suffer the effects of the dysfunction of the structural arrangements of society. This being the case, they are both dependent on service personnel, be they social workers, real estate brokers, accountants, or attorneys, to help them cope with a complex social environment whose demands exceed the resources of any single individual.

For the service beneficiary, client-worker equality means having a share in the planning and management of social welfare institutions. For the service provider, it means having a direct personal stake in the outcome of his practice. The benefits to be derived from an institutional-structural approach to social welfare do not accrue for the client alone; the profession and the institutions through which it operates are enhanced as well, because conjoint planning by service beneficiaries and service personnel leads to the provision of more relevant service to a more substantial proportion of the population. Institutional-structural perspectives, then, provide the social work profession and social work organizations with a context within which they can embrace, rather than resist, the inevitable trend toward full client participation in agency life. They provide a context within which self-interest and common interest coincide.

---

[5]Charles F. Grosser and Edward V. Sparer, "Legal Services for the Poor: Social Work and Social Justice," *Social Work*, 12:81–87 (January, 1967).

INSTITUTIONAL APPLICATIONS

The current debate within the field of social work has in part revolved around proposed new organizational forms for bringing social work services to recipients. Voluntary and public agencies have been examined and found wanting. Some commentators have suggested an entrepreneurial system, based on private practice, as a solution. The virtues[6] and shortcomings[7] of this solution have also been publicly discussed at some length. And it is clear that the proposal to resolve the dilemma of organizational dysfunction by eliminating the organization and to guarantee the integrity of social work by exploiting the attributes of the individual practitioner is essentially a residual strategy. An institutional-structural view, however, calls for an organizational solution, a permanent change in the auspices of practice that vests responsibility for maintaining professional integrity in the group that has the greatest stake in it, the clientele; such a solution calls for the initiation of devices to make the agency responsive to client needs — devices that bring the agency under client control, in large measure. Such control of the service-distribution system is the only way in which social welfare can hope to cope with the disbursement of the myriad individual services endemic to an urban industrial welfare state. Law and medicine are moving away from private entrepreneurial practice toward socialized and group arrangements.[8] Other service fields, such as pharmacy, education, and even the arts, have similarly been forced to seek collective structural devices in order to maintain themselves effectively in our changing society. The sensitivity of commerce and industry to this trend has been noted in the remark that our nation has become one where there is socialism for the middle class and laissez-faire for the poor.

Institutional solutions may also help to resolve some of the wider problems that beset the social work field today — for example, the charge of racism, which has been recently legitimized and made public by the Kerner Commission report.[9] In this instance clients

[6]Irving Piliavin, "Restructuring the Provision of Social Services," *Social Work*, 13:34, 41 (January, 1968).

[7]Alvin L. Schorr, "New Left and Old Right," editorial, *Social Work*, 13:2, 144 (April, 1968).

[8]Schorr, "New Left . . .," 2.

[9]*Report of the National Advisory Commission on Civil Disorders* (Bantam Books, New York, 1968).

have, indeed, set policy, for social work's mandate to deal with the fact and consequence of a racist society—and to do so now—has been issued, not by the profession but by the black community. The profession's principal strategy for serving black clients has been a long-range residual one: to the recognition that social distance between practitioner and beneficiary inhibits, distorts, and may even preclude the effective provision of benefits,[10] the response has been to attempt to maximize the number of minority group practitioners through existing institutions of recruitment, education, job placement, and practice. Although the attempt is fully justified in its own right, it is a solution of which the effects will be felt, if at all, far in the future, perhaps after our cities and nation have been irreparably damaged. Merely mitigating the ethnic gap between client and worker cannot redress the class and cultural and economic difference that inhibits relationships. Nor does it deal with the inequality between practitioner and beneficiary that residualism establishes and maintains. A structural solution, however, makes use of existing resources and opens vistas for more immediate results by dealing directly with inequality through client control of the welfare-disbursement system in which the social work practitioner is employed: a white middle-class practitioner who works for an agency controlled by its black lower-class clients will be responsive to the needs of those clients despite his differences from them. What inhibits service, in other words, is inequality, not differences; and it is power, in the form of client control, that will eliminate the inequality and thereby mitigate the differences. There is evidence that further exploration of the effects of client control will produce findings that will have profound consequences for all aspects of social work practice.[11]

Structurally institutionalizing social welfare services may have the unanticipated result of exposing the false dichotomy between individual and community services, for the debate between the actionist and the clinician derives, essentially, from an abjuration of the client. Social work practice offered under beneficiary control and constructed on the premise of client-worker equality will be unable to ignore individual needs in the name of social cause or to subvert individual needs to preconceived notions of treatment. How can a

---

[10]See, for example, John M. Martin, "Social-Cultural Differences: Barriers in Casework with Delinquents," *Social Work*, 2:22–25 (July, 1957); and Julia B. Bloch, "The White Worker and the Negro Client in Psychotherapy," *Social Work*, 13:36–42 (April, 1968).

[11]Bertha Capen Reynolds, *Social Work and Social Living: Explorations in Philosophy and Practice* (Citadel Press, New York, 1951), 13–132.

worker who is himself a client, or who is directly accountable to his clients, choose between social reordering directed at prevention and treatment directed at cure? To pursue either goal exclusively is to betray the vested rights of citizen-clients. Such a betrayal is much less likely to take place when the social work profession and its organizations are integrated within the structure of a democratic welfare state.

CONCLUSION

It appears, at least for the present, that the regular, mass structural integration of welfare service is the operational priority of the welfare state. No other possibilities seem to be capable of deflecting increasing inequality in a society of proliferating wealth. Nevertheless, as is implicit to the arguments offered in this article, another era—perhaps only a decade away—will demand new formulations to deal with new problems, for social solutions inevitably produce social problems, which, in turn, require new solutions.

· 37 ·

DORCAS D. BOWLES

Making Casework Relevant to Black People: Approaches, Techniques, Theoretical Implications

Historically, casework has been the technique most admired and respected among social work specialties. This is largely because the casework technique is the most fully developed; its style and con-

SOURCE: Reprinted from *Child Welfare*, Vol. 48, No. 8 (October, 1969), pp. 468–75.

cepts are easily articulated and transferable to the other social work methods.

Recently, social work has been under fire because of ineffectiveness in working with disadvantaged and deprived families. Paradoxically, the very persons to whom the social work profession has a historic commitment are the persons to whom casework methods have least to offer. Thus, many of the persons most in need of help are not being reached.

Many say that caseworkers, as well as members of other helping professions (psychologists, psychiatrists, teachers), have tried to work with poor families, but that they are "untreatable" and "unmotivated." Before we call this group of people unmotivated, we should take a hard look at traditional casework techniques, and seriously question them.

Are caseworkers committed to rigid techniques and methods that are inappropriate? If we are to meet the needs of poor people, we must design treatment appropriate to these people living in their own life situations, rather than impose techniques appropriate to other people. The recent findings of the President's Commission on Civil Disorders, and their implications for our field, make this matter urgent. This paper deals with experiences and impressions in my work with a small group of disadvantaged, deprived black families.

POPULATION AND PHYSICAL SETTING

The group comprised 40 mothers, each with a 4-year old child attending a research preschool center housed in four ground-floor apartments in a housing project extension near Chicago's West Side. The extension houses 745 families in three- to five-bedroom apartments. The majority of the mothers migrated to Chicago from the South as teenagers. Some had not completed grammar school; many were high school dropouts. The fathers are unskilled or semiskilled; a few of the mothers of intact families work in restaurants and factories, or as domestics. In father-absent homes, most of the mothers receive AFDC support.

The physical environment is the same for all the families. There are garbage, paper, discarded household furnishings, broken bottles, and other debris in the areas immediately approaching the apartments. The neighborhood stores carry poor-quality merchandise at high prices. Play space is inadequate and some of the playground equipment is unsafe. The littered ramps or porches are often used by children for playing.

In the building entrances, there are broken mailboxes. Nowhere do the occupants' names appear, adding to the sense of anonymity and depersonalization. Elevators are often dirty, and smell of urine. (There is no public washroom on the first floor, so that children in the playground must take the elevator to their apartments. It is obvious that some can't always make it in time.) Ventilation is poor. Floors and walls are scarred and dirty, garbage is scattered near incinerators that are too small for the accumulated refuse. There are no doorbells for the individual apartments. Stairways are dark and dirty, lights are often broken, and after dark many of the women are afraid to leave their apartments.

Even professionals sometimes assume that people in housing projects have stereotyped characteristics and behavior. Such assumptions are inaccurate. Despite the similar living conditions, these people cannot be reduced to one type, either family or individual. There is wide variation in childrearing practices and philosophies, family organization, functioning levels, interpersonal styles, and values and goals generally, as well as a wide range of human interests, talents, and potentialities. Discrimination in jobs and housing, of course, has forced people to accept less than their capabilities would produce were they not members of a minority. A small percentage of the group under study fulfills the stereotyped images, but many of the housing residents are not content with their lot, and dream of a better future for themselves and their children.

The similarities among these families end with the physical environment; the people form a continuum of personal functioning, with a wide variety of life styles. To talk meaningfully about the range of behaviors observed, however, it is helpful to define subgroups.

POPULATION SUBGROUPINGS

The groupings are based on the families' assumptions about their place in the social order, that is, do they believe that they can move up, or that they must remain in their current status. The first group consists of stable, upwardly mobile families. The second group comprises families on the periphery of the most deprived, hard-core group, but moving toward the stable, upwardly mobile group. These families have both strengths and weaknesses, and could potentially move in either direction. The third group comprises the disorganized, hard-core, deprived families.

UPWARDLY MOBILE FAMILIES

Families moving upward see their stay in the housing project as temporary, and make plans to move into better neighborhoods. They are interested in their children's development. The fathers, if present, are involved with the children, and weekends are spent in activities as a family — visiting relatives, going to places of amusement, or taking auto rides. These homes have parental standards and the children are affectionately and carefully supervised and differentiated. The mothers try to understand the child's experiences and needs, and to deal with each child as an individual.

Upwardly mobile mothers talk freely. They describe their children as good or bad, but the tone is positive, warm, and gentle. In the first and second interviews the mothers could relate to me, and involve the children in their communication. They were not embarrassed by the child's asking questions and they explained things freely to the children. These mothers can participate in and learn from planned group meetings with speakers, films, crafts, or from general discussion.

DEPRIVED HARD-CORE FAMILIES

Characteristic of the disadvantaged, deprived, hard-core families are passive acceptance and a sense of resignation in dealing with persons associated with power structures, that is, stores, schools, welfare, and so forth. Even when an active role is taken, the parent often feels that chance is the major factor. This is related to poor self-image and to expectation of criticism and punishment. Thomas Pettigrew, in *Profile of the Negro American*, referred to the expectation of mistreatment, combined with a feeling of helplessness, as the "oppressive phobia."

On one occasion, I made a routine home visit to a mother. One of the children let me in, and I saw and heard the public school truant officer talking to the mother in an angry, condescending, and threatening manner. The mother, crumpled on a couch, made no attempt to defend, question, or reply. The truant officer, not acknowledging my presence, warned the mother she would have to "do something" about her child's behavior. Then she left abruptly, without saying goodbye. The child, Denise, against whom the tirade was directed, stood in a corner, her head half turned to the wall, an angry, sullen look on her face.

The mother was immediately defensive about my presence. She asked what wrong her 4-year-old had done at preschool to bring me. I explained my visit, mentioned the positive aspects of the child's behavior at school, and initiated a discussion of the scene I'd just witnessed. The mother immediately began to discuss "how bad" Denise was, how many times she had been suspended from school.

The mother had not asked the truant officer the specifics of the suspension. She was surprised when I insisted she had a right to these facts. I asked Denise if she would like to talk with me and see if together we could help her to get along better in school. She agreed, and did not miss a single appointment during a 3-month period in which I saw her weekly. Two weeks before ending sessions with Denise, I visited her at home. Her mother showed me "the best report card Denise ever brought home." A note from her teacher indicated that, because of good grades, Denise and two of her classmates had been selected to visit the zoo with the teacher on a Saturday. Denise summed it up: "Well, like you said, if I behaved and was good, the teacher would be good to me. After I started to act better, she started to care, not as much as you, but at least she wasn't picking on me all the time."

In the disorganized homes, actions are unpredictable and inconsistent. Activities are very largely impulse-determined, so that, psychologically, there is an absence of internalization of both clear ideas and consistent, flexible controls. One day a mother may stay in bed until noon and insist her children do likewise, or permit the children to run around unsupervised. The next day the mother may be up at 6 o'clock, feed and dress the children, and have the house in order by 8:30. Children and adults are never sure what to expect.

The Wright family consists of Mrs. Wright, 24; Mr. Wright, 26 and unemployed; Angela, 6; Harry, 5; Joyce, 3; and Marie, 2. The family is on AFDC, at $206 a month. Mrs. Wright's inconsistent handling of the children was reflected in Harry's and Angela's school attendance. Mrs. Wright sent Harry to school one day, kept him out the next, even after I agreed to transport Harry. She vacillated between having the door open and waiting for me with coffee prepared, and not answering the door even though she was in the house. The children never knew when their mother would be in a good mood, prepare breakfast, dress them, and send them to school, or when their needs would be unmet.

In the most disorganized, deprived homes, mothers cannot discriminate among the children. Children seem to have no individuality in the mother's view. Asked in a first or second interview, "What is Johnnie like?", these mothers would say, "He's like his brother," or "He's like his sister," or "He's like any other 4-year-old child." "What toys does Johnnie like to play with?" The answer is, "Anything." There is no involvement of mothers in children's activities. They are guarded, suspicious. Relationships are shallow and tenuous. In describing how they punish their children, these mothers use such words as "beat" or "whip," in contrast to the stable families, where mothers say "talk" and "spank."

These mothers answer questions in brief, abbreviated fashion. When a child hurts himself, the mothers seldom inquire about the nature of the injuries or offer comfort. They tend to blame the child for the accident. It is often said, "I'm glad you hurt yourself; now maybe you'll listen to me." Curiosity and exploration by the children are greatly curtailed. Thus, in the parent-child relationship, the alternatives of action and thought open to the child are restricted. The mothers are depressed, "worn out" physically, and depleted emotionally. Their own needs for support and nurturance are unmet, so that they are incapable of meeting the needs of their children. Their negative self-image is reinforced by their children's lack of growth and responsiveness.

In these homes, the children become self-reliant and assume adult responsibilities at an early age. The 4- and 5-year-olds are often left in charge of younger siblings, including feeding and diapering and protecting. Being forced to relinquish the dependency relationship of childhood is the rule rather than the exception. At an early age, the child learns to keep secrets from adults, school officials, social workers, and police, and generally to cover up for parents. The orientation is to be able to outsmart the other person, to be stronger, slicker, and faster.

In these homes, the mothers' needs take precedence over the needs of their children. There is a great deal of displacement of anger from one person onto another. Once when I went to pick up Harry Wright, he was not dressed. Mrs. Wright said she would have to keep him from school because he had to take care of the younger children while she shopped. There was no thought of arranging things for Harry's convenience. After I focused on Harry's need for nursery school and the gains he had made, Mrs. Wright agreed to let Harry come to school.

On another occasion Mrs. Wright was angry because Angela, the 6-year-old, was ill and she had been up most of the night tending her. When I arrived for Harry, Mrs. Wright said that Harry could not go to school, since she was taking all the children to the doctor, even though only Angela was sick. I stressed how tired Mrs. Wright must be as a result of a sleepless night, and the difficult task she had of dressing the children in winter clothing to go to the doctor's office. I agreed to drive her to the doctor's, since Angela was very sick and Mrs. Wright had only bus fare, and would have to wait on the corner for a bus. I suggested that she let Harry come to school, since this would mean one fewer child to undress and dress, and Harry would not have to miss school. Mrs. Wright agreed; we all walked with Harry to school, after which I drove Mrs. Wright and the other children to the doctor's office.

Most deprived mothers cannot talk freely if the worker listens passively. If the mother is busy and the worker is involved in the activity, the mother is freer to discuss personal and family problems. If a mother is cutting a pattern or folding clothes, I often suggest that she continue, while I assist her in some manner. As we busy ourselves, the mothers often speak freely.

The most seriously deprived mothers want the best for their children. Their difficulty is due to psychological disorganization and general lack of knowledge of child care and norms for behavior at various ages. Families bring from their past, and perpetuate, some deprivations and inconsistencies, and many myths. Psychologically, the disorganized mothers are immature, and much like children themselves. But if some of their basic needs are met, they can proceed to a more developmental orientation toward their children. They can learn to get pleasure from their children and from contacts with other families in group activities in school.

If work with deprived black lower-class families is to succeed, casework techniques must be adapted to their values, beliefs, and life styles. The examination of life styles, values, and attitudes in interviews and contacts must not be done in a manner to suggest these values are not so "good" as middle-class values. These values and life styles match a way of life that helps one to cope with the realities of the environment.

The present caseworker image is largely that of a therapist. Thus casework is confined to a therapeutic function, to influencing the intrapsychic structure. In work with deprived black families, my role has been multifunctional: I have been therapist, teacher, transporter of children to school, family helper, an occasional babysitter, budgeter of time and finances, a referral service, or a sympathetic ear. But in all functions, the main concern has been the individuals served, by attempting to meet their needs, by being involved in their lives, by showing concern for them as people who care and who are interested in their children, as people who are motivated and treatable.

Work with a deprived mother must be focused on helping her sense that her energies can affect and determine to some extent what happens to her and to her children.

It must give mothers a sense of stability about and trust in the future.

SUGGESTED TECHNIQUES

There are special techniques in working with these families.

1. There must be casualness, and a "down-to-earth" approach. This encourages an exchange of ideas. In most visits, I open the discussion with some remark about the weather, a news event, or a general area of interest. This sets the tone of the interview, and helps establish contact with a mother who may be hesitant and distant. After several visits, most mothers feel comfortable, and there is a continuing discussion. Following a "warming-up" period, one can shift to more meaningful material.

2. Use of familiar words and terms is important. One must not, however, "talk down" to the parent or use language and mannerisms that are forced or unnatural. Condescending, patronizing, or insincere attitudes employed in this approach hinder meaningful relationships.

3. Areas of competence in the mother should be pointed out to her. This helps to broaden self-esteem and enhance self-image, and shows interest in the mother. The worker aligns herself with the mother's wish to be a good parent. A mother's selection of colors in furniture and accessories, her choice of curtains, rearrangement of furniture, special food she has prepared, a dress she has made, and a host of other things can be mentioned. Attention to such matters can give a mother a sense of self-worth. A compliment often is followed by a mother's showing increased interest in a hobby, giving more attention to her physical appearance and to the care of her children.

4. One must serve as a model for the mother. In the home, one can demonstrate verbally and in action how situations can be handled. As interest in parents and their children as people is shown, the

basis for a relationship is established. A worker's handling of an incident with the children may make the mother aware of how different the approach is from her own. This is especially true when the worker is firm, explains to the child without anger, and the child responds. It is fascinating to observe a mother, under similar circumstances, use the worker's words and gestures with similar success. Next, it may become part of the mother's response pattern.

In most instances, there is a period of testing until the worker is seen as a stable, consistent individual sincerely interested in the mother and the family. These mothers must test to see if they will again experience rejection from a person in authority. Thus, continued interest and concern serve as a corrective emotional experience, with authority in a positive, supportive role.

5. The caseworker must relate to the mother as the key person, and at the same time be sensitive to other family members. This is especially important for creating conditions that can be advantageously influenced. When the older children are present, ask their names, and how they are getting along in school. If the child says he is not doing well, and the mother confirms this, I ask both, "Why?" This helps both mother and child to explore causes, interpersonal conflicts, and family relationships, and encourages communication of ideas. Whenever possible, I raise questions that focus on what they can do to ease the situation. This enables the family members to pay special attention to suggestions. Often, the meaning of such an incident is related to other situations. Sometimes a child or a mother tells me after a visit that certain changes were observed; they are able to carry this over into other situations.

Not only family members "aggressive" enough to encourage and solicit communication should be involved. It is important to include the quiet, shy child. Such manipulation shifts the family composition, and may help the family to perceive this child in a different light and modify its way of dealing with him.

6. The worker can use appropriate toys and projects with a parent on a one-to-one basis. The toy can serve as a vehicle for communication, until rapport is established. As parents and children experience success in toys and projects, and through discussion between worker and parent concerning the toys and projects, changes can be brought about in the parents' overall orientation toward child-rearing, as well as in the children's rate of development. The home is a natural laboratory for teaching developmental differences through siblings. With the worker's help, the parent can understand norms for behavior and can see the child as passing through phases that

require varying approaches; she can see the need to differentiate the children on the basis of needs and age. Parents and children alike come to value the process of learning and to view it as being fun as well as educational. The experience of success enhances self-image and is extremely important to the child's ability to learn and the mother's feeling that, as a parent, she can help the child to learn and to be happy.

The mothers feel they are important to the child's growth; the child is pleased that his mother is showing interest, and so a feedback system is established. Once rapport is there, the parents bring up concerns to discuss with the worker. In all the families where developmental toys were introduced, there was an initial focus on the toys. This has now changed, and more time is spent discussing children's fears of separation and how a mother can help the children; how to explain a family death to children; how to discuss sex; problems with teenagers; marital difficulties, and so forth.

7. With the more deprived mothers, the one-to-one approach in the home setting is important. These mothers cannot be expected, at least initially, to come to the school voluntarily and become involved in group meetings around specific problems. The one-to-one approach is necessary to break through feelings of disillusionment, mistrust, and suspicion that isolate the deprived mothers from school personnel and institutional authority.

The worker can help the mothers to examine viable alternatives that can have some effect on their environment. This paves the way for participation in group activities.

8. There must be flexibility in timing and place of interviews. In relating to life styles, it is important to regulate time. If a mother is upset or is open and productive, it is desirable to have a long session (1 1/2 hours). If a mother seems closed and generally nonproductive, a 10–15 minute session is adequate. One may choose to deal with silence and lack of productivity at the next meeting. A caseworker must also be willing to respond to needs as they arise, to be ready if crisis strikes, and to have communicated to the mother that he is always available to assist her.

Except for tradition, convenience, and a narrow view of the function of caseworkers, there is no reason that counseling should take place only in the office or in the home setting. The housing project is close to the shopping area. During the day I frequently meet my parents at stores, on elevators, in halls or on porches. The parents begin to talk with me. Some of the most meaningful information has been imparted to me as I walked from an apartment building with a parent. If an issue that obviously requires further attention is brought up, it is important to continue the discussion at the office or at home.

As one goes about the community, one begins to feel a part of it, and this is closely linked to how the parents begin to relate to you. At first, I made all the initial contacts on seeing mothers in a store, or on the street. Now, as I make my rounds, mothers come up to me, or call me when I do not see them, or seek me out if they hear me talking to someone else in the laundry room or somewhere else in the building.

9. The worker must be able to bridge the gap between his usual method of verbal communication and the communication styles of the families with whom he works. Verbal statements, in and of themselves, are never adequate. These parents express a great deal through movements, gestures, and facial expressions. In an agency setting, it was most unlikely that I would embrace a client; I found that I could spontaneously and freely put my arm around a mother in the housing project setting.

10. It is important to point out the universality of these women's feelings as mothers and wives. This helps to lessen feelings of isolation and to bridge the social class gap. In so doing, one also bridges the gap between the client and the worker, who is viewed as middle class.

11. The worker must be constantly alert to rephrasing and enlarging on a mother's use of words, labeling of feelings, and focusing on her ego strengths. Many of these mothers think that they must "control" their children to be defined as "good mothers" and be accepted by the worker. If a mother says her child is "mean" and "stubborn" and "will not listen" to her, it must be explained that for him to learn to respect others, his mother must be patient and help him develop some awareness of "the other guy."

12. Mothers should be involved in social action, so that they experience participatory democracy. This gives them a sense of power, a feeling that they have some control over their environment, through involvement in groups.

13. The worker must see himself as a warm, giving human being first, and a caseworker second. His technical skills are secondary to his impact as a person. It is important for the worker to have confidence in himself as an effective force. His expectation has to be that he can and will have a positive effect on people. If the worker feels incompetent, he cannot help other people who feel incompetent.

BATTLE FATIGUE

Persons working with disadvantaged populations can expect to experience some "battle fatigue"—periods of mild depression and weariness and feelings of helplessness and pessimism. This can be eased by an occasional day off or a long weekend, by vacations, and by discussions with other personnel with expertise in working with disadvantaged persons. A caseworker who has experienced "battle fatigue" is more sensitive to the feelings of parents who live in conditions of poverty.

IMPLICATIONS OF TECHNIQUES

There are many who say these approaches are merely supportive and not insightful, and therefore, will not bring about permanent change. An insightful approach does not necessarily rule out supportive techniques. A worker being supportive in one area may explore another area on a deeper level. Whatever the approach, one must be aware of underlying causes and dynamics. An educational approach is sometimes sufficient to modify a general pattern of behavior. How permanent changes will be depends largely on the psychological stress involved and whether the person has developed sufficient strength to cope effectively. But, this is true of any therapy. The casework techniques appropriate to deprived black populations are applicable to lower-class populations generally. These approaches require a commitment to involve oneself totally; to get to know the most deprived families, to be a part of them. This kind of engagement makes significant impact in the attempt to achieve modification of behavior.

CONCLUSIONS

Evaluation of the approaches suggested in this paper must await their application in other settings. We do know, however, that programs that involve parents and have observable impact on the home are of extreme importance for long-range gains. It is essential to develop long-term programs for work with families and their children from birth, with continuity of service as the youngsters grow up.

No casework is more challenging than that with the families in our society who most need our help. Although the frustrations are great, the potential rewards and social satisfactions and the individual growth for the worker, as well as the clients, warrant continued vigorous effort in this area.

· 38 ·

FRED W. CHRISTIE

The Gang Fight

As we drove in the neighborhood, Blackie, the Wildcats member, pulled up beside us in his car. When we stopped to talk he said, "Manuel wants to fight me, and I hear he's got a gun. I've got a gun, too." I asked him where Manny was, and he said, "At Joe's." (A local restaurant.) I told him to follow me to the Boys' Club, then I took him to the office and told him to wait there until I returned. I asked Mr. Simon, the program director of the Club, to keep him in the office. I then drove to Joe's and found Manny. I asked him to come outside to talk with me for a moment. In the car, I asked if he were looking for a fight with Blackie and he said, "Yes." I asked him if he had a gun, and he said, "I know where I can get one." When I asked what it was all about, he said Bill, his brother, had loaned Blackie a battery for his car several weeks ago. Bill, in the meantime, had bought a car, and when he asked Blackie for the battery, Blackie told him he had sold it.

I asked him if this was worth shooting someone, and he said, "No, I just want to fight him, but I know he has a gun."

I then told him Blackie was at the Boys' Club, and I asked if he would be willing to go over with me and we could all sit down and talk about it.

SOURCE: Reprinted from Irving Spergel, *Street Gang Work*, 1966, Addison-Wesley Publishing Co., Reading, Mass., pp. 110–112.

Manuel said, "No, there's nothing to talk about; I'll beat his ass when I see him."

I said, "I won't stop you from fighting, but why don't you sit down and first know what you're fighting about?" He said, "Okay." I asked him if they did fight, would they do it in the ring at the Club. He said, "I don't know. Maybe."

At the office, Manuel, Blackie, Mr. Simon, and I talked for about 15 minutes. Bill, Manuel's brother, was called in to confirm the story. Several times while we were talking, the real cause for the fight came out. Manuel felt that Blackie, a relatively new member, had challenged his position as the toughest guy in their group. Manuel remarked, "The other guys consider me the bad boy," and when Mr. Simon asked, "What do you mean?" he said, "I'm the toughest guy in the group, and Blackie, being new, plays the role of the tough guy. I've let him push me around in school and other places, but I'm not going to anymore."

When Simon asked Manuel directly if the real cause of the fight was that he felt that Blackie challenged his role as the toughest, Manuel said, "Yes." It was quite apparent that our talking with the boys would not dissuade them from fighting, and I felt it best to let them go ahead and fight rather than prolong it. I asked Manuel if he would be satisfied with the outcome in the ring here at the Boys' Club. After thinking for a moment or two, Manuel said he would try.

The fellows went six two-minute rounds in the ring. They didn't box *per se*, only slugged wildly at each other; however, a good many blows did ring home. Up to the sixth round the fight was fairly even, but then, as Blackie landed a few good punches, Manuel stepped back, threw off his gloves, held up his bare fists and said, "I'm going to fight with these." Joe DeRose, staff member of the Boys' Club, who was refereeing the fight, said no. Manuel jumped out of the ring and shouted to Blackie, "I'll be outside waiting for you." Manuel picked up his shirt and shoes and walked out.

I should mention that while we were in the office, I had asked the two boys if they wanted the "Wildcats," who were at the club, to watch the fight. Blackie said he didn't care. Manuel, on the other hand, said, "I want them all there so they can see me beat his ass good." During the fight the Wildcats did not cheer. They sat back and waited for the outcome.

After Manuel walked out, I told Blackie to take his time getting dressed, then come outside. I then followed Manuel and talked to him in the street. I told him, "If you're going to fight outside, at least do it my way. Get in the car, and you, Blackie, and I will go somewhere and find an alley, and you two can have it out." He agreed and I put him in the back seat of my car. Blackie came out of the Club and said to me, "What do you want me to do?" I told him to get in the front seat which he did. I drove away with the two boys.

I didn't know exactly what I was going to do, but I knew the boxing match had already made them both very tired. Also, I felt sure that Blackie did not want to continue the fight. Manuel, on the other hand, would be a problem. I felt that Manuel did not really want to fight, but was compelled to because of the outcome of the first fight which was not particularly in his favor; he still felt his position in the group to be challenged. We drove down Simpson to Eastern Avenue, then I turned to them and said, "I'm sure you're both pretty thirsty; before we do anything, let's get a couple of cokes." Manuel smiled wearily, and Blackie said, "Okay." After we had cokes, I just drove around for half an hour. Neither boy spoke, and I didn't think we should say anything until we stopped. I pulled into an alley, off Darwin Drive, and stopped the car. We sat for about five minutes, not saying anything. I then turned to Blackie and asked him what he wanted to do. He said, "Nothing." I then looked at Manuel, and he said, "Fight." I talked to both boys, more directly to Manuel, for about 10 minutes.

The first thing I pointed out was that as things stood right now they had done a good thing for the Club. By fighting in the ring with gloves, and not in the street, they had set a good example for the others to follow; now, if they fought in the alley, they would destroy the good they had done. I pointed out to Manuel that many groups do not have just one fellow who is the toughest, but two or three guys who are equally tough. I pointed out that if they fought now there would be a winner and a loser, and this would split the club. Some of the fellows would side with Manuel and some with Blackie. I stopped talking for a minute and asked Manuel what he wanted to do. He replied, "Go in the alley." I said "Okay, let's go." As I got out of the car and came around between the two boys I said to them, it was a strange thing that they were both seniors in high school and that this was something I really would not expect from them. I asked Manuel if he knew what percentage of boys I worked with were seniors in high school. He said, "No," and when I told him it probably was less than ten percent he laughed. I then mentioned that for guys who had a chance to get a good job and have a family, this was not the type of thing I would expect.

I had delayed about as long as I could and was about ready to go back into the alley, when Blackie started to cry, "I'll quit the Club and give him a battery if he wants, but I don't want to fight any more." I looked at Manuel and he had his head down, scuffling his feet. Manuel then said, "I don't want him to quit the club; we need him for the door at socials." This remark by Manuel exposed his real feelings. I then hit him hard, asking, "How much more can you humiliate Blackie? You really want to rub his face in the dirt, don't you?" I told them both to get in the car and that I had to get some cigarettes and make a phone call, and then if they wanted to fight it was okay with me. I was through with them both: I acted as mad as I could, I slammed the door as I got into the car, and took off in a hurry.

I pulled into a Standard station and made my phone call. Back at the car I said to Manuel, "What alley do you want me to leave you in?" He kept his head down and said, "Let's go home." Needless to say I felt relieved. As I crossed the street I said to the fellows, "I'm glad the way things worked out, and I want you to know that I feel you're two of the finest boys I've worked with." I took Manuel home and Blackie back to his car.[1]

---

[1]This record was developed by Fred W. Christie of the *Chicago Youth Development Project*. By permission.

· 39 ·

B. HAROLD CHETKOW

So Go Fight City Hall:
A Community Work Record

This community action episode took place in a high population density, semisuburban area of a middle-sized metropolis. The spe-

---

SOURCE: Reprinted from John B. Turner (ed.), *Neighborhood Organization for Community Action* (New York: National Association of Social Workers, 1968), pp. 194–203.

cific neighborhood in question is located within the outer fringe of the inner city, is a racially mixed middle-class settlement, and is within a ten-minute automobile drive of downtown. Its houses are over forty years old, solidly built, with ample yards and physical amenities such as full-grown trees, sidewalks, paved streets, lawns and flower beds, street lights, and so on.

The neighborhood has twice the percentage of persons over 65 the county has, and double the county's average percentage of college graduates. Some parts of the area are predominantly renter-occupied. It contains less than half the county percentage of poor families. Since 1960 the in-mobility rate of the neighborhood has risen sharply above that of the county, especially with regard to younger Negro families with many children. The streets are jammed with parked cars at night and the schools are overcrowded.

One block within this neighborhood is the goal-setting group for the action process described in this case history. The over-all Neighborhood Association, mentioned repeatedly in the history, was organized in 1961. The action took place in the autumn of 1964, when all association activities were still done on a strictly volunteer basis.

The first-person narrative was related to the writer by one of the most active citizen-members of the association and is based primarily on this citizen's role in the events that took place. He was, of course, no ordinary citizen, bringing as he did a considerable postgraduate education and professional community planning background to his citizen role. His story has been left intact as much as possible.

PROCESS SUMMARY OF THE ACTION EPISODE

First Day

As block organization co-ordinator of the Neighborhood Association, I received a telephone call from Mrs. Cary, who had been referred to me by the director of the city's Human Relations Department. She had gone to the department to complain that her block, the 2800 block of B Street, was being torn up by a road construction company. Big chunks of cement had been left lying around, sidewalks were gone, stretches of roadbed were seas of water and mud, machinery was left unattended all night—these were dangers to the neighborhood children, raised dust, and created general mess and chaos. The residents had no place to park their cars at night. Mrs. Cary seemed genuinely upset, especially because no notice had reached the neighbors (mostly Negroes, marginal-income families, some public welfare recipients, and many renters). Property management firms that handled housing rental on the block also claimed that they had not received notice of this street repair. No one seemed able to find out why this was being done, or when it had been scheduled to begin. No attempt was made to discuss compensation for property frontages (as well as for shrubs, grass, trees, and so on) removed by scooping machines and bulldozers. The neighbors found it impossible to get any information from the crew or the foreman working on the block. In fact, these workmen were almost rude when approached for any purpose.

A midmorning telephone call to the president of the Neighborhood Association confirmed the facts of the situation. He had talked to the neighbors in this block over the past few weeks and had even driven a delegation of them downtown in his own car to confer formally with the city's chief engineer, who had contracted with the construction company now working in B Street. The interview had been a shambles. The chief engineer had been discourteous and evasive. Questions about replacement of shrubs were referred to the Parks Department (responsible for parkways and boulevards); of traffic speed limits, to the Traffic Department; and so on. The neighbors had been frustrated and angered by their experience. The association president gave me his blessing to take on the project and see what I could do. My own occupation and work schedule were flexible enough to allow me to spend the next few hours on this near-crisis situation.

A further telephone check with the Human Relations Department staff confirmed that Mrs. Cary had been there this morning. Her story was accurate. The city was extending a one-way traffic pattern through the block. The department director had advised her to contact me and ask the association to make a formal protest about this high-handed treatment of people. He was fairly certain that no violation of human or civil rights was involved, which ruled out action by his department.

I checked back with Mrs. Cary by telephone, agreeing to try to help. Since the association had not scheduled a membership meeting for another six weeks, we might have to rule out a general protest statement, but other courses of action would probably be possible. I suggested she try the local NAACP office, while I went further with some of my contacts within City Hall.

During the afternoon I made a phone call to a friend in the mayor's office (we had worked together professionally on the city's various poverty programs). She knew of Mrs. Cary, since both serve on the Poverty Action Board. As a known and trusted member of the Democratic party, I shared with her my concern about the way the B Street situation was being handled. I stressed that "we" might lose about one hundred Negro votes, as well as reap some negative mass-media publicity, if something remedial were not done soon. Since my friend was running for a county office in the forthcoming election, she was sensitive to these statements. Furthermore, she was able to generalize the problem into the immorality of running roughshod over human beings this way, and saw its negative implications for the mayor at a time when everyone was trying to help the poor. She asked me to continue "sitting on the lid," but also to call the chief engineer later—after she had an opportunity to go down to his office and discuss the entire matter with him.

Second Day

Early this morning I telephoned the chief engineer's office. Since he was in a meeting, I talked to his assistant. I introduced myself as a member of the Neighborhood Association and a friend of a certain person in the mayor's office. The assistant engineer was attentive and friendly, but evasive. He mentioned that there had been a public hearing some months ago regarding the block in question, attended by thirty to forty persons from the area. He took my message for the chief engineer and promised to ask the latter to phone me back later today. He also promised that the department's "field man" (really its right-of-way negotiator) would stop in the 2800 B Street area tomorrow or the next day and try to allay some of the neighbors' misgivings.

During the afternoon I tried to reach the Democratic county chairman and the ward chairman, but both men were out of town until next week. The wife of the county chairman, a family friend, promised to give the entire story to her husband as soon as he returned from Washington, D.C. In the meantime, the local NAACP office turned Mrs. Cary down with the statement that it did not see this case in terms of a race issue.

Fourth Day

I checked by telephone with Mrs. Cary. The field man had not turned up during the past days. Nothing had changed regarding the situation in the 2800 block of B Street.

The chief engineer returned my phone call Tuesday morning [the second day]. He expressed reluctance to do anything about the situation, since he had adhered to the letter of his responsibilities under the law. The project had been adequately advertised in the classified ads, a public hearing had been held in the prescribed manner, and he felt that the neighborhood had no cause to complain. His department has many such areas to fix up, and if it took time to listen to all complaints the work would never be done. He was not worried that people felt abused or that an active Neighborhood Association was now involved.

I finally said to him that we seemed to be wasting each other's time repeating the same issues and arguments. I had tried to alert him to a potentially explosive situation, but since he was not interested, I would hang up the telephone. However, I added, he should be aware that "from this point on, you are not likely to be pleased with what happens." For a few moments I could do nothing. Gradually I began to comprehend his tactics. Seething with indignation — controlled but real — I called my friend in the mayor's office. I apologized for bothering her again. She was very attentive when she sensed the anger in my voice, and I was careful not to suppress it completely. I told her that I felt, in the absence of the county chairman and my ward chairman, that she had to let responsible Democratic leadership know what might result from the chief engineer's attitude. I even used the metaphor that this man acted like an old-fashioned "highwayman," and was making it almost impossible for me to restrain the block much longer. In fact, I said that after my experience I felt like calling the newspapers myself.

She was immediately aware of the serious political implications of the situation. She asked me to keep B Street block calm a little longer and not to let the news media get involved. She finished with the words, "Let me see what I can do!"

Fifteen minutes later, an elated Mrs. Cary phoned me to ask, "What have you been able to do?" She had just received a polite call from the chief engineer himself, and he had sounded very uncomfortable (I guessed that the mayor's representative was standing beside him during the entire telephone conversation). He now volunteered to Mrs. Cary that if the neighbors had any questions and would write the questions in a letter, he would get answers for them within a few days. She was quite amazed at his seemingly total reversal and at the forced conciliatory tone she could detect in his voice. She was nevertheless pleased, and promised to have a list of questions for him by Monday.

I advised Mrs. Cary to take a short poll of her neighbors, including the two now threatening to sue the city, to find out from them precisely what concerns them at this time. She promised to do so, but asked me if I would help her write the letter to the chief engineer.

Fifth Day

When I approached Mrs. Cary's house, I was appalled at the chaotic conditions of the one-block area. There was serious danger to children from unremoved debris, large caverns in the roadbed, and huge machines that had been left unattended. The road and side-walks had been dug up well into the property line on both sides of the street. Some parts of the roadbed were under water and surrounded by mud.

My face-to-face meeting with Mrs. Cary was pleasant and heartening. Her home was neat and tastefully furnished. She has a teen-age son and a slightly younger daughter, both in high school. An AFDC mother, Mrs. Cary was attending a vocational retraining class, learning typing-receptionist skills. There was a rented typewriter on the dining room table, on which she and her daughter both practiced. She had done her poll well, and spoke from copious notes. Some of the questions, which I helped her articulate, are listed below:

If the new routing of B Street is a temporary experiment, why has the street been widened?

What will be the new traffic speed on this block? What kinds of signs will be put up (e.g., "Slow," "Watch for Children")?

When will the resurfacing be totally finished (and this muddy mess over with)?

Who is going to be responsible for replacing trees and shrubbery cut down because of the widening of the street?

How will this widened street and increased traffic contribute to the beauty of our block?

Will being on a high-traffic street make it harder to sell our houses or reduce the value of our property?

Where does the city's right-of-way end and a person's property begin? This matter is of much concern to some of the neighbors.

The realty company to which Mrs. Cary pays rent told her that the company did not receive notice of the coming change. How, then, are tenants to be informed about such things?

Some people want to know if retaining walls will be put in on properties that have been cut off. Also, will new sidewalks be built and how wide will they be?

Will the street lamp in the middle of the block, taken down Wednesday or Thursday, be replaced? This block is very dark without it.

What will the city engineer's department do to improve its way of dealing with other neighborhoods into which it is to put a new street? Their current public relations and interest in people affected by their work seems very inadequate.

Do you act as independently in all-white, middle-class suburbs as you seem to in our area?

On my advice Mrs. Cary mailed the questions to the chief engineer with a covering letter saying that she had also sent a copy to the mayor's office. I made thirty-five copies of these questions, which she distributed to all the neighbors on the block.

Eighth Day

The ward chairman having returned to town, I contacted him about the whole B Street matter. Since he lives on the southwestern tip of this exact area, he was already aware of what had happened during the two weeks he had been out of town. He was greatly shocked at the mess and well aware of the political dangers. As a lawyer, he had already taken on a suit against the construction company for one of his neighbors. He also tried to talk to the construction crew foreman, but had been given the usual runaround. He was especially suspicious that the construction company had taken more land than was in the city's legal right-of-way, pretending it was entitled to the extra ten feet or so, without paying compensation to anyone. He was going to check this matter when he got down to City Hall during the next few days. In the meantime, he had shaken up the foreman with some legal observations, with the result that he was treated with instant courtesy. At one point in the conversation, he reported with a chuckle, the foreman lapsed into frightened silence. The ward chairman also promised to visit Mrs. Cary at her home and offer his services to the cause.

Tenth Day

The ward chairman reported that he had checked the right-of-way issue and found his suspicions were accurate. He had also visited the chief engineer. The latter tried the same argument he had used in his telephone conversation with me during the previous week. He was reduced to sputtering in frustration at the warning that he was not going to get away with this sort of approach to voting citizens any more. He was told, in plain terms, that this ought to be a lesson to his department to change its method of working with citizens in all its future road-fixing projects. He was also advised that he had better put some restraints on the companies he contracts to do his work. The ward chairman particularly stressed the illegality of taking more land than was in the city's right-of-way, and the necessity of now mollifying and compensating the neighbors.

End of Second Week

Toward the end of the week Mrs. Cary telephoned to express her amazement at how things were moving. Both the mayor's representative and the Democratic ward chairman had been in the B Street area, going from house to house and personally inviting everyone to a new formal hearing at City Hall on Thursday, at 9:30 A.M. The residents of the 2800 block also received similar invitations by official letter. Mrs. Cary thought there would be a sizable turnout, despite the early morning hour, since most of the neighbors worked on night shifts.

She asked me directly if I would be present at the public hearing. This question gave me an opportunity to interpret to her the importance of my remaining invisible if I was to continue to be useful to her and to the neighborhood. She thought I deserved the credit for making this hearing possible. I thanked her, and reminded her of the courage and perseverance it took on her part to spark this whole episode (she was receiving Aid to Families with Dependent Children). If she wanted to thank me, she might concentrate on assuring a good turnout at the hearing and making certain that the Neighborhood Association received favorable mention. She seemed ready to be the spokesman for the block at the hearing, without my supportive presence.

In the meantime, not much actual change had taken place in the B Street block, although the crew and foreman acted less aloof than they had previously.

Middle of the Third Week

Mrs. Cary called me, elated, to relate the morning's events. The hearing had been a formal one, in front of the vice-president of the Board of Public Works. Some twenty-five B Street neighbors were present, both white and Negro, and each of the written questions was read out loud. People were further encouraged to ask questions not on the list, and did so without hesitation. Every question was answered, although some with less enthusiasm than others. City officials apologized over and over again to the people and listened to them attentively. The neighbors remarked later that they felt much better now that someone had listened to them. Promises were made that the department would not function in the future as it had in the 2800 block of B Street.

Furthermore, the citizens' group was promised that there would be compensation for damages to private property, new street lights would be installed, and alleys would be swept and fixed so that cars could at least be parked behind people's houses. Some plans were modified as a result of all this. The Neighborhood Association did receive favorable mention at the hearing. Mrs. Cary and I were both happy, but I cautioned her to remain skeptical and make sure that these promises were kept.

Fourth Week

One of the persons who had attended the hearing, without revealing his identity, was the head minister of a nearby church. He felt moved to write a letter to the city officials involved and to send me a carbon copy. Some days later, I called him to express gratitude for the gesture. I offered to distribute copies of the letter in the B Street block, and he liked the idea. Within a few days he sent me a supply of copies, and distribution was accomplished by the next weekend. Many of the block's residents were appreciative of this.

Thirty-fifth Day

The evening newspaper contained an article and picture on the troubles that another neighborhood was having with the chief engineer's department and the Board of Public Works. This gave me the idea that the Neighborhood Association should also write a formal letter to the board—especially to include a citation of the article and expressing the hope that the B Street situation would be different. The text of this letter follows:

Dear Mr. Y___ :

The Neighborhood Association, as you may know, has been active in helping residents of the 2800 block of B Street to put their grievances in writing and demand justice for themselves. We were pleased that the Board of Public Works could arrange to meet with the neighbors (although at a rather late date) to satisfy their doubts and lack of information. All reports confirm that you did a very fine job at the meeting. The association is glad to have played a role in preventing the crisis from splattering to other blocks or into the mass media.

It is our pleasure to tell you that the B Street neighbors were highly satisfied with the fine hearing conducted by yourself. However, on the basis of actual experience on their terribly messed-up block, they remain understandably skeptical. After reading about the T Avenue four-month fiasco in the August 12 issue of the *Morning Newsvoice*, their skepticism has not lessened.

We will continue to offer our assistance and counsel to the B Street neighbors throughout the destruction-reconstruction of their street and sidewalks.

May we respectfully suggest that the Board of Public Works, and its director and staff, consider developing regular procedures for effective neighborhood participation in this sort of matter—rather than presume that taxpayers and voters have nothing to contribute. Such procedures would likely prevent future frustration all around, and could very well expedite the important work of your board.

We also hope that once a project is begun, it is worked at fully, every day, so that it can be completed in a reasonable time and at minimum inconvenience to the citizens affected. Days of delay or inaction, while the mess simply continues untouched, are guaranteed to raise everyone's ire.

If the association can be of any service to you in planning your neighborhood approach, please feel free to call on us.

Please enter into the record our continued interest regarding the B Street situation at your next board meeting.

cc. County Chairman, Democratic Party
    Mayor's Assistant
    Mrs. Cary

After clearing the letter with members of the association's Executive Committee, the secretary dispatched it. The letter was never acknowledged or answered, although it was received.

Sixth and Following Weeks

Mrs. Cary telephoned in a panic to tell me that earlier this evening a 10-year-old girl had tripped over some dislodged concrete stairs and had fallen onto rusty pipes that had been excavated during the previous week. She had been rushed to the hospital in an ambulance, and required about one hundred stitches (this might be a bit of exaggeration) to save her arm. We agreed that Mrs. Cary would call the mayor's office while I called the ward chairman.

In my call, I asked in a tone of disciplined bitterness, "How many kids have to be maimed or killed before the city gets around to enforcing what it had promised a group of responsible citizens almost a month earlier?" The ward chairman asked me to calm down, and promised that the matter would be "handled." Within the subsequent three weeks (by the end of the ninth week), the 2800 block of B Street progressed from unleveled mud and dirt to a completely paved street with new sidewalks. Mrs. Cary reported that not only was the construction company apparently frantic to get this block done, the crews had become solicitous, and no debris was left around at the end of a workday. The night watchman would occasionally inquire, not without a note of humor in his voice, if all was okay tonight.

The street was not opened to through traffic for another twelve weeks, but residents could get to their homes in safety and could park their cars in front of their homes during these twelve weeks. Mrs. Cary was certain that "we had won."

Interestingly, as of the seventeenth week, two other blocks that were part of the over-all city project had not been completely paved. Cement-pouring had been under way in these two blocks since the eighth week, but had not been completed by the twentieth week after the fateful Tuesday morning when B Street was turned upside down.

40

FRANCES FOX PIVEN and RICHARD A. CLOWARD

How the Federal Government Caused the Welfare Crisis

In the mid-1960s, welfare rights emerged as a national issue. A vast array of groups—social workers, churchmen, lawyers, civic organizations, public welfare employees, private foundations, activist students, antipoverty employees, civil rights organizations, settlement house and family agencies, not to speak of organizations of the poor themselves—began to batter the welfare system. What is not generally understood is that this upsurge of pressure—and the welfare explosion which resulted—was largely stimulated by the federal government through its Great Society programs.

Nor was this the first time that a national government had stimulated a relief explosion. During the 1620s in England, the Privy Council investigated the administration of parish relief and then insisted on improved relief arrangements, with the result that the rolls rose to unprecedented levels; in 1933, when the New Deal Administration launched a massive program of federally subsidized relief and required the states and localities to participate, the result was that millions obtained relief. Early in 1960, the federal government once again adopted a posture of concern for the poor (and the black), calling for institutional reform in the name of these "forgotten men."

But when the federal government intervened in local relief arrangements in the 1960s, it did so in a novel way—not by directly liberalizing the existing welfare system through legislative amendments to the Social Security Act, but indirectly, through a series of new measures (particularly the antipoverty program) which had the consequence of mobilizing pressure against local relief restrictions. In retrospect, federal intervention occurred along three main lines:

SOURCE: Reprinted from *Social Policy*, Vol. 2, No. 1 (May/June, 1971), pp. 40–49. With permission of *Social Policy*, 901 North Broadway, White Plains, New York 10603.

The establishment of new services, both public and private, that offered the poor information about welfare entitlements and the assistance of experts in obtaining benefits.

The initiation of litigation to challenge a host of local laws and policies that kept people off the welfare rolls.

The support of new organizations of the poor which informed people of their entitlement to public welfare and mounted pressure on officials to approve their applications for assistance.

This array of activities, we believe, had much to do with the abrupt welfare rise in the 1960s. As a result of mass protest, litigation, and new services—all focusing on welfare rights—relief agencies found themselves confronted with an unprecedented volume of applications and unprecedented pressures to approve the granting of benefits. We base this conclusion on detailed scrutiny of the specific activities of Great Society programs, activities which coincided with the welfare explosion itself. Before going on to describe the Great Society programs, let us note a few salient statistics on the welfare explosion.

The welfare rise occurred in the category called Aid to Families with Dependent Children (AFDC). The rise was not, as many people think, a response to the great economic deprivation inflicted on families as a result of agricultural modernization (especially in the South) and the continuing high unemployment in the cities to which these displaced poor migrated (between the end of the Korean War and the escalation of the war in Vietnam, black unemployment fluctuated between 10 and 13 percent). As a matter of fact, with millions migrating during the 1950s, the AFDC rolls rose by only 110,000 families, or 17 percent in an entire decade. Traditional restrictions kept the poor off the rolls—residence laws, employable mother rules, man-in-the-house provisions, an eligibility procedure so complicated as to constitute a bureaucratic design in deterrence, and decisions to deny assistance that were simply blatantly illegal. The result was that a great pool of people built up in the cities who were eligible for aid but were not receiving it.

But traditional relief restrictions were to collapse in the 1960s. While they were not legislated out of existence, we shall argue that their implementation was thwarted by pressures exerted on welfare agencies as a result of Great Society programs. As a result, from December 1960 to February 1969, some 800,000 families were added to the rolls, an increase of 107 percent in just eight years and two months. But to speak only of the magnitude of the rise is to overlook its most striking features: *that the rolls went up all at once* — by 31 percent in the first four years of the decade, but by 58 percent in the next four years and two months. Stated another way, fully 71 percent of the huge welfare increase during the first eight years of the 1960s took place in the four years after 1964. It was truly an explosion. And the timing of the explosion was concurrent with the initiation and rapid growth of a great variety of welfare rights activities.[1]

Before we begin our account of the ways in which the Great Society programs increased the welfare load, let us make it clear that we do not mean to suggest that national political leaders intended the relief rolls to rise; in fact, we suspect that public welfare was usually far from their minds. (Indeed, had they been asked, many would have said their object was to reduce the welfare rolls by educating and training the poor.) The political circumstances of the 1960s made it crucial, however, that blacks get something in order to solidify their allegiance to the national Democratic party, and to quiet them. With many southern Democratic voters turning to the Republicans or to "States Rights" parties, the Democrats had become especially dependent on the northern industrial states where black voters had come to be concentrated. But many black voters had moved away from the Democratic party in the elections of 1956 and 1960. Moreover, economic modernization in the South, migration, and urban unemployment were beginning to take their toll of black institutional life, diminishing the capacity of institutions such as the family to control people's attitudes and behavior. The result, especially among the young, was rising disorder in the cities — crime, protests, addiction, riots. These troubles in the cities had also become political problems and concessions had to be made.

---

[1]Between February, 1969 and October, 1970, a period of 20 months, the AFDC (and AFDC-UP) rolls rose another 55 percent. For the full decade ending in December 1970, the overall rise exceeded 225 percent, and the rolls are still rising. The main stimulus for the upsurge after 1969, we believe, was the Nixon Administration's anti-inflation strategy, which greatly increased unemployment. Under ordinary circumstances, however, increases in unemployment do not produce comparable increases in the welfare rolls, but the 1960s were no ordinary time. The onset of recession in 1969 occurred at a unique moment, one in which the welfare system was extremely vulnerable owing to the great weakening of traditional restrictions which had taken place during the preceding few years. Among other things, the proportion of applications being approved stood at the unprecedented level of 70 percent. Moreover, as a result of years of agitation, litigation, and publicity, people's attitudes toward going on welfare had changed; many had come to believe that they had a "right" to assistance. As the recession deepened, therefore, applications for welfare surged, and with the approval level high, a renewed explosion occurred.

As it turned out, welfare was the system that was made to do most of the conceding—partly, perhaps, because black constituents needed money; more importantly, because it was easier to give welfare than to press for concessions that would challenge the interests of other groups in the cities. When the families who showed up at a community-action agency asked for housing because they lived in rat-infested tenements, or for more money for rent because they were dislocated by urban renewal, or for jobs, what were agency staff to do? They could not provide low-rent housing when none was being built or break down discriminatory housing patterns, or create jobs, or overcome discriminatory hiring practices. But it *was* possible to badger the welfare department into putting families on the relief rolls.

In other words, while the Great Society agencies often attempted to make gains for blacks in housing and health care and education and employment, resistance was stiff and sometimes virulent, for other groups in the cities had major stakes in these services and resources. But there were few other major groups in the cities with direct and immediate interests in welfare. (Giving welfare was also cheaper, at least in the short run, than building housing, for example.) In other words, relief-giving turned out to be the most expeditious way to deal with the political pressures created by a dislocated poor, just as it had been many times in the past.

WELFARE RIGHTS ADVOCACY
AND INFORMATION SERVICES

The first federally sponsored welfare rights services were actually initiated before the Great Society era—namely, the relocation provisions in the urban-renewal program. However, while these provisions were inaugurated in the late 1950s, they were more vigorously enforced under Kennedy and Johnson than they had been before, and one consequence was that thousands of people were unearthed and referred to public welfare departments for financial assistance.

The city of Baltimore provides a dramatic illustration of this process. The relief rolls in Baltimore trebled between 1960 and 1966, accounting for about 75 percent of the increase in the entire state of Maryland, and leading HEW and the Maryland State Department of Public Welfare to join in an investigation of the rise. Urban-renewal and relocation services were, it turns out, an important cause. Some 14,000 units of low-rental housing had been destroyed over a ten-year period beginning in 1955, and equivalent numbers of poor households (with a median income of $2,600) were forced to relocate. With their living arrangements disrupted, many families could no longer manage on their marginal incomes. For example, extended families (a mother with children living with her parents) were often forced to break up because the residences to which they were moved had less space; if their combined income was insufficient to pay two rentals, the mother and children were referred for AFDC benefits. For other families, adequate housing simply could not be found at rentals they could afford, so they were sent to the relief agency to obtain supplemental income. In the words of the report, "Uncovering low-income families and forcing them to move eventuated in thousands of referrals by the Housing Agency to the Department of Welfare ... There can be no question but that the Urban Renewal effort during these years resulted in a substantial amount of 'case-finding' for the Welfare Department." Thus the urban-renewal agency solved its problems with the poor, not by modifying its clearance program, but by turning to the public agency that traditionally deals with the poor—public welfare.

Baltimore is not an isolated instance; relocation agencies in other cities also had to turn to public welfare. Considering the magnitude of urban-renewal programs since the late 1950s, it is likely that many tens of thousands of eligible families in the cities were led to apply for public assistance at the urging and with the help of relocation personnel.

The type of welfare-rights service that became most prevalent in the 1960s was the "storefront service center," staffed by social workers, lawyers, churchmen, students, and slum-dwellers themselves. Although other Great Society programs sponsored local centers, OEO's "community-action agencies" (CAAs) sponsored most of them—perhaps one thousand in all. Hundreds of thousands of poor people were served in these centers. Their main problem was lack of income—often, it turned out, because they had been denied aid by the welfare department or because they were given less than the law prescribed. In time, center personnel became effective advocates of the poor in dealing with welfare departments.

Direct evidence of the impact of these services is available from the Baltimore study mentioned earlier. The conclusion was reached that, in addition to the relocation services, the local OEO agencies were a major cause of the welfare rise. The researchers analyzed the impact on the welfare rolls one year after the first neighborhood service center was opened:

From September of 1965 to September of 1966 . . . (the) AFDC caseload in (a particular anti-poverty) area grew by 36.6 percent; the total City AFDC caseload, during the same period, increased by only 8.6 percent . . . All the (anti-poverty) agency did . . . was to make people aware of the availability of AFDC (and) to stimulate the use of (it).

A study by HEW in 1969 examined the relationship between antipoverty expenditures and AFDC caseload changes in eleven cities, with the following tentative results:

A statistically significant relation did exist between CAP expenditures and the *AFDC poor rate*—the higher the (per capita) expenditure the higher the rate (at which poor families were on the rolls). Although there is no direct evidence, CAP programs may have helped the poor understand their rights under existing public assistance policies and may have lowered the amount of *personal* stigma recipients felt. There is evidence showing that CAP programs are associated with reduced feelings of helplessness. CAP expenditures per 1,000 poor persons were inversely related to powerlessness (the more a city received CAP funds, the fewer the number of recipients feeling helpless).

The less helpless people felt in dealing with public agencies, this same study also tentatively concluded, the more likely that a higher proportion of the poor were on the rolls.

The federal programs were also responsible for an information explosion in public welfare. In the 1960s, organizations all over the country began to produce simplified welfare manuals for distribution in slums and ghettos. The community-action agencies themselves prepared handbooks in hundreds of cities and counties, and other organizations followed suit, partly in response to the demand for information created by the new advocacy services. Inner-city churches produced handbooks in Cleveland and Pittsburgh. The NAACP Legal and Education Defense Fund made up handbooks for use in some Deep South states. Civil liberties unions brought out manuals in a number of places, such as Wisconsin and the District of Columbia. A comprehensive handbook for New Jersey was produced by the Scholarship, Education and Defense Fund. Recently, the National Urban League prepared and distributed handbooks for use in a dozen northern states, each describing in detail the state general assistance programs under which fully employed but low-paid workers can obtain wage supplements. In Columbus and the District of Columbia, the first handbooks were prepared by settlement houses in 1966—and other settlement houses in other cities followed suit in subsequent years. A few family service agencies, especially in older suburban communities with central ghettos, have also put such material together.

Beginning in 1966, the National Welfare Rights Organization stimulated the development of manuals in dozens of places, in part by distributing sample copies of manuals that had been prepared by various antipoverty agencies. At one point in New York City, three different comprehensive handbooks were available: one prepared by an antipoverty agency known as Mobilization for Youth, another by the Citizen's Committee for Children, (a prestigious civic organization that had received a foundation grant for this purpose), and still another by the OEO-sponsored Center on Social Welfare Policy and Law at Columbia University. At the same time, local groups all over the city had made up more abbreviated welfare rights manuals — some were really flyers, only three or four pages in length — so it could fairly be said that dozens of different welfare guides were circulating throughout New York's slums and ghettos.

Unfortunately, there are no available statistical data that would enable us to describe the pervasiveness of welfare rights activity in the nation's neighborhood service centers. The difficulty arises from the fact that welfare rights services were conducted under other formal program categories — such as employment training or preschool education. From direct observation and a few published accounts, we do know that in some centers personnel did little else than handle welfare grievances, becoming specialists in dealing with welfare departments. In other centers, such activity was an incidental by-product of other programs: For example, "Head-Start" teachers who found their new pupils without adequate food and clothing sometimes responded by helping the family to get on the welfare rolls. A few even undertook to organize groups of welfare recipients that later affiliated with NWRO. The same can be said of social workers, employment counselors, lawyers, and other professionals working in the service centers, for great numbers of the poor people who came to them for help needed money, and public welfare was the only place to go for it.

It should be added that welfare rights did not have to be a primary activity in order to account for the welfare explosion; even if it had been the lowest-priority service in the centers, its magnitude still would have been unprecedented. About 15 percent of CAA expenditures were devoted to neighborhood service center programs; in fiscal 1965, that amounted to $24 million, and by fiscal 1968 the figure exceeded $132 million. Translating these dollars into personnel, neighborhood service centers hired more than 100,000 professionals and community residents in 1968. This horde of workers provided "outreach and referral" services and organized community groups. In the same year, applications for AFDC rose by 90,000 — up from 998,000 in 1967 to 1,099,000 in 1968. On the average, if each of the service center workers reached and referred only one family to public welfare during the course of an entire year, the increase in applications would be largely explained.

WELFARE RIGHTS LITIGATION

While welfare restrictions were being battered from below, they were also being weakened from above. A series of judicial decisions in the 1960s had the effect of undermining some of the regulations by which the relief rolls have been kept down. For decades, reformers had lobbied unsuccessfully for legislative repeal of residence laws, man-in-the-house rules, and employable-mother rules. But in the 1960s these foundation blocks of the "poor law" were washed away by one court decision after another.

The legal assaults that set this process in motion originated mainly with OEO's neighborhood legal services program. Lawyers do what they are paid to do. In the three years between 1966 and 1968, OEO spent about $85 million on legal services — a very considerable sum, as the following comparison by Levitan reveals.

One year after OEO was established, the budget of Legal Services was nearly double that of all the traditional legal aid societies affiliated with the National Legal Aid and Defender Association (20 million dollars as compared with 11.7 million dollars).

By fiscal 1968, OEO expenditures had reached $36 million. Some 250 legal services projects were established which operated about 850 neighborhood law offices staffed by about 1,800 attorneys.

OEO also altered practices in private legal agencies, for they either wanted grants or were influenced by the emerging climate of social reform. The impact on the National Legal Aid and Defender Association (NLADA) provides one conspicuous example. NLADA, naturally enough, argued that its program should be strengthened with OEO grants. But OEO felt that NLADA affiliates were dominated by conservative bar associations and business groups, thus making it unlikely that politically controversial advocacy would be undertaken (e.g., fighting wage-garnishment actions in suing public welfare departments). In the end, a compromise was reached, with some 40 percent of OEO's legal services projects being administered by NLADA affiliates; the rest were administered through CAAs. But a price was exacted from NLADA: to qualify for funds, any affiliate was required to decentralize its operation to slum and ghetto neighborhoods and to undertake new and controversial areas of representation, including test cases designed to promote law reform.

The inauguration of hundreds of new neighborhood legal services under CAA programs, together with the new efforts in NLADA programs, had a far-reaching effect on the practice of poor-law. Many private legal defense organizations soon shifted some of their resources into the poor-law field, including the NAACP Education and Legal Defense Fund, the Scholarship Education and Defense Fund for Racial Equality, and the American Civil Liberties Union (and its special division, the Roger Baldwin Fund). The Law Students Civil Rights Research Council began to recruit hundreds of law-student volunteers to work with welfare rights groups and to perform legal research for attorneys representing recipients.

Moreover, OEO created a new kind of legal personnel—nonprofessionals trained in specific facets of the law who were able to extend the reach of the neighborhood legal services programs. Hundreds of poor people were recruited and trained to perform various kinds of "lay advocacy" tasks. In 1964, for example, OEO established the Dixwell Legal Rights Association in New Haven for the express purpose of training such nonprofessionals. About four hundred graduates of the program have since been placed in neighborhood legal offices throughout the country, and in other organizations, such as churches, as well. As part of its program, Dixwell has produced and distributed about a dozen different simplified manuals dealing with such subjects as rights to welfare, to bail bond, to hospital care, to urban renewal relocation subsidies, to public housing, to bankruptcy proceedings (as a way in which poor people can overcome indebtedness). Trainees are schooled in the use of these manuals.

Law schools themselves have been responsive to these new influences. "During fiscal 1967," according to Levitan, "OEO pumped more than 2 million dollars into law schools for research, changes in curricula, and various projects dealing with the poor." For example, a Center on Social Welfare Policy and Law was established at Columbia University to conduct legal research, advise attorneys in the field, and prepare briefs in test cases. At Northwestern University School of Law, an Institute for Education in Law and Poverty was created which, among other things, publishes a monthly digest of current poverty-law cases and opinions—called the *Clearinghouse Review*—that is distributed to all OEO legal service attorneys and to other involved attorneys as well. Similar law centers and projects were established elsewhere in the country. The ferment also affected law school curricula—new courses in poverty law were introduced in dozens of universities, and some two thousand law students registered for them in the 1965-1967 academic years.

The effect of these widespread activities by private legal agencies on the welfare rolls cannot easily be measured. There is considerable evidence, however, of the impact of the OEO legal services programs themselves. According to available evidence, only about 3 percent of the activity in neighborhood legal services agencies was devoted to "state and local welfare," or about 8,000 cases out of the 282,000 cases taken in fiscal 1968. However, these figures obscure a fact of great significance. In dealing with public welfare cases, OEO attorneys tended to eschew case-by-case assistance to families; instead, they promoted "institutional change through law reform" by taking "test cases" whose outcomes affected existing or potential welfare recipients as an entire class. "Class actions" were also litigated in some other areas (e.g., the rights of public housing tenants), but the most conspicuous legal victories by far were achieved in the public welfare field. On June 19, 1967, a three-judge federal court in Connecticut declared that state's relief residency requirements unconstitutional. In 1968, a three-judge federal court in Atlanta struck down the employable mother regulation. In the same year, a suit initiated by ACLU challenging man-in-the-house and substitute-parent rules produced a lethal blow by the United States Supreme Court.

There is no way of measuring the exact impact of these major legal reforms on the welfare rolls; all that can be said is that it has been considerable. Persons knowledgeable in the public welfare field generally believe that at least 100,000 persons annually had been denied aid because of residence laws. Attorneys and welfare rights organizers in the South estimated that tens of thousands of families were denied aid under employable mother rules. Once such rules were weakened or abandoned, approval rates rose, and the rolls grew. Litigation against Alabama's substitute-parent rule provides an illustration. Court action was initiated in 1966, and after a series of appeals, the United States Supreme Court acted in 1968. The effect of this continuous and much publicized course of litigation was startling: in Mobile, for example, the caseload rose from 1,700 to

3,100 (an increase of 82 percent) in the brief period between June 1966 and February 1969.

Suits overturning exclusionary statutes, such as residence laws, have received a great deal of publicity, but successful challenges taken against arbitrary administrative procedures, although less publicized, may have done even more to expand the rolls. Welfare functionaries have always been allowed a wide range of discretion in deciding whether or not to give aid, and they have used that discretion to deter people from applying or to turn them down when they do apply or, if applicants get on the rolls, to cut them off arbitrarily. Legal action has gone far toward hampering these practices.

Arbitrary terminations, for example, have always been a conspicuous feature of the public assistance system. In 1967, a beneficiary under the Aid to the Permanent and Totally Disabled Program in Mississippi was abruptly notified that he was no longer medically qualified for assistance. No specific reasons were given, nor was a hearing held prior to the termination. The client, a thirty-year-old black man with a large family, quickly secured affidavits from prominent doctors confirming that his right hand had been amputated and that he had both pulmonary tuberculosis and sickle-cell disease (a type of anemia which leads to progressive weakening and, in this case, to a short life expectancy). The day before the court hearing, welfare officials visited the plaintiff to say that a mistake had been made and would be rectified. Nevertheless, the plaintiff insisted that the hearing be held, arguing that his benefits might be arbitrarily terminated at some later time unless the constitutional issues raised by termination procedures were ruled upon. Despite protests by attorneys for the state, the judge agreed that serious questions of due process were involved and held the matter over for trial.

This case was typical of many instituted elsewhere in the nation after 1964. One case finally reached the United States Supreme Court, and a favorable ruling was handed down on March 24, 1970. It asserted that welfare recipients have a constitutional right to a trial-like hearing, with trial-like constitutional safeguards, before officials may terminate benefits. During the proceedings, welfare officials warned that a favorable ruling could swamp the system with demands for hearings while ineligible people remained on the rolls. But the Court decided that the protection of recipients outweighed such fiscal and administrative problems. As a result of this and earlier procedural victories, welfare departments found it increasingly difficult to restrict access to benefits, if only because the process of denial came to be cumbersome.

All in all, the legal assault on welfare departments contributed to the collapse of restrictions, partly by overturning major exclusionary statutes, but perhaps more importantly by instituting procedural safeguards that hampered the arbitrary exercise of discretion by relief officials. Rather than devote themselves to the difficult and time-consuming task of defending their decisions, welfare functionaries more often acquiesced, with the result that more people got on the rolls and they were not so likely to be terminated capriciously.

GRASSROOTS PROTEST:
THE NATIONAL WELFARE RIGHTS ORGANIZATION

In the 1960s as in the 1930s, poor people banded together to attack the relief system. Just as unemployed groups sprang up during the Depression and eventually banded together in the Workers' Alliance, so in the late 1960s welfare rights groups began to appear and then banded together in a National Welfare Rights Organization. In some respects, these organizations bear little similarity to each other; the Alliance was composed primarily of unemployed white men, whereas NWRO is composed mostly of black women who are, practically speaking, unemployable in today's market. But there are also striking similarities: each arose in a period of widespread social and political upheaval occasioned by profound economic dislocation, and each flourished by capitalizing on disorder to obtain public aid for masses of families in financial distress.

The first welfare protest groups originated in the OEO agencies. But once such groups came into being, so did the possibility of building a national grassroots organization through relief protests. Some independent activists came to see this. Their interest was stimulated by a paper we circulated in late 1965 among antipoverty workers, organizers and activists entitled "Mobilizing the Poor: How It Can Be Done." It called upon those who were working with welfare recipients, as well as other activists, to form a movement with the express purpose of getting hundreds of thousands of families onto the relief rolls, for we had by then conducted sufficient research to establish that only half of the eligible poor were on the rolls. We also reasoned that campaigns to double and triple the relief rolls would produce significant pressure for national reforms in the relief system, perhaps along the lines of a national guaranteed minimum income. Rapidly rising rolls would mean procedural turmoil in the cumbersome welfare bureaucracies, fiscal turmoil in the localities where existing sources of tax revenue were already overburdened, and political turmoil as an alerted electorate divided on the question of how to overcome this disruption in local government. To deal with these problems, we argued, mayors and governors would call upon the federal government with increasing insistency to establish a federally financed minimum income. This call for the mobilization of a nationwide drive against relief agencies was subsequently published in *The Nation* under the title "A Strategy to End Poverty."

The most important activist to see these possibilities was Dr. George A. Wiley, a professor of chemistry who had joined the civil rights movement and become the associate national director of CORE. In the late spring of 1966, he left CORE to open the Poverty/Rights Action Center in Washington, D.C. Within several months, PRAC became the organizing vehicle for what was to become the National Welfare Rights Organization; and under Wiley's leadership, the organization has since burgeoned.

Wiley, with Edwin Day and later Timothy Sampson, began by making strenuous efforts to establish links with the scattered welfare groups that already existed around the country and to spur the staff of antipoverty agencies (as well as activists who were in limbo after the civil rights movement passed its peak) to concentrate on organizing in the field of welfare. The idea spread rapidly, especially among antipoverty staff. As new groups developed, Wiley established contact and urged them to affiliate with the national headquarters. In February 1967, 350 leaders representing 200 welfare groups in 70 cities of 26 states answered the call to attend the first national meeting. Participating groups ranged from "Mothers of Watts" to "Mothers for Adequate Welfare" in Boston; from Chicago's "Welfare Union of the West Side Organization," composed of unemployed black men, to Eastern Kentucky's "Committee to Save Unemployed Fathers," consisting of unemployed white miners. Most of the groups originated in antipoverty agencies, but some had been organized by churchmen, others by civil rights activists, and still others by Students for a Democratic Society. By 1969, NWRO claimed more than 100,000 dues-paying members in some 350 local groups.

The new organization first came to national attention in June 1966. On June 20, Rev. Paul Younger and Edith Doering, welfare rights organizers who had been hired by the Cleveland Council of Churches, led about forty welfare recipients out of Cleveland on the first lap of a 155-mile march to Columbus to lobby with the Governor for an increase in Ohio's welfare payments. On the morning of June 30, when they finally reached Columbus, the forty marchers were joined by two thousand recipients and sympathizers from other towns in Ohio. On the same day in New York, two thousand recipients massed in front of City Hall to picket in the hot sun while swarms of their children clambered over the iron railings to play on the grassy squares of City Hall Park. Groups of recipients in fifteen other cities, including Baltimore, Washington, Los Angeles, Boston, Louisville, Chicago, Trenton, and San Francisco, also joined demonstrations against "the welfare."

By now NWRO is fairly well known, especially in northern cities, where local groups have staged hundreds of demonstrations to protest various welfare restrictions. Thousands of welfare recipients and organizers have been jailed on charges from trespass to riot. In the South, storefront offices have been razed, and welfare rights leaders' homes have been burned. One of the largest demonstrations was mounted in conjunction with the Poor People's Campaign in the spring and summer of 1968. On May 12 of that year, Wiley and Coretta King, widow of the slain civil rights leader, led more than five thousand welfare recipients on a "Mother's Day" march through the riot-torn section of Washington, D.C. Perhaps the most widely publicized incident occurred in the fall of 1969, when one thousand recipients and university students took over Wisconsin's legislative chamber to protest a cutback in welfare appropriations. This past winter and spring, NWRO led a campaign to reinstate thousands of families who were abruptly cut off the rolls in Nevada.

Most day-to-day organizing across the nation has consisted of efforts to settle individual grievances. Organizers generally begin by preparing a simplified handbook of welfare regulations (which may first require staging a sit-in in order to get a copy of the official manual), and thousands of copies are distributed through welfare rights groups, churches, stores, and other outlets in the ghettos. The handbooks alert people to the ways in which the system typically and often illegally rejects applicants or reduces benefits—e.g., by failing to increase payments as children grow older or to give special utility allowances in rat-infested areas so that lights may be kept on at night. Arbitrary terminations have been a constant subject of grievance work. The practice of summarily terminating people from the rolls without a written reason or an opportunity for a hearing led the welfare rights groups in Boston to stage a welfare department sit-in in the spring of 1967. When the police beat the demonstrators, they screamed from the windows of the welfare department, and for three nights widespread rioting erupted in the streets — the first major riot in the violent summer of 1967.

Welfare rights groups have also mounted large-scale campaigns to obtain certain benefits which many people are entitled to but few receive. As we have observed earlier, for example, many welfare departments officially permit extra grants for special purposes, but people are rarely told about them and generally don't get them. Staging a "mass benefit campaign" requires less organizing effort than the laborious process of adjusting individual grievances and produces a far greater financial pay-off. School clothing lists, for example, are mimeographed and widely distributed in slum neighborhoods, together with an announcement of a forthcoming demonstration at the welfare center. When hundreds of people assemble with a common demand, welfare departments usually release the grants, especially in cities where public officials fear that repression will provoke outbreaks of violence in the ghettos.

Campaigns of this sort in New York City included week-long sit-ins and forced some district welfare centers to close down. As the system lost control over its discretionary giving, the costs of special grants zoomed from about $40 per recipient in 1965 to $100 in 1968. When the aggregate costs reached an annual rate of $100 million, *The New York Times* was moved editorially to call these campaigns a "threat to [New York City's] treasury." To blunt that threat, state officials — responding to increased white antagonism toward welfare costs — abolished the special grant. But in the meantime, a great many people had got a great deal of money that they would not otherwise have received.

These campaigns were greatly aided by the contagious effects of successful welfare rights activity. In May 1968, for example, thousands of Puerto Rican mothers and children who were not affiliated with NWRO unexpectedly appeared in the South Bronx relief centers demanding money. After week-long sit-ins, checks were disbursed. Relief administrations attributed this avalanche of requests to a clothing grants campaign being conducted at the time by the City-Wide Coordinating of Welfare Groups. But they were wrong. The relief offices were engulfed by this mass of people, it turned out, because a rumor of unknown origin had spread to the effect that a wealthy patron had died and left $50 million to the welfare department to be given to the poor. Nor could the rumor be dispelled. Within days, it spread to Spanish Harlem and then to Central Harlem, and the relief offices in those districts were flooded, forcing the

check-writing machines into a virtual 24-hour schedule. These un-
planned demonstrations were partly responsible for the fact that the
cost of special grants, which had totaled some $3 million in the same
month a year earlier, reached $13 million in June 1968. For, except
by calling the police and thus risking mass violence, how else was
the welfare department to clear its offices and restore control?

NWRO has also exerted some influence on acceptance and termination decisions, and that too contributed to larger rolls. Much welfare rights organizing occurred in the waiting rooms of local welfare
centers with the intention of attracting new members from among
those recipients who had come to negotiate grievances. But many of
those jamming the waiting rooms were not recipients—they were
new families hoping to get on the rolls. Welfare rights organizers
have often given on-the-spot assistance to these potential recipients
by helping them to negotiate the intake process. Moreover, the constant agitation in welfare centers by groups of recipients conducting
campaigns for special grants has also led some welfare workers to
take sides with applicants and intimidated many others. In this new
climate, many intake workers, the "gatekeepers" of the system, have
tended to make more liberal decisions. Acceptance rates rose sharply
in the mid and late 1960s, and client protests were undoubtedly one
cause.

NWRO's organizing activities, it should be pointed out, were conducted mainly to benefit people already on the welfare rolls, for
NWRO is an organization composed of recipients. To keep their
members interested and involved, NWRO organizers have been constantly under pressure to increase benefits for existing recipients
rather than to find and organize the nonrecipient poor for the purpose of getting them on the rolls. For this reason, NWRO's contribution to to the rising welfare rolls has been slum and ghetto families
who witness demonstrations over grievances and demands for special grants or for higher grants and become more aware of their own
rights and less fearful of applying for aid. This may be what HEW
meant when, after surveying the causes of welfare increases in elev-
en cities, it drew the following conclusion regarding the impact of
local welfare rights organizations (WROs):

There was evidence that the higher the number of AFDC recipients who
belonged to WRO's, the larger the number of poor persons using AFDC, but
the evidence was not statistically significant. However, the number of AFDC
women who reported that they belonged to WRO's was very small in all
cities. For example, only 4.1 percent of all AFDC women in New York City

belonged to the local WRO. These small percentages could, however, lead to false conclusions. A slight increase in the number of WRO members might have a great influence on the attitudes of all AFDC recipients. To illustrate, there was a strong inverse relation between the percentage of WRO members and the number of recipients who felt helpless (the more WRO members in a city, the fewer the number of recipients who felt powerless).

In many respects, the emergence of NWRO represents the most striking example one could give of the federal role in stimulating the welfare explosion. For what must be recognized is that the welfare poor came to form a coherent organization as a consequence of federal intervention in the cities—as a consequence of the Great Society social workers and VISTA volunteers who became the organizers of NWRO groups, of Great Society lawyers who brought NWRO legal suits, and of the Great Society rhetoric and protection that made attacks on local welfare agencies first imaginable and then feasible.

If NWRO developed as a by-product of federal intervention in the cities, it later came to have quite direct relations with the national government. In 1968, the outgoing Johnson Administration granted NWRO more than $400,000 through the Department of Labor, a sum roughly equivalent to the total amount raised from private sources after the organization formed in early 1966. The money was ostensibly to be used to monitor the local employment programs for AFDC mothers, which had been mandated by the congressional amendments of 1967, in order to ensure that participation in training would be fully voluntary. However, federal officials were aware that a substantial part of the money would go toward strengthening local relief groups. The fact that the national government openly financed an organization of America's poor which was harassing local welfare departments is dramatic evidence of the federal role in the welfare explosion in the late 1960s.

THE IMPACT OF THE
WELFARE RIGHTS MOVEMENT

It is not possible to calculate just how much each of the components of the broad-based, variegated welfare rights movement of the 1960s contributed to the doubling of the AFDC rolls. Legal services obviously had an impact as did advocacy services in neighborhood centers, and organized protests by groups of recipients were influential in some places. Like most movements, this one was ubiquitous, and constantly changing. Once it had gained momentum, unexpected things happened. The press, for example, often played a large, if inadvertent, role. News coverage and documentaries on the movement alerted people to their rights and to the possibilities of obtaining them. In the fall of 1967, the New York *Daily News*, which is read by millions of the poor in New York City, carried a three-part series on the clothing and household furnishings campaign being conducted by welfare recipient groups. By way of explaining the campaign to their readers, the authors of this series described the welfare regulations in great detail and acknowledged that most recipients were not receiving full entitlements; they even printed a half-page replica of the clothing and furnishings check-list being circulated by welfare rights groups. For weeks thereafter, the welfare waiting rooms were filled with people carrying copies of the page with the check-list (much to the dismay of the *Daily News* editors, one suspects, who were writing hostile editorials throughout this period deploring the rise of a "new 'come-and-get-it' movement").

Taken as a whole, there is little reason to doubt that the many-faceted welfare rights movement had a crucial impact on the rolls. The report cited earlier on the causes of the extraordinary AFDC rise in Baltimore reaches the same judgment: *the rolls had risen primarily because families of long-standing eligibility had been led to apply for public aid in unprecedented numbers as a result of a great variety of welfare rights activities.* Thus the report observed:

When poor people are everywhere encouraged to make use of these re-sources (e.g., public welfare)—by publicity, by action workers on their own block, by teachers of their children in schools, by their doctors and by any social agency they happen to have contact with—a surge of response must be expected. It is the contention of this report that the increase of AFDC caseload reflects this response to the antipoverty effort, and that the poor families of this State through a combination of some changes in their alterna-tive forms of maintenance and perhaps for the major part encouraged by the national effort to do something about poverty have responded to the use of public services, including welfare, in numbers heretofore unequalled.

It is no exaggeration to speak of the poor applying for assistance "in numbers heretofore unequalled." Nationally, applications rose from 588,000 in 1960 to 1,088,000 in 1968, an increase of 85 percent. Moreover, the average annual volume of applications *after* 1964 was about 29 percent larger than the average annual volume in the early years of the decade. As the volume of applications rose, the proportion accepted also rose—from 55 percent in 1960 to 70 percent in 1968. In the Northeast, the acceptance rate reached 78 percent, and in some northern cities it exceeded even that level. Furthermore, the average annual acceptance rate after 1964 showed a 12 percent increase over the average in earlier years. All at once, in a mere four years, relief restrictions collapsed.

In summary, agricultural modernization, migration, and urban unemployment contributed to a growing pool of "eligible" families in the 1950s and 1960s. Nevertheless, the relief rolls did not rise until the 1960s. When they did, it was largely as a result of governmental programs designed to moderate widespread political unrest among the black poor. One consequence of these programs was that the poor were suddenly stimulated to approve applications in unprecedented numbers. The result was the relief explosion of the late 1960s. The terms in which that crisis must be explained are economic disruption, large-scale migration, mass volatility, and electoral responses—a sequence of disturbances leading to a precipitous expansion of the relief rolls.

We conclude, then, that because the 1960s were a time of profound disorder among the black poor, government responded with measures to ease that disorder. Blacks got a little more from some government agencies and suffered a little less at the hands of others, although, considering the magnitude of the political disturbances, it is remarkable to see how few and how modest these concessions were, and how often they turned out to be merely symbolic. Now that ghetto unrest has subsided (at least as of this writing), the liberalization of relief practices stands out, for without that concession the victims of agricultural modernization and of persisting unemployment in the cities would remain perilously close to starvation—as so many did in the late 1940s and the 1950s. And although the processes by which the relief expansion occurred were sometimes covert and circuitous, the moral seems clear: a placid poor get nothing, but a turbulent poor sometimes get something.

41

MYRTLE R. REUL

A Preview of the Migrant
as a Rehab Client

In order for rehabilitation services to be effectively offered to and made use of by migrant farm workers, it is essential for counselors and other rehabilitation workers to know something of the migrant life style. It is necessary to know how migrants travel, how they live and work, how they view their world, and how their world is viewed by non-migrant people.

A few years ago, my husband and I spent 54 weeks as migrant farm workers, traveling in all parts of the United States. We stayed in all types of housing. We worked in the fields, in orchards, and in packing sheds. We traveled in trucks and in a bus from border to border. We slept in our car, stranded in strange communities. We saw many things that would adversely affect communication between migrants and non-migrants and would affect how migrants might be expected to react to illness, disability, or some other crisis in their lives.

It is hard to say who the migrants are or how many migrants travel this country each year in search of work. Within the migrant streams can be found all races and most ethnic groups. There are migrants whose ancestors were among the earlier colonists of this country and those who were born in Mexico or the West Indies. There are migrants who are aged and those who are newborn. There are migrants who are physically handicapped, who have respiratory infections, intestinal parasites, diabetes, rheumatic fever, tuberculosis. There are those who are in need of all kinds of dental care. There are those who have defective vision, impaired hearing, deviated nasal septa, and diseased tonsils, and there are those who are reasonably strong and well nourished.

I think a description of workers waiting for their buses in Belle Glade, Florida, is fairly typical, except for racial differences of work-

SOURCE: Reprinted from *Rehabilitation Record*, Vol. 10, No. 6 (November–December, 1969), pp. 1–7, with minor corrections by the author.

ers found in the Eastern Stream, the Western Stream, and throughout the central section of the country. The open square in the center of the Negro quarter in Belle Glade at 6:30 in the morning of a winter day is a teeming cross section of migrant workers. It is to this vacant area that the buses come to pick up the vegetable workers who will harvest the beans, celery, or sweet corn in fields 20 to 60 miles away. In the early morning, the workers collect and mill in groups waiting for the 7 o'clock whistle, the signal for the buses to leave. Later these same migrants will follow the Eastern Stream north to the potatoes of New York and the apples of Virginia.

These are Negro workers of all ages. There are young men in their late teens who saunter nonchalantly toward a group of giggling girls and then stop a few feet away to engage a latecomer in a loud conversation for the girls' benefit. Men and women of varied ages cluster around a bus driver to hear his inducements that seek to persuade them to go with him to pick beans in south Palm Beach County. They laugh with each other and then move on toward some other bus, or they disperse to stand with new groups.

A lone man whose oversized clothes hang loosely on his wasted body staggers through the crowd, pausing to drain the last drops of cheap wine from a bottle he nurses against his chest. His glazed eyes slide over the others, seeming not to see. He doffs his frayed straw hat in a sweeping gesture, mumbling an apology as he bumps against the fender of a bus and ambles off across the square.

There are young mothers—carrying tiny infants and leading half asleep toddlers still in their night clothes—who scurry toward a baby sitter in some other part of the quarter. Their children seldom see them except for these hurried trips across the square in the early morning and back again after dark when the buses return from the distant fields.

Here and there are hucksters—old men whose bent bodies push lopsided grocery carts—calling out their wares of apples, peanuts, and potato chips for lunch in the field, spotted and bruised fruit, items too old to be sold in the local market but which may bring some slight income to those who are too old to work in the beans. There are those who come to watch, who have no intention of going to work. They may try to persuade a friend to take a day off and fish in the canal or start a crap game. Sometimes they come to the fields and encourage workers to go home early. Such people, whether men or women, are known as "deadbeats" and are looked upon with disfavor by the majority of workers who go every day to the fields and who try to earn as much as they can.

Migrants, regardless of race, represent all personality types. Migrant camps are like a cross section of any city with the most obvious feature being that of poverty — but a poverty more extreme, more secretive, more insidious than that found in the ghetto of any city.

If one word were used to describe the migrant workers, that word would need to be isolation.

There is an aloneness for the seasonal worker created by the temporary status of his employment. The two greatest factors which motivate his becoming a migrant worker are limited work near his own home and the promise of work or better opportunities in some other sections of the country. The average migrant worker is highly motivated to support himself and his family. He does not join the migrant stream out of dissatisfaction with his home area, as much as he is driven into this type of work because of necessity. His stay in any community can be determined by a whimsical change in the weather. A freeze, a windstorm, or hail can wipe out an entire crop, and he and his family are forced to move on, searching for another job.[1]

The principal migration of agricultural migrant workers is along five main streams. They follow the crops from the South to the North and back to the South. Workers also move from low wage areas to higher wage areas, seeking better working conditions. The streams of those looking for work constantly change. Men and women who picked strawberries in California last year may come to New Jersey for peppers or blueberries this season or to the cherries of the Midwest or the vegetables of south Florida.

The East Coast Stream leads from the Everglades of Florida up the Atlantic seacoast. Branches thrust as far west as Lake Erie and northward into New England. This stream is made up mainly of southern-born Negroes with larger numbers of Puerto Ricans and black and white "day haul" workers who come to the fields from Philadelphia and other northern cities.

The Central River Stream, largest of all, originates in south Texas and moves northward on both sides of the Mississippi River. The western workers in this stream thin sugar beets from Nebraska to Idaho and Montana; the eastern workers pick fruit and harvest vegetables from Missouri to Wisconsin and Michigan. These migrants are mainly Mexican American with some southern Negroes and Caucasians.

---

[1]Myrtle R. Reul, "Isolation of Farm Workers," *The Michigan State Economic Record* (June, 1967), p. 3.

The third stream moves up and down the West Coast staying mainly in California. These migrants are Mexican Americans, Caucasians, Indians, Negroes, and Orientals. The fourth stream is found in the Southwest working in the crops of Arizona, New Mexico, and southern California. The predominant culture here is Mexican American—with some Mexicans, Indians, and a very few Negroes and Caucasians.

The fifth stream is concerned only with wheat, oats, rye, and barley harvesting. It includes workers, mainly Caucasian, who originate in Texas and Oklahoma. These are the aristocrats of the migrant workers. They travel mainly with house trailers or stay at motels and for the most part do not experience the discrimination known to the "stoop laborers," who thin lettuce or pick strawberries.

Rehabilitation counselors working with migrants should be aware of cultural differences in family roles. Spanish Americans, mainly from a Mexican heritage, make up the largest number of migrants in the United States. Many of these have more traditional families than those usually found in urban centers. "In the Spanish culture the strongest feeling of belonging is in the family. This is not the nuclear family—it is the kinship or extended family. When the Spanish American speaks of his family, he means his spouse, his children, his parents, his in-laws, aunts, uncles, cousins, and god-parents."[2] In the traditional Spanish American home—whether Mexican, Puerto Rican, or Cuban—the man is the head of the household. He is the one who makes decisions as to whether his wife or children are ill enough to go to the doctor. He should always be part of the rehabilitation plan for his family. It is an insult in his culture to enter his home without his permission. It is an insult to his manliness to exclude him from plans concerning his family.

Among the Negro migrants, the woman, especially the grandmother, plays a more dominant family role. Divorce, separation, common-law marriages, or unwed parenthood are the usual reasons for the female family head, although there are some migrant families where the legal husband is present and yet the woman makes all of the major decisions. There are also many "adopted" children or relatives being raised by nonfamily members. Although these may be rather loosely defined family relationships, these adults—whether biological parents, step-parents, or self-adopted parents—seem to have a good deal of love and affection for the children in their care.

---

[2]Myrtle R. Reul, *Sociocultural Patterns among Michigan Migrant Farm Workers,* Rural Manpower Center, Michigan State University, 1967, p. 5.

There is less of the common-law marriage among white migrants. Family membership is along extended family lines, with the grandmother playing a dominant part. While the man is the head of the household, the woman is often the one who actually makes decisions in regard to the educational or medical needs of the children.

While many of the migrants travel in large crews in a convoy of inspected trucks or buses, still others are "free wheelers" who provide their own transportation and make their own contacts with the growers. There are also buses and trucks which may meet the bare minimum standards for inspection or which are driven over back roads to avoid inspection points.

Pedro Ordaz, a Mexican American migrant whom we came to know very well, was a person who owned such a mode of transportation. Pedro struggled with the unyieldingness of the heavy old bus. He told us that all the way from Texas there had been too much play in the steering wheel, and he had fought to keep the vehicle from straying toward the curb. The man who sold him the bus said the wheels had just had an alignment, but something was wrong. The mechanic at a service station said it sounded like a worn steering column, but Pedro could not afford to have him look. When the cucumbers were harvested then perhaps he would have money for the garage, but for now he would do well to get to Wisconsin.

His back ached between his shoulder blades and he shrugged in an attempt to relieve the tension. The pain in his back did not distract from the hurt of his foot and leg. There was a new raw spot near his ankle, an open sore that seeped a bloody ooze. The first sore had started a year ago when he trimmed a corn on his middle toe and the razor slipped. The spot had never healed. The sores and swelling had spread and other open ulcers had appeared until now his foot and leg were so swollen and inflamed he could not wear a shoe.

His leg had never bothered him so much as it did on this trip. He wished Manuel could drive, but Manuel was only 12 and small for his age. At least he was wiry and strong; he could help in the cucumbers and could help Marina with the younger children. Marina was pregnant again with their eighth child, but she too was strong and seldom went to the doctor. She would work in the cucumbers until the baby was born and perhaps the baby would be late this time and the cucumbers would all be picked. At any rate, Marina was strong and only stayed away from the fields a few days whenever she had a baby.

Pedro was more worried about the bus and how it handled than about anything else. Without the bus, he and his family could not find work. He had worked for the Clarks three years and had prom-

ised that he would be back to pick their cucumbers this year. Perhaps he was foolish to buy the bus and try to make it on his own.
Other years, he and his family had gone to Wisconsin with a crew.
When the man talked with him about buying the bus, it sounded like
a good idea. It sounded like a way to save money and to someday
have something for Manuel and the others. Perhaps someday Pedro
would have his own crew. The Anglo who sold him the bus made
him a good deal. It was only a few dollars down and the rest later
after many crops were picked. Pedro had always paid his bills. His
credit was good, but his leg hurt and his back was tired.

Maybe when he got to Wisconsin he could sleep in the bus while
Manuel and Marina and the younger children picked cucumbers. He
would rest, take it easy, and they would manage. In the ways of his
people, he would shrug his shoulders and say *ni modi* ("it can't be
helped"), and he, as they, would forget any discomfort he might have
and he would sing while he fought the wheel to hold the lumbering
weight of the bus in a straight track down the highway.

Later, we worked in the Wisconsin cucumbers with Pedro's family. Part of the first day, he hobbled up and down rows, bending in
the torrid heat to strip the tiny gherkins from the scratchy vines. His
leg became increasingly swollen and the flies "bothered." Pedro
covered the open sores with cigarette papers but the flies continued
to pester and finally he crawled into the bus and elevated his foot.
Someone told him to soak it in strong Epsom salts, but he understood
they were saying salt water. After one application of damp table salt,
his leg was even more inflamed.

We found Pedro's situation was not unique among migrants. We
were working in the strawberries in Washington when one of the
children fell out of a truck and broke his leg. A routine examination
at the hospital as preparation for the administration of an anesthetic
showed that this child had a malformed heart, rickets, a serious
respiratory infection, and scalp ringworm.

Prolonged illness or disability is a crisis situation for anyone, but it
becomes even more complicated for a migratory farm worker and his
family. Living circumstances often mean delayed medical attention
or total lack of attention at the onset of even an acute illness.

"Unless too sick to tolerate the motion of a car, bus, or truck, a
migrant worker will not try to see a doctor" . . . "The sick keep going
until such a time as they recover, or they worsen to the point of
requiring immediate hospitalization, or they even die."[3]

We were in Virginia working in apples when one of the young

---

[3]Myrtle R. Reul, *Where Hannibal Led Us* (New York: Vantage Press, 1967).

pickers was hospitalized with a ruptured appendix. For three days he had been doubling up in the orchard, but after stretching out on the ground would return to his ladder. His friends thought he had cramps from eating too many apples.

Even when medical facilities are available, financial pressure or travel demands may interfere with carrying out the physician's recommendations. A special diet may not be feasible. A prescription may never be filled because the migrant must choose between medicine, in which he has little faith, and food for his family.

In the tomatoes of Ohio, a physician diagnosed the pain in Joseph's chest as rheumatic fever. He recommended rest and limited physical activity. Months later, in Texas, we worked in the tomatoes with Joseph. He still had severe pains in his chest. His 15-year-old son threw the crates onto the truck and Joseph stopped for a few minutes at the end of each row. Joseph was not trained for any work less strenuous than harvesting crops. He could not follow the physician's recommendations.

With many migrants, regardless of race or ethnic background, there is a fear of doctors and hospitals. There is also superstition about the causes of illness, and it is often difficult, especially among Indians and Spanish Americans, to accept the fact that the illness or disease can be contagious. Within these two cultures, the family wants to be with the ill person. Sending him to the hospital is an act of rejection unless his relatives can come along.

Migrants are confused by medical terms, prescriptions, and hospital forms. They often nod their heads and say "yes" as an indication they are listening or because they think some reply is expected, not because they necessarily understand what they have been told.

On one occasion, we talked to a white migrant who came originally from the mountains of Tennessee. He was incensed with a young doctor at the clinic where he had gone for a "ringin'" in his head. He told the doctor it was "jest a bad case of catarrah o' the head." The physician said he had never heard of such a thing. He prescribed for a severe sinus infection, but the migrant refused to use the medication because he did not believe " 'hat was much of a doc when he never he'rd of anything so common as catarrh o' the head."

Still another time, we met a stranded migrant family whose five-year-old had his arm in a cast. His mother explained, "the doc said 'twas a broken clavicle." She looked concerned and added that she hoped the "doc has sit the right one, 'cause my baby brother once broke his collar bone and his 'peared just the same." The physician who put her youngster's arm in a cast had used the medical term "clavicle," never realizing the mother was confused because she did not recognize that clavicle and collar bone were one and the same.

It is paramount that the counselor accept the migrant or his family at the point where they are in understanding the illness or the service of the agency. What may appear to be resistance to service can actually be fear of being ill or fear of being alone or dependent.

In order to work effectively with members of another culture or subculture, it is not only necessary to understand something of the values of that culture but it is necessary to convey respect for it. This is done more at the nonverbal level, through attitudes and action, than at the verbal level.

Migrants are distrustful of the spoken word. Because they have known discrimination, because they are consistently at the mercy of those who are glib of tongue, they have come to perceive the sincerity behind the spoken word. They are sensitively aware of unspoken attitudes and feelings. The migrant, at a very young age, must learn to be intuitively aware of his surroundings in order to survive. He can accurately sense the prejudice, the distrust, or the dislike that others often have toward him.

The migrant inevitably is going to be suspicious of any helping person regardless of the profession represented. If the migrant senses that the helping person is contemptuous and does not respect him as a fellow human being in his own right, then it is exceedingly doubtful that a real working relationship can be developed.

All of the fears and dependency needs which illness or disability bring out in every individual are magnified for the migrant. While the basic human needs of the migrant are the same as those for any ill person, his experiences are uniquely different. His concept of self has been affected; he does not feel he really belongs. His lack of education or understanding of treatment procedures, the inadequacy of his convalescent experience, his feelings about illness and his fear of hospitals and agencies must be understood by the rehabilitation counselor. If he is patient and understanding, the counselor can open avenues for the migrant to a better way of life.

· 42 ·

HETTIE JONES

Neighborhood Service Centers

At the corner of Stanton and Ridge streets, toward the bottom of Manhattan Island, is a small store. On the door someone has scrawled "The Elegants," but the lettering on the window describes the place as Centro de Servicio al Vecindario, Neighborhood Service Center. A venetian blind on the inside of the door says "open/abierto" when the slats are turned one way and "closed/cerrado" when they are turned the other way. Even when the "closed" sign is out, though, people usually knock or try the door just to make sure.

Stanton and Ridge are narrow streets, so narrow that, even though the buildings rise no more than five stories, they seem to shut out the sky. If you look out the window from the waiting room of Neighborhood Service Center South, the whole street seems small and cramped. When the sofa and chairs are filled, there are cushions in the window, or in summer and spring you can sit on the one radiator. The workers' offices are not visible from the waiting room; they are tiny partitioned spaces, each large enough to hold a desk and chair for the worker and a chair for the client. If the client brings her children, as is often the case, they must sit on her lap or play on the floor or wander through the labyrinth of cubicles.

Appointments are not required here. When a client arrives, he is asked only his name. It was suggested at first that clients not be required to give their names directly upon presenting themselves, in order that the agency appear as nonbureaucratic as possible. But it soon became evident that it was not the giving of their names that mattered to people but the way in which they were asked for this information and the way the name was used or pronounced by those who had presumably come to serve the community.

SOURCE: Reprinted from *Individual and Group Services in the Mobilization for Youth Experience,* ed. H. H. Weissman (New York: Association Press, 1967), pp. 33–53.

In this center, as in the three others opened by MFY elsewhere in its service territory, the emphasis from the first was on the creation of an atmosphere of mutual respect in direct, daily contact with the people of the neighborhood. Within the context of respect, along with concrete aid such as homemaker help, legal assistance, emergency loans, etc., a social-casework approach was to be the major technique of changing clients' ways of perceiving and responding to their circumstances. Like other aspects of MFY's activity, the neighborhood service centers were conceived as a way of reducing or eliminating self-defeating attitudes and behavior on the part of the urban poor.

Of course, many people in the urban slums *do* have severe emotional and psychological disturbances which render them functionally unable to take advantage of social, educational, or vocational opportunities. For most slum dwellers, however, self-defeating behavior is very largely a matter of economics, personal attitudes, and the limitations imposed by their life situation. Some people may defeat themselves because of simple lack of information. Services may be available somewhere in the community of which these people know nothing. Or self-defeating attitudes may develop and persist because people lack the basic skills for making an alternative adjustment—budgeting, purchasing, etc. Or people may suffer continuously because they do not have access to anyone with the power to intervene for them when they get into trouble with employers or schools or law-enforcement agencies. The neighborhood service centers were meant to provide significant, direct help with these problems while using such aid as the basis for ongoing casework counseling.

The Proposal justified the emphasis on concrete services as follows:

Groups cannot be helped if they cannot be reached. It is generally conceded that lower class persons are drawn to agencies which have concrete services to offer. Their social and economic problems are both concrete and overwhelming, and they are quite naturally in search of equally concrete ways of solving these problems. For another thing, they tend to define these problems as the consequences of external, arbitrary, capricious and malevolent forces. One detects in these groups powerful if subtle emphasis upon fate, upon the evil and immutable nature of man, upon man as the victim of superior or innate natural and social forces. For these and other reasons, members of these groups may regard the notion that a person in trouble can improve his circumstances through a better understanding of himself and the way in which he contributes to creating his own problems as alien and impractical.

A further reason for our emphasis upon concrete services is our conviction that such services, if imaginatively employed in the context of a casework relationship, can be a powerful force for change in human behavior. For one thing, services which relieve environmental pressures may thus release blocked energies for investment in areas of family and occupational activity which were previously neglected. Secondly, some persons who experience overwhelming environmental pressures may become capable of using specialized therapeutic relationships once the external pressures are reduced. What we wish to stress is the reconstruction of the individual's social conditions through a casework process so that he can then experience new pressures which exert a direct influence on him for change in a preconceived direction. We assume that significant social and psychological growth takes place as one becomes enmeshed in and is forced to grapple with changed social circumstances.[1]

The aim was something akin to a new casework. The centers, as we have noted, were to include an inquiry service, a liaison-resource service, and a social-planning service. The same social workers, conceived of as general practitioners, were to be responsible for all of the services, with the aid of appropriate consultants — lawyers, housing experts, etc. In addition, there was a projected category of under-one-roof services — a social caseworker, public-health nurse, visiting homemaker, escorts, and baby sitters — who were to provide the enabling social resources: the concrete services to relieve the environmental pressures that often prevented the social and psychological adjustment of deprived and overburdened people.

It was expected that the inquiry service would provide "immediate practical information in response to inquiries about housing, education, public welfare, legal problems, consumer problems, and the like." The liaison resource service, composed of representatives of various municipal departments and an employment service would rotate among the various centers and be available to anyone in case of emergency. The liaison personnel were to function as a team which, it was hoped, would relieve people of the strain of having to deal with many offices in connection with a single problem.

The social-planning service was projected essentially as a casework service for those who might benefit from a lengthy casework relationship. Emphasis would be on recognition and treatment of

---

[1] *A Proposal for the Prevention and Control of Delinquency by Expanding Opportunities* (New York: Mobilization For Youth, 1961), pp. 356–57.

social as well as psychological problems, with appropriate attention to the cultural milieu of the client.

EARLY PROBLEMS

Neighborhood Service Center South (or No. 1) which opened on November 13, 1962, originally housed the staff of two neighborhood service centers plus a student unit. In early 1963, three more store-fronts were opened, two south of Houston Street and one north.

The professional caseworkers who opened the first center, the branch director relates, had "different perceptions of what was to be accomplished . . . in a neighborhood service center," and most of their ideas were soon found to be "untrue or not feasible." The physical facilities were more cramped than anyone had anticipated, the staff (all professional) was considerably smaller, and none of the proposed under-one-roof services was available. A few weeks of formal and informal meetings and conferences served only to reveal the differences of opinion about what the casework role in such a setting was supposed to be, and how to deal with a population thought to be traumatized emotionally and psychologically.

For practical purposes, cases were classified in two ways. So-cial-broker cases were those which required immediate, concrete service. The term "broker" was not mentioned in the Proposal; in practice, however, it replaced the designation "generalist" or "gen-eral practitioner." Social-planning cases were those which required contact with the client over a long period of time. However, the social brokers were also the social planners, since all staff was re-quired to perform all the functions of the agency. The problem of labeling the workers' role was part of the whole problem of defining service.

It became apparent, for example, early in the operation of the neighborhood service centers that to provide a social-planning ser-vice for all the clients who needed it would not be possible with the small staff available. After a few months, workers were allowed to carry only 10 percent social-planning cases, the remainder being broker cases. According to staff, however, the social-planning cases sometimes differed little from the broker cases in the amount of the worker's time and attention they required. By this time the word was out: "Go to the NSC if you're in trouble."

A survey of NSC activities indicated that by early 1963 the centers had already served more families and more individuals than anyone had anticipated. From January 1 to April 1, 1963, 482 families were served and 3,833 acts of service rendered. This was accomplished by a staff of ten.

What constituted an act of service? An office or field interview, a home visit, a telephone discussion, correspondence with clients or family or agency (public or private) or with another MFY division. The same survey mentioned that "heavy amounts of time are devoted to intervention for the satisfaction of basic survival requirements such as food, housing, and clothing." Workers, instructed to be available to all, were terribly overburdened, not only because of the large numbers of clients but also because most of the clients had so many problems that it was difficult to know where to begin. Mary Williams, a NSC worker, expressed some of this frustration:

I wonder if we can give the comprehensive, protracted services which deal with the many problems which prevail, one intensifying the other. Can we deal with the problems of substandard housing, medical, financial, recreational, and dietary needs? We attack one, perhaps two, of these problems, leaving others which are just as debilitating, eventually pulling the family back into preservice patterns and problems. After decades of deprivation, the deprived person is not necessarily impressed by the fact that his housing has been improved if he continues to be hungry or poorly clothed. So much remains to be resolved. . . .[2]

It was obvious that, if any of the problems were to be solved, there would have to be some limitation on the service, to focus the program and to further refine the worker's role, but also to isolate what was most needed by the target population, or, as one director called it, "what it is that people suffer most about."

Soon after service was begun, it became evident that part of the responsibility for people's problems lay with the very institutions on which they had to rely for their existence. A good many clients lacked the basic survival requirements. Many people, whose welfare was supposed to be the responsibility of public agencies, were walking around in various states of crisis. Since, as we have noted, there had to be some limitation on the services offered by the centers, the Services to Individuals and Families administration decided that the neighborhood service centers would serve only clients with prob-

---

[2]Mary Williams, "Detailed Notes of a Professional Social Worker in a Mobilization For Youth Neighborhood Service Center" (mimeographed, New York Mobilization For Youth, undated), pp. 8–9.

lems centering around the use of public and private agencies in the areas of welfare, health, education, housing, employment, and legal services. Those presenting other problems would be referred elsewhere for service. Whether a client was seen on a continuing basis or for merely brief contact was, then, no longer relevant; it was the nature of the problem, not of the client, that defined the duration of the contact.

An early series of taped interviews with workers and clients at one of the neighborhood service centers gives some idea of the reasons for this shift.

No one cares and you are like a stone on the sidewalk. What can you do if we are not lucky enough in the richest city in the world? We've got to go on welfare and have the welfare worker come up to see us and tell us how to live, and then she looks in the ice box at what we have. They want to know what kind of clothes you have, and when they see a telephone, they want to know who is paying for it and why that money isn't being used for food. They try every way to get you. They make it hard for you, and they don't want you to know from nothing. But they get a big salary every week. Before you get the first check, you wait three or four weeks, and when you get it, you don't know what to do first. They should have on their bones how much they give you. But you've got to make the best of it. One of these days I'll go up to the top of the Brooklyn Bridge, yell, "Here I go!" and then jump off. And you know what? Nobody will know! Nobody will care! Nobody will miss me.

Mr. L. had practically finished a TV repair course when illness intervened. He has not been able to afford the balance of the tuition and is now on welfare. Bitter and confused, he says, "Welfare won't pay for my schooling and if I pay ten dollars a week from what they give me, they'll close my case. But actually they'd save money by sending me to school, because then I could get a decent paying job and we wouldn't have to be on welfare. That's proof that they don't want you to get ahead. They want you to stay where you are."

Mr. R. complains about his slum tenement. "Every day when I come out of the building through a broken door and the filthy hall and see that abandoned car sitting in the garbage-littered snow, I feel as if I am living in a dump, one for which I am not responsible. I think to myself that the City of New York has abandoned me and my children, and I'm sad and ashamed. People who come to visit us look around with disgust and some have stopped coming. How can the city do this? It doesn't care about its residents or sanitation—not down here at least. But I've heard that it's different on Fifth Avenue. It's clean. The city thinks that something is being done because they have inspectors. But they don't know that the landlord pays off the health inspector or that the policeman on our beat lets the numbers man operate right out of our hall."[3]

The staffs had been engaged in a running battle with the Department of Welfare almost from the opening of the neighborhood service centers; this battle now took on larger and more consistent proportions. The policy of the centers toward the organizations and institutions they had to deal with mirrored the response of one client who said about Welfare: "They're quick to cut you off and slow to put you back on. When you're in need, the department takes its time, but when it's to their advantage, they can work fast. In other words, they can be efficient when they want to be."

STABILIZATION OF THE PROGRAM

By May 1963 it had become clear that many of the social-broker functions did not have to be handled by someone with a master's degree in social work, and a number of case aides were added to the staff. The liaison-resource service described in the Proposal was never put into effect, since the money allocated for it was used to hire additional case aides and caseworkers. In 1964 the Visiting Homemaker Service[4] was discontinued, and several of the homemakers were assigned to the neighborhood service centers to help in providing escort, translation, shopping, and other services.

By January 1964 the program of the neighborhood service centers had crystallized. The distinction between social-broker and social-planning cases in effect did not exist; there simply was no time for the long-term counseling envisioned in the Proposal for the social-planning cases. The Services to Individuals and Families divisional report of 1964 notes that limiting service to the provision of concrete aid in dealing with community agencies did not reduce the number of cases at the four centers. At that time the average case load per worker was thirty-two, and a client might be seen anywhere from one to five or six times a week. There was no question that the neighborhood service centers had reached the low-income population of the MFY area: Seventy-four percent of the cases were

---

[3]Sherman Barr, "Poverty on the Lower East Side" (mimeographed, New York Mobilization For Youth, 1964).

[4]See chapter on "The Use of Indigenous Personnel" in this volume for a description of this program [not reprinted here].

Puerto Rican, 20 percent Negro, 6 percent White. Seventy-five percent were known to the Department of Welfare, and 70 percent of the families were living in tenements.

A study commissioned by the Services to Individuals and Families chief to clarify the program called for "systematic cultivation of the welfare 'generalist' who is a resource specialist, mediator, service supplier, coordinator, caseworker, group worker, community organization worker, housing and welfare expert, social action specialist and diplomatic envoy with the establishment at one and the same time."[5] The role of the caseworker in practice was quite as complex as that outlined above but it was less than systematically cultivated.

In rendering concrete service, the worker acted in any one or a combination of several roles. People who came to the NSC became dependent on their workers to intervene for them with the service systems (Welfare mainly); workers performed this intervention over and over, acting in behalf of the client instead of enabling the client to make the necessary connections himself. There was too little time, and there were too many clients, for the service to be directed more consciously toward overcoming self-defeating behavior. In addition, there was a new awareness on the part of the workers of where the fault really lay; they questioned whether changing the client's behavior was possible or necessary, given what they had learned about their clients and the service systems with which they were in steady contact.

Mary Williams summed up these ideas as follows:

We observe the phenomena of dependency and denial on many avenues of service, and it may, in part, account for the difficulty deprived persons have in accurately assessing or accepting the planful roles they need to play to break the chain of circumstances by which they are surrounded. Accompanying this is the fact that their appraisal of [social systems] which have operated to freeze them into a given socio-economic mold, which . . . in turn establish the bulk of their life experience . . . leads them to the . . . denial-projection mechanism. For, in fact, they have demonstrable evidence which supports their [feeling of] blamelessness. . . .

Enhancing the blameless-helpless-hopeless syndrome are daily encounters with systems which appear more concerned with smooth operational procedures than the needs of the deprived. The denigrating responses of the systems' reactions to the problems and needs of the deprived may be discerned when a welfare investigator curtly replies, "I'm too busy to send you

---

[5]Frances G. King, *A Study of Services to Individuals and Families Within Mobilization For Youth* (New York, Mobilization For Youth, 1963), p. 41.

clothing"; when the hospital admonishes them to be there at 9:00 A.M., only to keep them waiting until 2:00 P.M. for the doctor; when the dietician "hasn't gotten a chance to send special diet forms to welfare"; when they receive no response whatever to complaints made to a city building department; when the landlord never seems able to get around to repairing the plumbing, the rat holes, the radiators, or the windows; when a new employee is hired, in the same job classification, and earns more than those with tenure (and a Spanish accent); when UIB [Unemployment Insurance Board] summarily denies benefits because the employer, who forced them to resign, describes them as an "involuntarily quit"; when the health station is seldom clear about why they must make tedious arrangements for the care of the other children in order to take one child in for what looks like a "weigh in"; when the teacher berates them about their "lack of interest" in Johnnie's reading problems when managing the problem of feeding and clothing Johnnie seems to be quite enough for them to handle; when there just isn't time for the "free lawyer" to explain to them exactly how it is that Joe, who's been in jail for three months, hasn't been sentenced yet; when everyone tells them not to pay exorbitant credit charges yet they can most easily secure credit in times of need only from those vendors whose credit charges are exorbitant; when they come to New York City in pursuit of "the American Dream" only to be told that they are "undeserving" and must return to the place of their legal residence; or, when welfare insists that employed teen-agers, whose hope for an improved existence has not been destroyed, contribute the lion's share of earnings toward the support of the family.

To draw this together, I would submit that there is an apparent consistency between the world of the deprived and their perceptions of it as a hostile, withholding, powerful, aggressive milieu in which they must fashion firm, pragmatic, self-protective coping devices to survive in this milieu. Unfortunately, the coping devices may be largely self-defeating.[6]

If the neighborhood service centers had had the facilities and the

---

[6]Mary Williams, "Direct Work with the Severely Deprived: Some Basic Considerations" (mimeographed, New York, Mobilization For Youth, 1964), pp. 4–6. She continues: "These devices include dodging the corner grocer to take their credit to another grocer, moving before rent is due in order to enjoy some 'extra' monies, selling their furniture and telling welfare that it was repossessed and must be replaced, throwing a 'rent party,' going to the local bar with the last $3.00 '. . . 'cause everybody eats somehow'; giving up a plan for marriage because 'at least welfare sends the money regular,' applying home remedies except when there is no choice but to seek medical attention, and moving from one extra-legal marital relationship to another. . . . This apparent fluidity and 'dealing' appears to contribute to the emergent or survival nature of the requests presented to the practitioner. By the time the problems are presented . . . the situation has so deteriorated that the deprived .iew immediate service as essential. . . . The sense of blamelessness appears to contribute to their sense of helplessness and hopelessness. These compound entrapments appear to damage clearly feelings of security and compromise greatly an investment in planful activity."

staff to provide each client with an extended casework relationship, some have contended, a new kind of casework could have been devised. Yet it is more likely that such a casework could only be developed when caseworkers can get the series of systems, which now fail to maintain people adequately, to respond to their needs. Since at that time, this was not possible, workers were urged to abandon the psychological side of casework services.[7]

The planned rectification of self-defeating patterns of behavior through psychotherapeutic techniques and environmental manipulation simply had to take a back seat. The individual's motivation to change his life hardly matters if a rat is scampering over his feet. A mother cannot be expected to bring her child to school if the child has no shoes. And most of the time neither the rat-infested apartment nor a lack of shoes is due to client behavior.

Workers still gave some psychological help to some clients, but by and large they were not expected to do so. The emphasis was on giving service related to the basic matters of existence. An important aspect of this decision, which has had far-reaching consequences, was the conviction that the good adjustment of NSC clients would have meant a good adjustment to poverty and to the constant violation of their rights by community agencies. The need for choice was clear, and the choice that was made was clearly the only one to be made in the circumstances, at that time, by socially conscious people.

THE ROLE OF THE ADVOCATE

By mid-1964 the social workers in the neighborhood service centers had assumed the title "advocate." The title reflected less a method than an attitude, a stance. For people had begun to see the NSC as their sole means, not only of communicating with service institutions but of obtaining a measure of justice from them. They had become aware that it was possible to gain access to power—power they did not view themselves as possessing—to confront an institution which was depriving them of their rights. Quite simply, it was a great relief to many people to be able to go somewhere where a phone call would be made that literally meant the difference between suffering and the cessation of suffering for a period of time.

---

[7]The provision of psychological services, for which there is still a very great need, is discussed in the paper "Psychological Help for the Poor" in this volume [not reprinted here].

Consider the following two cases, which are not atypical of life on the Lower East Side:

A fifty-four-year-old woman has been living in her one-room flat for three months with no lights. She cannot pay the electric bill, and the Department of Welfare, even after repeated requests, will not put her on its rolls because she cannot establish the legitimacy of her New York residence to its satisfaction. One day she complains of feeling ill and goes to the hospital; the hospital sends her home. She goes again when, after a few days, she feels worse, and is again sent home. Nothing is wrong; nothing shows on the x-rays. Three days later she returns to the hospital with a worker from NSC South. It is now noticed that the woman has a large tumor in her chest and is dying of bone cancer. Is it the three days' wait that has located the illness or the magic of the worker's demand, the power she wields as the representative of a social agency? And on whose conscience do those three months of darkness lie?

A woman whose son has been wounded in Vietnam wants to find out where he is and how he is. She has no address; she knows only that he has been taken from the Philippines to a hospital in Japan. She calls the Red Cross and is told that it is not possible to obtain such information. She comes to NSC South. A worker phones the Red Cross for her and is given an address to which one may write for the desired information. Where is the magic this time? Where is the failure?

Advocacy, as applied to a social worker, has been defined as the willingness to intervene with a government agency on behalf of a low-income person. It does not mean helping the poor man to help himself or enabling him to better manage his transactions with the governmental department. It means filling in the power deficit on his side of the transaction by providing him with a defender who has specialized knowledge of the rules and regulations of the system. (This includes its informal and therefore unstated inner workings, which may be of major significance in how decisions get made and how they can get changed.) But most of all advocacy means a readiness to become an adversary, to pit oneself against the system with whatever means are at hand, whether persuasion, manipulation, or straightforward pressure.[8]

Relative to their advocate designation, workers were called upon

---

[8]Richard M. Elman, "Neighborhood Service Centers" (mimeographed, New York, Mobilization For Youth, undated), p. 41. From Mobilization, the concept of a neighborhood service center assuming an advocacy stance on behalf of clients spread through New York City and the country.

to promote institutional change, with the Department of Welfare as the special target. Their methods and techniques were essentially the same as those conventionally called upon to effect bureaucratic change. There are the telephone and the letter, irritation on single cases. There is the more direct pressure of walking in a picket line in front of welfare headquarters, along with welfare recipients, to demand larger school-clothing allotments.

Sherman Barr, director of the neighborhood-service-center program, has referred to the advocate as a gadfly. This is a very adequate metaphor if one sees institutions that serve the poor as a herd of immobile cattle faced with the problem of a lot of sudden bites. When the animal finally realizes that no amount of tail-switching is going to do away with the irritation, he just may reason that it would be better to change position or deal with the problem another way. (Services to Individuals and Families was sometimes asked by such institutions: Why don't you people behave like other agencies? Why don't you be good and stop bothering me?)[9]

The advocate worker had to amass a considerable array of information on community resources, more than would suffice for a worker in a traditional family-service agency. A few workers became experts in housing or in health; everyone had to have a special knowledge of welfare. With regard to welfare, in fact, SIF innovated a welfare bulletin which was kept absolutely up-to-date by an experienced consultant. Thanks to the bulletin, NSC workers often had information in advance of Department of Welfare workers themselves—some of whom, as time passed, would call to find out the latest regulations. This bulletin became in great demand all over the city and country, as did information on the advocate role.

The public image of the NSC worker as advocate has refined relations with the Department of Welfare and, to a lesser degree, with other institutions. Since the emphasis is on rights rather than on undue demands, certain channels have been created, and a measure

---

[9]Agency personnel often complained bitterly that MFY clients were lying and cheating. There is little doubt that in some instances they were correct. But as Sherman Barr has pointed out (*op. cit.*, p. 11), "The poor do not and cannot understand bureaucratic problems. Use of the Welfare Department requires a level of knowledge and sophistication which is impossible for the bulk of the poor to learn and employ. For instance, the concept of appeal is unheard of. Service systems are seen by the poor as systems which must be manipulated if decent service is to be obtained. Methods and techniques for beating the system are disseminated." Mobilization's point of view was that, if the system were operating correctly, there would be a lot less cheating. Dealing with the problem on a client-by-client basis would only be attacking the effect and not the cause.

of understanding has been arrived at through negotiation as well as pressure. MFY Legal Services Unit has also been involved in dealings with the Department of Welfare, and this social worker-lawyer alignment has been invaluable.[10]

LATER DEVELOPMENTS

From October 1962 through March 1965, the SIF program served 18,500 persons (16 percent of the total MFY-area population) in 3,700 families. In mid-1965, in order to provide more effective service, two centers were closed and their staff redistributed to NSC's South and North.[11]

As the months passed, it became clear that the advocacy stance of the workers was successful in achieving concrete gains for the vast majority of clients, but was not particularly useful in bringing about broad changes in the policy of the Department of Welfare. At this point the decision was made to organize groups of clients to seek changes in the department's procedures and policies through concerted community action.[12] The reason for this partial shift in emphasis in the neighborhood service centers was twofold. First, staff was convinced that such action was necessary if bureaucratic service institutions were to be made more responsive to people's needs. Second, there was the desire to experiment with implementing the hypothesis that participation in social action is therapeutic to the client.

In December 1965, the policy was instituted to gear intake more sharply to public-welfare concerns. Workers were advised that in no case should they "spend an inordinate amount of time on areas not related to income maintenance, health, safety, housing, and concrete problems of welfare clients." In addition, the out-of-area cases, which had formerly constituted 15 percent of the total caseload, were closed and no more out-of-area cases were to be accepted without supervisory approval. With the availability of additional funds a third

---

[10]See the chapter on, "Legal Challenges to Formal and Informal Denial of Welfare Rights" in Vol. 4, *Justice and the Law.*

[11]The space already secured in one of the area's low-income housing projects, which became NSC North, was the first nonstorefront center to be put in operation. By this time, however, the lack of "visibility" made little difference. Within a short time NSC North had many more cases than had been anticipated.

[12]The chapter on "Organizations of Welfare Clients" in Vol. 2, *Community Development,* describes the history of these organizations in detail.

center was opened in 1966 (NSC West), located in three small store-fronts. In addition to the service provided in the other two centers, NSC West provided adult employment counseling.

RANGE OF SERVICES

Although the emphasis in the neighborhood service centers has been increasingly geared toward welfare problems, considerable assistance has been rendered in other areas.

In 1966, a public-health nurse was hired to provide group-teaching services to staff and clients, make home visits in emergencies, interpret and follow up treatment plans with clients, and intervene on behalf of staff with clinics and hospitals.

Active and aggressive intervention by NSC staff saved several clients from being hastily and incorrectly admitted to mental wards, saw to it that children of tubercular mothers were x-rayed without the usual delay, and forced reevaluation of hasty judgments about retardation, thus avoiding unnecessary institutional commitment.

Ancillary services were provided to make medical care possible. MFY escorts helped get frightened clients to clinics and interpreted the medical situation and hospital structure. Hundreds of dollars were made available annually, specifically for use as carfare to take young children to clinics or make regular visits to a prenatal clinic. Funds were also granted for eyeglasses, summer-camp physical examinations, emergency dental care, and the like when it became apparent that unreasonable delays would further increase social disorganization in the family and deterioration in the health situation of the client—particularly the young child.

The child-care service provided short-term baby-sitting while mothers were away from their homes for any number of reasons. This brief relief for the mother went far toward lessening the tensions and strains of everyday living. Although the service was essentially custodial, this service was used to uncover unmet needs. It was surprising and shocking to find children under the age of three who were legally blind or almost deaf or retarded and whose parents were not aware of the situation. Child care also enhanced the use the mother made of clinic visits. Placing well children in the care station during such a visit enabled a mother to give individualized attention to a sick child and eliminated the psychological wear and tear of disciplining children in the difficult environment of a clinic waiting room.

The services provided in relation to housing were also notable. Staff filled out scores of applications for low-cost housing projects and attempted to interpret the many confusing reasons given for rejections. A very important aspect of housing work related to the Department of Welfare. Workers took a strong stand to insure that the department moved quickly to provide security deposits and rent when an opening did become available for housing. Quick action often made the difference between a family's success or failure in securing a new apartment.

And finally the center staff served as friends and neighbors to the community:

Working mothers leave keys for their children: dogs are kept for short periods of time; addicts drop in to sleep off a high; emergency first aid is dispensed; money is held for clients who are afraid of being burglarized; policemen stop in for a cup of coffee; derelicts drop by to sit in the air-conditioned lobby during the summer; children drop in for a dime to buy some soda pop on a hot day; delinquent-prone youngsters check with us on the wisdom of "copping a plea" or going to trial; people drop in and preface their remarks by saying, "They told me that if you couldn't help me, no one could."[13]

THE NSC EXPERIENCE

From one point of view the neighborhood service centers can be regarded as a return to the political clubhouse style of help, with social workers instead of politicians dispensing the aid. From another point of view, they went far beyond the clubhouse into the realm of the institutional ombudsman, functioning as the watchdogs of public agencies.

A new casework, however, was not developed. In an early appraisal of the centers it was felt:

The casual voluntaristic nature of the present neighborhood service center program (largely walk-ins and informal referrals) precludes any systematic appraisal of the entire family in its total situation. Although gains doubtless have been achieved with these clients through the provision of concrete services ... serious problems continue in many of these families, gains tend

---

[13]Excerpted from Sherman Barr, "New Directions in Social and Medical Services for Young Children: A Review of the Mobilization For Youth Program," paper presented at the Conference on Changing Patterns of Health Services for Preschool Children (mimeographed, University of Minnesota, September, 1965), pp. 19–24.

to be lost, and some of the children become progressively more endangered. These outcomes would suggest that the segmented, crisis-oriented approach may not be the method of choice for families entrenched in the poverty status.[14]

Several factors accounted for the lack of development of the new casework. First, by agreeing to meet the needs of the clients as they themselves defined them, the centers soon became bogged down in giving service. Available staff time was insufficient to develop casework relationships. Second, and more important, Mobilization consciously chose to demonstrate how inadequately the institutions of society were functioning for poor people. Thus the concern of the centers was with institutional rather than personal change.

At a certain level of poverty, the demands of merely staying alive are so great and overwhelming that an attempt to form a psychologically oriented therapeutic relationship has little chance of success without the provision of concrete services. Since the centers wanted to serve as many people as possible (and had to depend on other institutions, like the Welfare Department, which controlled the significant concrete resources), there was neither the time nor the real possibility of developing the new casework techniques as originally intended.[15]

It is also reasonable to conclude that many people could have benefited from efforts to teach them to advocate for themselves. Some workers feel that advocacy puts the client on a treadmill: With such help readily available he will simply keep returning without ever attempting to assume an advocate stance himself. Others feel that advocacy is necessary, that clients will change only when the system is changed and until then will keep needing this help. Beyond a few individual workers' experiments, there were no systematic attempts to develop new methods and techniques for working with multiproblem families who might be involved in a casework relationship. Except for channeling clients to the welfare groups — which worked well — no systematic attempts were made to involve clients in advocacy or to train them to act as advocates for themselves.[16] That the neighborhood service centers' advocacy for

[14]Freda Taran, "Neighborhood Service Centers" (New York, Mobilization For Youth, undated), p. 7.

[15]It is also clear that the agency underestimated the difficulty of the task, first in not acknowledging the degree of training and conceptual ability required of staff for the task as well as its ability to restrict service to provide time to do the conceptual job.

[16]Of course, many clients learned how to advocate for themselves just by observing the workers. And most workers tended to urge clients to try to advocate for them-

their clients has created dependency is arguable. The risk of giving help is dependency. It is reasonable not to worry about this risk until clients are no longer faced with the broader risks of lack of food, clothing, and shelter.

The case record of Mrs. J. speaks to the point:

Mr. J. works and is out of the home from 8:00 A.M. to 6:00 P.M. Mrs. J. works and is out of the home from 5:00 P.M. to 11:00 P.M. From 5:00 P.M. to 6:00 P.M. the eight children are scheduled, in Mrs. J.'s words, "like the Marine Corps." The rest of her life is just as disciplined. She knows exactly which door to use in which department store on which day for which purpose. She travels from the Bronx to Brooklyn to save a few pennies on meat. She knows personally the owner of every second-hand clothing store on the Lower East Side. Her sons get their haircuts at the Bowery barber schools, where she saves one dollar over the regular price. She would never move from her small apartment to a different project because she is now living adjacent to a middle-income development populated largely by Jews, and where the Jews are, she says, you can find better schools, better police protection, better shopping, better recreation, and better support for various civic improvements. She knows which police station to go to for Christmas toys, which social agency for money, and which church offers more clothing. . . . In other words, she is everything some people in our society want poor people to be, thrifty, disciplined, and organized. However, after the seventh interview, she blurted out that all wasn't what it appeared to be. Occasionally she and her husband engage in violent battles which sometimes result in the police being called in. "Something has to give," she said, "something just has to give."[17]

Another projected intention for the neighborhood service centers was not realized—that the centers would coordinate the efforts of a variety of agencies and institutions into a coherent neighborhood service system. The liaison unit of city-agency personnel was never put into operation. By becoming advocates the center staffs became engaged in controversy, and this made cooperation—as envisioned in the idea of the liaison unit—impossible. But it seems likely that at the time the centers would have achieved a good deal less with most institutions had they avoided controversy and used friendly persuasion.

---

selves. But to be effective, advocacy must be backed up by power. Clients, acting alone, do not have the power to secure their legitimate demands when these are arbitrarily denied. The caseworker could threaten and follow through with picketing, legal action, etc.

[17]Barr, *op. cit.*, p. 6.

By the spring of 1966, the neighborhood service centers had four identifiable functions: (1) to provide information and referral services to assist people in the use of established agencies; (2) to act as an advocate to protect the client's interests and rights with respect to other agencies and to seek changes in those agencies' procedural policies that will become precedents for similar situations; (3) to provide concrete services directly to individuals and families; and (4) to organize and mobilize groups for collective action on behalf of the residents of the neighborhood.[18]

The Perlman-Jones report on the NSC's, compiled for the Department of Health, Education and Welfare, concludes with the following admonition:

It is important to recognize the limitations of neighborhood service centers in order to grasp what their appropriate role can be. At present they are being expected to compensate for and bring about changes in social conditions and social services, tasks which are beyond their unaided resources. They are, in effect if not in intention, being used as a way of avoiding the more radical action concerning social conditions and social provisions which the situation now requires. In the future they can take a more modest place as an essential part of a system of basic social provisions which insures humane and effective help to all people.[19]

While Perlman and Jones are correct in writing that the more adequate provisions of services deals only with the effects of poverty and will not change its causes, the neighborhood service centers have provided a base from which social-action organization can agitate for more basic changes. In any event, it is clear that, given the nature of the various institutional bureaucracies with which the poor must interact, there is a compelling need for a neighborhood-service-center operation which carries on an information-giving as well as an advocacy function for clients.[20] Certainly every settlement house in the country, as well as every citizens' organization located in a low-income area, should have a neighborhood service center.

One of the case aides characterized NSC clients as follows: "A third need only information, a third need support and advocacy, and

[18]Robert Perlman and David Jones, *Neighborhood Service Centers* (Washington, D.C.: Department of Health, Education and Welfare, 1967), p. 1.

[19]*Ibid.*, p. 80.

[20]The dramatic decrease in rejections for home relief in New York City from 66 percent in 1962 to 31 percent in 1967 is clear evidence of the need for these centers.

a third need long-term counseling." Low-income areas are in great need of a dependable, available source for information, advocacy, counseling, and social action, buttressed by such concrete services as baby-sitting, homemaking, escort, legal aid, and emergency loans.

In less than five years of operation (October 1962 to June 1967), the centers served 43,064 individuals in 10,487 families. Some 70 percent of the presenting problems involved the Welfare Department. The majority of problems were related to residents' eligibility, unmet needs – including clothing, household goods, beds and bedding – inadequate allowance for family size, late checks, incorrect computation, unserved cases, no worker for several months. About 40 percent of those who had welfare problems also had problems involving housing, health, schools, courts, etc. The remaining 30 percent of non-welfare problems were roughly divided into school, health, and miscellaneous category including addiction, employment, child neglect, emotional illness, housing, and housekeeping.

The amount of help these figures indicate is staggering, especially when one considers that most of it would not have been available had the service centers not been in operation. Without question, the neighborhood service centers discovered a vast pool of need which society's welfare institutions had been ignoring – largely because those institutions had been permitted to develop their policies and procedures with little or no accountability to the clients whom they served. The NSCs provided the means to begin a reversal of this process.

· 43 ·

H. JACK GEIGER

Medical Services:
Digging Wells and Building Privies

... We think we are able to give very adequate medical services. We have been able to recruit the necessary staff from all over the United States to the Tufts faculty. We have a full complement of physicians, nurses, technicians and others. Our definition of health, as you will see, is by design, a much broader one than many of the conventional ones. We dig wells, we build privies, we help people tear down old shacks and use the material to build new privies. We dig drainage ditches. We provided a tool bank for those who are well enough to repair their own houses, we make soap.

Mr. Choate mentioned some of this need. We teach other people how to make soap because that is the only way some of these needs can be met. We are deeply involved in community organization. There are now involved in Northern Bolivar County 10 local autonomous health associations, with 4,000 active members. For many of the black populations, it is the first organizational participation they ever had other than the Baptist Church. Each with its own set of priorities, clean water in one, healthy children in another, care of the elderly in another; each developing its own contact center, meeting hall, conference room, a dictionary, a few books, a telephone.

These are very innovative things to be appearing in black communities in Bolivar County and very often they are the first that are there. Working out programs that are their own, strong community organizations in their own communities, our partners; represented overall on a thing called the North Bolivar County Health Council.

These people with limited educational backgrounds, experience, and skills in 2 years have moved to the point where very recently

---

SOURCE: Reprinted from Statement made before Subcommittee on Employment, Manpower, and Poverty of the Committee on Labor and Public Welfare, U.S. Senate, 91st Cong. (April-June, 1969), pp. 267–71.

when we came to budget renewal they sat down and said, "Well, we would like to put in for a budget of our own, a program of our own, and we have done some work in figuring out what some of our needs and priorities are. Maybe you can give us a little help in the cost and then we think we can do them."

Their proposals were first of all that they develop a transportation system. They came to us and said, "Nobody could be doing as lousy a job as you are doing on getting these patients in from a 500 mile area and back out over the 500 miles. We have been living here a long time and we know something about what might be the reasonable way of getting around the county. We think we can do a better job than you can."

And they can. They budgeted themselves to do it, using buses and small vehicles that will come to the medical center, and also be the base of a public system, for tasks like getting to the county seat and getting food stamps.

They budgeted for youth guidance and career programs. They are concerned about the outmigration of children, and about their ill preparation for contemporary life.

They asked for and helped to design a Government agency grant and legal services program. That is the best name we could give it. In 2 years they have discovered that there are all kinds of existing Federal and State programs that are supposed to be offering services to them about which they knew nothing, from which they were systematically shut off, for which they didn't have the technical assistance to make application even if they knew, nor having made application would they have had the leverage to push it through.

Things like water systems, sewer systems, paved streets, and other kinds of economic development grants and the like which just don't go to black communities in Mississippi because they have never even heard of them. They recognize the need for technical assistance in going after what is available.

And finally they planned to take over our own modest funds for emergency relief and the administration of emergency relief. They have pointed out to us that they are in the best position to know whose needs are most acute and beyond that we haven't produced a social worker yet that knows how to make out a budget for 15 people to live on $30 a week, but they do, because they have had that experience.

I think the most important thing we have done, and "we" here refers to the black people of Bolivar County, not to myself and others from Tufts, is our response, together with the support of OEO's emergency food and medical care demonstration program, with regard to what was an overwhelming program, and that was hunger and malnutrition. It was an overwhelming problem in several ways.

We saw it first as a straight medical problem, as a kind of thing which we saw continually related to continuing infections, stunted growth, and now to these kinds of arrested developments in children. It was an overwhelming priority concerning the population themselves. In community after community as we organized health associations and health councils, sat with people, went door to door, people said, "Sure, health services are great and health care is great, it is important to share this, but for the love of God, isn't there some way you can share some food because we don't have any?"

We looked at the relationship between nutrition and the diseases we were seeing, and we started stocking food in the pharmacy. That was at the health center. There was some question about this, and I pointed out that the last time I looked in the book, the specific therapy for malnutrition was food, and in this situation I thought food belonged in the health center. But that is a clumsy mechanism.

Next we started to write prescriptions for food that could be honored out of our drug budget at local stores. It worked a little better but that was still a clumsy system. So, together with the people in this 500 square miles, we backed off and took a longer look at the situation, and what we saw was an agricultural people displaced by mechanization, unemployed and hungry, sitting on some of the richest land in the United States which was either in cotton, which you can't eat, or in nothing, which is also inedible, under the acreage restriction program. There seemed to us to be, and to them to be, a better way to put this package together. We started talking about a vegetable garden, and 800 families applied to belong to the vegetable garden. We realized that we were in a different ballpark. We sat down and talked it through again and said, "How about a farm cooperative?"

As far as I know, it is the first farm cooperative of landless people. This is not the usual getting together of small farmers with 40-acre patches. They don't have land.

We said, "How about if people got together, borrowed, rented or did whatever to get idle land, pooled their labor and worked for some cash and shares in the food that they could grow, and tried to do it all in one place?"

They could come from different parts of the county to this place. They could grow food instead of cotton. They said that sounded like a sensible plan and they knew something about doing that, and they would like to join. They made a rule that membership would be open initially only to people with a per capita income of $200 a year or less, because they wanted the poorest, the neediest people, in first and on the ground floor. They formed 10 autonomous co-op clubs and merged them into a farm co-op. We started with $5,000 of borrowed money and a borrowed tractor and some borrowed land.

At about that point we turned around to OEO and went to the emergency food, hunger, and medical services office. In effect, we said, "We think this is something that you should back. Here is a new way to do something about emergency food and hunger needs. We think it is a good nutrition demonstration. Can you help us?"

We got a grant to the Northern Bolivar County Farm Cooperative in association with the health center for $152,000. That enabled us to proceed with 120 acres. The members of the North Bolivar Farm Cooperative got a late start. This was last year. They didn't really get going until late March and early April. They didn't have all the equipment they needed. All they did, in a short growing season, was grow 1 million pounds of food: green beans, snap beans, red beans, kidney beans, turnips, collard greens, sweet potatoes, irish potatoes, black-eyed peas, and other crops.

I don't know what I am talking about because I am a city boy who grew up on the streets of New York. But they knew what they were doing and they grew it. It was enough food to end hunger in Northern Bolivar County and have a surplus.

They identified, rented, and remodeled a food freezer locker to keep the food through the winter. In 5 days, with the help of our sanitarians, they built a food freezing processing line inside it. When the first year's work was done, they started to plan for what they were going to do this year.

I would like to say a little bit about what happened this winter, still with the support of OEO emergency food and medical care.

The farm cooperative leadership and membership is all local, with its own elected board and its own central management, even though the members are scattered over 500 square miles, they come to one place for farming or for management, for distribution.

In this past winter they visited model experimental farms, canneries, and freezing plants. They have had 23 conferences with experts from the food industry. The Farm Co-op Board did cost analysis and worked out the advantages of joint ownership and centralized management. It has sought and obtained technical assistance from Mississippi State University, Iowa State University, Massachusetts Institute of Technology, the Federation of Southern Cooperatives, the University of Wisconsin, the General Foods Corp., and others.

Having digested all of this, these people with 6th and 7th grade, possibly 8th grade Mississippi Negro school education, turned to the Ford Foundation for help and back to OEO for some more help. Now they have a central tract of 347 acres that they own, and pretty soon it will be up to 500. That is enough, with irrigation and triple-cropping this year, to grow millions of pounds of food. They have drawn detailed plans for a commercially viable cannery and they are actively seeking investment funding for it.

The Board has decided that the co-op must have one of its own as at least a trainee in every managerial position. The co-op has identified the market, the ethnic market for southern soul food among all the Southern Negroes who have gone north. We even have a label figured out, "The Jolly Black Giant." The co-op farm manager, an ex-sharecropper with a fourth grade education, is studying the latest techniques for growing vegetables. The co-op director, a 30-year old black woman, is going to Israel this summer to study co-op management. She has five children. These people are in on the ground floor of the whole economic direction of the Mississippi Delta, which is out of cotton and into food production and processing. We think they are on their way.

I think it has to be added at the same time that the co-op and the food represents more than this. If it were possible to eat, many people will feel that voting and other forms of civic participation would be safer and more possible. You are a damn sight likelier to take the risk involved in that if you know you are going to eat and your children are going to eat, and you have some security as to the house over your head.

Persons now blocked from taking advantage of new training opportunities would have some way of feeding older and disabled relatives dependent on them but not recognized by the system as being dependent. With their own food supply, there would be means of feeding babies born out of wedlock and their mothers. In a very real sense, then, the co-op's food is freedom food. It is more than a source of food.

So are the health associations and the councils and the center. The idea has caught on—that if you get together and form new kinds of organizations and work together and get technical assistance, maybe you can really start to meet some of your own needs. Maybe the co-op can figure out a way to provide day care services for mothers who work in the fields. Maybe the co-op can find a way, and it is now looking into it, for a co-op owned, very low cost rural housing program.

There is no Federal program or housing market that will provide a house for people that make $900 a year, but it is possible to do that with co-op ownership of central, very low cost housing tracts, particularly looking at experimental techniques. That is in the works now, among very many other things.

The co-op is seen as a way even, perhaps, of helping people get to school. Maybe afterward, helping some people get to college and come back to provide the kinds of technically trained leadership that this population now knows and understands it needs.

I think the health center has had other effects than the narrowly medical effects. That is why I am emphasizing these, because I think they are among the most important. One of those I think I am proudest of is what we call training and human development. Six young black men and women, most from Mississippi, are now either in the freshman class at Tufts Medical School or starting in next September's freshman class, and others are getting into medical schools elsewhere. Two of our local staff members begin social work school this fall. Three of our local black staff have already passed the examination as public health sanitarians and one begins school in the fall in environmental engineering.

One is studying for certification as a medical record librarian. One is completing training for the registered nurse degree, and three others are beginning such training. One is headed for graduate training in hospital administration. Six, while working with us, are completing college at local colleges on work study programs. Almost the whole health center staff that has less than a high school education, grade school in general, is studying at night while working with us by arrangement with another local OEO funded program, the STAR program for adult education and training, to get their high school equivalency certificates.

Six have been assisted to enter college, either directly or the transitional year programs.

Mr. Choate mentioned some of the problems of medical students learning about nutrition. Well, there are going to be 26 medical students from 14 different schools in the United States at the Tufts-Delta Health Center and the Community Hospital this summer. They will have a very good opportunity to learn something about malnutrition. They have a commitment to put their developing professional talents at the disposal of the community's social purpose. We hope during the coming year that there will be 40 medical students from all over the United States taking part of their training at the Tufts-Delta Center.

Again, let me emphasize the importance of the development of this kind of institution. What kind of institution are we? We are, by my description, and I always leave out some of the words in the list: a well digging, privy building, co-op organizing, food growing, community organizing, health association forming, housing developing, soap making, ditch digging, youth guiding, transportation developing, cannery building, job training, professional training, income raising, government agency bugging health center.

My point is that it is just this new kind of multi-purpose institution extended over the full range of human need, based under one roof, rooted in the principles of community organization and local participation and human development that is needed to meet the problems of poverty. There is no point in just giving medical care. There is no point in just distributing food, essential and desirable as these things are.

One has to meet the full range of human needs and one has to do it all at once.

One must do it with an eye to how it can take off on its own. It would be impossible to do this if we had to go to 17 different Federal agencies with 17 separate funding applications to put it together.

In all the government, so far as I know, there is one agency, OEO, that has the flexibility, the range of services, the courage and willingness to experiment and innovate to make such a development possible.

· 44 ·

ROLAND CHILTON°

The Consequences of Florida's Suitable Home Law: A Study of Ineffective Intervention

Sharp criticism has often been aimed at the aid to families with dependent children (AFDC) program. Much of the criticism has suggested that the parents of many if not most AFDC children are unworthy of help because they are irresponsible, dishonest, and immoral.[1] Though State legislative action has accompanied or followed public criticism, much of the restrictive legislation has been prompted by budgetary and racial considerations independent of public criticism.[2]

Regardless of motivation, the AFDC program will very likely continue to attract criticism. If the experience of recent years is an indication of the direction the opposition to public assistance will take, attacks on current programs will be based not on fact but on the assumption that AFDC parents are undeserving of public assistance because of their conduct. The changes suggested by critics will probably be directed at reducing the cost of welfare by limiting

SOURCE: Reprinted from *Welfare in Review*, Vol. 7, No. 5 (September-October, 1969), pp. 17–23.

°The findings and conclusions in this article are based on a final report of the study, "The Consequences of a State Suitable Home Law for ADC Families in Florida," conducted with a grant (No. 155) from the U.S. Department of Health, Education, and Welfare, Social and Rehabilitation Service, under the Cooperative Research and Demonstration Grants program. The project was directed by Professor Lewis M. Killian.

[1]See Alvin L. Schorr, "Problems in the ADC Program," *Social Work*, Apr., 1960, pp. 3–15, and "ADC–What Direction," *Child Welfare*, Feb., 1962, pp. 72–78. For an openly hostile article, see Charles Stevenson, "Children Without Fathers: The Shocking Truth About the ADC Program," *Reader's Digest*, Nov., 1961, pp. 72–80. For a less critical article, see Leonard Gross, "Are We Paying an Illegitimacy Bonus?" *Saturday Evening Post*, Jan. 30, 1960, p. 30.

[2]For a discussion of the role of race in the development of social control legislation, see Julius Paul, "The Return of Punitive Sterilization Proposals: Current Attacks on Illegitimacy and the AFDC Program," *Law and Society Review*, Aug., 1968, pp. 77–106.

access to the program through legislative or administrative rules and regulations.

Distinct "suitable home" policies can be traced to developments, primarily in the South, between 1950 and 1960.[3] Beginning with "substitute parent" legislation in South Carolina intended to make the "man in the house" legally responsible for the support of his "stepchildren," several Southern States moved through a series of laws culminating in the "suitable home law" of Mississippi, Louisiana, and Florida. Although in 1952 Georgia public assistance officials set a policy holding that the birth of a child out-of-wedlock raised the question of the existence of a substitute father and of the suitability of the home, Mississippi passed the first formal legislation using the birth of a child out-of-wedlock as evidence of unacceptable conduct. By 1960 several other States had enacted similar laws limiting public assistance to children in "suitable homes."

So far, most systematic examinations of these laws and regulations have focused on their logic or legality. The study on which this article is based examined the consequences of a "suitable home law" for some of the families it affected. Its central question involved the extent to which the loss of assistance, as a result of the legislation, decreased "illegitimacy" and "discouraged" matriarchal family life.[4]

FLORIDA'S "SUITABLE HOME" LAW

In 1959 Florida amended the statutes governing eligibility for AFDC to specify that assistance should be granted to any dependent child living in a "suitable home" and that the State Board of Public Welfare should evaluate the suitability of the home when determining eligibility. The amendment lists seven "conditions" any one of which could make the home "unsuitable."[5] Most concern the abuse, neglect, or exploitation of children, but the mother's "having an illegitimate child after receiving a welfare payment" is also presented as a "condition" making the home "unsuitable"[6] and is the crux of the amendment. Other conditions include such acts by the parents as extramarital sex activity—whether or not it results in the birth of a

---

[3]For a detailed discussion of suitable home policies in the United States, see Winifred Bell, *Aid to Dependent Children*, New York, Columbia University Press, 1965.

[4]The term *matriarchal family life* is used loosely here, as it is in some public assistance publications, to refer to female-centered, one-parent families.

[5]Florida Statutes (1965), Sec. 409.18.

[6]*Ibid.*

child—and repeated convictions for disorderly conduct. In addition, the law recommends that the Department of Public Welfare try to improve the "conditions" of an "unsuitable home." If the effort fails, the children are to be placed by voluntary or court action in "suitable homes" with relatives or other persons.

The threat of placement and the Department's ruling that its responsibility for the suitability of a home (as defined by the law) ends when the mother withdraws from the program, gave the law force and made it a mechanism for discriminatory social control.[7] Rather than risk the loss of their children, several thousand mothers withdrew from AFDC between 1959 and 1961 when their homes were questioned for suitability.

Whatever the intent, the law resulted in the loss of assistance to over 7,000 families with more than 30,000 children during its first 2 years of operation. In most cases the children affected were living in homes meeting all AFDC eligibility requirements except "suitability." The homes were considered "unsuitable" because one or more children had been born out-of-wedlock, or the mother's conduct, as reported by the family caseworker, was not "acceptable."[8] In effect, assistance funds were used to censure the previous conduct and to control the future conduct of mothers in families needing public assistance.

THE STUDY METHOD

The study was possible because case records were compiled and kept by the State Review Team, a body set up in the Department of Public Welfare to examine homes for "suitability."[9] The Team kept files on about 18,000 of the homes questioned under the law and on another 1,800 in which the mother withdrew from the program after questioning but before a Team decision about suitability. From these lists, a representative sample of mothers was selected for in-

---

[7] The staff felt that the law precluded them from continuing to work with these families. Their decision to keep records of such cases and their request for an investigation on the effect of the law indicates their concern for the welfare of the families involved.

[8] In practice, an "illegitimate" child was taken to mean any child not fathered by a woman's legal husband, including children born from common law marriages, unless the marriage was registered as provided by law.

[9] The Department of Public Welfare set up the Review Team to decide on the "suitability" of homes considered questionable by local welfare workers to take advantage of the staff, to make record-keeping easier, and to keep arbitrary and prejudicial judgments at a minimum.

terviewing: mothers in "suitable homes," mothers in homes placed on trial, and mothers in "unsuitable homes"—generally homes that had lost assistance.[10] The study also included a group of mothers receiving AFDC shortly before the interviews as a sample of active cases. A total of 1,610 respondents were interviewed in all sections of the State during 1964 and 1965. The analysis of information from the interviews centered on answers to specific questions and on comparisons of answers given by mothers in specific categories.

FINDINGS AND CONCLUSIONS

In general, the results of the analysis suggest these conclusions:

• The economy provided by suitability practices is questionable.
• Changes in "immoral" sexual conduct were probably minimal.
• Views about boyfriends and sex were apparently unaffected by the law.
• An increase in the availability of information about contraceptives would probably have more effectively lowered the number of additional children born to the women in the sample than the attempt to control their conduct by discontinuing or threatening to discontinue assistance.

Estimates of the amount of money saved through the "suitable home law" are based on a projection of the trend in the number of AFDC children in Florida for the 6 years preceding the enactment of the law and on a comparison with the trend for the United States for the same years. Assuming that percentage increases over 1955 in the number of children in Florida's AFDC program would have paralleled similar increases in the United States and that the average amount of assistance per child per year would have remained at about $240, the savings that might have accrued to the State would have been about $1 million a year and the savings to the Federal Government, another $4 million a year.

As to actual per capita expenditures, the total State and Federal expenditures dropped from $4.15 per resident to $3.38 in 1961 and remained at about $3.50 for the years 1961-66. However, this reduction does not mean the law achieved a corresponding reduction in dependency. In fact, if continuing dependency is defined as receipt of assistance, the interview information suggests that 42 percent of the children whose homes were classified as "unsuitable" were still

---

[10]The preservation of these records reflected the concern of the Department for dependent children even when they ceased to be active cases. Without these lists and the cooperation of the Department, the study would not have been possible.

TABLE 44 – 1

Estimate of the Extent of Dependency at the Time of Interview for 3,894
Minor Children Whose Homes Were Found Unsuitable

Dependency estimate	Basis for classification as unsuitable			
	Card file only[1]	Self-report only[2]	Both card file and self-report	Total
Dependent				
Public assistance	822(46)	201(43)	625(38)	1,648(42)
No public assistance, no husband, pay under $25 a week	286(16)	114(24)	371(23)	771(20)
Total number of dependent children	1,108(62)	315(67)	996(61)	2,419(62)
Not dependent				
Husband	271(15)	34(7)	157(10)	462(12)
Common law husband	102(6)	29(6)	149(9)	280(7)
Pay $25-$39 a week, no husband	226(13)	61(13)	266(16)	553(14)
Pay over $40 a week, no husband	75(4)	34(7)	71(4)	180(5)
Total number of children not dependent	674(38)	158(33)	643(39)	1,475(38)
Total number of minor children in "unsuitable" homes	1,782(100)	473(100)	1,639(100)	3,894(100)

[1] *Dispositions by the Department of Public Welfare of trial, placement, court referral, and unsuitable are included.* [2] *Answers to the question about the reason given
for discontinuing related to birth out-of-wedlock or promiscuity were used to classify
these mothers as unsuitable.*

dependent at the time of the interviews. And, if the children of
women not receiving assistance payments but with incomes under
$40 a week are classified as dependent, the number of children still
dependent in 1962 rises sharply (Table 44– 1).

The extent to which Florida's reduction of AFDC expenditures
represents actual savings depends on the extent to which the reduction increased the cost of other State and county services. Such costs
are speculative, of course. But, if the law did increase the number of
undernourished, undereducated, or unsupervised children, it did not
result in sound economy.

We have, however, much clearer answers to questions about the
effect of the law on the conduct of AFDC mothers. The law created
this situation: women who had not borne a child out-of-wedlock and
who did not disclose information about their sex lives to caseworkers

were in a better position to be considered as having "suitable homes" than those who were less fortunate or less discreet. An examination of the ages of the women in "suitable homes" and of the respondents' statements about use of contraceptives suggests this very clearly.

Of the women 50 years of age or over, 64 percent had "suitable homes." Of the women under 30, only 25 percent had homes classified as "suitable" (Table 44–2). The larger proportion of older women in "suitable homes" suggests that an unexpected consequence of the law was the continued provision of assistance to older women for whom the question of sexual morality as expressed in the birth of an out-of-wedlock child was less relevant. Therefore, comparisons of answers to questions about sexual activity must take into account the ages of the women interviewed.

TABLE 44 –2
Age of Respondent, by Suitability Classification

Suitability classification	Age				
	Under 30	30 - 39	40 - 49	50 and over	Total
Unsuitable and trial[1]	270 (75)	455 (73)	242 (62)	83 (36)	1,050 (66)
Suitable, active, and other[2]	89 (25)	171 (27)	147 (38)	150 (64)	557 (34)
Total	359 (100)	626 (100)	389 (100)	233 (100)	1,607(100)

[1] *Includes 696 cases of homes classified as "unsuitable" (age missing for three women), 281 cases where the recipients withdrew because of the suitability law, and 73 homes classified as unsuitable but assistance continued for a trial period.* [2] *Includes 201 homes found suitable, 331 cases selected from a list of recipients for May 1964, and 25 mothers who withdrew for reasons other than suitability.*

Among other questions about sexual experience, the respondents were asked whether they were pregnant or were using some form of birth control. Because answers of "yes" to either question could be taken as indication of sexual activity, these questions provided important indications of the effect of the law on sexual conduct.[11]

---

[11]An affirmative answer did not necessarily mean illicit relations because 19 percent of the women were married and living with their legal husbands. However, 80 percent of the women who said they were practicing birth control or were pregnant were either single or living in common law relationships. The 41 common law marriages are included in the total because the children of such unions are classified as "illegitimate" by the Department of Public Welfare.

To the extent that the answers to these questions are indicative of the proportion of women who were having sexual relations with men not their husbands, it appears that the "suitable home law" did not effectively reduce illicit sexual relations. Of the women in "unsuitable homes," 37 percent were willing to report that they were using contraceptives or were pregnant though they were not living with their husbands.[12] For women living in "suitable homes," the percent is about 19. In addition, 34 percent of all women living with their husbands answered "yes" to one of these questions.

Although answers to these questions probably understate the amount of illicit sex relations, they do provide some indication of the sexual conduct of women whom the law was intended to reach. There is no way of knowing what their answers would have been before the law was passed, but it is apparent the law did not repress sexual activity.

Information about the number of children born out-of-wedlock to each woman provided a practical way to estimate the effect of the law on sexual conduct. Each mother was asked whether she was married to the father of each of her children at the time she became pregnant. The information obtained was checked against the Department's file on women whose AFDC grants were discontinued or whose suitability was questioned and as an indication that the right woman had been contacted. The information also allowed a comparison of the number of children born out-of-wedlock before and after the law was passed. The assumption was that less sexual activity should have resulted in fewer children under 6 than children between 6 and 12 born out-of-wedlock.[13] But no great difference appeared. Table 44–3 indicates that women in the sample who were over 19 and under 40 reported having 1,179 children, age 12, born out-of-wedlock, and 1,004 children under 6 born out-of-wedlock. Also, 43 reported they were pregnant by men not their legal husbands.

---

[12]A total of 772 women either had homes designated as "unsuitable" or withdrew because of the law. Of them, 286 who said they were living alone or in a common law relationship reported using contraceptives.

[13]It would, of course, be naive to assume that the number of out-of-wedlock children is a sufficient indication of fewer extramarital sexual unions because of the obvious importance of contraceptives in the prevention of pregnancy. There might be substantially fewer out-of-wedlock children after passage of the law because of increased use of contraceptives without a decrease in extramarital sexual unions. However, the answers to questions about contraceptive practices indicated how seldom these mothers used contraceptives or how little they knew about them. With this in mind, the comparison seems acceptable.

TABLE 44–3

Number of Children Born Out-of-wedlock under 6 Years Old and Between 6 and 12, Reported by 953 Respondents, by Age of Respondent

Age of Respondent	Number of respondents	Number pregnant no husband	Number of out-of-wedlock children under 13, by age				
			Under 1	1-5	Total under 6	6-12	Total under 13
20-24	91	6	19	108	133(72)	52(28)	185(100)
25-29	247	13	33	282	328(49)	339(51)	667(100)
30-34	334	14	41	302	357(44)	447(56)	804(100)
35-39	281	10	16	203	229(40)	341(60)	570(100)
Total	953	43	109	895	1,047(47)	1,179(53)	2,226(100)

Nor was the law more successful in controlling the conduct of the women whose assistance was discontinued. As Table 44–4 indicates, 41 percent of out-of-wedlock children under 6 were living with mothers who reported that their assistance was discontinued for "unsuitability." Roughly 30 percent of these children were living with mothers whose homes were found "unsuitable" but whose assistance had not been cut off. Another 29 percent were living in homes that had never been questioned. The over-representation of women whose assistance had been discontinued among mothers of out-of-wedlock children under 6 years of age suggests that discontinuing assistance was not successful in discouraging the birth of additional out-of-wedlock dependent children. The effect of the selection factor that brought about the loss of assistance again appears. About 45 percent of the out-of-wedlock children, age 6–12, were living with mothers whose homes had been classified as "unsuitable" and whose assistance had been discontinued. This is slightly higher than the 41 percent of the out-of-wedlock children under 6 living with mothers in that category. Both percentages reflect the fact that women were in this category because they had children born out-of-wedlock. Table 44–4 suggests they did not stop having children after they lost assistance.

Indeed, the percentage of children under 6 living with mothers in each age and suitability group is similar to the percentage of children, ages 6–12, in each age and suitability category. Thus, when the mothers' ages were considered, the proportion of children living with mothers in each category was roughly the same whether they were born before or after the suitable home law was passed.

The number of children born after the Review Team had finished its work differed slightly. Information concerning this matter was obtained by comparing the names and ages of the children reported

TABLE 44-4

Number of Children Born Out-of-wedlock, by Age of Children, Age of Respondents, and Suitability Classification

Age of respondent	Number of children born out-of-wedlock under 6 years of age			
	Unsuitable discontinued[1]	Unsuitable continued	Suitable	Total
20-24	27(21)	54(43)	46(36)	127(100)
25-29	112(35)	88(28)	115(37)	315(100)
30-34	154(45)	110(32)	79(23)	343(100)
35-39	122(56)	51(23)	46(21)	219(100)
Total	415(41)	303(30)	286(29)	1,004(100)

	Number of children born out-of-wedlock 6-12 years of age			
	Unsuitable discontinued	Unsuitable continued	Suitable	Total
20-24	12(23)	23(44)	17(33)	52(100)
25-29	119(31)	104(31)	116(34)	339(100)
30-34	209(47)	141(31)	97(22)	447(100)
35-39	193(57)	72(21)	76(22)	341(100)
Total	533(45)	340(29)	306(26)	1,179(100)

[1] *Includes those whose homes were classified as "unsuitable" and who reported loss of assistance for reasons related to suitability.* [2] *Includes those whose homes were classified as "unsuitable" but who reported no loss of assistance for reasons related to suitability.*

to the interviewers with the names and ages of the children listed in the homes the Team questioned. This comparison provided these findings: of the 694 women in "unsuitable homes," 51 percent had one or more children after a final Team decision (Table 44-5). Of the women whose homes were put "on trial," about 25 percent had one or more "new" children. And about 14 percent of the women in "suitable homes" had children born after the decision. The lower percentage of mothers in the "suitable" category probably indicates that public assistance workers and administrators were able to screen out recipients likely to have more out-of-wedlock children fairly well. It may, therefore, appear that the law helped reduce the number of out-of-wedlock births. However, if the women who dropped out continued to have "new" children, as did half of the women interviewed in "unsuitable homes," the procedure was really a re-

TABLE 44–5
Number of Children Born to 985 Respondents after Their Files Were Closed
by the State Review Team

Suitability classification	Number of children			
	None	One	Two or more	Total
Unsuitable[1]	341(49)	170(25)	183(26)	694(100)
Trial[2]	53(75)	11(15)	7(10)	71(100)
Suitable[3]	167(86)	24(12)	4(2)	195(100)
Other[4]	20(80)	3(12)	2(8)	25(100)
Total	581(59)	208(21)	196(20)	[5] 985(100)

[1] Cases of "unsuitable" homes. [2] Home classified as "unsuitable" but assistance continued for trial period. [3] Home found suitable. [4] Includes women whose assistance was discontinued for reasons other than suitability. [5] Number of children missing for 10 respondents.

definition of the persons to be served and did not prevent additional out-of-wedlock births.

As for stabilizing the home, the law seemed not to have a notable effect. Of the 1,610 women interviewed, 313 indicated that they had married and were living with their husbands since the law was passed. Another 79 said they were living in a common law relationship, but only those women who said they were legally married were classified as having stable marriages. To find out how many of the 313 had married as a result of the law, we had to take into account those women who were married before 1960 and those who gave marriage as the reason for the discontinuance of the AFDC grant. Of the 313 married at the time of the interview, 151 had been married after 1959; 155 before.[14] However, 28 of these marriages occurred before assistance was discontinued and marriage was given as the reason for discontinuance. Another 48 said they had not been "cut off," eight said no reason was given for discontinuance, and 30 said assistance was discontinued because it was no longer needed.[15]

The exact number of marriages that may be attributed directly to

[14] The year of marriage was not obtained in seven interviews.

[15] This procedure for estimating the number of marriages occurring before or after passage of the law provides only a rough approximation of the number occurring after discontinuance of assistance because some respondents did not lose assistance until 1960 or 1961.

the operation of the law is, of course, impossible to ascertain. It is reasonable to assume that a certain number of marriages by women whose homes were found unsuitable would have occurred regardless of the finding. However, the suitable home law could not be said to have produced a sizable number of stable marriages. Apparently, it was necessary to discontinue assistance to about 9,000 families to produce somewhere between 450 and 1,500 marriages. It is very unlikely the law could have produced more than this number, and very likely the number directly attributable to the law was much smaller.

Another 5 percent of the mothers reported they took boyfriends or established a nonlegal union when their assistance was discontinued.[16] When applied to the number whose assistance was discontinued or who withdrew because of the law, this percentage indicates that from 220 to 400 nonlegal unions may be attributable to the effects of the law.

The answers to questions such as "What did you do to make up for the check you stopped getting from ADC?" and "What difference did it make in the way you lived when your ADC check was cut off?" provide some indication of the economic consequences of the loss of AFDC. About 19 percent of those who lost their assistance said it made no difference; 63 percent said it made some difference; and 18 percent said it made a "lot" of difference. The least effect was felt in the families where the mother had married or had entered into a common law relation. It had the greatest effect on the families where mothers were forced to seek employment.

For the 683 respondents who said loss of assistance made a difference, some mentioned falling behind in the payment of bills; others, less money for food, clothing, and school supplies; 2 percent said they had to move to other housing. About 37 percent mentioned combinations of these. For at least a fourth of those whose assistance was discontinued, economic hardships increased. These mothers also had to spend more time at work, with the result that they had less time to care for and train their children.

However, one potential consequence of the law did not materialize; relatively fewer children were taken from their mothers than might have been expected. The nine women who said they gave up their children in response to the loss of assistance were only about 1

---

[16]Responses to a question about their action after loss of assistance suggested that 8 percent of all those whose assistance was discontinued married to make up for the lost payment, in addition to the 5 percent who entered into nonlegal unions.

percent of the women in the sample whose assistance had been discontinued. Perhaps another 1 percent of the children were removed from their homes by court action. Most of the children in "unsuitable" homes were still living with their mothers at the time of the study.

In addition to the information discussed above, the study provided answers to questions about the women's feelings concerning their first and last pregnancies, what they were doing to avoid pregnancy, and their desire to have additional children. Their answers suggest that most of them did not want to have as many children as they had, though there were many indications that the children were loved and wanted after they were born. Most of the women did not have information about effective birth control methods and others were apparently indifferent to the probable consequences of sexual activity, perhaps because they had been very young when they started dating and having sexual experience.

DISCUSSION

The information gathered by this study from interviews conducted in 1964 and 1965 suggests that legislation of this type may be among the least effective methods of social control. The law, though administered constructively and conscientiously by the Department of Public Welfare for at least 18 months, apparently did not result in any large number of stable, independent, two-parent families. It did not noticeably reduce the number of out-of-wedlock children, nor did it discourage illicit sexual relations by the women whose assistance was discontinued or even by those whose assistance was not cut off.

The practical effect of the law was to remove from the AFDC rolls for different lengths of time a large number of children who were otherwise eligible. In some cases the result for the families was severe. At the time the study was conducted, the homes were no more "suitable" than they were when the law was passed. Instead of accomplishing its purpose, the law set up an additional eligibility requirement that could not be administered fairly and caused children to be treated differently for reasons outside their need as dependent children, thus negating the purpose of the AFDC program.

There are, however, legislative and policy alternatives to the problems of rising AFDC caseloads and the continuing adverse consequences of poverty, including these:

• Direct money payments such as a guaranteed annual income or a negative income tax to bring all families up to a subsistence level.
• A children's allowance to all families based on the number of children in the family.
• Free family planning information available on request to all public assistance recipients.
• Adequate social service programs such as day-care centers, nursery schools, and after-school recreation and study programs readily accessible to all AFDC children whose mothers want to work outside the home.

Any of these suggested programs, if put into effect, might increase the possibility that AFDC children could rise above the poverty in which more than 26 million Americans are now trapped. However, if future attacks on public welfare programs produce similar attempts to control sexual conduct and shape family life through legislation, the experience of Florida's AFDC recipients and public assistance officials suggests that the results will not be effective social control but merely additional unnecessary hardship for the poorest people in the Nation.

· 45 ·

URIE BRONFENBRENNER

Damping the Unemployability Explosion

There was a time when society could find a place for its less capable members in millions of jobs requiring nothing more than unskilled labor. That day is rapidly passing. Already our major prob-

SOURCE: Reprinted from *Saturday Review*, January 4, 1969, pp. 108–110. Copyright © 1969 Saturday Review, Inc.

lem of manpower is not one of unemployment but of unemployability. Hundreds of thousands of jobs are available, but those who need them lack the requisite abilities and skills. Some of these men and women can be trained or retrained, but many others cannot. They are not only unemployable, but also untrainable for the level and type of work most needed by the society.

Moreover, unless appropriate countermeasures are taken, the proportion of unemployables in our nation is likely to grow at an increasing rate in the decades ahead. With continuing technological development, the number of jobs that can be filled by persons of limited cognitive capacity will become smaller and smaller. Unless present trends are reversed, long before the major impact of the population explosion is felt, this nation will have to cope with the explosion of the unemployables.

An explosion implies an event both massive and destructive. So the unemployability problem is likely to be. Available evidence indicates that when human beings are brought up in deprivation, experience little humanity at the hands of others, and grow into adults of limited competence — unable to find work, forced to live on leavings while the majority of citizens enjoy prosperity — the impulse to violence is high and hard to control.

But the unemployability explosion need not occur. It is susceptible to control by measures far less costly than its consequences. The weight of scientific evidence, particularly that accumulated in recent years, indicates that much of the incapacity of our citizens is not inborn but man-made during the early years of life.

The greatest damage is done at the very beginning. A growing body of research findings shows that, from the moment of conception onward, a mother's exposure to nutritional deficiency, illness, fatigue, or emotional stress can be far more damaging to her child than was previously thought. The neurological disturbances thus produced persist through early childhood into the school years, where they are reflected in impaired learning capacity (including reading disability) as well as behavioral disorders.

Second only to the onslaughts of prenatal and perinatal damage is the deadening impact of an unstimulating environment on a young child. A short two decades ago, most students of childhood believed that the early experiences of the infant and young child were of minor importance for his future development. Psychological growth was seen as a process of natural unfolding, predetermined by inexorable genetic forces. Today we know that early experiences can be decisive not only for the child's mental health, but also for the ability to learn. Scientific evidence both from laboratory and field studies demonstrates that mental development occurs primarily through interaction with adults in an encouraging atmosphere.

Fortunately, the same scientific evidence that reveals the damaging effects of human indifference also discovers the healing power of human intervention. We need not wait for a genetic miracle to improve the quality of our population. It is already within our capacity to reduce appreciably the number of persons in our nation who are mentally retarded, who fail to profit from school, who are unable to take a productive and responsible role in society. We need simply to insure American parents and their children those modest services and conditions of life that permit the human family to exercise its natural functions.

It is significant that, up to the present time, there has been no single body of legislation in America concerned with the total needs of children. At the federal level as at the local level, attention to these needs is fragmentary—scattered over thousands of statutes in hundreds of acts pertaining principally to other matters. The time has come to acknowledge the primacy of children in the national concern through enactment of a body of law specifically addressed to the total needs and rights of the child in our society. I therefore propose the drafting of an Act in Behalf of Childhood Development and, under its provisions, the establishment of an office for Family and Children's Services headed by an Assistant Secretary in the United States Department of Health, Education, and Welfare. I suggest that this Office for Family and Children's Services be given responsibility, authority, and financial resources to coordinate all existing programs relating to children—such as those of the Children's Bureau of the Labor Department, the National Institute of Child Health and Human Development, and the Head Start program of HEW. The Office for Family and Children's Services also should be empowered to initiate new programs through other federal government agencies such as the Department of Housing and Urban Development, and to work with state and local governments to see that appropriate programs and services are instituted in behalf of children and that the rights of children are protected.

To insure popular understanding and support of this new approach to the welfare of our future citizens, and to prevent capture of the initiative by bureaucrats or professional special pleaders of one kind or another, the Congress should authorize and the President of the United States should order the designation of a national Commission for Children.

In the following paragraphs, regular readers of *Saturday Review* will recognize that I am here attempting a prescription for the social sickness I described in these pages fifteen months ago under the heading "The Split-Level American Family" (*SR*, Oct. 7, 1967). As I pointed out then, it is the narrowing of the adult world surrounding the child that poses the most serious threat to his development. This is particularly true for impoverished families, for in these the two parents—or, in many cases, mothers alone—are thrown entirely on their own meager resources. In such an alienated world, parents cannot function as parents. They and their children need the help and active involvement of others; they need a functioning community in which parents and children have a place together.

All the services required by poor families—medical, economic, educational, and social—must be provided in such a way as to help restore the family and the community as constructive forces in the lives of children. Without such a restoration of the social fabric, no amount of money or professional service can enable children to function usefully in the society they will inherit.

It is my unhappy conclusion that many of the ways we now employ to help children fail in this vital regard. Rather than building the family, the neighborhood, and the community, we pass them by and even abet their fragmentation. One important reason for fragmentation is that the services themselves are fragmented. The needs of the child and the family are served by different agencies, operating in different locations, with seldom coordinated and sometimes contradictory activities. Economic assistance must be sought in one quarter, medical service in another, psychological help in a third, and legal aid elsewhere. Each agency is concerned with a restricted aspect of the family's problems. No one of them has responsibility for all of the minimal needs of the child.

The problem is compounded by a too-exclusive reliance on professional help. Since professional help is in short supply, little happens. Yet many of the supports and services which children and families need most could be provided by non-professional personnel with minimal training, working under professional supervision.

Finally, and most important of all, the approaches we typically employ involve intervention from the outside. There is no concerted effort to summon the inner rehabilitative resources of the community—groups of parents, neighbors, and older children. After minimal training, often simply by observation, they could perform many of the functions needed to stabilize and enrich the lives of children.

Activities by persons or in settings from outside the child's subculture must be heavily interlaced with participation from the child's own world by representatives who manifestly cooperate in the total effect. This implies close working relationships of mutual respect between workers from within and outside the child's own milieu. Mutual respect is essential not merely for the purpose of maintaining a viable learning atmosphere but more importantly to further the constructive development of the child's sense of identity and worth as a member of society. In the end, the significance of total community involvement in the life of the disadvantaged child lies in the fact that many of the problems he faces and the possibilities for their solution are rooted in the community as a whole and are, therefore, beyond the reach of segmental efforts at the level of the neighborhood, the school, or the home.

If every community had at least one Commission for Children (big cities might well have many), the commission members could hold the child's protective social structure together. A commission would have as its initial charge the task of finding out how, where, and with whom the children in the community spend their time. The commission would not keep this knowledge to itself but would report its findings to appropriate executive bodies and to the public at large. This revelation of the total pattern of life of children in the community would be sufficiently sobering in itself to generate concerted action. In this connection, I am impressed by remarks made in August by LBJ's last Secretary of Health, Education, and Welfare, Dr. Wilbur J. Cohen, in summing up his forty years of experience as a federal government welfare administrator:

> One very useful mechanism for narrowing the gap between knowledge and policy is a Presidential Commission or an advisory council to a secretary, a governor, or a mayor. Commissions and councils heighten public awareness of the need for action and focus debate on specific legislative proposals. And, if they are broadly representative, they can encourage the process of dialogue and coalition.

The Commissions for Children that I have in mind would be set up as quasi-public corporations. They would be formed at various levels of government down to county, school district, and village. The establishment of such commissions should be furthered through matching funds either by the federal government or possibly state governments. The purpose of matching funds would be both to stimulate the establishment of the commissions and to prevent them from becoming a purely political apparatus by requiring the inclusion of representatives of various segments of the community including the disadvantaged, local businessmen, the school system, welfare agencies, the police, parents, and teen-age children. Ideally, a commission would include the superintendent of schools, the chief public health officer, the director of welfare, the director of recreation. The public members should be appointed by the mayor or comparable local executive and should constitute less than half the membership. Non-public members would have to be appointed at first, but some mechanism should be developed to elect them later. Each commission would elect its own chairman and appoint an executive officer and staff to assist in developing and maintaining neighborhood Centers for Parents and Children.

Creation of these centers would be authorized by the Act on Behalf of Childhood Development which I have proposed. Each center would function as an opener of all doors through which the neighborhood child and his parents must pass for help. Consultation would be available on problems of health (including family planning, maternal and child care, nutrition, accident prevention, etc.), household management, and child rearing. Referral and active assistance would be provided for children requiring social and other special services (e.g., protection from neglect or abuse) available elsewhere. In such instances, the center would act not only as a referral agency but also as an active intermediary in behalf of the child and his parents to insure that needed services were in fact provided.

The center would offer cooperative group care and educational experience for children from early infancy through preschool age. The principal purpose would be not to free the mother from the child but to involve her more in the child's life at higher levels of understanding. For example, the child and his parents would enroll together, the mother being expected to participate much of the time. The schedule would be so arranged that parents could leave the center temporarily to do shopping, housework, etc. To compensate for loss of income in a job, parents would receive modest remuneration.

The Centers for Parents and Children would be so programed as to involve not only parents but also other adults. Under supervision, older children could be enlisted, both as individuals and groups, for activities with younger children both within and outside of school. Such activities might include reading to children, escorting them on outings, playing games, tutoring, etc. In the course of these activities, the development of friendships between older and younger children

would be encouraged. Even delinquent teen-agers have been known
to be dependable and helpful in the care of children.

The Centers for Parents and Children would not be directly operated by but would be guided, supported, and protected by the Commissions for Children of their respective communities.

The program I have proposed here is, I recognize, demanding.
Any program commensurate with the need must be demanding.
Many components of my proposals can be implemented by existing
funds but many others will require new expenditures. The initial
appropriations need not be large. Indeed, it would be better if they
were not too large, since it is sounder to extend proposals like these
on the basis of experience than to risk imposing an untried pattern
nationwide. Still, in the end, the financial commitment will be massive. But if we choose not to meet the cost now, we shall eventually
pay a far higher price. To deprive our children of their human
potential is to deny that generosity, neighborliness, gentleness and
compassion, zest and adventure are the American heritage.

· 46 ·

AMITAI ETZIONI

"Shortcuts" to Social Change?

In 1965, when New York City was hit by a "crime wave" (which
later turned out to be, in part, a consequence of improved
record-keeping), the city increased the number of lights in
crime-infested streets. Two of my fellow sociologists described the
new anti-crime measure as a "gimmick": it was cheap, could be
introduced quickly, was likely to produce momentary results, but

SOURCE: " 'Shortcuts' to Social Change?", *The Public Interest*, Vol. 12 (Summer,
1968), pp. 40–51. Copyright © National Affairs.

would actually achieve nothing. "Treating a symptom just shifts the expression of the malaise elsewhere," one sociologist reminded the other, reciting a favorite dictum of the field. Criminals were unlikely to be rehabilitated by the additional light; they would simply move to other streets. Or, when policemen are put on the subways, there is a rise in hold-ups in the buses. So goes the argument.

The same position is reiterated whenever a shortcut solution, usually technological in nature, is offered to similar problems which are believed to have deep-seated sociological and psychological roots. Because of a shortage of teachers, television education and teaching machines have been introduced into the schools. But most educators call this a "gimmicky" solution, for machines are "superficial" trainers and not "deep" educators. Or, in the instances of individuals who suffer from alcohol or drug addiction, blocking drugs (which kill the craving) and antagonistic drugs (which spoil the satisfaction) are now used. (Among the best known are, respectively, methadone and antabuse.) But, it is said, the source of the addiction lies deep in the personalities of those afflicted and in the social conditions that encourage such addiction. If a person drinks to overcome his guilt or to escape temporarily the misery of his poverty, what good is antabuse to him? It neither reduces his guilt nor his poverty; the only effect it has is to make him physically ill if he consumes liquor. Dr. Howard A. Rusk, who writes an influential medical column in *The New York Times*, stated recently:

One of the most dangerous errors in medicine is to treat symptoms and not get at the underlying pathology of the disease itself. Aspirin and ice packs may lower the fever but at the same time allow the underlying infection to destroy the vital organs of the body. So it is with social sickness.

Until a few years ago, I shared these views. But I was confronted with the following situation: The resources needed to transform the "basic conditions" in contemporary America are unavailable and unlikely to be available in the near future. So far as dollars and cents are concerned, Mayor John V. Lindsay testified before Congress that he needed $100 billion to rebuild New York's slums; at the present rate, it would take forty years before such an amount would be available to eliminate *all* American slums. And that is housing alone! With regard to all needs, a study by the National Planning Association calculated that if the United States sought, by 1985, to realize the modest goals specified by the Eisenhower Commission on National Goals, it would (assuming even a 4 percent growth rate in GNP) be at least $150 billion a year short.

But even if the economic resources were available, and the political will to use them for social improvement were present, we would
still face other severe shortages, principally professional manpower.
In the United States in 1966 there were an estimated four to five
million alcoholics, 556,000 patients in mental hospitals, and 501,000
out-patients in mental health clinics. To serve them there were about
1,100 psychoanalysts and 7,000 certified psychotherapists. If each
therapist could treat fifty patients intensively, a staggering figure by
present standards, this would still leave most alcoholic and mental
patients without effective treatment. Today most of those in mental
hospitals are not treated at all: only 2 percent of the hospital staffs in
1964 were psychiatrists, only 10 percent were professionals of *any*
sort; most of the staff are "attendants," more than half of whom have
not completed high school and only 8 percent of whom have had any
relevant training.

Thus, we must face the fact that either some shortcuts will have to
be found, or, in all likelihood, most social problems confronting us
will not be treated in the foreseeable future. Forced to reconsider
the problem, I decided to re-examine the utility of "shortcuts." For
example, do criminals really move to other streets when those they
frequent are more brightly illuminated? Or do some of them "shift"
to lesser crimes than hold-ups? Or stay home? Do shortcuts deflect
our attention from "real issues" and eventually boomerang? In my
re-examination,[1] I found some facts which surprised at least me.

DECISIONS WITHOUT FACTS

Take, first, the question of crime. It turned out that the sociologist
who asserted that, when more guards were put on the subways,
criminals shifted to buses, was merely making luncheon conversation; he simply "assumed" this on the a priori proposition that the
criminal had to go somewhere. He had neither statistics nor any
other kind of information to back up his proposition. I found that the
same lack of relevant information held for *all* the situations I examined. One can show this even in such a "heavily researched" area as
alcohol addiction.

Alcoholism is very difficult to treat. Most psychoanalysts refuse to
treat alcoholics. The rate of remission is notoriously high. Tranquil-

---

[1]The study is based on work conducted with the help of the Russell Sage Foundation. For additional discussion, see Amitai Etzioni, *The Active Society* (New York:
The Free Press, 1968).

izers are reported to be effective, but when I asked doctors why they are not used more widely, they suggested that these drugs provided no "basic" treatment and that patients became addicted to tranquilizers instead of alcohol. Searching for the source of this belief, I was directed to a publication of the United States Public Health Service entitled *Alcohol and Alcoholism*, a very competent summary of the knowledge of the field which is heavily laced with references to numerous studies. Here I found the following two statements:

(Tranquilizers) are highly effective, but some alcoholics eventually become addicted to the very tranquilizers which helped them break away from their dependency on alcohol.

For most patients . . . [tranquilizers] can produce lasting benefit only as part of a program of psychotherapy.

I wrote to the Public Health Service. Their reply was that

the bases for both of these statements are "social information" rather than substantive research. It is the clinical experience of many physicians (and some therapists) that some alcoholics have a tendency to become dependent on (whatever that means) other substances in addition to alcohol. There is, however, considerable disagreement on the extent to which this is a problem.

Thus, the Public Health Service really does not know if tranquilizers are only a "symptomatic treatment" which results in the shift of the problem from one area to another; it does not know what proportion of alcoholics can be "deeply" helped by these drugs, or even if those who remain addicted to tranquilizers, instead of alcohol, may not be better off than before.

THE CASE OF DRUGS

The same confusion exists about drugs. Until 1925, the regulation of drug addiction in the United States was largely in the hands of the medical profession; then it was declared to be a police matter and turned over to the Federal Bureau of Narcotics. The change drove the addicts underground, pushed up the price of narcotics, and prompted the large number of "secondary crimes" (to finance the habit) which are associated with addiction in this country. Drug users were involved in 22.4 percent of crimes involving property committed in New York City in 1963. While this is less than the more often-cited figures—that addicts are responsible for "half of all crimes"—it is a staggering cost paid for the partial suppression of addiction.

What body of evidence, medical or sociological, led to this rather far-reaching policy change? In fact, the chief reasons had little to do with evidence at all. The central fact was the ambition of the Federal Bureau of Narcotics (formerly the Narcotics Division of the Treasury Department) and of its former head, Harry J. Anslinger. He and his men conducted a systematic and effective campaign—in the courts, Congress, and the press—in favor of the punitive and against the medical approach to addiction because they viewed addicts as criminals.

Or, take the problem of distinctions among drugs. Over the years, many narcotic users, some medical authorities, and several leading social scientists have pointed out that the American drug laws do not distinguish between marijuana and heroin. Marijuana apparently has fewer effects than liquor; several experts argue that, unless one is in the proper company and mood, one does not even gain a "high" feeling from it. Alcoholism causes 11,000 deaths in the United States each year, not counting the thousands of fatalities inflicted by drunken drivers; marijuana per se causes none. Marijuana almost surely is less harmful than cigarettes. Some persons have smoked marijuana for years without visible effects. (Fifty-eight-year-old Mrs. Garnett Brennan, an elementary school principal in Nicasio, California, stated that she had smoked marijuana daily since 1949. Her suspension brought her to the attention of national television and press. She showed none of the symptoms widely expected in persons who have been on narcotics for long periods.) Yet the laws against the *possession* (not just the sale) of marijuana and heroin are equally severe—up to a forty-year jail sentence in some states.

Several authorities in the field have called for legalizing the consumption of marijuana. Those who object argue (1) that marijuana's effects are more severe, especially in accumulation, than has been acknowledged by those who favor its legalization, and (2) that the use of marijuana leads to the use of heroin, in a search for higher "highs," or through the mixing of heroin and marijuana by "pushers." Lawmakers, police authorities, opinion-makers, campus deans, and citizens continually make decisions on these matters, yet our information is, at best, quite spotty. Despite police attention to drugs for more than forty years, and the extensive attention focused on drug addiction in recent years, Robert Reinhold reported in *The New*

York Times, following about two weeks of experts' testimonies in a 1967 Boston trial of two youths accused of possessing marijuana that

The most striking impression to emerge from the Boston testimony is that there is a paucity of scientific evidence regarding the drug. Witness after witness offered opinion, based on personal observation and anecdotal evidence rather than on scientific experimentation.

On October 17, 1967, James L. Goddard, Commissioner of the United States Food and Drug Administration, stated: "Whether or not marijuana is a more dangerous drug than alcohol is debatable—I don't happen to think it is." He added: "We don't know what its long term effects are." A few days later, citing no more evidence than Dr. Goddard, Sir Harry Greenfield, chairman of the United Nations Permanent Central Narcotics Board, rejected the "tendentious suggestions" that marijuana was not "very dangerous." Nor has research settled the question whether continuous use of heroin is physiologically debilitating, or whether the symptoms usually associated with the use of heroin are actually the effects of withdrawal. And neither do we know whether a user's inability to function in a social setting is a cause or an effect of his use of heroin.

The main point I wish to make, though, concerns not marijuana but "shortcuts." And the common characteristics of this and other such situations is that the decision-makers *and* experts do not have the information needed to provide the answers. We could, as a shortcut, reduce much of the drug problem by legalizing marijuana. *That* we do know. The rest is conjecture.

OF TAXIS AND FIRE ALARMS

Many other questions I have examined are in the same condition. Neither the New York City Police Department nor any other city agency knew what had happened to the criminals who were driven off the lighted streets or off the subways. More recently, there was (or was believed to be) a crime wave in the form of hold-ups of taxi drivers. The police department initiated a new policy which permitted off-duty policemen to "moonlight" as taxi drivers. They were allowed to carry firearms and exercise their regular police prerogatives. This led to a rapid reduction in the number of taxi hold-ups. Good news—unless, as some claim, these muggers were now driven to robbing old ladies. We know that they are not back on the subways (which is relatively easy to establish). Whether they are operating elsewhere in New York City, in other cities, in other illegitimate pursuits, and whether these are less or more costly to society than mugging, or even if they have switched to *legitimate* undertakings, no one knows. The one thing we do know is that the original "symptom" has been reduced.

False fire alarms plague the cities; there were 37,414 such calls in New York City in 1966. In the summer of 1966 the New York City Fire Department installed a whistle device, which is activated when the glass is broken, to call attention to persons who pull the trigger of an alarm box. This, it was believed, would reduce the number of false alarms. "Gimmick," one may say; the exhibitionists who set the alarms now create some other mischief, such as causing real fires in order to see the fire trucks racing at their say-so. But nobody knows if these were actually exhibitionists and what they now do. Have they turned arsonists—or are they taking more tranquilizers? In this case it is not clear if the "symptom" was handled; in 1967 there were more false alarms than in 1966, but the device was not yet universally introduced and not publicized, so it could not deter.

EMOTIONS AND POLITICS

Although almost everybody wants "facts" on which to make decisions, the obvious point is that facts are frequently less powerful in shaping a decision than the long-held prejudices of a person. Many a decision-maker in effect says, "I don't care what the facts are; I am against 'it' because it is evil." In the case of drugs, the methadone programs are a revealing case in point. There is fairly good evidence that methadone kills the craving for heroin (persons on methadone have shot themselves with as much as sixteen units of heroin without attaining a "high"), removes the physiologically debilitating effects of heroin (if it has any) without introducing such effects of its own, and that this treatment enables those who take methadone to function socially more effectively than when they were on heroin.[2] Methadone thus is a "shortcut" *par excellence* because while it solves at least part of the problem, addiction, it does not change the personality which craves for an addicting drug (if there is such a personality), nor does it alter the social setting which encourages the craving.

---

[2] I benefited from a discussion with Dr. Vincent P. Dole and a visit with his patients on methadone at the Rockefeller University.

Although each of the preceding statements in favor of shifting patients from heroin to methadone is not unquestionably substantiated, the critics of the program stress somthing else: the fact that, in the end, the person is still addicted. A person who regularly takes methadone does seem to become addicted to *it;* at least, it is believed that if a heroin addict stops taking methadone, the craving for heroin will reassert itself. Dr. Robert W. Baird, Director of the Haven Clinic for heroin addicts in New York City, has said that using methadone is "like giving the alcoholic in the Bowery bourbon instead of whiskey in an attempt to get him off his alcoholism." Professor Bernard Barber in his recent book, *Drugs and Society,* reports that in the past the United States Public Health Service "has not accepted any treatment of addicts that left the patient dependent on another drug." Methadone is still legally considered a narcotic and Section 151-392, Regulation No. 5 of the Bureau of Narcotics decrees that treatment by the use of such a drug is by definition not a treatment and hence technically illegal.

Now, if the argument that a person addicted to methadone is still not able to function in society, or not as well as a fully rehabilitated person (a position taken by some experts), we then have a question of fact: do they or don't they? But the antagonism to such a resolution will not even permit such a question to be seriously raised. The puritanical tradition is still sufficiently strong in American culture so that the use of any substitute drugs, even if less harmful, is regarded as an indulgence. When the American Medical Association in November announced the launching of a year-long scientific study of the effects of marijuana to test the question of its harm, AMA president Dr. Rouse Milford added — before the first day of research — "No good can come from its (marijuana's) use. It's an hallucinogenic drug." Many Americans seem to hold that persons who are attracted to a narcotic should view this as a weakness of the flesh which they should fight and overcome. Similarly, the Food and Drug Administration is not particularly friendly to efforts to find "safe" cigarettes, or blocking antagonist medication for smokers. It keeps stressing that "Will Power Is the Only Smoking Remedy." Americans, at least when speaking collectively, seem to value a strong person, one able to function without narcotics (however stress-provoking his social environment) and one who seeks a life of achievement and enterprise, not "artistic" existence or nirvana.

Often the underlying prejudice sneaks through when the method of treatment is discussed. When one hears those who prefer the harsh "cold turkey" withdrawal over the painless transition from heroin to methadone, one gains the impression that the heroin users are viewed as sinners, who are to be penalized (or who have to undergo penance) before they are to be considered pure enough to be allowed to return to the flock.

Where there are emotions, politics is not far behind. Politicians have a high sensitivity to voters' sentiments and a low tolerance for risk. If the voters have (or seem to have) puritanical sentiments, a politician prefers "cold turkey" (despite the known fact that 85 to 95 percent of all of those thus treated return to the use of heroin once released from supervision) over "soft belly" methadone (despite the fact that the remission rate is *much* lower).

And there is intra-professional politics as well. Were the facts cut and dry, few experts would support an ineffectual program or question one which "works." But as the merits of various approaches are almost always contested, battles rage over funds, prestige, and missions, as for example between the Synanon people (who believe in complete rehabilitation via a version of group therapy), the therapeutic professions (psychiatry, psychotherapy) which have little sympathy for "sheer" chemical-medical treatment, and the methadone doctors and their supporters. Similar battles are fought in other fields, for instance between those who would use teaching machines and television to help alleviate the shortage of teachers and those who consider these "gimmicks" and favor high raises in teachers' salaries and improvement in the teachers' working conditions and status to attract more men and women into the field.

"FRACTIONATING" THE PROBLEM

Often a solution to a long-raging controversy over the more effective treatment of a social ill becomes possible once we realize that we have asked the wrong question. Similarly, when we ask whether "shortcuts" really work, we approach the problem in an unproductive way by lumping together too many specific questions.

First, the question must be answered separately from a societal and from a personal vantage point. Some shortcuts "work" for the society, in the limited sense at least that they reduce the societal cost of the problem (not only the dollar and cents cost, but also ancillary social effects), but not the personal costs. For instance, between 1955 and 1965 the number of patients in state mental hospitals declined from 558,922 to 475,761. This decline, however, was not the result of new, therapeutic-oriented, community mental-health centers, but mainly caused by introduction of massive use of tranquilizing drugs, "which do not 'cure' mental illness and often have been called 'chemical straitjackets.' " Tranquilizers obviously do not change personalities or social conditions. Patients, to put it bluntly, are often so drugged that they doze on their couches at home rather than being locked up in a state mental hospital or wandering in the streets. How effective the shift to "pharmaceutical treatment" (as the prescription of sedatives is called) is depends on the perspective: society's costs are much reduced (the cost of maintaining a patient in a state mental hospital is about seven dollars a day; on drugs — an average of fifteen cents). Personal "costs" are reduced to some degree (most persons, it seems, are less abused at home than in state mental hospitals). But, obviously, heavily drugged people are not effective members of society or happy human beings. Still, a device or procedure which offers a reduction of costs on one dimension (societal *or* personal) without *increasing* the costs on others, despite the fact that it does not "solve" the problem, is truly useful — almost by definition.

It may be argued that by taking society "off the hook" we deflect its attention from the deeper causes of the malaise, in this case of mental illness. But this, in turn, may be countered by stating that because those causes lie so deep, and because their removal requires such basic transformations, basic remedial action is unlikely to be undertaken. *Often our society seems to be "choosing" not between symptomatic (superficial) treatment and "cause" (full) treatment, but between treatment of symptoms and no treatment at all.* Hence, in the examination of the values of, many shortcuts, the ultimate question must be: is the society ready or able to provide full-scale treatment of the problem at hand? If no fundamental change is in sight, most people would favor having at least ameliorations and, hence, shortcuts. Moreover, the underlying assumption that amelioration deflects attention may be questioned: studies of radical social change show that it often is preceded by "piecemeal" reforms which, though not originally aimed at the roots of the problem, create a new setting, or spur the mobilization for further action.

Second, shortcuts seem to "work" fully — for sub-populations and for some problems. It is wrong to ask: "Are teaching machines effective substitutes for teachers?" We should ask: "Are there any teaching needs which machines can effectively serve?" The answer then is quite clear: they seem to function quite well as routine teachers of mechanical skills (typing, driving) and of rudimentary mathematics and language skills. Similarly, machines may be quite effective for those motivated to learn and ineffective for those who need to be motivated. A recent study which compared 400 television lectures with 400 conventional ones at Pennsylvania State University showed the television instruction to be as effective on almost all dimensions studied. It freed teachers for discussion of the television lecture material and for personal tutoring. After all, books are not more personal than television sets.

To put it in more general terms, "gimmicks" may be effective for those in a problem-population whose needs are "shallow," and much less so for those whose problems are deep; and most problem-populations seem to have a significant sub-population whose ills or wants are "shallow." Critics of methadone have argued that it works only for those highly motivated addicts who volunteer to take it. But this is not to be construed as an indictment; while such a treatment may reduce the addiction problem "only" by a third, or a quarter, this constitutes a rather substantial reduction.

The same may be said about procedures for training the hard-core unemployed. These are said to "cream" the population, focusing on those relatively easy to train. Such an approach is damaging only to the extent that the other segments of the unemployed are neglected *because* of such a program and on the assumption that they too can be as readily helped. Otherwise, much can be said in favor of "creaming," if only that it makes most effective use of the resources available.

Debates, indeed fights, among the advocates of various birth-control devices – pharmaceutical means (pills), mechanical devices (especially the IUD), sterilization, and the rhythm method – are often couched in terms of one program against all others, especially when the advocates seek to influence the government of a developing nation on the best means of birth control. The Population Council, at least for a while, was "hot" on the IUD. Some drug manufacturers promote the pill. The Catholic church showed more than a passing interest in a rhythm clock (a device to help the woman tell her more from her less fertile periods). In such battles of the experts and "schools," the merits and demerits of each device are often explored without reference to the persons who will use them. Actually, though, merits and demerits change with the attributes of the "target" sub-population. The rhythm methods may be inadequate for most, but when a sub-population for religious reasons will not use other birth control devices, some reduction in birth may well be achieved here by the "gimmicky" rhythm clocks. Pills seem to work fine for "Westernized," routine-minding, middle-class women who remember to use them with the necessary regularity. They are much less effective in a population that is less routine in its habits. The IUD may be best where persons who are highly ambivalent about birth control can rely on the loops while forgetting that they are using them.

It is in the nature of shortcuts to be much less expensive in terms of dollars and cents and trained manpower than "deeper" solutions. The HEW cost-benefit analyses reported in *The Public Interest*, No. 8 (Summer, 1967) are a case in point. While PPBS is far from a "science of decision-making," it occasionally does provide new ihsights and raise fresh considerations. If we assume that the following statistics are *roughly* correct, even allowing for a margin of error of 30 to 50 percent, we still see the technological devices are much less expensive—per life saved—than the "deeper," educational, approaches. The problem was the effectiveness of rival programs in the prevention of "motor vehicle injuries." When various programs were compared in terms of their cost-effectiveness, it was found that the use of technical devices was most economical: $87 per death averted by the use of seat belts and $100 per life saved by the use of restraining devices. The cost of motorcyclist helmets was high in comparison—$3,000 per man; but it was low when compared to the "fundamental" approach of driver education. Here, it is reported, $88,000 is required to avert one death. Of course we may ask for both technological devices *and* education; and the benefit of technological devices by themselves may be slowly exhausted. Still, this data would direct us then to search for more and improved mechanical devices (e.g., seat belts which hold the shoulders and not only the abdomen) rather than spending millions, let us say, on "educational" billboards ("Better Late Than Never"). I am willing to predict—a hazardous business for a sociologist—that the smoking problems will be much reduced by a substitute cigarette (not just a tarless but also a "cool" one, as the hot smoke seems to cause some medical problems) rather than by convincing millions to give up this imbedded symbol of sophistication and—for teenagers—protest.

THE POWER OF FORMULAS

Not all shortcuts are technological. There is frequently a social problem which can be treated if social definitions are changed; and this can be achieved in part by new legislation. This may seem the most "gimmicky" of all solutions: call it a different name and the problem will go away. Actually, there is much power—both alienating and healing—in societal name calling, and such redefinitions are not at all easy to come by. After years of debate, study, and "politicking," homosexuality was "redefined" in Britain in 1967; it became less of a problem for society and for the homosexuals after Parliament enacted a law which defined intercourse between consenting adults of the same sex in privacy as legal and, in this sense, socially tolerable. The remaining stigma probably more than suffices to prevent "slippage," i.e., even broader tolerance for other kinds of homosexuality, e.g., those affecting minors.

The extent to which such social definitions of what is legitimate, permissible, or deviant can be more easily altered than personality and social structure is an open question; at best, as a rule, only part of a problem can be thus "treated." This approach is superficial or worse when it defines a social or personal want so as to make it non-existent (e.g., reducing unemployment by changing the statistical characterization). It is not a "gimmick" in that the problem was created by a social definition — by branding a conduct as undesirable or worse when actually it was one of those "crimes without victims."

GUNS, FOR INSTANCE

There is one area of social conduct where, for reasons which are unclear to me, the blinders fall off, and most social scientists as well as many educated citizens see relationships in their proper dimensions and are willing to accept "shortcuts" for what they are worth. This is the area of violent crime and gun control. Usually, progressive-minded people scoff at gimmicks and favor "basic cures." But it is the conservatives who use the anti-shortcut argument to object to gun control as a means of countering violent crimes. On August 10, 1966, on the tower of the University of Texas, Charles Whitman killed, with his Remington rifle, thirteen people and wounded thirty-one. This provided some new impetus to the demand to curb the traffic in guns. About sixty bills were introduced in Congress following President Kennedy's assassination, but none has passed; it is still possible to order by mail for about $27 the same kind of weapon, telescopic lenses included, which Lee Harvey Oswald used. The National Rifle Association spokesmen typically argue that criminals would simply turn to other tools — knives, rods, or dynamite — if no guns were available.

But actually this is one of the areas where the value of shortcuts is both logically quite clear and empirically demonstrable. Logically, it is a matter of understanding probabilities. While motives and modes of crime vary, most murders are not carried out in cold blood but by highly agitated persons. Out of 9,250 so-called "willful" killings which took place in the United States in 1964, only 1,350 were committed in the course of committing some other crime such as robbery or a sex offense. The others, 80.1 percent, were committed among friends, neighbors, and in one's family, by "normally" law-abiding citizens, in the course of a quarrel or following one. Obviously, if deadly weapons were harder to come by, the chances of these quarrels being "cooled out," or a third party intervening, would have been much higher and most fatalities would have been averted.

Second, the damage caused is much affected by the tool used. While it is correct to assume that a knife may be used where there is no gun, the probability of *multiple* fatalities is much lower. And a policeman can learn to defend himself from most assaults without having to use a firearm. Most policemen who are killed on duty are killed by guns; all but one of the fifty-three killed in the United States in 1965, according to official statistics. Hence if the population is disarmed, the fatalities resulting from arming the police can also be saved. Here, as in considering other devices, one must think in terms of multi-factor models and probabilities. No one device, such as a gun-control law, can *solve* the problem. But each additional device may well reduce the probability that a violent act will cause a fatality. This is a "shortcut" in the right direction—even if it doesn't lead you all the way home. Not because I don't want to go all the way at once; but because such trips are often not available.

MARY RABAGLIATI and EZRA BIRNBAUM

The Campaign for Minimum Standards

With the termination of the winter-clothing campaign, a new issue came up, the question of budgets. Many of the families receiving welfare either had never been given a copy of their budget, listing what they were receiving money for, or were not kept up to date by their caseworkers on changes made in their budgets. It became evident that the real issue was those items that were not included in the regular checks — that is, everything other than food, rent, and utility allowances. These unincluded items comprised clothing, furniture, household goods, and various special allowances for articles which the department was expected to provide and replace at reasonable intervals. It was discovered that families lacked enough beds for their children, enough chairs, pots and pans, cutlery, and cleaning equipment. Many families were clearly not living at the minimum level provided for in welfare regulations. On this basis, the Committee of Welfare Families began a campaign around the issue of minimum standards. This became the issue through which the Committee of Welfare Families and other organizations were able to attract and mobilize thousands of welfare recipients.

By this time it was evident that the membership, and particularly the most active participants, wanted a durable organization, and that they wanted to play an important part in it. A number of Negroes and Puerto Ricans had become very militant through the efforts of the worker and through the opportunities which were becoming open to them for speaking out and taking action. A committee of four had been elected and were now conducting the mass meetings and encouraging the others to stand up for their rights. Thus, the Com-

SOURCE: Reprinted with permission from *Community Development in the Mobilization for Youth Experience*, ed. H.H. Weissman (New York: Association Press, 1969), pp. 112–122.

mittee of Welfare Families evolved into a fairly structured organization with leadership, both elected and voluntary, which served many purposes for the members.

In the eyes of the Committee of Welfare Families organizer, training was the most important element in a welfare organization. The welfare recipients who were to take a leading part in the organization would not only have to learn the welfare laws and regulations and keep abreast of any changes, but also become acquainted with what an organization could do to alter the welfare system. This meant knowing how to mobilize and use large numbers of people, which officers in the bureaucracy held what responsibilities and power, and how to cope with the daily events and chores of an organization. The worker conceived a series of training programs through which the necessary knowledge could be imparted. He felt that training should be geared specifically to the ongoing action programs of the committee.

The training program took place between January and April. Eight sessions were held covering a variety of subjects. An average of ten persons was present at each session. The subjects and speakers ranged from staff members of the Welfare Department and the caseworkers' union, who explained their work and their positions in relation to a welfare-client organization, to Columbia University professors, who taught the law and how welfare clients could bring pressure on the Department of Welfare to enforce it.

For those who attended the sessions—not always the same people, except for a hard core of four or five among the leadership—the program was useful. They learned more about the law of the New York State Welfare Department; they learned something of what client organizations had done in other states; they learned that the Social Service Employees' Union could help them and they could help the union by participating in preparing a welfare manual for clients; they discussed the welfare budget in detail and knew how much was supposed to be allotted for food, furniture, and other items according to the size of the family.

However, the program ended with an unfortunate incident. A disagreement developed between the staff and some participants who wanted a graduation party and various other symbols of their achievement. In the end they got none of these, and the program fizzled out without ever ending officially.

The conflict over the graduation party is illuminating in that it illustrates low-income perspective on participation. Agency staff were appalled at the demands of the women for party dresses and various funds for the graduation ceremony. The women for their part wanted more status and recognition. The idea of doing something for the community or for others on welfare was not the only significant reward that some of these women sought. Their desire for recognition and status was to come up again in a very significant way a few months later.[1]

The campaign for minimum standards officially commenced with a mass meeting attended by about a hundred people, attracted by flyers and posters in neighborhood stores as well as by word of mouth.[2] There had been publicity in the press, on radio and television, and the presence of television cameras and microphones no doubt contributed to the general excitement and enthusiasm of the meeting. The campaign was explained; people were told that the organization would help hundreds of individuals and families to obtain from the Department of Welfare every household and personal item that the welfare laws allowed. This meant, for example, one chair per person, a certain number of beds according to the sexes and ages of the children, and specific items for cooking and housework, many of which were known to be missing in the homes of most welfare recipients. When the list of items was read out, it was evident that most of the people present did not possess many of these items and were overwhelmed at the long enumeration.

The leaders asked people to talk about what they had or did not have, and suddenly people were on their feet telling everyone – the other recipients, the social workers, the television cameras, the newspapermen – what they had and how their requests had been ignored or refused by their caseworkers. A mother of four told of having only one bed for the whole family; an elderly lady living alone in a dark basement described how she had been refused extra money for electricity; another woman said she kept her light burning all night to keep away the rats and took the money for the electricity out of the food budget; another complained that her children could not attend school because they lacked sufficient clothing particularly in the winter. None of these tales was new to the listening clients of the Department of Welfare.

Before long the emotional atmosphere was such that any proposed action was immediately cheered and approved. The procedure of the

---

[1] Later graduation parties were paid for by the agency, though the amounts expended were very modest. The request for new dresses was not raised again. The worker felt that this request was an attempt to con the agency.

[2] Attendance at subsequent meetings during the campaign reached 225.

campaign was decided and put into effect at this first meeting. Letters demanding that recipients be brought up to the minimum standards prescribed by the department regulations were to be sent to
local centers, and a copy as well as petitions asking that the department heed the requests were to be sent to the commissioner of
welfare. For the next month regular mass meetings of the same type
took place, and many of the participants helped the leadership in
getting petitions signed and finding willing recipients who would be
prepared to ask for what they needed.

At this point the campaign was heading for a meeting between the
Committee of Welfare Families delegates and the commissioner at
the Department of Welfare main office. The organization prepared
itself for this occasion. At a couple of meetings the group held
role-playing sessions, rehearsing what they would say to the investigators who would come into their houses to check on the requested items. It was recognized that many people, alone in their
homes with a caseworker, without the protection and enthusiasm of
the group, would either deny their once-asserted needs or would
agree to reduce their original demands. This did happen in a few
cases, but the majority apparently stood firm when investigated; it is
also very possible that the Department of Welfare caseworkers themselves were more liberal when they knew their client was backed by
a strong organization. During the campaign, workers tried to find
common complaints; individual grievances were referred to one of
the neighborhood-service-center social workers or, if necessary, to a
lawyer. The search for complaints which were common to the majority resulted in the presentation of a list to the commissioner with the
petitions for minimum standards.

On April 5, eighty welfare recipients went down to 250 Church
Street to meet with Commissioner Ginsberg on minimum standards.
They had decided beforehand that the line outside was to be orderly
and dignified and that those on the line were not to respond to any
remarks made by onlookers or caseworkers.

As it happened there was no trouble or heckling, and despite the
cold weather people stayed in line for two hours waiting for the
delegation to report on the meeting with Ginsberg. After a long wait
the delegation appeared and reported jubilantly that they had been
well received by the commissioner, that their demands had been
approved and answered with the promise to either enforce the regulations immediately or investigate their complaints. A time limit of
two weeks for answering demands to be brought up to minimum

standards had been proposed by the recipients and accepted by the commissioner. The press again reported favorably on the activities of the organization.

Following the meeting with Ginsberg, the campaign for minimum standards was taken up on a city-wide basis by other welfare groups. At the beginning of May, the executive committee met again to discuss their forthcoming activities. Their agenda included a conference of welfare-client groups, a fashion show, and newsletter. The latter did not materialize immediately, but the conference did. Participation in a city-wide demonstration at City Hall with other client organizations and a summer program were next to be included in the organization's program.

It is interesting to note that the Committee of Welfare Families worker argued strenuously against the conference but was overruled by the executive committee. The women were concerned lest a city-wide organization of welfare organizations, the City-Wide Coordinating Committee of Welfare Groups, gain more recognition and status than the Committee of Welfare Families.[3] The conference was intended to uphold their status. (The same concern was evident in the graduation-ceremony dispute.) City-Wide was actually a rather weak organization at this time, and the worker was afraid that some of the Committee of Welfare Families leaders might attempt subtly to discredit it. Actually the conference strengthened City-Wide. Letters were sent out to other groups, stating that the reason for meeting together was that "our children must have the same advantages, the same education, the same hospital services, the same opportunities as other children." Four workshops were set up to discuss clients' rights, how to organize neighborhood groups, how to lead the normal social life promised by welfare laws, the new budget, and the welfare client in relation to the city hospitals. On May 21, when the conference met, thirty-two groups were represented, and 240 individuals were present. The groups came from the Bronx, Brooklyn, and Manhattan, including a small delegation from Harlem. The morning session was devoted to introducing the Committee of Welfare Families, explaining how and why welfare clients were or should be organizing, followed by an address by a lawyer on the rights of welfare recipients. The afternoon workshops provided an opportunity for welfare clients from different parts of the city to meet in small groups and discuss more specialized problems. Although few decisions came out of these workshops, they did provide a

---

[3]MFY staff had in fact been instrumental in forming this city-wide organization.

means of communication and exchange. Before the conference broke up, all the participants met together to hear reports on the workshop discussions.

During the last minutes of the conference, a question was raised about the new welfare budget which was due to come into effect on July 1 of that year. Most people had heard that allowances were to be increased as well as some change made in the distribution of clothing grants, but few understood exactly what was going to happen. One of the MFY social workers in the audience explained the new budget in detail. The change that would affect them most was the inclusion of the clothing grants, which had previously been given at specific times of the year, in a lump sum in the regular check so that people would have to put aside funds for the clothing from a budget that was too small in the first place. When this was explained, there was a general uproar, which did not subside until a representative from the newly formed City-Wide Coordinating Committee of Welfare Groups offered the suggestion that this be made one of the first issues for a city-wide effort. The speaker invited everyone to participate in a demonstration at City Hall in June, at which a list of grievances was to be presented to the mayor and the commissioner of welfare. The new budget could be one of the major points on the list. The idea was accepted with cheers, and the conference ended on an optimistic note.

During the month of June the minimum-standards campaign continued and was climaxed by the planned demonstration at City Hall, organized by the City-Wide Coordinating Committee; a police estimate set the participation at two thousand welfare recipients. By spring the Committee of Welfare Families had been granted more support by MFY in the form of a storefront, a secretary, and some petty cash, and later a part-time social worker was added to take care of some of the details that the organizer would not have time for. They also started proceedings to incorporate and open their own bank account. This move for independence came about as a result not only of the members' wish to have their own organization, but also as a conscious intention of the organizer, who felt that he could more easily resist pressure to tone down the group if the committee were relatively independent.[4]

For the months of July and August, the Committee of Welfare Families obtained $19,000 from the New York City Office of Eco-

---

[4]It was also useful to MFY to have the groups independent so that pressure to tone them down could be resisted. The agency's stance in such cases was that organizations of adults may do anything which is legal.

nomic Opportunity (OEO) for a summer program, and thus had its first opportunity to operate as an independent body, responsible only to OEO for their actions on this program. Although the proposal was written rather hastily by the professional staff, the program was taken in hand by the committee members themselves, in particular the leadership. Having been assured of a grant which would pay for a training program, a children's program, and family and adult outings, the committee set about hiring the professional staff required by OEO. Applicants were interviewed by the executive committee—a board of eight members—who questioned and evaluated each applicant, and then took the responsibility of hiring the person they considered to be most suitable.

In all, four professionals were hired—a director for the whole program, a training-program director, and a young couple who were jointly to direct the children's program. Each of these had a member of the committee assigned to him as an assistant over a ten-week period.

The training-program director was a young man from the neighborhood who did not have a social-work degree but who had had experience with MFY summer programs and was well liked and respected. He organized a training program in which the participants were taught how to interview, how to fill out questionnaires such as a receptionist in a public agency might be faced with, how to do elementary filing, and how to deal with unexpected situations during work with other people. For practical experience, they participated in the follow-up of the minimum-standards campaign—knocking on doors, introducing themselves and the Committee of Welfare Families, and asking questions. In the course of this experience they met with the same refusals, slammed doors, time spent in listening to other people's problems, and aching feet that the social worker or professional interviewer encounters every day. They were not told how to deal with stereotyped situations but were instructed to use their initiative and common sense; then they were given an opportunity to discuss with the whole group any problems or questions they had and how such situations might best be dealt with.

At the end of the training period, there was a graduation ceremony at which certificates were distributed. Invited officials from MFY and the city Office of Economic Opportunity gave short speeches and congratulated the trainees on what they had achieved during their training, stressing the jobs they could look forward to and what the Committee of Welfare Families expected of them in the future.

Of the fourteen who participated, three found temporary work as interviewers with either MFY or the Salvation Army, and five were enrolled in English or math classes. An observer of these ten weeks would have noticed that, despite the apparent chaos of the program, it achieved what it had set out to do. Children took advantage of the children's programs; families went on family outings; adults visited the theaters and museums. Ultimately, thirty women received five weeks of training,[5] after which a number were able to get jobs and leave the welfare rolls, if only temporarily. During this time, no extra professional staff was added except those provided for in the proposal, and many members who were not hired gave their services voluntarily, some of them every day throughout the program.

These and the earlier training sessions had special importance in the mind of the Committee of Welfare Families organizer.

An organization only a few months old cannot draw hundreds of people into a strong identification with it. Therefore, it was necessary to evolve a concept of membership where people can come and go, where you don't preach or berate people for coming in and getting what they need and walking out and not coming back. One thing led to another; the need for a great number of people in the campaign led to the evolution of the relationship of member to organization as one of extreme looseness. What we came up with was the concept of membership participation whereby I concentrated on a relatively small number of people whom I brought into leadership and whom I tried to educate as leaders to entice them toward participation at a high level.

The training group was evolved as a way of latching on to the people with a high participation ratio, the people who were already acknowledged leaders and spokesmen, and further educating them and further giving them the status and prestige of being one of the chosen few in the training program. The training program was an idea that I had to fight for very hard over the objections of my supervisors. Both of them at the beginning or even toward the middle of the program doubted its importance. (Part of their inability to see the value of the training sessions may have been that their concept of community organization was one that tries to bring every member of the group into the fullest degree of participation. While they would acknowledge that this is extremely difficult, they nevertheless would not take the tack of purposely setting up two different levels of organizational membership.)

Social workers have an Achilles' heel. The social worker's Achilles' heel is that what the clients want to do is a sacrosanct thing. If a group of clients makes a decision which is a group decision, then self-determination and democracy come in, and it becomes quite difficult for the agency to turn

---

[5]There were two training periods.

aside what the group wants to do. This causes two problems. First, the group may make the wrong decision and destroy itself. Second, the agency has real problems controlling the group, especially if the worker wants to chart an independent course. If in certain situations supervisory people said, "Well, you can't do that," I could always point to the social-work ideal and say, "Look, the group wants to do it, just ask them." By training a small group of people in the total problems of welfare, it became much more likely that these people would take independent action and feel very strongly about their decisions.

From the very beginning I had no idea whether or not the agency was going to support me. So from the very beginning I tried to set up a situation where there was some kind of barrier between what the group wanted to do and a possible attempt on the part of the top people in the agency to stop something. This mechanism did not have to be used, because I continued to get excellent support, more than I expected.

The development of the summer program had a great effect on the Committee of Welfare Families. Even before this program, members of the organization were constantly pressing the organizer to find jobs for them so that they could get off the welfare rolls. The leadership women had friends and knew people who were working for Mobilization in various capacities. They felt that they could be just as effective as those who had been hired. The organizer was well aware that, if people got jobs, they would leave the organization, and the precious leadership he had developed would be siphoned off, thereby weakening the organization.

We simply cannot set up a situation where you keep your leadership people on welfare when it's possible for them to get jobs. Morally and professionally we can't do this, and the members wouldn't permit us anyway. What we have to do is set up some structure which feeds new leaders into spots which become vacated when people graduate from being on welfare; the training sessions and action campaigns are the way to do it.

I think the summer program forever changed the nature of our group, in that now the idea of getting jobs and getting off welfare will be as important a focus of the group as helping people to live decently under a welfare system. . . . The major reason for our putting in the proposal was not so much for the content of the programs as for the organizational value and prestige that would accrue to the group by handling and managing its own funds. I was concerned about the effect of their having complete control over their own funds as a responsible neighborhood group and what this would mean to the leadership. I expected this would build pride in the organization and give the leaders prestige and a name in a wider circle. What was finally written was a combination of the members' generally vague comments about what it would be nice to do during the summer, plus ideas which I had of using money which would train neighborhood people for the kinds of jobs they could get through the antipoverty programs, at the same time paying them money, being able to use these very same people for organizing purposes in our own campaigns.

The Committee of Welfare Families organizer tended to look at all programs first from the point of view of their effect upon the organization, and only then from the point of view of their effect on the individual members. His organizational perspective on programs was the main factor which distinguished him from the other organizers and his group from other MFY organizations.

BOOK MANUFACTURE

The Practice of Social Intervention: Goals, Roles and Strategies: A Book of Readings in Social Work Practice was composed by Allied Typesetting, Dexter, Michigan, with printing and binding by Kingsport Press. The paper is Perkins & Squier Company's Glatfelter Special Book L. Charles Kling & Associates designed the cover. F. E. Peacock Publishers, Inc., art department designed the interior. The type is Caledonia with Bodoni.